D&AD 12

TASCHEN

Contents

I have always loved D&AD and it's an incredible honour to be president in the 50th year.

D&AD is the reason I have a job in advertising, as from my very first contact with 'The Book' I knew this was what I wanted to do.

So it gives me special pleasure to actually come up with the idea for this year's Annual, ably helped by the wonderful Michael Johnson – one of my very favourite designers and a real pleasure to work with.

I wanted something that would reflect the numerous inspiring, talented, creative people who have made D&AD the peak of excellence it is today, so I asked 50 of the best practitioners to come up with their ideas for the cover. I then asked for the signed artwork so we could auction the pieces off, with all the proceeds going into the D&AD Foundation.

As I hoped, there are some outstanding and thought-provoking pieces. I hope you enjoy identifying who came up with what.

I also wanted to reintroduce photographs of the hard working jury members (as a tribute to their hard work). All this and keep the book as sustainable as possible.

Whoever said women were multi-taskers was right.

Rosie Arnold
D&AD President

Ich habe D&AD immer geliebt, und so ist es mir eine unbeschreibliche Freude, im 50. Jahr die Präsidentschaft innezuhaben.

D&AD ist der Grund, warum ich in der Werbebranche arbeite. Durch meinen ersten Kontakt mit „The Book" wusste ich, dass ich genau das machen wollte.

Also habe ich die ganz besondere Ehre, die Idee für das diesjährige Jahrbuch vorzustellen, wobei mir einer meiner Lieblingsdesigner, der wundervolle Michael Johnson, tatkräftig geholfen hat. Mit ihm zu arbeiten ist eine wahre Freude.

Ich wünschte mir etwas, das die zahlreichen inspirierenden, talentierten und kreativen Menschen repräsentiert, die D&AD zu jenem Sammelpunkt für Spitzenleistungen gemacht haben, der er heute ist. Also forderte ich 50 der besten Fachleute auf, Ideen für das Cover vorzuschlagen. Dann bat ich um ihre signierten Werke, damit wir sie versteigern konnten. Alle Einnahmen kamen der D&AD-Stiftung zugute.

Wie ich es erhoffte, trafen eine ganze Reihe hervorstechender und geistig anregender Werke ein. Ich hoffe, Sie haben Spaß daran herauszufinden, zu wem welche Arbeiten gehören.

Außerdem wollte ich, dass wieder die Fotos unserer hart arbeitenden Jurymitglieder im Buch erscheinen – als Würdigung der vielen, vielen Stunden, die sie investiert haben. All das sollte Berücksichtigung finden, und überdies sollte das Buch so nachhaltig wie möglich produziert werden.

Wer auch immer gesagt hat, Frauen wären multitaskingfähig, hat recht.

Rosie Arnold
D&AD President

J'ai toujours aimé D&AD, et c'est un honneur incroyable d'en être la présidente en cette 50e année.

D&AD est la raison pour laquelle je travaille dans la publicité, car dès mon premier contact avec « Le Livre » j'ai su que c'était cela que je voulais faire.

C'est donc un plaisir tout particulier pour moi d'avoir trouvé l'idée pour l'album de cette année, avec l'aide compétente du merveilleux Michael Johnson, l'un de mes designers préférés, avec qui j'ai eu grand plaisir à travailler.

Je voulais quelque chose qui représenterait dignement les nombreuses personnes talentueuses, créatives et stimulantes qui ont fait de D&AD le modèle d'excellence que cette institution est devenue aujourd'hui. J'ai donc demandé à 50 des meilleurs professionnels de soumettre leurs idées pour la couverture. Puis je leur ai demandé des œuvres signées, afin de pouvoir les vendre aux enchères et reverser les gains à la fondation de D&AD.

Comme je l'avais espéré, ce processus a donné lieu à des œuvres remarquables et intrigantes. J'espère que vous aurez plaisir à identifier leurs auteurs.

Je voulais aussi réintroduire les photographies des membres du jury (en hommage à leurs longues heures de dur travail). En plus de tout cela, je voulais aussi que le livre s'inscrive autant que possible dans le respect de l'environnement.

Qui a dit que les femmes savent faire plusieurs choses à la fois avait bien raison.

Rosie Arnold
Présidente de D&AD

This is a mean book, put together by a mean organisation.

There are 568 pieces of work in it; 112 Nominations, 65 Yellow Pencils, one Black.

This year's wonderful President, Rosie Arnold, encouraged the jury foremen at Olympia back in April to be rigorous, but also generous. This is our 50th year, she said. We must make sure that the 50th D&AD Annual is a true record of the year's best work from around the world.

They responded by enthusiastically excluding anything that didn't meet their very high standards.

And, of course, they were quite right to do so. If we didn't make it so unbelievably difficult to get in the Annual – let alone get a Nomination or a Pencil – creative people around the world wouldn't want it quite so much. And D&AD wouldn't be able to contribute as much as it does to stimulating creative excellence in communication and design, or contribute as much to creative education.

We have exciting plans to expand our presence and influence around the world. But here is not the place.

This is the place to thank and salute the creative people who made the work in this book, the hard-to-please jury men and women who judged it and their impossibly high standards.

In a world awash with awards that can often seem harder not to win than to win, mean is good.

Tim Lindsay
D&AD CEO

Dies ist ein unverschämtes Buch, zusammengestellt von einer unverschämten Organisation. Darin finden sich 568 Arbeiten, 112 Nominierungen, 65 Yellow Pencils und ein Black Pencil.

Rosie Arnold, unsere wunderbare Präsidentin in diesem Jahr, forderte seinerzeit im April die Jury in Olympia auf, nicht nur rigoros, sondern auch großzügig zu sein. Bei unserem 50. Jubiläum, meinte sie, hätten wir darauf zu achten, dass das 50. D&AD-Annual ein wahrhaftiges Dokument der besten Arbeiten aus der ganzen Welt sei.

Die Jury reagierte darauf, indem enthusiastisch alles ausgeschlossen wurde, das nicht die sehr hohen Qualitätsstandards erfüllte.

Und natürlich haben sie völlig richtig gehandelt. Wenn wir es nicht so unglaublich schwer machen würden, in dieses Jahrbuch aufgenommen zu werden – ganz zu schweigen davon, eine Nominierung oder einen Pencil zu erhalten –, dann wäre das Annual für die kreativen Köpfe der Welt nicht in dieser Weise erstrebenswert. Und D&AD wäre nicht in der Lage, zu so umfassend kreativen Höchstleistungen in Kommunikation und Design zu stimulieren oder derart viel für die kreative Aus- und Weiterbildung zu bewirken.

Wir arbeiten an spannenden Plänen, um unsere Präsenz und unseren Einfluss weltweit auszubauen. Doch darum geht es an dieser Stelle nicht. Hier wollen wir uns bei all den kreativen Menschen bedanken und sie feiern, die die Werke in diesem Buch geschaffen haben. Wir bedanken uns bei den schwer zufriedenzustellenden Frauen und Männern der Jury mit ihren unsäglich hohen Ansprüchen, die alles beurteilt und eingeschätzt haben.

In einer Welt, die überflutet wird von Auszeichnungen und Preisverleihungen – bei denen es scheinbar oft schwerer ist, sie nicht verliehen zu bekommen –, ist es schon sehr gut, unverschämt zu sein.

Tim Lindsay
D&AD CEO

Ceci est un méchant livre, réalisé par une méchante organisation.

Il contient 568 projets, 112 nominations, 65 prix Yellow Pencil, et un prix Black Pencil.

La merveilleuse présidente de cette année, Rosie Arnold, a encouragé les membres du jury à être rigoureux mais aussi généreux dans leurs délibérations, qui ont eu lieu en avril à Olympia. C'est notre 50e année, a-t-elle rappelé. Nous devons faire en sorte que le 50e album annuel de D&AD reflète fidèlement les meilleurs projets du monde entier pour l'année.

Ils ont obtempéré avec enthousiasme, en excluant tout ce qui ne satisfaisait pas à leurs critères extrêmement exigeants.

Et, de toute évidence, ils ont eu bien raison. Si nous n'avions pas fait en sorte qu'il soit aussi incroyablement difficile de se faire une place dans l'album annuel (et encore plus de décrocher une nomination ou un prix), les créatifs du monde entier ne seraient pas aussi déterminés à essayer. Et D&AD ne serait pas en position de contribuer autant à l'excellence créative dans la communication et le design, ou à l'éducation des créatifs.

Nous avons des projets électrisants pour étendre notre présence et notre influence dans le monde entier. Mais ce n'est pas ici que j'en parlerai.

Ici, je veux remercier et saluer les créatifs qui sont à l'origine des projets présentés dans ce livre, les jurés pointilleux qui les ont jugés, et leurs critères presque impossibles à satisfaire.

Dans un monde inondé de récompenses qui peuvent souvent sembler plus faciles à gagner que le contraire, la méchanceté peut avoir du bon.

Tim Lindsay
D&AD CEO

D&AD Executive Committee

President
Rosie Arnold
BBH London

Deputy President
Neville Brody
Research Studios

Mark Bonner
GBH
Andy Cheetham
CheethamBell JWT
Bryan Clark
University College Falmouth
Bruce Duckworth
Turner Duckworth
Joe Ferry
IHG
Vince Frost
Frost Design
Laura Gregory
Great Guns
Flo Heiss
Dare
Nat Hunter
Steven Johnson
Laura Jordan Bambach
Dare
Simon Manchipp
SomeOne
Andy Sandoz
Work Club
Mike Stephenson
Moon
Alexandra Taylor
Mrs McGuinty Ltd
Sean Toal
The Creative Rebellion
Tom Uglow
Google

Chairman
Dick Powell
Seymourpowell

Treasurer
Graham Stewart
Inside Out Search

Chief Executive Officer
Tim Lindsay
Chief Operating Officer
Dara Lynch

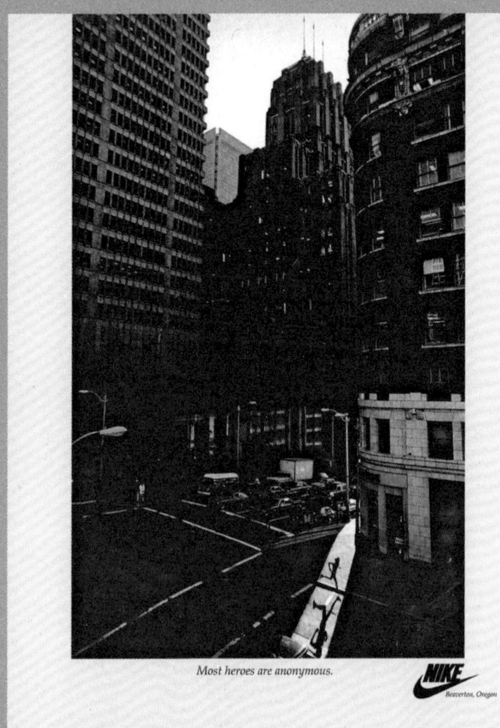

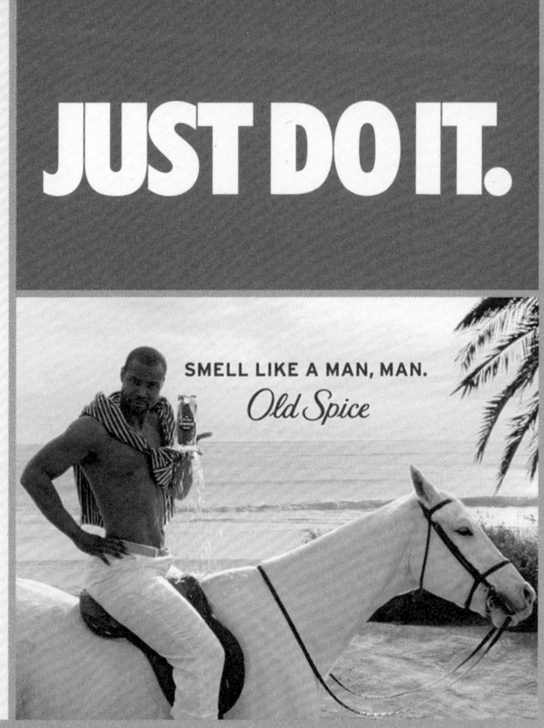

Most heroes are anonymous.

JUST DO IT.
SMELL LIKE A MAN, MAN.
Old Spice

President's Award

Dan Wieden is one of the most inspirational advertising brains of our age. His spirit remains restless and free, and he continues to champion independent thinking and behaviour. His work and that of his now numerous agencies lead the way across all disciplines. I've lost count of how many times I've seen a piece of work that has surprised and delighted me, and made me run up and down the corridors at work showing it to other creatives, only to discover it came from Wieden+Kennedy. So when I asked myself if I should give Dan my President's Award, I told myself, 'Just Do It'.

Rosie Arnold
D&AD President

Auszeichnung der Präsidentin

Dan Wieden gehört zu den inspirativsten Köpfen der Werbebranche unserer Zeit. Als rastloser und freier Geist tritt er stets für unabhängiges Denken und Verhalten ein. Seine Werke und die seiner mittlerweile zahlreichen Agenturen führen quer durch alle Disziplinen. Ich kann gar nicht mehr zählen, wie oft ich schon eine Arbeit gesehen habe, die mich derart überrascht und erfreut hat, dass ich sie flurauf und flurab anderen Kreativprofis gezeigt habe, nur um dann zu entdecken, dass sie von Wieden+Kennedy stammte. Als ich also überlegte, ob ich Dan Wieden meinen President's Award verleihen sollte, sagte ich mir: „Tu es einfach."

Rosie Arnold
Präsidentin des D&AD

Prix du Président

Dan Wieden est l'un des cerveaux les plus intéressants de notre époque dans la publicité. Il a su conserver un esprit insatiable et libre, et il continue de défendre l'indépendance dans la pensée et les actions. Son travail, et celui de ses nombreuses agences, défriche de nouveaux territoires dans toutes les disciplines. J'ai perdu le compte du nombre de fois où j'ai vu un projet qui m'a surprise et charmée, et m'a fait courir dans les couloirs au bureau pour le montrer aux autres créatifs, pour ensuite découvrir qu'il venait de Wieden+Kennedy. Alors quand je me suis demandé si je devais décerner mon prix de la présidence à Dan, je me suis dit « Just Do It ».

Rosie Arnold
Présidente de D&AD

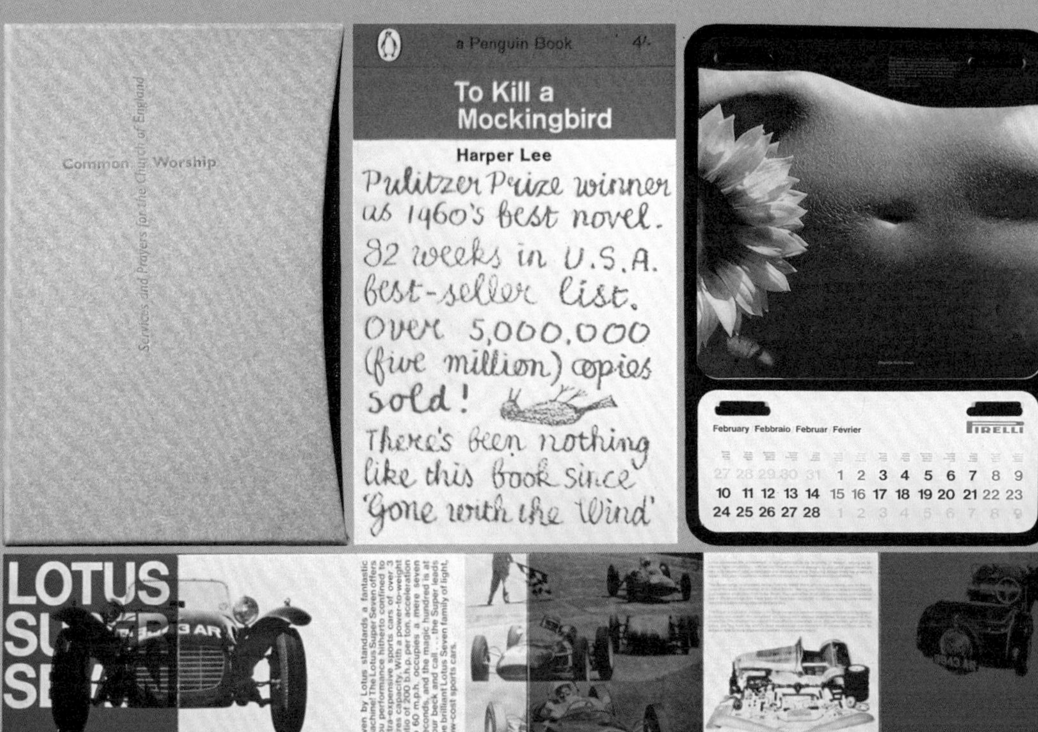

President's Award

Derek Birdsall defies description. He was the opinionated young lion whose 1961 Association of Graphic Designers, London's exhibition '17 Designers' caught the attention of his industry peers and clients and became the catalyst for design's involvement in the formation of D&AD. His impeccable work in editorial, identity, exhibition and education, as well as every other challenge graphic design can throw at us, spans all five decades of D&AD's existence. He is still at it. Numerous projects including the Pirelli calendar that set the bar, Penguin jackets that define an era, and his Book of Prayer perfection for the Church of England, were all overlooked by the organisation he did so much to define. Somehow, D&AD recognition has always eluded Derek, until now, in its 50th year. It's the D&AD board's proud decision that Mr 'Black Hat, White Space' finally gets the special gold he so richly deserves.

Mark Bonner
Trustee, D&AD Executive Committee

Auszeichnung der Präsidentin

Derek Birdsall trotzt jeder Beschreibung. Er war jener eigensinnige junge Löwe, dessen Londoner Ausstellung „17 Designers" der Association of Graphic Designers von 1961 in der Branche für Furore sorgte. So wurde er zum Katalysator für die Einbindung des Designs in die Strukturen des D&AD. Seine tadellose Arbeit für Editorial Design, Identitäten, Ausstellungen, Schulungen und alle anderen Bereiche des Grafikdesigns umspannt die fünf Jahrzehnte des D&AD. Dennoch wurden seine Projekte wie der Pirelli-Kalender, der zum Maßstab wurde, die Penguin-Cover, die eine Ära definieren, und die Vollendung des „Book of Prayer" für die Church of England von jener Organisation übersehen, für die er so viel getan hat, um sie zu definieren. Die Anerkennung des D&AD für Derek ließ stets auf sich warten – in diesem 50. Jahr ist Schluss damit. Das D&AD-Gremium verkündet stolz, dass Mr. „Black Hat, White Space" endlich die hochverdiente Gold-Auszeichnung verliehen wird.

Mark Bonner
Kurator im D&AD-Führungsgremium

Prix du Président

Derek Birdsall échappe aux définitions. Il est le jeune lion dont l'exposition « 17 Designers » à l'Association of Graphic Designers de Londres en 1961 devint le catalyseur du rôle du design dans la formation de D&AD. Son travail impeccable dans l'édition, l'identité, les expositions et l'éducation, ainsi que dans tous les autres secteurs du graphisme, couvre les cinq décennies de D&AD. Ses nombreux projets, entre autres le calendrier Pirelli, qui a établi un nouveau standard, les couvertures des livres Penguin, qui définissent une époque, et son parfait Book of Prayer pour l'Église anglicane, ont tous été négligés par l'organisation qu'il a tant contribué à définir. D&AD n'a jamais récompensé officiellement Derek, jusqu'à aujourd'hui pour la 50e année de l'organisation. Le comité de D&AD a le grand honneur de décerner enfin à « M. Chapeau Noir, Espace Blanc » la décoration en or qu'il mérite tant.

Mark Bonner
D&AD, membre du comité exécutif

Student of the Year

Open Brief
for Interbrand

Electronic Arts' Peace Day
The brief was to help make Peace Day an international day of recognition. On Christmas Day 1914, all along the western front, British and German soldiers put down their guns, climbed out of their trenches, and played football. For Peace Day, we would team up with Electronic Arts to get videogamers to do the same. On 21 September, players of Battlefield 3 would be asked to play a demo version of FIFA 12, using their Battlefield character, on a war zone pitch. We would promote this using in-game advertising and social media teasers. As an incentive, gamers who participated in Electronic Arts' Peace Day would receive medals to unlock bonus levels in Battlefield 3.

Students
Martin Headon
Olly Wood
Tutors
Chris Hill
Blair Jarvis
Marc Lewis

College
School of Communication Arts 2.0

Yellow Pencil

Open Brief
for Interbrand

Peace Books
The brief was to help make Peace Day an international day of recognition. According to Nigerian poet and novelist Ben Okri, 'Stories are the secret reservoir of values: change the stories individuals and nations live by and you change individuals and nations'. Our idea was to promote the observance of Peace Day through a collaborative grassroots campaign. Every year, celebrity supporters will campaign through social media to a worldwide audience to get people to write Peace Books – children's books about peace. Publishers working not-for-profit with organisation Peace One Day will choose the best of these books for global release. Reading a Peace Book on Peace Day will become a much loved universal tradition.

Students
Andy Dexiang Xu
Violaine Hemery
Amelie Kam Pei Wen
Goh Ting Yu
Fleur Vella

Tutor
Chen Kai'En

College
Chatsworth Medi@rt Academy

Yellow Pencil

Advertising
for Channel 4

LookFour
The brief was to promote Channel 4's new over 60s channel. I created the LookFour identity, a sequence of abstract and elegant typography that relies on reflective surfaces to come to fruition. My TV campaign uses a viral strategy in which the sequenced identity claims ownership of programming due to appear on LookFour. The idents emerge from reflective surfaces within the scheduled footage. After the viral strategy of week one, the official idents would be gradually introduced to the advertising campaign.

Student
Chris Nuelle
Tutors
Martin Coyne
Phil Jones

College
The Arts University College at Bournemouth

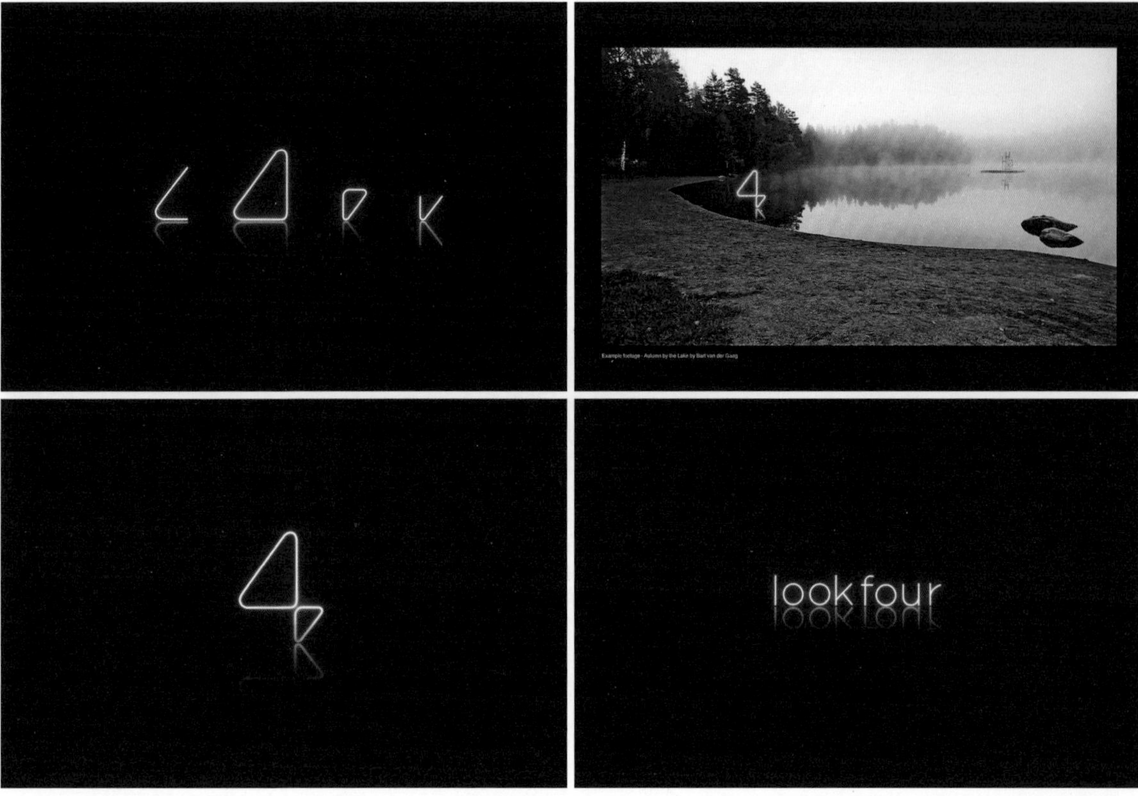

Yellow Pencil

Advertising
for Channel 4

4Prime
The brief was to promote Channel 4's new over 60s channel. Retired and free to do as they please, the 60+ audience represents the new prime of life. This mature audience has an expectation of quality programming, so I called the channel 4Prime. Referencing the abundance of family pictures found in older people's homes, my campaign for 4Prime highlights how the viewer has grown up alongside Channel 4. It also reminds the viewer how much Channel 4 has shown them already, rekindling an interest in the channel's offering. The commercial concludes with the message that there is still so much left to see and 4Prime is the only place to see it.

Student
Stephen Pierce
Tutor
Richard McElveen

College
University of Ulster

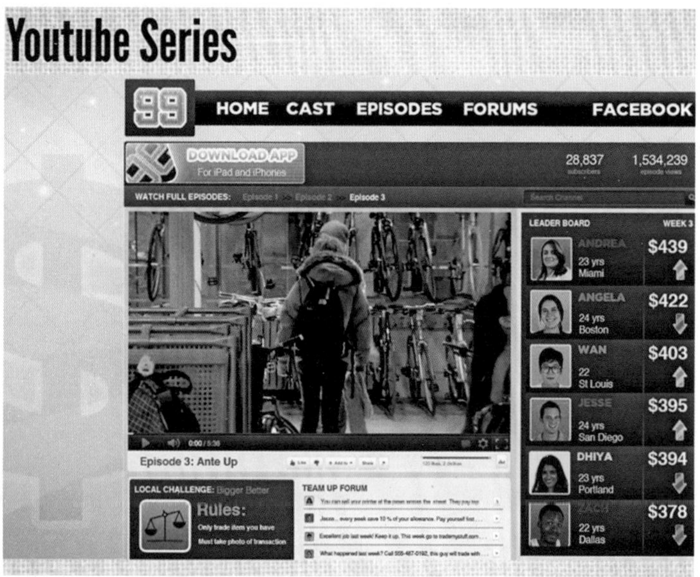

Yellow Pencil

Open Advertising
for Aviva

Aviva 99
The brief was to encourage 18-25 year olds to save for their financial future. In these hard economic times, convincing young people to start saving can seem daunting. What teen would listen to a big insurance company telling them what to do? Rather than beat our target over the head with a message, we thought of a better place for it to come from: themselves. Branded online entertainment acts as a platform for young people to share information on smart financial practices. By creating an engaging medium that encourages participation, we allow Generation Y to stand on its own. They gather strength from their connections and use it to face the future together.

Students	College
Matthew Kern	Miami Ad School
Westley Taylor	Miami
Tutor	
Serena Berra	

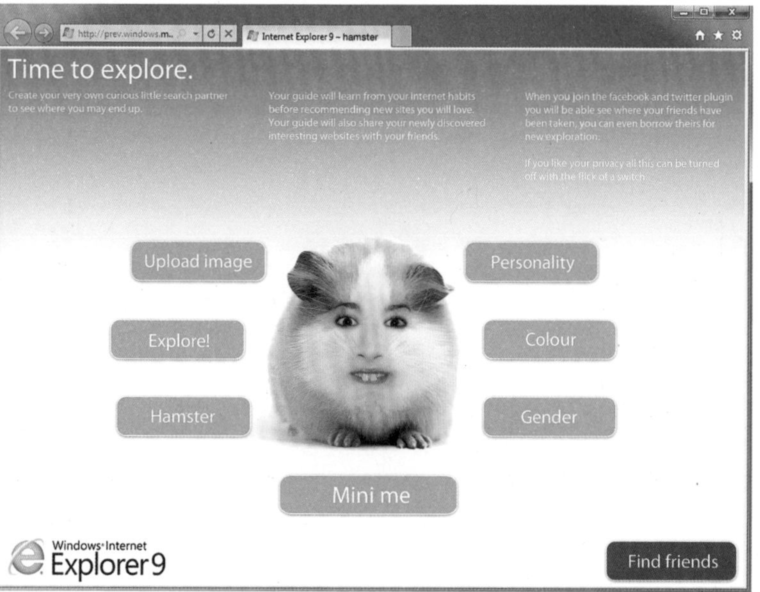

Yellow Pencil

Advertising
for Internet Explorer 9

Hamsterize
The brief was to promote IE9 by inspiring people to become internet explorers.
As internet customers, we are stuck in a rut, turning the wheel in the same direction, visiting the same websites day in, day out. Hamsterize is a software tool that enables the discovery of new websites based on your browsing history. Hamsterize yourself, step off the wheel, out of that cage and freefall into the exciting world of online exploration. Let your curiosity run free to discover the unseen, online universe. Your little search partner is very intuitive; he knows what you like and where you've been and will take you to places he knows you'll love. You can even swap pets with friends and see where each of you has been.

Students	College
Emma Leamore	University of Salford
Michael Pollard	
Tutors	
Leonie Clements	
Christopher Morris	
Kostas Zochios	

Yellow Pencil

Advertising
for Internet Explorer 9

Sorb
The brief was to promote IE9 by inspiring people to become internet explorers instead of being stuck in an internet rut. Sorb is a mobile app that uses keywords from the different locations on your phone's GPS to gather internet content you can check out later when you are home. For example, the app could 'sorb' an article about the coffee trends while you are at your local java joint, pick up fashion blogs while you're walking by clothing stores or even get you an invitation to a VIP concert at a venue you didn't know you passed. When you get home and open IE9, your Sorb homepage will pop up to let you know what you've discovered that day.

Students
Fernando Barcelona
Juan David Manotas
Tutors
Jan Jaworski
Thomas Kropp

Colleges
Miami Ad School
Brooklyn, Miami
and San Francisco

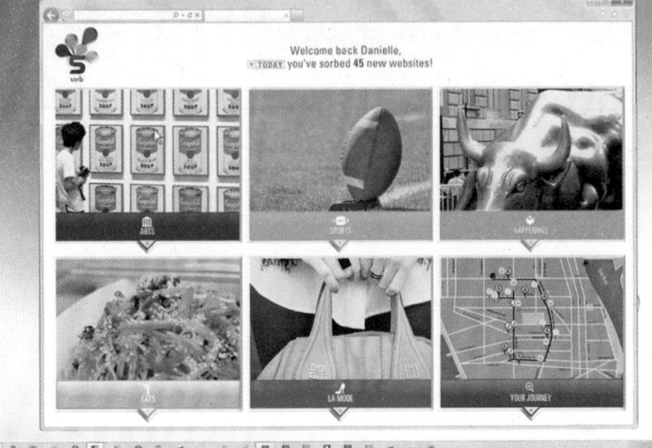

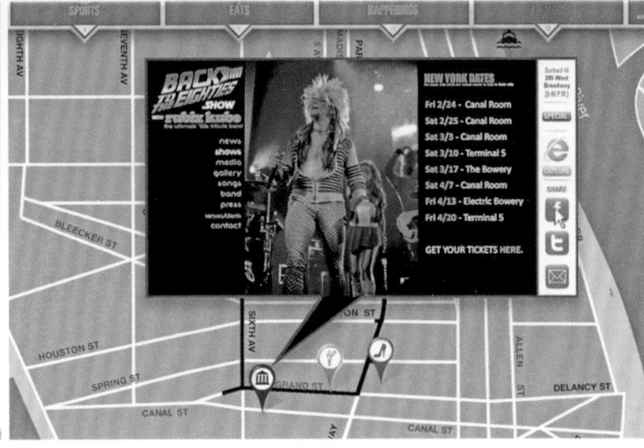

Yellow Pencil

Advertising
for Internet Explorer 9

Top Explorer
The brief was to promote IE9 by inspiring people to become internet explorers instead of being stuck in an internet rut. In the online community, the ability to 'get there first' is associated with prestige. We decided to add a feature to IE9 that lets you mark your territory all across the internet. Every time you find something you believe has potential, you can mark it. If that topic, website or video later becomes viral, you'll earn points. The users who gather the most points are presented as 'Top Explorers' on the IE9 start page. So every time any IE9 user opens a new window or tab, the Top Explorers and their discoveries are promoted.

Students
Fredrik Broander
Adam Gäfvert
Jesper Stein
Tutor
Annika Berner

College
Beckmans College
of Design

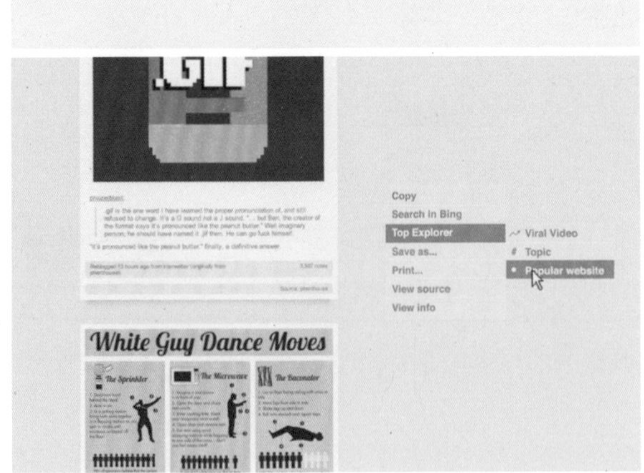

Cavendish & Harvey Fruit Drops
We won't pause until your brand sounds better pitchandsync.com
P&S™
sounds like a good idea

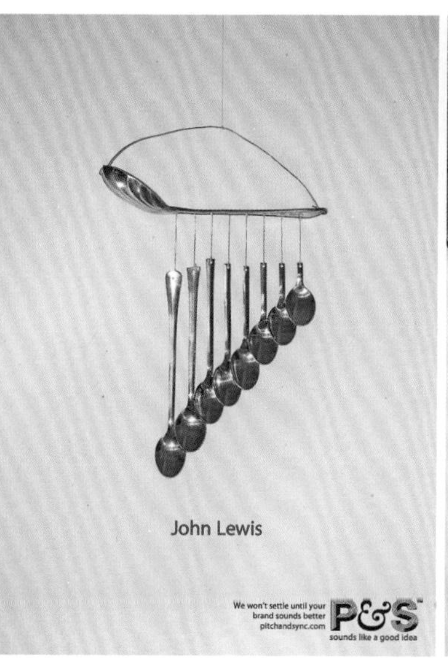

John Lewis
We won't settle until your brand sounds better pitchandsync.com
P&S™
sounds like a good idea

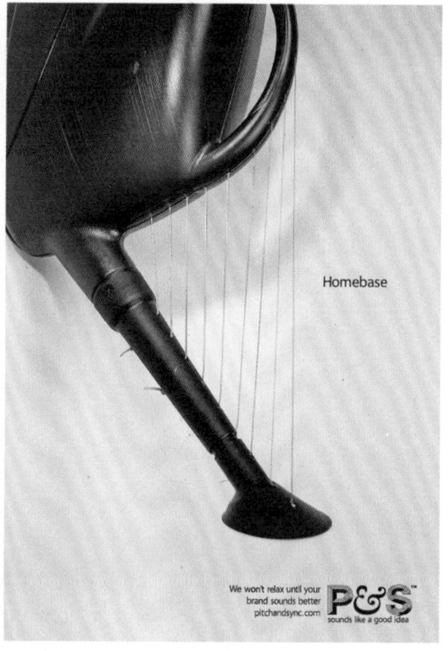

Homebase
We won't relax until your brand sounds better pitchandsync.com
P&S™
sounds like a good idea

Yellow Pencil

Advertising
for Pitch & Sync

Brands into Sounds
The brief was to create a campaign to help creative noisemakers Pitch & Sync amplify their business to the next decibel. Our campaign uses visual metaphors in a fun and innovative way to illustrate how Pitch & Sync can bring out the music in every brand idea.

Students
Louise Flanagan
Naomi Hodgson
Tutor
Frank Cookson

College
University of Central Lancashire

Yellow Pencil

Advertising
for Pitch & Sync

Viral Madness
The brief was to create a campaign to help creative noisemakers Pitch & Sync amplify their business to the next decibel. These ads aim to show how crucial music is to creating and enhancing the right atmosphere. This point is made by running clips of well-known children's TV shows and inserting unlikely tracks. Viewers are surprised to witness Sooty and Sweep moshing to Datsik, Rosie and Jim joined by Judas Priest and Elmo from Sesame Street breaking out into Trahison by Vitalic. These short ads were made with the intent to go viral, using juxtaposition to alter and parody the original videos and push the Pitch & Sync name out there.

Student
Steven Kelly
Tutor
Paul Goodfellow

College
Northumbria University

Yellow Pencil

Radio Advertising
for RAB

Office Dramas
The brief was to get people listening to radio at work via the Radioplayer, the web platform that allows you to listen to the radio online. 'Office Barbecue' is part of a campaign of three radio spots called 'Office Dramas'. Imagine a typical day at work. You have a big, scary stressball of a deadline to meet. All you need is a bit of peace to get on with it. But every time you try to settle down and work, some office drama kicks off around you, cracking your concentration. My radio spots position Radioplayer as a perfect solution to the problem; an entertaining and welcome escape from even the most dramatic of office distractions.

Student
Caitlin Breeze
Tutors
Rob Kitchen
Chris Waite

College
University College
Falmouth

Office Barbecue

Gary Hey hey, Mickeyboy. Take a break from work for some lunch? Ooh, is that BBQ I smell – let's get summa that!

Mike Not barbecue, mate. It's Francine.

Gary From HR? Always sending round sodding pointless mass emails?

Mike People'd had enough of her clogging up their inboxes, so they tied her to the projector n' are burning her at the stake. (As an afterthought) She made quite a racket. Didn't you hear?

Gary Nah, been plugged into Radioplayer all morning – in a world of my own.

SFX Crackling flames become audible.

Gary Shame. She was quite fit.

Mike Yeah.

Gary Yeah. Wanna get a burger?

MVO (Light, friendly and lively male voice) At radioplayer.co.uk, you'll find all of your favourite stations in one place. So, whatever the distraction, you'll find it easy to tune out from office dramas.

Yellow Pencil

Digital Advertising
for Spotify

Friends FM
The brief was to spread Spotify's musical conversation to Facebook's 800 million users. When Facebook and Spotify joined forces, they added a ticker to the live feed so people could see what their friends were listening to in real time. But the ticker revealed everyone's guilty pleasures; people turned the whole thing off and stopped sharing their music. Friends FM is Facebook's own radio channel where people can listen to what their friends are listening to in real time, without revealing who is listening to what. Friends FM is a feature available to everyone on Facebook who has friends with Spotify – reaching out to all the Facebook users who don't yet have a Spotify account.

Students
Caroline Ekrem
Sara Marie Hodnebo
Tutors
Astrid Brodtkorb
Anse Kjersem
Tom Kvisle

College
Westerdals School
of Communication

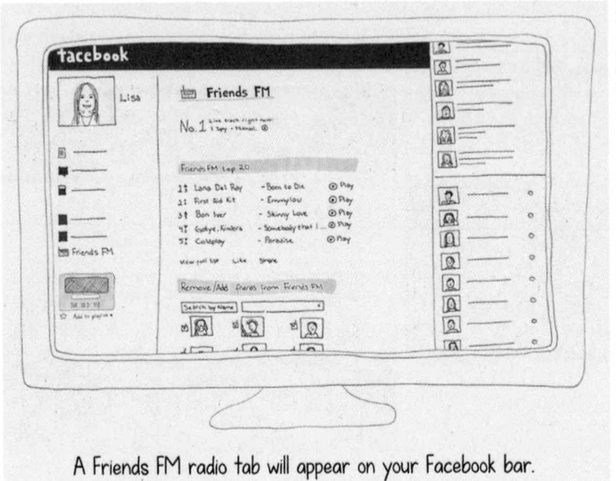

A Friends FM radio tab will appear on your Facebook bar.

And you can add and remove friends who influence your Friends FM

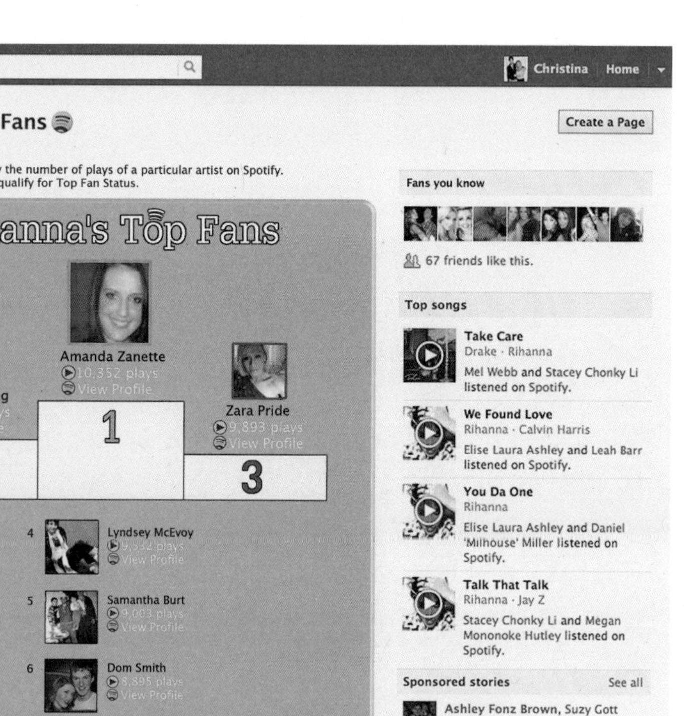

Yellow Pencil

Digital Advertising
for Spotify

Top Fans

The brief was to spread Spotify's musical conversation to Facebook's 800 million users. With our solution, die-hard fans can show their passion for music and finally settle the debate of who really is the most devoted, by simply playing the songs of their favourite artist on Spotify more than anyone else. Top Fans will get exclusive rewards such as gig tickets and pre-release tracks, all published on Facebook for everyone to see. Music artists will even write on Top Fans' profile pages to really get to know them. So Facebook and Spotify become the new way to bring music artists and fans together.

Students
Christina Smith
Claire Stokes

Tutors
Mike Belton
Gyles Lingwood

College
University of Lincoln

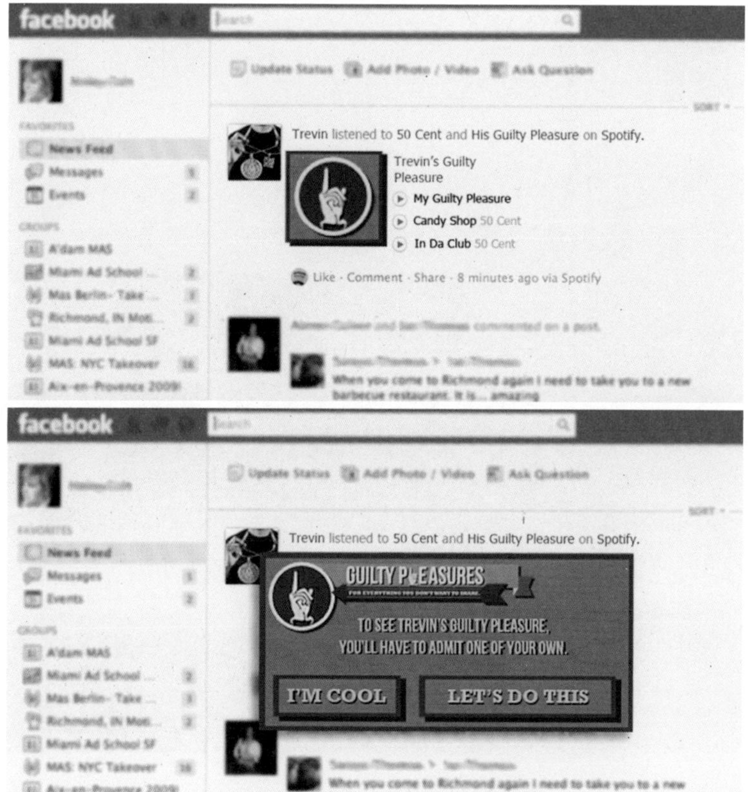

Yellow Pencil

Digital Advertising
for Spotify

Guilty Pleasures

The brief was to spread Spotify's musical conversation to Facebook's 800 million users. We identified that the shame of revealing the songs they hate to love to their friends stops users from being more interactive with Spotify on Facebook. With Guilty Pleasures, users can single out the embarrassing songs in their library, so that when they share music, instead of appearing with their real titles, these shameful songs are simply presented as 'guilty pleasures'.

Students
Laura Cabello Molina
Haley Cole
Olimpia Muñoz Clare
Eiluned Prowse
Martina Ricciardi

Tutors
Manolo Garcia
Alvaro Sotomayor
Erik Wunsch

Colleges
Miami Ad School
Amsterdam, Madrid
and San Francisco

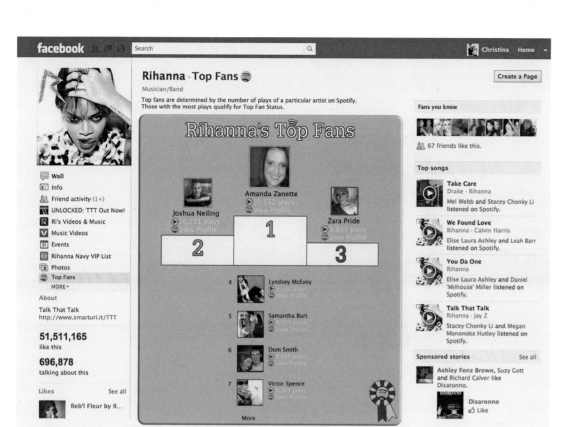

Yellow Pencil

Make Your Mark
Brief set by D&AD

The Online Intern
The brief was to choose your dream employer, and present yourself to them. The Online Intern was a six week project, created to solve some of the problems faced by students trying to gain an internship in the advertising industry. It took the problems of money, accommodation and visas out of the equation and proved that internships could also be done online. A website was designed and advertising via social media asked agencies to get involved. Each week (over a period of six), a different internship was completed, with agencies such as Poke, JWT, DDB, TMW and StrawberryFrog responding to the ads. Briefs and mentoring occurred over Skype and email and the progress was aired over Twitter, Facebook and a daily blog. It was a great success, not only allowing me to make my mark, but also achieving the potential to grow into a platform which other students could use.

New Creative
Joy Ayles

THE ONLINE INTERN
Home
About
Briefs
Live
Blog
Contact
The Online Intern
Industry – Advertising.
One week, One brief, One agency.
9.00 – 16.00, Monday – Friday
Anywhere in the world
Every week for 5 weeks.
Email me a brief, Skype me a challenge,
Tweet me your lunch, Tag me in a photo
- or, if you fancy, mix it up a little.
My challenge, the above.
Your challenge, keep me busy.
THE ONLINE INTERN
Copyright © 2011 by Joy Ayles | Website Authoring by Przemyslaw Bobak

Yellow Pencil

Make Your Mark
Brief set by D&AD

Constructive Procrastination
The brief was to choose your dream employer, and present yourself to them. We wanted to make our mark, get noticed and maybe even get a job in advertising. But with so many other things to do instead of actually sitting down and working, that wasn't going well. The only thing to do was work with what we had – a lot of ways to procrastinate. We made the problem the solution, literally. We created a set of 50 engraved pencils to ensure that procrastination resulted in ideation. The pencils offer you 50 common time-wasting, stalling and pussyfooting techniques, so each time you indulge in a good bit of dilly-dallying, just use that pencil to write down one idea. By uniting delay tactics with an idea recorder/pencil, you can drag your heels all the way to that deadline. This was 'disruptive' enough to get the attention of TBWA\Hunt\Lascaris – we work there now.

New Creatives
Chad Goddard
Kyle Jacobson

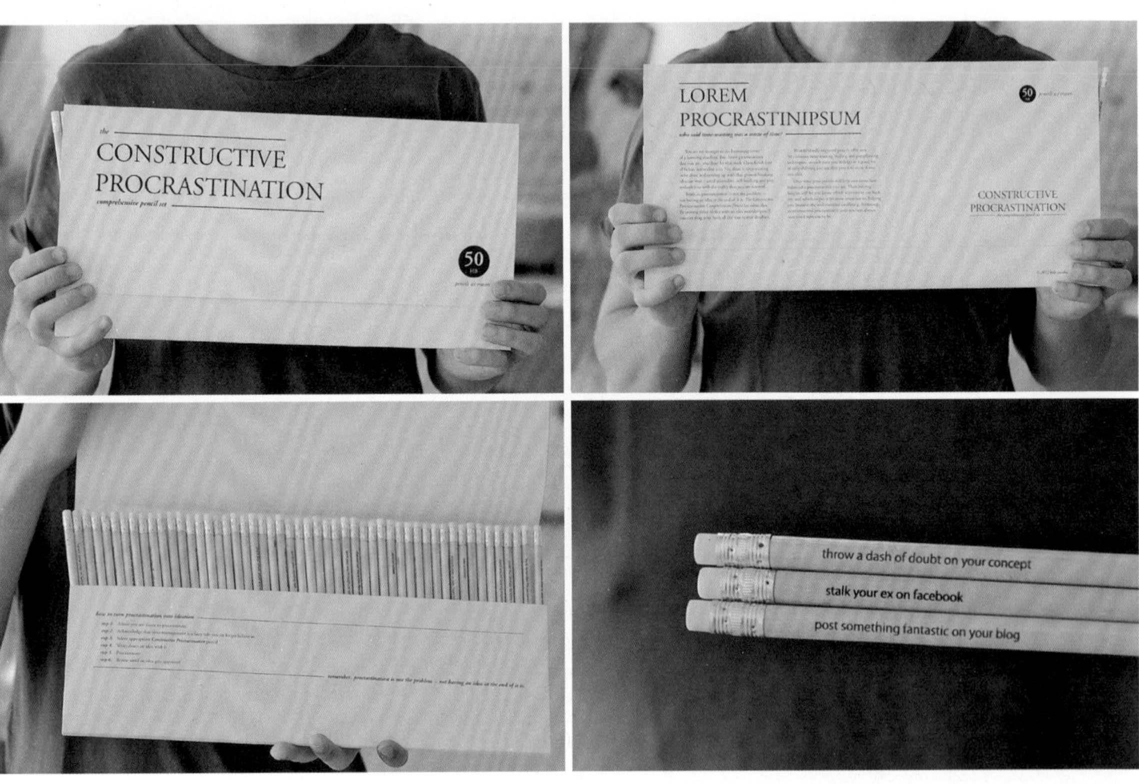

Yellow Pencil

Integrated Communications
for 17

Make-up School

The brief was to promote the Boots 17 cosmetics range to sassy young women. The usual problem for young girls is that their parents don't allow them to wear make-up. Our concept is based on special packaging for 17's products that makes them look like school supplies, not cosmetics.

Students	College
Kseniya Apresyan	British Higher School
Arina Kiseleva	of Art and Design

Tutors
Dmitry Karpov
Anton Yarusov

Yellow Pencil

Branding
for Venture Three

The City

The brief was to rebrand the City, telling the story of how it has changed, to bring back a sense of pride to the community. The City of London connects a mass of people, businesses and international assets. It also harbours a rich cultural heritage alongside cutting-edge modernity. Based on these observations, we decided to focus our rebranding on the idea of the City as a point of connection. We used a simple and universal typographic symbol, the colon. 'The City:' can be inserted in company logos or business cards, showing connections to the City of London across the globe.

Students	College
Jay Jung Hyun Yeo	London College of
Hwasoo Shim	Communication, UAL

Tutors
Monica Biagioli
Siân Cook
David Phillips

Yellow Pencil

Digital Design
for Windows Phone

Senses

The brief was to create a multi-screen experience for Windows 7 that will enhance the personal or professional life of users. Most of the contemporary digital interactions we see today take users out of their physical context, and force them into the confines of digital space. We propose a deeper integration of our digital and physical spaces that spans across devices and environments. Using projections and Windows Phone, we bring digital technology out into the physical environment. Using digital services no longer means interacting with discrete devices, but engaging with a pervasive network of screens and sensors.

Students
Kenneth Au-Yeung
Sarah Fung
Stanley Lai
Yu-Chuan (Felix) Lai
Justin Lim

Tutor
Andres Wanner

College
Simon Fraser University

changing how you
wake up every morning

We have all experienced being rudely awakened by our screaming alarm clocks. Besides giving us a nasty start to the day, it is unnatural and disruptive to our sleep rhythms. Our Windows Phone would act as the centerpiece of the room, where spatial specific settings allow the phone to customize room settings specific to the individual user. Once the user decides how he/she wants to wake up, the rest will be taken care of by the system. Through the play of lights, blinds, music and temperature, we are uniting both the physical and the digital intimately to help improve the experience of waking up every morning.

Yellow Pencil

Graphic Design
for Pentagram London

Live from The Typographic Circle

The brief was to design a supplement for The Typographical Circle that focuses on a series of talks from typography designers. Our concept takes the structure of the talks and uses typography as a vehicle for recreating the events. The speech is transcribed exactly as it has been given. Pauses and laughs are included, questions are 'thrown' in when asked and pictures appear whenever they are shown. Two different fonts distinguish between speaker and audience, and a third is used on the cover to demonstrate that we're stepping in and out of the event. These techniques shape our reading of the text in a way that replicates the live event.

Students
Josefin Janson
Nicole Kärnell
Elin Mejergren

Tutor
Annika Berner

College
Beckmans College of Design

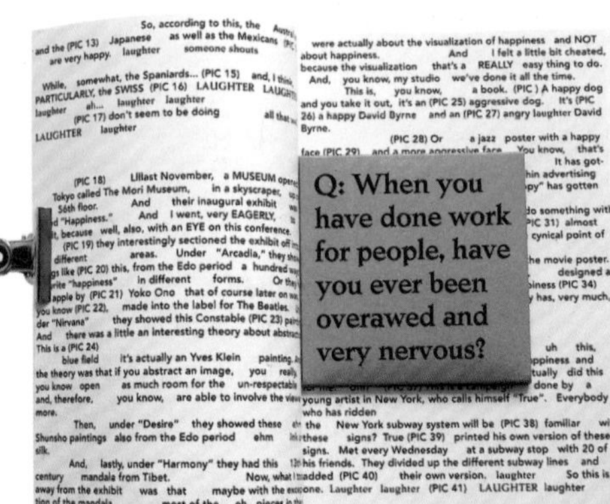

Yellow Pencil

Packaging Design
for Design Bridge

WLTM Whisky
The brief was to design packaging for a 21st Century scotch that challenges category conventions and appeals to an international female consumer. WLTM whisky doesn't use conventional or obvious Scottish imagery, instead it uses humour to connect with the female consumer. The use of personal ads softens the whisky's image as a male drink by making it more vulnerable in looking for the love of a woman.

Student
Melissa Preston
Tutors
Mick Dean
Myrna Macleod

College
Edinburgh Napier University

MCKENZIE

My dad always said that making whisky was a man's job.

I learned everything there was to know, but I was not a son.
So the world called, and I left.
I learned balance in Japan; poetry at Oxford and design in New York.
As fate will have it, I had to return to Scotland with the passing of my father.
Suddenly I was the sole owner of a business I was never destined to have.
But then I realised something very important:

I cannot make whisky like a man; I can make it better.

Yellow Pencil

Packaging Design
for Design Bridge

McKenzie Scotch Whisky
The brief was to design packaging for a 21st Century scotch that challenges category conventions and appeals to an international female consumer. In my solution, the texture and look of the whisky bottle distinguish it from its competitors on the shelf and at the bar. The accompanying ads can also be written in different languages and vary according to culture, giving flexibility and depth to the brand story.

Student
Batya Raff
Tutors
Jonathan Cane
Shakera Kaloo

College
Vega School of Brand Leadership

Yellow Pencil

Product Design
for Oakley

Click & Switch
The brief was to design the next generation of Oakley eyewear that will allow an athlete to enhance their performance. The purpose of these sunglasses is to enhance the sailor's performance by adjusting rapidly and easily to the frequently changing light conditions when sailing. The athlete simply needs to pull the lenses down and rotate them to fit on the glasses' arms. This allows users to switch colours or lens type. The visible lenses turn the eyewear into a futuristic and extreme looking product. This illustrates Oakley's brand statement, 'beyond reason'.

Student
Lise Charpentier
Tutor
Paul Sayers

College
Central Saint Martins College of Art and Design

Yellow Pencil

Environmental Design
for IHG

Urban Nest
The brief was to design a blue-sky vision of a hotel room of the future for one of IHG's hotels. This room was designed for people who don't have the time to get away to the countryside, but still want to experience it. The Urban Nest brings a sense of calm and serenity to the city for the busy public to experience.

Student
Elizabeth Beal
Tutors
Paul Blindell
Penny Sykes

College
University of Huddersfield

Yellow Pencil

Environmental Design
for IHG

Hermitage
The brief was to design a blue-sky vision of a hotel room of the future for one of IHG's hotels. Hermitage is a transient hotel solution offering mobile rooms that enable a high-end experience in areas that are normally inaccessible by conventional hotels. The rooms are moved to different locations according to guests' requirements. The idea is a response to current techno-social trends in combination with a more holistic analysis of trends in the hospitality market. Hermitage capitalises on an emerging market for techno-escapism combined with the predicted increase in value of sensitive, natural areas as access to them decreases.

Student
Daniel Sunden
Tutors
Elio Caccavale
Don McIntyre
Mil Stricevic

College
Glasgow
School of Art

Yellow Pencil

Environmental Design
for IHG

Algae Suite
The brief was to design a blue-sky vision of a hotel room of the future for one of IHG's hotels. My aim was to create a clinical yet natural design for a city hotel room where guests would revitalise. The building's façade is made out of a glass pipe structure that resembles the network of veins in a leaf. These pipes are filled with water, and inside algae microorganisms grow and produce oxygen, biomass and biofuel. This energy is used to fuel the building, making it self-sufficient. The structure is a natural haven, sealed in an urban environment. The Algae Suite's comfortable and revitalising atmosphere would give guests an experience they want to repeat and recommend to friends.

Student
Linda Halaszova
Tutors
Karl Foster
Valerie Mace

College
London College of
Communication, UAL

Yellow Pencil

Installation Design
for Coutts

The Coutts Canvas
The brief was to create an installation that showcases the extraordinary Coutts archive. My installation is an interactive wall-hung art piece, which uses IR and CMOS motion sensors to respond to the movements of those walking past. It is designed to arouse the curiosity of the user, by instilling a sense of play in the way the assets are revealed. The innovative approach uses new technologies to engage the user with the Coutts archive, revealing the company's rich history within a modern context. The concept behind the canvas brings value to the newly designed logo and reinforces the Coutts brand within the user's mind.

Student	College
Giles Pearson	University College Falmouth
Tutors	
Bryan Clark	
Jon Unwin	

Yellow Pencil

Social Design
for Helen Hamlyn Centre for Design

Agil
The brief was to design a product, service, communication or environment to help someone who has suddenly become dependent on help for everyday tasks in their own home. Walking is a basic need of our locomotor system. For elderly people or those recovering from injuries, it is excellent exercise to stay fit and healthy. Agil is an adaptive walking aid with responsive and flexible polymer support structures designed to maintain a high level of freedom and sensitivity during walking. Agil allows for a natural walking motion since it enables a more even distribution of body weight, thus creating an equilibrium that reduces the chance of falling. With Agil, walking can remain dynamic and spirited, thus promoting health or supporting a recovery process.

Student	College
Sebastian Reichel	Weißensee School of Art Berlin
Tutors	
Prof Helmut Staubach	
Prof Carola Zwick	

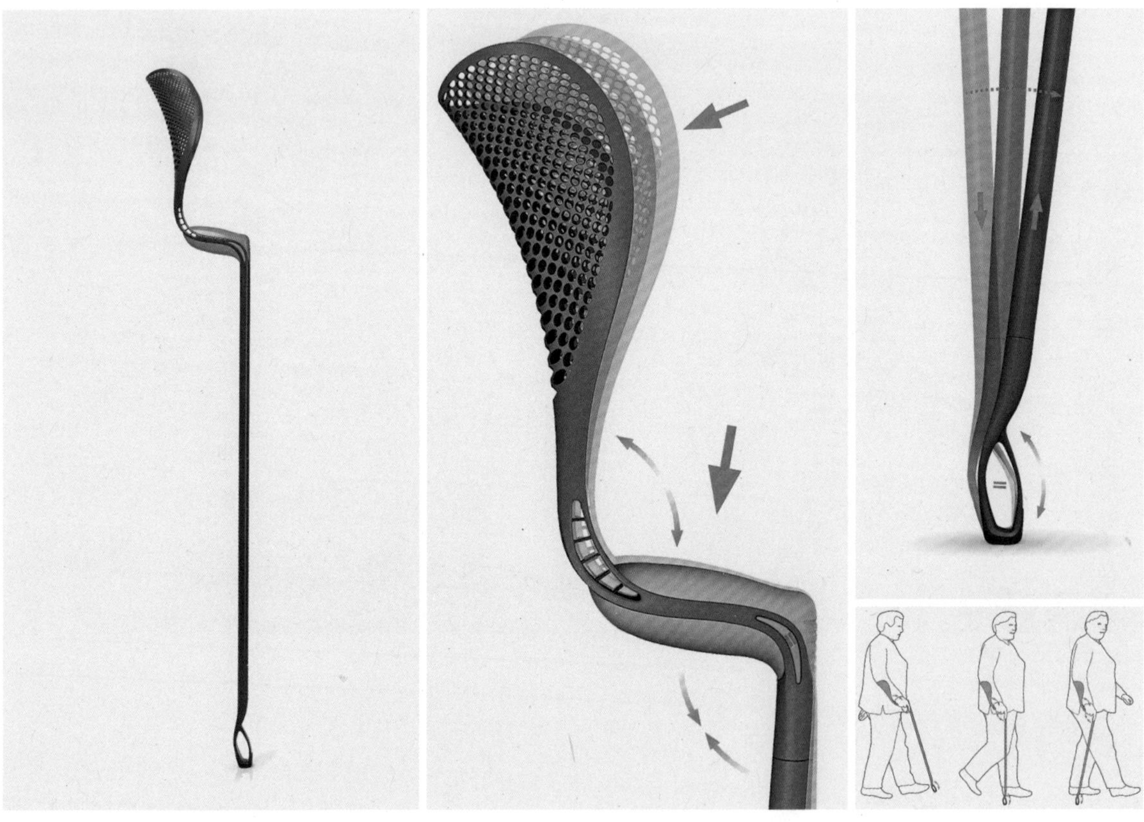

Yellow Pencil

Moving Image
for HP

Love is Not for Sale?
The brief was to create a moving image piece to bring to life people's creative workstations. We decided to make a 'mockumentary'. The movie was made using mobile technologies and by asking people around the world to share their experience, feelings and thoughts about modern ways of creating. We were fascinated to hear things that are so true; that laptops and other devices are not just pieces of plastic and iron – we love them, and we have relationships with them.

Students
Yana Mironova
Zhanna Nosova
Lidia Velles
Tutors
Dmitry Karpov
Anton Yarusov

College
British Higher School of Art and Design

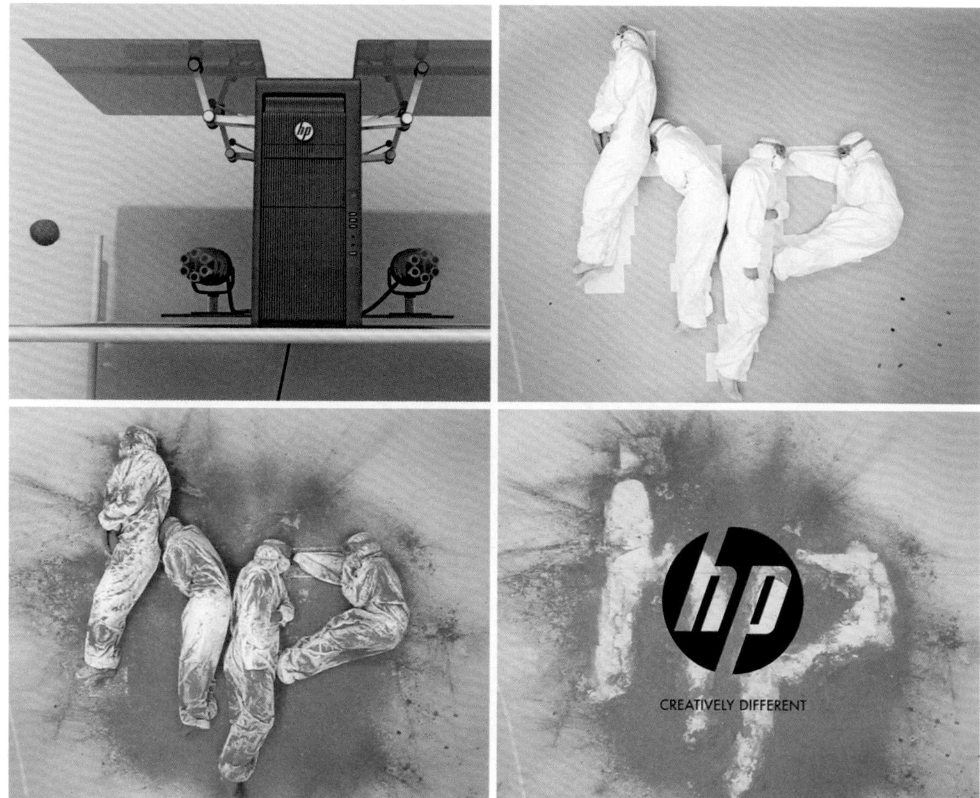

Yellow Pencil

Moving Image
for HP

HP Creatively Different
The brief was to create a moving image piece to bring to life people's creative workstations. HP Creatively Different is a fun, out of the box approach to how designers can use HP Workstations to aid ideas within the design process. Our piece of moving image shows an HP Workstation unfold to reveal paint-ball firing missiles. We follow the paint balls until they explode on white suited bodies – creating the HP logo.

Student
Martin Craster
Tutors
Gary Peploe
Tash Willcocks

College
University of Salford

Yellow Pencil

Illustration
for Little White Lies

The Tinker Tailor Soldier Spy Issue
The brief was to create the cover for Little White Lies magazine choosing one of 2011's five biggest films. This illustration for Tinker Taylor Soldier Spy focuses on the secrecy and distorted perception surrounding George Smiley's character. This led to a decision to incorporate the theme of being 'hidden in plain sight'. The smoke represents both the conceptual and visual styling of the film and, in conjunction with the typography, the idea of revealing information is reinforced. The hand-rendered style, using white pencil on black paper, was chosen to reflect the 'old-school' nature of Smiley's investigative methods. The illustration's composition ultimately aims to portray Smiley's intense nature and determination.

Student
Francesca Hotchin
Tutors
Fabio Fragiacomo
Alan Oliver

College
University of Leeds

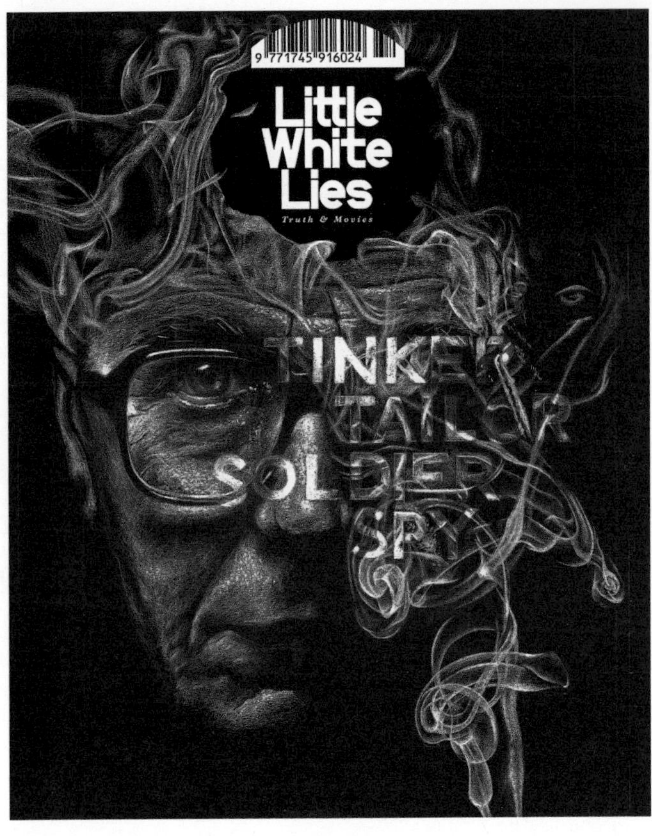

Yellow Pencil

Illustration
for Little White Lies

The Black Swan Issue
The brief was to create the cover for Little White Lies magazine choosing one of 2011's five biggest films. I chose the movie Black Swan. With this image I was aiming to capture the beauty but also the surreality of the main character Nina's transformation in the film. I wanted to present a striking image that was quietly dramatic without trying to recreate the melodrama of the film itself.

Student
Rupert Smissen
Tutor
Glyn Brewerton

College
Norwich University
College of the Arts

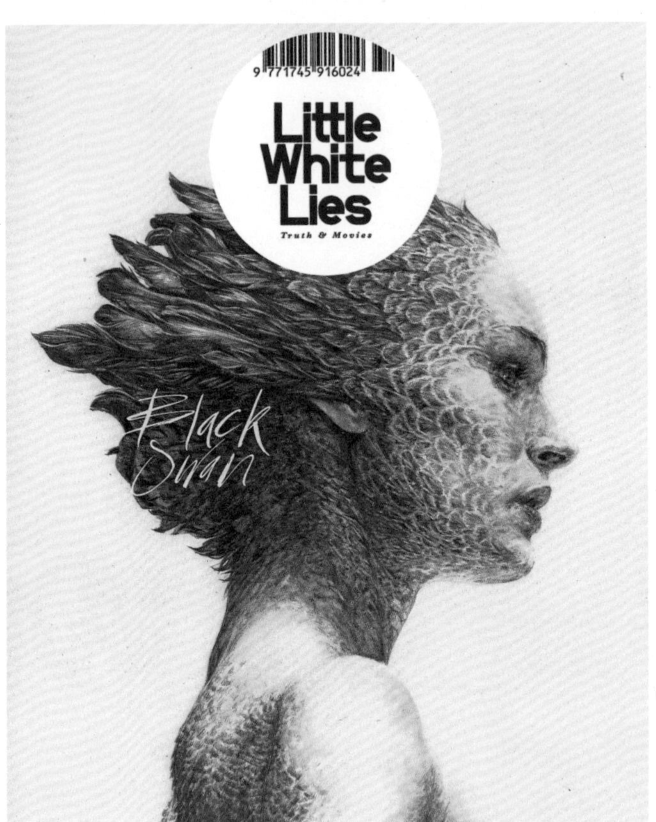

Yellow Pencil

Photography
for Rankin

Clothes Wearing Humans
The brief was to bring to life a 2D image using texture. The world of fashion is natural and close to humans. It's a reflection of our inner world, state of mind, charisma, identity and self-expression. Skin is the appearance of a person; in fact, it is clothing for our body. The material as a skin covers our body and has an intimate relationship with the wearer. This provocative collection represents a mystical world in which the roles are changing, where the structure is absolutely different: a world where clothes wear humans.

Student
Michael Skachkov
Tutors
Laura Parke
Tim Simmons

College
British Higher School of Art and Design

Yellow Pencil

Photography
for Rankin

Landmark
The brief was to bring to life a 2D image using texture. In the densely populated city of Hong Kong, buildings move vertically up towards the sky. On these vertically extending planes, the hidden landmarks of the city can be found. These imaginative shots take an unusual angle and explore architectural identities by comparing the textural qualities revealed.

Student
Eason Page
Tutor
Jeffy Leung

College
City University of Hong Kong

Black Pencil in Direct

Direct Response/Ambient
LOWE/SSP3
for the Ministry of Defence, Colombia

Rivers of Light

The Rivers of Light campaign of December 2011 was a nationwide endeavour to persuade the river-based guerrilla fighters of Colombia to demobilise. We asked friends and relatives of the fighters to send letters and gifts, inviting the rebel soldiers to leave their weapons and come home for Christmas. In a carefully planned military operation, the messages were sealed in airtight, solar powered capsules, and placed in nine rivers in guerrilla-occupied areas across Colombia. By nightfall, LEDs in the capsules began to glow and illuminated the rivers as they floated downstream toward the rebel camps. Testaments from former fighters indicated that Christmas was an important time, even for revolutionaries, and it was hoped that the Rivers of Light would stir a longing for home. The president and people of Colombia also contributed personal messages and a total of 6,823 capsules reached the combatants. Between December and January, one guerrilla fighter demobilised every six hours and returned home to reunite with their family.

Art Director
Carlos Andres Rodriguez Monroy
Copywriters
Mario Lagos
Sergio Leon
Creative Director
Jaime Duque
Executive Creative Director
Jose Miguel Sokoloff
Advertising Agency
LOWE/SSP3
Account Handlers
Emiliano Arango
Juan Pablo García
Client
Ministry of Defence, Colombia

VOTE TO CLOSE
TROY LIBRARY
AUG. 2nd
BOOK BURNING
PARTY
AUG. 5th
facebook.com/BookBurningParty

TOUCH THE RAINBOW

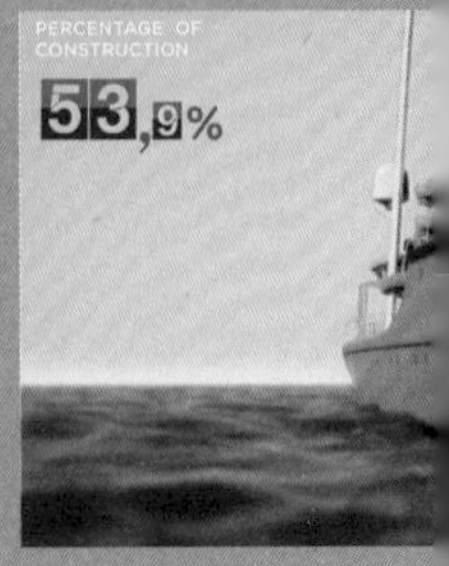
PERCENTAGE OF
CONSTRUCTION
53,9%

KAISER CHIEFS

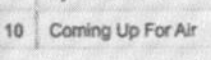
YOUR ALBUM
1 Child Of The Jago
2 I Dare You
3 Fly On The Wall
4 Dead Or In Serious Trouble
5 Saying Something
6 When All Is Quiet
7 Starts With Nothing
8 Things Change
9 My Place Is Here
10 Coming Up For Air

YOU CAN STILL
FORWARD
THIS MESSAGE
TO ALL YOUR OTHER FRIENDS WITH OUR EMAIL TOOL

pepsi

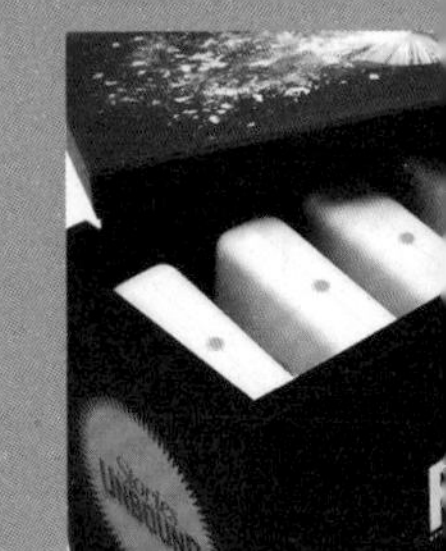

John M. Brannan
1865-1882
John Pope
1882-1886
Alfred Terry
1886-1888

TA FOR
THE
EXTRA
DAY
OFF

A.R.

sky ATLANTIC HD

DRAWING HERE
Peter Pen
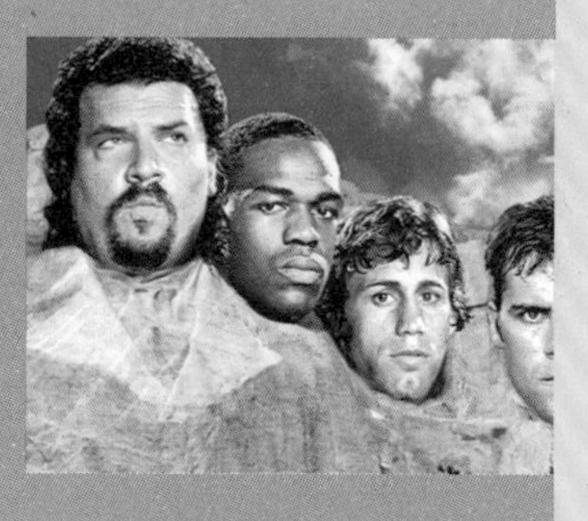

Advertising

2355

1

2

3

4

5

6

7

8

9

10

11

12

13

14

15

16

Jury Foreman
1. Robert Greenberg
R/GA New York

2. Valerie Cheng
JWT Singapore

3. Juliana Constantino
AgenciaClick Isobar

4. Ben Mooge
Work Club

5. Jon Dranger
DDB Stockholm

6. Koichiro Tanaka
Projector Tokyo

7. Abi Ellis
LBi

8. Russ Tucker
Tequila\Digital Sydney

9. Jan Pautsch
Aperto

10. Rob Schwartz
TBWA\Chiat\Day
Los Angeles

11. Dominic Goldman
BBH London

12. Ian Kerrigan
Gyro

13. Pepa Rojo
Grey Group Madrid

14. Michael Tabtabai
Wieden+Kennedy
Portland

15. Natalie Lam
McCann Erickson
New York

16. Tiffany Rolfe
Crispin Porter +
Bogusky Los Angeles

facebook
Search
SHOP SMALL
SM
SMALL BUSINESS SATURDAY.
NOV 26
AMERICAN EXPRESS

Small Business Saturday® ▸ Get Involved
Company
Are you a Small Business Owner? Get free tools for the day.
PLEDGE YOUR SUPPORT FOR
SMALL BUSINESS SATURDAY.
NOV 26

First there was Black Friday, then Cyber Monday. **Now, there's the 2nd annual Small Business Saturday,** the day people support small businesses. Pledge to Shop Small℠ on Nov 26th. If millions of Americans shop small, it could be huge.
"I PLEDGE TO SHOP SMALL"
Tell your friends where you'll shop on Nov 26
SHARE THIS
★ SHOP SMALL AND GET $25 BACK ★

2012
Barack Obama
Follow
@BarackObama
Today, support small businesses in your community by shopping at your favorite local stores. #SmallBusinessSaturday.

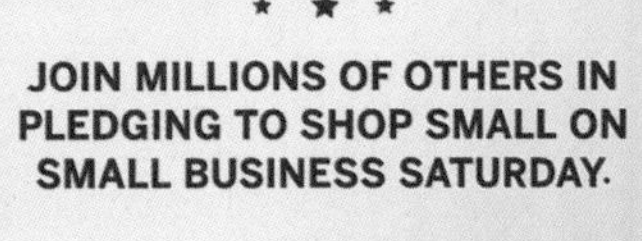

JOIN MILLIONS OF OTHERS IN PLEDGING TO SHOP SMALL ON SMALL BUSINESS SATURDAY.

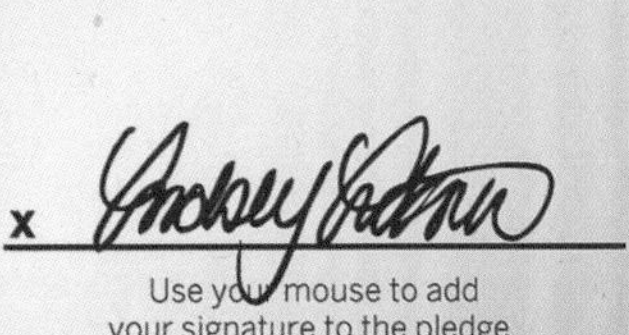

x
Use your mouse to add your signature to the pledge.

Yellow Pencil in Digital Advertising

Integrated Digital Campaigns
Crispin Porter + Bogusky Boulder
for American Express

Small Business Gets an Official Day

In 2010, American Express created Small Business Saturday, a new shopping day right after Black Friday. For 2011, the goal was clear: to cement Small Business Saturday as an official shopping day. American Express rallied business owners, consumers, and public officials to help. They created tools to help business owners reach more customers and to help customers find small businesses to shop at. Businesses were given everything they would need to promote the day, including badges, posters and social marketing tools. A digital kit featured a YouTube video maker for businesses to make their own ads, a Facebook page builder, and a way to launch online Shop Small deals through Foursquare. Ultimately, 103 million Americans shopped small, and the US Senate declared it an official day, cementing Small Business Saturday as an official part of the holiday shopping season.

Creative Directors
Matt D'Ercole
Dan Ligon
Tom Miller
Allen Richardson
Atit Shah
Executive Creative Director
Mark Taylor
Group Creative Director
Chris Kindt
Chief Creative Officers
Lincoln Bjorkman
Rob Reilly
Art Directors
Mike Blanch
Daniel Burke
Josh Gross
Laura Potsic
Directors
Robert Rakowitz
Leela Ramdeen
Wade Rifkin
Seth Spievogel

Copywriters
Adrian Alexander
Kelly McCormick
Jens McNaughton
Senior Producer
Matt Hantz
Advertising Agency
Crispin Porter + Bogusky Boulder
Strategic Director
Andrew Teagle
Account Director
Shaunn D'Alessandro
Marketing Directors
Roger Box
Alex Jacobs
Mark Kiernan
Client
American Express

Yellow Pencil in Digital Advertising

Digital Solutions & Use of Social Media
Wieden+Kennedy London
for the Kaiser Chiefs

The Kaiser Chiefs Bespoke Album Creation Experience
Conversation between Oli, from Wieden+Kennedy, and Ricky, from the Kaiser Chiefs, over fish and chips:
'Can we make people LOVE albums again?'
'Anybody ever done a bespoke one?'
'Somebody must have.' (Check Google.)
'Nope.'
'Well, let's do that then.'
'Let's write 20 songs and let people pick ten.'
'They could make their own artwork.'
'What if they could SELL their unique albums?'
'People share stuff anyway. Let's pay them.'
'£1 per album.'
'We could give them tools to sell it on social media.'
'Their own websites.'
'Banner ads for their blogs.'
'Posters.'
'Reward the top sellers.'
'Is any of this even possible?'
'We'll need a website.'
'Can it look old-fashioned?'
'Yes.'
'OK.'

Creative Director
Oli Beale
Executive Creative Directors
Tony Davidson
Kim Papworth
Interactive Director
Andy Cameron
Creative Technologist
Joao Wilbert
Designer
Jon Harris
Director
Andy Bruntel
Producer
Rachel Dargavel
Interactive Producers
Chris Binks
Michelle Cox
Agency Executive Producer
Danielle Stewart

Creative Agency
Wieden+Kennedy London
Production Company
Somesuch & Co
Interactive Production Company
Specialmoves
Planners
Alex Franklin
Jennifer Lewis
Project Manager
Alex Franklin
Account Director
Hanne Haugen
Public Relations Manager
Lois Newcombe
Client
Kaiser Chiefs

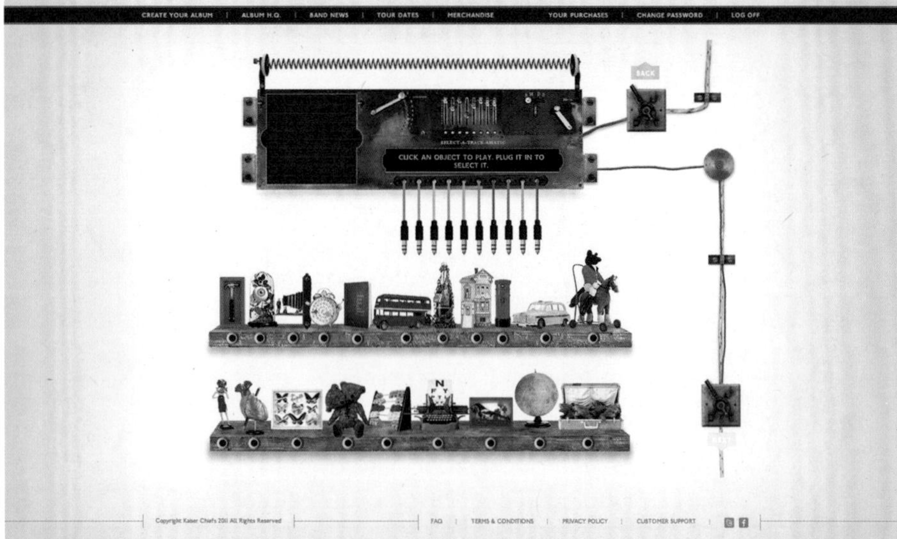

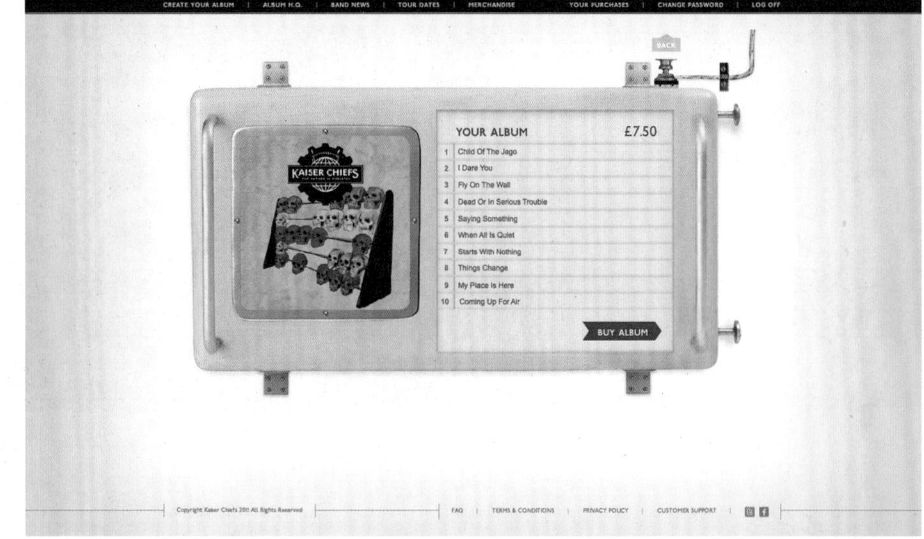

Yellow Pencil in Digital Advertising

Web Films
72andSunny USA
for K-Swiss

K-Swiss: MFCEO
In the 2010 campaign, K-Swiss signed controversial fictional 'athlete' Kenny Powers to an endorsement deal. In the 2011 campaign, Kenny took over K-Swiss as MFCEO (Mother F***ing Chief Executive Officer), reshaping the company in his image and enlisting the world's baddest athletes to help him unsuck the sports world.

Director
Jody Hill
Copywriter
Matt Heath
Designer
Jay Kamath
Creative Directors
Barton Corley
Matt Murphy
Chief Creative Officer
Glenn Cole
Agency Producer
Danielle Tarris
Executive Producer
Michael Sagol
Photographer
Mike Piscitelli

Editors
Matt Murphy
Graham Turner
Production Company
Caviar LA
Visual Effects Company
Animal
Advertising Agency
72andSunny USA
Editing
Final Cut
Los Angeles
Brand Director
Matt Rohmer
Client
K-Swiss

Nomination in Digital Advertising

Integrated Digital Campaigns
Leo Burnett Detroit
for the Troy Public Library

Book Burning Party
The city of Troy in Michigan couldn't afford to sustain its library, so it scheduled a vote for a tax increase. A strong anti-tax group waged a dominating campaign against it. Posing as a political group, we posted signs around town that said, 'Vote to close Troy Library August 2nd, book burning party August 5th'. We invited everyone to our Facebook page, adding Twitter, Foursquare, online classified ads, flyers and more to drive engagement. The campaign became international news as outcry over the idea of burning the library's books drowned out the opposition and galvanised support for the library – which won by a landslide.

Creative Directors
Glen Hilzinger
Bob Veasey
Executive Creative Director
Peter McHugh
Art Directors
Derek Tent
Bob Veasey
Copywriters
Mike Davis
Glen Hilzinger
Rob Thiemann
Agency Producers
Tony Booth
Erik Zaar
Creative Technologist
John McClaire
Advertising Agency
Leo Burnett Detroit
Project Manager
Jennifer Samra
Client
Troy Public Library

Nomination in Digital Advertising

Campaign Sites
Hakuhodo
for Google

OK Go – All Is Not Lost
We developed a music video unlike any other: an immersive, interactive, multi-window rendering of OK Go's 'All Is Not Lost', showcasing HTML5 and Google Chrome. A music video where you can enter a message and see it brought to life by dancers within the video. OK Go and Pilobolus dancers are filmed through a clear floor, making increasingly complex shapes, and eventually words. Different shots are rendered in different browser windows that move, resize and realign throughout the piece. Original message cards and videos are generated, which users can share with the world.

Interactive Design Agency
TYO Interactive Design
Digital Design Agency
Kaibutsu
Digital Production Companies
1→10 design
FutureK

Advertising Agencies
Aoi Advertising
Promotion
Hakuhodo
Client
Google
Brand
Google Chrome

Nomination in Digital Advertising

Web Films
BBDO Canada
for Wrigley Canada

Touch the Rainbow
We invited people to see what happens when they touch the rainbow. To do that, we didn't invent new touchscreen technology, or anything for that matter. We just asked people to touch their computer screens and watch as their finger played a starring role in five interactive online commercials. In the process we did manage to invent one thing: a completely new way to interact with an interactive medium.

Directors
Jeff Low
Chris Woods
Art Director
Mike Donaghey
Writer
Chris Joakim
Executive Creative Directors
Peter Ignazi
Carlos Moreno
Associate Creative Directors
Mike Donaghey
Chris Joakim
Producer
Dwight Phipps
Agency Producer
Ann Caverly
Digital Producer
Amy Miranda
Editors
Griff Henderson
Raj Ramnouth
Sound Designer
Rocco Gagliese
Digital Strategist
Zach Klein
Production Company
OPC
Digital Production Companies
Lunch
Pixel Pusher
Visual Effects Company
AXYZ
Advertising Agency
BBDO Canada
Colour Correction
Notch
Editing
PosterBoy Edit
Account Executive
Bhreagh Rathbun
Account Manager
Chitty Krishnappa
Marketing Manager
Laura Amantea
Marketing Director
Dan Alvo
Client
Wrigley Canada
Brand
Skittles

Cat

War Finger

Hitch Hiker

Skittles Girl

Cage Cop

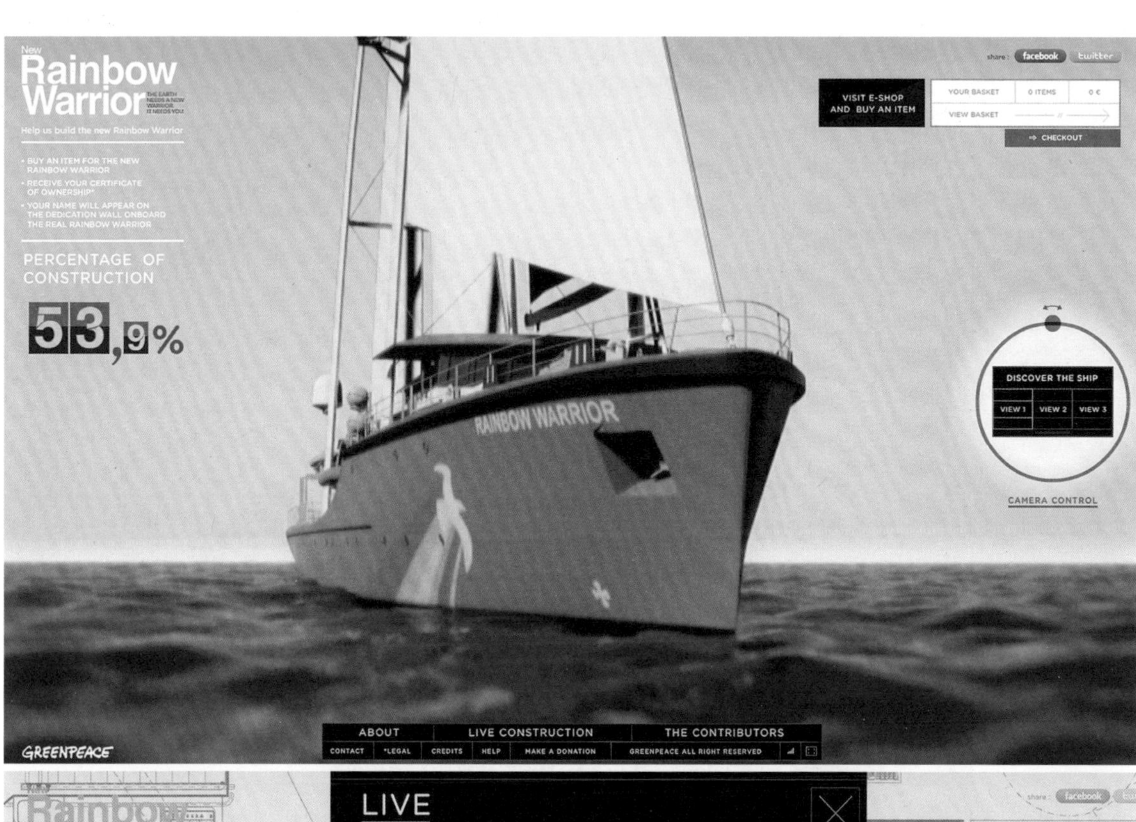

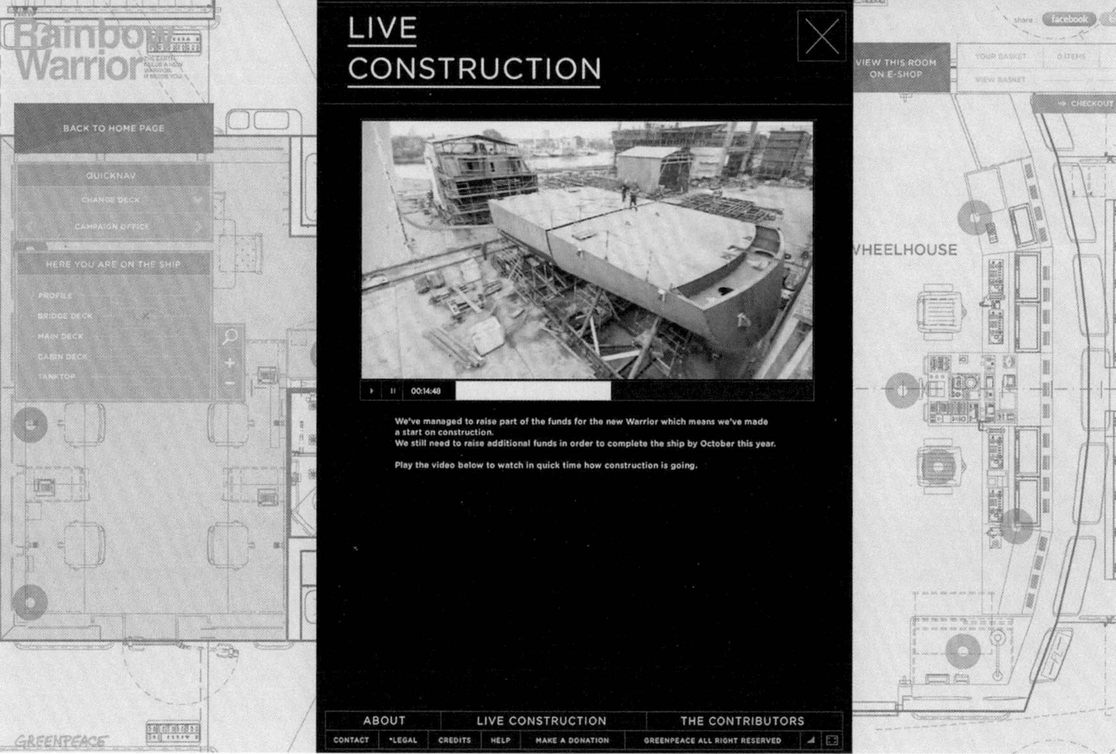

Nomination in Digital Advertising

Digital Solutions & Use of Social Media
DDB Paris
for Greenpeace

A New Warrior
Since 1978, the Rainbow Warrior allowed Greenpeace to gain numerous victories for the protection of our planet. But Greenpeace needed to replace it. The new Rainbow Warrior is the first ever purpose-built environmental campaigning vessel. It will play a key role in Greenpeace's future campaigns. We wanted to raise funds to finance its construction and involve all the people who want to be part of this story. We made people purchase and own a piece of the new Rainbow Warrior by launching an e-commerce website: anewwarrior.com. 400,000 items went on sale, ranging from 1€ to 7,000€. After payment, buyers received a certificate of ownership – thousands of these were posted on social networks, creating a media burst. The new Rainbow Warrior has now been constructed and was officially launched on 14th October 2011.

Art Director
Benjamin Marchal
Executive Creative Director
Alexandre Hervé
Copywriter
Olivier Lefebvre
Production Company
Make Me Pulse
Digital Production Company
Les 84

Advertising Agency
DDB Paris
Visual Effects Company
Virtek
Sound Design
Panarama
Account Managers
Paul Ducré
Xavier Mendiola
Client
Greenpeace

Nomination in Digital Advertising

Animation & Illustration for Digital Advertising
kempertrautmann
for edding International

Wall of Fame
On the occasion of its 50th anniversary, pen manufacturer edding wanted to bring the brand to the attention of illustrators and creative types alike, and become a topic of conversation in a place where these people spend most of their time: online. The 'Wall of Fame' is an interactive live drawing board that features ten pens with which you can immortalise yourself. In the first six months alone, a collaborative piece of art was created consisting of more than 150,000 drawings by people from over 150 different countries. And the wall continues to grow.

Animation
LIGA_01
COMPUTERFILM
Creative Directors
Christoph Gähwiler
Simon Jasper Philipp
Stefan Walz
Gerrit Zinke
Art Directors
Simon Jasper Philipp
Florian Schimmer
Stefan Walz
Associate Art Directors
Tobias Lehment
David Scherer
Copywriters
Christoph Gähwiler
Michael Götz
Samuel Weiß

Interactive & Digital Production Company
demodern | digital design studio
Post Production
flavouredgreen/ PX Group
Advertising Agency
kempertrautmann
Sound Design
Supreme Music
Account Managers
Andrea Bison
Elisabeth Einhaus
Niklas Kruchten
Client
edding International
Brand
edding

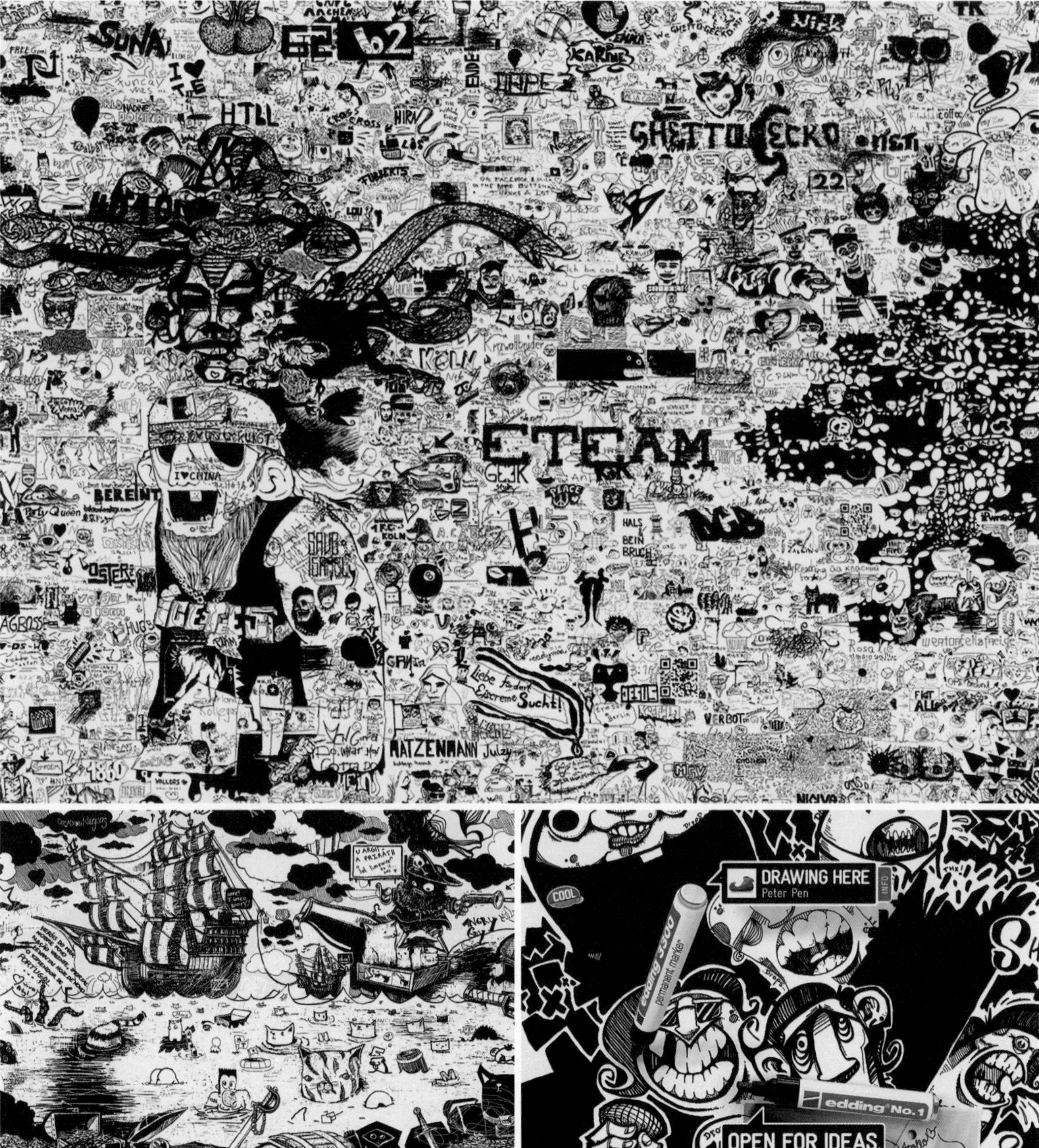

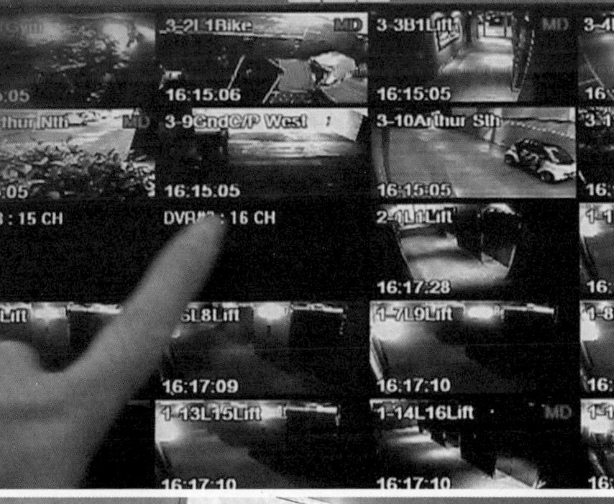

Integrated Digital Campaigns
Naked Communications Australia
for the Art Series Hotels

Steal Banksy
The Art Series Hotels in Australia is an art themed hotel chain. Inspired by Melbourne's history of art theft and the fact that thefts from hotels are quite common, we hung a Banksy and challenged people to 'Stay the night. Steal the art'. The signed Banksy was 'No Ball Games', which was once stolen off the streets of London using an angle grinder. Clues were seeded via social media, theft attempts were recorded and journalists documented their own attempts. The Banksy was eventually stolen and tracked via a GPS chip hidden in the art to announce the successful thieves.

Creative Directors
Seehan Moodley
Paul Swann
Designer
Gerard Hindle
Digital Producer
Lach Hall
Strategic Directors
Matt Houltham
Jono Key

Account Executive
Aliya Hassan
Public Relations Manager
Larissa Rembisz
Planner
Adam Ferrier
Client
Art Series Hotels

Integrated Digital Campaigns
Ogilvy & Mather New York
for IBM

Smarter City
For the first time in history, half the world lives in cities. So how do we keep traffic flowing? Protect citizens while protecting their privacy? The technology to solve these problems exists. But without public support, our governments can't initiate these changes. Smarter City is an immersive, interactive experience designed to show how cities all over the world are using advanced technology to help address some of the biggest problems facing our planet. Here, visitors can watch IBM's best documentaries, download reports, explore product demos, and share with colleagues.

Creative Directors
Ryan Blank
Mike Hahn
Executive Creative Director
Susan Westre
Flash Programmer
Guojian Wu
Flash Developers
Gicheol Lee
Tim Murray
Art Director
Sarah Nguyen
Copywriter
Andrew Mellen
Illustrator
Thomas Porostocky
Computer Graphics Artists
Joe DiGerolamo
John Dretzka
Robert Paynter
Jason Shevchuk
Digital Producers
Aneela Idnani
Tracy Moore
Music Producer
Karl Westman
Advertising Agency
Ogilvy & Mather New York
Project Manager
Ian Crowley
Client
IBM

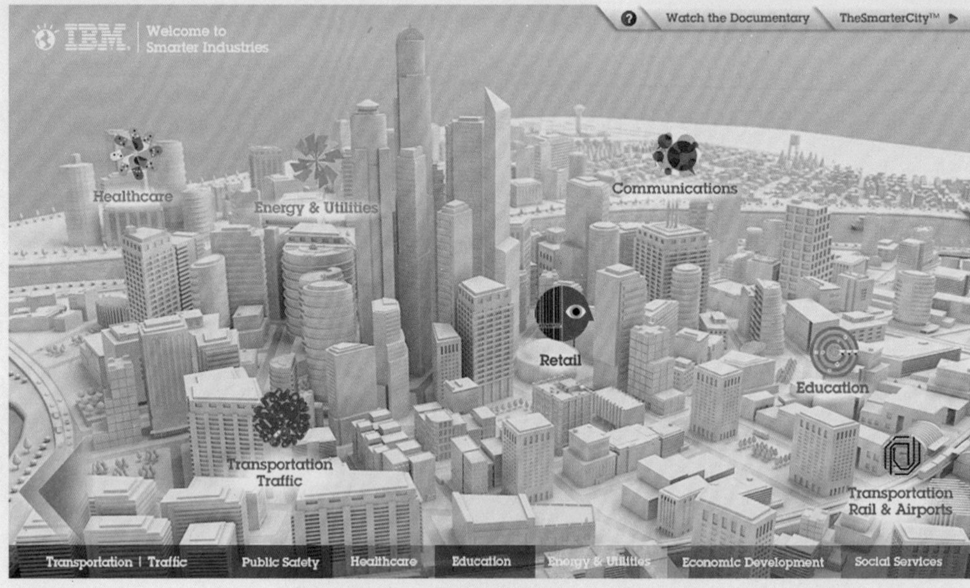

Digital Advertising
JWT New York
for Kraft Foods

Be Ridiculously Long Lasting
We created a simple, yet addictive game that challenged people to be as ridiculously long lasting as Stride chewing gum. Players have to hold their mouse down on a moving red button, while a member of the Stride marketing team moves the button around the frame with increasing speed. While participants muster every ounce of dexterity and concentration to stay on the button, they must also resist rolling off to click on cute cat and baby videos. A combination of challenging game play and silly content got many to spend a ridiculously long time (67 minutes in one case) with a ridiculously long lasting brand.

Creative Director
Mason Hedgecoth
Executive Creative Director
Tom Christmann
Chief Creative Officer
Peter Nicholson
Technical Director
William Mincy
Flash Developer
Matt Severin
Art Director
Kevin Li
Copywriter
Ethan Schmidt
Digital Producer
Vanessa Scanlan
Head of Interactive Production
Pam Scheideler
Production Director
Matt Anderson
Digital Strategist
Dan Bennett
Director of Photography
Aaron Platt
Content Producer
Angela Buck
Editor
Blake Bogosian
Advertising Agency
JWT New York
Post Production
Impact
Sound Design
JWTwo
Media Agency
MediaVest
Business Director
Christian Hughes
Account Executive
Greg Ahern
Account Manager
Mona Munayyer
Account Director
Lauren Hanin
Project Managers
Elias Kakomanolis
Scott Kogos
Client
Kraft Foods
Brand
Stride

Digital Solutions & Use of Social Media
Whybin\TBWA\Tequila Sydney
for Mars Petcare

Dog-A-Like
It's amazing how many dog owners look like their dogs. Based on this insight, we custom-built a canine analysis engine for a phone and Facebook app called 'Dog-A-Like'. It not only matches your facial features perfectly with a dog from the live Pet Rescue database, it also lets you adopt them when they would otherwise be put down. Sadly, over 100,000 shelter dogs are euthanised every year in Australia because people think they are damaged and find it difficult visiting shelter homes to adopt. If we couldn't bring people to the shelter dogs, we decided to bring the shelter dogs to the people.

Executive Creative Directors
Dave Bowman
Matty Burton
Digital Creative Director
Russ Tucker
Technical Director
David Cox
Designers
Aliza Nordin
Prentice Porter
Art Director
Hannes Ciatti
Copywriter
Dean Hamilton
Digital Producer
James Kavanagh
Agency Producer
Chris Rollings
Advertising Agency
Whybin\TBWA\Tequila Sydney
Account Director
Andrea Byrne
Client
Mars Petcare
Brand
Pedigree

Digital Solutions & Use of Social Media
Projector
for Intel

The Museum of Me
'The Museum of Me' is an interactive online experience that reveals who you are as a reflection of your Facebook activities. We created this personalised museum exhibit to promote Intel's smart new processor.

Creative Director
Koichiro Tanaka
Design Director
Toru Hayai
Technical Director
Seiichi Saito
Interactive Designer
Ken Murayama
Director
Eiji Tanigawa
Programmers
Hirohisa Mitsuishi
Hajime Sasaki
Designers
Mitsuhiro Azuma
Yuuki Nemoto
Hiroshi Takeyama
Takashi Yasuno
Art Director
Masanori Sakamoto
Writer
Lilia Silva
Producer
Satoshi Takahashi
Video Producer
Keisuke Nishina
Music Producer
Yoko Hata
Music Composer
Takagi Masakatsu
Production Manager
Yoshinari Hama
Project Manager
Shimpei Oshima
Creative Agency
Projector
Production Companies
DELTRO
MountPosition
Rhizomatiks
TAIYO KIKAKU
Client
Intel

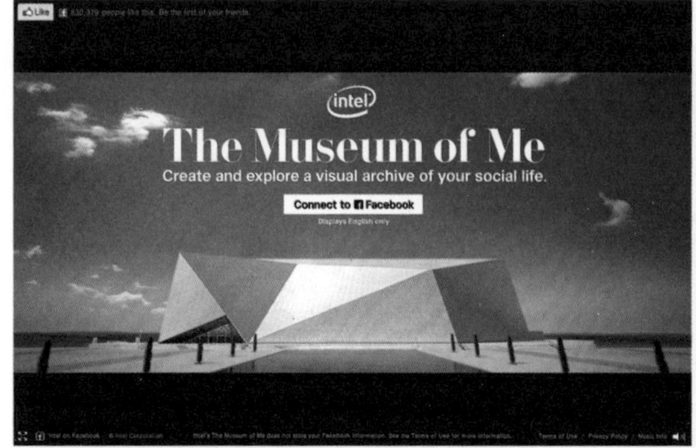

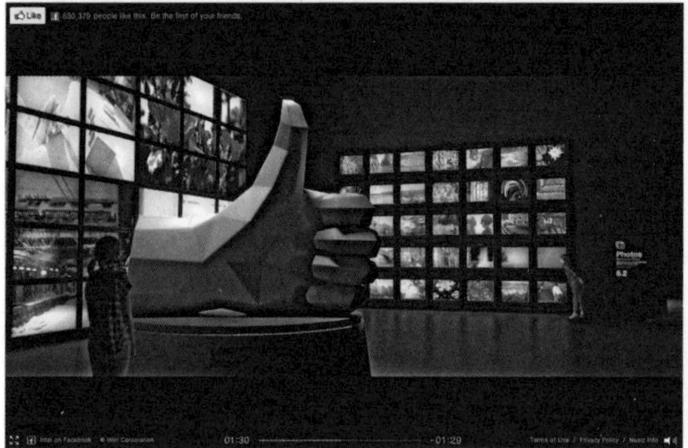

UNDERHEARD
IN NEW YORK
@albert 814
@jessie 550
@putodanny
@awitness 2011
awitness2011
It is raining and cold outside. I dinned in the subway to the sounds of saxaphonist. I am now on my way to an employement interview.
about 6 hours ago via txt
It is raining and cold outside. I had lunch in the subway while listening to the sounds of saxaphonist. I am now on my way to an employe ...
about 6 hours ago via txt
Greetings everyone, I'm pressing towards the mark..
about 24 hours ago via txt
Greetings to all, I am at the employement center hopefully something will come through soon.
3:01 PM Mar 14th via txt
@jenn2173 I think it is a great thing your going back to school. keep going I'm in your corner.
7:39 PM Mar 7th via txt
@jenna2179 Oh the joys of family life, I miss it so.
9:16 AM Mar 6th via txt

Digital Solutions & Use of Social Media
BBH New York
for the NYC Rescue Mission

Underheard in New York
Underheard in New York was created to help the NYC Rescue Mission's ignored homeless residents. We identified four homeless men and gave them prepaid mobile phones to tweet via SMS thoughts and anecdotes from their daily lives. The project built a community of over 18,000 Twitter followers who sent more than 9,000 messages to the men within a single month. Followers volunteered gifts both financial and priceless, from metrocards and part-time jobs, to reconnecting a man with his daughter after eleven years apart. Twitter even voted one of the men's tweets the third most important tweet of 2011.

Creative Directors
Zac Sax
Jessica Shriftman
Technical Director
Brian Moore
Art Director
Willy Wang
Editor
Mark Block
Advertising Agency
BBH New York

Strategic Directors
Heidi Hackemer
Robert Weeks
Account Handler
Saneel Radia
Account Manager
Rosemary Melchoir
Account Director
Dane Larsen
Client
NYC Rescue Mission

Digital Solutions & Use of Social Media
Ogilvy & Mather Sydney & Wunderman Sydney
for Coca-Cola South Pacific

Share a Coke
To help Coca-Cola reconnect with Australians, we printed the 150 most popular Australian names on Coke bottles and invited Australians to 'Share a Coke', helping people come together with the best conversation starter of all – a first name. In just three months, we saw young adult consumption increase by 7% and Facebook traffic increase by 870%.

Creative Directors
Boris Garelja
Brian Merrifield
Executive Creative Director
Chris Ford
Art Directors
Luke Acret
Liam Hillier
Jakub Szymanski
Copywriters
Omid Amidi
Alex Stainton
Producer
Claire McDonald
Advertising Agency
Ogilvy & Mather Sydney

Digital Agency
Wunderman Sydney
Media Agency
Ikon
Account Handlers
Suzie Baker
Vickie Mogensen
Adam Lee
Planners
Gerry Cyron
Damian Damjanovski
Public Relations
One Green Bean
Sales Promotion
Momentum
Client
Coca-Cola South Pacific

Web Films
Cundari Toronto
for BMW Canada

1M Launch Films
BMW had been promoting the joy of driving for a few years. However, the launch of the BMW 1 Series M Coupé, 1M, provided the perfect opportunity to communicate the raw essence of the brand: high performance. This campaign featured films that pushed the limits of possibility with the intention to spark discussion. Part one, 'Walls', showcased the 1M's unbelievable precision driving by threading the needle through silhouettes cut into concrete walls. Part two, 'Helipad', featured the 1M drifting atop the world's highest helipad.

Director
Mike "Mouse" McCoy
Art Director
Raul Garcia
Copywriter
Brian Murray
Creative Director
Brent Choi
Producer
Ryan Slavin
Agency Producer
Daryn Sutherland
Executive Producer
Jeff Rohrer
Special Effects
Sean Cushing
Lance Holte
Stephen Lawes

Editor
Jacob Rosenberg
Sound Designer
Jamey Scott
Advertising Agency
Cundari Toronto
Account Handlers
Ranjan Gill
Daryn Sutherland
Client
BMW Canada

Walls

Helipad

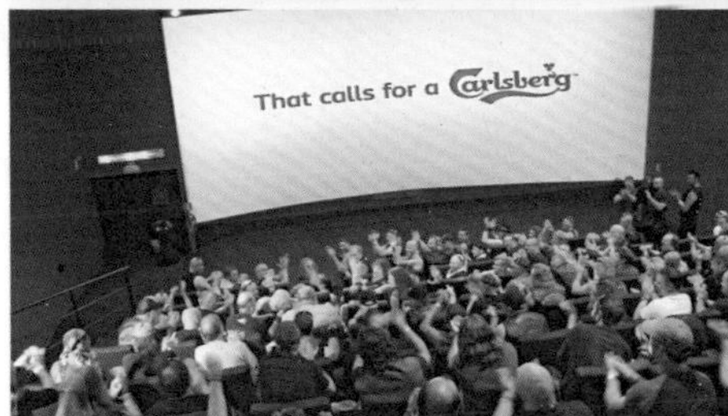

Web Films
Duval Guillaume Brussels
for Carlsberg

Bikers
The launch of Carlsberg's new global strapline, 'That calls for a Carlsberg', positions Carlsberg as a reward for people showing courage. This web film shows how we promoted the brand through directly targeting the brave. A series of unsuspecting couples bought tickets at the Kineopolis Cinema in Brussels, only to find as they walked into the theatre that they were surrounded by hard-core bikers, and only two seats were left. Those that stayed were rewarded with a Carlsberg.

Director
Cecilia Verheyden
Art Director
Koenraad Lefever
Copywriter
Dries De Wilde
Creative Directors
Katrien Bottez
Geoffrey Hantson
Producer
Tatiana Pierre
Production Company
Monodot

Advertising Agency
Duval Guillaume Brussels
Account Handlers
Elke Janssens
Jonathan Moerkens
Brand Managers
Bart Creemers
Igor Nowé
Client
Carlsberg

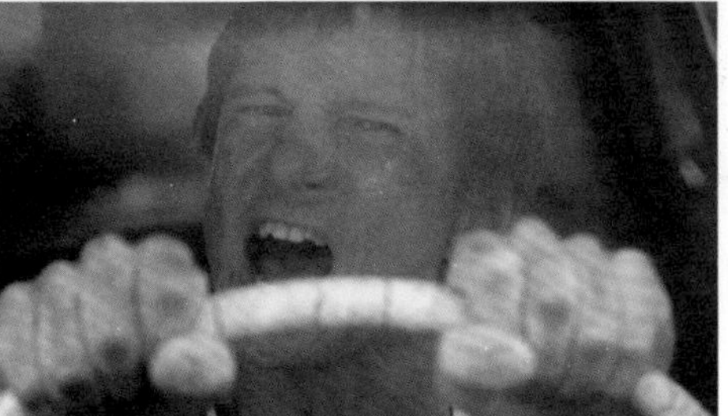

Web Films
Tool of North America
for Little Monster

Take This Lollipop
'Take This Lollipop' was a self-promotional piece by ad agency Little Monster. Fourteen days before Halloween, a Facebook app launched showing a lollipop on screen and the words: 'I dare you'. Once you grant permission, you're taken down into a dark basement, where a sweaty, lurid man logs onto your Facebook page. He scrolls through your profile page, fixated on what he sees. He studies your personal photos, examines your friends list and his grimy hand moves his mouse through your news feeds and personal information (the site is plugging your personal data right into the story). It's an ominous, disturbing and thought-provoking experience... a sort of twisted and frightening fairy tale, personalised.

Director
Jason Zada
Executive Producers
Dustin Callif
Oliver Fuselier
Brian Latt
Developer
Jason Nickel
Digital Production Company
Tool of North America

Advertising Agency
Little Monster
Music Remix
Future Perfect
Client
Little Monster

Web Films
john st.

Catvertising
In November 2011, john st. released a short promotional video announcing the launch of an entirely new advertising model: Catvertising. The video received a million views in just ten days and made Time magazine's 'Top Ten Everything of 2011' list. Even better, it sparked several new business inquiries and a flood of resumes from cat wranglers, cat whisperers and cat talent coordinators. Interviews are still pending.

Directors
Will Beauchamp
Jamie Cussen
Art Director
Kyle Lamb
Copywriter
Kurt Mills
Creative Directors
Stephen Jurisic
Angus Tucker
Producer
Dale Giffen
Production Company
Aircastle Films
Advertising Agency
john st.
Editing
Relish Editorial
Music Arrangement
Vapor Music
Account Manager
Madison Papple
Client
john st.

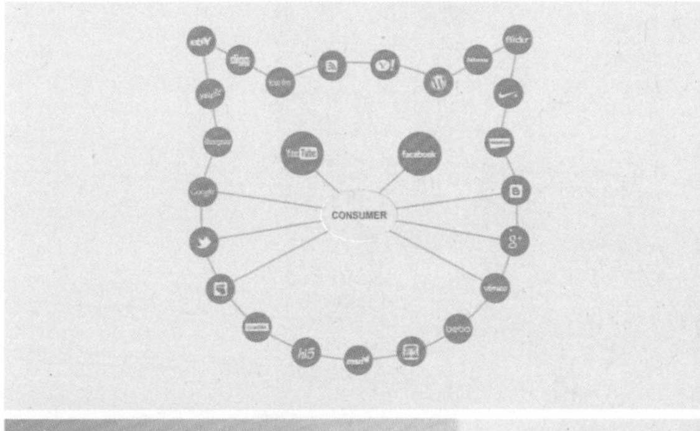

Sound Design & Use of Music
for Digital Advertising
KNARF
for Moment of Silence

The Steve Jobs Moment of Silence
'The Steve Jobs Moment of Silence' is an eight-second silent audio file launched on iTunes and downloadable for 99 cents. The eight seconds symbolise the eight years Steve Jobs fought pancreatic cancer. This small break in our iTunes library reminds us to never forget the man who brought us so much, including the very devices this moment of silence will be played on. All proceeds are donated to several pancreatic cancer organisations.

Creative Director
Frank Anselmo
Designers
Frank Anselmo
Bryan Wolff
Schoemaker
Hyui Yong Kim
Interactive Designer
Yong Wolff
Art Directors
Bryan Wolff
Schoemaker
Hyui Yong Kim
Copywriters
Bryan Wolff
Schoemaker
Hyui Yong Kim
Advertising Agency
KNARF
Client
Moment of Silence

The Steve Jobs Moment of Silence
PAY HOMAGE TO STEVE JOBS WHILE FIGHTING PANCREATIC CANCER

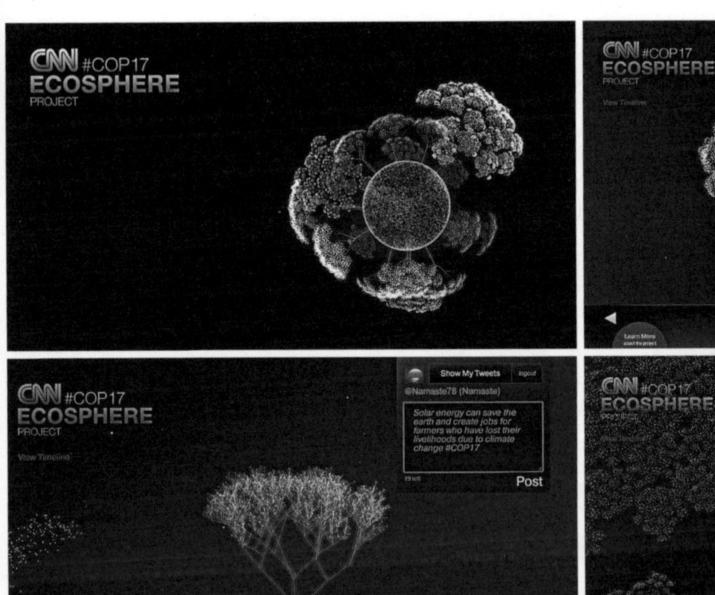

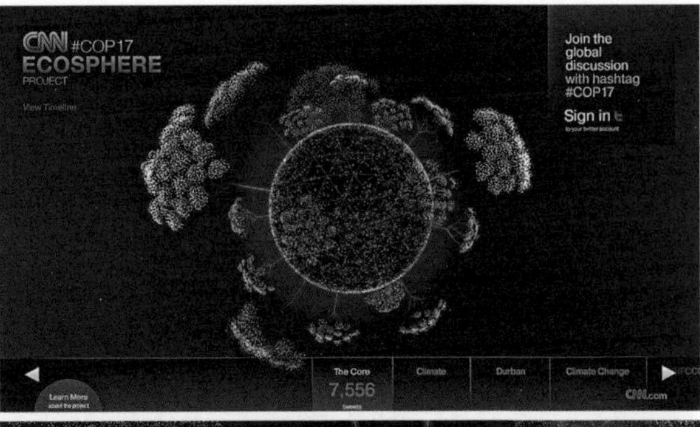

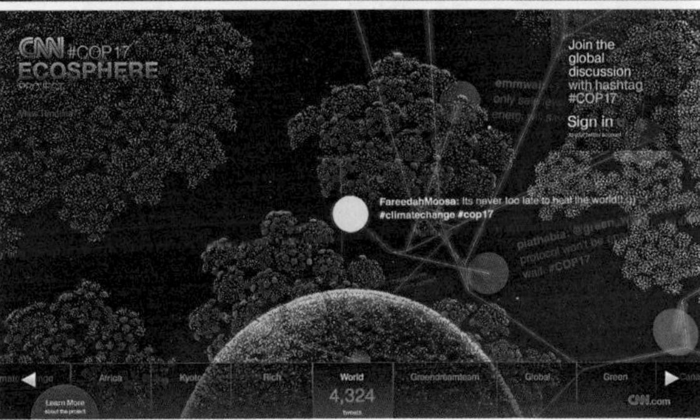

Art Direction for Digital Advertising
HEIMAT Berlin
for Turner Broadcasting System Deutschland

The CNN Ecosphere
The CNN Ecosphere is a digital ecosystem growing from tweets using the hash tag #COP17. It is a living 3D visualisation of the global climate change discussion around the UN COP17 Conference held at the end of 2011. Every tweet tagged with #COP17 becomes part of one of the numerous plants representing topics like sustainability or carbon. Tweets mentioning similar issues were grouped together on branches, while new thoughts were planted as seeds, waiting to grow. Topic plants emerged and withered as trends shifted in the discussion, offering the user a real-time view of the evolving conversation.

Art Directors
Jue Alt
Luc Schurgers
Creative Directors
Guido Heffels
Myles Lord
Designers
Jue Alt
Alexander Suchy
Copywriters
Martien Delfgaauw
Ramin Schmiedekampf
Agency Producer
Jessica Valin
Digital Agencies
Minivegas
Stinkdigital
Advertising Agency
HEIMAT Berlin
Brand Manager
Jörg Buddenberg
Client
Turner Broadcasting System Deutschland
Brand
CNN

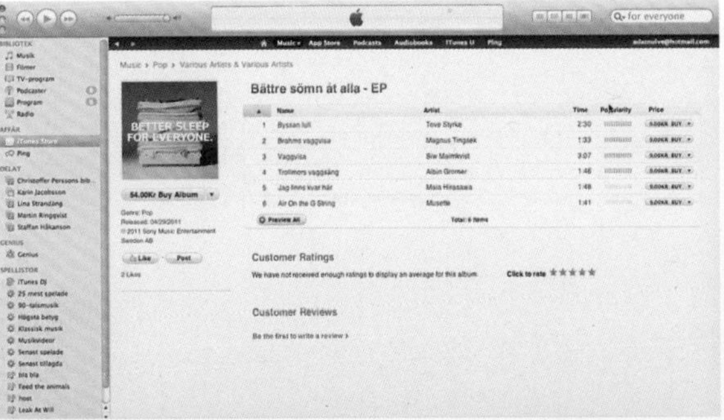

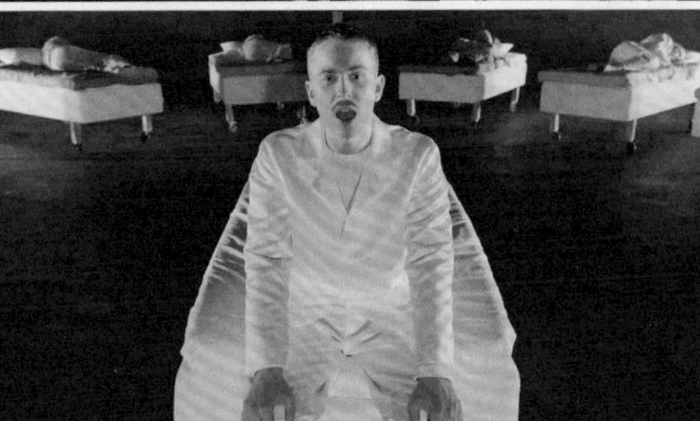

Art Direction for Digital Advertising
Forsman & Bodenfors
for IKEA Sweden

Lullabies
IKEA wanted to revitalise the long running claim for its bed offer: 'Better Sleep for Everyone'. We asked six of Sweden's most talented musicians to compose modern interpretations of classic lullabies. We turned the songs into six music videos each featuring an artist in a bed. We created a site to host the videos and released the songs on an album. With a cover that looked, surprisingly, a lot like a banner for IKEA. Of course, we could follow people as they logged into iTunes and bought our commercials.

Art Directors
Andreas Malm
Adam Ulvegärde
Designer
Christoffer Persson
Copywriters
Elisabeth Christensson
Fredrik Jansson
Agency Producer
Alexander Blidner
Web Producer
Stefan Thomson
Advertising Agency
Forsman & Bodenfors
Production Companies
Kokokaka
Social Club
Music Composition
Music Super Circus
Account Executive
Hans Andersson
Account Manager
Katarina Klofsten
Planner
Tobias Nordström
Client
IKEA Sweden
Brand
IKEA

Jury Foreman
1. Terry Hunt
Institute of Direct
& Digital Marketing

2. Marco Versolato
DM9DDB Brasil

3. Martin Riesenfelder
Wunderman Germany

4. Selina Ang Sze Woon
OgilvyOne Malaysia

5. Philippe Meunier
Sid Lee Montreal

6. Nicky Bullard
LIDA / M&C Saatchi
London

7. Tony Clewett
Draftfcb

Well-read European seeks accommodation in Perth.

Give the new IKEA catalogue a home, and you'll get monthly rent cheques to spend at the IKEA Store. Sign up at **www.IKEA.com.au**

Terms and conditions apply. See website for details.

Yellow Pencil in Direct

Direct Integrated Campaigns
303Lowe
for IKEA

Rent
The IKEA catalogue is often discarded by consumers shortly after reading it, but more catalogues in homes equals more sales. How do you keep the 2012 catalogue in Aussie homes for the whole year? Our idea was the first catalogue that pays you rent for being in your home. Visits to ikea.com.au went up 30% and sales 59% in the first week; we achieved 50,000 sign ups in the first three weeks; $2million in rent cheques have been mailed; 6.8% of households signed up. So far IKEA has rented 5km² worth of space in Australia.

Art Directors
Darren Borrino
Michael Sequeira
Copywriters
Dav Tabeshfar
Stuart Turner
Executive Creative Director
Simon Langley
Associate Creative Director
Richard Berney
Director
Rob Forsyth
Interactive Director
Nic Chamberlain
Technical Director
Aaron Collyer
Producer
Francesca Hope
Agency Producer
Holly Kemp
Digital Producer
Michelle Bunday
Artworker
Helen King
Advertising Agency
303Lowe
Account Manager
Kate Somerford
Account Director
Jane Orchard
Client
IKEA

Nomination in Direct

Direct Integrated Campaigns
Clemenger BBDO Melbourne
for the National Australia Bank

Break Up
Australians have always believed their four biggest banks work together, eliminating competition. As a result, for two years they refused to notice NAB, the National Australia Bank, becoming fairer and more competitive. Instead of fighting this perception of 'togetherness', we embraced it, letting Australia witness NAB breaking up with the other banks. The break up exploded simultaneously across different media, surprising the nation. It received $5million earned media in a single day and completely transformed the perception of NAB.

Art Director
Darren Pitt
Copywriter
Rohan Lancaster
Designer
Kim Buddee
Creative Directors
Tom Martin
Julian Schreiber
Executive Creative Director
Ant Keogh
Creative Chairman
James McGrath
Agency Producer
Sonia Von Bibra
Interactive Producer
Karina De Alwis
Executive Interactive Producer
Sasha Cunningham
Executive Producer
Michael Ritchie
Head of Projects
Josh Mullens
Senior Editor
Luke Crethar
Sound Designer
Paul LeCouter
Music Producer
Karl Richter
Print Producer
Sharon Adams
Director of Digital Innovation
Eaon Pritchard
Technical Lead
Daniel Zabinskas
Advertising Agency
Clemenger BBDO Melbourne
Planning & Insights Director
Paul Rees-Jones
Group Account Director
Simon Lamplough
Digital Account Director
Tanya Garma
Account Manager
Kate McCarthy
Account Director
Kelly Richardson
Business Director
Tim McColl
Client
National Australia Bank

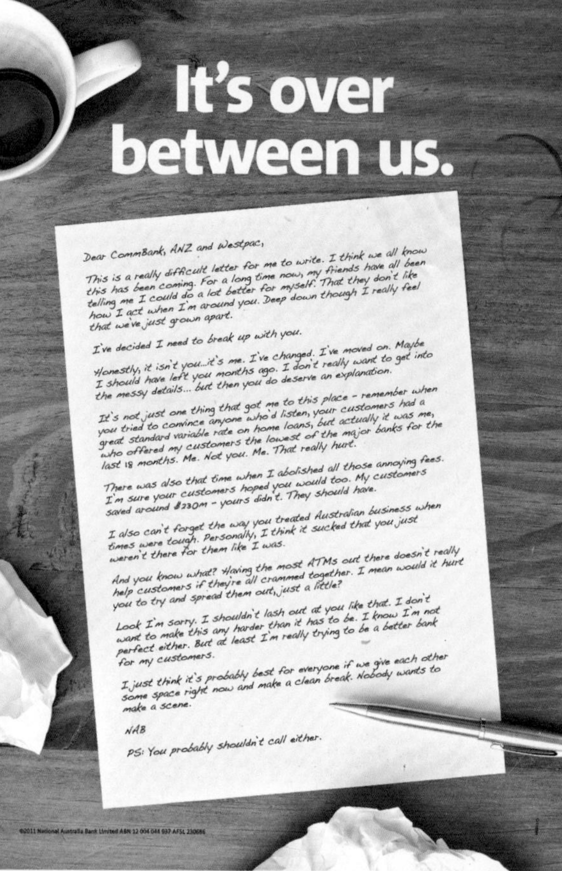

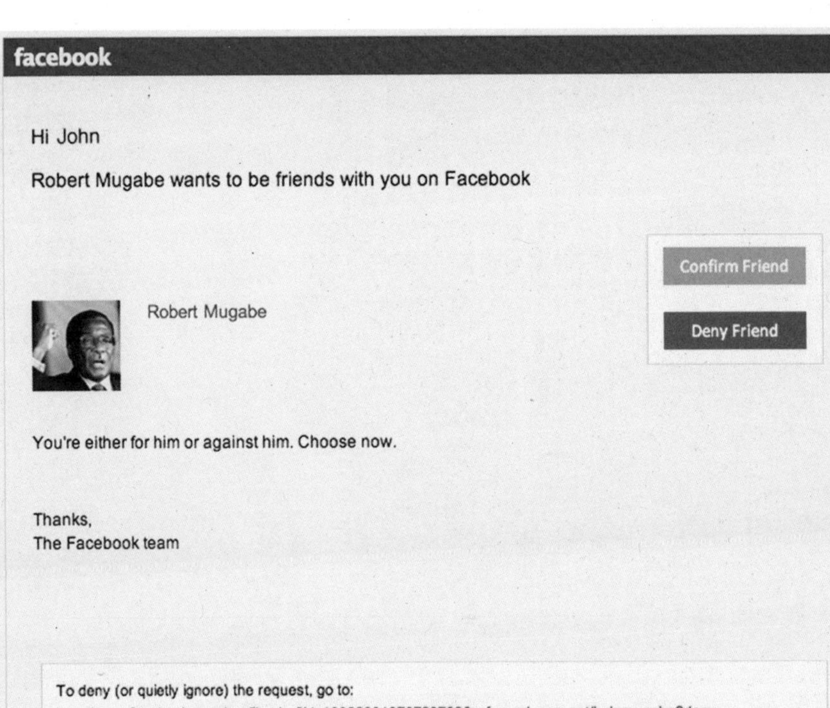

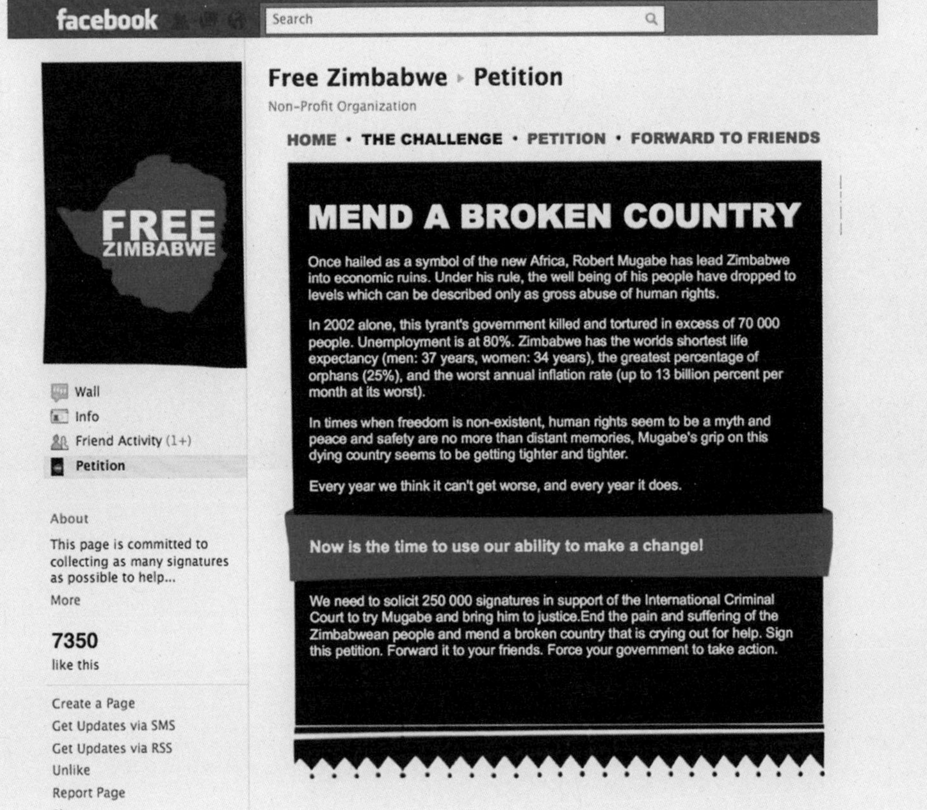

Nomination in Direct

Direct Response/Digital
Ireland/Davenport & Buynary
for Free Zimbabwe

Friend Request
To solicit signatures to bring free elections to Zimbabwe, we sent out personalised friend requests from 'Robert Mugabe'. The requests looked like regular Facebook notifications, giving recipients the option to accept or deny. Upon clicking deny, they were taken to a Facebook page where they could sign a petition for free elections in Zimbabwe, read about the goals of the campaign and help it to go viral by sending their own personalised requests. This campaign highlighted the fact that if you aren't a part of the solution, you're a part of the problem, and may as well be friends with Mugabe.

Art Director
Jean-Pierre De Villiers
Copywriter
Jenna Smith
Creative Directors
John Davenport
Philip Ireland
Digital Agency
Buynary
Advertising Agency
Ireland/Davenport
Client
Free Zimbabwe

Nomination in Direct

Direct Response/Digital
BBDO New York
for AT&T

You've Got a Case
AT&T wanted to help young people prove to their parents that they deserve a new 4G smartphone this holiday season. But kids aren't always the best at winning arguments. Meet high-powered internet attorney Kent Wesley. Kent thinks you deserve an AT&T 4G smartphone, and he's here to prove it with 'You've Got a Case'. Using information from your Facebook profile and a panel of 'experts', Kent creates a personalised case video, twisting everything about you into a convincing argument for why you deserve a 4G smartphone from AT&T. If you've got Kent, you've got a case.

Art Directors
Danny Adrain
Marcel Yunes
Director
Jonathan Krisel
Copywriters
Mark Anderson
Rick Williams
Creative Directors
Arturo Aranda
George Ernst
Executive Creative Director
Greg Hahn
Chief Creative Officer
David Lubars
Design Director
Brad Cohen
Agency Producer
Jeff Puskar
Executive Producer
Julian Katz
Interactive Producer
Clemens Brandt
Director of Photography
Damian Acevedo
Music Producer
Melissa Chester
Advertising Agency
BBDO New York
Interactive Production Company
The Famous Group
Production Company
Caviar LA
Editing
Arcade Edit
Account Executives
Marc Burns
Kara Carpentier
Mallory Hartline
Maryeliza Massengill
Shannon Schmidt
Doug Walker
Client
AT&T

Nomination in Direct

Direct Response/Press & Poster
Publicis Brussels
for Reporters Without Borders

Talking Poster
Reporters Without Borders created the first 'talking' poster. It showed a picture of Mahmoud Ahmadinejad, the president of Iran and a famous predator of press freedom, with a QR code in the bottom corner. By scanning this code and putting your iPhone on the mouth of the predator, you were directed to a movie showing the lips of a journalist describing what's really happening nowadays in Libya, Iran or Russia. It ends with the phrase: 'Because there are mouths that will never speak the truth. Reporters Without Borders. For press freedom'. This work was also selected in the 'Direct Response/Digital' category.

Art Director
Daniel Van den Broucke
Copywriter
Kwint De Meyer
Creative Director
Alain Janssens
Executive Creative Director
Paul Servaes
Video Producer
Marc Van Buggenhout
Advertising Agency
Publicis Brussels
Digital Production Company
Reed
Photography
Getty Images
Digital Strategist
Nadia Dafir
Planners
Vincent D'Halluin
Tom Theys
Account Manager
Mikaël Ogor
Account Director
Sébastien Desclée
Art Buyer
Laurence Maes
Brand Manager
Olivier Basille
Client
Reporters Without Borders

Direct Integrated Campaigns
Whybin\TBWA\Tequila Sydney
for Mars Petcare

Pedigree Adoption Drive
Sadly, over 100,000 dogs are needlessly euthanised every year in Australia because most people find it difficult visiting shelter homes to adopt. So if we couldn't bring people to the shelter dogs, we decided to bring the shelter dogs to the people. We embarked on the biggest pedigree adoption drive in Australia's history. Central to our campaign was a search engine that matches potential adopters with a dog from a pet rescue database. We used activity and communications across multiple channels, including a mobile phone and Facebook app, social networking, outdoor events and online branded content, as well as educational events and films.

Art Director
Hannes Ciatti
Copywriter
Dean Hamilton
Digital Creative Director
Russ Tucker
Executive Creative Directors
Dave Bowman
Matty Burton

Agency Producer
Chris Rollings
Advertising Agency
Whybin\TBWA\Tequila Sydney
Account Director
Andrea Byrne
Client
Mars Petcare
Brand
Pedigree

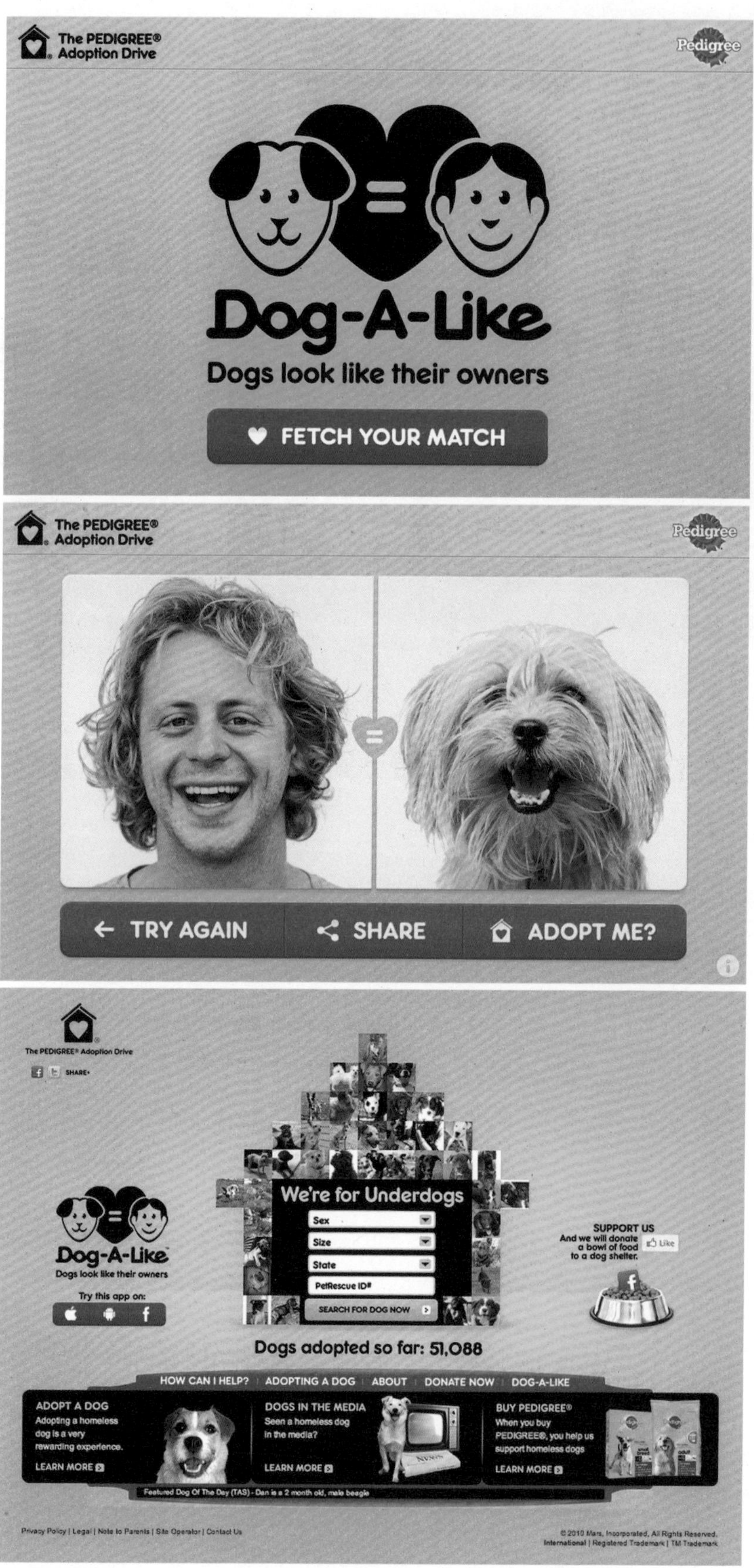

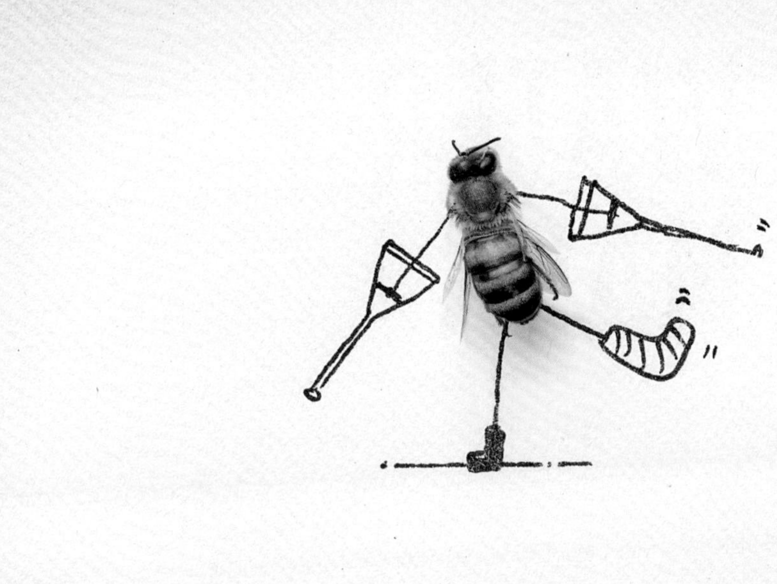

London's bees are in trouble.
Find out how you can help at
capitalgrowth.org/bees
MAYOR OF LONDON
Transport for London

Direct Integrated Campaigns
LIDA
for the Greater London Authority
& Sustain: the Alliance for Better
Food and Farming

Capital Bee: Saving London's Bees
Einstein said that if bees die out, we will die out. In just four years. With London's bee numbers declining rapidly, we set out to raise awareness amongst Londoners of the plight of the city's bees, soften the image of bees to encourage action, and drive Londoners online to discover simple ways to help. We took a risk. We used (already) dead bees to save live ones. Inspired by the dead fly art of Magnus Muhr, we portrayed the bees as 'little Londoners', characters in trouble, in real life situations that human Londoners would relate to, whose charm and cuteness inspired Londoners to want to help. This work was also selected in the 'Direct Response/Press & Poster' and 'Art Direction for Direct' categories.

Art Director
Chris Whitehead
Copywriter
John Fazio
Creative Director
Nicky Bullard
Photographer
Piet Johnson
Illustrator
Greg Lockhart
Advertising Agency
LIDA
Animation
Picasso Pictures
Account Director
Daniel Jenkins
Business Director
Camilla Patel
Clients
Greater London Authority
Sustain: the Alliance for Better Food and Farming
Brand
Capital Bee

Direct Integrated Campaigns
Leo Burnett Sydney
for Diageo Australia

Watermark

On 26 January 2011, the Australian state of Queensland was nearly wiped out by floods. Bundaberg Rum is a brand that has been lifting Queensland's spirit for over 120 years. When that spirit came under threat from the rising waters, Bundaberg Rum felt a duty to lift it up once again. So two days after the distillery was drained of floodwater, we created a product that would become a symbol of defiance and resilience, and rally the support of the nation. The product is Watermark – a rum crafted to mark the point where the floodwaters peaked; to mark the spirit in the towns on the road to recovery.

Art Director
Tim Green
Copywriter
Rupert Taylor
Designer
John-Henry Pajak
Creative Director
Tim Green
Executive Creative Director
Andy DiLallo
Editor
Angus Forbes
Advertising Agency
Leo Burnett Sydney
Planner
Warwick Heathwood
Account Handlers
Peter Bosilkovski
Sam McGown
Jodi McLeod
Client
Diageo Australia
Brand
Bundaberg Rum

WATER MARK

The Mark of Resilience.

This is the mark

JANUARY 2011

that marks the

point where the floodwaters peaked.

The mark that marks

the day when the

iron will of ordinary people gave

to others when their

own lives were tested.

The mark that marks the spirit in this

town and every town on

the hard road to recovery.

This is a day to mark in your memory.

When people came

and gathered together

had a drink, a laugh and kept going.

BUNDABERG DISTILLING CO

16 *April* 2011
facebook.com/*bundyrum*

ROM
Cremă Rom
TRY THE NEW ROM
PATRIOTISM WON'T FEED YOU
www.noulrom.ro

ROM
Cremă Rom
THE AMERICAN DREAM NOW IN THE ROMANIAN CHOCOLATE
TRY THE NEW ROM
www.noulrom.ro

Direct Integrated Campaigns
McCann Erickson Bucharest
for Kandia Dulce

American ROM
Romania's ROM is the traditional chocolate bar that all Romanians grew up with. Wrapped in the national flag, it had an ageing, nostalgic consumer base and was losing ground with young generations who preferred 'cool' American brands. We challenged young people's national ego by replacing ROM's packaging with an American version. The campaign started in stores, and we placed blunt messages in relevant outdoor locations in order to trigger a strong response from the population. Many of the panels were painted overnight by unknown individuals with patriotic messages asking for the return of the old ROM.

Art Directors
Andra Badea
Ionut Cojocaru
Laurentiu Stere
Copywriter
Florin Florea
Group Creative Directors
Catalin Dobre
Dinu Panescu
Chief Creative Officer
Adrian Botan
Video Producers
Tiberiu Munteanu
Ilinca Nanoveanu
Head of Broadcast
Victor Croitoru
Advertising Agency
McCann Erickson Bucharest

Planner
Ileana Seban Parau
Account Executive
Lavinia Vaduva
Account Manager
Ruxandra Savulescu
Account Director
Cristina Birleanu
Brand Communications Directors
Sorina Lordan
Ruxandra Vasilescu
Client
Kandia Dulce
Brand
ROM

Direct Integrated Campaigns
Euro RSCG Australia
for Reckitt Benckiser

Toilet Confessions
To boost sales of Harpic White & Shine, our client gave us the unenviable task of persuading consumers to clean the toilet every day, instead of every week. In research, women told us a simple truth: men make the mess and women clean it up. From this we created Harpic Toilet Confessions, where the men of Australia finally came clean about their toilet crimes. We launched the idea with traditional media and then encouraged men to visit our direct response website and create personalised apologies that were posted on social media and sent via email.

Art Director
Dave Ladd
Copywriter
Chris Johnson
Executive Creative Director
Steve Coll
Producers
Chris Hulsman
Emma Thompson
Editor
Beau Simmons
Heads of Broadcast
Sean Kruck
Monique Pardavi
Advertising Agency
Euro RSCG Australia

Account Manager
Josh Sandford
Account Director
Holly Ripper
Brand Managers
Nicole Chang
Amy Kitchener
Jennifer Osborne
Marketing Director
Chris Tedesco
Client
Reckitt Benckiser
Brand
Harpic White & Shine

A PUBLIC APOLOGY:

We, the men of Australia, would like to apologise for our daily toilet indiscretions.

For our bad aim, our failure to flush and for flushing too much.

For leaving the loo looking like a bombsite.
For forgetting to flick on the fan.

For our sprays, splashes and splatters.
For the miles and miles of wasted paper.

And for all the little surprises we leave behind.

Sorry.

Cleans up their act. Every time.

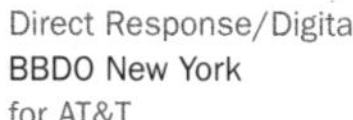

Direct Response/Digital
BBDO New York
for AT&T

Shout from the Mountain
AT&T needed to give people a personalised and individual way to say 'I love you' with its technology on Valentine's Day. It needed to live up to the brand promise: Rethink Possible. Our solution was to let users literally shout their love from a mountaintop by having a group of very loud mountain men do it for them. Anyone could submit love proclamations through Facebook or Twitter, then see the shouts streamed live on Valentine's Day. Afterwards, individual clips were posted on the Facebook walls of senders.

Art Director
Jaclyn Rink
Copywriter
Ashley Davis Marshall
Creative Directors
Arturo Aranda
Jeff Greenspan
Executive Creative Directors
Greg Hahn
Ralph Watson
Chief Creative Officer
David Lubars
Designers
Gene Na
Mike Sheppard
Director
Jorma Taccone
Agency Producer
Jesse Brihn
Executive Producer
Julian Katz
Interactive Producer
Jonathan Percy
Head of Interactive Production
Niklas Lindstrom
Director of Integrated Production
Brian DiLorenzo
Editors
Kim Bica
Will Hasell
Geoff Hounsell
Greg Scruton
Advertising Agency
BBDO New York
Production Company
Caviar LA
Digital Production Company
B-Reel
Visual Effects Company
Visual Creatures
Sound Design
740 Sound Studio
Editing
Arcade Edit
Client
AT&T

Direct Response/Digital
DDB Singapore
for Cisco Consumer Products

Flip Your Profile
Flip Video claimed the web's hottest real estate by creating the world's first Facebook profile video sharing platform. Flip Your Profile enables users to replace profile pictures with profile videos. The moving, breathing, sound-generating profile videos became powerful user-generated brand ads on Facebook. Users could share videos by recording directly via their computer's web cam, or by uploading a file, or, best of all, by shooting and sharing directly from a Flip Video device. The idea was not just one of a kind, but also on brand.

Creative Directors
Terrence Tan
Thomas Yang
Executive Creative Directors
Jeff Cheong
Joji Jacob
Chief Creative Officer
Neil Johnson
Technical Director
Yeo Wee Lee
Developers
Rosslyn Chay
Ng Chee Sheng
Boby Ertanto
Viknesk Kumarr
Copywriters
Naresh Kumar
Vinod Savio

Art Directors
Sham Nassar
Suhaimi Saadan
Creative Technologists
Augustine Low
Ciaran Lyons
Gerald Yeo
Head of Broadcast
Jackie They
Advertising Agency
DDB Singapore
Marketing Managers
Shaun Quek
Lit Yang Quek
Client
Cisco Consumer Products
Brand
Flip Video

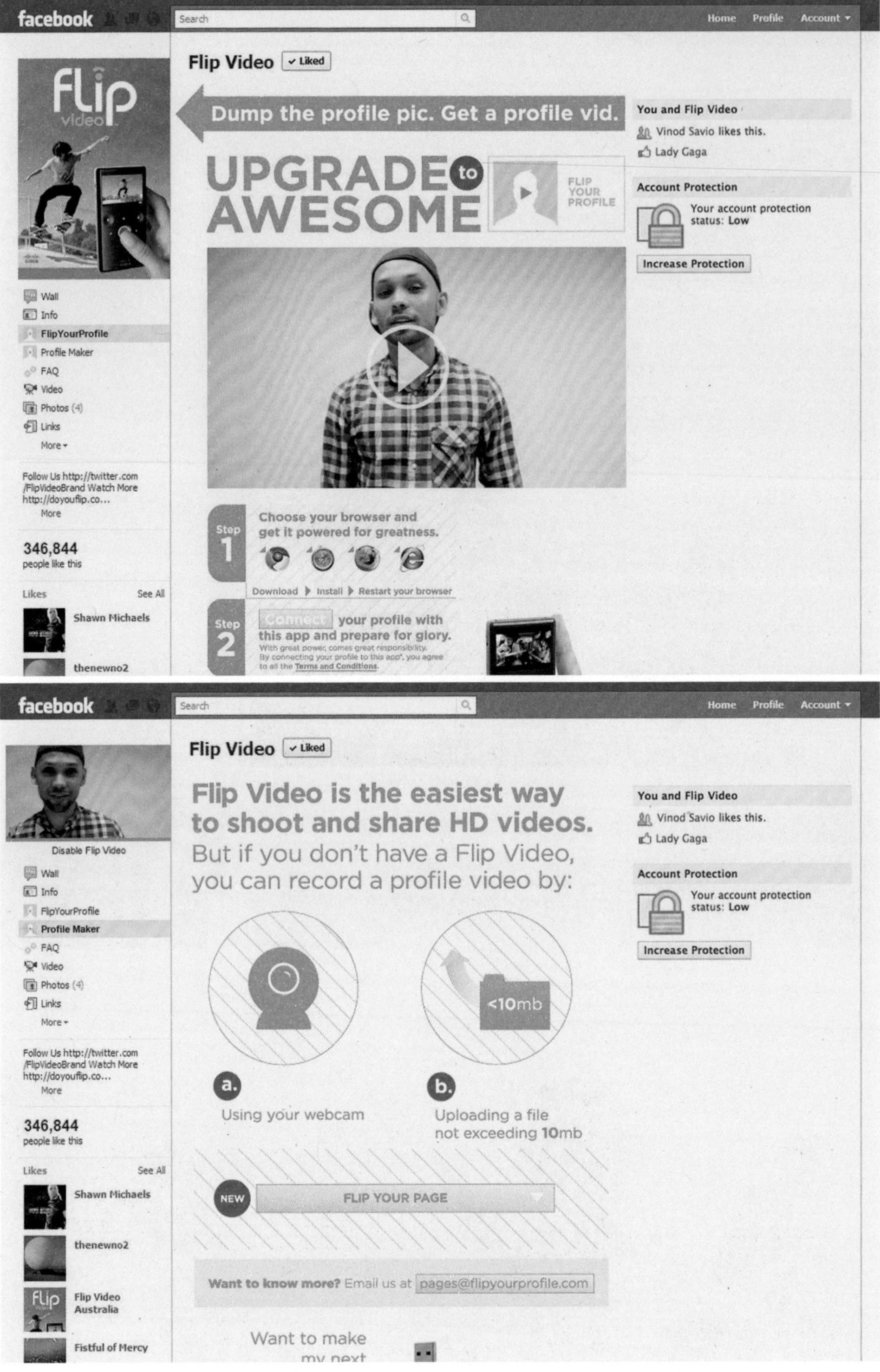

Direct Response/Digital
DDB Paris
for Greenpeace

A New Warrior
Since 1978, the Rainbow Warrior allowed Greenpeace to gain numerous victories for the protection of our planet. But Greenpeace needed to replace it. The new Rainbow Warrior is the first ever purpose-built environmental campaigning vessel. It will play a key role in Greenpeace's future campaigns. We wanted to raise funds to finance its construction and involve all the people who want to be part of this story. We made people purchase and own a piece of the new Rainbow Warrior by launching an e-commerce website: anewwarrior.com. 400,000 items went on sale, ranging from 1€ to 7,000€. After payment, buyers received a certificate of ownership – thousands of these were posted on social networks, creating a media burst. The new Rainbow Warrior has now been constructed and was officially launched on 14th October 2011.

Art Director
Benjamin Marchal
Copywriter
Olivier Lefebvre
Executive Creative Director
Alexandre Hervé
Production Company
Make Me Pulse
Digital Production Company
Les 84

Advertising Agency
DDB Paris
Visual Effects Company
Virtek
Sound Design
Panarama
Account Managers
Paul Ducré
Xavier Mendiola
Client
Greenpeace

Direct Response/Digital
Forsman & Bodenfors
for Comviq

Single Single Release
Swedish mobile provider Comviq asked us to launch 'Ringback Tones', a new service which lets you replace the tones people hear when calling you, with a song of your choice. We teamed up with Swedish pop star Veronica Maggio, who released her anticipated new single 'Välkommen in' exclusively as a ringback tone, and on one mobile number only. For two weeks, the only way to hear the new single was to call a number that belonged to an average Joe: Comviq user and Maggio fan Firat Strechim Delen. The campaign started with a mailer sent to journalists and bloggers. As soon as the number was out there, the phone started ringing. Every caller got a text explaining how to sign up for the service. The news about the single release spread even more, with radio stations calling to play the song, and praise from influential music writers. Aside from all the publicity for Veronica Maggio and Comviq, 56% of callers signed up for the new service.

Art Director
Annika Frankel
Copywriters
Marcus Hägglöf
Robert Lund
Designer
Axel Söderlund
Agency Producer
Magnus Kennhed
Web Producers
Peter Gaudiano
Stefan Thomson
Music Composer
Veronica Maggio

Advertising Agency
Forsman & Bodenfors
Production Company
ACNE Production
Public Relations
Spotlight PR
Account Executive
Stefan Rudels
Account Manager
Sanna Kander
Client
Comviq

Direct Response/Ambient
Ogilvy & Mather Argentina
for TEDx

Spread the TEDx
In Latin America, TEDx talks are still far removed from ordinary people. If we wanted to spread these ideas, we needed a more personal approach to promote TEDx. So we called the city's most remarkable speakers: taxi drivers. Fifty of them were invited to TEDx Buenos Aires, so that they could spread these outstanding ideas all over the city. The creation of this link between TEDx and passengers put them face-to-face with some of the most inspiring and fascinating ideas. We spread the TEDx.

Art Director
Ignacio Flota
Copywriter
Nicolás Vara
Executive Creative Directors
Gastón Bigio
Maximiliano Maddalena
Javier Mentasti
Head of Art
Diego Grandi
Producer
Patricio Alvarez Casado
Advertising Agency
Ogilvy & Mather Argentina
Client
TEDx
Brand
TED

Direct Response/Ambient
AlmapBBDO
for Casa do Zezinho

Share with Those in Need

We used this ambient idea to generate donations for Casa do Zezinho, a charity which guarantees basic necessities for children in need. We asked consumers to pay full price for half of the product, with half of their money going to Casa do Zezinho.

Art Directors
Daniel Manzi
Vinicius Sousa

Copywriter
Fabio Ozorio

Advertising Agency
AlmapBBDO

Client
Casa do Zezinho

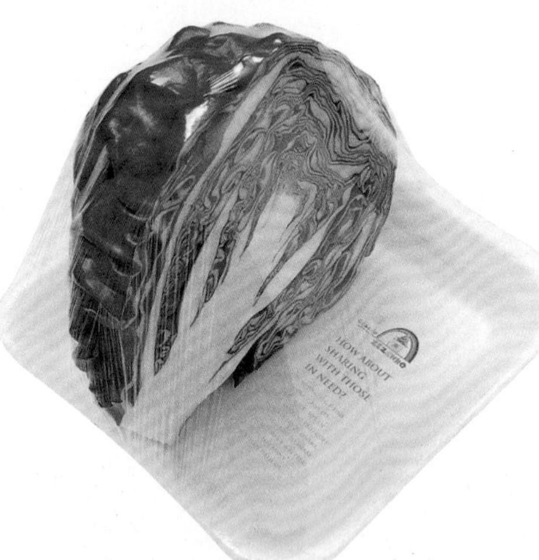

Direct Response/Ambient
Santa Clara
for Festival El Ojo de Iberoamérica

El Ojo Beer
How do you talk to the Brazilians – and only the Brazilians – at Cannes? That's what we needed to do to promote El Ojo de Iberoamérica, an advertising festival made exclusively for Ibero-Americans. We created and submitted a spot for a beer that doesn't exist. It was narrated in Portuguese with fake English subtitles. The audio talked about the festival, while the subtitles deceived the English-speaking audience, making them believe it was just a lame beer spot. This way, during the longlist exhibition in the Palais, we aired our commercial and talked to all of our hermanos.

Art Directors
Thiago Grossi
Maso Heck
Ronaldo Tavares
Copywriters
Leo Avila
Fernando Campos
Caio Lekecinskas
Raphael Quatrocci
Creative Director
Fernando Campos
Director of Photography
Luiz Fernando Gaio
Producers
Regina Knapp
Thieny Prates

Advertising Agency
Santa Clara
Editing
Fantástica Filmes
Music Arrangement & Production
Play It Again
Account Handler
Mariana Zavanella
Client
Festival El Ojo de Iberoamérica

Direct Response/Ambient
Euro RSCG Australia
for Reckitt Benckiser

Sponsor the White House
Detergent advertising isn't known for getting people talking. So at the height of the US debt crisis, Vanish NapiSan sent a delegation to Washington DC with a giant cheque for $25million to sponsor the most famous white building in the world: the White House. In five days we created 12 online films as we lobbied media, politicians, celebrities and the American public. Of course, President Obama was always going to say no. When he did, we used the publicity to kick-start our real campaign – a nationwide promotion culminating in Vanish NapiSan sponsoring an Aussie family's white house instead.

Art Directors
Gavin Maloney
Scott Sparks
Copywriter
Peter Maniaty
Executive Creative Director
Steve Coll
Director
Dan Reisinger
Agency Producer
Amy Friend
Producers
Brian Hegedus
Anna Marie Pittman
Nick Simkins
Jenny Webb
Post Producer
Sarah Brown
Sound Designers
Alex Mills
Anthony Smith
Sound Producer
Larissa Couple
Editors
Brad Hurt
Beau Simmons
Head of Broadcast
Monique Pardavi

Advertising Agency
Euro RSCG Australia
Public Relations
Cake/Workman Entertainment
New York
Grayling
Washington DC
Red Agency
Account Managers
Natasha Carroll
Elizabeth McKenzie
Josh Sandford
Account Director
Holly Ripper
Brand Manager
Jennifer Osborne
Marketing Director
Chris Tedesco
Public Relations Manager
James Wright
Client
Reckitt Benckiser
Brand
Vanish NapiSan

'Arizona' by Ruth O'Leary
ARIZONA'S TIME IS LIMITED.
SO IS THIS PRINT.
Help save her by bidding for this one-off print at SDCH.org.au

Direct Response/Press & Poster
M&C Saatchi Sydney
for the Sydney Dogs and Cats Home

Limited Edition
Australian law dictates that shelters are only required to keep an animal for 14 days. Due to lack of funds, on the 15th day many healthy animals are put down. Their time is limited. Our objective: save them. To convey the message that animals have limited time left, 21 of Australia's best photographers captured 63 limited edition portraits, which ran as roadside posters in high traffic areas around Sydney. The public could view the entire exhibition online, bid for a print on eBay, adopt the animal or donate to the Sydney Dogs and Cats Home. All 63 posters were sold. All 63 animals were saved.

Art Directors
Gavin McLeod
Joshua Rowe
Jason Woelfl
Copywriters
Gavin McLeod
Joshua Rowe
Jason Woelfl
Photographers
Juli Balla
Toby Burrows
Terence Chin
Michael Corridore
Tamara Dean
Toby Dixon
Marc Gafen
Florian Groehn
Amelia Hawkins
Gary Heery
Jeremy Hudson
Nic Ingram
Ingvar Kenne
Adrian Lander
Tom Luscombe
Jonathan May
Michael Miller
Ruth O'Leary
Andreas Smetana
Adam Taylor
Julian Wolkenstein

Creative Directors
Michael Andrews
Gavin McLeod
Joshua Rowe
Executive Creative Directors
Tom McFarlane
Ben Welsh
Print Producer
Ben Nash
Advertising Agency
M&C Saatchi Sydney
Client
Sydney Dogs and Cats Home

Direct Response/Press & Poster
McCann Erickson Thailand
for Clean Plus Thailand

Office / Service Apartment / Factory
Dust accumulates but it can't be seen, so people don't use a cleaning service as often as they should. To let our target market know it's time for cleaning, we let the dirt speak. We created posters covered with clear glue, and placed them in the offices, service apartments and factories of our customers. As time passed, the sticky parts of the posters would capture dirt and form shapes of office appliances, furniture or factory icons. The dirt would also stick to a headline that said: 'It's cleaning time. Call us'.

Art Director
Winna Kiao-on
Copywriter
Arnicknard
Krobnoparat
Creative Director
Chinnawut Awakul
Chief Creative Officer
Martin Lee
Retoucher
Chalermpol
Kiatpatananukul
Producer
Pittkanya Poonlumlert
Advertising Agency
McCann Erickson
Thailand
Planner
Apichaya
Taechamahapun
Business Director
Opapen Kittipanyakul
Client
Clean Plus Thailand

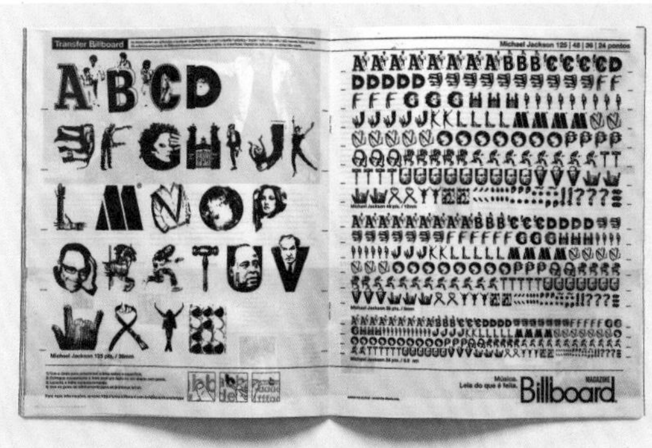

Direct Response/Press & Poster
AlmapBBDO
for Billboard Brasil

Transfertype
Six artists were chosen for this campaign for Billboard Magazine. Fonts were created for each, based on the artists' styles. The fonts were reproduced on transfer paper as double page magazine ads. Each letter tells a part of the story of each artist: influences, record covers, music videos and their biography. A campaign with details worth discovering.

Art Directors
Marcos Kothlar
Marcos Medeiros
Copywriter
Andre Kassu
Illustrator
Marcos Medeiros

Advertising Agency
AlmapBBDO
Client
Billboard Brasil

Direct Mail
JWT London
for Nestlé

Chunky Mail
To communicate the chunkiness of Kit Kat Chunky and drive trial, we created a mailer that looked just like the cards postmen leave behind when they're unable to deliver a package. The real cards often state that the package couldn't be delivered because it is 'too big for your letterbox'. Our tongue-in-cheek card claimed that we couldn't deliver a Kit Kat Chunky because it is 'too chunky for your letterbox'. Recipients were directed to collect their free Kit Kat Chunky from their local newsagent.

Art Director
Matt Leach
Copywriter
Jess Oudot
Designer
Casa Hamid
Creative Director
Jason Berry
Executive Creative Director
Russell Ramsey

Advertising Agency
JWT London
Project Manager
Stuart Heyburn
Account Handler
Christopher Godfree
Client
Nestlé
Brand
Kit Kat

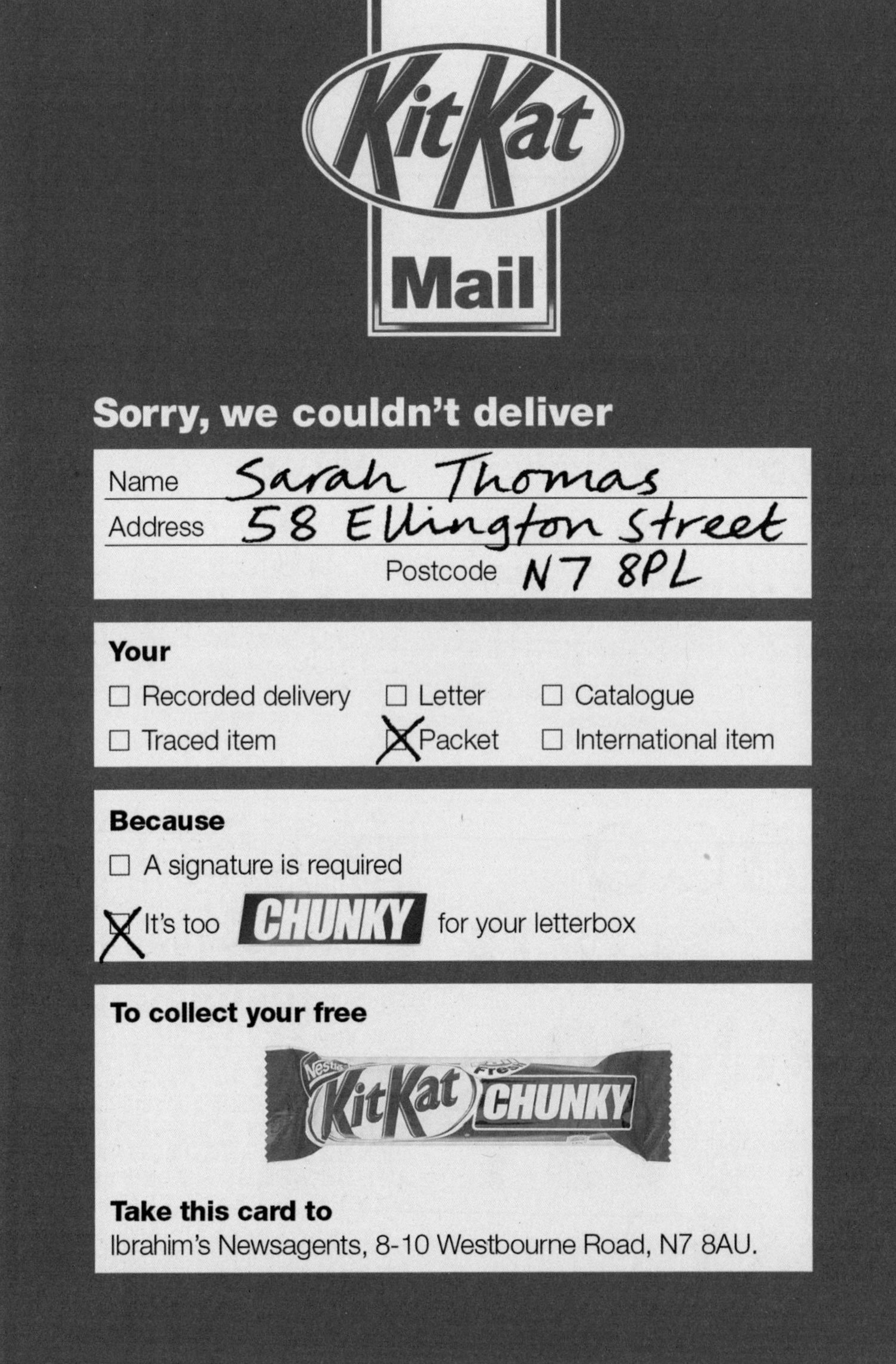

Direct Mail
JWT Cape Town
for Kalahari.net

Shoe / Beer / Burger
Being a student at university can be tough on the pocket, especially when the price of textbooks leaves you with even less money to spend on the little things in life. We sent direct mailers to student representatives in South Africa to show how they could make cash for things that are important to students, like shoes, beer and burgers, by selling their old textbooks on Kalahari.net. The mailers helped Kalahari.net reach record targets for first and second semester sales. Not to mention helping students to afford the essential things in life.

Art Directors
Mpumelelo Ngewu
Annelie Nothnagel
Executive Creative Director
Conn Bertish

Advertising Agency
JWT Cape Town
Client
Kalahari.net

Direct Mail
JWT London
for Anti-Slavery International

Victorian Newspaper
Slavery is seen as something from the past, abolished long ago. We wanted to communicate to Londoners that little has changed. Up to 5,000 people in London are made to work under conditions reminiscent of a Charles Dickens novel. Since slavery is a 'hidden' problem, we decided to write an 'expose', but blur the boundaries between the past and present to emphasise that slaves continue to work in a way that our ancestors would think had been outlawed. The four-page Victorian illustrated newspaper was placed inside 100,000 copies of 'The Sunday Telegraph' and sent to a targeted mailing list.

Art Director
Anita Davis
Copywriter
Jonathan Budds
Typographer
Casa Hamid
Illustrator
John Spencer
Designer
Casa Hamid
Executive Creative Director
Russell Ramsey

Advertising Agency
JWT London
Account Handler
Jonny Kanagasooriam
Account Director
Hamish Goulding
Client
Anti-Slavery International

No.1214 — VOL. XXIII. DECEMBER 2011. LONDON EDITION

READ ABOUT SLAVERY TODAY AND YOU MIGHT WONDER WHICH CENTURY YOU'RE LIVING IN

You have no control over your life. You are little more than another person's property. You are threatened, abused, employed in a degrading job and paid a pittance, if you are paid at all. Your humanity has been stripped away.

This is what slavery meant in the past and what it still means today.

Because one hundred and seventy-eight years after this barbaric practice was outlawed, it continues. Although it seems like something from that dark, misguided period in our history when British ships carried millions of Africans to the Americas, this year, 2011, will see over five thousand people – fifteen every day - brought into the UK and made to work in a way that defines them as slaves.

Inevitably, many of them end up in London. It seems difficult to believe that these abuses go unrecognised in a city so wealthy, so lawful and so conscious of human rights.

The work they do in our capital is varied, but almost always takes place in the worst of conditions. Many women are employed as domestic maids in private houses where they find themselves sleeping on basement floors and treated with less consideration than the family pet. Others are trafficked into the sex industry, working in brothels and massage parlours and watched over by brutal pimps. Men are forced to do menial jobs on construction sites or in hotels.

Hours are long and movements restricted: often, passports are taken and withheld. Contact with family is minimal at best.

These are slaves. People who have no options in their lives. People who, to their employers, are nothing more than objects. People who do not feel like people.

In the following pages, you will find several personal stories of men and women in London forced to become involved in slavery today. Please help to make sure that for this unlawful and cruel practice, there is no tomorrow.

WINTER 2010

1.30 A.M. A DOMESTIC WORKER HAS TO DO THE HOUSEHOLD SHOPPING HAVING WORKED 18 HOURS.

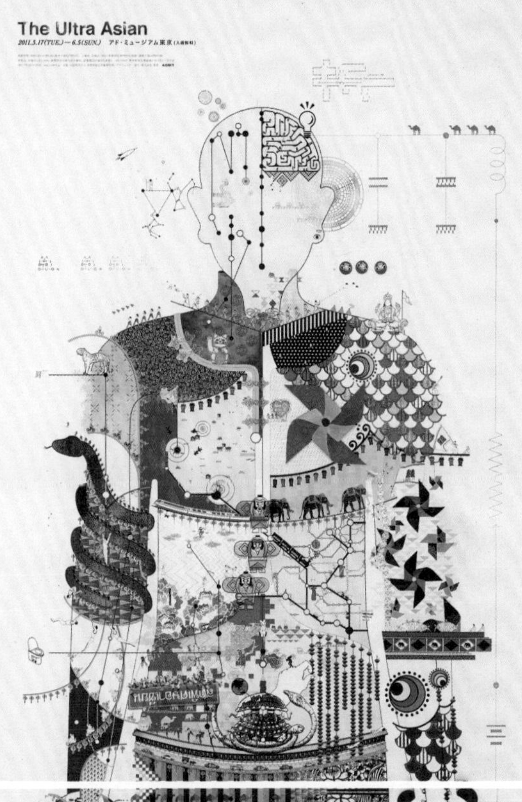

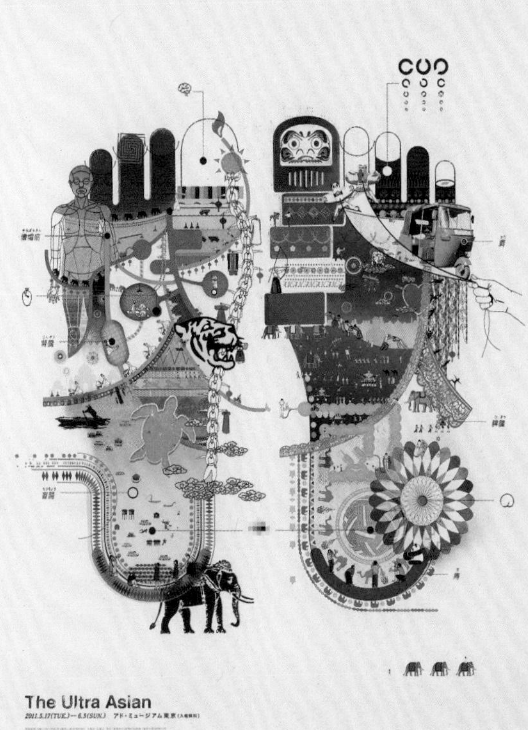

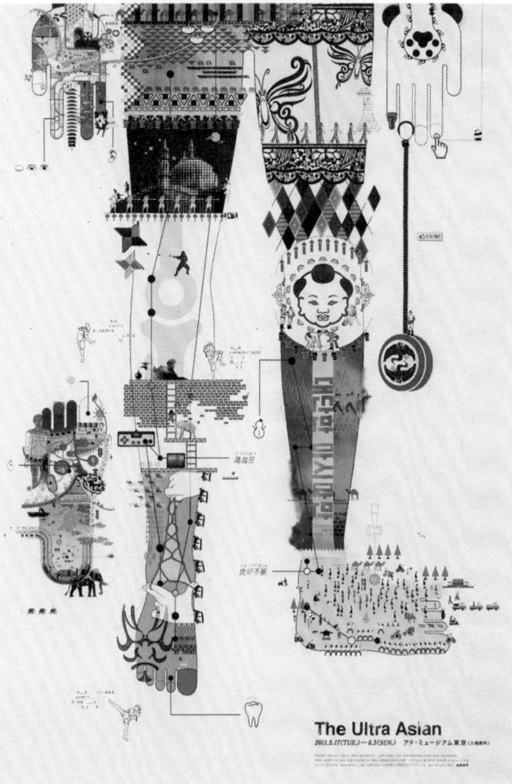

Art Direction for Direct
Dentsu Tokyo
for the Yoshida Hideo Memorial Foundation

The Ultra Asian
These pieces were created to promote the ADFEST 2011 Exhibition. We developed the concept of a 'life-sized Asian'. We wanted to show the history, culture, technology and trends of Asia becoming the flesh and blood of an Asian. A giant palm leads visitors into the exhibition hall, where they are welcomed by a giant Asian, who looks dynamic from a distance, but delicate at close range. Visitors could experience the Asian feel from the overall exhibition design while viewing the exhibited work. The number of visitors doubled, and the life-sized posters received a lot of praise.

Art Director
Yoshihiro Yogi
Copywriter
Haruko Tsutsui
Photographer
Takaya Sakano
Illustrator
Minami Otsuka
Designers
Minami Otsuka
Kazuaki Takai
Executive Creative Director
Yuya Furukawa

Advertising Agency
Dentsu Tokyo
Project Manager
Yoshiko Tomita
Client
Yoshida Hideo Memorial Foundation
Brand
ADFEST 2011

Art Direction for Direct
Serviceplan München
for Austria Solar – Verein zur Foerderung der Thermischen Solarenergie

The Solar Annual Report 2011
Solar energy is the main business of our client Austria Solar. That's why we thought about how we could put this energy to paper. The result: the first annual report powered by the sun. Its content remains invisible until sunlight falls on its pages.

Art Director
Matthäus Frost
Copywriter
Moritz Dornig
Designer
Mathias Nösel
Creative Directors
Christoph Everke
Cosimo Möller
Alexander Nagel
Print Producer
Melanie Dienemann

Advertising Agency
Serviceplan München
Account Handler
Diana Günder
Brand Manager
Roger Hackstock
Client
Austria Solar – Verein zur Foerderung der Thermischen Solarenergie

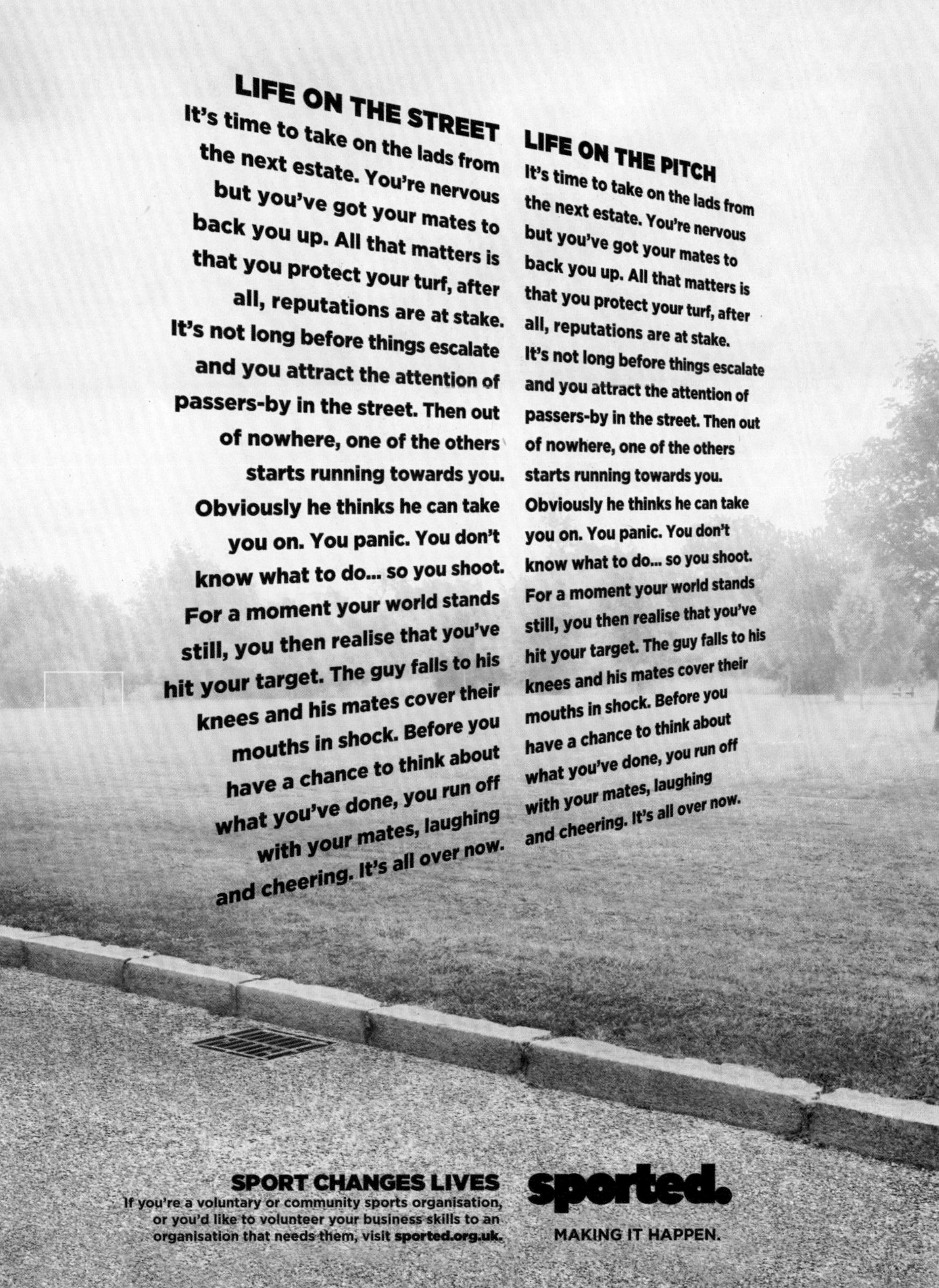
LIFE ON THE STREET
It's time to take on the lads from the next estate. You're nervous but you've got your mates to back you up. All that matters is that you protect your turf, after all, reputations are at stake. It's not long before things escalate and you attract the attention of passers-by in the street. Then out of nowhere, one of the others starts running towards you. Obviously he thinks he can take you on. You panic. You don't know what to do... so you shoot. For a moment your world stands still, you then realise that you've hit your target. The guy falls to his knees and his mates cover their mouths in shock. Before you have a chance to think about what you've done, you run off with your mates, laughing and cheering. It's all over now.
LIFE ON THE PITCH
It's time to take on the lads from the next estate. You're nervous but you've got your mates to back you up. All that matters is that you protect your turf, after all, reputations are at stake. It's not long before things escalate and you attract the attention of passers-by in the street. Then out of nowhere, one of the others starts running towards you. Obviously he thinks he can take you on. You panic. You don't know what to do... so you shoot. For a moment your world stands still, you then realise that you've hit your target. The guy falls to his knees and his mates cover their mouths in shock. Before you have a chance to think about what you've done, you run off with your mates, laughing and cheering. It's all over now.
SPORT CHANGES LIVES
If you're a voluntary or community sports organisation, or you'd like to volunteer your business skills to an organisation that needs them, visit sported.org.uk.
sported.
MAKING IT HAPPEN.

Writing for Direct
Draftfcb London
for Sported

Cross the Line
Summer 2011 saw some of the worst civil unrest ever in Britain's cities. Of the 1,715 people arrested, 73% were aged between 10 and 24. Sported is a charity that exists to help young people find an alternative to the culture of street violence. Set up by Olympic bid leader Sir Keith Mills, it now establishes sports projects in inner cities to turn negative energy into positive energy. The riots gave Sported an opportunity to promote itself as a proven solution. To encapsulate this, the agency wrote an emotive press ad that shows what happens when you cross the line from street to sport.

Copywriter
James White
Art Director
Henry Finnegan
Photographer
Kulbir Thandi
Creative Director
Alistair Ross
Executive Creative Director
Mark Fiddes
Advertising Agency
Draftfcb London
Client
Sported

1

3

6

8

4

9

2

7

5

Jury Foreman
1. David Droga
Droga5 New York

2. Christina Yu
Red Urban Canada

3. Guga Ketzer
Loducca

4. Steve Back
Ogilvy & Mather
Singapore

5. Graham Lang
Y&R South Africa

6. James Hilton
AKQA London

7. Agnello Dias
Taproot India

8. Neil Dawson
BETC London

9. Laura Jordan
Bambach
Dare

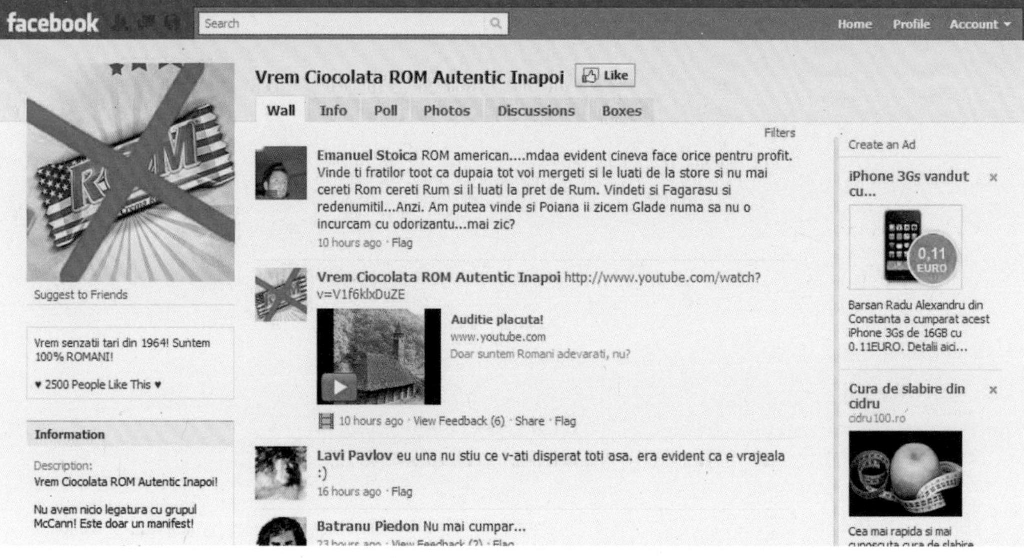

Yellow Pencil in Integrated & Earned Media

Integrated
McCann Erickson Bucharest
for Kandia Dulce

American ROM
Romania's ROM is the traditional chocolate bar that all Romanians grew up with. Wrapped in the national flag, it had an ageing, nostalgic consumer base and was losing ground with young generations who preferred 'cool' American brands. We challenged young people's national ego by replacing ROM's packaging with an American version. The campaign started in stores, and we placed blunt messages in relevant outdoor locations in order to trigger a strong response from the population. Many of the panels were painted overnight by unknown individuals with patriotic messages asking for the return of the old ROM.

Art Directors
Andra Badea
Ionut Cojocaru
Laurentiu Stere
Copywriter
Florin Florea
Group Creative Directors
Catalin Dobre
Dinu Panescu
Chief Creative Officer
Adrian Botan
Video Producers
Tiberiu Munteanu
Ilinca Nanoveanu
Head of Broadcast
Victor Croitoru
Advertising Agency
McCann Erickson Bucharest
Planner
Ileana Seban Parau
Account Executive
Lavinia Vaduva
Account Manager
Ruxandra Savulescu
Account Director
Cristina Birleanu
Brand Communications Directors
Sorina Iordan
Ruxandra Vasilescu
Client
Kandia Dulce
Brand
ROM

Yellow Pencil in Integrated & Earned Media

Integrated
Wieden+Kennedy London
for the Kaiser Chiefs

The Kaiser Chiefs Bespoke Album Creation Experience

Conversation between Oli, from Wieden+Kennedy, and Ricky, from the Kaiser Chiefs over fish and chips:
'Can we make people LOVE albums again?'
'Anybody ever done a bespoke one?'
'Somebody must have.' (Check Google.)
'Nope.'
'Well, let's do that then.'
'Let's write 20 songs and let people pick ten.'
'They could make their own artwork.'
'What if they could SELL their unique albums?'
'People share stuff anyway. Let's pay them.'
'£1 per album.'
'We could give them tools to sell it on social media.'
'Their own websites.'
'Banner ads for their blogs.'
'Posters.'
'Reward the top sellers.'
'Is any of this even possible?'
'We'll need a website.'
'Can it look old-fashioned?'
'Yes.'
'OK.'

Designer
Jon Harris
Digital Designer
Chi Li
Creative Director
Oli Beale
Executive Creative Directors
Tony Davidson
Kim Papworth
Director
Andy Bruntel
Interactive Director
Andy Cameron
Producer
Rachel Dargavel
Interactive Producers
Chris Binks
Michelle Cox
Agency Executive Producer
Danielle Stewart
Creative Technologist
Joao Wilbert
Creative Agency
Wieden+Kennedy London
Production Company
Somesuch & Co
Interactive Production Company
Specialmoves
Public Relations Manager
Lois Newcombe
Project Manager
Alex Franklin
Planners
Alex Franklin
Jennifer Lewis
Account Director
Hanne Haugen
Client
Kaiser Chiefs

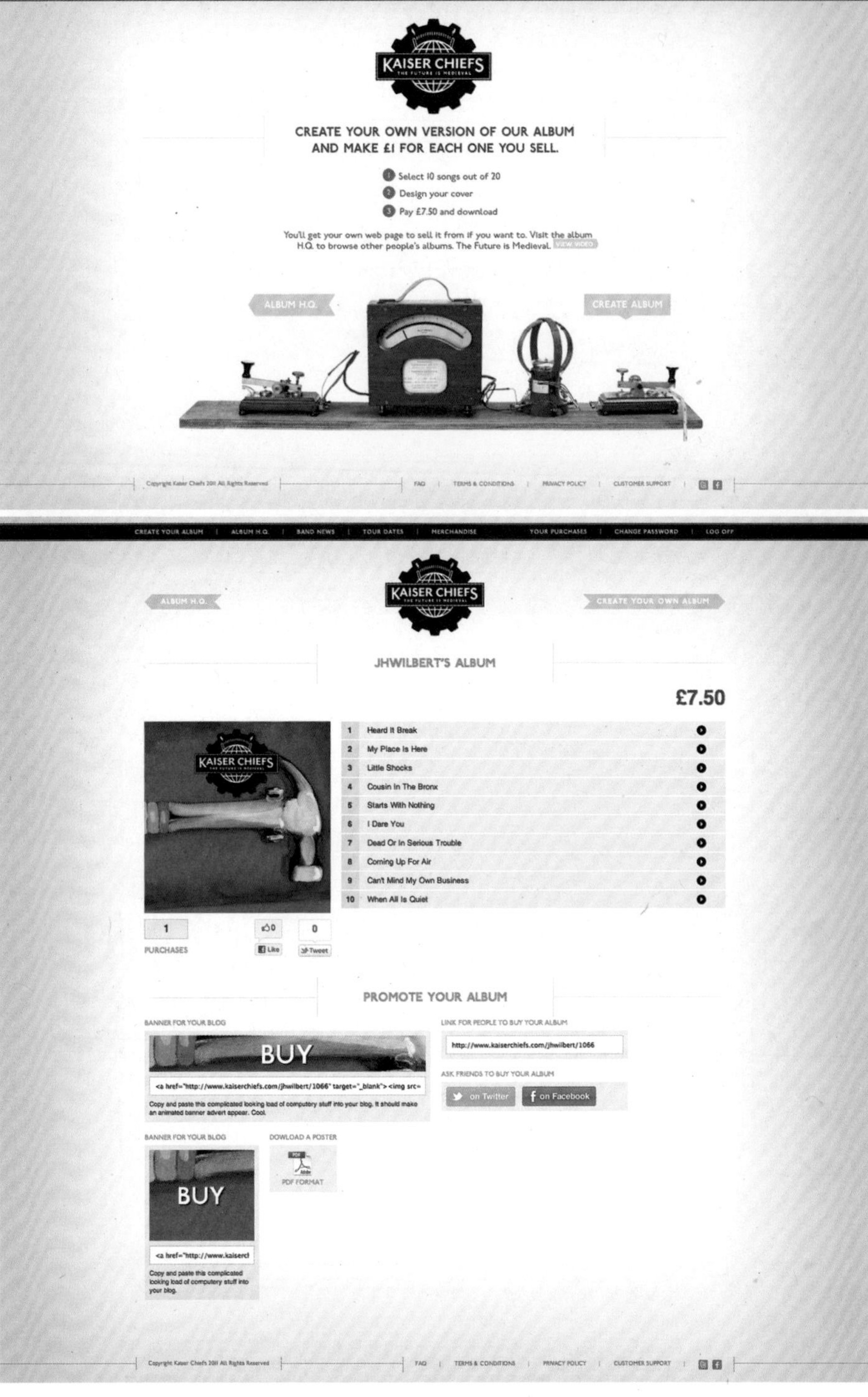

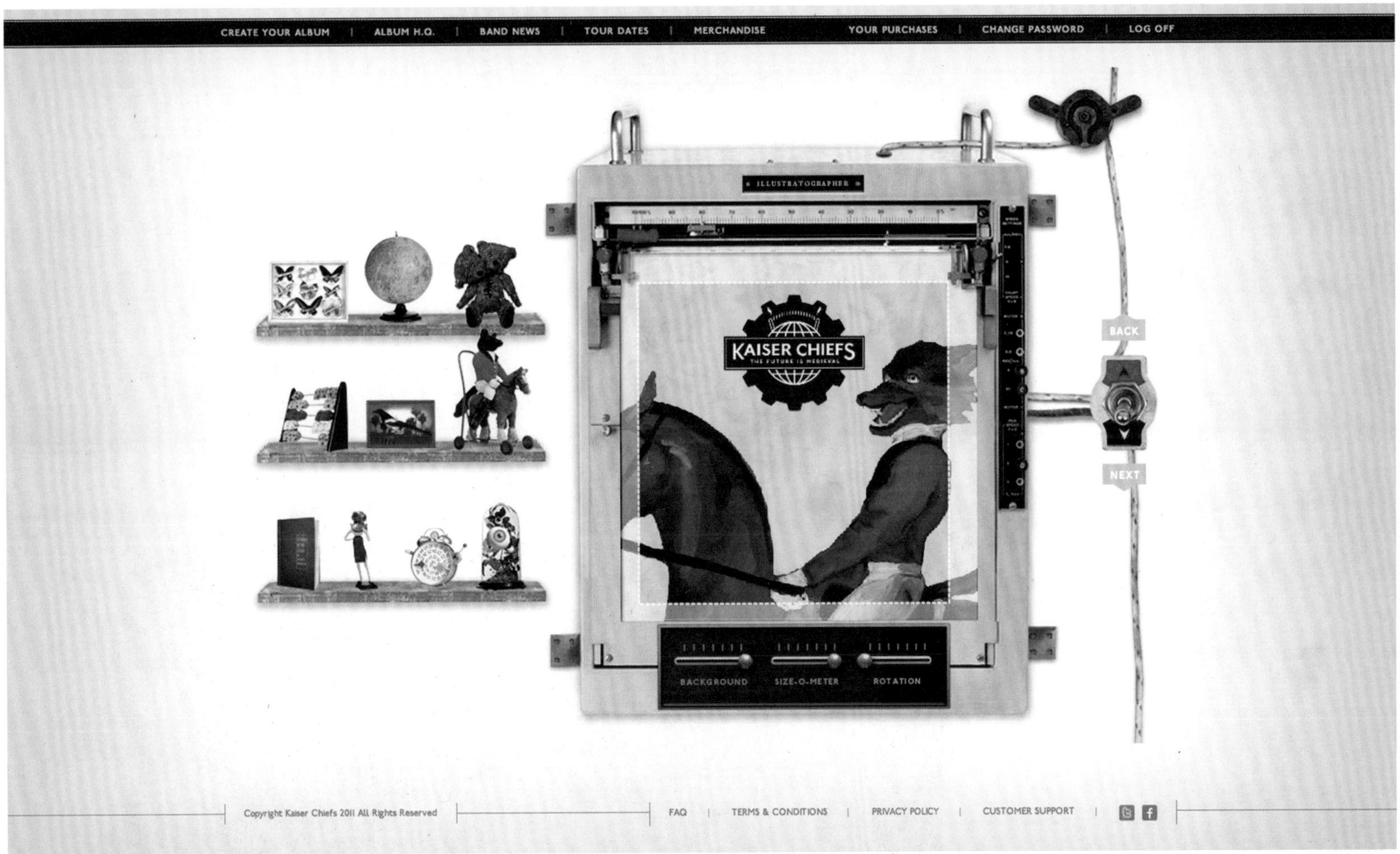

CREATE YOUR ALBUM | ALBUM H.Q. | BAND NEWS | TOUR DATES | MERCHANDISE YOUR PURCHASES | CHANGE PASSWORD | LOG OFF

ILLUSTRATOGRAPHER

KAISER CHIEFS
THE FUTURE IS MEDIEVAL

BACK

NEXT

BACKGROUND SIZE-O-METER ROTATION

Copyright Kaiser Chiefs 2011 All Rights Reserved

FAQ | TERMS & CONDITIONS | PRIVACY POLICY | CUSTOMER SUPPORT

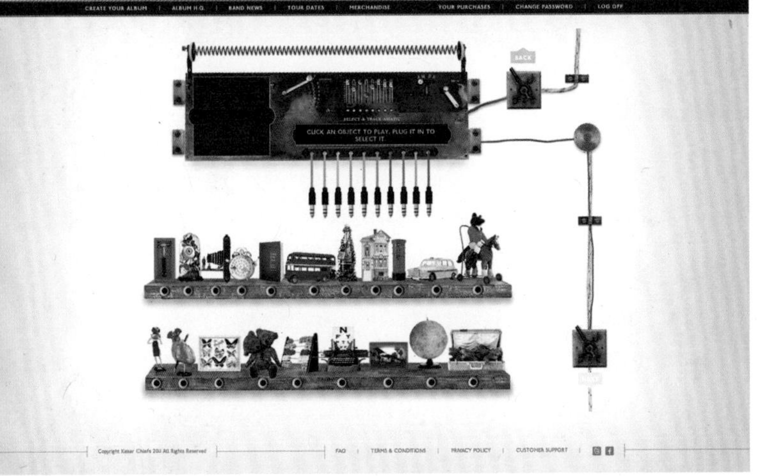

Yellow Pencil in Integrated & Earned Media

Earned Media Campaign
Clemenger BBDO Wellington
for the New Zealand Transport Agency

Ghost Chips
Drink driving is a big problem in New Zealand, particularly with young Maori guys. When they're out partying, the last thing they want to do is kill the vibe by telling a mate not to drive home drunk. We tackled the issue with 'Ghost Chips', a campaign based on a film that portrayed the audience in a cool, aspirational way. We used humour to break through and laced the content with catchphrases. A couple of lines in the film quickly became part of the Kiwi vernacular, giving our audience the tools they needed to speak up and stop their mates from drink driving. The campaign was a massive viral success, resulting in countless mentions in social media, video mash-ups and the biggest New Zealand meme of the year.

Art Director
Brigid Alkema
Copywriters
Mitch Alison
Brigid Alkema
Philip Andrew
Steve Ayson
Executive Creative Director
Philip Andrew
Director
Steve Ayson
Producer
Larisa Tiffin
Agency Producer
Martin Gray
Editor
Peter Scribberas
Sound Engineer
Jon Cooper
Music Composer
Mahuia Bridgman-Cooper
Advertising Agency
Clemenger BBDO Wellington
Account Directors
Julianne Hastings
Linda Major
Brand Managers
Paul Graham
Rachel Prince
Client
New Zealand Transport Agency

World Record Jump Testing
Hot Wheels Test Facility
April 2011

Nomination in Integrated & Earned Media

Integrated
Mistress
for Mattel

Hot Wheels for Real
The Hot Wheels for Real campaign revolved around the mysterious Hot Wheels Test Facility, where cars and tracks are tested on a life-sized scale. Also featured was Team Hot Wheels, a real team of the world's best drivers. The campaign consisted of over 30 pieces of content. This included an online promotion, a global brand TV commercial, an integrated online media buy that teased a live event (a world-record-breaking vehicle jump) and a half-hour TV show. Exclusive content from the show and the identity of the driver were then released via a transmedia activation on Facebook.

Art Director
Brittany Riley
Copywriters
Damien Eley
Scott Harris
Melissa Stefanini
Creative Directors
Damien Eley
Scott Harris
Design Director
Blake E Marquis
Director
Mike "Mouse" McCoy
Producers
Kay Lynn Dutcher
Lyra Rider
Executive Producer
Jeff Rohrer
Editor
Jeff Tober
Visual Effects Producer
Sean Cushing
Line Producer
Ryan Slavin
Design Vice President
Felix Holst
Digital Media Manager
Travis Harding
Social Media Manager
Lindsey Chen
Creative Agency
Mistress
Production Companies
Bandito Brothers
Laissez Faire Presents
Visual Effects Company
Cantina Creative
Mixing
Lime Studios
Public Relations
Ketchum
Strategic Directors
Christian Jacobsen
Jens Stoelken
Brands Executive Vice President
Tim Kilpin
Marketing Vice President
Simon Waldron
Marketing Senior Manager
Heather Miller
Public Relations Vice President
Sara Rosales
Client
Mattel
Brand
Hot Wheels

Integrated
Whybin\TBWA\Tequila Sydney
for Mars Petcare

Pedigree Adoption Drive
Sadly, over 100,000 dogs are needlessly euthanised every year in Australia because most people find it difficult visiting shelter homes to adopt. So if we couldn't bring people to the shelter dogs, we decided to bring the shelter dogs to the people. We embarked on the biggest pedigree adoption drive in Australia's history. Central to our campaign was a search engine that matches potential adopters with a dog from a pet rescue database. We used activity and communications across multiple channels, including a mobile phone and Facebook app, social networking, outdoor events and online branded content, as well as educational events and films.

Art Director
Hannes Ciatti
Copywriter
Dean Hamilton
Digital Creative Director
Russ Tucker
Executive Creative Directors
Dave Bowman
Matty Burton

Agency Producer
Chris Rollings
Advertising Agency
Whybin\TBWA\Tequila Sydney
Account Director
Andrea Byrne
Client
Mars Petcare
Brand
Pedigree

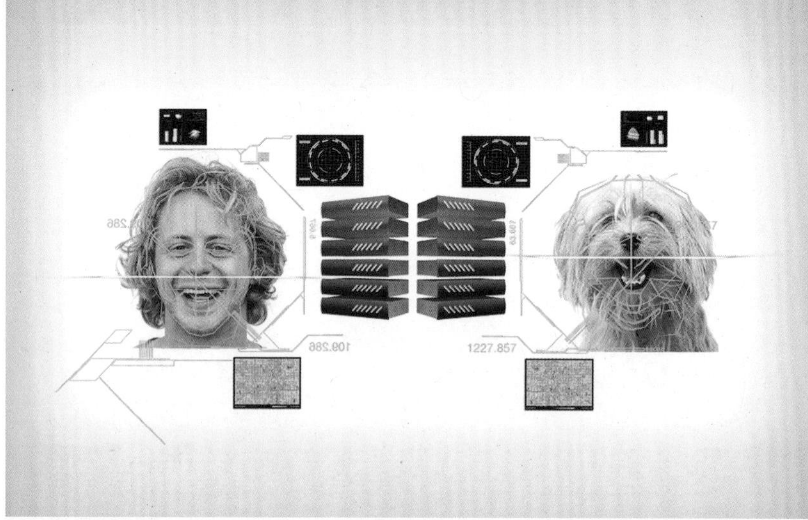

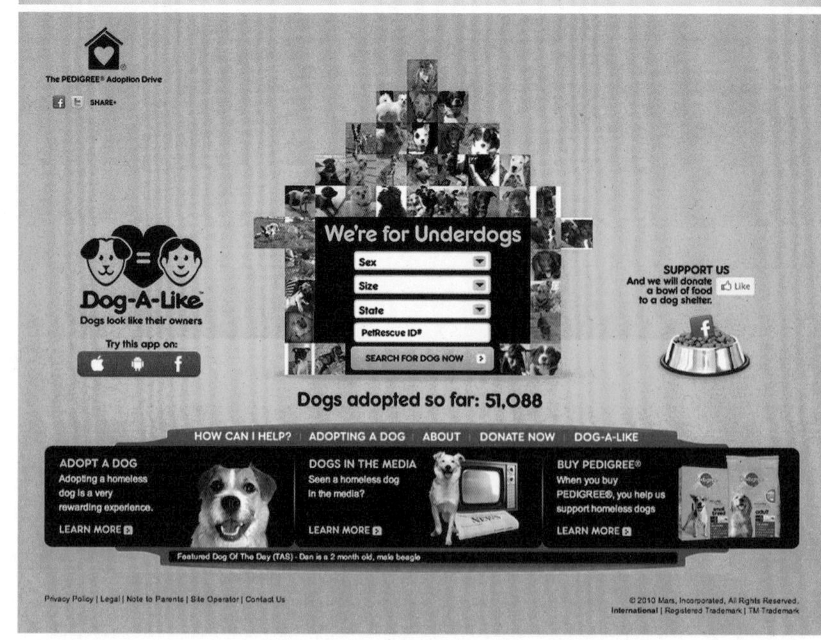

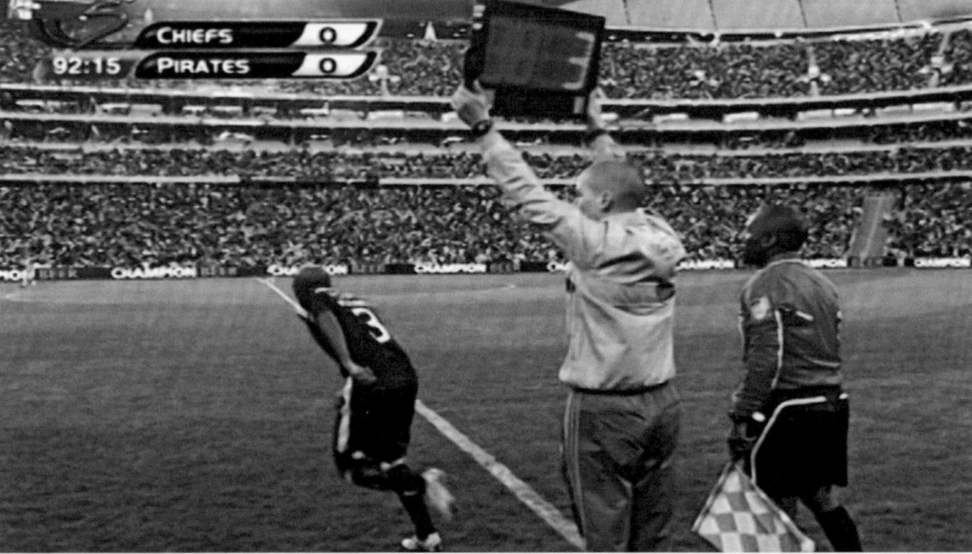

Integrated
Ogilvy Cape Town
for South African Breweries

Be the Coach
Carling Black Label wanted to leverage its upcoming sponsorship of a football match and use it as a way to attract new consumers. For the first time ever, fans could use their mobile phones to vote for the players in the Carling Black Label Cup between Orlando Pirates and Kaizer Chiefs. They could literally be the coach by selecting the players and making a live substitution on the day of the game. We received more than 10.5 million votes in seven weeks and generated over $12.2million of PR for the brand. Over 80,000 fans watched the game live, and Carling Black Label saw growth in a declining market.

Art Directors
Delano Chengan
Jonathan Lang
Benjamin de Villiers
Copywriters
Logan Broadley
Tommy Le Roux
Yazeed Solomons
Digital Designer
Alex Van Niekerk
Creative Directors
Jonathan Lang
Tommy Le Roux
Nicholas Wittenberg
Executive Creative Director
Chris Gotz
Head of Interactive Production
Umar Jakoet
Agency Producer
Bronwyn Henry

Advertising Agency
Ogilvy Cape Town
Mobile Marketing Agency
Brandtone
Production Company
Platypus Productions
Sound Design
The Workroom
Account Director
Paul Grater
Business Director
Luca Gallarelli
Client
South African Breweries
Brand
Carling Black Label

Integrated
Publicis Mojo Auckland
for Greenpeace

Oil on Canvas
The MV Rena oil spill was New Zealand's worst maritime disaster. Greenpeace wanted to use it as a warning against the much greater threat posed by deep-sea oil drilling. Using actual dead birds and oil from Rena, we created a series of handmade prints to be used as street posters with a petition call. We also created a number of canvas artworks for galleries and pop-up exhibitions around the country. The price of entry? To sign the petition. We sent out prints as direct mail to celebrities and media, inviting them to the exhibition launch. Images of the prints were also aired in a TV commercial and web film.

Art Director
Mike Barnwell
Copywriter
Guy Denniston
Executive Creative Directors
Mike Barnwell
Lachlan McPherson
Director
James Solomon
Producer
Angela Da Silva
Advertising Agency
Publicis Mojo Auckland
Production Company
Flying Fish
Marketing Manager
Michael Tritt
Client
Greenpeace

THIS OIL PRINT WAS MADE USING AN ACTUAL BIRD KILLED IN THE 'RENA' DISASTER.

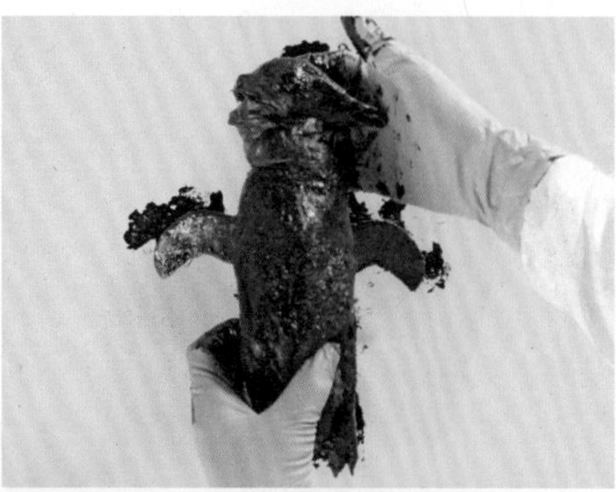

Integrated
Draftfcb San Francisco
for Electronic Arts

Your Mom Hates Dead Space 2

Electronic Arts' graphic, violent and terrifying video game 'Dead Space 2' was set to be a certain hit amongst a small but loyal audience. Our task was to make it resonate with everyone else. And to get people to listen, particularly our target of cynical 18 year olds, we needed a credible voice. So, we turned to moms – because a mother's disapproval has always been an accurate measure of what's cool. We showed the worst moments in the game to over 200 moms and recorded their horrified reactions. And with that content, the campaign was born.

Art Director
Justin Hargraves
Copywriter
Eric Molina
Digital Designer
Mike Squibb
Creative Directors
Colin McRae
Tony Vazquez
Executive Creative Director
Tom O'Keefe
Director
Charles Jensen
Agency Producer
Jeremy Arth
Editors
Tim Brooks
Kevin Jardin
Connor McDonald
Advertising Agency
Draftfcb San Francisco
Account Handler
Isaac Clemens
Business Director
Dominic Whittles
Client
Electronic Arts

Integrated
Forsman & Bodenfors
for IKEA Sweden

Lullabies

IKEA wanted a campaign that would revitalise the long running claim for its bed offer: 'Better Sleep for Everyone'. So we asked six of Sweden's most talented musicians to compose modern interpretations of classic lullabies. We turned the resulting songs into six music videos each featuring an artist in a bed. We first aired the music videos on TV, then created a website where you could watch them and read more about the artists and their respective beds. We also released the songs on an album. With a cover that looked, surprisingly, a lot like a banner for IKEA. We could also follow people as they logged into iTunes and bought our commercials for 99 cents each.

Art Directors
Andreas Malm
Adam Ulvegärde
Copywriters
Elisabeth Christensson
Fredrik Jansson
Designer
Christoffer Persson
Agency Producer
Alexander Blidner
Web Producer
Stefan Thomson
Advertising Agency
Forsman & Bodenfors

Production Companies
Kokokaka
Social Club
Music Composition
Music Super Circus
Planner
Tobias Nordström
Account Executive
Hans Andersson
Account Manager
Katarina Klofsten
Client
IKEA Sweden
Brand
IKEA

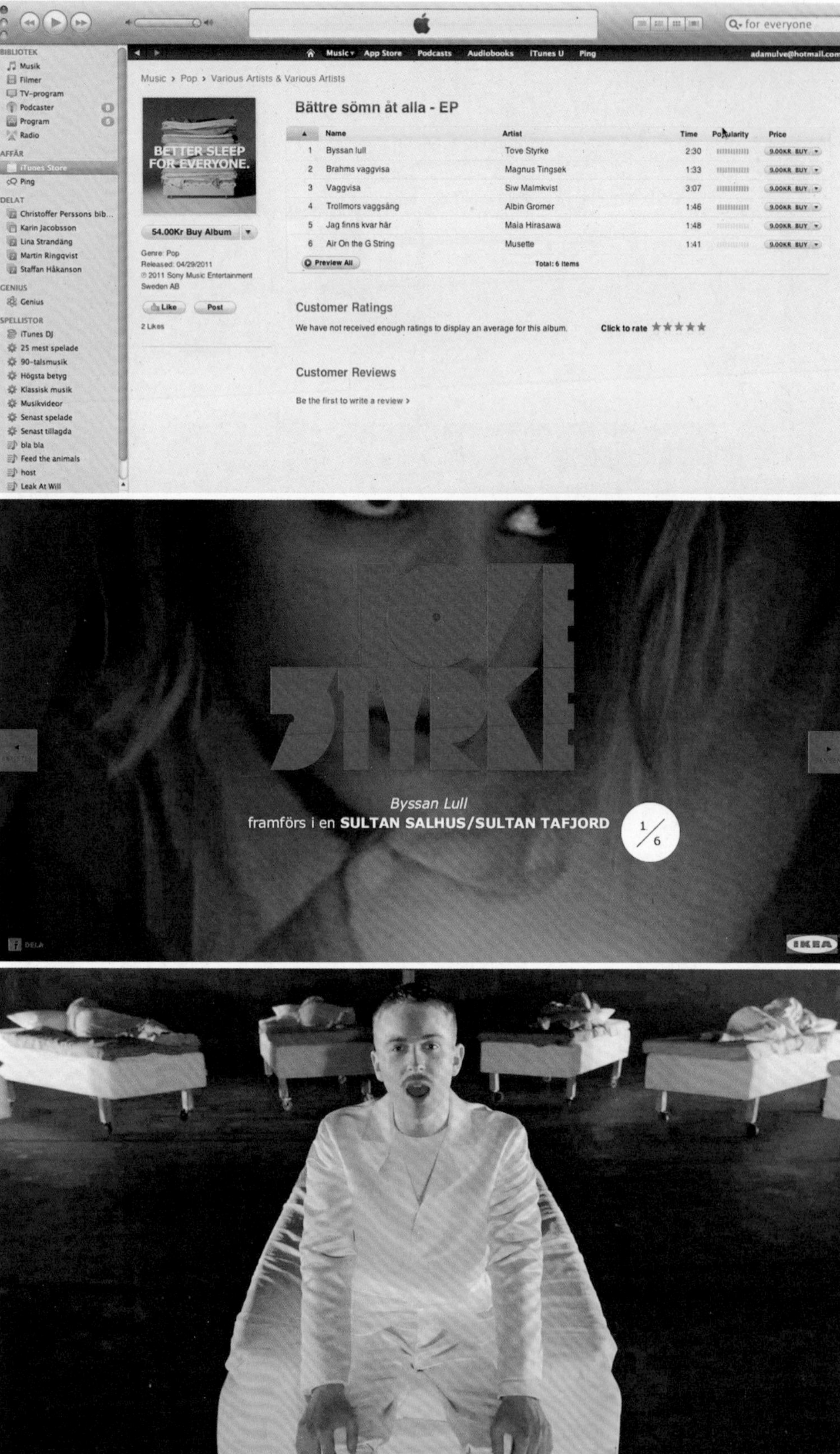

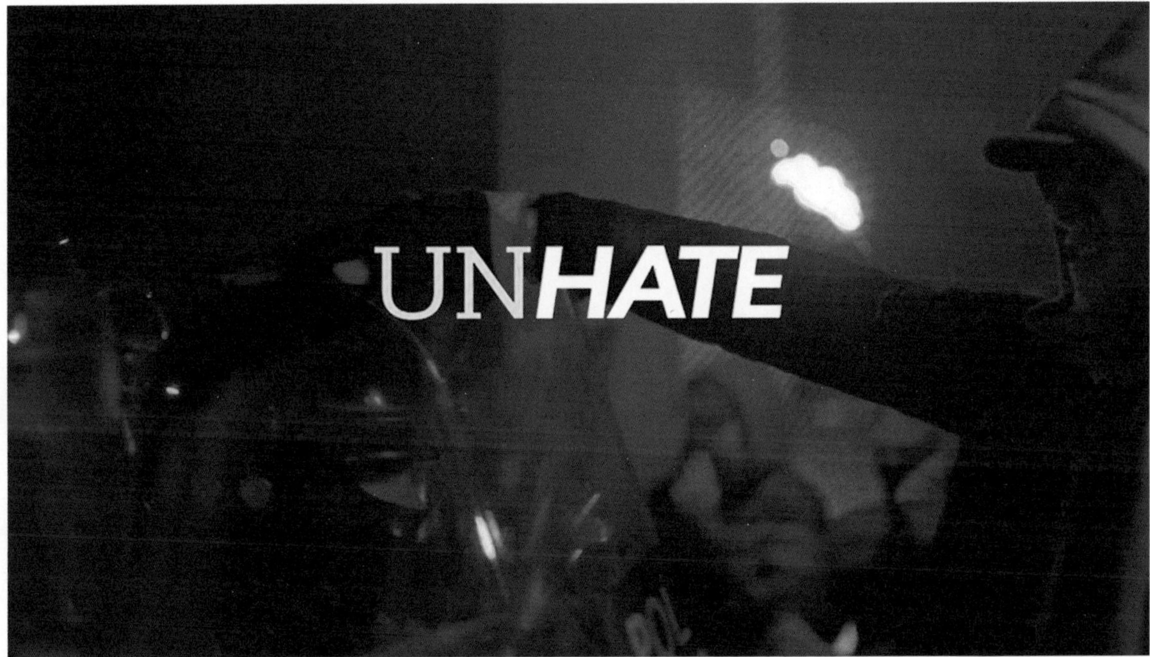

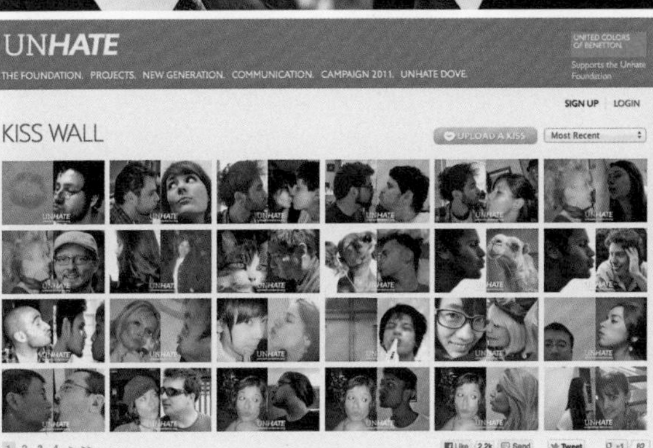

Earned Media Campaign
72andSunny & Fabrica
for United Colors of Benetton

Unhate
In a year of crisis, government distrust, war, and social and religious turmoil, we decided to deliver a simple and powerful message of tolerance and peace; a new expression of Benetton's original values and credo. An expression to put people in a new state of mind: Unhate. Unhate is a message that invites us to consider that hate and love are not as far away from each other as we think. The two opposing sentiments are often in a delicate and unstable balance.

Designer
Wendy Richardson
Creative Directors
Carlo Cavallone
Paulo Martins
Robert Nakata
Erik Ravelo
Executive Creative Director
John Boiler
Chief Creative Officer
Glenn Cole
Director
Laurent Chanez
Agency Producers
Sam Baerwald
Ellen Pot
Print Producer
Maria Perez
Advertising Agencies
72andSunny NL
72andSunny USA
Fabrica
Production Company
Identity
Brand Manager
Frederic Point
Brand Director
Judson Whigham
Client
United Colors of Benetton

Earned Media Campaign
BBH London
for Aaron Biber

Keep Aaron Cutting
The 2011 London riots lost thousands of people their livelihoods and belief in their fellow man. Social media was blamed, with many calling it a negative force. But we believed social media could do good. So we launched a campaign to help 89-year old barber Aaron Biber stay in business after his shop was ransacked. People responded via the Internet, donating over £35,000 in 72 hours and focussing the world's media on his little shop. The headlines truly changed too, celebrating social media for the rebuild of London. The problem child of social media had solved a problem and it kept Aaron cutting.

Creative Director
Pablo Marques
Executive Creative Director
Nick Gill
Creative Team
Sophie Browness
Mareka Carter
Björn Conradi
Omid Fard
Simon Pearse
Producer
Chris Watling
Advertising Agency
BBH London
Strategist
Ben Shaw
Public Relations Manager
Isobel Barnes
Communications Director
Sarah Pollard
Head of Administration
Andy Coppin
Client
Aaron Biber

Keep Aaron Cutting

Aaron Biber, 89, had his barbershop destroyed by the rioters.

Wednesday, 10 August 2011

Aaron's Story

"I will probably have to close because I haven't got insurance and I can't afford the repairs," - Aaron

Aaron has been in the Tottenham area for 41 years and at 89 is devastated by the damage to his livelihood.

Let's use the internet, spread this and all donate a couple of quid so Aaron can get his shop back up and running so he will not have to worry how he's going to make a living at his old age.

Photo courtesy of Getty Images, taken by Dan Kitwood
Aaron's shop was wrecked by the rioters

Aaron lost his wife last year. Born in Cable Street, he built up his businesses in Tottenham High Street over several decades and is a popular figure in the local community.

Thank you all

£35,000 has been raised for Aaron.

Who's behind this?

We are interns at BBH, a London advertising agency, and were touched by Aaron's story and wanted to help. We wanted to use this opportunity to show that youth and technology can be a force for good.

We are currently part of the first round of BBH Barn's interns.

All the money donated will be given directly to Aaron to help him get his Barbershop up and running again.

Thanks for your support,

Björn, Sophie and Omid

Read more about the Barn and the Project

Share it

Like Mareka Carter, Olivia Muus and 13,684 others like this.

Tweet 9.2

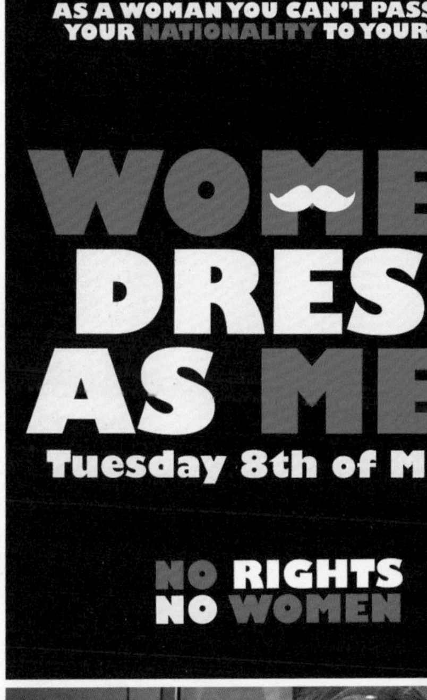

Earned Media Campaign
Leo Burnett Beirut
for No Rights No Women

No Rights No Women

We were approached by a group of Lebanese women fighting for women's rights, to create a campaign for their new organisation. Under Lebanese law, men and women are not equal. For example, Lebanese women have no right to pass their nationality onto their children. Because men have more rights than women, we asked women to give up their womanhood. We aimed to engage the largest number of people with a simple act. Four weeks before International Women's day, women became men online. On Facebook, women changed both their profile pictures and gender to become men. Hype was building up online until March 8th, when the movement hit the real world, and women dressed as men filled offices and workplaces around the city.

Art Directors
Natasha Maasri
Lea Salibi
Copywriters
Dalia Haidar
Rana Khoury
Creative Director
Areej Mahmoud
Executive Creative Director
Bechara Mouzannar

Advertising Agency
Leo Burnett Beirut
Account Handler
Nada Abi Saleh
Marketing Manager
Rana Ismail
Client
No Rights No Women

Earned Media Campaign
Ogilvy & Mather Sydney
for Coca-Cola South Pacific

Share a Coke
Coca-Cola needed to reconnect with young Australians. After 125 years of printing 'Coca-Cola' on every bottle, we invited Australians to 'Share a Coke', by replacing the brand name on the packaging with 150 of the most popular names in Australia. Coca-Cola was bringing people together with the best conversation starter of all – a first name. In just three months, we saw young adult consumption increase by 7% and Facebook traffic increase by 870%, making us the most talked about page in Australia.

Art Directors
Luke Acret
Liam Hillier
Jakub Szymanski
Copywriters
Omid Amidi
Alex Stainton
Creative Directors
Boris Garelja
Brian Merrifield
Executive Creative Director
Chris Ford
Producer
Claire McDonald
Print Producer
Sonia Ebrington
Advertising Agency
Ogilvy & Mather Sydney
Digital Agency
Wunderman Sydney
Media Agency
Ikon
Kiosk Manufacturer
Urban
Public Relations
One Green Bean
Sales Promotion
Momentum
Planners
Gerry Cyron
Damian Damjanovski
Account Handlers
Suzie Baker
Adam Lee
Vickie Mogensen
Client
Coca-Cola South Pacific

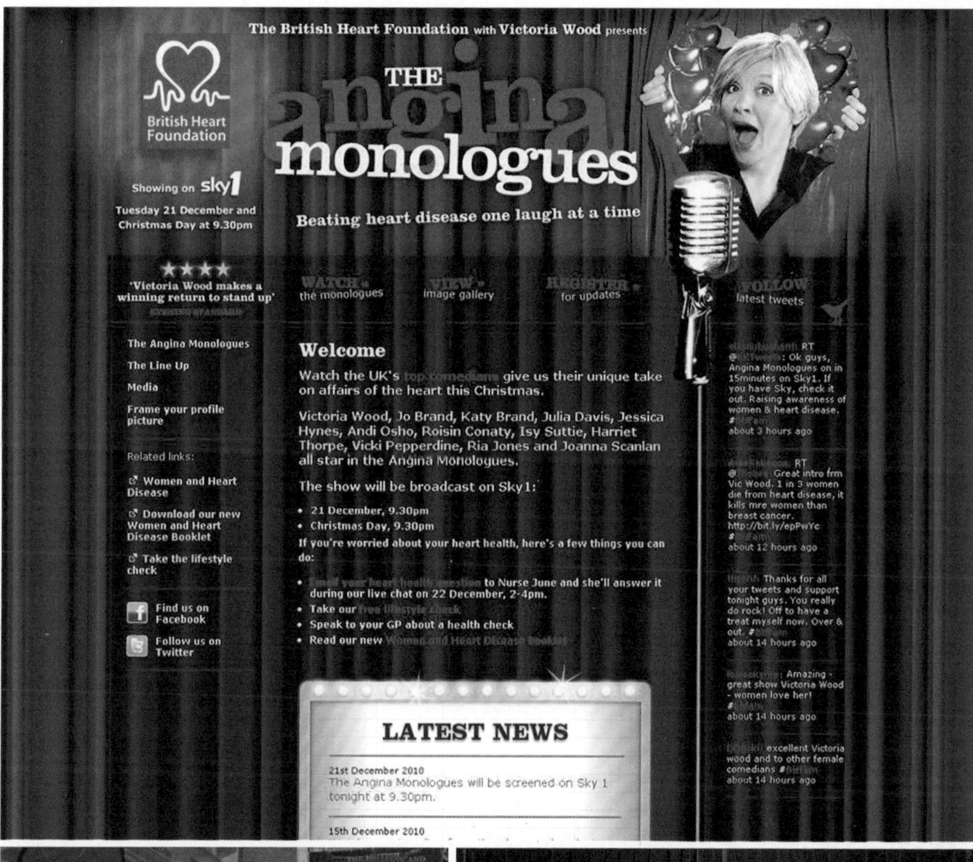

Earned Media Campaign
Grey London
for the British Heart Foundation

The Angina Monologues
Coronary heart disease is the biggest killer of women in the UK, yet breast cancer is seen as a bigger health threat. Women are constantly inundated with health scares – but what if we could make them engage with this unpleasant truth, by choice? We enrolled the nation's funniest women, led by Victoria Wood, and created 'The Angina Monologues', a comedy show and special TV event to raise awareness of heart disease amongst women. This hugely successful event saw Victoria Wood win 'Best Female Comedian' at the prestigious 2011 British Comedy Awards for her involvement in 'The Angina Monologues'.

Art Director
Scott Bradley
Creative Directors
Dan Cole
Andy Garnett
Vicki Maguire
Executive Creative Director
Nils Leonard
Producers
Martin Dance
Hazel Stocker
Executive Producers
Lucy Ansbro
Simon Wells
Victoria Wood
Agency Producers
James Covill
Francesca Mair
Leon McComish

Audio Producer
David Woolley
Advertising Agency
Grey London
Media Agencies
Drum
PHD
Planner
Nick Hirst
Account Manager
Sophie Fredheim
Client
British Heart Foundation

1

2

3

4

5

6

7

Jury Foreman
1. Scott Seaborn
XS2

2. Rik Haslam
RAPP

3. Mark Freeman
Movement

4. Thea Frost
Somewhat_

5. Masaru Kitakaze
Hakuhodo

6. Kim Lenox
Interaction Design
Association

7. Richard Ting
R/GA New York

Select a Wireless Network
! UGLY DUCKLING
* GETS BEAK-JOB.
+ SNARES RICH
< MALLARD.
> Melb Writers Festival
> Stories Unbound
Cancel
space
Search
123

Select a Wireless Network
! DRAGON SLAYER
* PURSUED BY
+ ANIMAL RIGHTS
< ACTIVISTS.
> Melb Writers Festival
> Stories Unbound
Cancel

Select a Wireless Network
! SHOTGUN WEDDING
* BACKFIRES; TURNS
+ INTO JOB-LOT
< FUNERAL.
> Melb Writers Festival
> Stories Unbound
Cancel

Yellow Pencil in Mobile Marketing

Mobile Campaigns & Mobile Advertising
JWT Melbourne
for the Melbourne Writers Festival

Wi-Fiction
Wi-Fiction is an entirely new digital medium of storytelling that works by hijacking the 'available networks' pop-up window on mobile devices. A box containing a set of Wi-Fi routers was placed in Federation Square, Melbourne's cultural epicentre and Australia's biggest free Wi-Fi hotspot. When anyone nearby used a smartphone, iPad or laptop, they saw the list of network names had seemingly conspired to create short, humorous stories. During the festival, over 65,000 visitors were exposed to over 20 different Wi-Fiction stories, bringing to life the festival theme, 'Stories Unbound'. This work was also awarded a Yellow Pencil in the 'Writing for Mobile Marketing' category.

Creative Director
Jim Ritchie
Executive Creative Director
Richard Muntz
Copywriters
Deborah Frenkel
Jim Ritchie
Advertising Agency
JWT Melbourne
Planner
Anuj Mehra
Account Handlers
Melissa Benavides
Prue Tehan
James Wright
Marketing Manager
Juliette Kringas
Client
Melbourne Writers Festival

Yellow Pencil in Mobile Marketing

Mobile Interaction & Experience
AKQA London
for Heineken

Heineken Star Player
Heineken Star Player is the world's first multi-platform live dual-screen football game. Created for the premium beer that aims to make watching the best football in the world even better, Heineken Star Player engages fans and takes watching football on TV to the next level. Fans play along live with their favourite teams, predicting the outcome of key moments as the match unfolds to earn points and compete with friends.

Creative Director
Miles Unwin
Executive Creative Director
Nick Bailey
Associate Creative Director
Kevin Russell
Chief Creative Officer
James Hilton
Executive Creative Development Director
Andy Hood
Associate Creative Development Director
Paddy Keane
Art Director
Jamen Percy
Senior Copywriter
Tessa Hewson
Technical Designer
Christopher Marsh
Head of Technical Architecture
Neville Kuyt
Technical Delivery Manager
Gareth Scrivens
Developer
Lewis Corbett
Creative Developer
Wanja Stier
Senior Web Developers
James Lelyveld
Andrew Smith
Senior Software Engineer
Rob Gilks
Technical Architect
Christopher Marsh
User Experience Architect
Joanne Alden
Editor
Ellen Woolridge
Quality Assurance Manager
Ellen Woolridge
Senior Strategic Analyst
Lewis Corbett
Advertising Agency
AKQA London
Project Manager
Carolyn Mangan
Project Director
Hanna Gray
Group Account Director
James Scott
Client
Heineken

Nomination in Mobile Marketing

Mobile Campaigns & Mobile Advertising
Ogilvy Cape Town & Brandtone
for South African Breweries

Be the Coach

Carling Black Label wanted to leverage its upcoming sponsorship of a football match and use it as a way to attract new consumers. For the first time ever, fans could use their mobile phones to vote for the players in the Carling Black Label Cup between Orlando Pirates and Kaizer Chiefs. They could literally be the coach by selecting the players and making a live substitution on the day of the game. We received more than 10.5 million votes in seven weeks and generated over $12.2million of PR for the brand. Over 80,000 fans watched the game live, and Carling Black Label saw growth in a declining market.

Creative Directors
Jonathan Lang
Tommy Le Roux
Nicholas Wittenberg
Executive Creative Director
Chris Gotz
Art Directors
Delano Chengan
Jonathan Lang
Benjamin de Villiers
Copywriters
Logan Broadley
Tommy Le Roux
Yazeed Solomons
Digital Designer
Alex Van Niekerk
Agency Producer
Bronwyn Henry
Head of Interactive Production
Umar Jakoet
Mobile Marketing Agency
Brandtone
Advertising Agency
Ogilvy Cape Town
Production Company
Platypus Productions
Sound Design
The Workroom
Account Director
Paul Grater
Business Director
Luca Gallarelli
Client
South African Breweries
Brand
Carling Black Label

Nomination in Mobile Marketing

Sound Design & Use of Music
for Mobile Marketing
AMV BBDO
for Wrigley

The Night Jar
The brief was to develop a brand awareness campaign for 5 Gum, aimed at 18 to 24-year-olds, using the proposition: 'Stimulate your senses'. So we created an experience that stimulated their senses for real. We identified mobile gaming as the most relevant platform for the audience, and created an unexpected experience: a video game with no video. It uses groundbreaking 3D binaural sound technology to create a world of sound, through which you must navigate using only hearing and touch. It is a chilling sci-fi horror game where users have to escape an alien infested spaceship.

Creative Directors
Mark Fairbanks
Thiago de Moraes
Art Director
Thiago de Moraes
Copywriters
Neil Bennun
Mark Fairbanks
Executive Creative Director
Paul Brazier
Technical Architects
Jean Phillipe Altier
Adam Hoyle
Developer
Trevor Klein
Programmer
Daniel Jones
Designers
Neal Coghlan
Paul Grizzell
Thiago de Moraes
Harry Osborne
James Townsend
Directors
Paul Bennun
Nick Ryan
Tassos Stevens
Producers
Kelly Casey
Esther Cunliffe
David O'Donnell
Information Architect
Pete Law
Advertising Agency
AMV BBDO
Production Company
somethin' else
Production Manager
Laura Nix
Client
Wrigley
Brand
5 Gum

Nomination in Mobile Marketing

Sound Design & Use of Music
for Mobile Marketing
Society 46
for Carlsberg Sweden & Pepsico

The Sound of Football
For this Pepsi Refresh project, we accepted the challenge to invent a new way for visually impaired people to play football. We used augmented reality sound to guide them in real time on the field. They could hear where the ball was, as well as the other players, the goals, and the side lines. The project was released as open source, and Society 46 is now collaborating with scientists in the field. Discovery Channel did a documentary about the project, which has been featured in 'Fast Company'.

Sound Designer
Jon Pontén
Creative Directors
Martin Cedergren
Kalle Thyselius
Art Director
Björn Kusa
Copywriter
Patrick Dry
Developers
Jonas Stattin
Ellen Sundh
Designer
Robin Lantz
Directors
Fredrik Forrest
Henrik Gyllenskiöld
Producers
Kristina Nilsson
Alex Picha
Karl Rosander
Marcin Tallmarken
Production Company
Society 46
Clients
Carlsberg Sweden
Pepsico
Brand
Pepsi

Mobile Campaigns & Mobile Advertising
Colenso BBDO Auckland
for Westpac New Zealand

Impulse Saver
What if we could save as impulsively as we spend? Imagine a red button, and every time you press it you save. Now imagine that button in your pocket. We developed Westpac's Impulse Saver iPhone app, the world's first impulse saving product from a bank. Simply by pressing the button, customers can save a predetermined amount by sending it from a transaction account to a savings account.

Digital Creative Director
Terry Williams-Willcock
Creative Chairman
Nick Worthington
Art Director
Sarah Frizzell
Copywriter
Tom Paine
Designer
Kate Slavin
Digital Designer
Pablo Dunovits
Creative Technologist
Mathew Tizard
Developer
David Wilcox
Director
Adam Good
Digital Producers
Oli Moorman
Amanda Theobold
Advertising Agency
Colenso BBDO
Auckland
Strategic Director
James Hurman
Account Directors
Marcelle Baker
Lou Kuegler
Rebecca Richardson
Account Manager
Krystel Houghton
Client
Westpac
New Zealand
Brand
Westpac

Mobile Interaction & Experience
Brand New School & Venables Bell & Partners
for eBay & Toys for Tots

Give-a-Toy Store
For the 2011 holiday season, eBay teamed up with charity Toys for Tots to launch Give-a-Toy Store, an interactive window display in both New York and San Francisco, which lets you donate a toy by scanning its tag with the eBay mobile app. Once scanned, the animated toys come to life, encouraging passers-by to get into the holiday giving spirit. To accommodate those who couldn't stop by in person, we created the Give-a-Toy Store that lived on eBay.com and Facebook, allowing people to donate whenever they felt inspired.

Creative Directors
Lee Einhorn
Tyler Hampton
Executive Creative Directors
Will McGinness
Paul Venables
Art Director
Brad Kayal
Copywriter
Kelly Diaz
Director
Robert Bisi
Producer
Jeanette Etchebehere
Executive Producer
Jason Cohon
Interactive Directors
Justin Bakse
Heather Wischmann
Visual Effects Supervisor
Marco Maldonado
Director of Integrated Production
Craig Allen
Advertising Agency
Venables Bell & Partners
Digital Design Agency
Brand New School
Art Buyer
Jacqueline Fodor
Clients
eBay
Toys for Tots

1

2

3

4

5

6

Jury Foreman
1. Andy Morahan
Great Guns

2. Phil Clandillon
FOAM / Sony Music UK

3. Dougal Wilson
Blink

4. Oscar Romagosa
Canada / Partizan

5. Ross Anderson
Nice&Polite

6. Tom Lindsay
Trim

Yellow Pencil in Music Videos

Music Videos
El Niño & Irene
for Kitsuné

The Greeks

This music video is a graphic representation of war using children and toy guns. We used a new After Effects plugin called 'Crazy Akira', which generates random 2D blood and explosion SFX animations. For the shoot we used a new device called 'Automatic Director', a sort of drone with a video camera that flies randomly around the actors and finds the best angles to film them. The actors are generated with a new 3ds Max plugin called 'Frank Einstein', which generates ultra realistic characters that you can download in real life using a 3D biological printer.

Direction
Megaforce
Artist
Is Tropical
Sound Designer
Laurent D'Herbecourt
Production Companies
El Niño
Irene

Music Production
Kitsuné
Animation
Seven
Sound Design
Tranquille le Chat
Record Company
Kitsuné

Yellow Pencil in Music Videos

Music Videos
Division & Les Télécréateurs
for Dim Mak Records

No Brain
'If someone was to pass you a video treatment that read something like '90s rave visuals, fluro pixel explosions and a fat dancer', you'd most likely wipe your ass with it and call it a day. This, however, is proper psychedelic mun, a stunning, woozy trip you can safely take from the comfy confines of your office cubicle.' – Modular People. 'Here comes a corker. Étienne de Crécy's 'No Brain' is a massive, unapologetic slab of thumping retro-electro, and Fleur & Manu's video is an awesome exercise in appropriately head-frying psychedelic CGI – with a surprising and equally nutty live action ending.' – Promo News.

Directors
Fleur & Manu
Artist
Étienne de Crécy
Production Companies
Division
Les Télécréateurs

Post Production
Mathematic
Record Company
Dim Mak Records

Yellow Pencil in Music Videos

Special Effects for Music Videos
PRETTYBIRD
for Columbia

Simple Math
A horrific car accident has Manchester Orchestra frontman Andy Hull going through the calculus of his life in this fractured and ambitious video. It's a story about a 23-year-old who questions everything from marriage to love to religion to sex. Despite the video's fairly low budget, it has received huge amounts of critical acclaim. This work was also nominated in the 'Music Videos' category.

Visual Effects
Daniels
Direction
Daniels
Art Director
Sophie Kosofsky
Executive Producer
Candice Ouaknine
Video Producer
Gaetano Crupi Jr

Artist
Manchester Orchestra
Director of Photography
Jackson Hunt
Production Company
PRETTYBIRD
Record Company
Columbia

Music Videos
PRETTYBIRD
for Warp Records

My Machines

The Daniels wanted to experiment with shooting a video in what appears to be a seamless take. The video tells the story about a guy falling slowly and dramatically down the up escalator at a mall, never able to get up or to reach the bottom. Battles and Gary Numan rock out unconcernedly around him. It's a sort of modern-age Sisyphean parable disguised as a low-budget music video.

Direction
Daniels
Executive Producer
Candice Ouaknine
Artist
Battles
Video Producer
Jonathan Wang
Director of Photography
Larkin Seiple
Production Company
PRETTYBIRD
Record Company
Warp Records

Music Videos
Partizan
for Warp Records

Ice Cream

From directing collective Canada comes the Battles 'Ice Cream' music video, which is more like an inner-space, free-form journey through what goes on inside a melting ice cream cone, as seen through the eyes of a 19-year-old girl. She enjoys the clash of hot and cold in her mind and body while seated inside a bath tub licking some chocolate ice cream.

Direction
Canada
Art Director
Roger Belles
Producer
Alba Barneda
Executive Producer
Oscar Romagosa
Artist
Battles
Director of Photography
Marc Gomez del Moral
Stylist
Xenia Gasull
Production Company
Partizan
Editing
Canada
Record Company
Warp Records

Music Videos
Partizan
for Epic Records

White Nights
Canada's 'White Nights' video effortlessly cuts between different environments, dimensions and states of mind – from a bright bedroom, to distant forests, to a blocky geometric space, to Oh Land leaping from a cliff into a lagoon. The video features charming choreography from Tuixen Benet, and is meticulously captured with beautiful cinematography by long-time collaborator Marc Gomez del Moral.

Direction
Canada
Art Director
James Hatt
Producer
Oscar Romagosa
Executive Producer
Jeff Pantaleo
Artist
Oh Land
Director of Photography
Marc Gomez del Moral

Editor
Luis Cervero
Choreographer
Tuixen Benet
Production Company
Partizan
Record Company
Epic Records

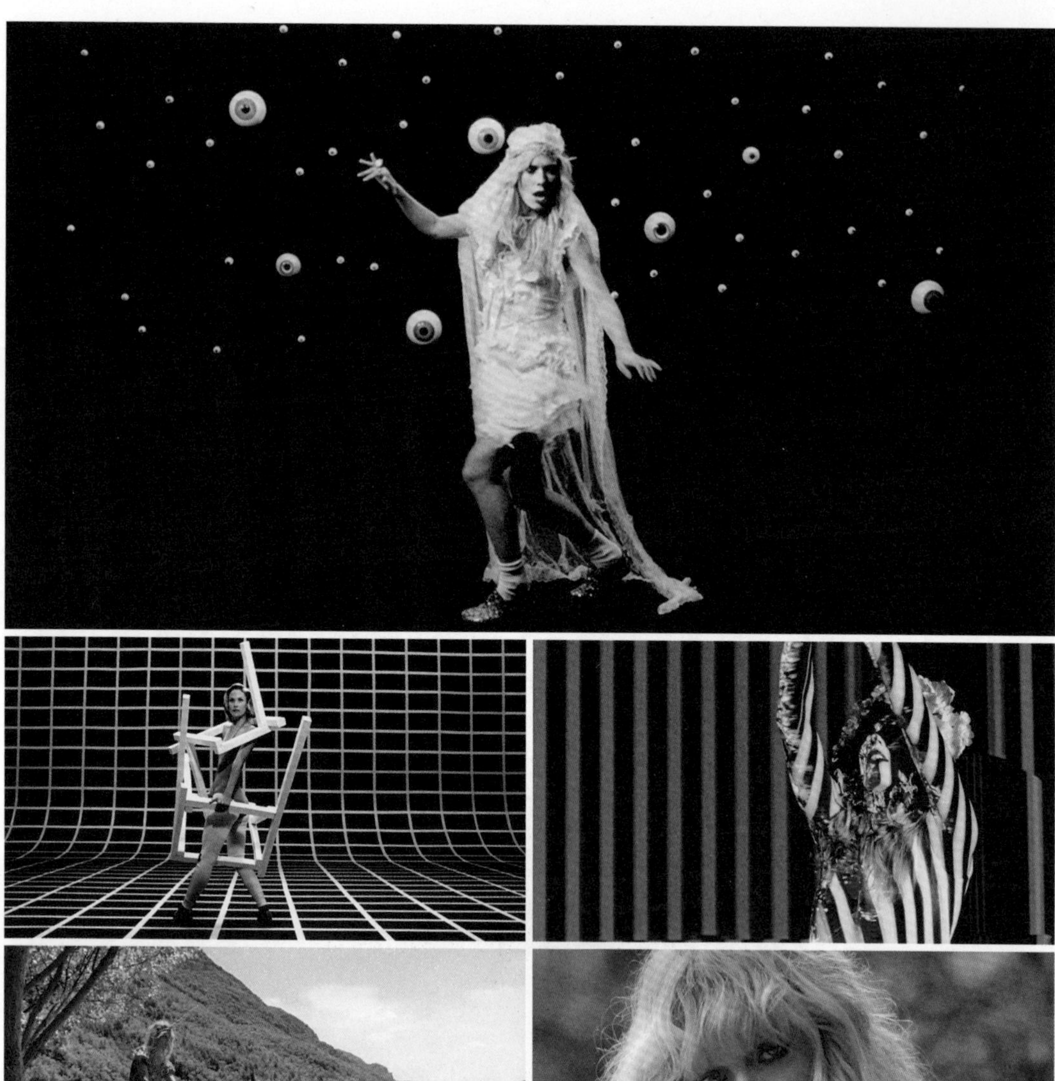

Music Videos
Colonel Blimp
for Because UK

The Bay
David Wilson turned the English Riviera into a tropical paradise for Metronomy's hit 'The Bay' with the help of some swimsuit-clad ladies and tongue-in-cheek imagery. Clever 80s-inspired editing is combined with humorous choreography and glamorous characters to accompany the band's signature electro-pop sound. It's a glorious tribute to summertime, complete with palm trees, white suits and sparkling turquoise pools. It makes Torquay look more like Miami than a seaside town in Devon.

Director
David Wilson
Art Director
Tim Gibson
Producer
Patrick Craig
Executive Producer
Tamsin Glasson
Artist
Metronomy
Colourist
James Bamford
Stylist
Cynthia
Lawrence John

Director of Photography
Richard Stewart
Editor
James Rose
Production Company
Colonel Blimp
Post Production
Munky
Editing
Cut+Run London
Record Company
Because UK
Video Commissioner
Jane Third

Music Videos
Somesuch & Co
for 3Beat

Big Bad Wolf
'Big Bad Wolf' is outrageous and hilariously funny, capturing Schofield's absurdist concept 'crotch faces'. A carefully crafted gag, 'Big Bad Wolf' enters the parallel universe of its characters in which they are ambushed and possessed by crotch faces.

Director
Keith Schofield
Producer
Tash Tan
Executive Producer
Tim Nash
Artist
Duck Sauce
Director of Photography
Damien Acevedo

Editor
Keith Schofield
Production Company
Somesuch & Co
Record Company
3Beat

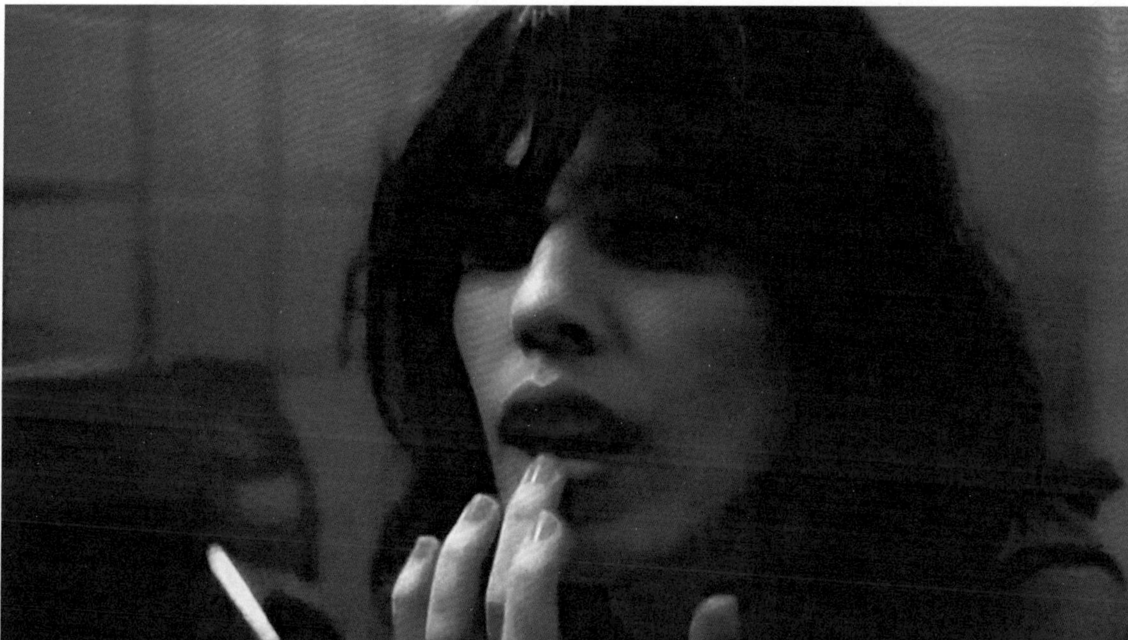

Music Videos
El Niño
for EMI

The Saboteur
Surrender Monkeys' video for The Kooks 'The Saboteur' sees an infectious smile spread throughout a nightclub, resulting in a rather disconcerting punch-up.

Direction
Surrender Monkeys
Producer
Jules Dieng
Executive Producers
Zico Judge
Norbert Phelut
Artist
The Kooks
Director of Photography
Cosmo Campbell
Sound Designer
Ed Downham
Post Producer
Glendon Percival
Editor
Ed Cheesman
Colourist
Ricky Gausis
Production Company
El Niño
Special Effects
Mathematic
Record Company
EMI

Cinematography for Music Videos
Orange Films
for One Louder

Control
'Control' is a 'darkwave township house' cover of the Joy Division classic 'She's Lost Control'. It's the fourth single to be taken from South African producer/DJ Spoek Mathambo's album 'Mshini Wam'. The video was a collaboration between one of South Africa's most influential photographers, Pieter Hugo, and cinematographer Michael Cleary. The video was shot in Langa, Cape Town using a cast of kids from the local dance troupe, Happy Feet.

Directors of Photography
Michael Cleary
Pieter Hugo
Directors
Michael Cleary
Pieter Hugo
Producer
Jon Day
Artist
Spoek Mathambo
Production Designer
Mike Berg
Production Company
Orange Films
Editor
Richard Starkey
Record Company
One Louder

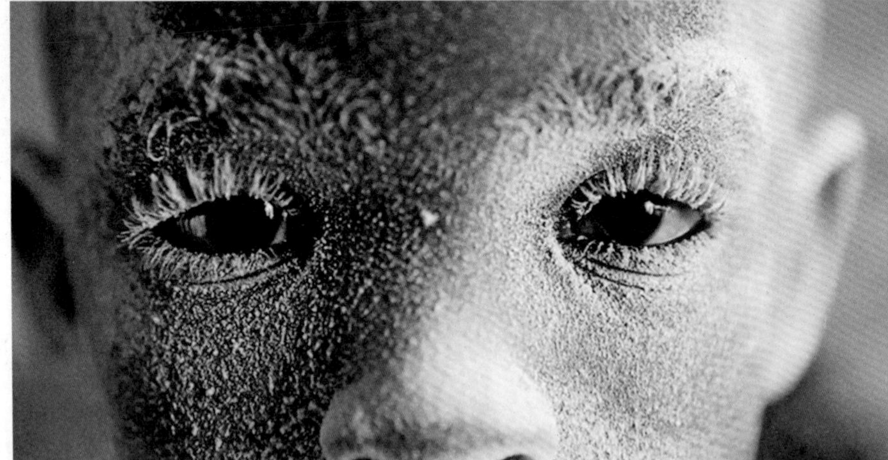

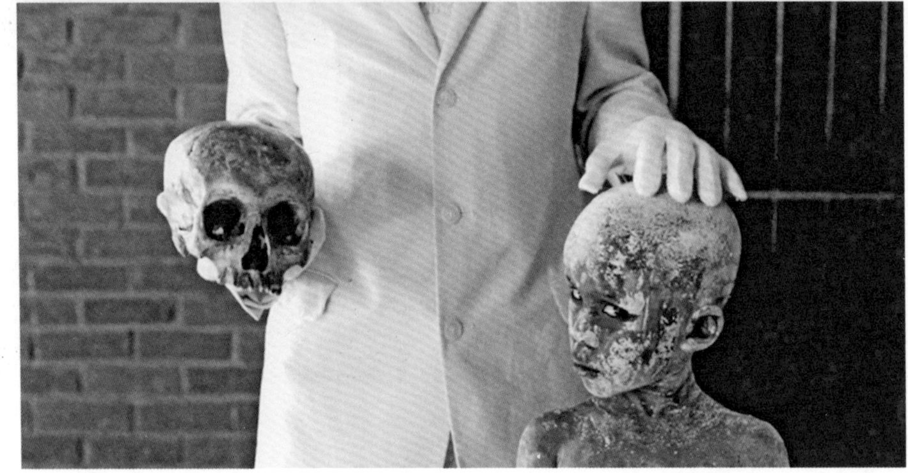

Cinematography for Music Videos
A+/Academy Films & The Lift
for Polydor Universal

The Bad in Each Other
Martin de Thurah and long time collaborator Kasper Tuxen spent five days shooting in Mexico City for Canadian chanteuse Feist. 'The video captures glimpses of something human', Martin says. 'It opens up a world of relations between people – could be loss, longing or love. A lot of things that are about being a human being. It is told in a way where it opens up more aspects than it concludes. We get a peek inside something real between people. Maybe something we can't grasp, but it points at it or touches it and leaves us with different kinds of emotions.'

Director of Photography
Kasper Tuxen
Director
Martin de Thurah
Producers
José Barrera
Morgan Clement
Executive Producers
Avelino Rodriguez
Dominic Thomas
Artist
Feist
Editor
Mikkel E G Nielsen
Colourist
Jonas Drehn
Production Companies
A+/Academy Films
The Lift
Video Commissioner
Jannie McInnes
Record Company
Polydor Universal

Jury Foreman
1. John O'Keeffe
WPP

2. Roberto Fernandez
JWT São Paulo

3. Mareka Carter
BBH London

4. Simon Langley
303Lowe Australia

5. Connie Lo
Leo Burnett Hong Kong

6. Alex Schill
Serviceplan Group

7. Simon Dicketts
M&C Saatchi London

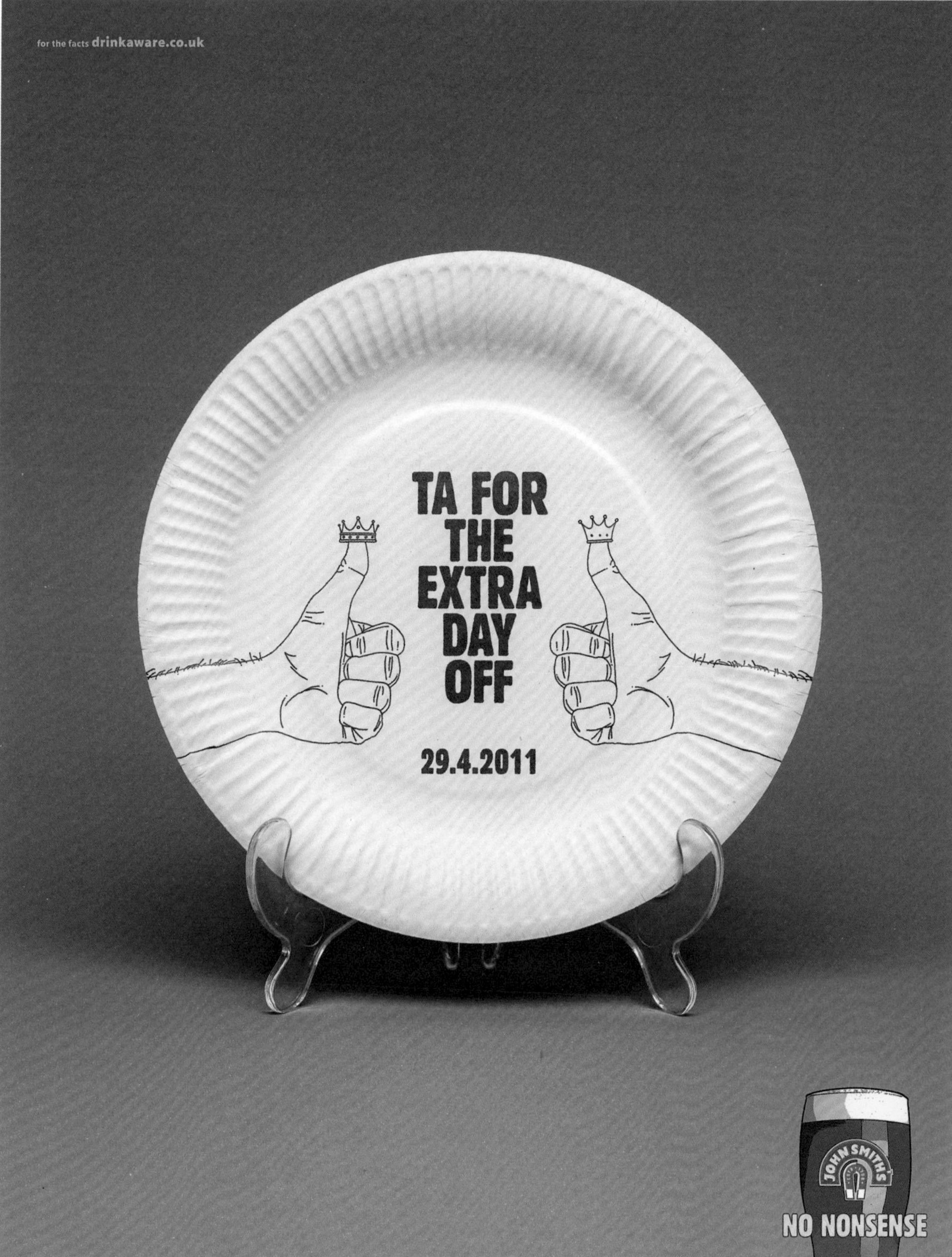

Yellow Pencil in Outdoor Advertising

Poster Advertising/Free Format
TBWA\London
for Heineken

Commemorative Plate
The British love a commemorative plate, especially for a royal wedding. But in typical no nonsense style, our commemorative plate was made of paper and celebrated the day off. Not the poncy wedding.

Art Director
Paul Pateman
Copywriter
Mike Nicholson
Illustrator
Paul Pateman
Photographer
Eugenio Franchi
Executive Creative Director
Andre Laurentino

Advertising Agency
TBWA\London
Account Handler
Ahmad Salim
Client
Heineken
Brand
John Smith's

Yellow Pencil in Outdoor Advertising

Ambient
LOWE/SSP3
for the Ministry of Defense, Colombia

Operation Christmas
We discovered that Christmas is an emotional time of year for guerrillas, because they are away from their homes and loved ones. So we created a four-day operation that brought Christmas to the Colombian jungle. Along a strategic guerrilla route through the jungle, we chose a 25m tall tree to decorate with lights. When guerrillas approached the tree, movement sensors made it light up and a banner announced the following message: 'If Christmas can come to the jungle, you can come home. Demobilise. Everything is possible at Christmas'. Nine more trees promoted demobilisation across different rebel zones in the country.

Art Directors
Carlos Andres
Rodriguez Monroy
Copywriter
Sergio Leon
Chief Creative Officer
Jose Miguel Sokoloff
Advertising Agency
LOWE/SSP3

Account Handlers
Emiliano Arango
Juan Pablo Garcia
Client
Ministry of Defense, Colombia

SI LA NAVIDAD PUDO LLEGAR HASTA LA SELVA,
USTED TAMBIÉN PUEDE LLEGAR HASTA SU CASA.
DESMOVILÍCESE. EN NAVIDAD TODO ES POSIBLE.

Yellow Pencil in Outdoor Advertising

Poster Advertising/Existing Sites
JWT Shanghai
for Samsonite

Heaven and Hell
The task was to produce print ads and outdoor communication for the Samsonite Cosmolite suitcase. The selling point is its ultra-durability. The creative idea is a vivid contrast between how 'heavenly' it is in first class for the passenger, but 'hellish' down below where the suitcase is being handled. And yet the suitcase emerges sparkling after the torture.

Art Directors
Rojana Chuasakul
Danny Li
Haoxi Lv
Surachai
Puthikulangkura
Copywriter
Marc Wang
Illustrators
Surachai
Puthikulangkura
Supachai U-Rairat
Creative Directors
Hattie Cheng
Rojana Chuasakul
Executive Creative Directors
Elvis Chau
SheungYan Lo
Yang Yeo
Production House Producers
Somsak Pairew
Anotai Panmongkol
Advertising Agency
JWT Shanghai
Production House
Illusion
Account Handlers
Michelle Xiao
Lily Zheng
Maggie Zhou
Account Directors
Tom Doctoroff
Sophia Ng
Client
Samsonite

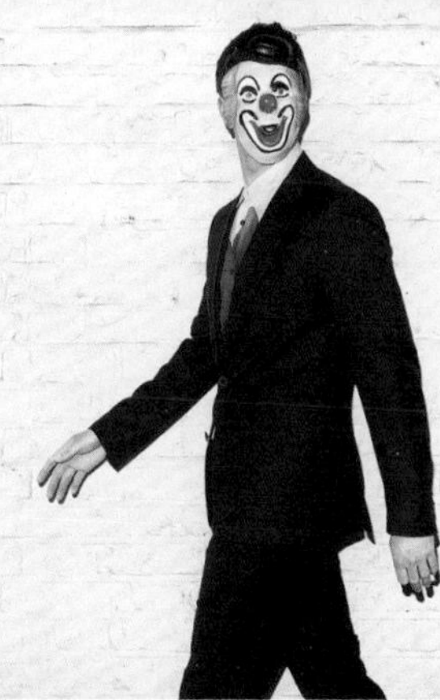

Nomination in Outdoor Advertising

Poster Advertising Campaigns
DDB UK
for Harvey Nichols

Daylight Robbery
This press and poster campaign is to announce the launch of the Harvey Nichols summer sale and remind people that they can get their hands on the most gorgeous fashion items at a fraction of their usual price. The campaign shows how getting your hands on those items at sale prices will feel like you've committed daylight robbery. It's a steal! 'Clown' and 'Stocking' were also selected as single executions in the 'Poster Advertising/ Free Format' category.

Art Director
Victor Monclus
Copywriter
Will Lowe
Photographer
Frederike Helwig
Designer
Pete Mould
Creative Director
Grant Parker
Executive Creative Director
Jeremy Craigen
Head of Art
Grant Parker
Retoucher
Andrew Walsh
Advertising Agency
DDB UK
Project Manager
Sophie Simonelli
Account Manager
Charlotte Evans
Art Buyer
Sarah Thomson
Business Director
Paul Billingsley
Client
Harvey Nichols

Nomination in Outdoor Advertising

Poster Advertising Campaigns
Leo Burnett Hong Kong
for Casablanca

Deep Sleep

We wanted to promote a new product, the I-Pillow. Instead of showing another beautiful shot of someone sleeping, we decided to dramatise what happens when you sleep really well. People who sleep poorly toss and turn. People who sleep well stay very, very still. The single execution 'Dominos' was also selected in the 'Poster Advertising/ Free Format' category.

Art Directors
Nateepat Jaturonrasmi
Martin Tong
Copywriters
Nutchanun Chiaphanumas
Spring Liu
Creative Director
Nutchanun Chiaphanumas
Executive Creative Director
Connie Lo
Computer Graphics Artist
Surachai Puthikulangkura

Advertising Agency
Leo Burnett Hong Kong
Photography
Illusion
Account Handler
Alan Ng
Client
Casablanca
Brand
I-Pillow

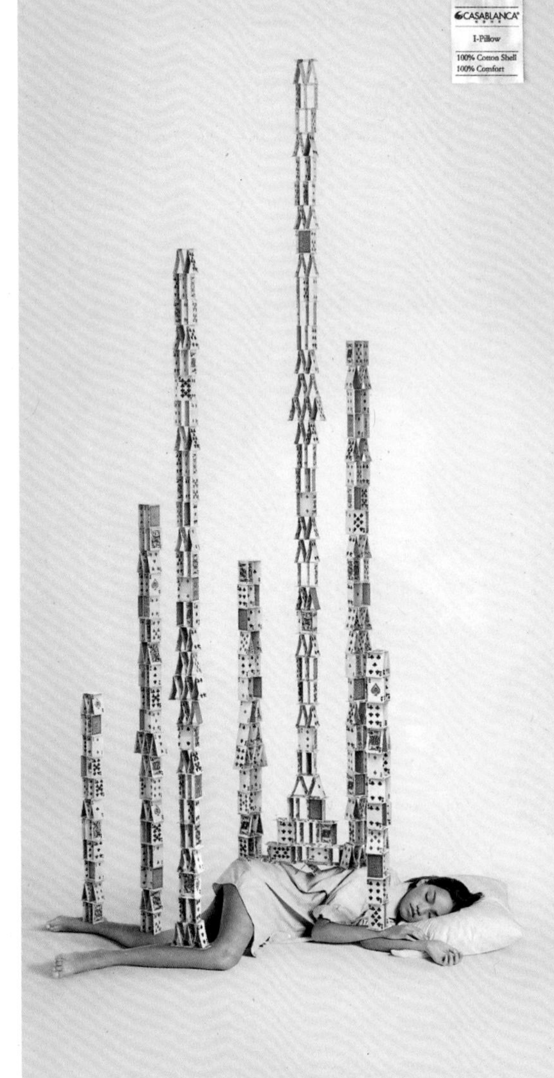

YOU ARE LOOKING AT EVERY WATTLED CRANE LEFT IN SOUTH AFRICA.

To save the last 235 visit ewt.org.za
ENDANGERED WILDLIFE TRUST

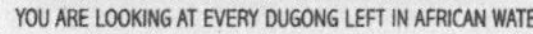

YOU ARE LOOKING AT EVERY DUGONG LEFT IN AFRICAN WATERS.

To save the last 153 visit ewt.org.za
ENDANGERED WILDLIFE TRUST

YOU ARE LOOKING AT EVERY RIVERINE RABBIT LEFT ON THE PLANET.

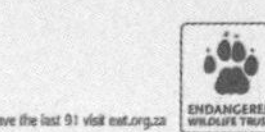

To save the last 91 visit ewt.org.za
ENDANGERED WILDLIFE TRUST

YOU ARE LOOKING AT EVERY NORTHERN WHITE RHINO LEFT ON THE PLANET.

To save the last 8 visit ewt.org.za
ENDANGERED WILDLIFE TRUST

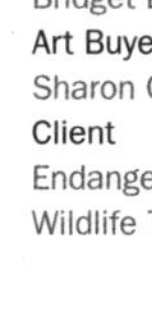

Nomination in Outdoor Advertising

Poster Advertising Campaigns
TBWA\Hunt\Lascaris Johannesburg
for the Endangered Wildlife Trust

The Last Ones Left
The Endangered Wildlife Trust is a conservation group providing vital awareness about endangered species. Statistics have become prevalent in the mass of information people face every day, and are easy to ignore. The public was no longer responding to the statistics the EWT was releasing. To increase the funds essential for wildlife conservation, we had to bring back the stopping power of statistics. Behind every number that makes up a statistic, there is a living animal. We had to make people see the animals behind the information. And it was from this insight that we conceptualised our idea: to put faces to the figures. 'Riverine Rabbit' and 'Northern White Rhino' were also selected as single executions in the 'Poster Advertising/Free Format' category.

Art Director
Lizali Blom
Copywriters
Lizali Blom
Jared Osmond
Photographer
Mari Keyter
Creative Directors
Miguel Nunes
Adam Weber
Executive Creative Director
Damon Stapleton
Production Director
Craig Walker
Production Manager
Robert Mackenzie
Advertising Agency
TBWA\Hunt\Lascaris Johannesburg
Account Manager
Katiso Maarohanye
Account Director
Bridget Langley
Art Buyer
Sharon Cvetkovski
Client
Endangered Wildlife Trust

Nomination in Outdoor Advertising

Poster Advertising Campaigns
AlmapBBDO
for Volkswagen do Brasil

Beep-beep
Parking a car a little too far back can cause accidents. The Park Assist technology from the new Voyage can avoid situations similar in risk to the ones illustrated in this campaign.

Art Director	Advertising Agency
Pedro Rosa	AlmapBBDO
Copywriter	Client
Ana Carolina Reis	Volkswagen do Brasil
Creative Director	Brand
Luiz Sanches	Voyage

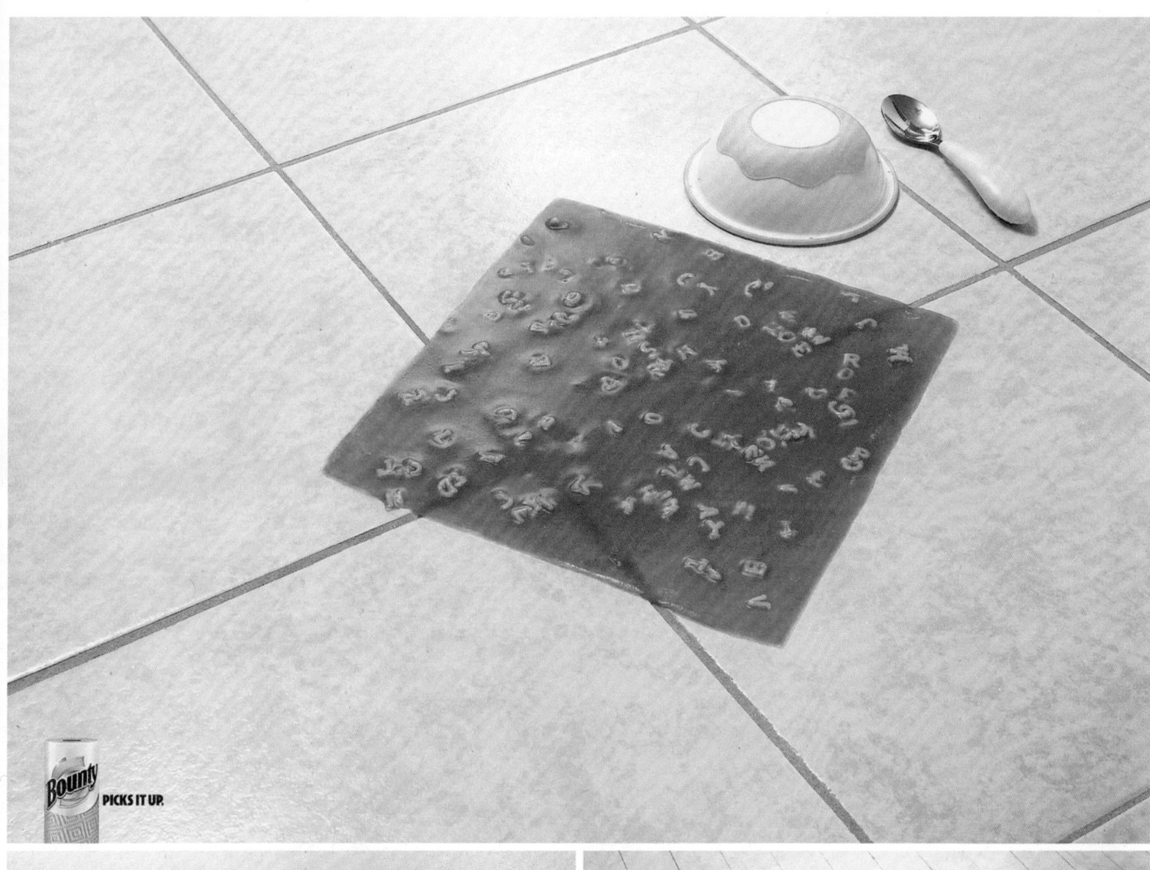

Nomination in Outdoor Advertising

Poster Advertising Campaigns
Leo Burnett Toronto
for Procter & Gamble

Bounty Picks it Up

Bounty is a premium priced paper towel brand; it wanted to attach benefit to those extra few dollars consumers pay. The benefit amounts to a single sheet that does more. It cleans more mess, picks up liquids more easily and lasts longer. This print campaign displayed the extent of 'wipe-up quality' with simple visuals. The campaign helped maintain Bounty's superiority in the market by telling consumers: 'No matter the mess, Bounty picks it up'.

Art Director
Anthony Chelvanathan
Copywriter
Steve Persico
Photographer
Mark Zibert
Creative Directors
Heather Chambers
Lisa Greenberg
Chief Creative Officer
Judy John
Print Producer
Anne Peck
Advertising Agency
Leo Burnett Toronto
Planner
Jose Daniel
Account Executive
Dan Koutoulakis
Account Directors
Millie Alicea
Kim Koster
Samantha Pollock
Art Buyer
Leila Courey
Client
Procter & Gamble
Brand
Bounty

Ambient
Y&R South Africa
for LG Appliances

Rugby Tunnel
To launch and demonstrate the capacity of LG's 11kg washing machines, we placed them in front of players' tunnels at Super Rugby games. At the beginning of the game, fans watched players run out of the washer clean. At half-time players ran into the washer dirty, changed into fresh kits and ran back out of the washer clean again.

Art Directors
Steve Dirnberger
Bruce Murphy
Copywriters
Katherine Glover
Eric Wittstock
Creative Director
Ian Franks
Executive Creative Director
Liam Wielopolski
Advertising Agency
Y&R South Africa
Client
LG Appliances

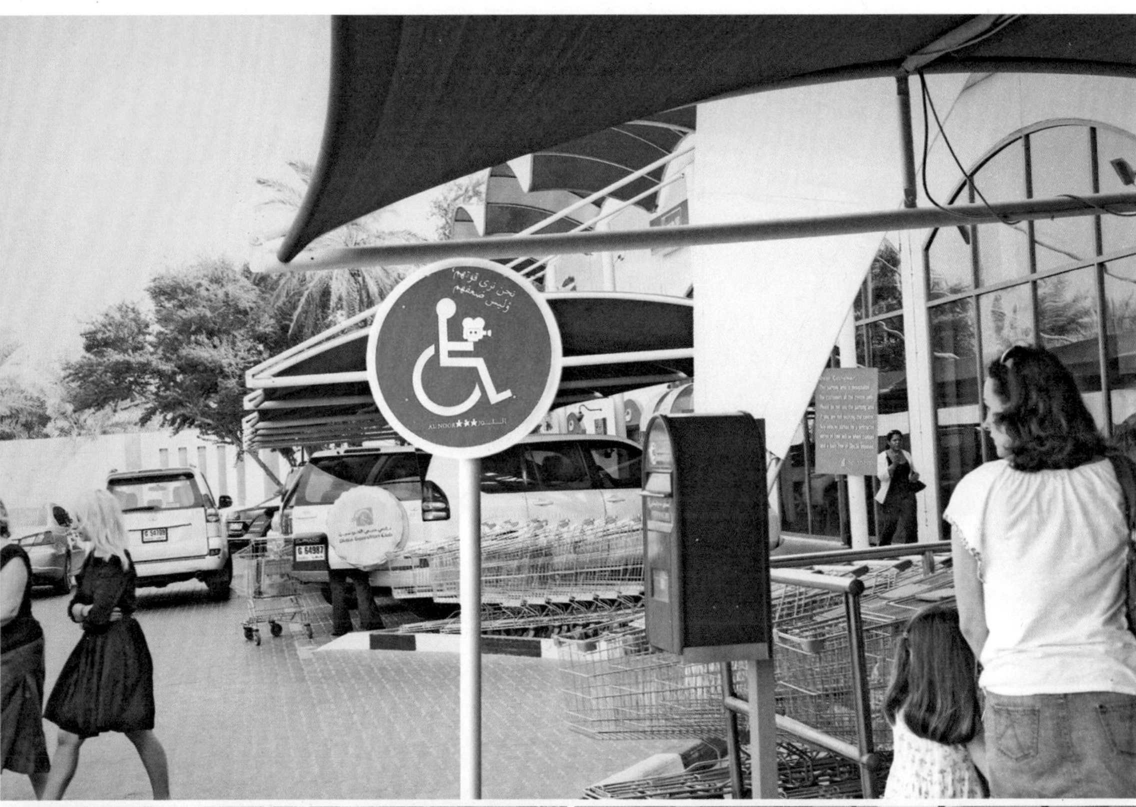

Ambient
Y&R Dubai
for the Al Noor Training Centre

See Potential
With no budget, we had to find an ingenious way to use media and create awareness about the Al Noor Training Centre, a school for children with special needs. To achieve this, we made innovative use of the globally recognised disabled sign. We designed stickers that, when stuck on disabled signs around the city, turned the familiar symbols into visuals of a film director, cook, singer and so on. We managed to turn disability into potential, simply and effectively. Disabled signs across the city became mini billboards driving home the centre's message.

Art Director
Husen Baba
Copywriter
Wilbur D'Costa
Designer
Husen Baba
Creative Directors
Husen Baba
Wilbur D'Costa
Shahir Zag
Producer
Amin Soltani

Advertising Agency
Y&R Dubai
Account Handler
Uday Desai
Brand Manager
Isphana Al-Khatib
Client
Al Noor
Training Centre

Ambieht
Del Campo Nazca Saatchi & Saatchi
for BGH

Big Noses
BGH wanted to launch its new line of air conditioners with five air filtering stages, providing the purest air of all. For the launch, BGH decided to help those who need pure air the most: big noses. If you had a big nose, BGH gave you a 25% discount. Identifying whose nose is big and whose isn't is a very delicate matter, so we created the nose-o-meter – a device capable of measuring the length of a nose. If your nose reached the sensor, a siren went off and you won the discount.

Art Director
Ignacio Ferioli
Copywriter
Diego Medvedocky
Designers
Sebastian Beretta
Guido Fusetti
Creative Directors
Ignacio Ferioli
Diego Medvedocky
Directors
Diego & Vlady
Executive Creative Directors
Maxi Itzkoff
Mariano Serkin

Executive Producer
Alejandro De Michele
Agency Producers
Adrian Aspani
Paz Landeyro
Advertising Agency
Del Campo Nazca Saatchi & Saatchi
Account Executive
Mariano Cafarelli
Account Director
Juan Manuel Aralda
Client
BGH

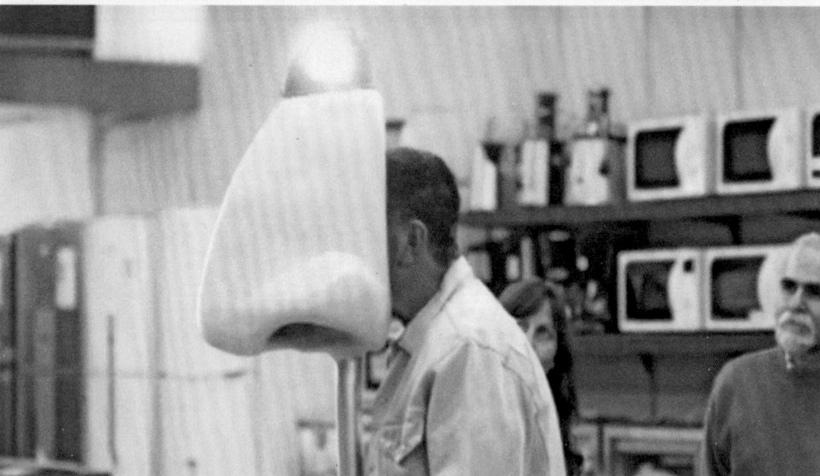

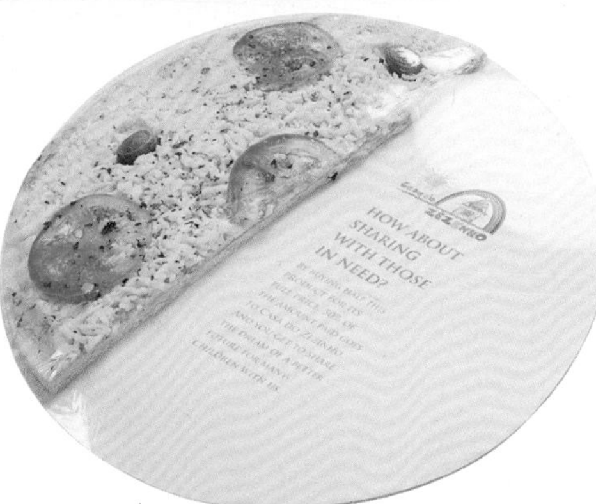

Ambient
AlmapBBDO
for Casa do Zezinho

Share with Those in Need
We used this ambient idea to generate donations for Casa do Zezinho, a charity which guarantees basic necessities for children in need. We asked consumers to pay full price for half of the product, with half their money going to Casa do Zezinho.

Art Directors
Daniel Manzi
Vinicius Sousa
Copywriter
Fabio Ozorio

Advertising Agency
AlmapBBDO
Client
Casa do Zezinho

Ambient
Ogilvy & Mather Mexico
for Mattel México

Speedway
Two giant child-shaped structures were placed on both sides of the Mexico-Cuernavaca speedway, so drivers could experience being inside a Hot Wheels car.

Art Directors
Iván Carrasco
Francisco Hernández
Sergio Díaz Infante
Copywriters
Sergio Díaz Infante
Carlos Meza
Photographer
Diego Arrigoni
Creative Director
Iván Carrasco
Executive Creative Directors
José Montalvo
Miguel Ruiz
Head of Art
Iván Carrasco

Producers
Ereth Bolaños
César Gama
Ernesto Herrera
Juan Pablo Osio
Ezequiel Schnabel
Advertising Agency
Ogilvy & Mather Mexico
Account Handler
Ma Pilar Troconis
Client
Mattel México
Brand
Hot Wheels

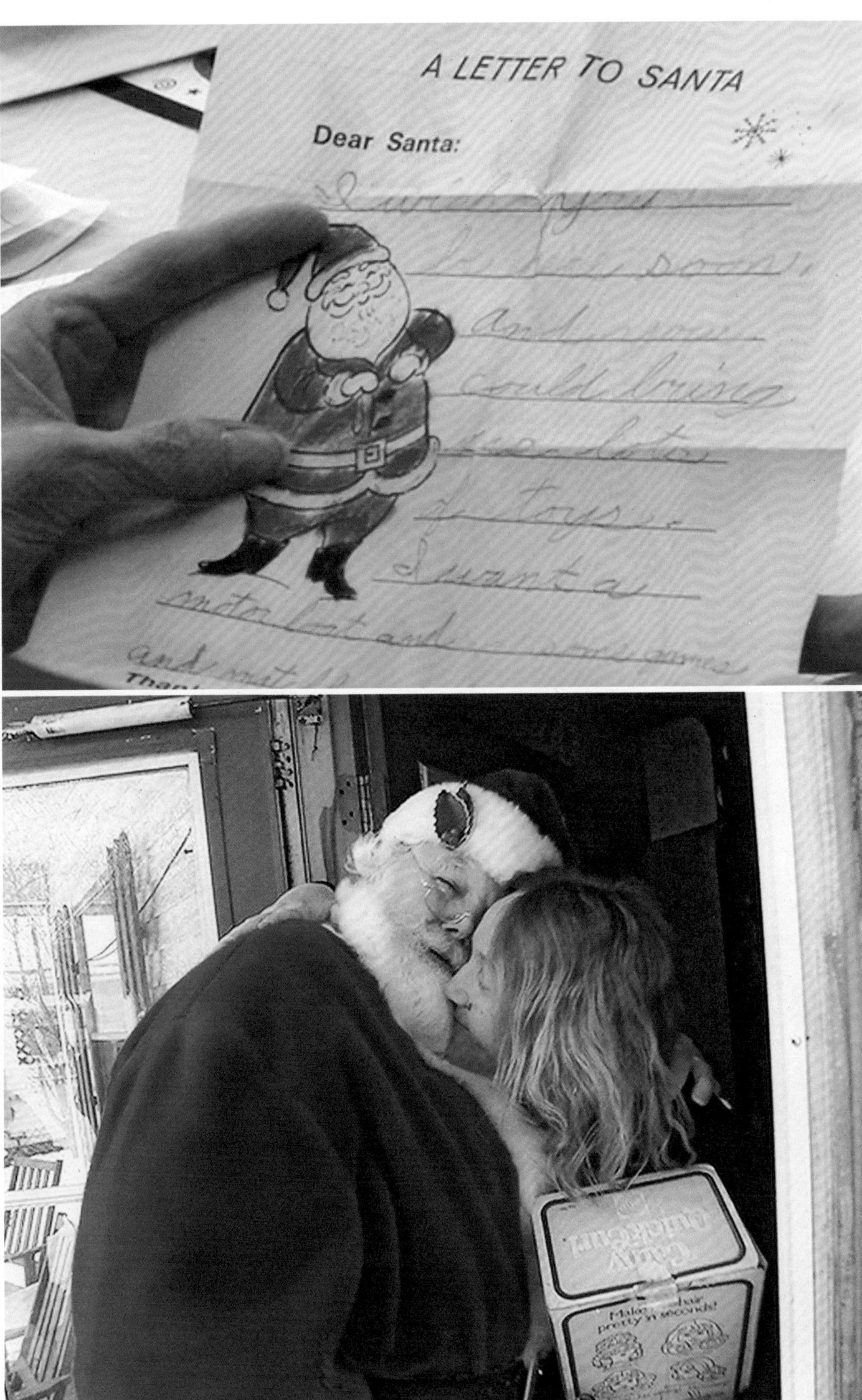

Ambient
Ogilvy Brazil
for The Coca Cola Company

Santa's Forgotten Letters
Children all over the world write letters to Santa, but not all of them get what they ask for. We decided to find Santa's forgotten letters and grant their wishes now, many years later. We searched the world and in the little town of Santa Claus, Indiana, found the Santa Claus Museum, a place that keeps letters to Santa dating back to the 1930s. A few weeks later, Santa visited the homes of some of the authors, wish lists and presents in hand.

Art Directors
Izabella Cabral
Pedro Izique
Copywriters
Fred Aramis
Megan Farquhar
Creative Director
Claudio Lima
Executive Creative Director
Anselmo Ramos
Directors
Alex Mehedff
Ricardo Mehedff
Animator
Rubens Angelo
Editor
Ricardo Mehedff
Producers
Nana Bittencourt
Alex Mehedff
Susanne Shropshire
Music Producers
Andres Goldstein
Daniel Tarrab
Advertising Agency
Ogilvy Brazil
Production Company
Hungry Man
Account Handlers
Claudia Bastos
Luis Carlos Franco
Ana Paula Perdigão
Marketing Manager
Guido Rosales
Client
The Coca Cola Company
Brand
Coca Cola

Ambient
Ogilvy & Mather Argentina
for TEDx

Spread the TEDx

In Latin America, TEDx talks are still far removed from ordinary people. If we wanted to spread these ideas, we needed a more personal approach to promote TEDx. So we called the city's most remarkable speakers: taxi drivers. Fifty of them were invited to TEDx Buenos Aires, so they could spread these outstanding ideas all over the city. The creation of this link between TEDx and passengers put them face-to-face with some of the most inspiring and fascinating ideas. We spread the TEDx.

Art Director
Ignacio Flota
Copywriter
Nicolás Vara
Executive Creative Directors
Gastón Bigio
Maximiliano Maddalena
Javier Mentasti
Head of Art
Diego Grandi
Producer
Patricio Alvarez Casado
Advertising Agency
Ogilvy & Mather Argentina
Client
TEDx
Brand
TED

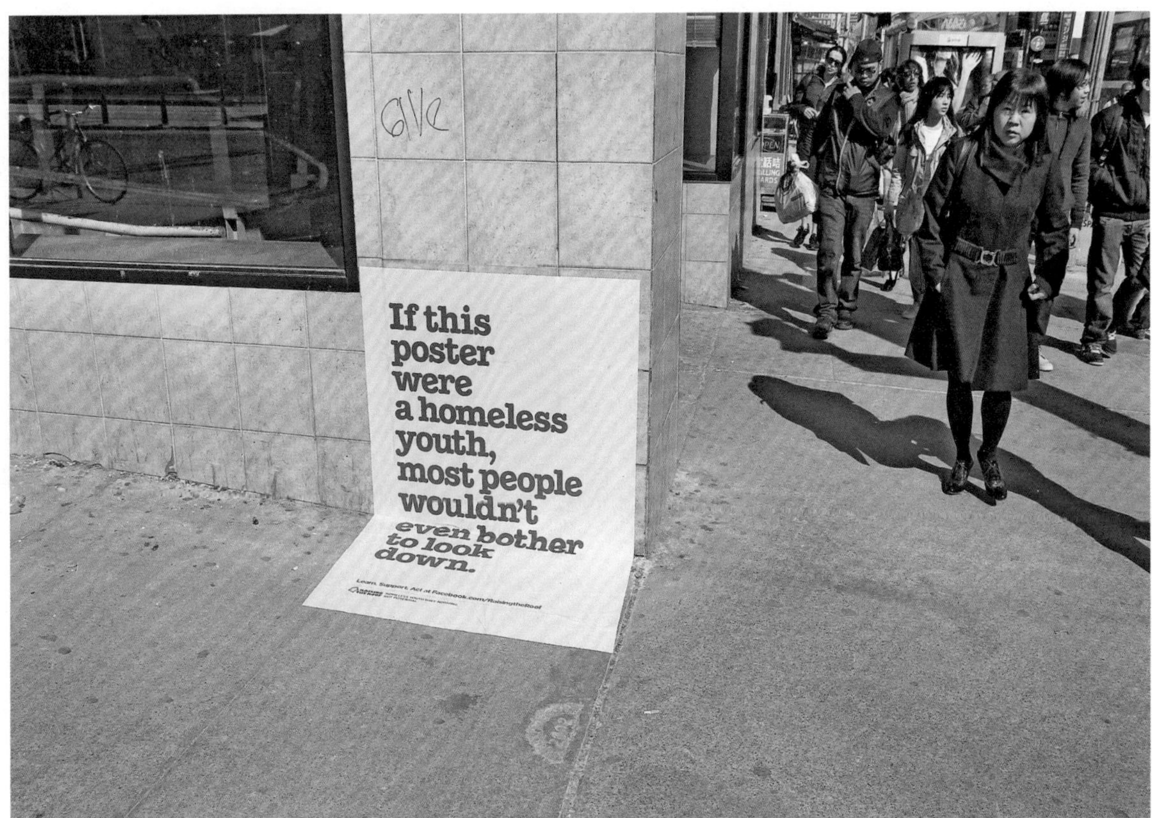

Poster Advertising/Enhanced Posters
Leo Burnett Toronto
for Raising the Roof

Look Down

We were challenged to get people to stop and think about how they consider homeless youth. If we could make them conscious of this, chances are they would then begin to see the issue of homeless youth as something they could play a part in changing. The end goal: get them to see the potential in homeless youth and donate or act. This poster (along with the rest of the campaign) helped Raising the Roof reach well beyond its goal of engaging 65,000 people to donate or act.

Art Director
Anthony Chelvanathan
Copywriter
Steve Persico
Creative Director
Lisa Greenberg
Chief Creative Officer
Judy John
Print Producers
Gladys Bachand
Kim Burchiel
Advertising Agency
Leo Burnett Toronto
Planners
Brent Nelsen
Ian Westworth
Account Director
Natasha Dagenais
Art Buyer
Leila Courey
Client
Raising the Roof

Poster Advertising/Existing Sites
RKCR/Y&R
for Land Rover

Passport Stamps

The Land Rover Defender is a vehicle that can tackle almost anything. Used in the most demanding situations around the world, the Defender is as tough as they come. This ad is an expertly crafted collage, featuring passport stamps that are built up in the shape of the vehicle. The suggestion is that the Defender is ready for your next adventure, no matter how challenging the environment.

Art Director
Tim Brookes
Copywriter
Phil Forster
Photographer
Carl Warner
Typographer
Lee Aldridge
Creative Directors
Graham Lang
Mark Roalfe
Advertising Agency
RKCR/Y&R
Account Handler
Glynn Euston
National Communications Manager
Les Knight
Client
Land Rover
Brand
Defender

Poster Advertising/Free Format
Grabarz & Partner
for Volkswagen

Parking Precision
Precise parking has always been an enormous challenge for a lot of drivers. That was yesterday. Today, with the new Park Assist electronic parking system from Volkswagen, there's absolutely no need to worry about whether your car fits into a tight space or not. Park Assist is always a reliable friend when you need to park precisely, no matter how full your garage may be.

Art Director
Tim Hartwig
Copywriter
Christian Moehler
Photographer
Patrice Lange
Creative Directors
Christoph Breitbach
Tom Hauser
Christoph Stricker
Timm Weber
Executive Creative Director
Ralf Heuel

Advertising Agency
Grabarz & Partner
Account Handlers
Katja Fredriksen
Reinhard Patzschke
Peter Stroeh
Art Buyer
Anna Simdon
Client
Volkswagen

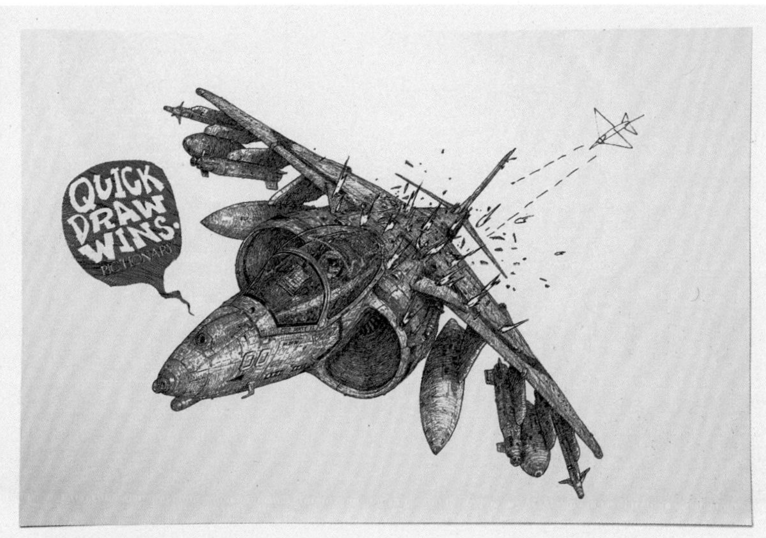

Poster Advertising Campaigns
Ogilvy Malaysia
for Mattel Malaysia

Quick Draw Wins
The brief was to promote Pictionary, the game in which players guess words from drawings. We recreated the fun of playing Pictionary, where winning depends on how quickly you can draw, through ads featuring drawings. Guess them right and you'll get the message. These posters were placed in toy stores to help Pictionary stand out from the sea of games on the shelves.

Art Directors
Tan Chee Keong
Gavin Simpson
Yee Wai Khuen
Copywriters
Adam Chan
Donevan Chew
Illustrators
Milx
Yee Wai Khuen
Designer
Lian Ee Wern
Creative Directors
Tan Chee Keong
Executive Creative Director
Gavin Simpson

Advertising Agency
Ogilvy Malaysia
Photography
Studio DL
Account Executives
Joanne Lee
Amy Yep
Account Director
Sharon Khor
Client
Mattel Malaysia
Brand
Pictionary

Poster Advertising Campaigns
Fuel Lisbon
for Amnesty International

Mugshots
To mark the 30th anniversary of Amnesty in Portugal, Fuel has created a press and poster campaign called Mugshots. In this campaign, we see file photos from the PIDE (the secret police when Portugal was under dictatorship) showing political prisoners. Under these, we see the same people photographed in the present day – alive, thanks to the intervention of institutions such as Amnesty. The campaign was inspired by the book 'For Your Free Thought' by Portuguese photographer João Pina, who photographed and interviewed dozens of Portuguese political prisoners.

Art Director
Pedro Bexiga
Copywriter
Marcelo Lourenço
Photographer
João Pina
Creative Directors
Pedro Bexiga
Marcelo Lourenço
Agency Producers
Miguel Barbosa
Pedro Silva

Advertising Agency
Fuel Lisbon
Account Executive
Joana Gomes Pedro
Account Director
Sérgio Resende
Brand Manager
Irene Rodrigues
Marketing Manager
Pedro Krupenski
Client
Amnesty International

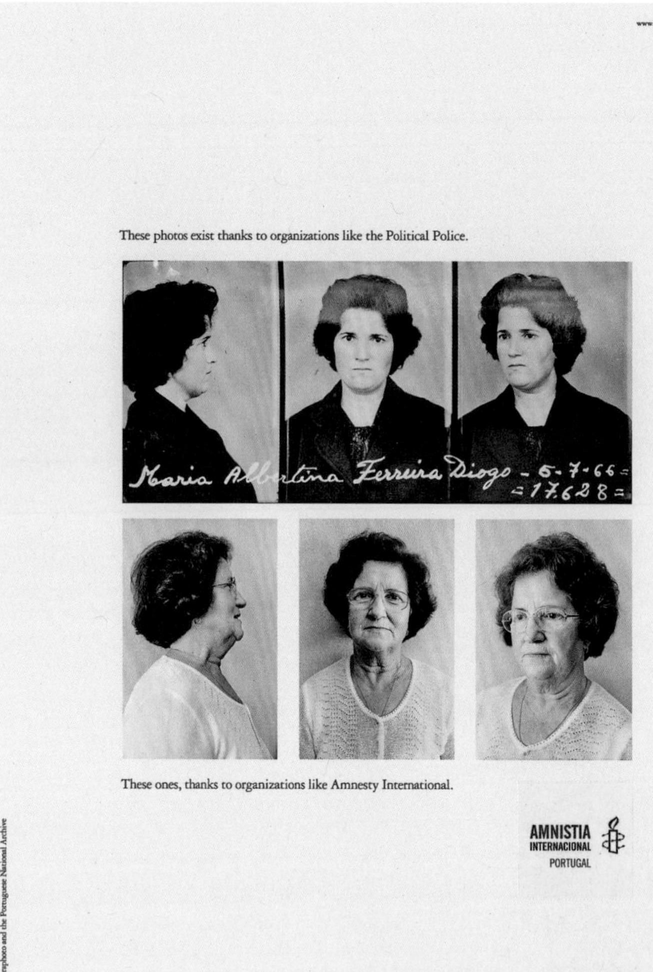

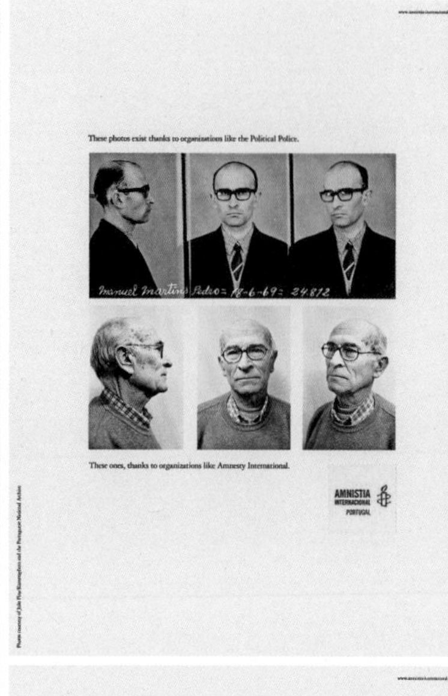

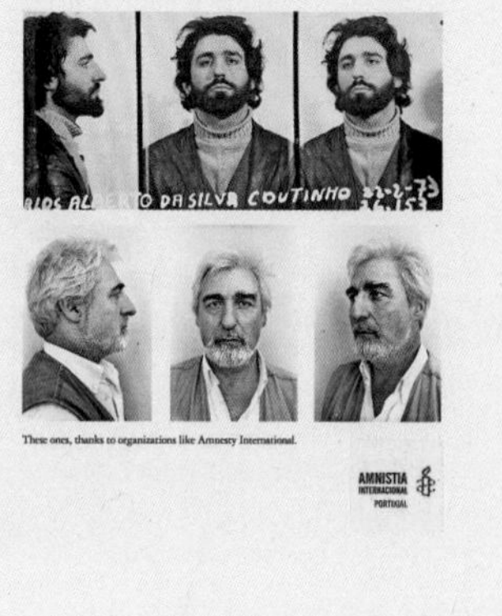

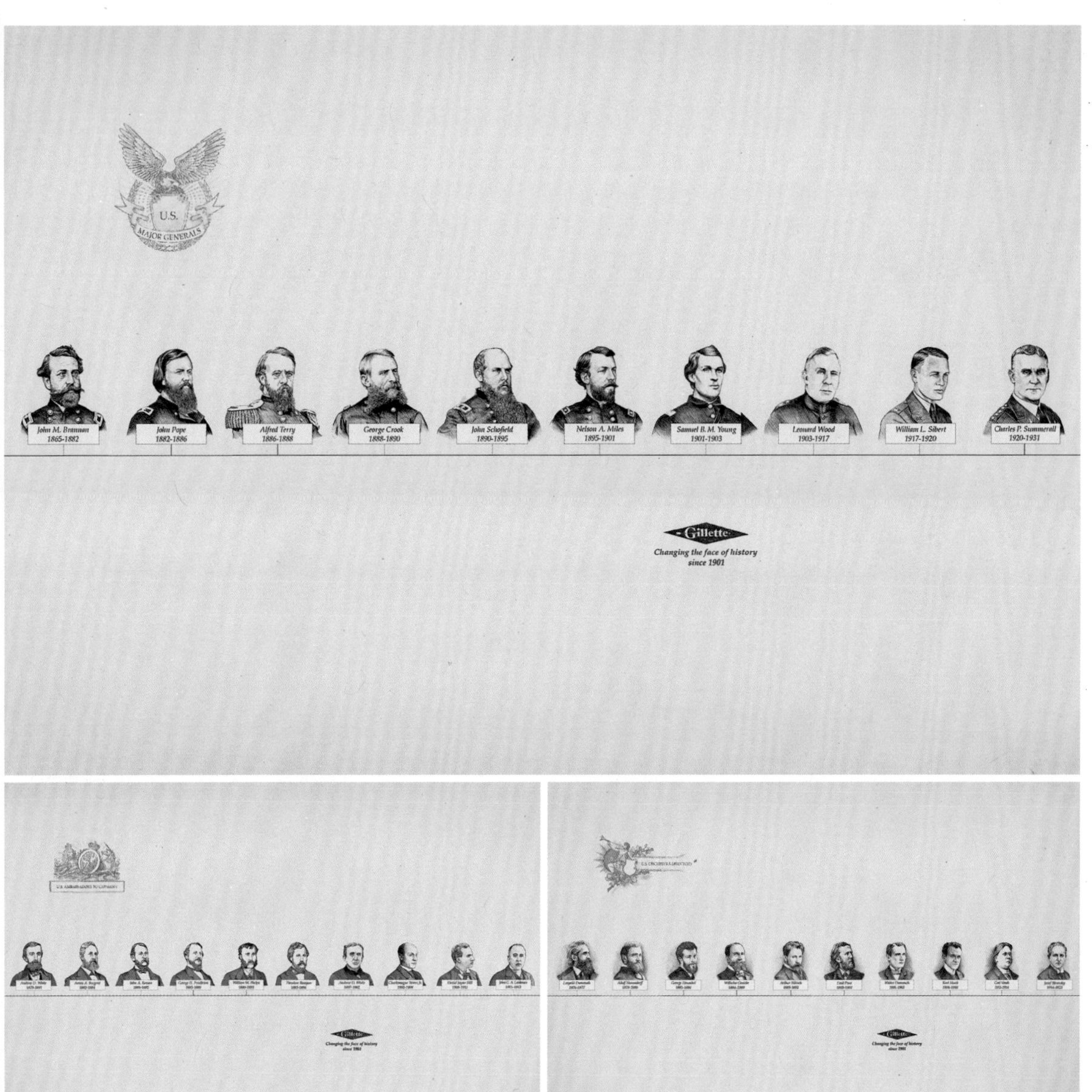

Poster Advertising Campaigns
BBDO New York
for Procter & Gamble

True Stories
If you study portraits of prominent men of the 20th Century – whether it's US orchestra conductors, generals or ambassadors – a recognisable shift takes place in 1901. That's the exact year King C Gillette invented his safety razor with disposable blades. (Note: all names and dates in this campaign for Gillette are accurate.)

Art Directors
Nick Klinkert
Jens Waernes
Copywriters
Oliver Handlos
Tom Kraemer
Illustrator
Sam Kerr
Creative Directors
Oliver Handlos
Nick Klinkert
Tom Kraemer
Jens Waernes
Executive Creative Director
Toygar Bazarkaya

Chief Creative Officer
David Lubars
Retoucher
Steve Lakeman
Advertising Agency
BBDO New York
Account Executives
Henrie Clarke
Dylan Green
Cassi Pires
Art Buyer
Betsy Jablow
Client
Procter & Gamble
Brand
Gillette

Poster Advertising Campaigns
DDB Argentina
for Volkswagen Argentina

Drive Carefully
Our challenge was to communicate the drama of a car accident without resorting to the usual clichéd horror. Inspired by the wit and humour that have been a part of the brand's communication for the past 50 years, we had the idea of measuring the speed of common household accidents – building on the uncertainty of 'what if' instead of explicitly showing the consequences of an accident on a person.

Art Director
Alejandro Hara
Copywriter
Emilio Yacon
Creative Directors
Lisandro Grandal
Fernando Tchechenistky
Executive Creative Directors
Pablo Batlle
Hernan Jauregui

Agency Producer
Nelson Zeljkovich
Advertising Agency
DDB Argentina
Account Executive
Agustina Iparraguirre
Account Director
Graciela Combal
Brand Manager
Martin Sorrondegui
Client
Volkswagen Argentina

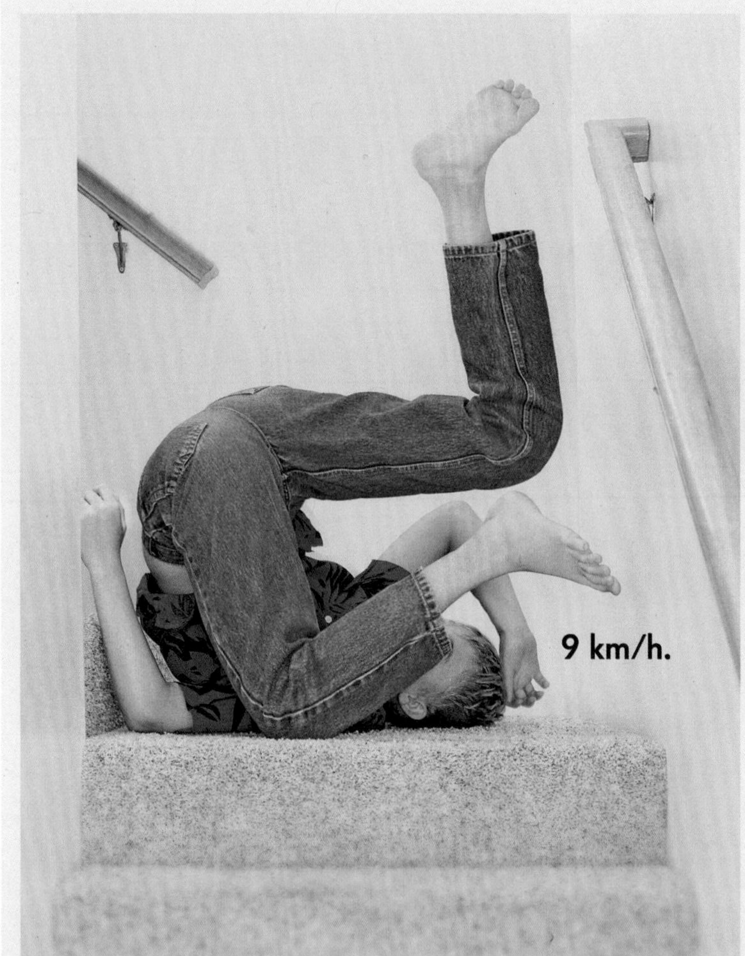
9 km/h.

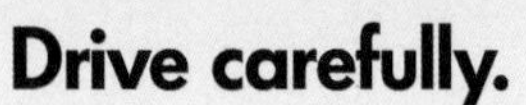
Drive carefully.

Das Auto.

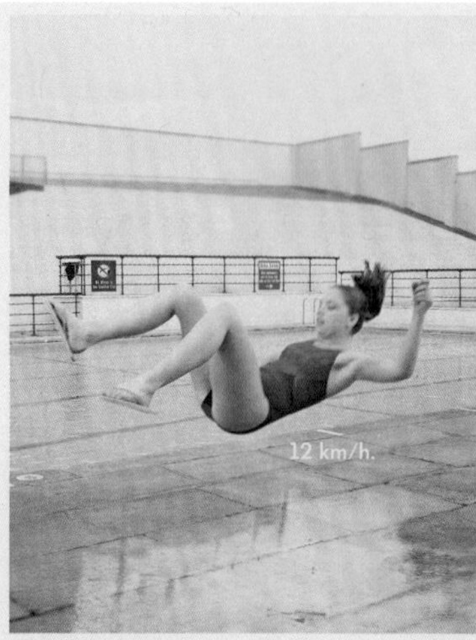
12 km/h.
Drive carefully.

7 km/h.
Drive carefully.

foot-see wun-hun-dred

say it to get it
Google voice search for mobile

tak-see num-buhz

say it to get it
Google voice search for mobile

res-tront ree-vyooz

say it to get it
Google voice search for mobile

Poster Advertising Campaigns
BBH London
for Google

Say it to Get it
This is a series of location-specific posters to highlight that you can now search using your voice with the Google voice search mobile app.

Art Direction
BBH London
Google Creative Labs
Copywriting
BBH London
Google Creative Labs
Typography
BBH London
Creative Direction
BBH London
Google Creative Labs
Strategy
BBH London
Print Production
BBH London
Advertising Agency
BBH London
Planning
BBH London
Account Management
BBH London
Client
Google

Poster Advertising Campaigns
Publicis Mojo Aukland
for Greenpeace New Zealand

Oil on Canvas
The MV Rena oil spill was New Zealand's worst maritime disaster. Greenpeace wanted to bring the reality of the disaster home to those who live miles away from it and create an emotional drive to sign the petition against deep-sea oil drilling. We created hundreds of handmade oil prints from the oil-covered bodies of birds killed during the disaster. These were put up as street posters with a call to sign the petition. They served as both a memorial to the 20,000 birds that died during the spill and a warning against the much larger threat of deep-sea oil drilling.

Art Director
Mike Barnwell
Copywriter
Guy Denniston
Director
James Solomon
Executive Creative Directors
Mike Barnwell
Lachlan McPherson
Producer
Angela Da Silva

Advertising Agency
Publicis Mojo Auckland
Production Company
Flying Fish
Marketing Manager
Michael Tritt
Client
Greenpeace New Zealand
Brand
Greenpeace

THIS OIL PRINT WAS MADE USING AN ACTUAL BIRD KILLED IN THE 'RENA' DISASTER.

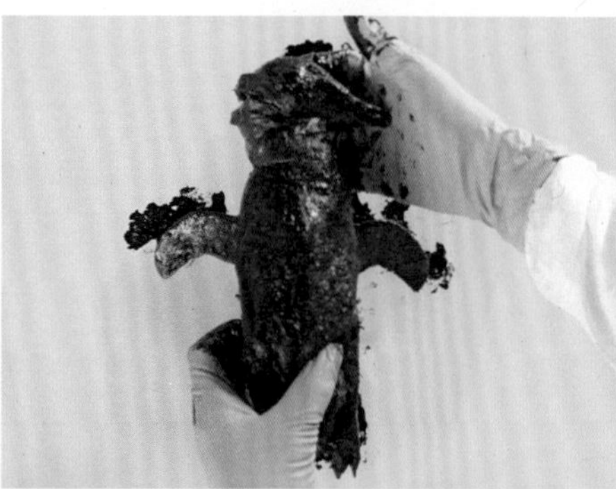

Poster Advertising Campaigns
SPILLMANN/FELSER/LEO BURNETT
for SwissLife

Life's Turn in a Sentence
The SwissLife pension and life insurance solutions are flexible and adapt to life's twists and turns. So we created a headline campaign dramatising this, and pointing out that life sometimes does take unexpected turns.

Art Directors
Daniele Barbiero
Reto Clement
Copywriters
Thomas Schöb
Simon Smit
Executive Creative Director
Peter Brönnimann

Advertising Agency
SPILLMANN/FELSER/LEO BURNETT
Client
SwissLife

I never want children are great.

For all life's twists and turns:
Flexible financial plans.

I love my house now belongs to my ex-wife.

For all life's twists and turns:
Flexible financial plans.

I'm not interested in getting married in church is more romantic.

For all life's twists and turns:
Flexible financial plans.

She's my everything went wrong.

For all life's twists and turns:
Flexible financial plans.

I like working with you is impossible.

For all life's twists and turns:
Flexible financial plans.

You're the only woman I love a man now.

For all life's twists and turns:
Flexible financial plans.

Poster Advertising Campaigns
Serviceplan München
for Barmer GEK

The Fat Posters
People eat too much fat. Health insurance company Barmer GEK asked us to make people aware of how much fat their food contains. So we created posters made out of fat. In a complex chemical process, we extracted the fat from popular dishes and airbrushed it on white paper. The result: fat posters. The fat of one product for one poster – no more, no less.

Art Director
Roman Becker
Copywriter
Andreas Schriewer
Graphic Designer
Felix von Pless
Executive Creative Directors
Maik Kaehler
Christoph Nann
Chief Creative Officer
Alexander Schill
Programmer
Steffen Knoblich
Producer
Bianca Schreck
Advertising Agency
Serviceplan München
Account Executive
Ines Herbold
Client
Barmer GEK

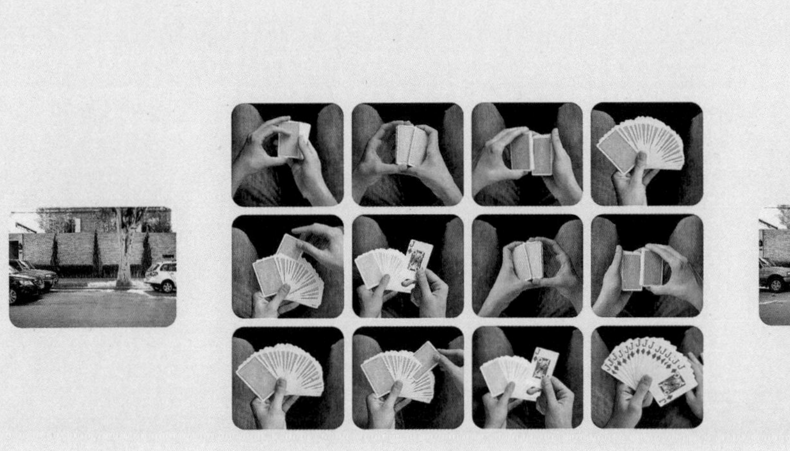

Cinto de segurança salva vidas.
Estacione sem usar as mãos. Tiguan, agora com Park Assist.
Das Auto.

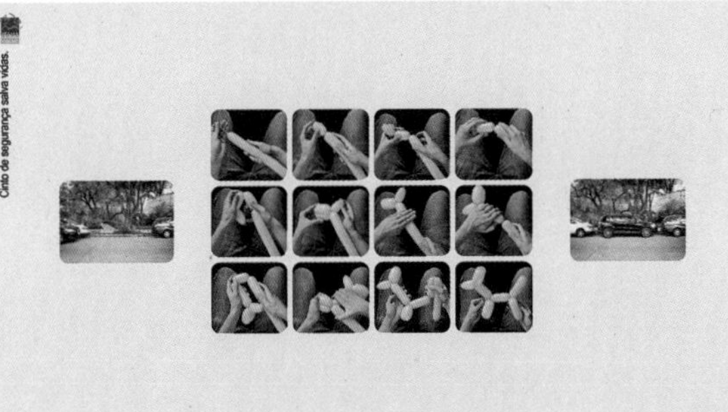

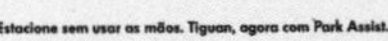

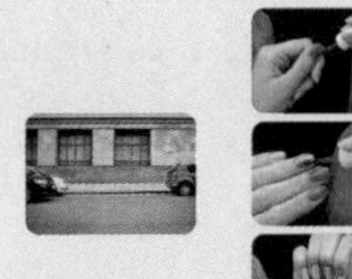

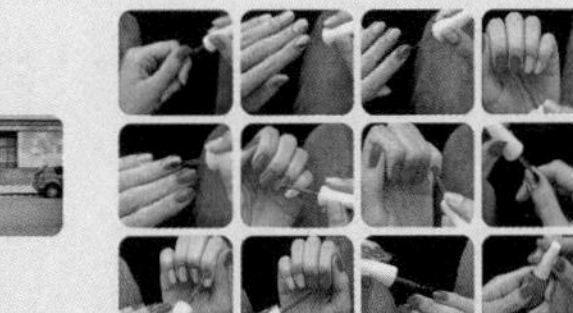

Poster Advertising Campaigns
AlmapBBDO
for Volkswagen do Brasil

Hands-free Parking System
With Park Assist, owners of the Volkswagen Tiguan can park their cars without using their hands. So we asked ourselves: what would people do with their hands while the car parallel parked by itself?

Art Director
Bruno Prosperi
Copywriter
Renato Simoes
Advertising Agency
AlmapBBDO

Client
Volkswagen do Brasil
Brand
Tiguan

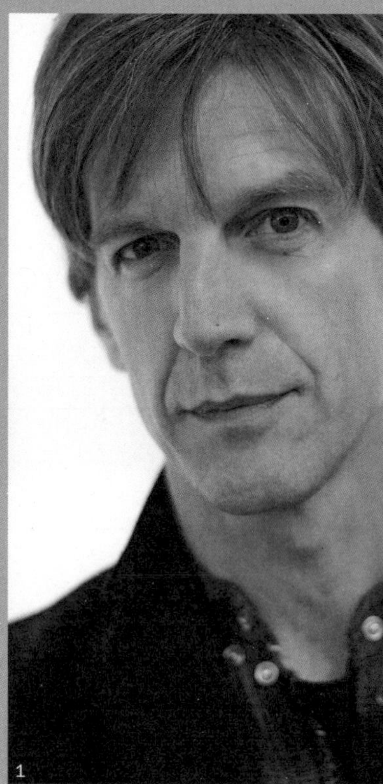
1

2

3

4

5

6

Jury Foreman
1. Graham Fink
Ogilvy & Mather China

2. Alexandre Hervé
DDB Paris

3. Marcos Medeiros
AlmapBBDO

4. Jack Steers

5. Rachel Heathfield
EHS 4D

6. Marcus Rebeschini
Y&R Asia

Yellow Pencil in Press Advertising

Press Advertising
JWT Shanghai
for Samsonite

Heaven and Hell
The task was to produce print ads and outdoor communication for the Samsonite Cosmolite suitcase. The selling point is its ultra-durability. The creative idea is a vivid contrast between how 'heavenly' it is in first class for the passenger, but 'hellish' down below where the suitcase is being handled. And yet the suitcase emerges sparkling after the torture.

Art Directors
Rojana Chuasakul
Danny Li
Haoxi Lv
Surachai
Puthikulangkura
Copywriter
Marc Wang
Illustrators
Surachai
Puthikulangkura
Supachai U-Rairat
Creative Directors
Hattie Cheng
Rojana Chuasakul
Executive Creative Directors
Elvis Chau
Sheung Yan Lo
Yang Yeo
Production House Producers
Somsak Pairew
Anotai Panmongkol
Advertising Agency
JWT Shanghai
Production House
Illusion
Account Handlers
Michelle Xiao
Lily Zheng
Maggie Zhou
Account Directors
Tom Doctoroff
Sophia Ng
Client
Samsonite

Nomination in Press Advertising

Press Advertising Campaigns
Ogilvy Malaysia
for Mattel Malaysia

Quick Draw Wins
The brief was to promote Pictionary, the game in which players guess words from drawings. We recreated the fun of playing Pictionary, where winning depends on how quickly you can draw, through ads featuring drawings. Guess them right and you'll get the message. These posters were placed in toy stores to help Pictionary stand out from the sea of games on the shelves.

Art Directors
Tan Chee Keong
Gavin Simpson
Yee Wai Khuen
Copywriters
Adam Chan
Donevan Chew
Illustrators
Milx
Yee Wai Khuen
Designer
Lian Ee Wern
Creative Director
Tan Chee Keong
Executive Creative Director
Gavin Simpson

Advertising Agency
Ogilvy Malaysia
Photography
Studio DL
Account Executives
Joanne Lee
Amy Yep
Account Director
Sharon Khor
Client
Mattel Malaysia
Brand
Pictionary

THI$ I$ A PAID ADVERTI$EMENT. YEAH, THAT'$ RIGHT. I BOUGHT THI$ ON A WHIM. THAT'$ WHAT BALLER CEO$ DO. $UCK IT.

I became the K-Swiss CEO in a swift, but unviolent, coup. Then I brought in the most badass athletes to help me run the company. Light Heavyweight Champion Jon "Bones" Jones keeps employees in line as the Director of HR. All-Pro quarterback Matt Cassel runs my high-powered marketing offense, humiliating our competition. I also got the incredibly nurturing Jillian Michaels to be our Director of Community Outreach.

MF'N BUSINESS INNOVATION

With my staff in place, my next job was to reinforce K-Swiss as an innovator in the sports industry. I focused my genius ways on K-Swiss Tubes, our most advanced training shoe ever, breaking all Federal Shoe Administration limits of breathability and comfort.

They say that an artist knows he has reached perfection, not when there is nothing left to add, but when there is nothing left to take away. Now, I don't know what that means, but that's why you never trust artists.

Tubes ARE perfect: Lightweight. Breathable. Death-proof.

$$$$$$$$$$$$$$$$$$$$$$$$$

ACCORDING TO AN INDEPENDENT STUDY, K-SWISS HAS SOLD "OVER INFINITY" PAIRS OF TUBES.

$$$$$$$$$$$$$$$$$$$$$$$$$

I lorded over my team of scientists night and day like a cruel, but just, dictator, tweaking, refining, crafting the design of Tubes until they met my unwavering standards. When I demanded lighter shoes, the scientists made them lighter.

When those scientists said I was pushing the shoe technology too far, I fired them. Then I hired a group of Soviet shoe-scientist defectors to push the lightness even farther, eventually

Kenny's autobiography, "I'm the CEO. You Shut Up," is currently unavailable due to unprecedented demand.

PWNING THE SPORTS WORLD

Now that I broke apart the corporate ladder and beat the world into submission with it, I'm putting the mamby-pamby sports world on notice. I'm making it more badass, more wild, more lethal.

I'm talking about settling lockouts MMA-style, in the ring. Legalizing genital text-message pics. Making post-game press conferences offensive/interesting again. Forcing a playoff system on college football. Basically, making sports be the thing that everyone in the world has been wanting it to be: not sucky.

Am I the most powerful man in the sports world? A less humble man would say yes. But, for the sake of clarity, let's just say that the second most powerful man in sports is in my rearview mirror, basically wishing he was Kenny Powers.

THE FINAL WORD

I'm the CEO. You shut up.

Press Advertising
72andSunny USA
for K-Swiss

K-Swiss: MFCEO
In the 2010 campaign, K-Swiss signed the controversial fictional 'athlete' Kenny Powers to an endorsement deal. In the 2011 campaign, Kenny took over K-Swiss as MFCEO (Mother F***ing Chief Executive Officer), reshaping the company in his image and enlisting the world's baddest athletes to help him unsuck the sports world.

Copywriter
Matt Heath
Photographer
Mike Piscitelli
Designer
Jay Kamath
Creative Directors
Barton Corley
Matt Murphy
Chief Creative Officer
Glenn Cole
Print Producer
Natalie Flemming
Advertising Agency
72andSunny USA
Brand Director
Matt Rohmer
Client
K-Swiss

What a quaint little kitchen, also known as the heart of the Anderson's home. Did you notice the one cupboard doesn't close? Marge does. In fact, since that day little Tina bent the hinges, it's the only thing she ever sees. "Imperfections give character", she reassures herself a gazillion times a day. And yes, it is a real number, just ask Marge.

Rather have the party at our place.

Kids Parties

Press Advertising
DDB South Africa
for McDonald's South Africa

Kids' Birthday Parties
The aim of the ad was to remind parents why McDonald's is the perfect venue for their kids' parties. We all know kids' parties are a nightmare, so have the party at McDonald's, where they'll take care of everything for you. We created an ad that highlighted the frightening consequences of hosting a kid's birthday party at home. It can go pretty pear-shaped. So seriously, have the party at McDonald's.

Art Directors
Jade Manning
Hital Pandya
Greig Watt
Copywriters
Vincent Osmond
Kenneth van Reenen
Creative Director
Phil Mailer
Executive Creative Director
Grant Jacobsen
Advertising Agency
DDB South Africa
Client
McDonald's South Africa

Press Advertising
TBWA\Hunt\Lascaris Johannesburg
for the Endangered Wildlife Trust

The Last Ones Left
The Endangered Wildlife Trust is a conservation group providing vital awareness about endangered species. Statistics have become prevalent in the mass of information people face every day, and are easy to ignore. The public was no longer responding to the statistics EWT was releasing. To increase the funds essential for wildlife conservation, we had to bring back the stopping power of statistics. Behind every number that makes up a statistic, there is a living animal. We had to make people see the animals behind the information. And it was from this insight that we conceptualised our idea: to put faces to the figures.

Art Director
Lizali Blom
Copywriters
Lizali Blom
Jared Osmond
Photographer
Mari Keyter
Creative Directors
Miguel Nunes
Adam Weber
Executive Creative Director
Damon Stapleton
Production Manager
Robert Mackenzie
Production Director
Craig Walker
Advertising Agency
TBWA\Hunt\Lascaris Johannesburg
Account Manager
Katiso Maarohanye
Account Director
Bridget Langley
Art Buyer
Sharon Cvetkovski
Client
Endangered Wildlife Trust

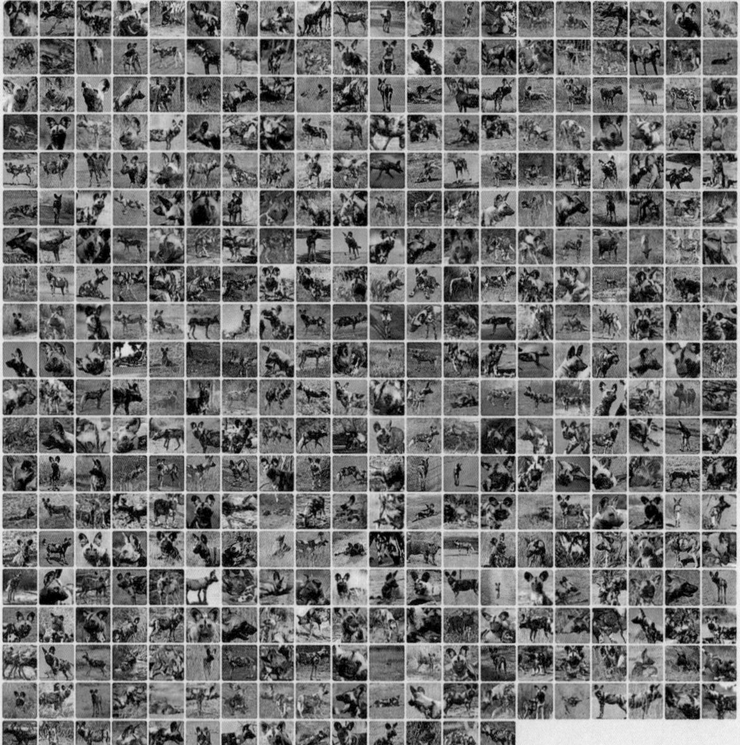

YOU ARE LOOKING AT EVERY WILD DOG LEFT IN SOUTH AFRICA.

To save the last 394 visit ewt.org.za

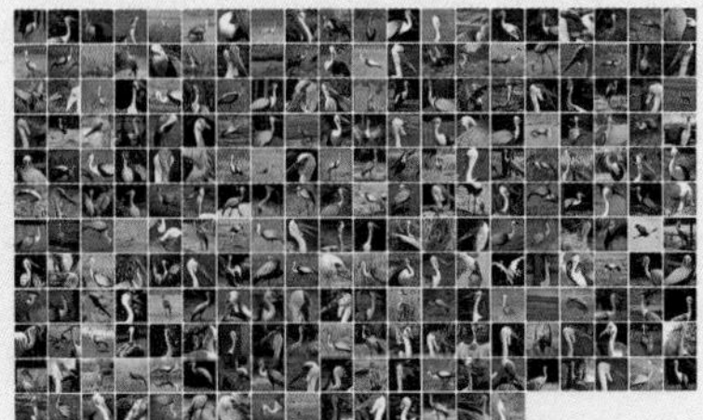

YOU ARE LOOKING AT EVERY WATTLED CRANE LEFT IN SOUTH AFRICA.

To save the last 235 visit ewt.org.za

YOU ARE LOOKING AT EVERY BLUE SWALLOW LEFT IN SOUTH AFRICA.

To save the last 36 visit ewt.org.za

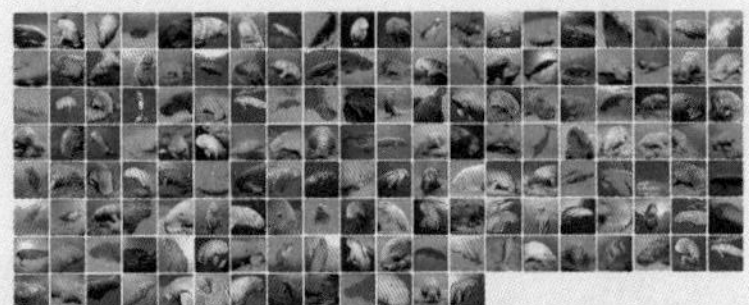

YOU ARE LOOKING AT EVERY DUGONG LEFT IN AFRICAN WATERS.

To save the last 153 visit ewt.org.za

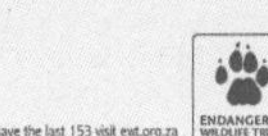

YOU ARE LOOKING AT EVERY NORTHERN WHITE RHINO LEFT ON THE PLANET.

To save the last 8 visit ewt.org.za

Press Advertising Campaigns
BBDO GUERRERO
for Bayer Philippines

Persistent Headache
This is a campaign for Saridon, a pill that works against persistent headaches. The press ads show our target market's repeated headaches coming to life and attacking them while they work non-stop.

Art Directors
Gary Amante
Peepo David
Copywriters
David Guerrero
Rey Tiempo
Photographers
Abet Bagay
Paolo Gripo
Creative Directors
Gary Amante
Rey Tiempo
Executive Creative Directors
David Guerrero
Brandie Tan
Retouchers
Oliver Brillantes
Vilma Magsino
Manny Vailoces

Print Producer
Al Salvador
Advertising Agency
BBDO GUERRERO
Project Manager
Cindy Evangelista
Account Handler
Iking Uy
Brand Managers
Christian Galvez
Edward Go
Client
Bayer Philippines
Brand
Saridon

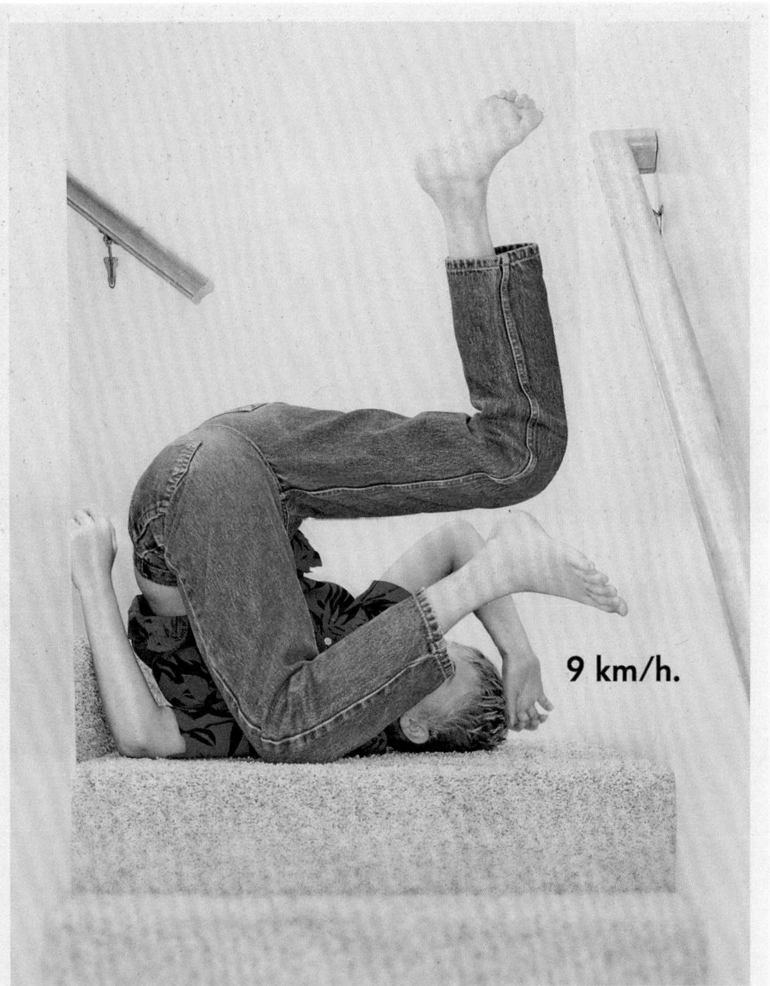
9 km/h.

Drive carefully.
Das Auto.

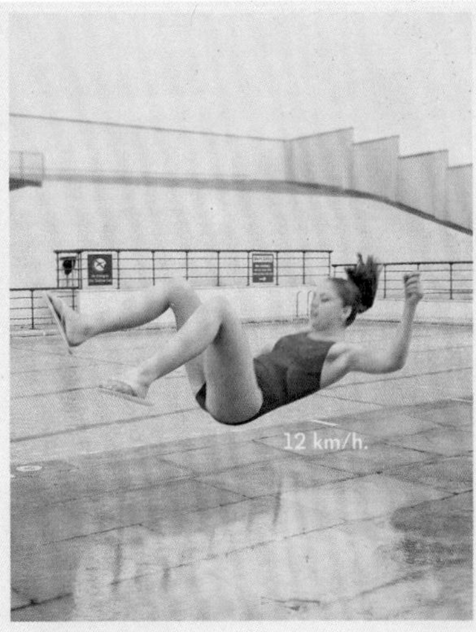
12 km/h.
Drive carefully.

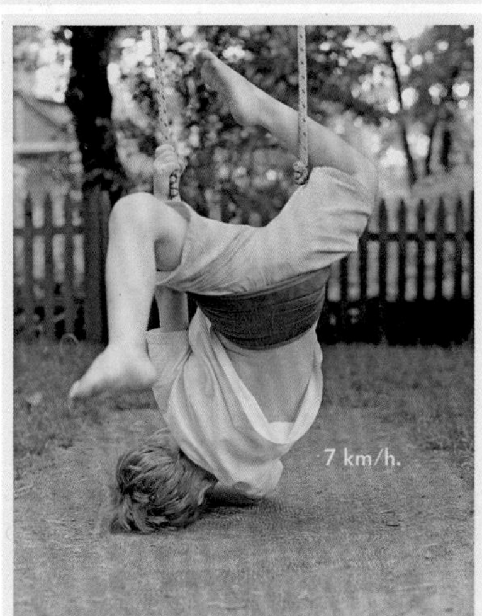
7 km/h.
Drive carefully.

Press Advertising Campaigns
DDB Argentina
for Volkswagen Argentina

Drive Carefully
Our challenge was to communicate the drama of a car accident without using the usual clichéd horror. Inspired by the wit and humour that have been a part of the brand's communication for the past 50 years, we had the idea of measuring the speed of common household accidents – building on the uncertainty of 'what if', instead of explicitly showing the consequences of an accident on a person.

Art Director
Alejandro Hara
Copywriter
Emilio Yacon
Creative Directors
Lisandro Grandal
Fernando Tchechenistky
Executive Creative Directors
Pablo Batlle
Hernan Jauregui
Agency Producer
Nelson Zeljkovich
Advertising Agency
DDB Argentina
Account Executive
Agustina Iparraguirre
Account Director
Graciela Combal
Brand Manager
Martin Sorrondegui
Client
Volkswagen Argentina

Press Advertising Campaigns
Memac Ogilvy & Mather Dubai
for Reporters Without Borders

Pixelated Truth

The biggest problem with censorship is not the suppression of information, but the fact that it distorts the truth and tells the wrong story. Reporters Without Borders fights for press freedom – and this campaign helped spark a worldwide discussion about the issue. Google hits for 'censorship tells the wrong story' before the campaign launch were 0; after the launch, hits reached 24.5 million.

Art Directors
Leonardo Borges
Sascha Kuntze
Rafael Rizuto
Copywriter
Sascha Kuntze
Creative Director
Ramzi Moutran
Executive Creative Director
Steve Hough

Advertising Agency
Memac Ogilvy & Mather Dubai
Photography
Associated Press
Client
Reporters Without Borders

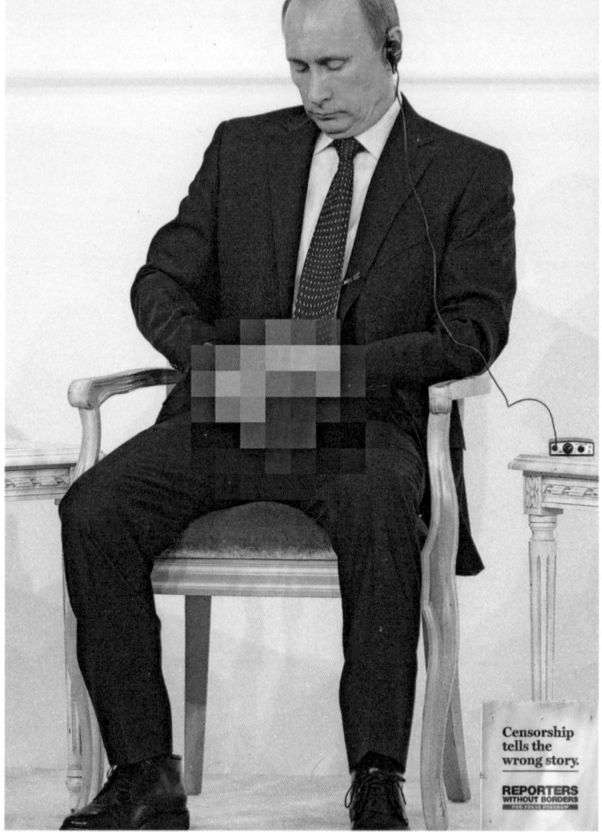

Press Advertising Campaigns
Grey Worldwide
for MTV Networks Switzerland

Sexidents
MTV wanted to remind its sexually active audience to use a condom – always. The idea: 'Sex is no accident. Always use a condom'. By showing absurd situations ending in intercourse, these print ads prove that sex is indeed never an accident, so there's no excuse for not using a condom.

Art Directors
Alphons Conzen
Frederico Gasparian
Reto Oetterli
Copywriter
Janus Hansen
Illustrator
Gary Davidson
Creative Directors
Moritz Grub
Regner Lotz
Executive Creative Directors
Andreas Henke
Sacha Reeb

Print Producers
Peter Engel
Mathias Renner
Advertising Agency
Grey Worldwide
Account Handler
Marco Koeditz
Art Buyer
Sabine Campe
Client
MTV Networks Switzerland

Press Advertising Campaigns
Ogilvy Brazil
for BandSports

BandSports 24/7
We wanted to advertise the fact that people can watch the best sports programming 24 hours a day on BandSports. We came up with a simple and funny campaign showing an awful truth: whatever the occasion, Brazilian men just can't miss a second of BandSports 24-hour sports channel – even during the most important family moments!

Art Director
Eduardo Doss
Copywriter
Hugo Veiga
Creative Director
Fred Saldanha
Executive Creative Director
Anselmo Ramos
Print Producer
Antonio Carlos

Advertising Agency
Ogilvy Brazil
Account Handlers
Evandro Guimarães
Carolina Vieira
Art Buyer
Nanci Bonani
Marketing Manager
Alexandre Bortolai
Client
BandSports

Press Advertising Campaigns
SPILLMANN/FELSER/LEO BURNETT
for SwissLife

Life's Turn in a Sentence
The SwissLife pension and life insurance solutions are flexible and adapt to life's twists and turns. So we created a headline campaign dramatising this, and pointing out that life sometimes does take unexpected turns.

Art Directors
Daniele Barbiero
Reto Clement
Copywriters
Thomas Schöb
Simon Smit
Executive Creative Director
Peter Brönnimann

Advertising Agency
SPILLMANN/FELSER/LEO BURNETT
Client
SwissLife

I never want children are great.

For all life's twists and turns:
Flexible financial plans.

I love my house now belongs to my ex-wife.

For all life's twists and turns:
Flexible financial plans.

I'm not interested in getting married in church is more romantic.

For all life's twists and turns:
Flexible financial plans.

She's my everything went wrong.

For all life's twists and turns:
Flexible financial plans.

I like working with you is impossible.

For all life's twists and turns:
Flexible financial plans.

You're the only woman I love a man now.

For all life's twists and turns:
Flexible financial plans.

Inserts & Wraps for Press Advertising
Y&R São Paulo
for Telefônica & TVA

Maps
Telefônica launched its fibre optic service in 2011. Our challenge was to rapidly raise awareness and increase its penetration, focusing only on the neighbourhoods where it was already available. To reach these potential consumers directly, we combined 'Época' magazine coverage and Google Earth technology to produce more than 5,000 different subscribers' magazine covers with a customised image of their streets and houses. The message reinforced the exclusivity, as each magazine cover informed the reader that their street already had Telefônica's fibre optic cables.

Art Director
Guilherme Rácz
Copywriters
Lucas Casão
Evandro Soares
Creative Directors
Rui Branquinho
Flavio Casarotti
Jorge Iervolino
Victor Sant'Anna
Chief Creative Officer
Rui Branquinho
Print Producers
Elaine Carvalho
Rodrigo Cassino

Advertising Agency
Y&R São Paulo
Photography
Yes Mobile Media
Planners
David Laloum
Eliana Yamaguchi
Account Manager
Marcelo Moreno
Account Director
Claudia Menezes
Clients
Telefônica
TVA

Inserts & Wraps for Press Advertising
The Jupiter Drawing Room Johannesburg
& Matchworld
for Absa

Team of Millions
For Absa bank's sponsorship of South Africa's national rugby team, the Springboks, we wanted to make fans feel they really were a part of the team. We set out to create the world's biggest team picture with the players asking fans to have their photos taken at kiosks in shopping centres. Over two days, eight photographers shot more than 10,000 fans. Retouchers then put fans into Springbok jerseys and added them to the team. On the weekend before the Springboks' first World Cup match, the Sunday press ran with 1.3 million posters featuring all the fans who had taken their place in the Team of Millions.

Art Directors
David Blakey-Milner
Gareth Pretorius
Copywriters
Eyrton Hayes
Darren Kilfoil
Photographer
Michael Lewis
Executive Creative Director
Tom Cullinan
Chief Creative Officer
Brad Reilly
Retoucher
Nick Robinson
Advertising Agency
Matchworld
Creative Agency
The Jupiter Drawing Room Johannesburg
Client
Absa

Jury Foreman
1. Warren Brown
BMF Australia

2. John Altman

3. Bob Winter
Y&R Chicago

4. Stephanie Pigott
Pirate Toronto

5. André Laurentino
TBWA\London

6. Rob McLennan
Net#work BBDO
Johannesburg

7. Torsten Hennings
Studio Funk Hamburg

Nelson Mandela

Nelson Mandela: During my lifetime, I have considered dedicating myself to this struggle of the African people.

I have thought perhaps I should fight against white domination and perhaps even fight against black domination. But I have my career to consider. Don't get me wrong, it is an ideal many of my people hope to live for and to achieve, but it's not my problem and it is certainly not an ideal for which I'm prepared to die.

MVO: If Nelson Mandela made this speech at the Rivonia trial in 1964 who knows where we'd be today. One voice can make a difference. Use yours and help us take the Nelson Mandela legacy forward.

Visit: nelsonmandela.org

Martin Luther King Jnr

Martin Luther King Jnr: I had a dream, but freedom will never reign from Stone Mountain of Georgia nor any hills or mole hills of Mississippi. The life of a negro is crippled by the chains of discrimination. We will have neither rest nor tranquility. The truth is there will never come a day when all of God's children will be able to join hands and sing in the words of the old negro spiritual: 'Free at last, Free at last'. I say to you today my friends we shall never ever be free.

MVO: If Martin Luther King Jnr delivered this message to civil rights supporters in 1963 who knows where we'd be today. One voice can make a difference. Use yours and help us take the Nelson Mandela legacy forward.

Visit: nelsonmandela.org

Yellow Pencil in Radio Advertising

Sound Design & Use of Music for Radio Advertising
Grey South Africa
for the Nelson Mandela Foundation

Nelson Mandela & Martin Luther King Jnr
The Nelson Mandela Foundation wanted to inspire ordinary people to take responsibility and help realise Nelson Mandela's ideal of a just society. We adapted Nelson Mandela's iconic closing statement at the Rivonia Trial in 1964, before he was sent to prison for 27 years. We changed his words to challenge listeners to imagine a world where no one, not even Mandela, has the guts to take a stand for what is right. We used the same approach with Martin Luther King's celebrated 'I Have a Dream' speech, made to civil rights supporters in 1963. Both spots were also selected as single executions in the 'Radio Advertising over 30 seconds' category.

Sound Designer
Lorens Persons
Copywriters
Wihan Meerholz
Wynand Prinsloo
Executive Creative Director
Cath Ireland

Advertising Agency
Grey South Africa
Strategic Director
Sizakele Marutlulle
Client
Nelson Mandela Foundation

Yellow Pencil in Radio Advertising

Writing for Radio Advertising
Net#work BBDO Johannesburg
for Mercedes-Benz

Attention Assist
Sometimes when you're driving, your brain takes a little leave of absence from your body. Maybe it visits a beach or lives out a bizarre fantasy moment while your body drives your car on autopilot. Mercedes-Benz Attention Assist is a nifty feature that brings you back from your daydream to the very important task of driving. This work was also selected in the 'Radio Advertising Campaigns' category.

Copywriters
Jenny Glover
Brent Singer
Creative Director
Rob McLennan
Agency Producer
Tanja Rae
Recording Engineer
David Law
Sound Designer
David Law

Advertising Agency
Net#work BBDO
Johannesburg
Recording Studio
First#Left
Account Handler
Karen Carr
Client
Mercedes-Benz

Cabo

MVO 'I'll have a slippery nipple' said the brain to the barman as he surveyed the beach and contemplated new ways of making an international cretin of himself. Yes, the brain was in Cabo baby, partaking in bro-times and general nincompoopedness with men known only as Bruski and Von Dudenstein. Brain found itself saying shameful things like 'Appletini's all round' and 'I have a Speedo just like that'. Rest assured, if brain had a fist, it would be pumping it. 'Last one in's a bed wetter' brain shouted, as it prepared to do a running bomb into the hot tub. Yes, and while brain is signing up for the world beach bat championships, your body, well, your body drives unsupervised down an endlessly long road. Lucky for you, Mercedes-Benz Attention Assist is designed to bring brains quickly back from Cabo, right to the here and now. 'Pull my finger' said brain, as he suddenly returned to the present – 'Oh, there's a bend in the road, good thing I noticed.'

Boss

MVO 'This is for making me apply ointment to your thigh eczema' cried brain as he emptied four months worth of carefully collected dry heal shavings into the water dispenser. Brain had snuck into his boss's office and was exacting his revenge for 10 years of humiliation and bad pay. He cologned himself extravagantly with single malt before releasing the feral tomcat onto the carpet. 'There's a weak bladdered kitty, kitty' said brain as he rubbed his hands together repeatedly. Brain then began to methodically feed ripe sardines into the hems of his boss's curtains to the soundtrack of his own maniacal laughter. 'Mwa ha ha' boomed brain. And yes, while brain contemplated making anatomical adjustments to a priceless artwork, your body is merrily driving without any supervision down a treacherous stretch of road. Lucky for you, Mercedes-Benz Attention Assist is designed to bring brains quickly back from revenge fantasies, right to the here and now. 'No one is fooled by your hairpiece,' yelled brain, as he suddenly came to behind the wheel of his car.

Class Reunion

MVO 'I lickie, boom, boom, down' sang brain as he did the robot at his class of '91 high school reunion. 'Why yes, it's true, my pecks have officially been declared the hardest substance known to man,' confirmed brain to a sea of his old class mates. Brain was hip and cool and capable of melting panty elastic with a single look. When he said things like 'yo dawg' and 'smell you later', every girl in the room dreamt of pairing his socks and starching his shirts. And while brain was recounting the tale of how he invented the world wide interweb and vegetarian shoes to his adoring fans, it's worth noting that your body drives all on its own down a very busy highway. Lucky for you, Mercedes-Benz Attention Assist is designed to bring brains quickly back from imagined class reunions, right to the here and now. 'Facebook me' said brain as he returned to the present. 'Oh, right, I'm driving a car.'

Yellow Pencil in Radio Advertising

Radio Advertising Campaigns
bravo | y&r New York
for Leica

See Everything
This campaign is a showcase for the listener, demonstrating that with a truly powerful camera lens, you really do see everything.

Copywriter
Hugo Castillo
Creative Directors
Hugo Castillo
Markus Gut
Guillermo Vega
Producer
Clara Romero
Agency Producer
Maria Molina

Advertising Agency
bravo | y&r New York
Recording Studio
Audio Engine
Account Handler
Julia Kull
Client
Leica

Company Outing

MVO Everybody at the annual company summer outing.

SFX Photo snap/flash

MVO That's Jerry Richards.

SFX Camera zoom

MVO And that's a mustard stain.

SFX Camera zoom

MVO It marks him like the palpable disdain he has for his job.

SFX Camera zoom

MVO Where he shares a desk with Harry, a grown man who still says 'dude'.

SFX Camera zoom

MVO Harry encouraged Jerry to be a little less than honest on his tax return.

SFX Camera zoom

MVO Like back in 1983 when he asked Julia Van Crinkle to the school dance.

SFX Camera zoom

MVO He danced the mashed potato with a certain toadying waltz.

SFX Camera zoom

MVO But didn't then, and never has, owned a tax deductible yellow speedboat.

SFX Camera zoom

MVO The Leica V-LUX 20 with 24x optical super zoom lens.

SFX Camera zoom

MVO See everything.

MVO The Grand Canyon.

SFX Photo snap/flash

MVO That's Frank Beamer standing proudly.

SFX Camera zoom

MVO Frank proposed here 8 years ago, at that spot, to Amy Lewis.

SFX Camera zoom

MVO They married and assumed a $30,000 loan at 15% on a little 2-bedroom place.

SFX Camera zoom

MVO And adopted a Shih Tzu named Belvedere.

SFX Camera zoom

MVO They all came back to the Grand Canyon every summer for 7 years.

SFX Camera zoom

MVO Each year dining at a little Mexican restaurant called El Sombrero.

SFX Camera zoom

MVO Where his wife fell in love with a waiter named Miguel.

SFX Camera zoom

MVO Frank is single now.

SFX Camera zoom

MVO But happily dating a heavy-set German woman that makes a great Goulash.

SFX Camera zoom

MVO The Leica V-LUX 20 with 24x optical super zoom lens.

SFX Camera zoom

MVO See everything.

Yellow Pencil in Radio Advertising

Radio Advertising over 30 seconds
bravo | y&r New York
for Leica

Picture Day
This ad is a showcase for the listener, demonstrating that with a truly powerful camera lens, you really do see everything.

Copywriter
Hugo Castillo
Creative Directors
Hugo Castillo
Markus Gut
Guillermo Vega
Producer
Clara Romero
Agency Producer
Maria Molina

Advertising Agency
bravo | y&r New York
Recording Studio
Audio Engine
Account Handler
Julia Kull
Client
Leica

Picture Day

MVO The official company picture.

SFX Photo snap/flash

MVO That's Jane Mitchell from accounting.

SFX Camera zoom

MVO That's a big, white, happy smile.

SFX Camera zoom

MVO But her teeth are lacking a certain symmetry.

SFX Camera zoom

MVO Her spreadsheets also have slight flaws.

SFX Camera zoom

MVO She always forgets to carry the decimal point.

SFX Camera zoom

MVO Jane has a problem with the small details.

SFX Camera zoom

MVO Like state capitals and where she leaves her keys.

SFX Camera zoom

MVO And never remembers the names of men she meets online. Was it Richard? Or Dick?

SFX Camera zoom

MVO But she remembers the names of all her cats, all 37…

SFX Camera zoom

MVO …no, 39 of them.

MVO The Leica V-LUX 20 with 24x optical super zoom lens.

SFX Camera zoom

MVO See everything.

Watching

VO (In disguised voice, sounding low and scary)
You don't know it, but I'm watching you.

I know where you hang out.

The car you drive.

The clothes you wear.

I swear I'm going to get you.

And give you what you deserve.

I'm going to use them to do something terrible to you…

And watch you suffer.

FVO An anonymous tip. It's a scary thing to criminals. Call Crime Stoppers at 1-800-222-TIPS, to leave yours.

Not Safe

VO (In disguised voice, sounding low and scary)
You think you're safe… But you're not.

There are things I know about you.

Things you'd never realise I know.

But I do.

FVO An anonymous tip. It's a scary thing to criminals. Call Crime Stoppers at 1-800-222-TIPS, to leave yours.

Nightmare

VO (In disguised voice, sounding low and scary)
I am your worst nightmare. I know more about you than you can ever imagine.

You just don't realise it.

I'm watching.

Waiting…

And before you know it… I will make your life a living hell.

FVO An anonymous tip. It's a scary thing to criminals. Call Crime Stoppers at 1-800-222-TIPS, to leave yours.

Nomination in Radio Advertising

Radio Advertising Campaigns
DDB Canada, Toronto
for Toronto Crime Stoppers

Expose
Toronto Crime Stoppers promotes the fact that individuals who provide tips remain anonymous. The validity of this claim was being questioned by the public. Research showed that our primary target felt as though the tip line was not truly anonymous and feared being exposed to the police, or worse, to the offender. This radio campaign was created to address these concerns and demonstrate that the only person who should be fearful of a tip is the criminal.

Copywriter
David Ross
Art Director
Paul Wallace
Creative Directors
Todd Mackie
Denise Rossetto
Associate Creative Directors
David Ross
Paul Wallace
Audio Director
Stephanie Pigott
Agency Producer
Andrew Schulze
Audio Producer
Joanne Uyeyama
Voice Over Artists
Steve Gardiner
Tom Goudie
Mary F Moore
Terry O'Reilly
Recording & Mixing Engineer
Jared Kuemper
Advertising Agency
DDB Canada, Toronto
Sound Design
Pirate Toronto
Account Handlers
Reshma Lalany
Carly Sutherland
Client
Toronto Crime Stoppers

Nomination in Radio Advertising

Radio Advertising Campaigns
AMV BBDO
for the Metropolitan Police

Metropolitan Police Robbery Campaign
Street robbery is on the increase in London. This campaign aims to highlight these hotspots and make people think twice about where they take out their possessions. Most Londoners aren't aware that their everyday behaviour could be putting them at risk of street robbery. By simply explaining how this behaviour is seen through the eyes of a robber, we conveyed a powerful and important message.

Copywriter
Charlotte Adorjan
Art Director
Michael Jones
Creative Directors
Steve Jones
Martin Loraine
Executive Creative Director
Paul Brazier

Producer
Paul Burke
Recording Engineer
Chris Turner
Advertising Agency
AMV BBDO
Production Company
Jungle
Client
Metropolitan Police

Bus

MVO1 So I get off the bus and zip up my coat.

MVO2 You get off the bus and zip up your coat.

MVO1 I open my bag and bring out my mp3 player.

MVO2 You open your bag and bring out £200.

MVO1 I put in my earphones and choose a track.

MVO2 You shut off your hearing and hold up the cash.

MVO1 Then I set off down the street with my music pumping.

MVO2 You set off down the street, drawing everyone's attention.

End VO Thieves see your possessions differently, so take care where you take them out.

Here for London.
The Metropolitan Police service.

For more information visit met.police.uk

Jewellery

FVO I bump into my friend at the bus stop.

MVO You bump into your friend at the bus stop.

FVO I take off my pashmina and show her my new necklace.

MVO You take off your pashmina and show her £150.

FVO I play with the necklace as we talk.

MVO You play with the money as you talk.

FVO I say goodbye and walk home.

MVO You keep the money on show and walk home alone.

End VO Thieves see your possessions differently, so take care where you take them out.

Here for London.
The Metropolitan Police service.

For more information visit met.police.uk

Tube

FVO At the station I walk down the stairs.

MVO At the station you walk down the stairs.

FVO I walk through the exit and bring out my phone.

MVO You walk through the exit and bring out £300.

FVO I check my messages and make a call.

MVO You hold up the money and make sure everyone sees it.

FVO I chat on the phone and wait for my friend.

MVO You become totally distracted and stand away from the crowd.

End VO Thieves see your possessions differently, so take care where you take them out.

Here for London.
The Metropolitan Police service.

For more information visit met.police.uk

Nomination in Radio Advertising

Radio Advertising over 30 seconds
Ogilvy Germany
for The University of Music, Drama and Media Hanover

The Absolute Pitch

People with absolute pitch can identify every tone on the musical scale without any device. They can hear the tones C, D, E, F, G, A and H (German scale). With these tones, you can encode words that can only be identified by people with absolute pitch. To make sure that only the most talented young musicians apply for courses at Hanover's University of Music, Drama and Media, we developed an effective barrier: we produced a radio ad where the contact email address chef@hmtm-hannover.de ('chef' is German for 'boss') was encoded using tones. Our radio commercial became the first round of the qualifying examination.

Copywriter
Manuel Rentz
Creative Directors
Matthias Storath
Dr Stephan Vogel
Audio Producer
Stephan Moritz
Recording Engineer
Andy Schlegel
Advertising Agency
Ogilvy Germany
Record Company
Studio Funk Berlin
Account Handlers
Michael Fucks
Sophie Gudat
Client
The University of Music, Drama and Media Hanover

MVO Welcome to the first official application procedure of the University of Music Hanover. We are searching for students with an absolute pitch. If you can hear that this (piano sound A) is an A, and this (piano sound C) is a C, then we are looking forward to receiving an email from you. Just send it to (piano sounds C-H-E-F) @ hmtm-hannover dot (piano sounds D-E).

Once again, so you can write it down: (piano sounds C-H-E-F) @hmtm-hannover dot (piano sounds D-E).

Nomination in Radio Advertising

Radio Advertising over 30 seconds
DDB Colombia
for the Military Forces of Colombia

The Code

In Colombia, some policemen and soldiers have been held captive by guerillas for years with limited exposure to the news. To help the Military Forces of Colombia speak directly to their men, we created a song to be aired on the radio. The chorus included a tapping sound, which was a hidden Morse code message to boost morale. The voice of the Military Forces of Colombia broke enemy lines, and reached its men to give them strength and hope. This work was also selected in the 'Sound Design & Use of Music for Radio Advertising' category.

Copywriter
Alfonso Diaz
Art Director
Mario Leon
Creative Directors
Rodrigo Bolivar
Alfonso Diaz
Executive Creative Directors
Juan Carlos Espitia
Juan Carlos Palma
Chief Creative Officer
Rodrigo Davila
Producer
Carlos Portela
Sound Designers
Diego Bautista
Amaury Gutierrez
Advertising Agency
DDB Colombia
Production Company
Radio Bemba
Account Handlers
Luis Fernando Castilla
Claudia Fernandez
Client
Military Forces of Colombia

Morse code message
19 people rescued.
You're next.
Don't lose hope.

MVO The little girl lies peacefully on her bed of tarmac, a ruby red pillow cradling her head.

With her eyes still closed, she sucks the blood slowly back into her mouth.

Now her shattered legs become whole.

The shards of glass embedded in them fly out, like crystal butterflies, and become your headlights once more.

She leaps up gracefully from the road, and now she is a broken ballerina, twirling and twisting in mid-air. She travels five full metres, and lands on her two feet, her scattered schoolbooks falling neatly back into her satchel.

The sudden fear in her eyes fades.

And as you stop to let her cross safely, she smiles at you, almost as if you haven't just killed her.

Regret has no rewind button. If you respect life, respect speed limits. A community service message from Fly FM.

Writing for Radio Advertising
Bates Malaysia
for Fly FM

Rewind
The commercial describes, in poetic detail, a fatal accident in reverse. It illustrates an impossible scenario, conveying the message that regret has no rewind button.

Copywriter
Viknesh Chandra
Creative Director
Ajay Bakhshi
Agency Producer
Sandra Duarte
Sound Designer
Julian Lim

Advertising Agency
Bates Malaysia
Sound Design
Real Time Studios
Client
Fly FM

SFX Clock sound

MVO Maria won a college scholarship when she turned 18.

She graduated with a finance degree at 23.

When she was 25 she got her first job.

She got married at 29.

At 33, she was named group director.

At 33, she became a mum.

At 33, she had her second son.

At 33, she retired.

At 33, she celebrated her 25th wedding anniversary.

At 33, she became a grandmother.

Olay. Time stops whenever you want.

Radio Advertising 0-30 seconds
Badillo Nazca Saatchi & Saatchi
for Procter & Gamble

33
Olay's regenerative power is so great that ageing stops once you use it.

Copywriters
Cristina Burckhart
Pedro Perez
Fernando Suarez
Creative Director
Mariano German
Executive Creative Director
Juan Carlos Rodriguez
Agency Producer
Vanessa Ramirez de Arellano
Sound Engineer
Denes Pagan

Advertising Agency
Badillo Nazca Saatchi & Saatchi
Recording Studio
GPS Studio
Account Executive
Yisa Vargas
Account Manager
Mariam Zemuri
Client
Procter & Gamble
Brand
Olay

Radio Advertising Campaigns
FoxP2
for Frank.Net

What Isn't Coming: 2012 / Mall / Star Jumps
One thing is certain in life and that's death. Frank is a straight-talking life insurance company that tells it like it is, even when death is involved.

Copywriter	Advertising Agency
Gavin Williams	FoxP2
Creative Director	Sound Design
Justin Gomes	The Workroom
Agency Producer	Account Handler
Katherine Tripp	Kaylin Mendes
Voice Over Artist	Client
Adam Behr	Frank.Net

2012

MVO What isn't coming is a dishwasher designed specifically for your collection of plates, pots and pans.

What isn't coming is a billionaire crime fighter.

What isn't coming to Springs is your favourite band.

What isn't coming is the end of the world in 2012.

What isn't coming to cinemas near you is 2012. Part 2.

What is coming is death. But don't worry – when it does, Frank pays.

Frank.Net. Life cover made simple.

Frank.Net is a registered financial services provider.

Mall

MVO What isn't coming to your work is a convenient earthquake minutes before your spectacularly unprepared presentation.

What isn't coming to the mall is an exciting new store where that sign says: 'exciting new store coming'.

What isn't coming back is your hairline or another shot at glory.

What isn't coming to the 94th minute is an equalizer.

What isn't coming is a type of chocolate that tones your butt.

What is coming is death. But don't worry – when it does, Frank pays.

Frank.Net. Life cover made simple.

Frank.Net is a registered financial services provider.

MVO What isn't coming is
a dignified way to do
star jumps.

What isn't coming is a
photocopier with only one
button that says 'Photocopy',
which it then does.

What isn't coming is a simple
way to explain the offside
rule without using salt and
pepper shakers.

What isn't coming is a late
rally by the Zim dollar before
the closing bell.

What isn't coming is soaring
CD sales, door-to-door
encyclopedias or a firm
grasp on technology from
your parents.

What is coming is death.
But don't worry – when it
does, Frank pays.

Frank.Net. Life cover
made simple.

Frank.Net is a registered
financial services provider.

Radio Advertising Campaigns
McCann Erickson Malaysia
for BFM: The Business Station

Anytime: Audrey / Freda / Yameen
October 2011 was Breast Cancer Awareness Month in Malaysia. BFM 89.9 supported the larger initiative with this thought: since breast cancer can strike when least expected, can an awareness campaign also do the same? Our solution was to interrupt regular radio programming on the all-business channel BFM 89.9 with awareness messages, seamlessly delivered by newscasters or programme hosts themselves, read in exactly the same style as the news, daily updates or business coaching segments they were presenting.

Copywriters
Gavin E Hoh
Ean-Hwa Huang
Szu-Hung Lee
Oon-Hoong Yeoh

Creative Directors
Ean-Hwa Huang
Szu-Hung Lee

Advertising Agency
McCann Erickson Malaysia

Marketing Director
Malek Ali

Client
BFM: The Business Station

Audrey

Newscaster: Air Asia's Thai unit remains on target to sell shares in the fourth quarter through an initial public offering as the plan hasn't been affected by the flooding. CEO Tan Sri Tony Fernandes says the share sale plan is progressing well, and Thai Air Asia's earnings are strong. He adds that the company's fourth quarter may be affected a little bit by the flooding in Thailand, but the tendency to rebound is very strong.

Breasts today are their usual size and shape.

Both breasts show no visible distortion or swelling.

Nipples are pointed slightly upwards as they usually are.

Rolling nipples gently between the thumb and index finger causes no pain.

Much like this interruption to this programme, breast cancer can strike when you least expect it.

Follow these self-check instructions regularly and see your doctor early if you spot anything.

For more information, visit cancer.org.my

BFM in support of breast cancer awareness.

Hirotako's board of directors does not intend... (business updates continue)

Freda

Host: This is 'Raise your game on Enterprise', I'm here with action coach Jeevan Sahadevan, and we're talking about nine common mistakes managers make in managing departments and companies and how to avoid them. We've gone through the first two – refusal to accept personal accountability, and failure to equip people.

Now take off your blouse, then your bra if you're wearing one.

Turn on the light and stand in front of the mirror.

Gently touch your left breast, now your right.

Use your fingertips to feel your way around the sides of both breasts.

Touch every inch.

Much like the interruption to this programme, breast cancer can strike when you least expect it.

Follow these self-check instructions regularly and see your doctor early if you spot anything.

And for more information, visit cancer.org.my

BFM, in support of breast cancer awareness.

We're onto the third one, Jeevan.

Jeevan So of the first nine mistakes we've gone through, we're going through four today... (coaching session continues)

Yameen

ewscaster ...is on target to sell shares in the fourth quarter, through an initial public offering, as the plan hasn't been affected by the flooding. Petronas has clarified that there is no policy change on licensing systems for companies engaged in Malaysia's upstream oil and gas industry.

Men need to touch themselves more often.

They need to do this regularly and without shame.

Using their fingertips they should touch their chests, working their way closer to their nipples, and gently squeeze or tweak them.

There should be no pain, lumps or swollen spots.

Much like the interruption to this programme, breast cancer can strike when you least expect it.

Men are not immune and you too should follow these self-check instructions regularly and see your doctor early if you spot anything.

For more information, visit cancer.org.my

Tasek Corporation's earnings fell by 32.9%... (news updates continue)

Jury Foreman
1. Mark Tutssel
Leo Burnett Worldwide

2. Jo Wallace
Draftfcb London

3. Pelle Sjoenell
BBH LA

4. Nick Bell
DDB Europe

5. Lizie Gower
Academy Films

6. Alvaro Sotomayor
Wieden+Kennedy
Amsterdam

7. Anselmo Ramos
Ogilvy & Mather Brazil

8. José Miguel Sokoloff
LOWE/SSP3

It doesn't have to end like it began.

Yellow Pencil in TV & Cinema Advertising

TV Commercials 61-120 seconds
BBH London
for Barnardo's

Life Story
This film tells the story of Michael, a man with a family, job and everything to live for. He talks about his life. As he speaks he regresses back to a younger version of himself, so that we see the extraordinary journey he's been on. We discover that he was violent as a teenager and ready to give up hope. Then we see that he was beaten as a young boy, and had to hide from his mother's boyfriend. We also see the positive impact Barnardo's had on his life. Through belief and support, the charity helped turn his troubled life around. The film concludes: 'It doesn't have to end like it began'.

Director
Ringan Ledwidge
Art Directors
Rory Hall
Melanie Lynch
Copywriters
Rory Hall
Melanie Lynch
Executive Creative Director
Nick Gill
Producer
Sally Humphries
Agency Producer
Davud Karbassioun
Director of Photography
Theo Garland
Editor
Rich Orrick
Music Composer
Ludovico Einaudi
Production Company
Rattling Stick
Advertising Agency
BBH London
Post Production
The Mill London
Sound Design
Wave Studios
Account Handlers
Charlotte Bowden
Helen James
Strategic Director
John Harrison
Brand Director
Lindsay Gormley
Marketing Director
Diana Tickell
Client
Barnardo's

Yellow Pencil in TV & Cinema Advertising

TV Commercials 61-120 seconds
BETC Paris
for CANAL+

The Bear
A bearskin rug explains what it takes to become a great Hollywood director.

Director
Matthijs van Heijningen
Art Director
Eric Astorgue
Copywriter
Jean-Christophe Royer
Executive Creative Director
Stéphane Xiberras
Executive Producer
Yuki Suga
Agency Producers
David Green
Isabelle Menard
Director of Photography
Joost Van Gelder
Production Designer
Jan Houllevigue

Editor
Jono Griffiths
Music Producer
Eric Cervera
Production Company
Soixante Quinze
Advertising Agency
BETC Paris
Post Production
Mikros
Visual Effects Company
Mikros
Sound Design
GUM
Planner
Clarisse Lacarrau
Client
CANAL+

Nomination in TV & Cinema Advertising

TV Commercials 41-60 seconds
Loducca
for MTV Brasil

Balloons
In order to celebrate MTV's 21st anniversary in Brazil, we prepared a retrospective of the most important events in music, using stop motion animation with party balloons. The most memorable facts and characters in music history intertwine in an unconventional, yet faithful narrative, reinforcing the concept: 'The music never stops'.

Director
Dulcídio Caldeira
Art Directors
André Faria
Guga Ketzer
Copywriters
Dulcídio Caldeira
André Faria
Guga Ketzer
Producer
Karina Vadasz
Executive Producers
Ana Luisa André
Egisto Betti
Sid Fernandes
Photography Director
Alexandre Ermel
Production Designer
Daniel Semanas
Animator
Daniel Semanas
Illustrator
Daniel Semanas
Music Composer
Gioachino Rossini
Sound Designers
Fernando Forni
Hilton Raw
Advertising Agency
Loducca
Planners
Isabella Mulholland
Mariana Quintanilha
Account Executive
Sabrina Spinelli
Account Director
Carmen Assumpção
Client
MTV Brasil

Nomination in TV & Cinema Advertising

TV Commercials 41-60 seconds
Deutsch LA
for Volkswagen

The Force
A little boy discovers the force in the magic of his father's Volkswagen Passat.

Director
Lance Acord
Senior Art Directors
Ryan McLaughlin
Craig Melchiano
Senior Copywriter
David Povill
Group Creative Directors
Michael Kadin
Eric Springer
Chief Creative Officer
Mark Hunter
Producers
Mary Catherine Finney
Jim Haight
Executive Producer
Mary Ann Marino
Director of Integrated Production
Vic Palumbo
Director of Broadcast Production
Victoria Guenier
Editor
Jim Haygood
Sound Designer
Jeff Elmassian
Sound Mixer
Mark Meyuhas
Production Company
Park Pictures
Advertising Agency
Deutsch LA
Post Production
Company 3
Audio Post Production
Lime Studios
Editing
Union Editorial
Sound Design
Endless Noise
Account Planner
Douglas Van Praet
Account Director
Chris Carter
Group Account Director
Tom Else
Chief Strategic Officer
Jeffery Blish
Chief Executive Officer
Mike Sheldon
Client
Volkswagen

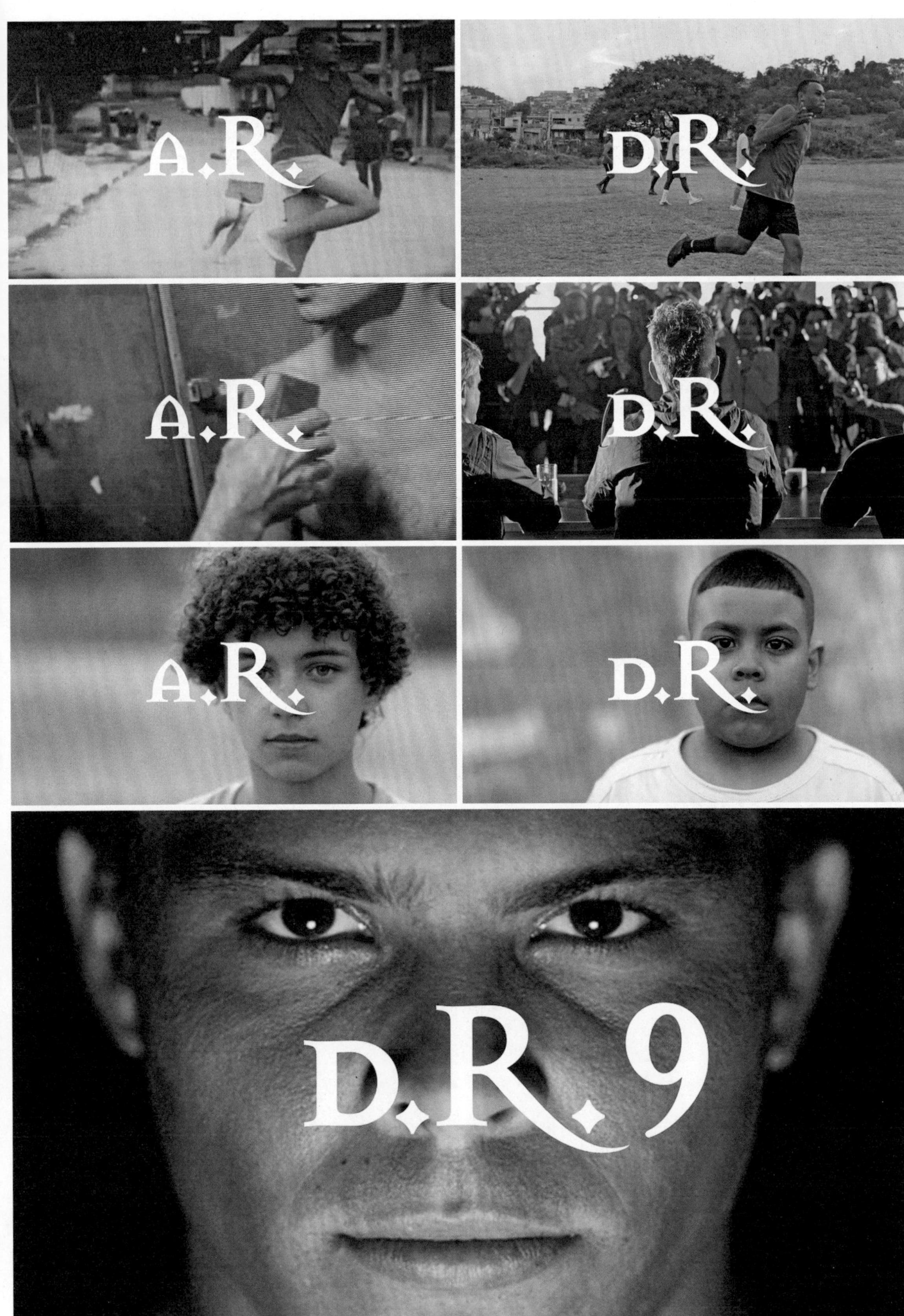

Nomination in TV & Cinema Advertising

TV Commercials 41-60 seconds
F/Nazca Saatchi & Saatchi
for Nike

Before and After
This commercial pays homage to ace football player Ronaldo in his friendly farewell game playing for the Brazilian All-Star Team against Romania. The film shows how Ronaldo has been able to divide the world of football into two eras: before and after Ronaldo. In just 60 seconds we get the general picture of Ronaldo's characteristic qualities, such as his fast and technical playing style, which has influenced thousands of new soccer players and rooters, creating an unprecedented aura of glory for Brazilian soccer.

Directors
Jones+Tino
Creative Directors
Fabio Fernandes
Eduardo Lima
Theo Rocha
Head of Art
João Linneu
Director of Photography
Andre Faccioli
Animation Director
Fernando Lanças
Illustrator
André Maciel
Production Company
Ioio Filmes

Advertising Agency
F/Nazca
Saatchi & Saatchi
Post Production
Tribbo Post
Sound Design
Satélite
Planners
Utymo Oliveira
José Porto
Account Handler
Marcello Penna
Client
Nike

Nomination in TV & Cinema Advertising

TV Commercials 41-60 seconds
Lowe Bull
for the Organ Donor Foundation

Leila
This ad opens on a girl in a hospital gown walking onto the scene of an accident. She reaches the driver, who is no longer alive, and lies down next to him. The ad illustrates a harsh reality: by not becoming an organ donor, you're potentially taking another life with you when you die.

Director
Tristyn Von Berg
Art Director
Brendan Hoffmann
Copywriter
Natalie Rose
Creative Director
Kirk Gainsford
Agency Producer
Riska Emeran

Production Company
Velocity Films
Advertising Agency
Lowe Bull
Account Handler
Arno Du Toit
Client
Organ Donor Foundation

If you're not an organ donor when you die

you take someone else with you

Nomination in TV & Cinema Advertising

TV Commercials 120-240 seconds
Deutsch LA
for Sony Computer Entertainment America

To Michael
Video game characters are the heroes and stars of the gaming industry. In this epic, live-action spot we turn the tables by showing the most iconic heroes in gaming honouring the true hero, the one who makes it all possible for them: the gamer.

Director
Simon McQuoid
Senior Art Director
Ryan Dickey
Copywriters
Sam Bergen
Josh Fell
Group Creative Directors
Mike Bryce
Jason Elm
Shannon McGlothin
Associate Creative Directors
Sam Bergen
Josh Fell
Chief Creative Officer
Mark Hunter
Producers
Kristina Iwankiw
Marisa Wasser
Executive Producers
Doug Halbert
Scott Ganary
Stephen Venning
Agency Producer
Marisa Wasser
Director of Integrated Production
Vic Palumbo
Director of Broadcast Production
Victoria Guenier
Director of Photography
Jan Velicky
Editor
Steve Gandolfi
Music Composer
Robert Miller
Sound Designer
Andrew Tracey
Sound Mixer
Mark Meyuhas
Production Company
Imperial Woodpecker
Advertising Agency
Deutsch LA
Post Production
The Mill Los Angeles
Audio Post Production
Lime Studios
Editing
Cut+Run Los Angeles
Sound Design
740 Sound Design
Stimmung
Account Director
Matt Small
Group Account Director
John McGonigle
Chief Executive Officer
Mike Sheldon
Client
Sony Computer Entertainment America
Brand
Sony PlayStation

Nomination in TV & Cinema Advertising

Cinema Commercials 120-240 seconds
AMV BBDO
for PepsiCo

Dip Desperado
Doritos is a sharing brand. But while its chips were flying off the shelves for social snacking, it seemed that consumers weren't buying Doritos dips to complete the experience. So we needed to put Doritos chips and dips together in the minds of consumers. We created a game around dipping chips into jars of salsa. To stand out in the app store, we did this in two ways. Firstly, we invented the Mexican sport of El Flicko – the art of flicking chips into salsa. Secondly, Esteban Ortega, the greatest chip-flicker who never lived, became the star of the commercial we subsequently produced. This work was also selected in the 'TV Commercials 120-140 seconds' category.

Direction
The Glue Society
Art Directors
Jeremy Tribe
Tim Vance
Copywriters
Paul Knott
Prabhu Wignarajah
Creative Director
Mark Fairbanks
Executive Creative Director
Paul Brazier
Producers
Jason Kemp
Suzy MacGregor
Digital Producer
Suzanne Melia
Editors
Adam Jenkins
Jeff Stevens
Production Company
Independent Films

Advertising Agency
AMV BBDO
Post Production
The Mill London
Digital Production Company
ACNE Production
Music Production
Human
Sound Design
750mph
Human
Planner
Tom White
Account Handler
Benedict Pringle
Client
PepsiCo
Brand
Doritos

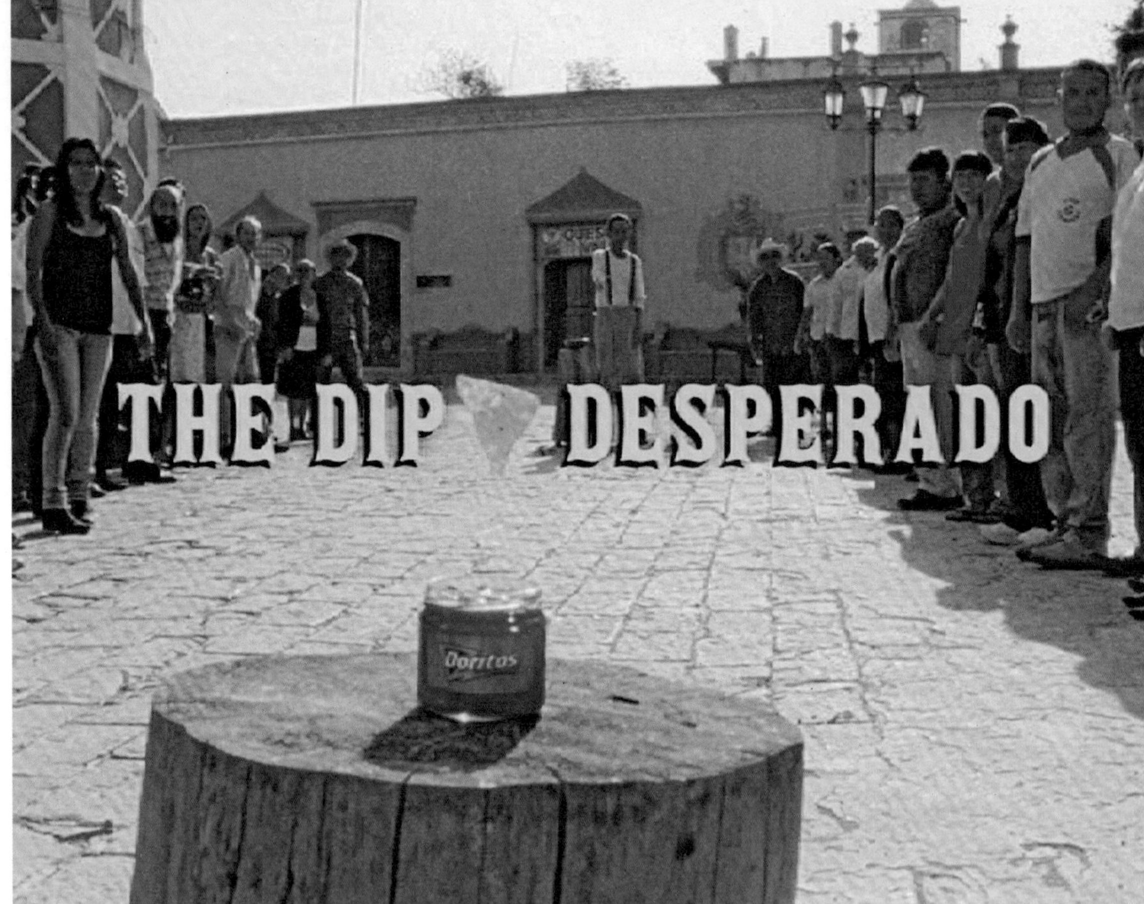

Nomination in TV & Cinema Advertising

Long Form Branded Content
Leo Burnett Bangkok
for TMB

Panyee FC

Leading Thai bank TMB launched a new brand vision, 'Make THE Difference', by creating a piece of communication that hopes to inspire people to start to make the difference in their own world. This film tells the story of a group of boys from Panyee island who pursued their dream of becoming world champions, despite having nowhere to practice. They made a football pitch out of rafts and learnt to play on the uneven, slippery surface. The team decided to take part in a one-day tournament and the rest of the village, admiring their determination, bought them new kits for the competition. They reached the semi-final and, through their inspirational success, football has become Panyee's number one pastime. Now they will have a smooth new pitch with no nails in it.

Director
Matt Devine
Art Directors
Sanpathit Tavijaroen
Sompat Trisadikun
Park Wannasiri
Copywriters
Chanwit Nimcharoen
Puttipong Pattanapongsagorn
Creative Director
Sanpathit Tavijaroen
Executive Creative Director
Keeratie Chaimoungkalo
Chief Creative Officer
Sompat Trisadikun
Producer
Alice Grant
Executive Producer
Michael Ritchie
Agency Producers
Sompetch Nuntasinlapachai
Jirateep Sangsuwan
Cinematographer
Geoffrey Simpson
Editor
Daniel Lee
Sound Designers
Paisan Chamnong
Jirasak Rungruengthanja
Direction
The Glue Society
Production Company
Revolver
Advertising Agencies
Arc Worldwide Thailand
Leo Burnett Bangkok
Account Executive
Phatarada Tritiprungroj
Account Director
Suthasi Sukpornsinchai
Client
TMB

TV Commercials 1-20 seconds
DDB Sydney
for Wrigley

Toll Booth

A man pulls up in his car to pay at the toll booth. We discover the attendant in the toll booth doesn't want to speak; however, when he opens his mouth, the window frosts up. He has seriously cold breath with Eclipse Ice from Wrigley.

Director
Nick Ball
Art Director
Ian Broekhuizen
Executive Creative Director
Dylan Harrison
Producer
Catherine Chapple
Agency Producer
Claire Seffrin
Production Director
Danny Ruhlmann
Production Company
Finch
Advertising Agency
DDB Sydney
Planner
David Chriswick
Business Directors
Rebecca Crawford
Matt Graham
Client
Wrigley
Brand
Eclipse Ice

TV Commercials 21-40 seconds
BBDO New York
for FedEx

AAAA Auto Repair

A mechanic chooses to name his company AAAAAAAAAA Auto Repair, so that he can 'get an edge' by being listed first in the phone book. His co-worker informs him that FedEx offers smarter ways to get an edge on the competition.

Director
Jim Jenkins
Art Director
Gianfranco Arena
Copywriter
Peter Kain
Creative Directors
Gianfranco Arena
Peter Kain
Executive Creative Directors
Greg Hahn
Mike Smith
Chief Creative Officer
David Lubars
Executive Producer
Elise Pavone
Director of Photography
Larry Fong
Editor
Ian Mackenzie
Production Company
O Positive
Advertising Agency
BBDO New York
Editing
Mackenzie Cutler
Account Executive
Julie Meyerson
Client
FedEx

TV Commercials 21-40 seconds
Wieden+Kennedy London
for Arla

Cats with Thumbs
'Cats with Thumbs' was created to jolt people out of a certain apathy towards milk and sweep them up in Cravendale's milk-enthusiasm. To stay prominent within the huge online world of cat-related content, we focused on an unfamiliar condition: polydactylism. This light-hearted ad shows Cravendale's superior taste and quality through a gang of ominous cats with thumbs, preparing to get hold of the milk they love.

Director
Ulf Johansson
Art Directors
Chris Groom
Sam Heath
Freddie Powell
Hollie Walker
Copywriters
Chris Groom
Sam Heath
Freddie Powell
Hollie Walker
Creative Directors
Chris Groom
Sam Heath
Executive Creative Directors
Tony Davidson
Kim Papworth
Producers
Josh King
Philippa Smith
Agency Producer
Lucy Russell
Visual Effects
Kamen Markov
Editor
Russell Icke
Sound Designer
Jack Sedgwick
Production Company
Smith and Jones Films
Creative Agency
Wieden+Kennedy London
Post Production
MPC London
Editing
The Whitehouse
Music Arrangement
Tonic Music
Media Agency
Carat
Planner
Theo Izzard Brown
Client
Arla
Brand
Cravendale

TV Commercials 21-40 seconds
King Solutions KB
for Expressen Newspaper

Expressen
Keeping an eye on powerful people makes them become less powerful. If tabloids like 'Expressen' didn't exist, the abuse of power would be more widespread. There would simply be less for state and business officials to be afraid of. In this ad, a group of powerful men decide to round off their meeting by visiting a porn club with tax payers' money, but when they think about 'Expressen' they suddenly change their minds.

Directors
Alex Brügge
Markus Ernerot
Art Director
Nima Stillerud
Copywriters
Jens Englund
Pontus Thorén
Producer
Sofia Wall
Cinematographer
Henrik Gyllensköld
Production Company
Esteban
Advertising Agency
King Solutions KB
Post Production
Riviera
Account Manager
Åsa Slättegård
Account Director
Mattias Bohlin
Client
Expressen
Newspaper
Brand
Expressen

TV Commercials 21-40 seconds
Bates Y&R
for Nupo

Eric
A woman comes home from work and finds her husband in the living room, drunk. He tells her that he has found some pictures of her with another man, and now he wants to know who he is. She replies: 'This is me and you in Greece in 1998'. Super: 'Get your shape back. Nupo. Low calorie diet products'.

Director
Michael Toft
Art Director
Thomas Fabricius
Copywriter
Thomas Fabricius
Creative Director
Thomas Fabricius
Agency Producer
Nya Bille
Photography Director
Sophia Olsson
Lighting
Cameraperson
Viggo Grumme
Editor
Leif Axel Kjeldsen
Advertising Agency
Bates Y&R
Post Production
Welcome
Editing
Welcome
Sound Design
Supersonic
Account Manager
Ida Emme
Account Director
Thomas Brandt
Business Director
Peter Wedelheim
Client
Nupo

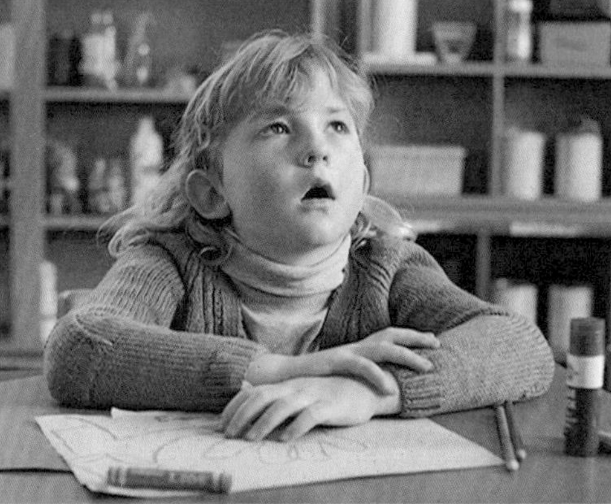

TV Commercials 21-40 seconds
Saatchi & Saatchi Carouge
for Novartis Consumer Health

You Look Dumber with your Mouth Open: Classroom Craft
A primary school teacher is distributing metal scissors to her class at craft time. A girl with a blocked nose is breathing deeply through her open mouth, so the teacher thinks she's a little special and hands her plastic safety scissors. Super: 'You look dumber with your mouth open. Otrivin Nasal Spray. The pleasure of breathing'.

Director
Sam Holst
Art Directors
Lucy Crudgington
Lisa Mcleod
Daniela Nedelschi
Copywriters
Boris Declerck
Maureen Mccabe
Creative Director
Leon Jacobs
Chief Creative Officers
Derek Green
John Pallant
Producer
Camillo Spath
Agency Producer
Scott McBurnie
Editor
Michael Londsdale
Sound Designer
Adam Iles
Production Company
The Sweet Shop
Advertising Agency
Saatchi & Saatchi Carouge
Planner
Carolyn Dateo
Account Managers
Mélanie Foucher
Cassy Ymar
Account Directors
Giuliana Mandelli
Stéphanie Rupp
Client
Novartis Consumer Health
Brand
Otrivin

TV Commercials 21-40 seconds
BBDO New York
for Mars Chocolate North America

Party
'Party' is the next chapter in 'You're not you when you're hungry' – the global campaign we launched for Snickers in 2010. The campaign idea is based on the insight that hunger can drastically change your personality. This commercial features Joe Pesci and Don Rickles as the hunger-induced angry alter egos of two young people at a house party.

Director
Jim Jenkins
Art Director
Gianfranco Arena
Copywriter
Peter Kain
Creative Directors
Gianfranco Arena
Peter Kain
Chief Creative Officer
David Lubars
Executive Producer
Amy Wertheimer
Director of Photography
Robert Yeoman
Music Producer
Loren Parkins
Editor
Ian Mackenzie
Production Company
O Positive
Advertising Agency
BBDO New York
Visual Effects Company
Mass Market
Editing
Mackenzie Cutler
Account Executive
Kathryn Brown
Client
Mars Chocolate North America
Brand
Snickers

TV Commercials 21-40 seconds
JWT Milan
for UNA Onlus

Hate
UNA Onlus asked us to create a campaign to raise awareness and funds for a life-threatening children's disease. The ad shows a father whispering hateful words into the ear of his sleeping son. His animosity is shocking at first before we realise he is addressing the child's cancer. The initial misreading of the father's intention only amplifies the emotions at play.

Director
Luca Lucini
Copywriter
Davide Boscacci
Creative Director
Davide Boscacci
Executive Creative Directors
Enrico Dorizza
Daniela Radice
Sergio Rodriguez
Production Company
Filmmaster
Advertising Agency
JWT Milan
Client
UNA Onlus

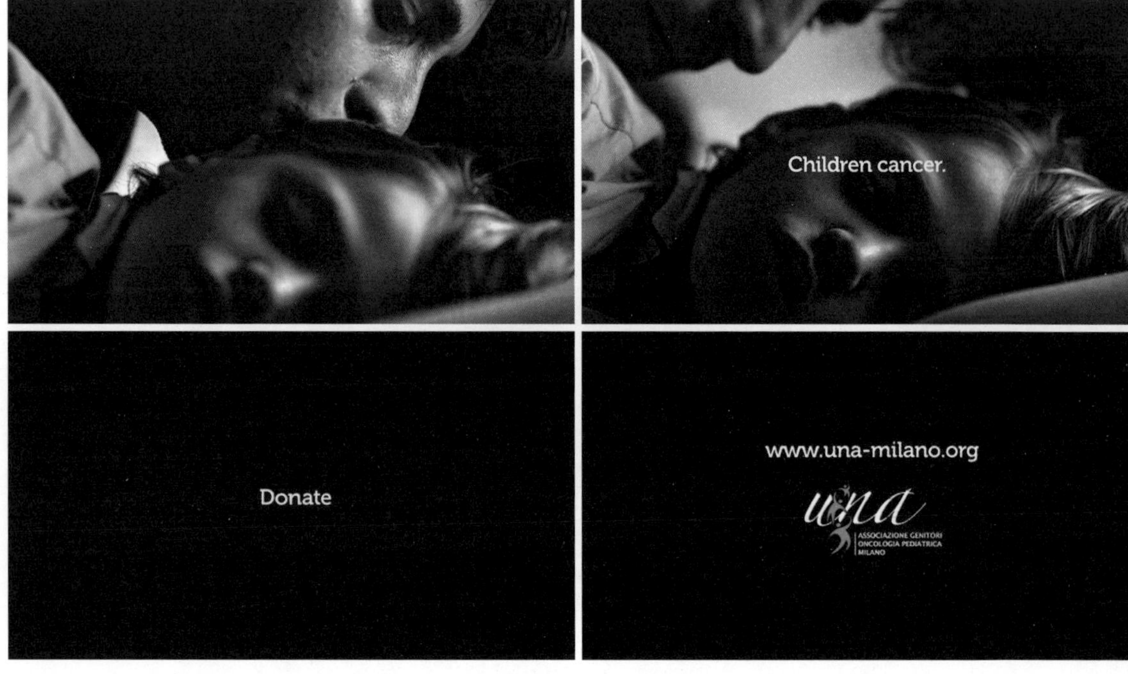

TV Commercials 41-60 seconds
StrawberryFrog
for Beam

Parallels
The bold choices we make, make us. In this anthem spot, we see actor Willem Dafoe as a young man faced with a choice: to boldly leave his small hometown, and head for the bright lights and long odds of an acting career in New York City; or to stay put, and let fate play a leading role in deciding his future.

Director
Dante Ariola
Copywriters
Todd Beeby
Josh Greenspan
Creative Directors
Josh Greenspan
Jason Koxvold
Chief Creative Officer
Kevin McKeon
Producer
Natalie Hill
Executive Producers
Jeff Scruton
David Zander
Agency Producer
Sherri Levy
Director of Photography
Emmanuel Lubezky
Production Designer
Christopher Glass
Editor
Adam Pertofsky
Production Company
MJZ Los Angeles
Advertising Agency
StrawberryFrog
Visual Effects Company
The Mill New York
Editing
Rock Paper Scissors
Sound Design
Human
Account Director
Sherri Chambers
Client
Beam
Brand
Jim Beam

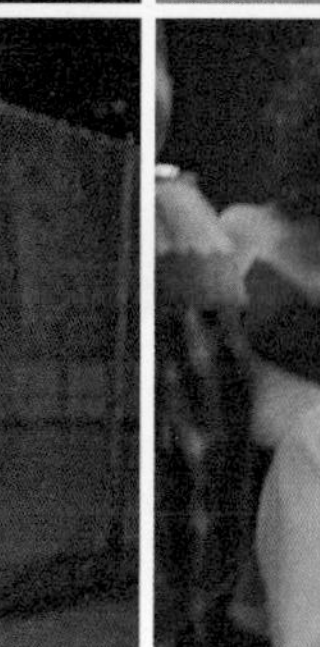

TV Commercials 41-60 seconds
Droga5
for PUMA

Pump Up

This spot takes one of the most familiar sport chants in the world and applies it to the After Hours Athlete, albeit with a PUMA Social twist, adding reverence to late night accomplishments, and treating social athletes in a manner that puts them on par with other sports athletes. Because, let's face it, karaoke can be hard.

Direction
Thirtytwo
Executive Creative Directors
Ted Royer
Nik Studzinski
Associate Creative Directors
Amanda Clelland
Tim Gordon
Creative Chairman
David Droga
Producer
Sarah Frances Hartley
Executive Producer
Ben Davies
Head of Integrated Production
Sally-Ann Dale
Production Company
Pulse Films
Advertising Agency
Droga5
Post Production
Absolute
Visual Effects Company
Smoke & Mirrors
Editing
Final Cut New York
Sound Design
Sound Lounge
Music Arrangement
Human
Account Director
Nick Phelps
Strategic Director
Ben Jenkins
Client
PUMA
Brand
PUMA Social

TV Commercials 41-60 seconds
Badillo Nazca Saatchi & Saatchi
for Toyota Puerto Rico

Letter

A man finds an old letter in the back of his Toyota. He returns it to the car's previous owner, who returns it to the owner before that, who gives the letter to the owner before him, who gives the letter to the man who sold him the car. This man returns the letter to an elderly couple, the car's original owners. The old lady sits down to read it... the letter is incriminating. Toyota – lasts a lifetime.

Director
Cali Ameglio
Art Directors
Cristina Burckhart
Fernando Suarez
Copywriter
Pedro Perez
Creative Director
Mariano German
Executive Creative Director
Juan Carlos Rodriguez
Producer
Nero Vargas
Production Company
Salado Montevideo
Advertising Agency
Badillo Nazca Saatchi & Saatchi
Account Executive
Yia Marini
Client
Toyota Puerto Rico
Brand
Toyota

TV Commercials 41-60 seconds
Wieden+Kennedy London
for Arla

Kitchen Odyssey
Lurpak encourages us to make uncompromising food decisions like choosing quality ingredients over ready meals. In this ad, whipping up an easy after-work dinner becomes a glorious odyssey.

Director
Martin Krejci
Creative Directors
Dan Norris
Ray Shaughnessy
Executive Creative Directors
Tony Davidson
Kim Papworth
Producer
Louise Gagen
Executive Producer
Blake Powell
Agency Producer
Anna Smith
Director of Photography
Stepan Kucera
Flame Artists
Jonathan Hairman
Tom Sparks
Web Producer
Sarah Hiddlestone
Production Company
Stink
Editors
Filip Malasek
Tom Spark
Sound Engineer
Aaron Reynolds
Creative Agency
Wieden+Kennedy London
Post Production
Framestore CFC
Wave Studios
Editing
The Whitehouse
Sound Design
Wave Studios
Account Director
Alice Von Oswald
Brand Manager
Thryth Jarvis
Client
Arla
Brand
Lurpak

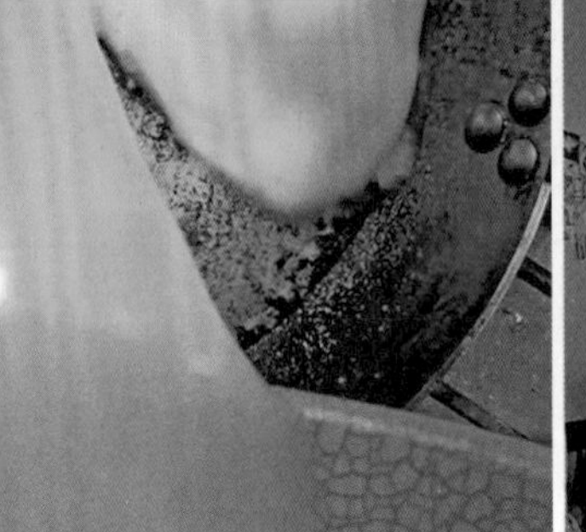

TV Commercials 61-120 seconds
Dare Vancouver
for the Whistler Film Festival

Princess
Hollywood movies are getting more and more predictable, with the same stories told time and time again. The Whistler Film Festival showcases films that tell original, unexpected stories. 'Princess' starts like a typical Hollywood animation in the world of Disney, but ends with a very unexpected twist.

Directors
tokyoplastic
Art Director
Rob Sweetman
Copywriter
Mia Thomsett
Creative Directors
Bryan Collins
Rob Sweetman
Executive Producers
Jane Bolton
Steve Lowe
Richard Price
Music Composer
Jamie Masters
Music Producer
Greg Moore
Sound Designer
Andrew Sherriff
Sound Engineers
Chris Hobbs
Wes Swales
Head of Broadcast
Mike Hasinoff
Advertising Agency
Dare Vancouver
Animation
Picasso Pictures
Music Arrangement
Adelphoi Music
Sound Design
Adelphoi Music
Mixing
Koko Productions
Account Manager
Tamara Bennett
Client
Whistler Film Festival

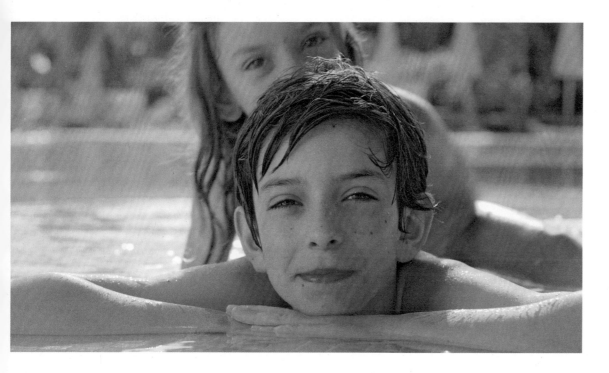

TV Commercials 61-120 seconds
Beattie McGuinness Bungay
for Thomson & TUI Travel

Time for a Holiday
We created this ad as a hard-hitting brand piece to establish Thomson as the category leader. We see families and couples enjoying their holidays, and a child reminds us of what's really important in life. The film has an effortless and natural beauty to it, which is complemented by a musical rearrangement of 'Where is My Mind' by the Pixies.

Director
Martin de Thurah
Art Director
Stephen Reed
Copywriter
Stephen Reed
Creative Director
Gavin McGrath
Producer
Lucy Gossage
Agency Producer
Jonathan Chads
Director of Photography
Lasse Frank
Editor
Mikkel Neilsen
Music Composer
Guy Farley
Sound Designer
Aaron Reynolds
Production Company
Academy Films
Advertising Agency
Beattie McGuinness Bungay
Post Production
The Mill London
Sound Design
Wave Studios
Planner
Caroline Bermingham
Account Handlers
Aimee Luther
Andrew Milner
Brand Managers
Rebecca Edwards
Jeremy Ellis
Clients
Thomson
TUI Travel

Book your winter holidays now

TV Commercials 61-120 seconds
SPILLMANN/FELSER/LEO BURNETT
for Switzerland Tourism

Ant Hill
Martin Horat is a real Swiss weather prophet, not an actor. His forecasts are based on his observations of nature. 'I see a great winter coming. How do I know that? Come and have a look. See these ants? They tell me how the winter will be. Holy cow! They've got legs like a ski racer!' He sits on the anthill, gets covered in ants. 'Hang on, what's that? An ant from the Netherlands! And some from England, France, Italy! They've come to us. They know why. That's a clear sign. That here in Switzerland we're gonna have a bloody great winter. With heaps of snow and sun. Come see us, we won't bite!'

Director
Xavier Koller
Copywriters
Peter Brönnimann
Martin Spillmann
Creative Directors
Peter Brönnimann
Martin Spillmann
Production Company
Plan B Film
Advertising Agency
SPILLMANN/FELSER/LEO BURNETT
Post Production
Plan B Film
Client
Switzerland Tourism

TV Commercials 61-120 seconds
adam&eve
for the John Lewis Partnership

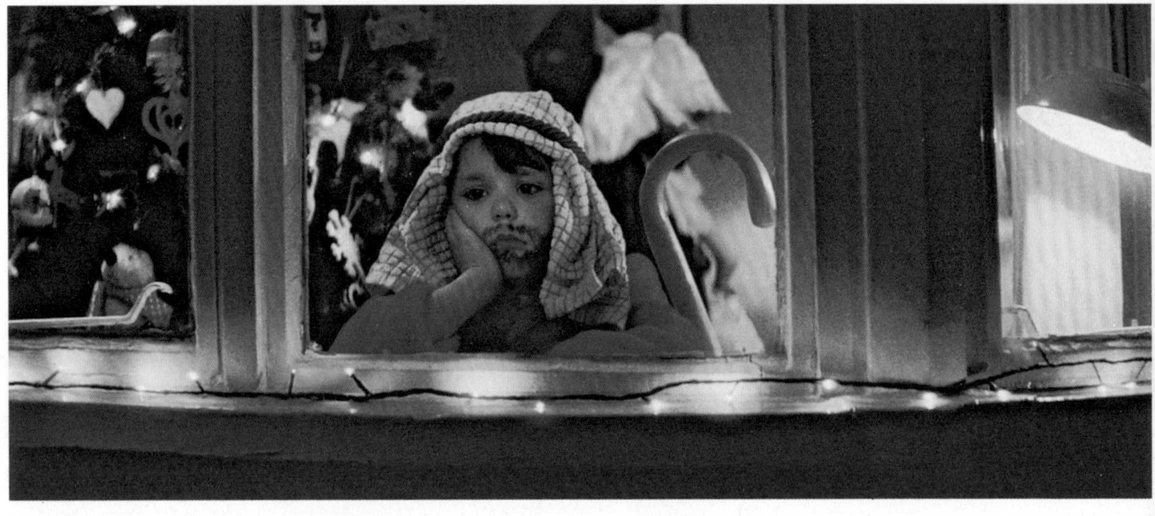

The Long Wait
This story follows a boy in the days leading up to Christmas. We see him wishing time away as he waits for the big day to arrive. But when he wakes on Christmas morning he ignores his own presents, and gets a gift he has crudely wrapped from his wardrobe. We finally realise that he has been excitedly waiting to give the perfect gift to his parents. The super reads: 'For gifts you can't wait to give'.

Director
Dougal Wilson
Art Director
Matt Gay
Copywriter
John Long
Creative Directors
Ben Priest
Emer Stamp
Ben Tollett
Producer
Ben Link
Agency Producer
Matt Craigie
Production Company
Blink
Advertising Agency
adam&eve
Client
John Lewis
Partnership
Brand
John Lewis

Cinema Commercials 21-40 seconds
Publicis Conseil
for the Fondation Pour L'Enfance

Fondation Pour L'Enfance: 3 Generations
A little girl is doing her homework while having an afternoon snack. Suddenly, she unintentionally spills her fruit juice over the table. Her mother instantly gets upset and gives her a slap. She starts crying. Her grandmother, who witnessed the scene from the kitchen, looks petrified. She finally walks to her daughter (the little girl's mother), gives her a hug and says sorry. The ad ends on the line: 'Parents who beat were often beaten as children. Let's educate without violence'.

Direction
Les Uns
Art Director
Jean-Marc Tramoni
Copywriter
Marc Rosier
Creative Director
Olivier Altmann
Producer
Antoine Daubert
Agency Producers
Pierre Marcus
Timothe Rosenberg
Sound Designer
Boris Jeanne
Advertising Agency
Publicis Conseil
Account Handler
Eleonore Mabille
Brand Managers
Didier Chanal
Arnauld Gruselle
Dr Gilles Lazimi
Dr Emmanuelle Piet
Client
Fondation Pour
L'Enfance

Cinema Commercials 41-60 seconds
DDB UK
for Harvey Nichols

Walk of Shame

The ad plays on the theme 'the morning after the night before'. We see different women the morning after a big Christmas party, going home, trying to ignore the disapproving stares of the 8am commuters. We culminate with our 'hero' girl walking back to her flat doing more of a 'stride of pride'. She clearly never made it home either, but something sets her apart from the others. Her Harvey Nichols outfit still looks fantastic and she walks with her head held high.

Director
James Rouse
Art Director
Rob Messeter
Copywriter
Mike Crowe
Executive Creative Director
Jeremy Craigen
Producer
Benji Hopkins
Agency Producers
Maggie Blundell
Chris Styring
Lighting Cameraperson
Alex Melman
Editor
Rachael Spann
Sound Designer
Mark Hellaby
Production Company
Outsider
Advertising Agency
DDB UK
Planner
Elisabeth Jamot
Account Directors
Paul Billingsley
Charlotte Evans
Marketing Manager
Julia Bowe
Client
Harvey Nichols

Cinema Commercials 41-60 seconds
Serviceplan München
for Sanyo Video Vertrieb

Santec Prison

We created a spot in which thieves literally experience how quickly they will end up in jail after being filmed by a Santec security camera. Thieves are shown robbing a house when the image on the CCTV screen freezes and a team of Santec workers enter the room. The scenery is quickly changed around them and, after the last worker leaves, the thieves find themselves trapped in a prison cell. Caught on camera, they can't escape jail anymore.

Director
Axel Laubscher
Art Director
Till Diestel
Copywriter
Marc Vosshall
Executive Creative Directors
Maik Kaehler
Christoph Nann
Chief Creative Officer
Alexander Schill
Producers
Tanja Bruhn
Pieter Lony
Bianca Schreck
Agency Producer
Christoph Koehler
Cinematographer
Sven Siegrist
Production Company
Cobblestone Filmproduktion
Advertising Agency
Serviceplan München
Account Executive
Florian Klietz
Client
Sanyo Video Vertrieb
Brand
Santec

Cinema Commercials 41-60 seconds
Y&R New York
for Land Rover

Pathological Liar
Land Rover drivers experience a feeling of safety that drivers of other vehicles don't. That's why this pathological liar chooses to be in a Land Rover 4 while confessing to his girlfriend that he's not exactly who she thinks he is.

Director
David Shane
Art Director
Michael Schachtner
Copywriter
Julia Neumann
Creative Directors
Graham Lang
Guillermo Vega
Steve Whittier
Executive Creative Director
Kerry Keenan
Executive Producer
Ralph Laucella
Senior Producer
Mara Milicevic
Agency Producer
Jona Goodman
Director of Photography
Antonio Calvache
Editor
Jason MacDonald
Heads of Broadcast
Nathy Aviram
Lora Schulson
Digital Production Company
O Positive
Advertising Agency
Y&R New York
Post Production
Number Six Edit
Sound Design
Sound Lounge
Client
Land Rover

Cinema Commercials 41-60 seconds
Mother London
for match.com

Ukulele
This spot is a classic tale of boy meets girl. It is set in a suburban train station, and shows a boy trying to catch the eye of the girl on the opposite platform by singing a spontaneous song about her. 'Ukulele' reminds people what it feels like to meet someone you're attracted to for the first time. It celebrates what match does every day – bringing people together to start their own love stories.

Director
Nacho Gayan
Art Directors
Craig Ainsley
Paddy Fraser
Fernando Perottoni
Copywriters
Craig Ainsley
Paddy Fraser
Fernando Perottoni
Creative Directors
Stephen Butler
Mark Waites
Producer
Toni Moreno
Agency Producer
Craig Keppler
Director of Photography
Manel Ruiz
Editor
Bill Smedley
Production Company
Stink
Creative Agency
Mother London
Post Production
MPC London
Sound Design
Factory Studios
Development
MediaMonks
Motim Technologies
Planner
Matt Andrews
Client
match.com

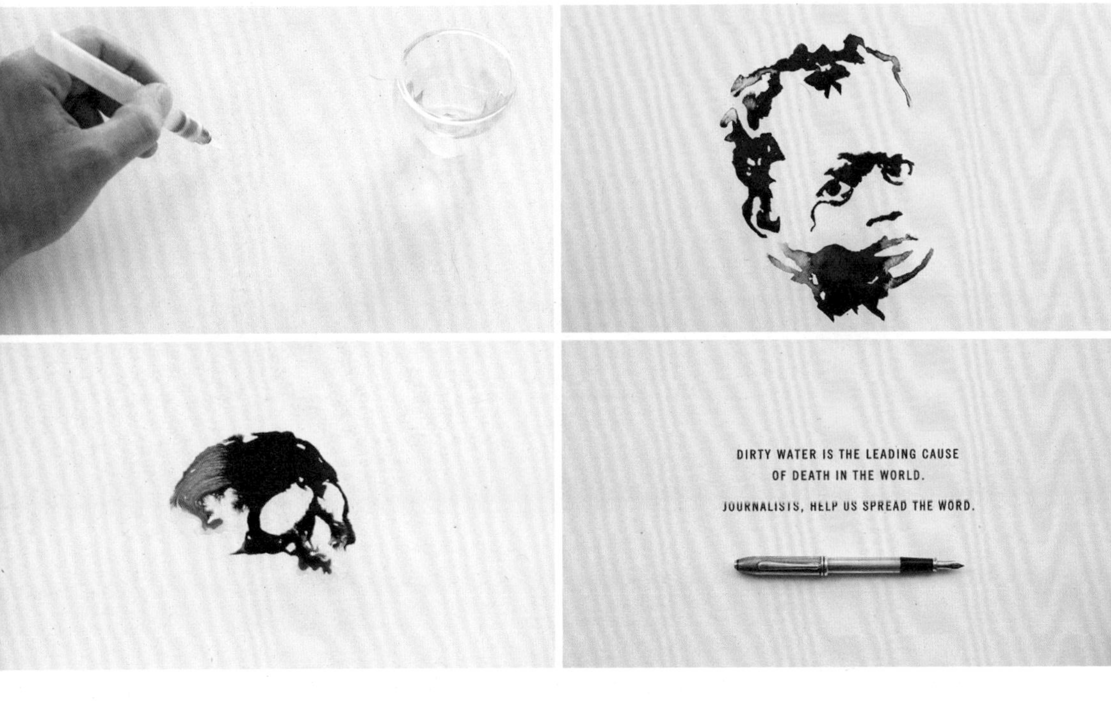

Cinema Commercials 61-120 seconds
BDDP Unlimited
for SOLIDARITÉS INTERNATIONAL

Water & Ink
To mark World Water Day on 22 March 2011, SOLIDARITÉS INTERNATIONAL decided to roll out a campaign to build awareness of the scourge of undrinkable water. The campaign calls on journalists to spread awareness of this blight and appeal to readers to sign the petition. To evoke the silent and invisible threat of unhealthy water, we opted for a minimalist creative approach that is both visually appealing and surprising, using water and ink exclusively.

Director
Clement Beauvais
Art Director
Fabien Nunez
Copywriter
Fabien Duval
Creative Director
Guillaume-Ulrich Chifflot
Producers
Arthur de Kersauson
Nicolas Lhermitte
Sound Designer
Elisa Hiscox
Production Company
Hush
Advertising Agency
BDDP Unlimited
Sound Design
Else
Planner
Christian Baujard
Account Handlers
Anne-Celine Bloch
Marco de la Fuente
Irache Martinez
Brand Managers
Alain Boinet
Constance Decorde
Patricia de Venevelles
Client
SOLIDARITÉS INTERNATIONAL

Cinema Commercials 61-120 seconds
Try
for Canal Digital

The Man Who Lived in a Film
A man tells a story about the strange things that happen to him. Increasingly, he ends up in a movie scene. He finds a man tied up in his trunk. He goes for a run in the park, but ends up in a Jane Austen movie. Death (from Bergman) seeks him out in a café; a taxi turns out to be a Transformers robot; he is suddenly in the middle of an intimidating social realism drama from the 70s. And in the end, a giant Tyrannosaurus Rex shows up outside his window. Canal Digital presents its film rental service named 'Go', with the payoff: 'We bring the movies to you'.

Director
Joachim Trier
Art Director
Egil Pay
Copywriter
Lars Joachim Grimstad
Producers
Helene Hovda Lunde
Mone Mikkelsen
Production Company
One Big Happy Family
Advertising Agency
Try
Visual Effects
Shortcut
Storm Studios
Account Executive
Marte Heiersted
Account Director
Lars Mitlid
Brand Managers
Bjørn-Inge Haugan
Torill Silkoset
Client
Canal Digital

TV Commercial Campaigns
Wieden+Kennedy Amsterdam
for Heineken

Open Your World
'The Entrance', the first installment of Heineken's global 'Open your World' campaign, demonstrates the ultimate party entrance. Charming his way past a coterie of unexpected guests, the film's hero ends up on stage performing with The Asteroids Galaxy Tour. 'The Date' follows the Heineken Legend, a 'man of the world', as he woos his girl on an epic date. The pair enters a restaurant-cum-theatre, kicking off a series of encounters between the duo and a cast of colourful characters. Our hero impresses his girl with his eel-taming skills as they stumble past an aquarium. They encounter a magician and are pursued by an overzealous Chinese dragon. Finally the Legend shows off his unique dance skills in the main hall of the venue.

Director
Fredrik Bond
Art Director
Alvaro Sotomayor
Copywriter
Roger Hoard
Creative Director
Mark Bernath
Executive Creative Directors
Mark Bernath
Eric Quennoy
Producer
Alicia Bernard
Executive Producer
Helen Kenny
Agency Producers
Niko Koot
Tony Stearns
Director of Photography
Mattias Montero
Editor
Tim Thornton-Allan
Music Composer
Mohammed Rafi
Sound Designer
Raja Sehgal
Head of Broadcast
Erik Verheijen
Advertising Agency
Wieden+Kennedy Amsterdam
Project Manager
Sharon Kwiatkowski
Planners
Stuart Parkinson
Martin Weigel
Account Manager
Dan Colgan
Account Directors
Jasmina Krnjetin
Clay Mills
Brand Communications Director
Cyril Charzat
Brand Manager
Sandrine Huijgen
Client
Heineken

The Entrance

The Date

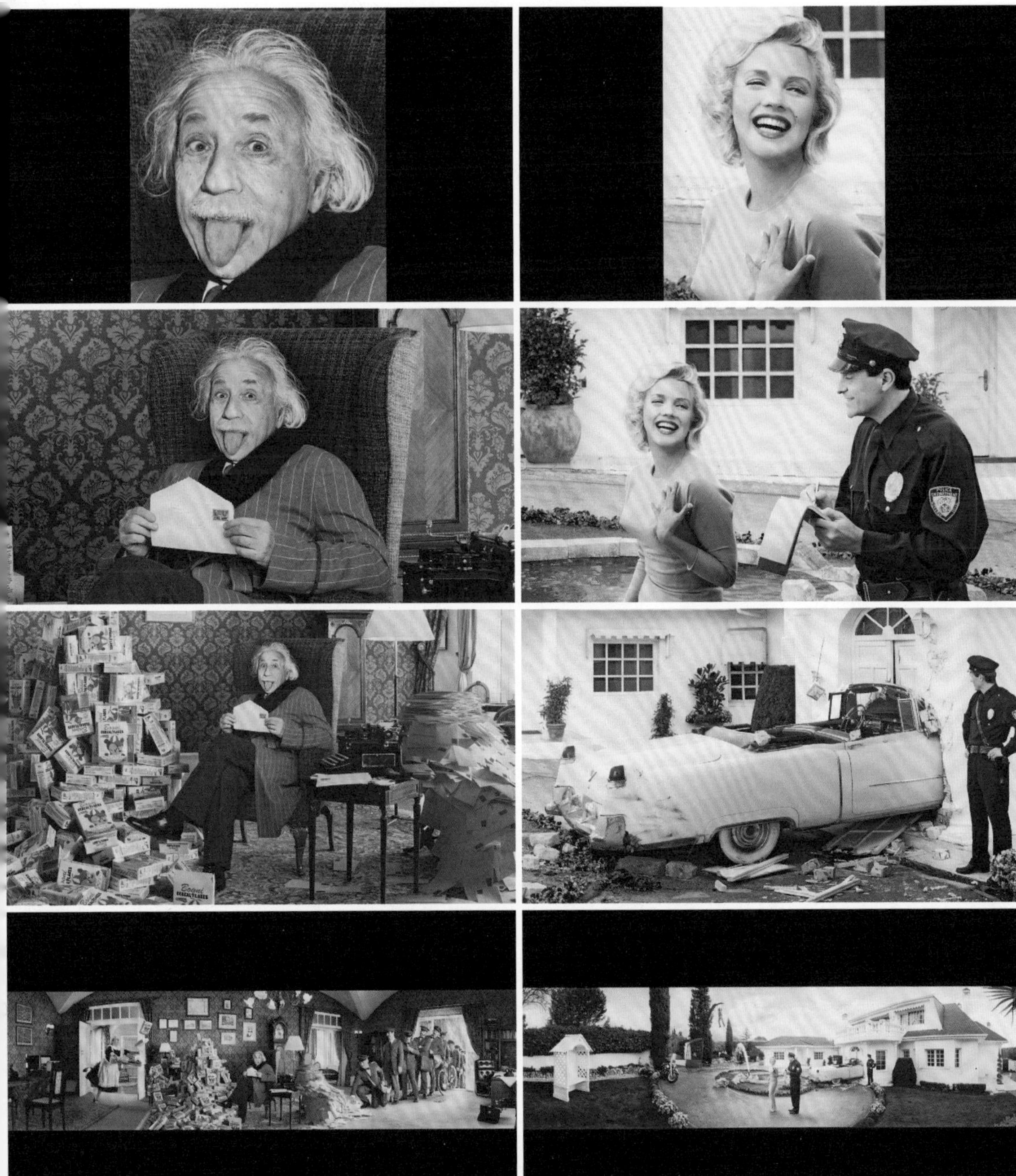

Einstein

Marilyn

TV Commercial Campaigns
Del Campo Nazca Saatchi & Saatchi
for Sony

Famous Pictures
To launch the new Cyber-shot with sweep panorama, we created a campaign that dramatised the true benefit of a camera that allows you to take panoramic pictures. In the ads, we see famous pictures and discover what was going on outside of the frame: funny stories that no one could see because the camera with which the picture was taken was not panoramic. The ads end with the conclusion that stories are better panoramic.

Director
Marcelo Burgos
Art Director
Ignacio Ferioli
Copywriter
Diego Medvedocky
Creative Directors
Ignacio Ferioli
Diego Medvedocky
Executive Creative Directors
Maxi Itzkoff
Mariano Serkin
Executive Producers
Alvaro Gorospe
Irene Nuñez Palma
Agency Producers
Adrian Aspani
Ezequiel Ortiz

Production Company
Garlic
Advertising Agency
Del Campo Nazca Saatchi & Saatchi
Account Executive
Reinier Suarez
Account Manager
Ana Bogni
Account Director
Joseph Baide
Client
Sony
Brand
Cyber-shot

TV Commercial Campaigns
Grey New York
for DIRECTV

Cable Effects
To highlight the problems people have with Cable TV – high prices, poor customer service, unreliable signals – we show the consequences of these issues and offer DIRECTV Satellite as the better alternative.

Director
Tom Kuntz
Art Director
Doug Fallon
Copywriter
Steven Fogel
Creative Directors
Doug Fallon
Steven Fogel
Executive Creative Director
Dan Kelleher
Chief Creative Officer
Tor Myhren
Producer
Jeff McDougall
Agency Producers
Andrew Chinich
Lindsay Myers
Cinematographer
Emmanuel Lubezki
Editors
Gavin Cutler
Nick Divers
Valerie Sachs
Sound Designer
Sam Shaffer
Production Company
MJZ Los Angeles
Advertising Agency
Grey New York
Post Production
Method Studios
New York
Editing
Mackenzie Cutler
Sound Design
Mackenzie Cutler
Project Manager
Joanne Peters
Account Executive
Kristen Stahl
Account Managers
Adam Clark
Josh Mandell
Account Director
Beth Culley
Client
DIRECTV

Stray Animals

Roadside Ditch

Dog Collar

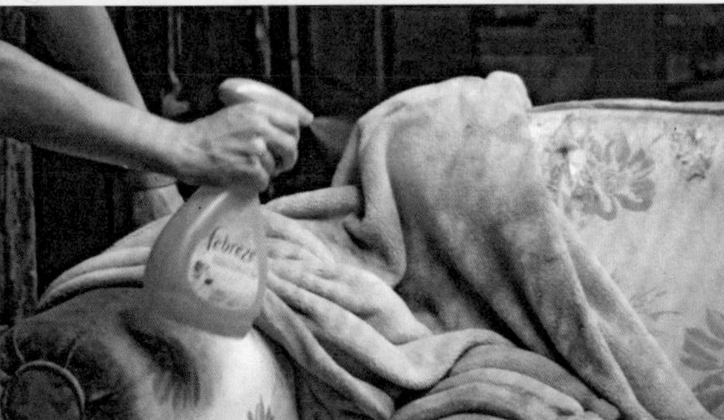

Febreze Couch

Febreze Hotel

Febreze Restaurant

TV Commercial Campaigns
Grey New York
for Procter & Gamble

Breathe Happy Social Experiment
Experiments were conducted to prove that Febreze could tackle even the toughest odour challenges. These experiments were then turned into TV spots. Taken right off the street, participants were blindfolded and exposed to smelly and dirty locations that had been sprayed with Febreze. They described the refreshing fragrance of their surroundings and appeared to be convinced of a luxurious environment. When their blindfolds were removed, they witnessed how effective Febreze really is.

Director
Sam Cadman
Creative Directors
Rob Lenois
Rob Perillo
Jeff Stamp
Executive Creative Directors
Jeff Odiorne
Per Pedersen
Associate Creative Directors
Marie Ronn
Erik Tell
Chief Creative Officer
Tor Myhren
Executive Producer
Elizabeth Krajewski
Agency Producers
David Cardinali
James McPherson
Angela Ong
Assistant Agency Producer
Zachary Flemming
Editors
Rebecca Beluk
Michael Elliot

Production Company
Station
Advertising Agency
Grey New York
Post Production
Beast New York
Account Executives
Emily Darby
Erin Lewis
Cassie Novick
Diana Silfen
Account Directors
Jean Donahue
Elizabeth Gilchrist
Elena Grasmann
Brand Communications Director
Rick Reilly
Client
Procter & Gamble
Brand
Febreze

TV Commercial Campaigns
Mullen
for Planet Fitness

Planet Fitness
These Planet Fitness spots were made to drive awareness of the mentality that members of this gym have. They are not meatheads, just people looking to get a good workout at a fair price. Our solution was to poke fun at the gym freak mentality and make people see that there is a place they can go to avoid all that, whilst also avoiding the high membership fees.

Art Director
Chris Toland
Copywriter
Brian Tierney
Creative Directors
Stephen Mietelski
Brian Tierney
Chief Creative Officer
Mark Wenneker
Producer
Mary Donington
Executive Producer
Zeke Bowman
Director of Integrated Production
Liza Near
Production Company
Hungry Man
Advertising Agency
Mullen
Visual Effects Company
Brickyard
Editing
Bikini Edit
Sound Design
Soundtrack
Client
Planet Fitness

Application

Bunny Ears

Lift Things Up

TV Commercial Campaigns
BBH New York
for Google

The Web is What You Make of It
No matter who you are, the web can help you do anything. So for Google Chrome's first global TV effort, we told stories with a simple message: 'The web is what you make of it'. The spots showcase the power of the web and demonstrate how anyone, anywhere, can use the Chrome browser and the web to make the most of life.

Advertising Agencies
BBH New York
Google Creative Lab
Client
Google

Brand
Google Chrome

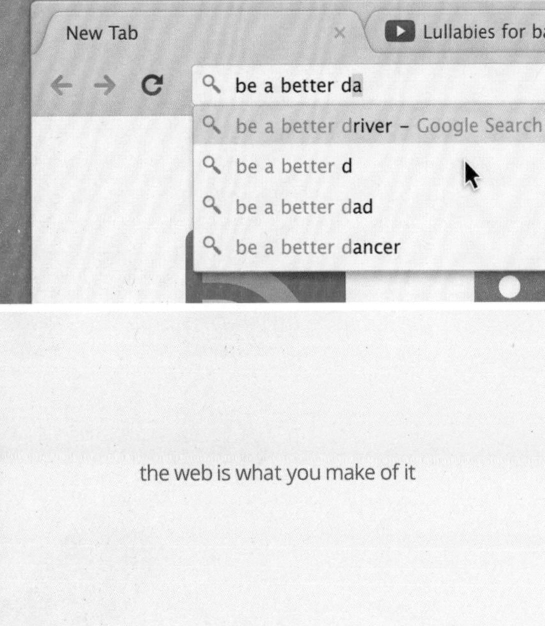

Make it Happen

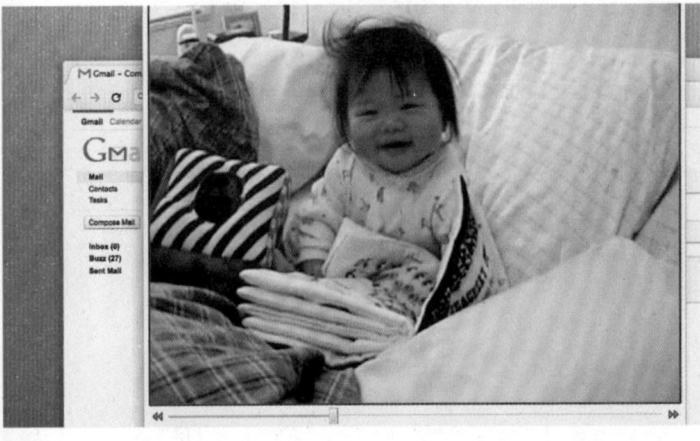

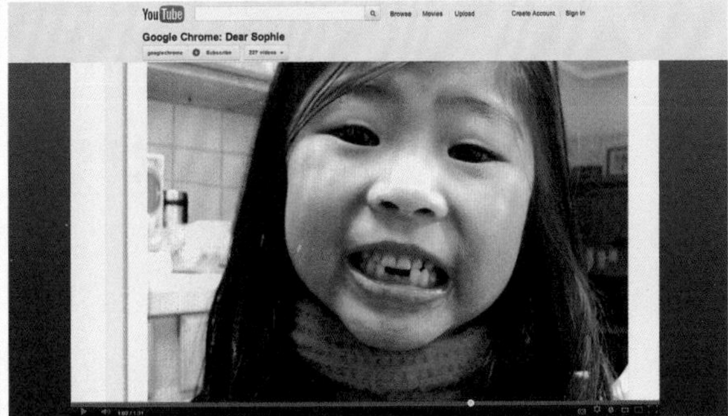

Dear Sophie

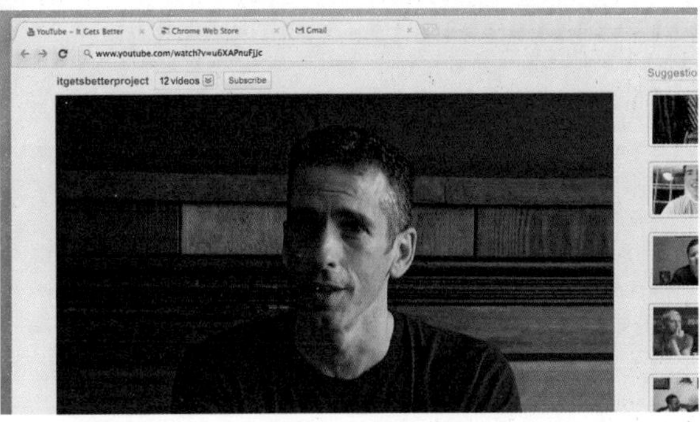

It Gets Better

Cinema Commmercial Campaigns
Ponce Buenos Aires
for Unilever

The Cleaner
The Cleaner is a man who cleans the traces of all-night parties. The first commercial shows a boy waking up at his house after a wild night. Feeling desperate, he phones The Cleaner who arrives promptly, cleans up the mess and teaches him to wipe the evidence off his body using Axe Shower Gel. The second commercial shows two young office workers calling The Cleaner. They need him to remove the traces of a party they held in the meeting room. On his arrival, The Cleaner not only cleans up but also teaches them how to scrub the remains of glitter from their bodies, leaving them with two clean suits to suggest nothing ever happened.

Director
Rafael Lopez Saubidet
Art Directors
Hernan Cerdeiro
Pedro Losada
Copywriters
Ariel Serkin
Nicolas Zarlenga
Creative Director
Mariano Jeger
Executive Creative Directors
Ricardo Armentano
Joaquin Cubria
Analia Rios
Chief Creative Officer
Hernan Ponce
Integrated Communications Director
Hernan Zamora
Production Director
Roberto Carsillo
Agency Producer
Elizabeth Crego
Production Company
Argentina Cine
Advertising Agency
Ponce Buenos Aires
Planner
Marina Pen
Brand Communications Director
Vanina Rudaeff
Brand Director
Luciano Landajo
Client
Unilever
Brand
Axe Shower Gel

Evidence 1

Evidence 2

Long Form Branded Content
TBWA\Chiat\Day Los Angeles
for Nissan & Sony PlayStation

GT Academy USA
With 'GT Academy', Nissan and Sony created a once in a lifetime opportunity to take a player's driving skills from virtual to reality and become a professional race-car driver. The platform meshed gaming, branded entertainment, events and social media, including a nationwide online gaming contest and reality TV series that aired primetime on Speed network.

Director
Jeff Zwart
Copywriters
Steve Bolton
Peter Von Sass
Creative Director
Tito Melega
Digital Creative Directors
Michael McGrath-Sing
Steve Savic
Associate Creative Directors
Jason Locey
Nik Piscitello
Chief Creative Officer
Rob Schwartz
Producers
Rachel Rudwall
Larry Struber
Executive Producers
David O'Connor
Frank Scherma
Agency Producer
Tim Newfang
Agency Executive Producer
Brian O'Rourke
Director of Integrated Production
Richard O'Neill
Production Company
@radical.media
Advertising Agency
TBWA\Chiat\Day Los Angeles
Digital Agency
Critical Mass
Editing
Venice Beach Editorial
Media Agency
OMD
Contractor
Laurence Wiltshire
Digital Strategist
Chrissie Graboski
Strategic Directors
Ed Beadle
Dario Raciti
Clients
Nissan
Sony PlayStation

1

2

3

4

5

6

7

Jury Foreman
1. Martin Lambie Nairn

2. Alice Tonge
4creative

3. Elspeth Lynn
M&C Saatchi London

4. Simon Wells
Drum PHD

5. Emma Starzacher
Mother New York

6. Charlie Mawer
Red Bee Media

7. Jasmine Huang
BBH China

Yellow Pencil in TV & Cinema Communications

Multi Platform Branding & Promotions
Ogilvy Johannesburg
for M-Net & Multichoice

MK is
MK is a South African TV channel that promotes only local music. It needed to connect with a far more influential youth audience to reclaim its cutting-edge image as the voice of the youth music scene. Using a blend of media, we made MK come alive as three different living characters. Their adventures unfolded 'live' as 60-second idents. These were linked to blogs with Facebook and Twitter feeds. In 60 days we gained a new youth fan base, four times more influential than the previous one. This work was also awarded a Yellow Pencil in the 'Channel Branding & Identity' category.

Director
Henrik Purienne
Art Directors
Mark Haefele
Frank van Rooijen
James Smith
Copywriters
Mark Haefele
Frank van Rooijen
James Smith
Creative Director
Mariana O'Kelly
Executive Creative Director
Fran Luckin
Producer
Julia Thorpe
Executive Producer
Daniel Siegler
Agency Producer
Lisa Wides
Editor
Jamie Taylor
Advertising Agency
Ogilvy Johannesburg
Account Managers
Caree Ferrari
Kay Motuba
Clients
M-Net
Multichoice
Brand
MK

Yellow Pencil in TV & Cinema Communications

Multi Platform Branding & Promotions
4creative
for Channel 4

Street Summer
Channel 4's 'Street Summer' season celebrates the best of British street culture. On air, the challenge was to seamlessly zoom in and out on each performer as the camera panned around the street itself, all the while maintaining a unified aesthetic. Alongside this we created Street Tag, an app that turns your iPhone into a can of spray paint using augmented reality. Using the iPhone's camera, it allows users to virtually graffiti any surface in real time. An identity stitched the entire campaign together and became the hero visual in our print campaign. This work was also selected in the 'TV Promotions & Programme Junctions' category.

Director
Neil Gorringe
Art Director
Alice Tonge
TV Promotions Art Director
Neil Gorringe
Copywriter
Alice Tonge
Creative Director
Tom Tagholm
Producer
Shananne Lane
Digital Producer
Syed Naqvi
Post Producer
Tim Phillips
Director of Photography
Tom Townend
Artworker
Jack Newman
Colourist
George K
Production Designer
Kave Quinn

Visual Effects
Sterling Archibald
Liam Griffin
Giacomo Mineo
Visual Effects Supervisor
Michael Gregory
Editor
Joe Guest
Sound Designer
Rich Martin
Stunt Coordinator
Marc Cass
Advertising Agency
4creative
Design Agencies
Brothers and Sisters
Magpie Studio
Project Manager
Gagan Rehill
Business Director
Stephen Johnstone
Marketing Manager
Gagan Rehill
Client
Channel 4

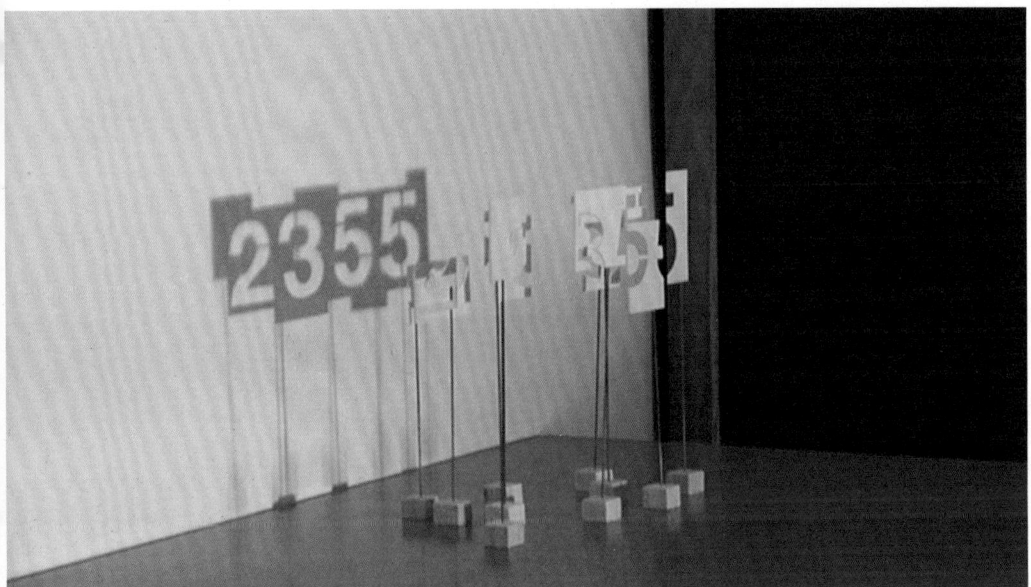

Light

Window

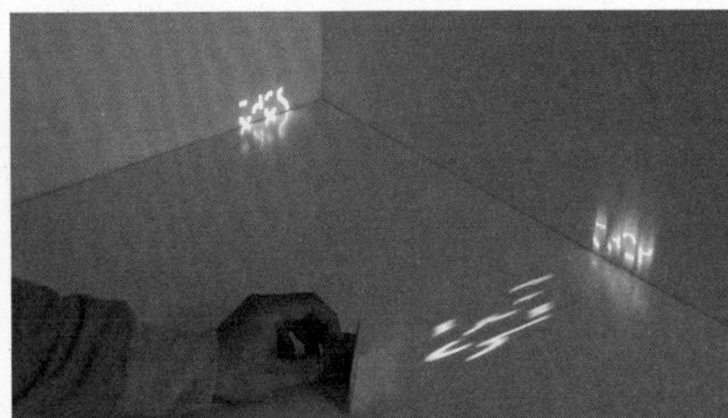

Projection

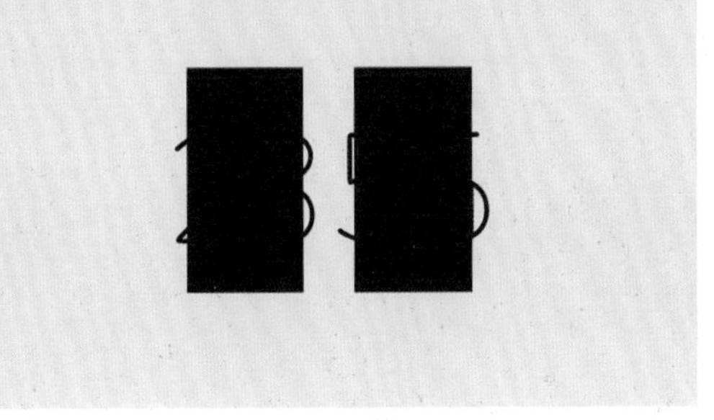

Hide

Yellow Pencil in TV & Cinema Communications

TV Promotions & Programme Junctions
Euphrates
for NHK

2355 ID
'2355 ID' is a series of short films used as teasers for '2355', a five-minute TV programme aired at 11:55pm every weekday on the educational channel of NHK, the Japan Broadcasting Corporation. The programme's aim is to make enjoyable viewing by airing a short composition of interesting features at the end of the day. The '2355 ID' teasers were aired between features and announced the programme's title, '2355', in different ways. Various techniques are used to create the number 2355, but they all have the same aim: to alert viewers to an interesting element inside each film.

Directors
Junya Hirose
Masaya Ishikawa
Tomoko Kaizuka
Ueta Mio
Ryo Oshima
Masashi Sato
Syun'ichi Suge
Akio Tokita
Masako Wakigawa
Kohji Robert Yamamoto
Hirofumi Yonemoto

Executive Creative Director
Masahiko Sato
Producers
Akiko Ie
Mitsuko Okamoto
Design Agency
Euphrates
Client
NHK

Yellow Pencil in TV & Cinema Communications

Cinema Title Sequences
Blur
for Sony Pictures

The Girl with the Dragon Tattoo
Featuring Trent Reznor and Karen O's visceral cover of 'Immigrant Song', the main title for David Fincher's portrayal of the internationally acclaimed, bestselling book is a glimpse into the psyche of heroine Lisbeth Salander. The sequence is a non-linear, impressionistic story featuring breathtaking imagery and special effects. It's a fever dream/nightmare that foreshadows the entire Millennium series.

Director
David Fincher
Art Director
Jerome Denjean
Designers
Jennifer Miller
Onur Senturk
Creative Director
Tim Miller
Producer
Tobin Kirk
Executive Producer
Al Shier
Lead Animator
Derron Ross
Visual Effects Supervisor
Kirby Miller
Editor
Franck Balson
Design Agency
Blur
Client
Sony Pictures

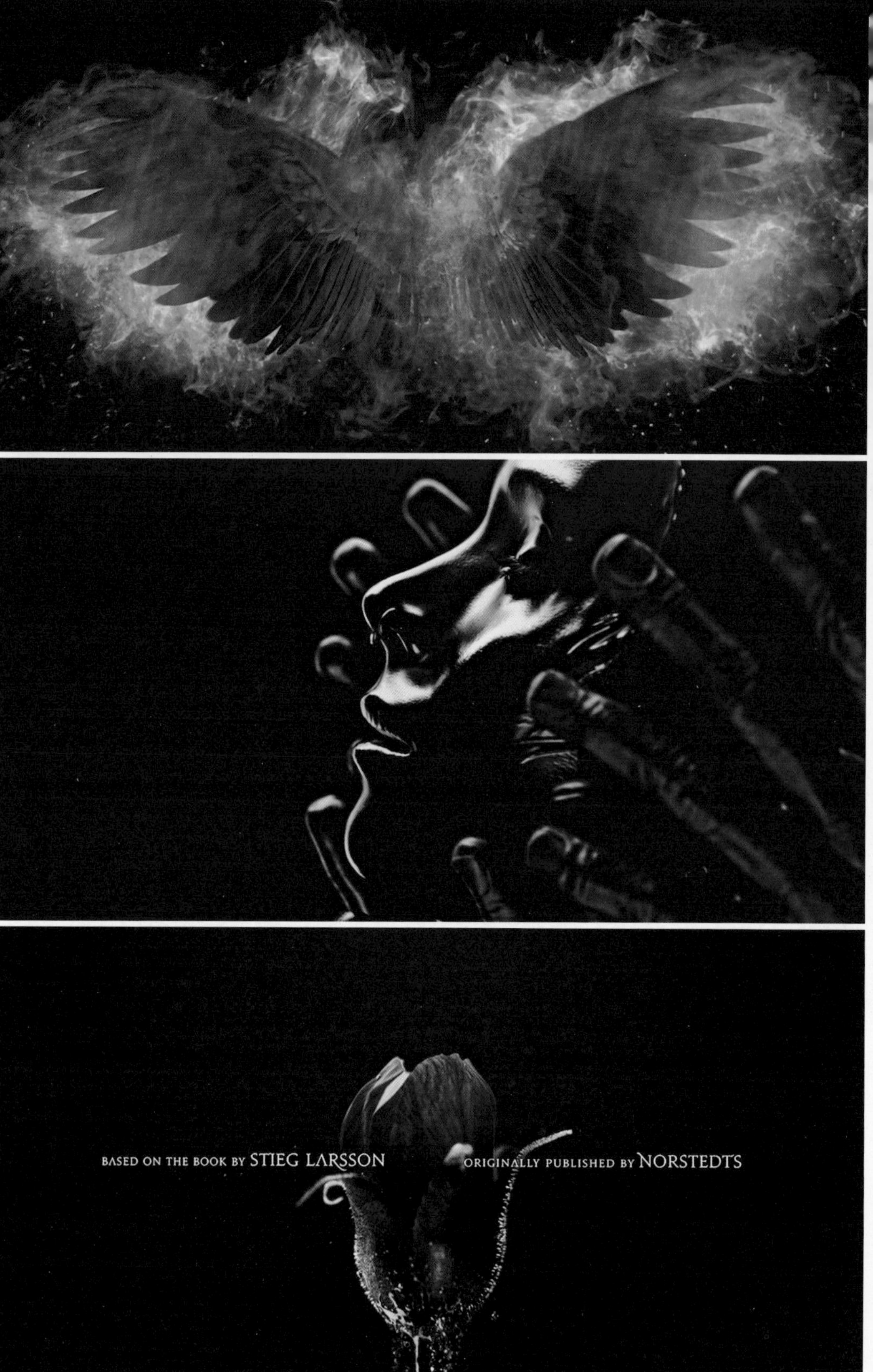

Nomination in TV & Cinema Communications

Channel Branding & Identity
Heavenly
for Sky Atlantic

Sky Atlantic Positioning, Naming & On-screen Identity

Sky Atlantic launched in the UK on 1 February 2011 with positioning, naming and on-screen identity by Heavenly. The five idents created by Heavenly to support the channel's launch were inspired by the belief that Sky Atlantic was the channel that bridges the best of US and UK culture. This was visualised by splicing together British and American locations and seeing them exist on screen at the same moment in time. The two sides complement and contrast to create a dynamic and distinctive representation of the channel's positioning.

Director
Thomas Napper
Music Composer
Colin Towns
Production Company
HSI London
Post Production
Prime Focus London

Branding Agency
Heavenly
Clients
BSkyB
Sky Atlantic

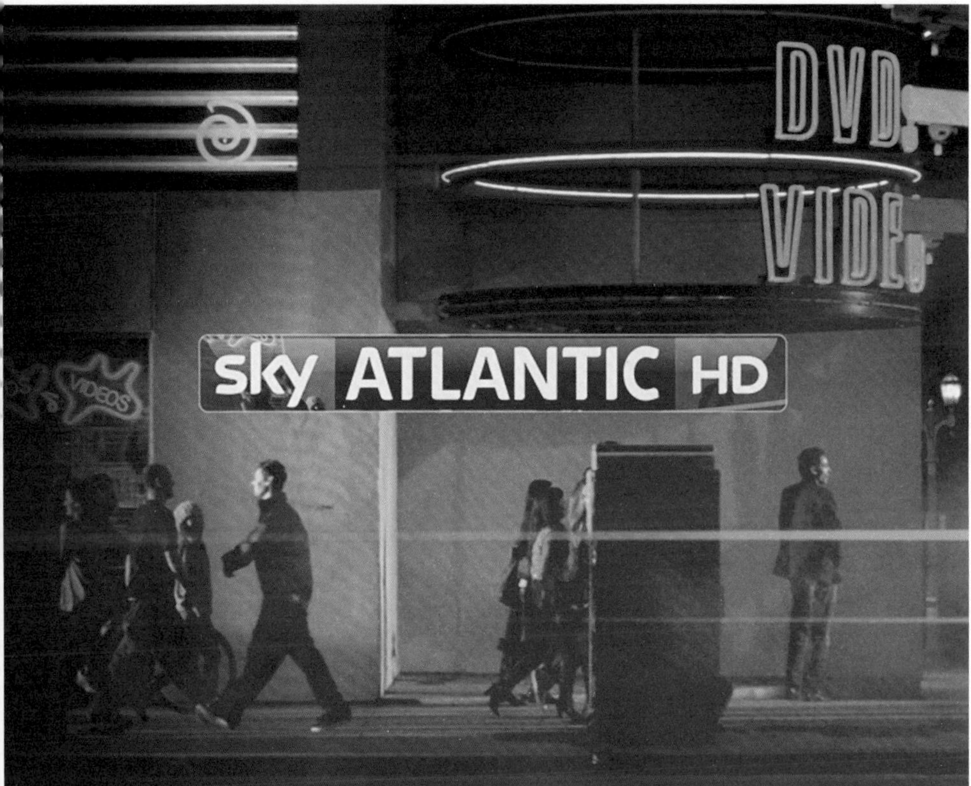

Bright Lights

Bridges

City Lab

Café Diner

Train

Nomination in TV & Cinema Communications

Channel Branding & Identity
4creative
for Channel 4

April Fools' Idents
Channel 4 forgets to include the 4 logo in its iconic idents for one special day only.

Director
Brett Foraker
Art Director
Russell Appleford
Creative Director
Tom Tagholm
Producers
Gwilym Gwillim
Shananne Lane
Post Producer
Tim Phillips
Director of Photography
Dan Bronks

Special Effects
Russell Appleford
Editor
Adam Rudd
Advertising Agency
4creative
Marketing Manager
Rufus Radcliffe
Client
Channel 4

Tokyo

City Skyline

Diner

Containers

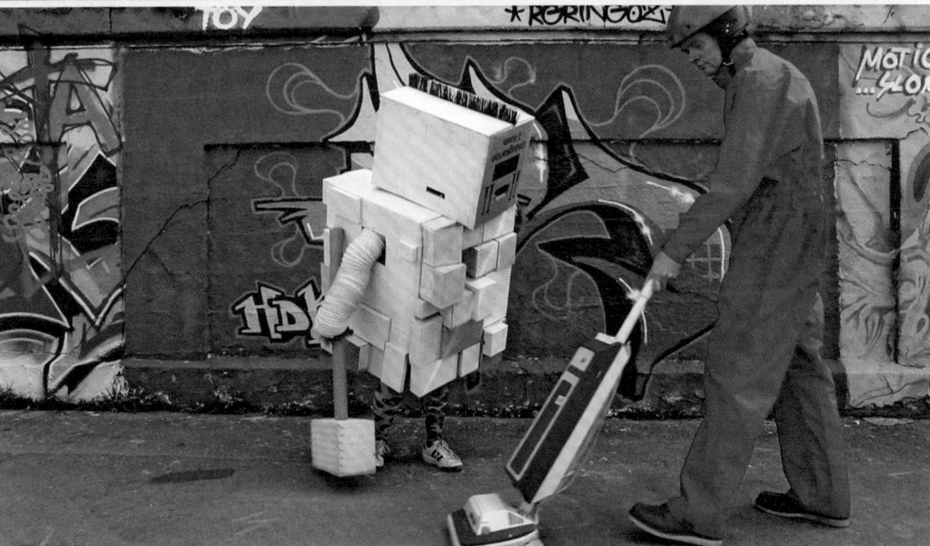

Nomination in TV & Cinema Communications

TV Promotions & Programme Junctions
Luxlotusliner
for zdf.kultur Germany

Pixelmacher
The Pixelmacher (German for Pixel Maker) is a format running on new pop culture orientated channel zdf.kultur. The programme contains all sorts of games, including new computer games. Game freaks can use this forum to gain access to the latest news on the gaming scene. We took the title of the format literally and created a pixel monster, which is 'pixelating' things. With a big latex hammer the Pixelmacher bangs on the objects of desire, which are immediately transformed into various big and colourful pixels. Inside the monster outfit was one of Luxlotusliner's managing directors.

Creative Director
Gabi Madracevic
Branding Agency
Luxlotusliner
Project Manager
Andrea Bednarz

Client
zdf.kultur
Germany

Nomination in TV & Cinema Communications

TV Promotions & Programme Junctions
Les Télécréateurs
for France 5

History of America
We were asked to create promos for the 'History of America' series airing on French TV channel France 5. When thinking about the history of the US, we realised our knowledge was very approximate and fuzzy. We were then just one step away from reversing the proposal and asking ourselves, what do they know about us? Hence the baseline: 'Just because they know nothing about us, doesn't mean we shouldn't know anything about them'. We interviewed people on the street in New York, and the answers we got were so funny that we edited four promos. The whole series became a hit in France, ending up on many blogs and generating over 70,000 views – a lot for a channel with a 3.2% market share.

Director
David Gray
Producers
Julien Chavepayre
Eric Nung
Production Company
Les Télécréateurs

Design Agency
Les Télécréateurs
Brand Manager
Eric Rinaldi
Client
France 5

French President

French Revolution

Louvre

Steak Tartare

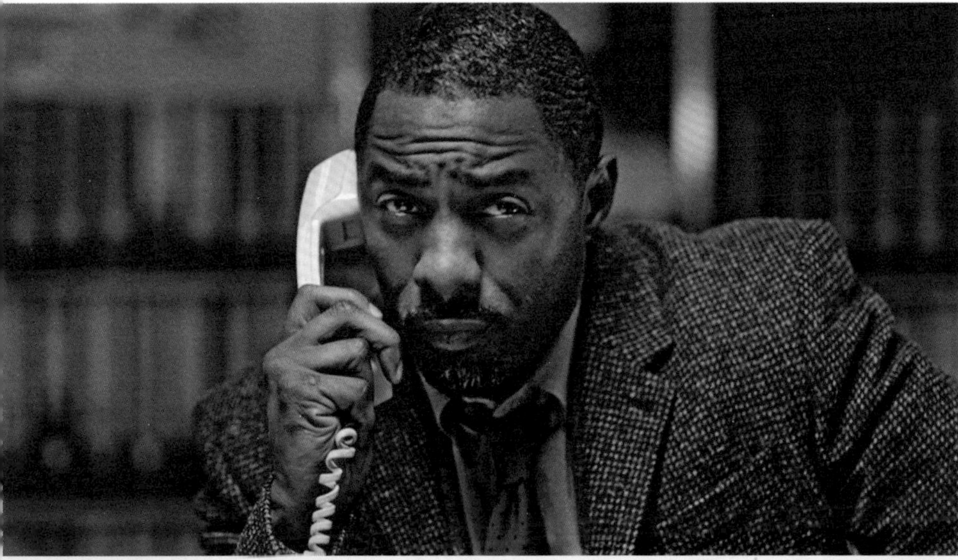

Nomination in TV & Cinema Communications

TV Promotions & Programme Junctions
Red Bee Media
for the BBC

Luther
Our challenge was to target 24–35 year olds and position action-packed psychological crime drama 'Luther' as an unmissable TV event. We also wanted to use 'Luther' to exemplify the new BBC Drama brand and cement BBC One's reputation for, and commitment to, edgy drama with world-class talent. Our solution was a creative idea that raised more questions than it answered, and stood out from other drama trails on BBC One and beyond. It was hugely successful in meeting the objectives of driving viewing, driving interaction online and creating an impact – ultimately driving credit back to drama.

Director
Caswell Coggins
Art Director
Frazer Jelleyman
Writer
Frazer Jelleyman
Group Creative Director
Frazer Jelleyman
Executive Creative Director
Charlie Mawer
Producer
Kate Woodhouse
Agency Producer
Tony Pipes
Creative Agency
Red Bee Media
Account Handler
Emma James
Client
BBC
Brands
BBC Drama
BBC One

Nomination in TV & Cinema Communications

TV Promotions & Programme Junctions
Serviceplan München
for ZDF

Witness to History
In these TV promos, people like you and me are telling historical stories as if they have experienced them for themselves. But really, they have just watched the exciting and realistic TV documentaries on ZDF History.

Art Directors
Sandra Loibl
Franz Röppischer
Copywriter
Frank Seiler
Executive Creative Director
Matthias Harbeck
Chief Creative Officer
Alexander Schill
Producer
Martin Schmid
Agency Producer
Maik Schmidt
Cinematographer
Casey Campbell
Advertising Agency
Serviceplan München
Sound Design
Supreme Music
Client
ZDF
Brand
ZDF History

Apollo

Kennedy

HEY LOOK, NO RUGBY.
FOUR
THE HOME OF NOT RUGBY
AMERICA'S NEXT TOP MODEL. FREEVIEW 4. SKY 012. FOUR.CO.NZ

IF YOU LOOK VERY CAREFULLY, YOU'LL SEE ABSOLUTELY NO RUGBY.
FOUR
THE HOME OF NOT RUGBY

SEE THIS. THIS ISN'T RUGBY.
FOUR
THE HOME OF NOT RUGBY
AMERICA'S NEXT TOP MODEL
FREEVIEW 4. SKY 012.
FOUR.CO.NZ

ROLL OVER TO UN-RUGBY THIS BANNER

FAMILY GUY SUNDAY, 8PM
FOUR
THE HOME OF NOT RUGBY

Multi Platform Branding & Promotions
Special Group
for MediaWorks

The Home of NOT Rugby
New Zealand is a rugby-mad nation. During the 2011 Rugby World Cup the game was everywhere – across nearly all New Zealand media, 24/7. But TV channel FOUR had no rugby content on its schedule whatsoever. So it positioned itself as 'The Home of NOT Rugby' – a destination where non-rugby lovers (or those suffering from rugby overload) could enjoy the latest award-winning TV shows. Viewership increased by more than 10% during the Rugby World Cup, while all other free-to-air channels lost viewers. Nice result.

Art Director
Tony Bradbourne
Copywriter
Kim Fraser
Creative Directors
Tony Bradbourne
Rob Jack
Advertising Agency
Special Group
Account Directors
Michael Redwood
Annabel Rees

Brand Manager
Renee Colquhoun
Marketing Director
Amanda Wilson
Client
MediaWorks
Brand
Channel FOUR

Multi Platform Branding & Promotions
BBDO San Francisco
for Comcast SportsNet Bay Area

Search for the World Series Baby

Following the 2010 San Francisco Giants World Series victory, Comcast SportsNet asked us to develop a low-cost idea that leveraged the Giants' big win to help build Comcast SportsNet Bay Area's online community. From this brief, the idea for the search for the 'World Championship Baby' was born. We promoted our contest during Giants games with a 30-second spot and in-game mentions, along with creating a homepage on CSN's website. In total, 921 mothers-to-be entered our contest and on 1 August 2011, the official nine-month anniversary of the Giants victory, the winning baby was born.

Art Director
Page Kishiyama
Copywriter
Jack Harding
Executive Creative Director
Michael McKay
Producer
Sam Barrett

Editor
Michael Schwartz
Advertising Agency
BBDO San Francisco
Account Handler
Jill Rohde
Client
Comcast SportsNet Bay Area

Channel Branding & Identity
Luxlotusliner
for zdf.kultur Germany

zdf.kultur
Zdf.kultur, the new pop culture orientated channel of the ZDF family, was launched in May 2011. The design focus is one of the playful treatments of culture. The high level of integration between the web and TV opens up new opportunities for two-way communication. The idents present imaginative scenes and installations relating to cultural topics. These are home-made constructions; everyday objects placed in unexpected new contexts. Following this principle, a number of visuals, programme packages and the promotion design were created.

Creative Director
Gabi Madracevic
Design Agency
Luxlotusliner
Project Manager
Andrea Bednarz

Client
zdf.kultur
Germany

Channel Branding & Identity
Red Bee Media
for the BBC

BBC Two Christmas Idents
Our challenge was to create idents that built an immersive Christmas world, signifying everything that is wonderful about BBC Two: bold creativity, wit, substance and pleasure. To create a counterbalance to Christmas clichés, we chose to celebrate the more magical, inspired and unexpected elements of Christmas. The idents received acclaim industry-wide and with audiences. The first BBC Two Christmas idents for four years cut through the usual Christmas clutter and were genuinely pleasurable to watch. They stand up to viewing time and time again.

Art Director
Ollie Parsons
Creative Directors
Frazer Jelleyman
James de Zoete
Executive Creative Director
Charlie Mawer
Producer
Laura Gould

Creative Agency
Red Bee Media
Animation
No Brain
Account Handler
Richard Stuart
Client
BBC
Brand
BBC Two

Sun and Moon

Turkeys

Scientist

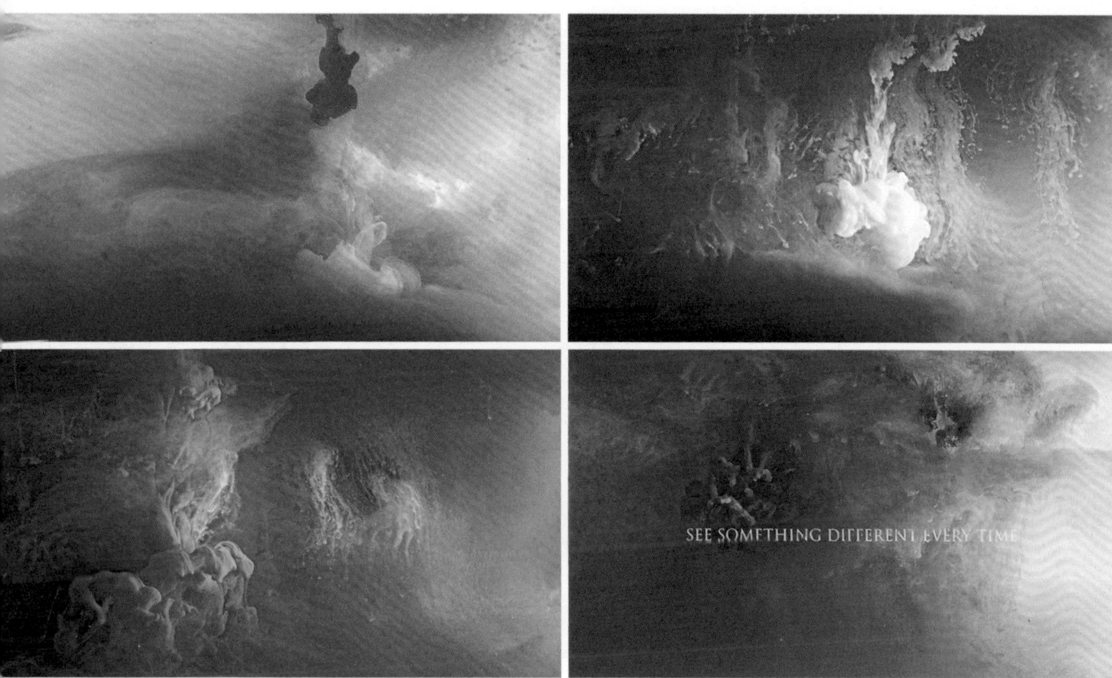
SEE SOMETHING DIFFERENT EVERY TIME

TV Promotions & Programme Junctions
Red Bee Media
for the BBC

Art Revealed
The BBC launched a website curating 200,000 paintings, until now held in private hands, for the public to enjoy for the first time. We wanted to create a campaign that delivered the same promise of discovery. Working with conceptual artist Giles Revell, we produced living paintings, constantly changing, evolving and developing. As with each visit to the site, the viewer would enjoy seeing something different every time.

Director
Giles Revell
Creative Director
Tony Pipes
Executive Creative Director
Charlie Mawer
Group Creative Director
Frazer Jelleyman
Producer
Deborah Stewart
Editor
Gerry Lindfield
Creative Agency
Red Bee Media
Client
BBC
Brand
BBC One

TV Promotions & Programme Junctions
4creative
for Channel 4

Derren Brown – The Experiments
Derren's experiments were to showcase how we are all capable of doing things that are extremely out of character; that everyone can be controlled in some way, including Derren himself. To suggest this lack of self-control, we cast Derren and his subjects as ventriloquist dummies within a dark, unsettling atmosphere. In a listless, brainwashed tone they pose the question 'what are the limits of human behaviour?'

Director
Phil Lind
Art Director
Claire Watson
Creative Director
Tom Tagholm
Producer
Tabby Harris
Production Designer
Adam Zoltowski
Director of Photography
Oliver Schofield
Editor
Dan Sherwen
Sound Designer
Rich Martin
Music Supervisor
Alice Godfrey
Advertising Agency
4creative
Marketing Manager
Charlie Palmer
Client
Channel 4

TV Promotions & Programme Junctions
4creative
for Channel 4

4oD – Jon Snow
The brief was to promote that 4oD, the TV on-demand service from Channel 4, was expanding into mobile devices. We wanted a progression from earlier ads that would retain their humour and character. The idea of content being delivered to users everywhere was a logical and fun evolution.

Director
Tom Tagholm
Art Director
Alice Tonge
Copywriters
Ben Edwards
Phil Lind
Creative Director
Tom Tagholm
Producer
Gwilym Gwillim
Production Designer
Simon Davis
Director of Photography
Luke Scott
Editor
Tim Hardy
Sound Designer
Rich Martin
Advertising Agency
4creative
Marketing Manager
Nick Gilmer
Client
Channel 4
Brand
4oD

TV Promotions & Programme Junctions
RKCR/Y&R
for BBC Digital Radio UK

Cry
We wanted to dramatise the emotional power of listening to BBC stations on digital radio. A man at his kitchen table listens to The Velvet Underground's 'Pale Blue Eyes'. The music evokes memories and he cries. We show the exact same scene again, only this time the radio plays BBC's live commentary of a football play-off final. The man's team are promoted. Now the tears rolling down his face are tears of joy.

Direction
Thirtytwo
Art Director
Jerry Hollens
Copywriter
Mike Boles
Executive Creative Director
Mark Roalfe
Producer
Louise Jones
Director of Photography
Natasha Braier
Editor
Leo Scott
Sound Designer
Parv Thind
Production Company
Pulse Films
Advertising Agency
RKCR/Y&R
Sound Design
Speade
Editing
Speade
Planner
Joanna Bamford
Account Director
Graham Smith
Business Director
Jo Bacon
Client
BBC Digital Radio UK

BBC 6Music

MORE STATIONS,
MORE TO MOVE YOU.

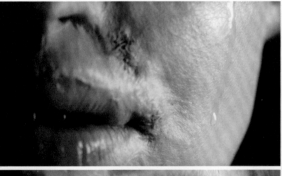

TV Promotions & Programme Junctions
4creative
for Channel 4

The World Sheepdog Trials 2011

We wanted to create a spot that would show the extraordinary skill and control involved in sheepdog trials. After weeks of searching we eventually found an exceptionally talented handler and sheepdog team, who through years of unrelenting dedication and somewhat unorthodox training methods could get a sheep to perform a 360-degree somersault. Once we met their outrageous terms, both financial and on-set demands, we got them in a field, turned the camera on, two takes, job done.

Director
Mick Arnold
Creative Director
Chris Wood
Producer
Louise Oliver
Visual Effects
Marcus Dryden
Production Designer
James Thompson
Director of Photography
Luke Scott
Editor
Nick Armstrong
Sound Designer
Rich Martin
Advertising Agency
4creative
Marketing Managers
Zoe Baker
Adam Young
Client
Channel 4
Brand
More4

TV Promotions & Programme Junctions
4creative
for Channel 4

My Beautiful Friends

Channel 4 wanted to promote a new series featuring Katie Piper as she helped people come to terms with their scars and turn their lives around. We showed the scars without any compromise, while listening to the individuals' positive stories, thoughts and feelings. The iconic metaphor of a reversing tear travelling up their cheeks symbolised the process of recovery. The tear returning into the eye illustrated the extent to which Katie has helped these people.

Director
Dahlan Lassalle
Art Directors
Milan Desai
Molly Manners
Copywriter
Martin Jeyes
Creative Director
Tom Tagholm
Producer
Tabby Harris
Production Designer
Simon Davis
Director of Photography
Lynda Hall
Visual Effects Producer
Peter Winslett
Visual Effects Supervisors
Marcus Dryden
James Smith
Editor
Kel McKeown
Advertising Agency
4creative
Marketing Manager
Ros Godber
Client
Channel 4

LETTUCE
CELERY
CHESTNUTS
MUSHROOMS
TRUFFLES
PUMPKIN
BEETROOT
CARROTS
POTATOES
SCORZONERA
TURNIPS
AUTUMN

DALEY&

AFRICAN
Some of Picasso's
Art was influenced
by African Art which

ファンから託された義援物資を震災
います。これから、相馬市と、30°

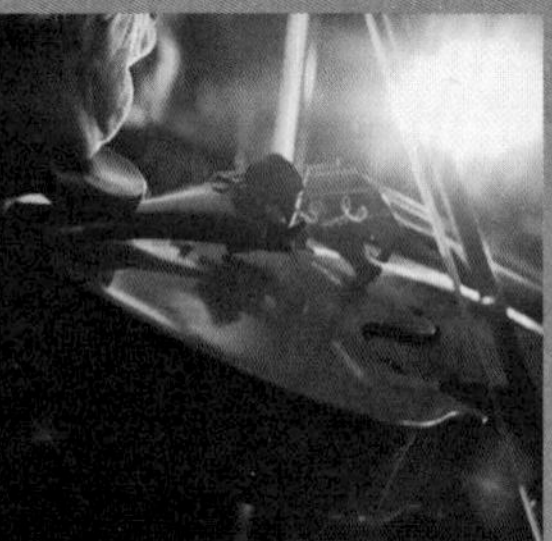
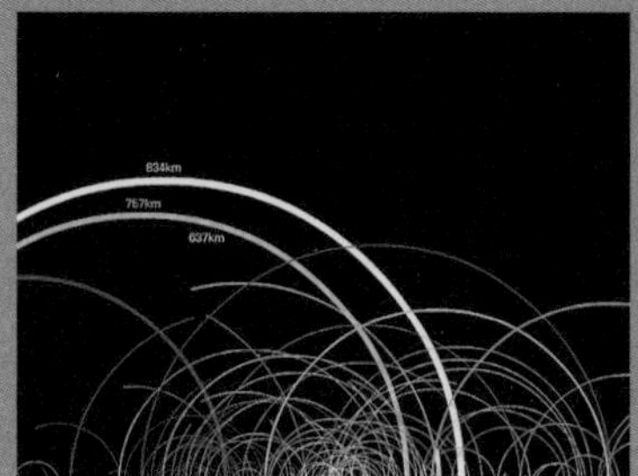
834km
767km
637km

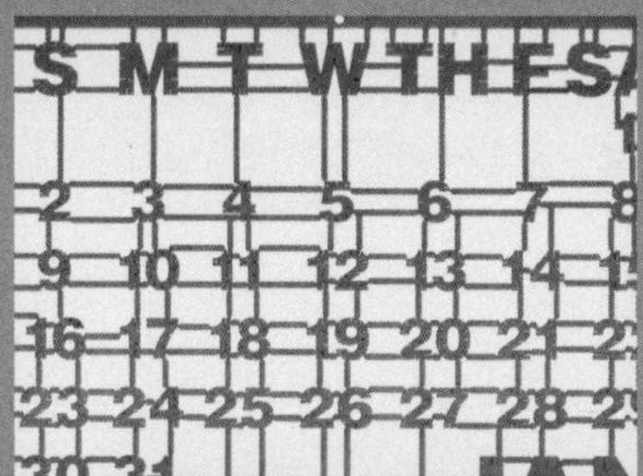
S M T W TH F S
2 3 4 5 6 7 8
9 10 11 12 13 14
16 17 18 19 20 21
23 24 25 26 27 28

the devil's in the detail
Fülle die Leere.
Einladung

DESIGN FEVER!

CURRENT

NEW YORK
One Day, Ten Years

YOUR LIFE
TORN OPEN

echo

Home
READING now
on page
104
of 492
NEW reads
I'll Walk Alone
by Mary Higgins Clark
Little Bee
by Chris Cleave
Fast Company
LAURA HILLENBRAND
UNBROKEN

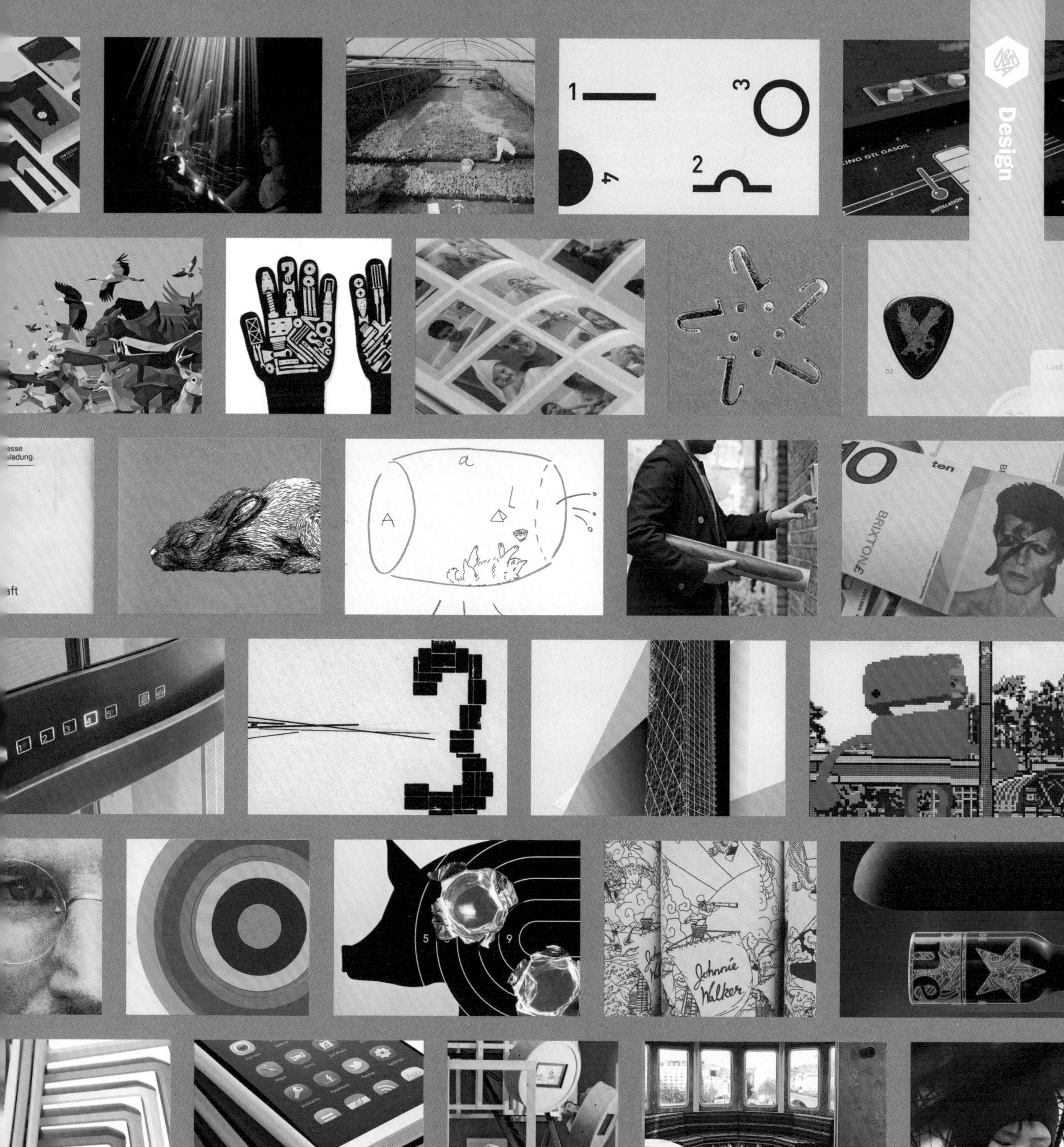
1
3
4
2
DISTILLATION
ten
BRIXTONE
Johnnie Walker

Jury Foreman
1. Irma Boom
Irma Boom Office

2. Mark Ecob
mecob design
& art direction

3. Josh Baker
TASCHEN

4. Johanna Neurath
Thames & Hudson

5. Stefanie Posavec

6. Melanie Mues
Mues Design

7. Coralie Bickford-Smith
Penguin Books

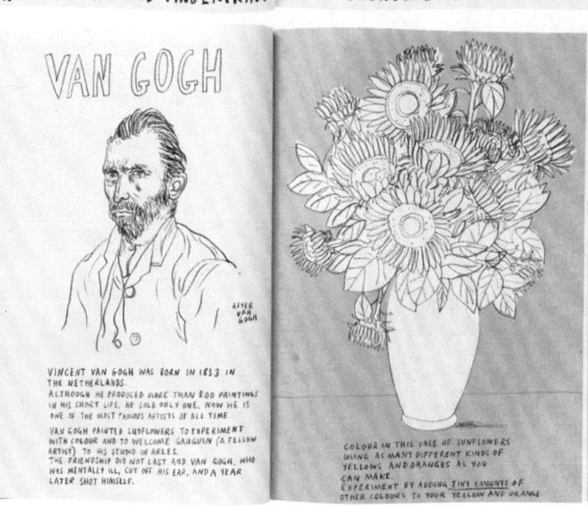

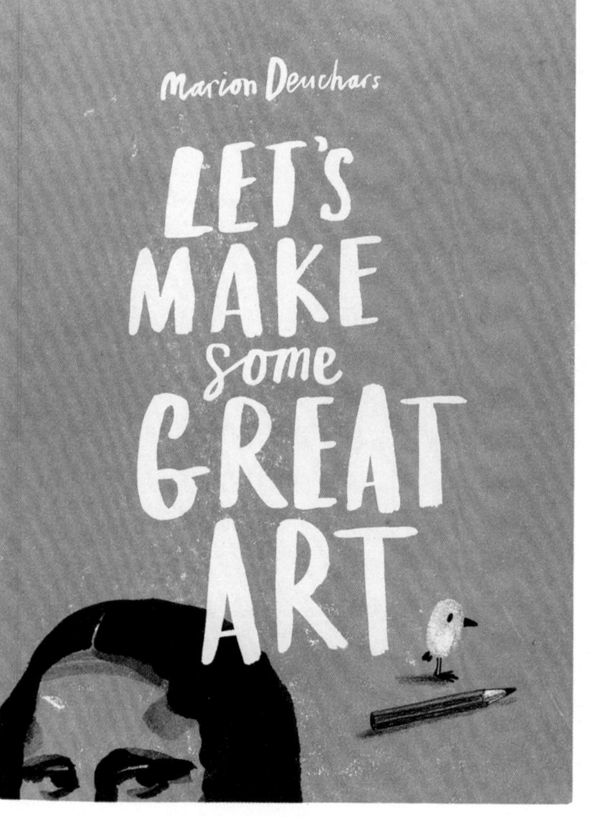

Yellow Pencil in Book Design

Entire Books
Laurence King Publishing

Let's Make Some Great Art
This book originated from a small promotional activity book for art material supplier Cass Art. The book was given away when someone purchased art materials in the children's department. One ended up at Laurence King Publishing and Laurence thought it was an idea worth developing into a book. The result: an interactive colouring and activity book. Marion Deuchars takes the broad canvas of art and fills it with drawings and activities that let the reader discover what art can be, how it can be made, what it can mean and what it has meant for people through the ages.

Art Director
Angus Hyland
Designer
Marion Deuchars
Illustrator
Marion Deuchars
Author
Marion Deuchars

Publishing Company
Laurence King Publishing
Client
Laurence King Publishing

Yellow Pencil in Book Design

Book Front Covers
INT Works
for Pan Macmillan Picador

Don DeLillo Series
Don DeLillo is one of America's greatest writers. What distinguishes him is his prophetic vision – the ability to see and chronicle his homeland like no one else. So when Rebecca Ikin at Picador commissioned INT Works to redesign his novels, his extraordinary gift for perception became the brief's focal point. INT Works saw in Noma Bar's illustrations the perfect vehicle to visually communicate DeLillo's work. Noma offers a bold image for each cover that might seem conventional at first, but reveals more with a deeper viewing. Design and content are perfectly matched.

Publisher
Paul Baggaley
Illustrator
Noma Bar
Artworker
Jonathan Pelham
Editor
Kris Doyle
Design Agency
INT Works
Publishing Company
Pan Macmillan
Picador

Production Manager
Amelia Douglas
Marketing Director
Rebecca Ikin
Clients
Don DeLillo
Pan Macmillan
Picador

DON DELILLO
WHITE NOISE
PICADOR
DON DELILLO
FALLING MAN
PICADOR
DON DELILLO
COSMOPOLIS
PICADOR
DON DELILLO
THE BODY ARTIST
PICADOR

Nomination in Book Design

Entire Books
Nippon Design Center
for Heibonsha & Takeo

Takeo Paper Show 2011 Book
This catalogue covers the contents of an exhibition that was held under the theme 'a paper book'. The catalogue consists of three chapters. Using words and images, chapter one answers the question 'What are books?'. Chapter two is a full-scale image of 'a paper book' that was presented by 78 experts just for this exhibition. Chapter three features comments on the exhibition from the 78 experts.

Art Director
Yoshiaki Irobe
Designers
Yoshiaki Irobe
Nozomi Morisada
Editor
Chinatsu Kuma
Editor in Chief
Keiichirou Fujisaki
Design Agency
Nippon Design Center

Editing
Takeo
Photography
amana
Publishing Company
Heibonsha
Clients
Heibonsha
Takeo

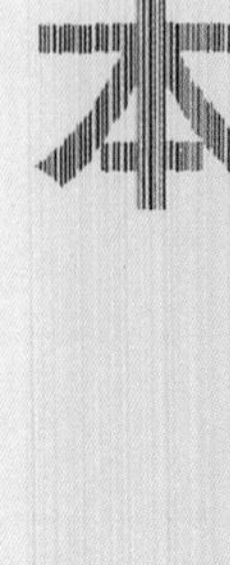

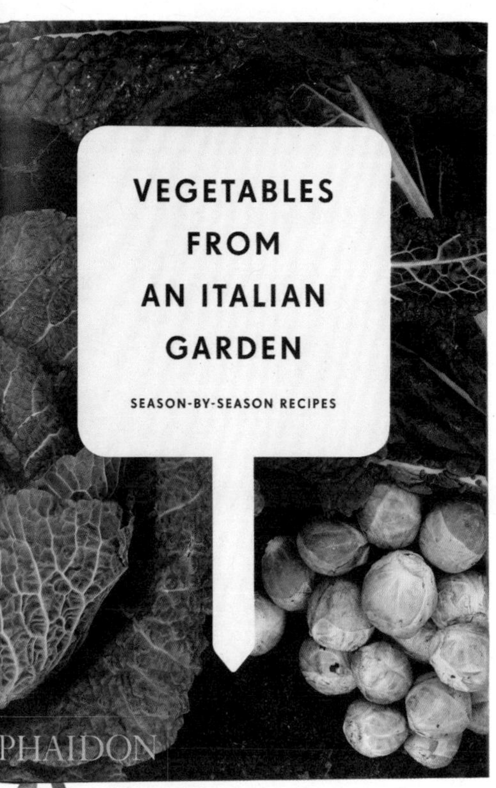

MUSHROOMS

FUNGHI

Italians are passionate about mushrooms and about harvesting them in the wild, where they will pick rich-flavoured porcini, also known as ceps, delicate yellow chanterelles, large parasols and clusters of honey fungus. Never pick wild mushrooms unless you are certain that you can identify edible species. Cooks in many other countries rely on cultivated mushrooms, which still have a concentrated earthy flavour, although not quite so intense as wild mushrooms.

Mushrooms are hugely versatile. They add texture to warm salads and deep flavour to dishes such as Tagliatelle with Mushrooms (see page 290) or a traditional Mushroom Risotto (see page 295). They work just as well in sauces, gratins, pies, fricassées, omelettes, timbales and flans. However, one of the easiest and most delicious ways to serve any kind of mushrooms is *trifolati*, cooked with oil, parsley and lemon juice.

Mushrooms should be firm to the touch and without slime. They should have a pleasant earthy smell. Do not wash cultivated mushrooms; simply wipe with damp kitchen paper. Gently brush grit and dirt from wild mushrooms, rinse very briefly and dry immediately.

IN THE GARDEN Mushrooms such as portobello, oyster and button can be grown in box kits or outdoor beds. Mushrooms should appear in a few weeks and you can get 2–3 harvests from a box. To grow outdoors, fill a bed in a shady area with straw, bark mulch or wood chips. Wet the organic material thoroughly, then spread the spore. Cover until mushrooms begin to emerge, then uncover and begin to harvest.

MUSHROOM RECIPES ON PAGES 289–300

AUTUMN 250

Nomination in Book Design

Entire Books
Studio Astrid Stavro
for Phaidon Press

Vegetables from an Italian Garden

This is a season-by-season guide to cooking vegetables the Italian way. The book is organised by season with each chapter featuring a garden journal and a collection of recipes. Each journal provides readers with profiles of vegetables within that season, highlighting best-known varieties, appearance, storage and preparation. Different colour codes are used for each season.

Art Director
Astrid Stavro
Designers
Marianne Noble
Astrid Stavro
Publisher
Richard Schlagman
Photographers
Steven Joyce
Andy Sewell

Editor
Emilia Terragni
Design Agency
Studio Astrid Stavro
Production Manager
Michelle Lo
Client
Phaidon Press

Nomination in Book Design

Entire Books
Leo Burnett Chicago

Where the Wind Blows
Leo Burnett Chicago's newly formed Department of Design had a problem. Designers were coming to town for a national conference but were not yet familiar with the design talent and output Leo Burnett had to offer. To showcase the department and celebrate our passion for design, as well as welcome weary travellers to our city, we distributed a promotional book based on the many Chicago things that inspire us. Since Leo Burnett is a Chicago institution, we found it fitting to show the city through our eyes.

Designers
Dan Forbes
Jason McKean
Kyle Poff
Design Director
Alisa Wolfson
Writers
Susan Credle
Jason McKean
David Schermer
Alisa Wolfson
Illustrators
Jason Frohlichstein
Natalia Kowaleczko
Casey Martin
Eing Omathikul
Kine Ugelstad
Luke Williams
Photographers
Jason Frohlichstein
Natalia Kowaleczko
Casey Martin
Eing Omathikul
Kine Ugelstad
Luke Williams
Chief Creative Officer
Susan Credle
Producer
Laura Stern
Design Agency
Leo Burnett Chicago
Client
Leo Burnett Chicago

Entire Books
M/M (Paris)
for TASCHEN

Stanley Kubrick's Napoleon:
The Greatest Movie Never Made

In 2009, TASCHEN published a collector's edition of the book 'Stanley Kubrick's Napoleon'. It was designed by M/M (Paris) and limited to 1,000 copies. The book featured a carved-out reproduction of an antique history book containing ten smaller books, each covering a category of material from the archive of the unmade 'Napoleon' movie, and a copy of the screenplay. To turn this art object into a smaller, affordable single-volume book, the designers retained the book's original form and reproduced all of the ten interior books as if they had been 'photocopied' onto the pages, with two books often running simultaneously on the same page.

Editor	**Publishing Company**
Alison Castle	TASCHEN
Managing Editor	**Production Manager**
Florian Kobler	Thomas Grell
Design Agency	**Client**
M/M (Paris)	TASCHEN

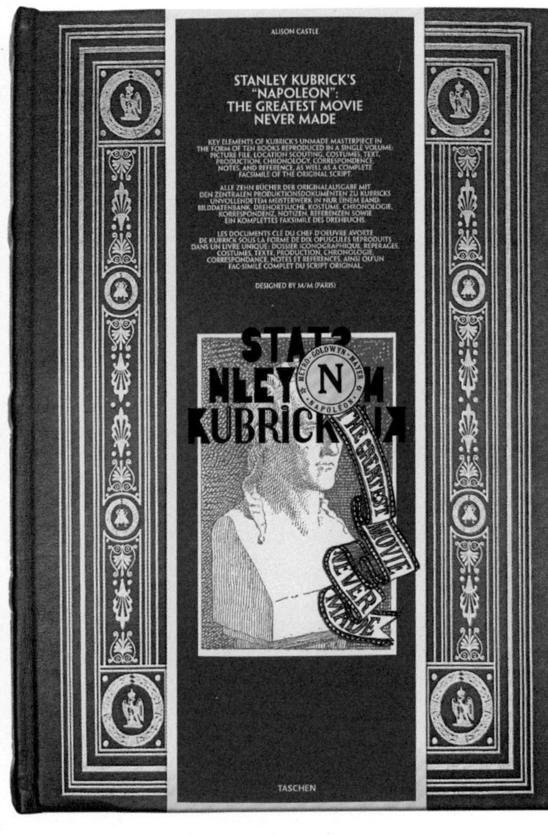

Entire Books
buero uebele visuelle kommunikation

No Detail: Michael Held 27 Houses
Architect Michael Held was a man of letters. He recorded his thoughts in notebooks where he made a collage of them together with tickets to exhibitions and all kinds of small treasures. There are photos clipped from magazines of items of clothing, bicycles, tables and above all, houses. This book presents his work in the same way that his diaries are arranged: as a multifaceted architectural landscape comprising narrative elements, drawings and colour. The material for this monograph of his work – a collection of plans, computer drawings, sketches and photos – has been assembled in blank 'diaries'.

Graphic Designers
Carolin Himmel
Katharina Moritzen
Felix Rabe
Andreas Uebele
Max Uebele
Design Director
Andreas Uebele

Design Agency
buero uebele visuelle kommunikation
Client
buero uebele visuelle kommunikation

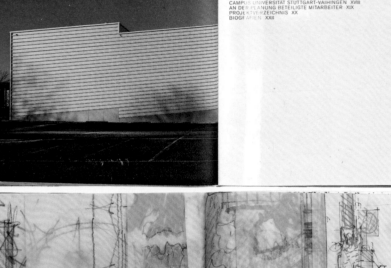

Entire Books
Shawati'
for the Abu Dhabi Authority for
Culture & Heritage

The Sheikh Zayed Grand Mosque
The limited edition of 'The Sheikh Zayed Grand Mosque' is a visual journey into one of the world's iconic modern Islamic buildings. The audience are affluent collectors of luxury coffee table books. The book was also intended to be a corporate government gift to heads of states and officials.

Creative Chairman
Sabah Al Abbasi
Project Manager
Laila Al Abbasi
Production Director
Abdallah Al Shami
Design Agency
Shawati'

Publishing Company
Shawati'
Client
Abu Dhabi Authority for Culture & Heritage

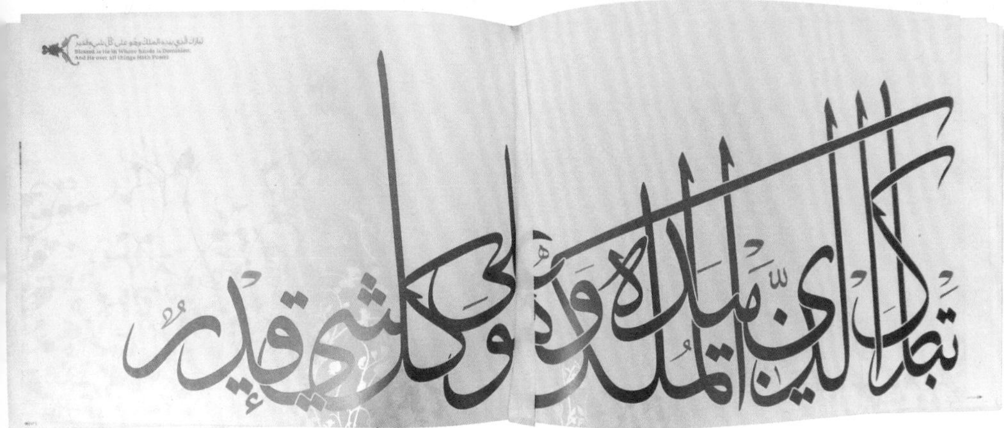

Entire Books
A Beautiful Design
for The Browsing Copy Project

For Browsing Only
The Browsing Copy Project focuses on unloved books, those that remain on the shelves unsold. These books were collected from local bookstores, then designers from around the world were invited to use them as canvases to express their creativity and give the books a second life. The 'before and after' results are documented. Only 300 copies were printed and circulated around the world's good bookstores, shops and design studios, just for people to browse. 'For Browsing Only' is not for sale. The condition of the books and the places they've been are documented on the website www.browsingcopy.com.

Designer
Roy Poh
Creative Director
Roy Poh
Copywriter
Roy Poh
Photographer
John Nursalim

Design Agency
A Beautiful Design
Client
The Browsing Copy Project

Entire Books
Gassner Redolfi
for Geninasca Delefortrie Architects

Singular Plural
This publication presents the architectural works of Geninasca Delefortrie Architects as an opportunity to reflect on the relationship between architecture and its geographical, cultural, economic and political context. Twenty projects are presented at length as concrete examples of how to clarify the ongoing relationship between architects, clients, contractors, public officials and society. A double page at the beginning collects and compares all the principal buildings, bringing out their richness of dimensions, variety of functions and typological complexity.

Graphic Designers
Reinhard Gassner
Andrea Redolfi
Photographer
Thomas Jantscher
Authors
Walter Angonese
Vincent Mangeat
Luca Merlini
Ignacio Rubino
Caspar Schärer

Editor
Alberto Alessi
Design Agency
Gassner Redolfi
Printers
Eberl Print
Client
Geninasca
Delefortrie
Architects

Entire Books
Music
for The National Literacy Trust

The Hand.Written.Letter.Project
Initially an exhibition, The Hand.Written.Letter. Project is an invitation to creative thinkers to make known their thoughts on the demise of the handwritten word in the form of a letter. This book catalogues the exhibition using experimental production methods. Each letter is a leaf of the book, mixing actual letterheads and reproductions across various stocks, finishes, inserts and sizes, all displayed chronologically and uninterrupted. Offering much more than a voyeuristic insight into the creative minds of those we revere, it represents a visual narrative on the cultural transition in which we all find ourselves.

Designer
Craig Oldham
Illustrator
Marion Deuchars
Artworker
Jon Hatton
Curator
Craig Oldham
Production Manager
Shelley Wood
Design Agency
Music
Publishing Company
Unified Theory
Of Everything
Printers
Team Impression
Clients
KK Outlet
The National
Literacy Trust

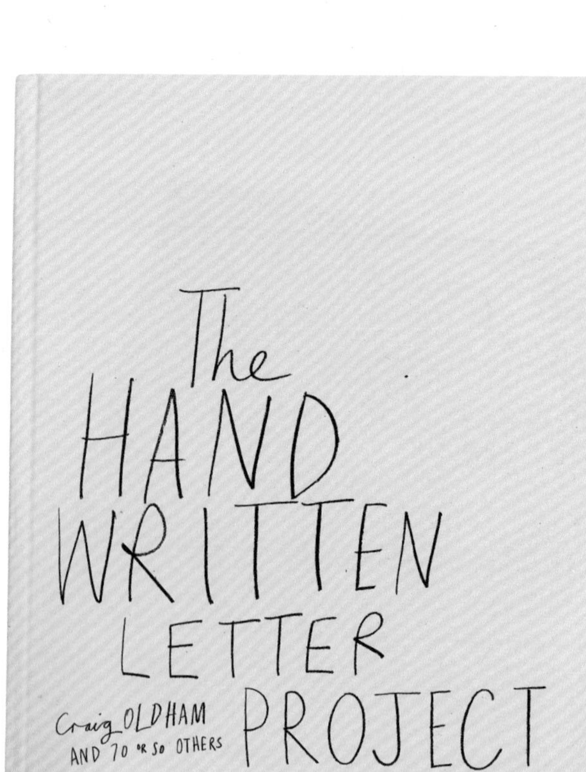

Entire Books
Non-Format
for Sternberg Press

The Opening
London-based artist Merlin Carpenter created all of the paintings documented in this book during a series of opening events staged at galleries in New York, Los Angeles, Berlin, Zurich, London and Brussels between 2007 and 2009. The front section of the book combines essays by Caroline Busta alongside a showcase of each event using grids of reportage photography, presented as though cropped from a larger document. The back section of the book catalogues each of the resulting paintings alongside an email exchange between George Baker, Merlin Carpenter and his publisher.

Art Directors
Kjell Ekhorn
Jon Forss
Designers
Kjell Ekhorn
Jon Forss
Publisher
Caroline Schneider
Author
Merlin Carpenter

Contributors
George Baker
Caroline Busta
Design Agency
Non-Format
Publishing Company
Sternberg Press
Client
Sternberg Press

Sunday
September
23
2007

Reena
Spaulings
Fine
Art
(New
York)

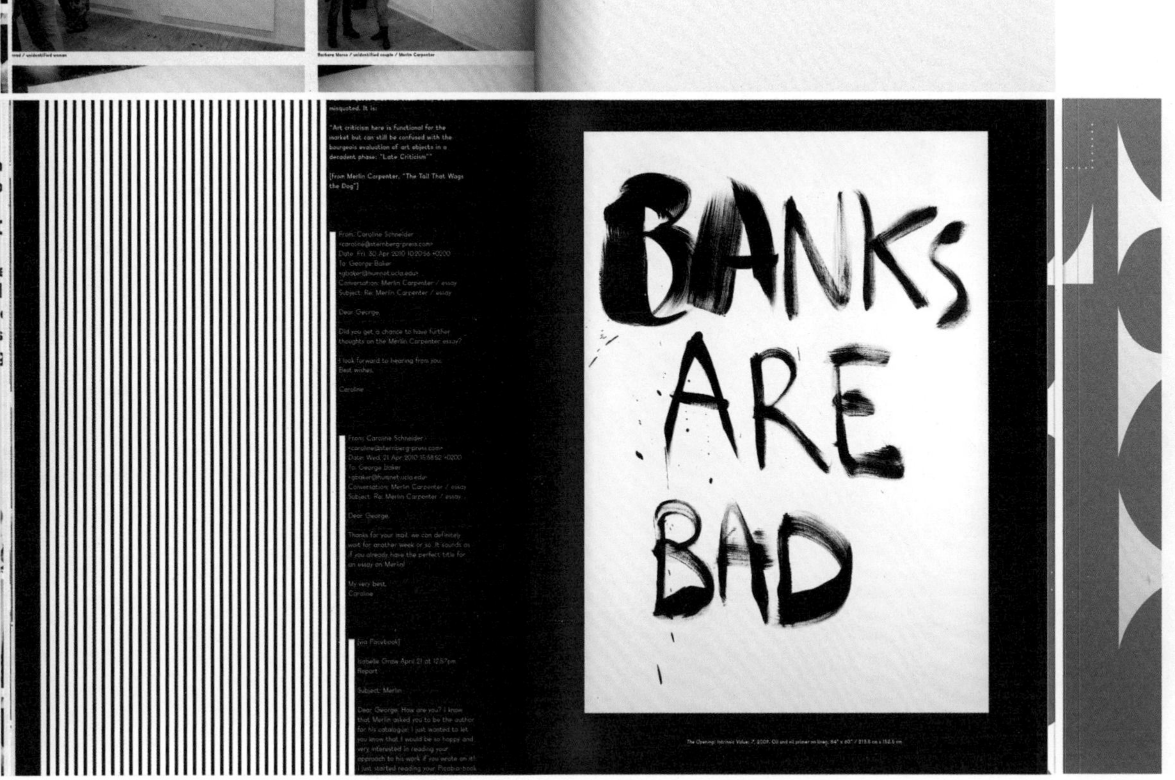

Entire Books
Loran Stosskopf Studio
for the Ecole d'Art de Mulhouse
& Les Presses du Réel

Faire Impression
This book is about the creation of French art schools in the 19th Century and their link with each region's industry. Mulhouse (Alsace) presents the story of these schools. Mulhouse was then renowned for its fabric printing industry. A drawing school was created to provide fresh designs. We used original students' drawings, found in the archives of the Fabric Printing Museum, to design the cover and title pages. Typography and pattern are merged down. The book size is the same as the annual books published by the Mulhouse Industrial Society. Fonts were designed by François Rappo, former typography teacher at the school.

Art Director
Loran Stosskopf
Designers
Alexandre Chapus
Clara Sfarti
Typographer
Loran Stosskopf
Type Designer
François Rappo
Design Agency
Loran Stosskopf
Studio

Publishing Company
Les Presses
du Réel
Clients
Ecole d'Art
de Mulhouse
Les Presses
du Réel

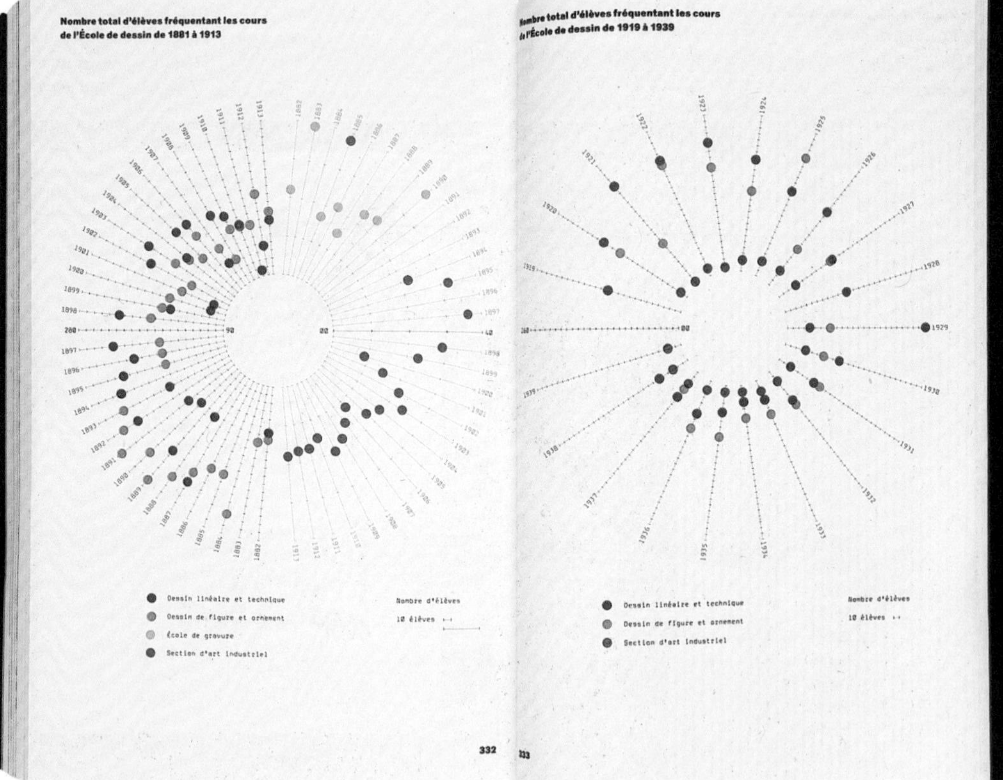

Entire Books
Sánchez/Lacasta
for AECID (Spanish Agency for International Cooperation and Development)

Africa.es: 7 African Views of Spain
This book gathers the works of seven African photographers who offer us their own personal vision of seven Spanish cities. The cover depicts, by means of a photograph, a printed African cloth. Photographs are arranged into files, one for each city.

Design Agency
Sánchez/Lacasta
Client
AECID (Spanish Agency for International Cooperation and Development)

Book Front Covers
Peter Saville Studio
for Penguin Books

The Quantum Universe: Everything That Can Happen Does Happen
Brian Cox and Jeff Forshaw wrote this book to help make the science of quantum mechanics accessible to absolutely anyone who wants to know. Peter Saville Studio advocated the rainbow as the perfect allegorical image for the cover of this book: a rainbow's creation is both a spectacular example of quantum mechanics at work and yet utterly familiar and beautiful to every one of us. Having sourced the rainbow photo from Flickr, the titling was rendered in holofoil to further manifest the division of light. The font was sourced by Paul Hetherington and designed by Radim Pesko and Karl Nawrot.

Art Director
Peter Saville
Designer
Jim Stoddart
Photographer
Tina Negus
Authors
Brian Cox
Jeff Forshaw

Design Agency
Peter Saville Studio
Publishing Company
Penguin Books
Client
Penguin Books
Brand
Allen Lane

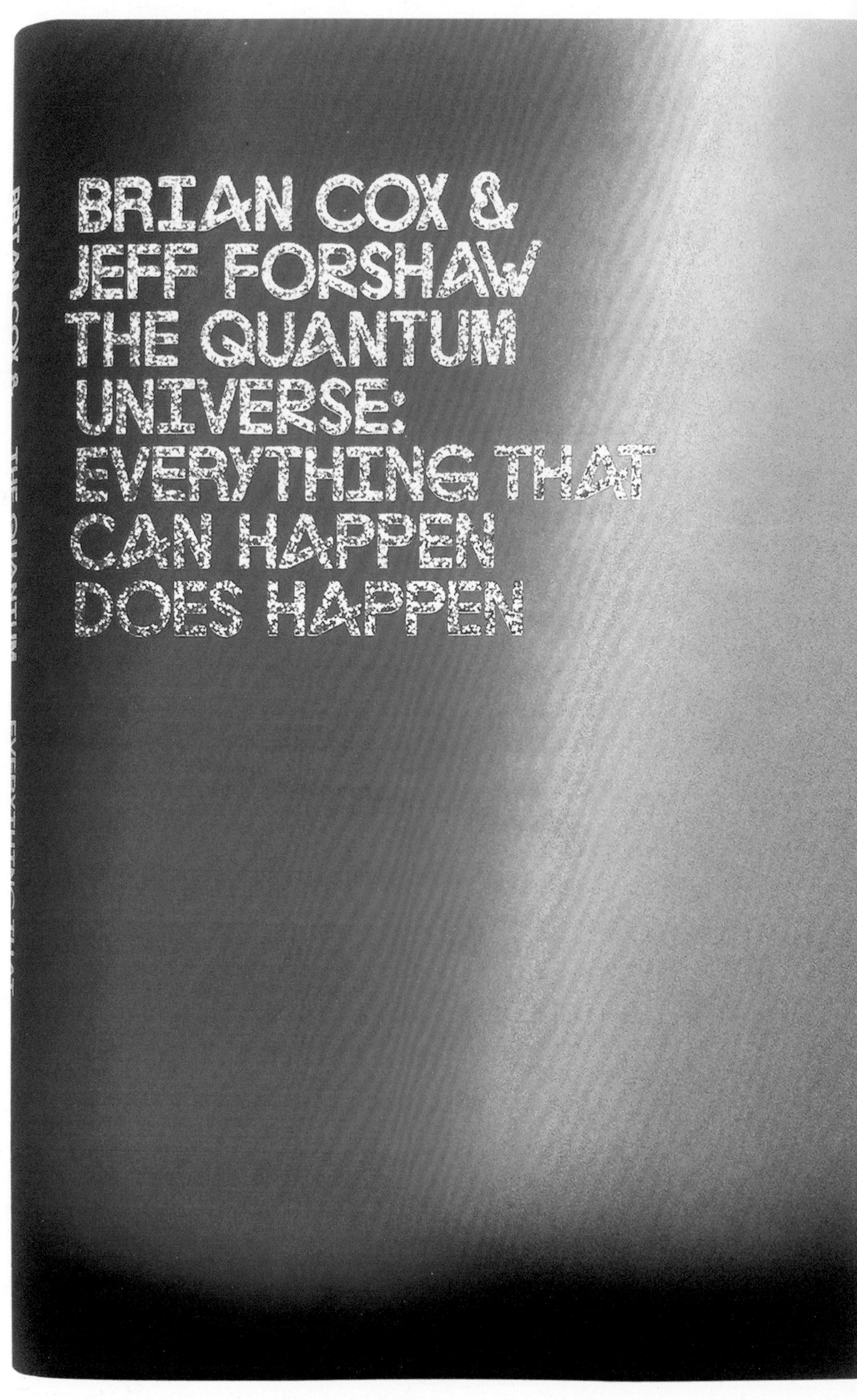

The Days and Nights
of London Now –
As Told by Those Who
Love It,
Hate It,
Live It,
Left It
and Long for It
LONDONERS
CRAIG TAYLOR

Book Front Covers
FUEL Design
for Granta Books

Londoners
Here are the voices of London – rich and poor, native and immigrant, women and men – witnessed by Craig Taylor, who has lived in the city for ten years, exploring its hidden corners and listening to its residents. From the woman who is the voice of the London Underground to the man who plants the trees along Oxford Street; from a Muslim currency trader to a guardsman at Buckingham Palace; from the marriage registrar at Westminster Town Hall to the director of the biggest Bethnal Green funeral parlour; together, these voices and many more paint a wholly fresh portrait of 21st Century London.

Art Director
Michael Salu
Design Agency
FUEL Design
Publishing Company
Granta Publications

Production Manager
Sarah Wasley
Client
Granta Books

Book Front Covers
Vintage Books

Oliver Sacks Series
Oliver Sacks has an unusual talent in that he can understand and piece together the far borderlands of neurological experience and the abnormalities of the human mind. The covers create a tableau to visually mirror Sacks's conceptual ideas of discovery. Arranged together, they create a powerful visual of a human head, while individual covers deftly convey in graphic shorthand the neurological idiosyncrasies Sacks describes in each book. Colour atop, the clinical black and white imagery represents the vibrancy Sacks discovers within his patients; the life that he finds where nothing was meant to exist.

Art Director
John Gall
Designer
Cardon Webb

Client
Vintage Books

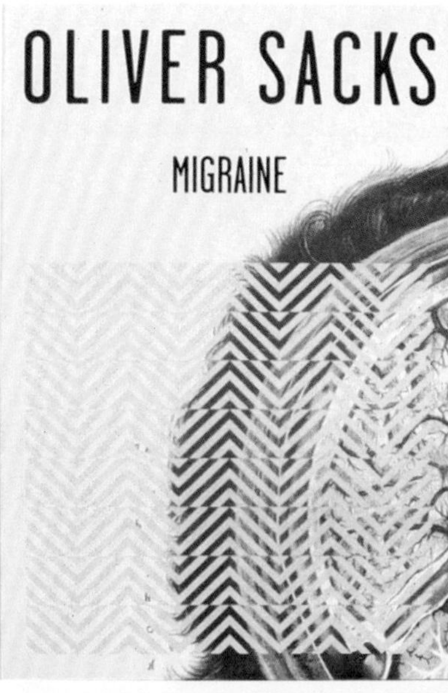

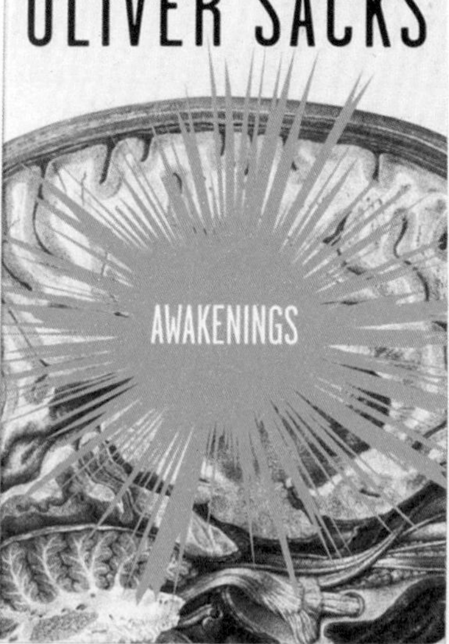

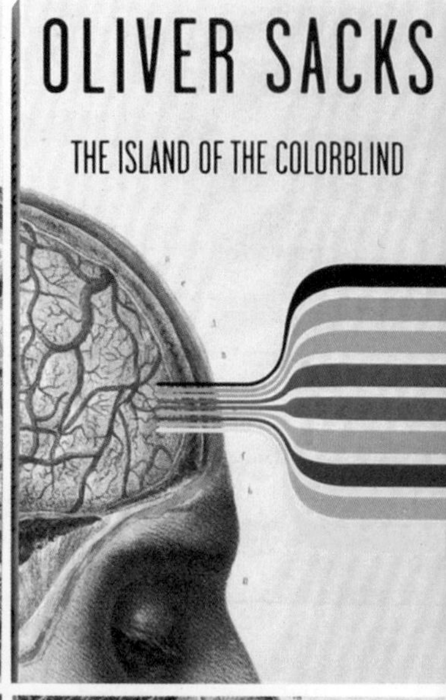

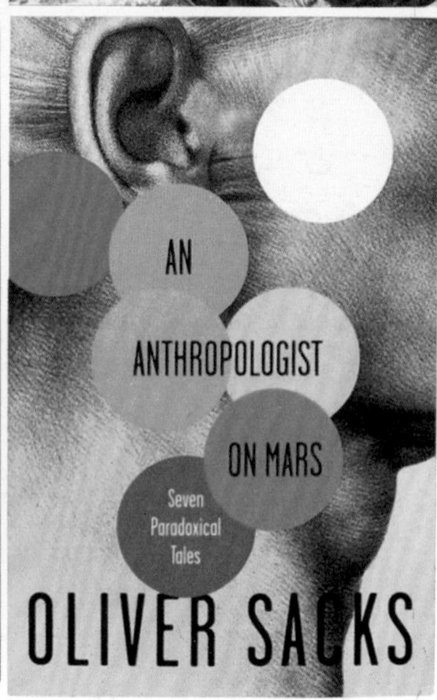

Reading analysis and eye-tracking data
courtesy of Interaction Laboratory,
Centre for Human Computer Interaction,
City University, London.
The Copy Book.
How some of the best advertising writers in the world write their advertising.
TASCHEN

Book Front Covers
This is Real Art
for D&AD & TASCHEN

The Copy Book
This is a book about writing for advertising. Good copy gets read. So the idea behind the cover design is all about reading. We visited an eye-tracking lab and recorded the eye movements of someone reading the book title. This data was overlaid on the title for the final cover design.

Designers
Rick Banks
Paul Belford
Creative Director
Paul Belford
Editor In Charge
Julius Wiederman
Editorial Coordination
Daniel Siciliano Bretas
Editorial Manager
Jana Labaki
Lithography Manager
Horst Neuzner
Project Manager
Natalie Wetherell
Design Agency
This is Real Art
Awards Director
Holly Hall
Clients
D&AD
TASCHEN

Book Front Covers
Paprika Communications
for the Montreal Museum of Fine Arts

The Fashion World of Jean Paul Gaultier: From the Sidewalk to the Catwalk

The Montreal Museum of Fine Arts organised 'The Fashion World of Jean Paul Gaultier: From the Sidewalk to the Catwalk', the first retrospective exhibition to be devoted to the famous fashion designer. The monograph accompanying it was not intended to be a conventional exhibition catalogue, but a true reference on Gaultier's work. The book cover is a nod to the French sailor sweater forever associated with Gaultier. It is enclosed in a navy and white striped plastic slipcase. The cover was designed to produce an optical effect, revealing striking images of the designer and his work as the book is removed from its case.

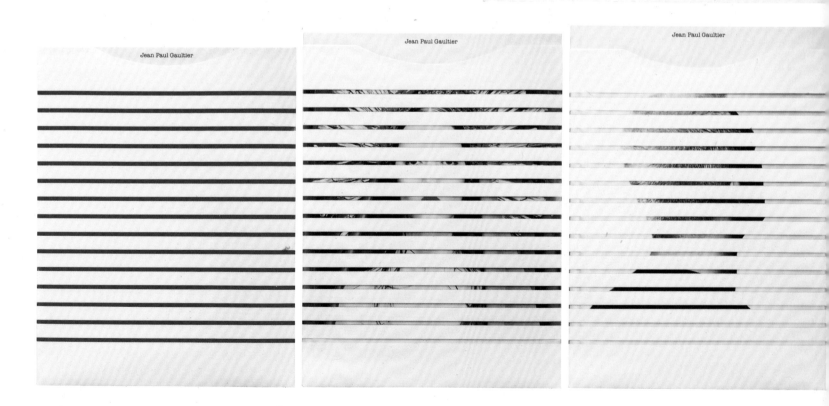

Art Director
René Clément
Creative Director
Louis Gagnon
Account Director
Jean Doyon

Design Agency
Paprika Communications
Client
Montreal Museum of Fine Arts

Jean Paul Gaultier

Jean Paul Gaultier

Jean Paul Gaultier

Jean Paul Gaultier

Dieter Rams:
As Little Design
as Possible

PHAIDON

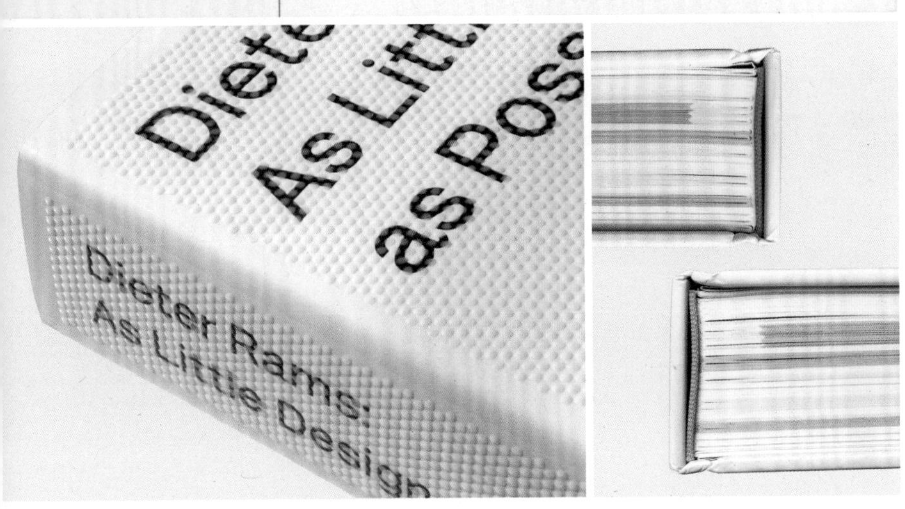

Book Front Covers
Kobi Benezri Studio
for Phaidon Press

Dieter Rams: As Little Design as Possible

A book on Dieter Rams called for a layout that was functional and effortless, yet elegant and developed to the last detail. A sensory mesh is silkscreened using clear ink on the front cover, back cover and the spine. The cover was inspired by Rams's emphasis on materials' tactility (concave stereo buttons, convex calculator smarties, shavers' grips). The mesh can't be seen clearly from a distance so the plastic feeling of it in your hand is a subtle surprise. The only touches of colour are the dark green type and the different coloured head and tail bands. The font, Lettera-Txt, was specially designed for this book.

Art Director
Kobi Benezri
Typographer
Kobi Benezri

Design Agency
Kobi Benezri Studio
Client
Phaidon Press

Jury Foreman
1. Marina Willer
Pentagram London

2. Jason Little
Re

3. Sasha Vidakovic
SVIDesign

4. Steve Edge
Edge Design

5. Garry Blackburn
Rose

6. Afonso Rebelo
de Sousa
adidas

7. Elsie Nanji
Red Lion Publicis
Mumbai

Yellow Pencil in Branding

Brand Experience & Environments
AMV BBDO
for GE

Living Masterpiece
To demonstrate GE's commitment to helping reduce the National Gallery's carbon footprint, we created the world's first 'living' masterpiece. Using over 8,000 plants, we recreated one of the National Gallery's most famous paintings, Van Gogh's 'A Wheatfield, with Cypresses'. Over a four-month period the plants were grown and then installed onto a huge 22-metre site outside the gallery in Trafalgar Square, London. The installation was seen by over 60 million people over six months.

Art Directors
Mike Bond
Antony Nelson
Copywriters
Bern Hunter
Mike Sutherland
Creative Director
Paul Brazier
Director
Jamie Maule-ffinch
Producers
Sam LeGassick
Ciara McGowan
Agency Producers
Chloe Robinson
Adam Walker
Advertising Agency
AMV BBDO
Account Handlers
Amber Glenister
Tim Rogowski
Client
GE

Nomination in Branding

Brand Experience & Environments
Leo Burnett Shanghai
for A.O.Smith China

Sun Bathing

To address the growing consumer trend towards low carbon energy sources, water-heating systems manufacturer A.O.Smith launched a solar powered water heater. In Shanghai, we constructed an A.O.Smith 'sun bathing' consumer experience: a self-contained lightproof shower room, with shower nozzle fitted into the ceiling. It looked just like any other dark tiled bathroom, except that it was rays of sunlight, not streams of water, that flowed through the showerhead. The resulting 23% increase in sales in Shanghai led A.O.Smith to make plans to roll out the 'sun bathing' experience across Nanjing and Hangzhou.

Designers
Xiao Kun
Eiffel Ma
Zhihui Tan
Art Directors
Chocolate Huang
Xiao Kun
Amanda Yang
Writers
Gordon Hughes
Jason Su
Amanda Yang
Creative Directors
Gordon Hughes
Amanda Yang
Forest Young

Production Manager
William Huen
Advertising Agency
Leo Burnett Shanghai
Account Handler
Claire Zhou
Client
A.O.Smith China
Brand
A.O.Smith

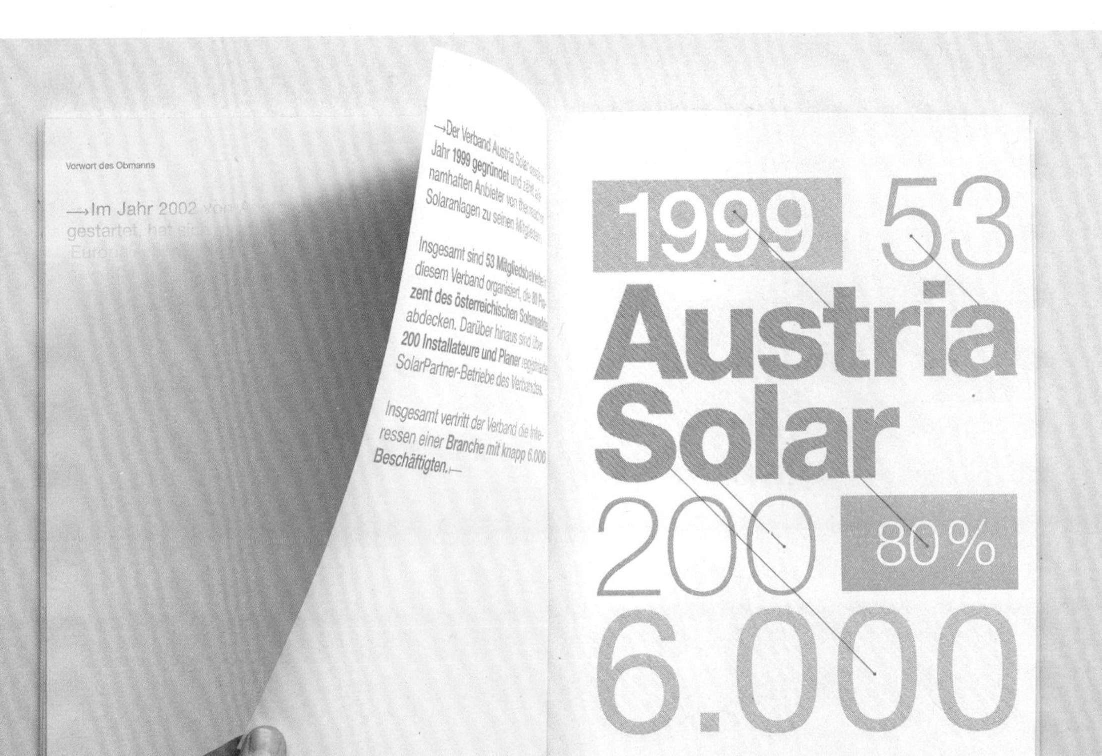

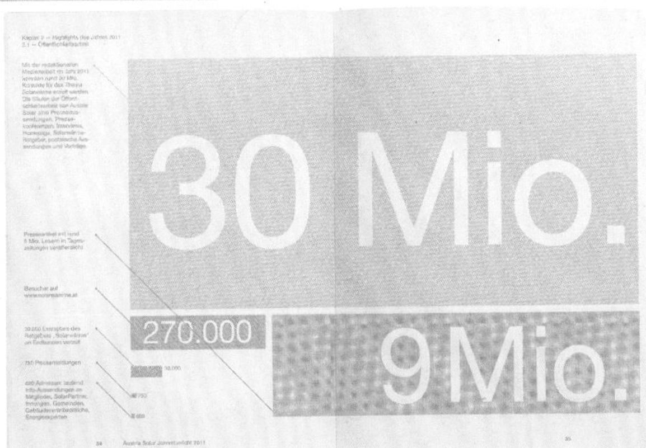

Nomination in Branding

Brand Expression in Print
Serviceplan München
for Austria Solar – Verein zur Förderung der Thermischen Solarenergie

The Solar Annual Report 2011
Solar energy is the main business of our client Austria Solar. That's why we thought about how we could put this energy to paper. The result: the first annual report powered by the sun. Its content remains invisible until sunlight falls on its pages.

Designer
Mathias Nösel
Art Director
Matthäus Frost
Copywriter
Moritz Dornig
Creative Directors
Christoph Everke
Cosimo Möller
Alexander Nagel
Print Producer
Melanie Dienemann

Advertising Agency
Serviceplan München
Account Handler
Diana Günder
Brand Manager
Roger Hackstock
Client
Austria Solar – Verein zur Förderung der Thermischen Solarenergie

Branding Schemes/Small Business
Alphabetical
for Penny Royal Films

Penny Royal Films Identity
Penny Royal is a film production company leading the field in animation, visual effects and direction for film, television and online. The directors of Penny Royal required a timeless identity heralding them as the leading production house for high-end film making. Inspired by the humble penny piece, the logo mark balances their initials, P and R, together to create a priceless monogram in copper foil, which appears at the same size as a penny coin across all applications.

Designers
Tommy Taylor
Robert Young
Design Agency
Alphabetical

Client
Penny Royal Films

Branding Schemes/Small Business
Landor Associates San Francisco
for Advanced Ice Cream Technologies

Bardot Identity
Advanced Ice Cream Technologies, a boutique ice cream purveyor from Mexico, came to us with dreams of sharing its artfully crafted ice cream bars with America. Unfortunately, its name sounded more like an innovator in cold storage than an artisan iced confectionery. Our goal was to create a name, identity and design system that conveyed the unparalleled decadence of its product, creating a sense of luxury, sensuality and desire. The product was delicious; our job was to make it beautiful.

Designers
Lia Gordon
Tosh Hall
Creative Director
Tosh Hall
Writer
Jen Jordan
Illustrator
Michael Goodman
Typographer
Jessica Minn
Design Agency
Landor Associates
San Francisco

Account Manager
Allison Hung
Account Director
Jean-Pierre Sabarots
Client
Advanced Ice Cream Technologies
Brand
Bardot

Branding Schemes/Medium Business
Tommy Li Design Workshop
for The Vietnam Woods

The Vietnam Woods Identity

Although most Vietnamese restaurants use typical Viet elements like a Vietnam hat or the pedicab, Tommy Li Design Workshop presented a Viet restaurant with a new angle. The Vietnam Woods indicates a joyful nature with simple and elegant interior design, which provides a cosy dining place for fast-paced urbanites. To emphasise the French colonial background of Viet cuisine, Tommy designed a few distinctive graphics that integrated some French and Ming Dynasty elements, presenting the integrated image in window-blind graphics.

Designer
Renatus Wu
Art Director
Thomas Siu
Creative Director
Wing Chuen Tommy Li
Design Agency
Tommy Li Design Workshop

Marketing Managers
Lancy Chiu
Sonia Lo
Client
The Vietnam Woods

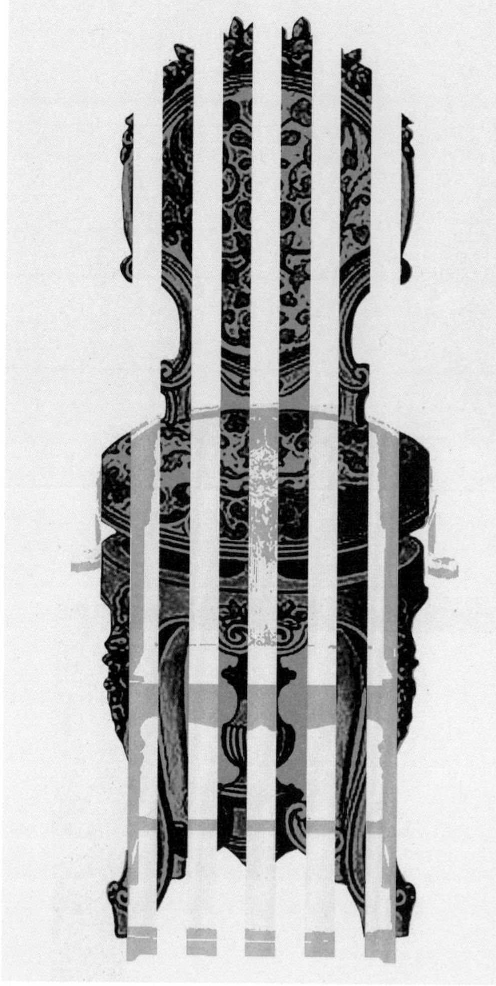

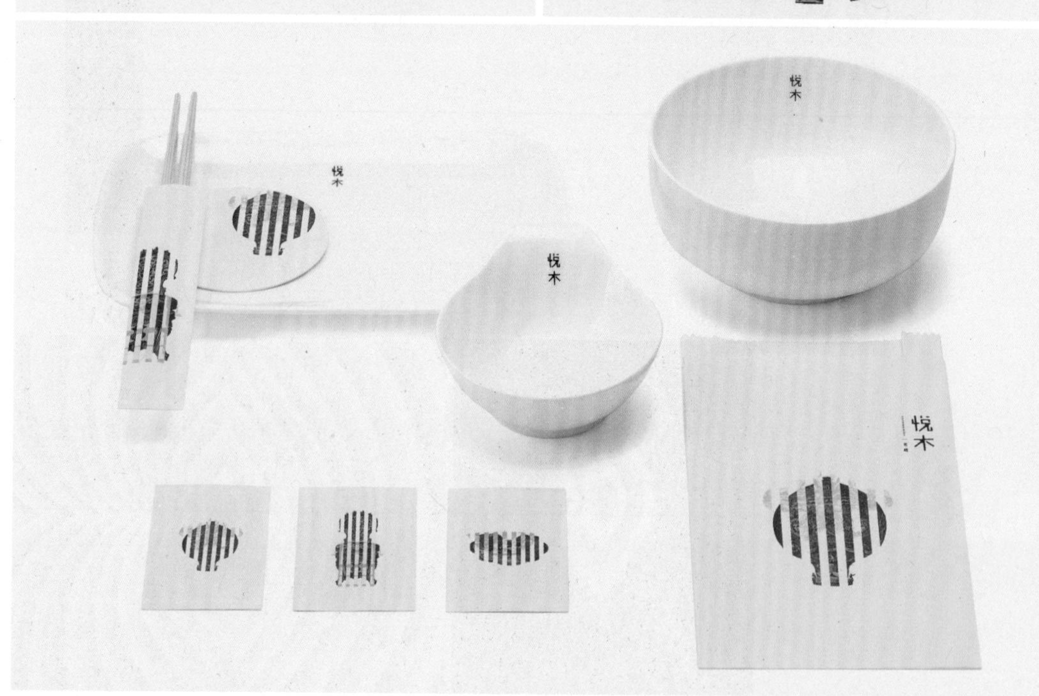

Branding Schemes/Large Business
BRANDHOUSE
for SABMiller

St Stefanus Identity
St Stefanus beer originates from the Augustinian order in Ghent and is brewed according to traditional principles dating back to 1295. All iconography and typography is inspired by the St Stefanus Monastery in Ghent. The logo is based on library manuscripts, and the crown visuals are taken from a stained glass window. The beer is brewed with three different yeasts and refermented in the bottle, enabling consumers to drink at varying stages of maturity according to personal taste. Each bottle of beer has a cellar release date and signature giving consumers the knowledge that they are drinking a truly handcrafted, premium drink.

Designers
Chris Nokes
Hamish Shand
Copywriter
Anna Hamill
Creative Director
David Beard
Photographers
Bronwen Edwards
Hamish Shand
Typographers
Peter Horridge
Hamish Shand
Design Agency
BRANDHOUSE

Project Manager
Crispin Reed
Production Manager
Alexa Cohen
Strategic Directors
Gabriel Collins
Anna Hamill
Brand Managers
Eva Velclova
Nicolas Versloot
Client
SABMiller
Brand
St Stefanus

Branding Schemes/Large Business
Turner Duckworth Design London
& San Francisco
for Levi Strauss

Levi's Identity
Levi's recently moved to a centralised global business model. With that came the need to create a clear and concise visual identity that celebrates Levi's heritage while positioning the brand for the future. We defined the brand architecture and then evolved all of the trademarks and icons that we felt would best communicate its brand story, including the Levi's iconic 'two horse' symbol, leather patch and house mark. The full visual identity system and guidelines were used to brief the global marketing team and regional stakeholders.

Designers
Britt Hull
Brian Steele
Creative Directors
Bruce Duckworth
Sarah Moffat
David Turner
Design Agencies
Turner Duckworth
Design London
& San Francisco

Client
Levi Strauss
Brand
Levi's

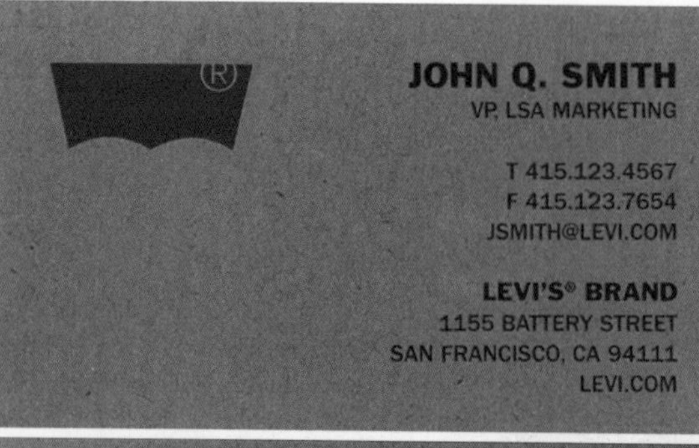

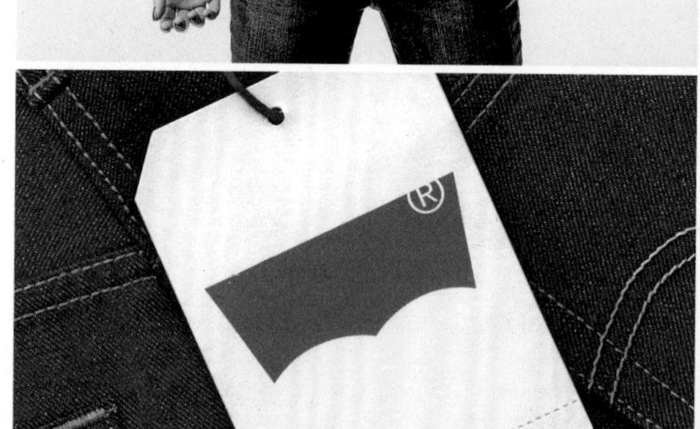

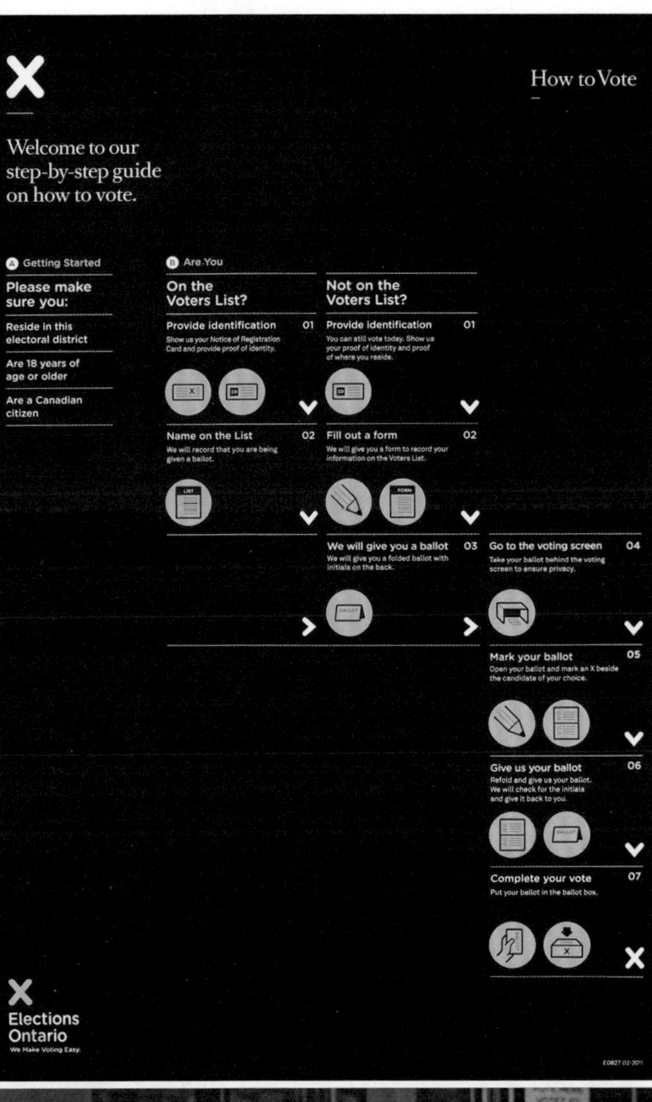

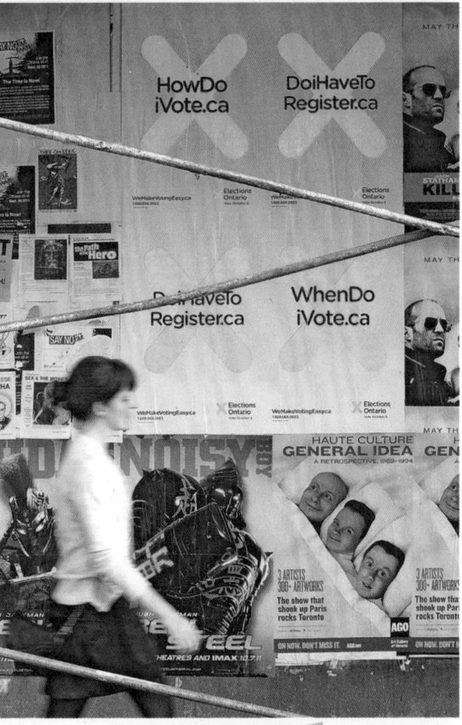

Branding Schemes/Large Business
Leo Burnett Toronto
for Elections Ontario

We Make Voting Easy

Elections Ontario's sole responsibility is to help the people of Ontario vote in Ontario's provincial election. Our sole responsibility was to help it do that. To make voting easy, Elections Ontario had to make all its material friendly and easy to understand, so we gave it a whole new friendly look in both print material and online. We redesigned everything from its voting handbooks and voter information guides, to the voter registration cards so they were easy to read. We extended this ethos to TV, outdoor advertising and a direct mail piece called 'the householder', which was distributed to every household in Ontario.

Designers
Chris Duchaine
Scott Leder
Tracy Ma
Kimberley Pereira
Jeff Watkins
Art Directors
Ron Cueto
David Federico
Brendan Good
Matthew Kenney
Scott Leder
Mike Morelli
Copywriters
Morgan Kurchak
Joy Panday
Len Preskow
Josh Rachlis
Creative Director
Lisa Greenberg
Chief Creative Officer
Judy John
Photographer
Jesse Senko
Illustrator
James Joyce
Creative Technologist
Felix Wardene
Agency Producer
Jacqueline Bellmore
Advertising Agency
Leo Burnett Toronto
Planner
Brent Nelsen
Account Executive
Danielle Iozzo
Account Director
David Buckspan
Client
Elections Ontario

Branding Schemes/Large Business
FutureBrand
for PromPerú & ProInversion

Perú Country Brand
At a time when Peru was showing impressive economic growth, a new national brand was needed. Selected via an international bidding process, a FutureBrand multinational team created a positioning based on three attributes: multifaceted, specialist and captivating. Following the subsequent idea that 'There is a Peru for every one', the new logo is reminiscent of the spiral, a symbol present in many ancient Peruvian cultures. One year after the launch, the brand has over 90% of public acceptance, and is widely present in the country.

Senior Designer
Alejandra Serra
Art Director
Mariano Barreiro
Creative Director
Gustavo Koniszczer
Branding Agency
FutureBrand
Brand Manager
Isabella Falco

Brand Director
Julia Viñas
Marketing Manager
Mariella Soldi
Clients
PromPerú
ProInversion

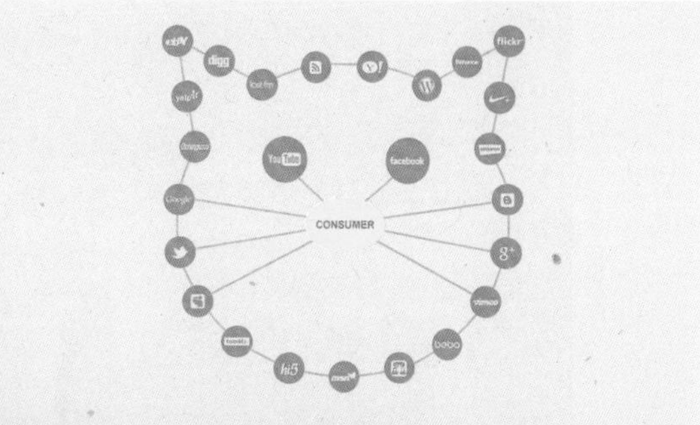

Brand Expression in Moving Image
john st.

Catvertising
In November 2011, john st. released a short promotional video announcing the launch of an entirely new advertising model: Catvertising. The video received a million views in just ten days and made Time magazine's 'Top Ten Everything of 2011' list. Even better, it sparked several new business inquiries and a flood of resumes from cat wranglers, cat whisperers and cat talent coordinators. Interviews are still pending.

Directors
Will Beauchamp
Jamie Cussen
Art Director
Kyle Lamb
Creative Directors
Stephen Jurisic
Angus Tucker
Copywriter
Kurt Mills
Producer
Dale Giffen
Production Company
Aircastle Films
Advertising Agency
john st.
Editing
Relish Editorial
Music Arrangement
Vapor Music
Account Manager
Madison Papple
Client
john st.

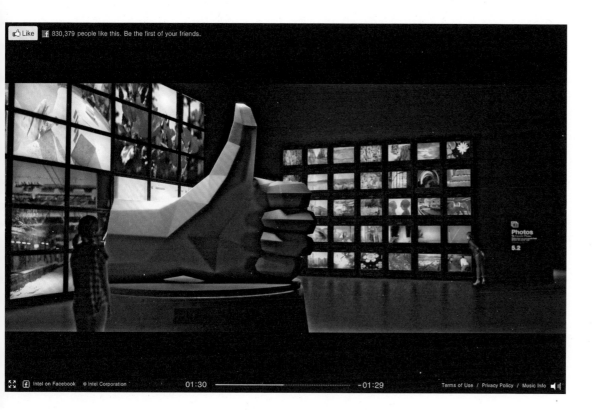

Digital Brand Expression
Projector
for Intel

The Museum of Me
'The Museum of Me' is an interactive online experience that reveals who you are as a reflection of your Facebook activities. We created this personalised museum exhibit to promote Intel's smart new processor.

Designers
Mitsuhiro Azuma
Yuuki Nemoto
Hiroshi Takeyama
Takashi Yasuno
Interactive Designer
Ken Murayama
Art Director
Masanori Sakamoto
Writer
Lilia Silva
Design Director
Toru Hayai
Creative Director
Koichiro Tanaka
Technical Director
Seiichi Saito
Director
Eiji Tanigawa
Programmers
Hirohisa Mitsuishi
Hajime Sasaki
Producer
Satoshi Takahashi
Music Composer
Takagi Masakatsu
Music Producer
Yoko Hata
Video Producer
Keisuke Nishina
Production Manager
Yoshinari Hama
Creative Agency
Projector
Production Companies
DELTRO
MountPosition
Rhizomatiks
TAIYO KIKAKU
Project Manager
Shimpei Oshima
Client
Intel

Digital Brand Expression
Mother London
for Anheuser-Busch InBev

The Green Box Project
The Green Box Project is a global cultural commissioning initiative that will support independent thinkers in creating 1,000 new works of art, fashion, design and music over the next three years. The project helps breaking art out of the gallery and presents a future perspective for outdoor advertising. Each work was experienced via the Beck's Key app, which was activated against physical green boxes located across the US, UK and Italy. In 2011, 30 artists were commissioned to create location-specific works, creating the world's largest networked augmented reality gallery.

Art Directors
Ana Balarin
Hermeti Balarin
Jason Bottenus
Ed Warren
Copywriters
Ana Balarin
Hermeti Balarin
Jason Bottenus
Ed Warren
Creative Directors
Stephen Butler
Mark Waites
Agency Producers
Marta Di Francesco
Nicolyn Marino
Jon Shanks

Producers
Tobias Gefken
Joris Pol
Creative Agency
Mother London
Planners
Matt Hardisty
Katie Mackay
Client
Anheuser-Busch InBev
Brand
Beck's

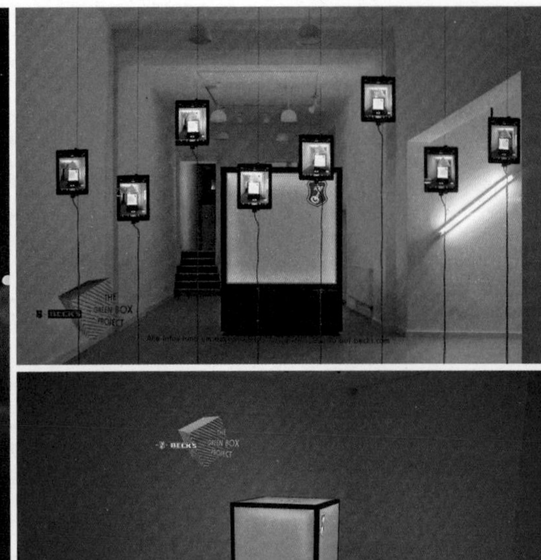

Digital Brand Expression
4creative
for Channel 4

Twist
Twist is Channel 4's cross-platform brand campaign that blurs the line between digital and on-air with audience participation at its heart. Using Channel 4's on-screen stars, participants created on-screen and online fridge magnet poems. Starting out with a batch of spots created by 4creative, viewers were encouraged to create their own personal and topical spots, the best of which were chosen each morning, put online by MPC, and put out on air that night. The campaign also diversified in the second stage, allowing viewers to create musical Twists.

Art Director
Tom Tagholm
Copywriters
Brett Foraker
Tom Tagholm
Creative Director
Tom Tagholm
Director
Tom Tagholm
Producer
Shananne Lane
Post Producer
Tim Phillips
Digital Producer
Tom Powell

Director of Photography
Luke Scott
Editors
Xavier Perkins
Adam Rudd
Advertising Agency
4creative
Post Production
MPC London
Marketing Manager
Rufus Radcliffe
Client
Channel 4

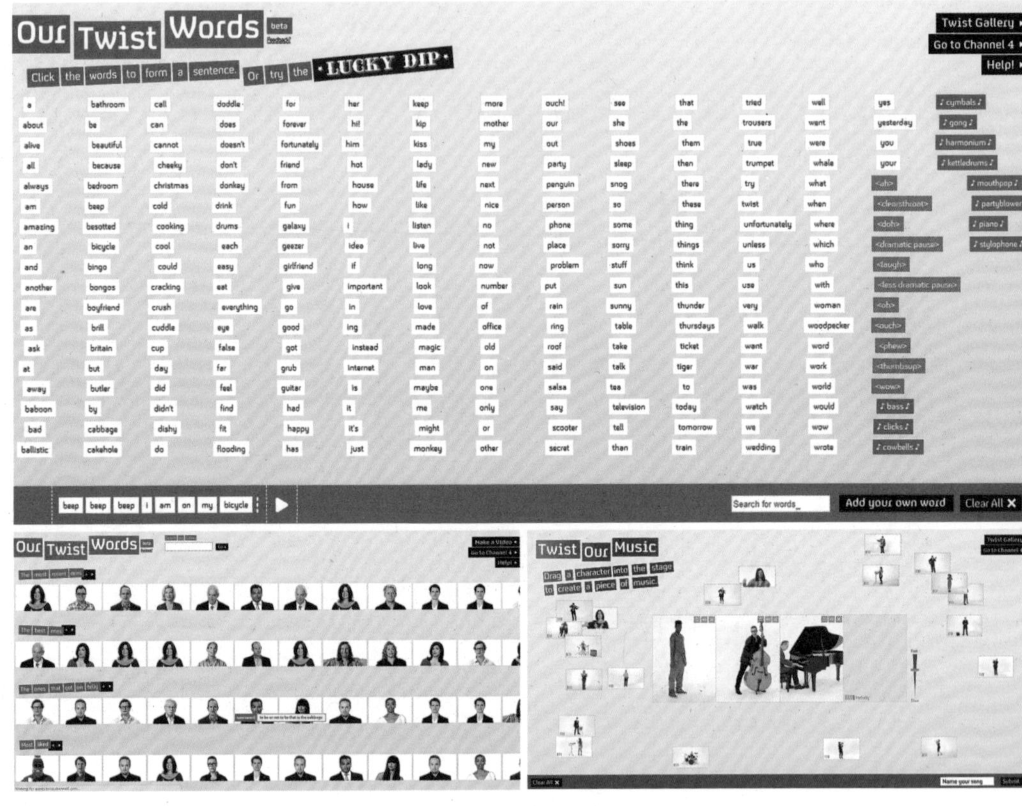

Brand Experience & Environments
Saatchi & Saatchi Beijing
for P&G

Ariel Big Stain
We wanted to demonstrate the cleaning power of Ariel on a scale that nobody had seen before. So we created large outdoor installations, and gave people technology that allowed them to have fun with stains, but also experience the satisfaction of getting rid of them.

Art Directors
Wendy Chan
Fan Ng
Liu Zhong Qing
Ocean Ye
Kobe Yu
Director
Eddy Chan
Copywriters
Wendy Chan
Andy Greenaway
Qi Lin
Creative Director
Wendy Chan
Executive Creative Director
Fan Ng
Interactive Creative Directors
Jonathan Ip
Fan Ng
Chief Creative Officers
Edmund Choe
Andy Greenaway
Producers
Wendy Chan
Dorothy Zeng
Interactive Producers
Tet Chen
Henry Chu
Zhao Yi
Photographer
Chen Xi Qiang
Interactive Production House
pill & pillow
Advertising Agency
Saatchi & Saatchi Beijing
Planner
Angie Ma
Account Executive
Sophia Peng
Account Supervisors
Neel Chaurasia
Ann Jingco
Account Managers
Polly Wang
Sam Wong
Client
P&G
Brand
Ariel

Brand Experience & Environments
DDB Shanghai
for Family Care For Grassroots
Community China

The Keyboard of Isolation
Family Care for Grassroots Community wanted to communicate its call for spending less time online and more time with family in a groundbreaking way. We recorded real scenes in families that had poor relationships due to the overuse of computers. We then made more than 100 figurines crafted in the likeness of these family members, recreating the scenes of their computer addiction. We put these figurines in glass jars arranged in the form of a five-metre-long keyboard. Through the installation we communicated our message: 'Less online time and more family time'.

Art Directors
Jody Xiong
Jack Xuan
William Zhang
Copywriters
Leo Liu
Jody Xiong
Design Director
Jody Xiong
Creative Directors
Michael Dee
Jody Xiong

Production Manager
James Chen
Advertising Agency
DDB Shanghai
Planner
Jenny Liu
Client
Family Care
For Grassroots
Community China

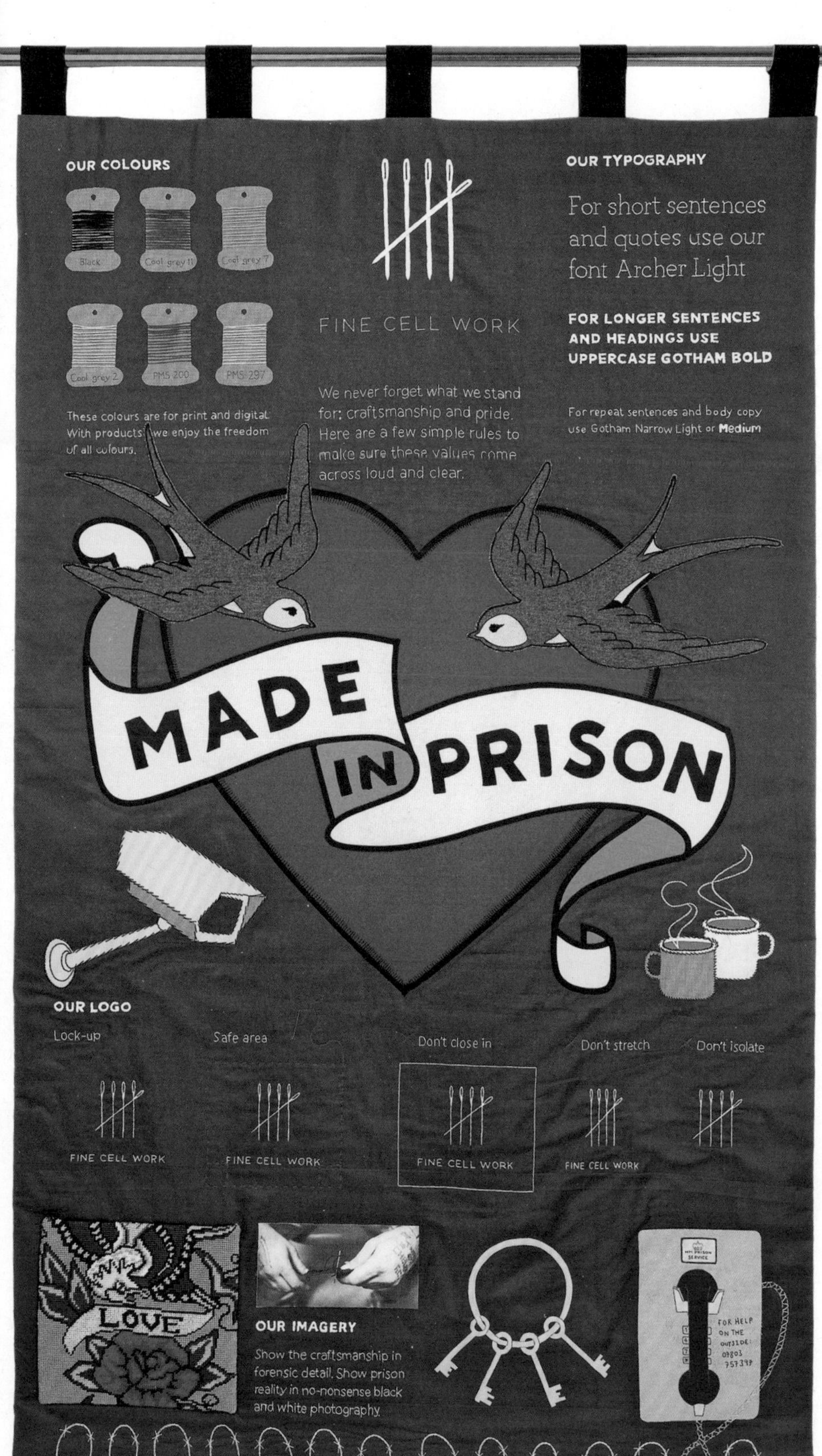

Brand Expression in Print
The Partners
for Fine Cell Work

Fine Cell Work Sewn Guidelines
Fine Cell Work is a prison charity that teaches needlework to inmates. Prisoners can channel their energies creatively and earn money from commissions. With marketing produced by a group of staff and volunteers in one London office, they needed guidance on creating consistent communications. Traditional guidelines weren't appropriate. Instead, a team of volunteers and prisoners helped create a set of guidelines like no other: a piece of embroidery to hang in Fine Cell Work's office. It was not only the rules of their identity but a statement of the passion they put into everything they do.

Senior Designer
Miranda Bolter
Creative Director
Greg Quinton
Embroiderers
Jessica Aldred
Genevieve Brading
HG
Kate Rolison

Design Agency
The Partners
Account Manager
Suzanne Neal
Client
Fine Cell Work

Jury Foreman
1. Simon Waterfall
Fray

2. Vivian Rosenthal
GoldRun

3. Daito Manabe
Rhizomatiks

4. Jiri Bures
Imagination London

5. Geoff Teehan
Teehan+Lax

6. Panja Göbel
Kin Associates

7. Gary Hoff
Cogapp

8. Toshiya Fukuda
777interactive

9. Robert Lindström
North Kingdom

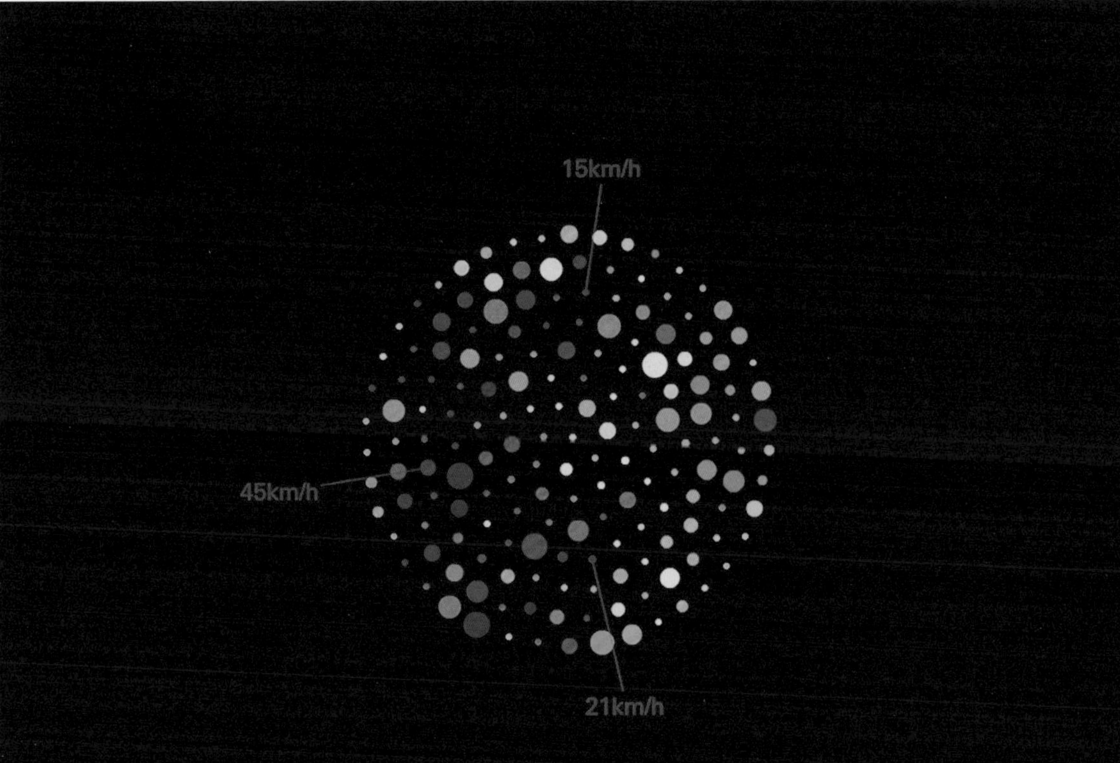

Yellow Pencil in Digital Design

Websites
Dentsu Tokyo
for Honda Motor

Dots Now
Honda Internavi is the world's first car navigation system that recommends routes based on real-time traffic data. The data is collected via the 3G network from other Internavi-equipped Honda vehicles across Japan. To make our target market aware of this highly complex system, the real-time information collected by Internavi was simply and beautifully visualised with a graphic theme of coloured dots and made available to the public online. User activity is reflected online every time they use Internavi. Furthermore, at events we displayed Internavi's multiple data feeds simultaneously on six large screens.

Designer
Takato Kanehara
Art Directors
Yu Orai
Kotaro Yamaguchi
Creative Director
Kaoru Sugano
Director
Toshiyuki Nagashima
Developer
Hiroki Hirano
Flash Developers
Ichitaro Masuda
Yosuke Seki
Creative Technologists
Kaoru Sugano
Kyoko Yonezawa
Information Architects
Tadafumi Nogawa
Aiko Sugawara
Copywriters
Nadya Kirillova
Sotaro Yasumochi
Producers
Haruhiko Ishikawa
Kazushige Mori
Sound Designer
Shuta Hasunuma
Advertising Agency
Dentsu Tokyo
Account Directors
Takao Kaburaki
Takuma Sato
Brand Manager
Takeshi Imai
Marketing Managers
Ken Imamura
Yuichiro Ishido
Akihiro Mikawa
Client
Honda Motor
Brand
Internavi

Yellow Pencil in Digital Design

Digital Design
Dentsu Tokyo
for Honda Motor

Connecting Lifelines
11 March 2011. Eastern Japan is rocked by a massive earthquake and tsunami. Traffic in and out of the region grinds to a complete halt. Within 20 hours, Honda responded to the critical situation by providing road information data collected in real-time via Internavi systems installed in vehicles. This downloadable data that visualises functioning roads on maps spread rapidly. Also, a documentary installation at events showed the spread of road repairs using data and a laser projector. Internavi contributed to rebuilding efforts by literally showing the road to recovery. This work was also nominated in the 'Animation for Websites & Digital Design' category.

Designers
Yusuke Nishida
Kotaro Yamaguchi
Art Directors
Ryuta Modeki
Yu Orai
Creative Director
Kaoru Sugano
Executive Creative Director
Takeshi Imai
Technical Director
Hiroyuki Hori
Programmers
Hiroko Ise
Yuhei Urano
Copywriters
Nadya Kirillova
Sotaro Yasumochi
Producer
Haruhiko Ishikawa
Digital Producer
Seiichi Saito
Creative Technologist
Kyoko Yonezawa

Information Architects
Tadafumi Nogawa
Aiko Sugawara
Software Engineer
Akira Hayasaka
Animators
Akira Hayasaka
Hiroyuki Hori
Sound Designer
Taeji Sawai
Advertising Agency
Dentsu Tokyo
Account Directors
Takao Kaburaki
Takuma Sato
Planner
Keisuke Arikuni
Marketing Managers
Ken Imamura
Yuichiro Ishido
Akihiro Mikawa
Client
Honda Motor
Brand
Internavi

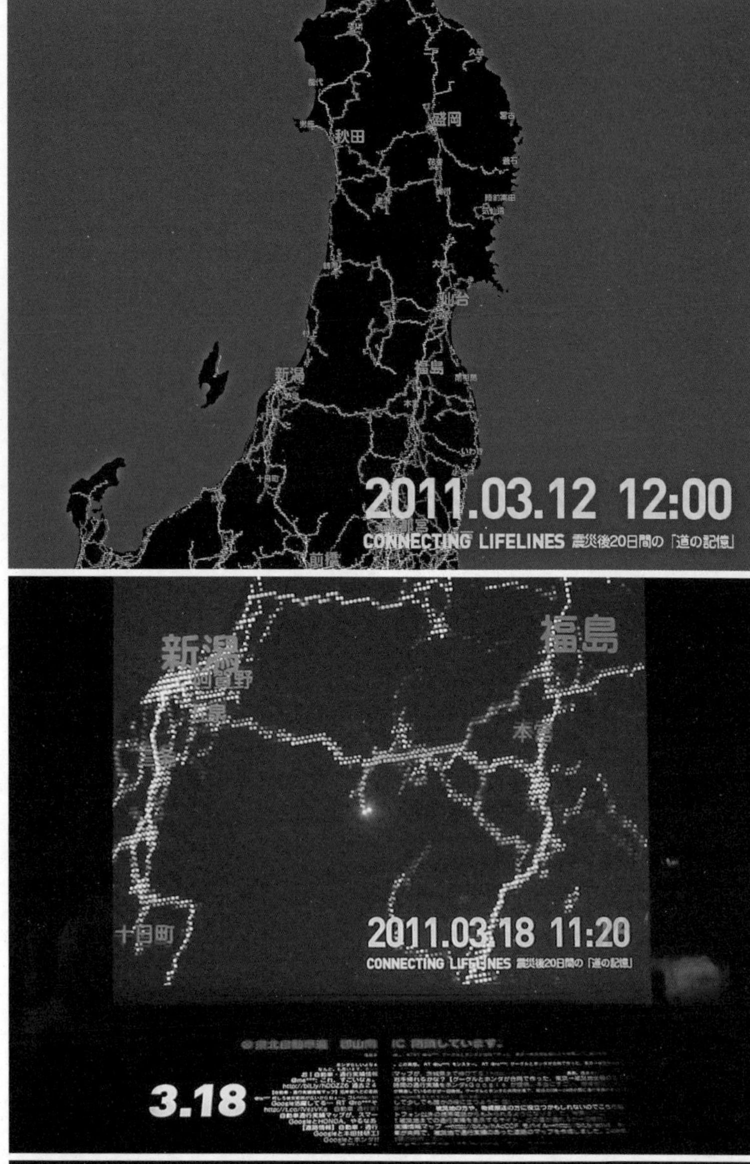

Yellow Pencil in Digital Design

Digital Design
B-Reel
for Hi3G Access

3LiveShop
3LiveShop is the live online shop and customer service solution of mobile service provider 3. This is where users can interact with a real salesperson face-to-face online, while products and service plans are displayed dynamically by a stroke of the salesman's fingertips. We designed a user-friendly interface for both salesperson and customer. The interface and underlying technology were all built in Adobe Flash. The system is capable of detecting multiple fingers and hands at the same time, allowing the salesperson to interact with products on the display while simultaneously recreating the visuals on the customer's screen.

Digital Agency
B-Reel
Client
Hi3G Access

Brand
3

Yellow Pencil in Digital Design

Digital Design
Forsman & Bodenfors
for Västtrafik

Tram Sightseeing App
Tourists in Gothenburg pay good money for sightseeing tours. Unnecessarily, we thought. So we created the app Tram Sightseeing. For the price of a tram ticket, Tram Sightseeing gives you a guided tour. You simply put your headphones on and listen to the app telling you about the sights as they pass outside the tram window. The sights are geotagged and, thanks to the GPS in your phone, the app knows exactly where you are. This work was also selected in the 'Interface & Navigation for Websites & Digital Design' category.

Art Directors
Staffan Forsman
Lars Jansson
Copywriter
Anders Hegerfors
Web Producer
Eva Råberg
Production Company
Mad In Sweden

Advertising Agency
Forsman & Bodenfors
Account Executive
Greger Andersson
Account Manager
Jenny Edvardsson
Client
Västtrafik

Yellow Pencil in Digital Design

Animation for Websites & Digital Design
Mirada
for Google

Rome – 3 Dreams of Black
'Rome – 3 Dreams of Black' is the first WebGL film ever created. It is a lucid dream-like narrative for Danger Mouse, Daniele Luppi, and Norah Jones' album 'Rome'. We used WebGL to weave film with 2D cell and 3D interactive animation, while showcasing the power of modern browsers such as Google Chrome. This interactive music video has been set to the song 'Black'. Since this project was developed from open source technologies, we shared all the code and assets on the site. 'Rome' got two million page views within the first week and 60% of the visitors used Google Chrome.

Technical Director
Mr.doob
Director
Chris Milk
3D Animation
Mirada
Conceptual Design
Mirada
Creative Agency
Google Creative Lab
Digital Production Company
Mirada
Interactive Production Company
North Kingdom
Production Company
@radical.media
Visual Effects Company
Mirada
Music Company
EMI Music
Project Manager
Thomas Gayno
Client
Google

Yellow Pencil in Digital Design

Interface & Navigation for Websites
& Digital Design
DDB Paris
for Greenpeace

A New Warrior
Since 1978, the Rainbow Warrior allowed Greenpeace to gain numerous victories for the protection of our planet. But after so many years in service, Greenpeace needed to replace it. The new Rainbow Warrior is the first ever purpose-built environmental campaigning vessel and will play a key role in Greenpeace's future campaigns. The objective here was to raise funds to finance the construction of the new Rainbow Warrior and involve all the people who want to be part of this story. Our idea was to let people purchase and own a piece of the new Rainbow Warrior by launching an e-commerce website: anewwarrior.com. 400,000 items went on sale, ranging from 1€ to 7,000€. After payment, buyers received a certificate of ownership – thousands of these were posted on social networks, creating a media burst. The new Rainbow Warrior has now been constructed and was officially launched on 14th October 2011.

Art Director
Benjamin Marchal
Executive Creative Director
Alexandre Hervé
Copywriter
Olivier Lefebvre
Advertising Agency
DDB Paris
Production Company
Make Me Pulse
Digital Production Company
Les 84
Visual Effects Company
Virtek
Sound Design
Panarama
Account Managers
Paul Ducré
Xavier Mendiola
Client
Greenpeace

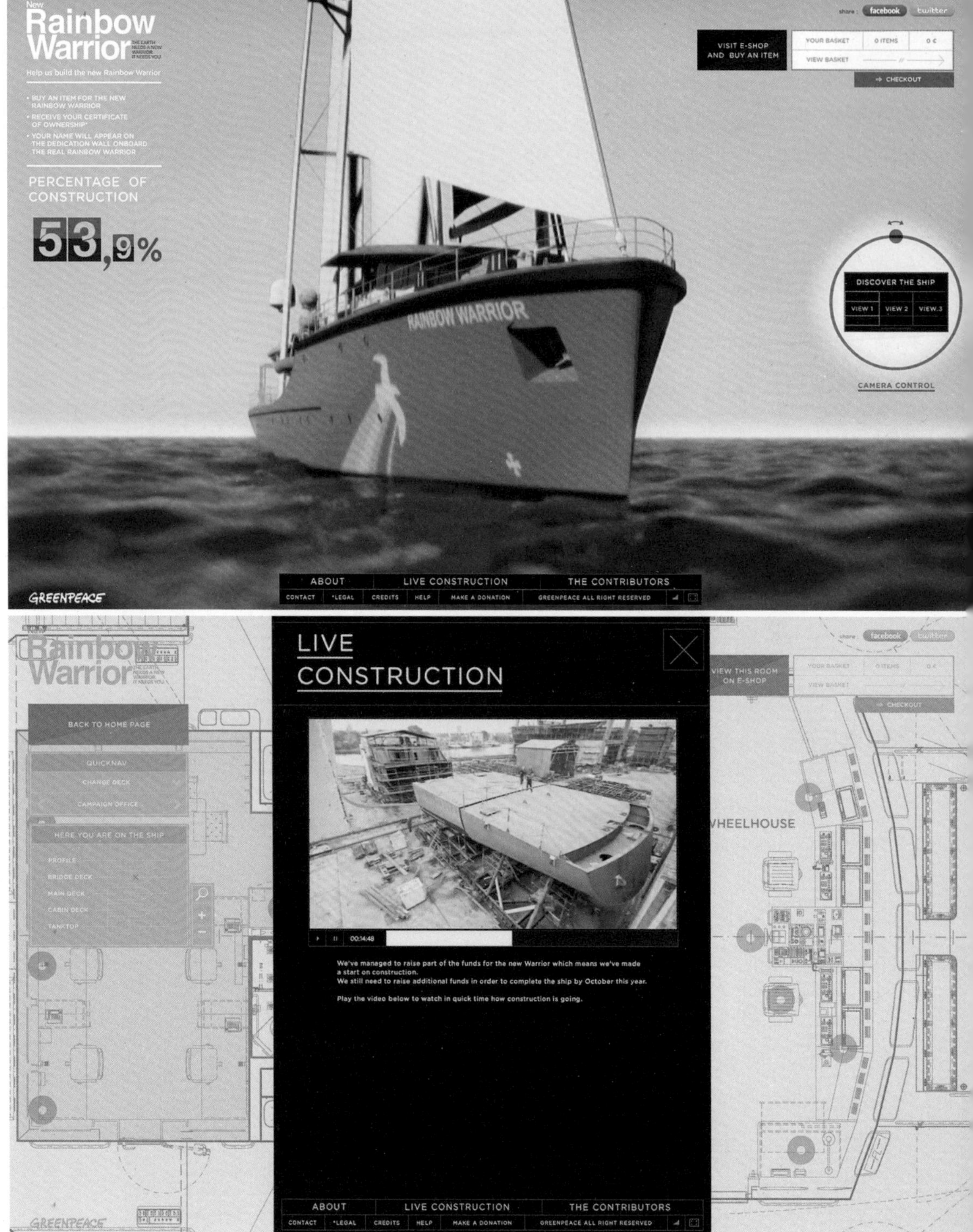

Yellow Pencil in Digital Design

Sound Design & Use of Music for Websites & Digital Design
Tribal DDB Amsterdam
for Philips

Obsessed with Sound
Philips Sound designs products for real music lovers, people to whom every single detail in music matters. Our job was to demonstrate that Philips is 'obsessed with sound' and claim that you can hear every detail with the brand's audio products. We collaborated with the Grammy Award-winning Metropole Orchestra, and recorded a specially composed piece in 55 separate music tracks. On the site, which can be accessed through Facebook, viewers can experience the music video as a whole, played by the entire orchestra, and are invited to single out each musician to hear every detail. This work was also nominated in the 'Interface & Navigation for Websites & Digital Design' category.

Music Composers
Berend Dubbe
Sonja van Hamel
Designer
Robbin Cenijn
Art Director
Bart Mol
Executive Creative Director
Chris Baylis
Technical Director
Jan Willem Penterman
Creative Technologist
Ian Bauer
Orchestra Conductor
Jules Buckley
Director of Photography
Matias Boucard
Copywriter
Pol Hoenderboom
Director
Rob Chiu
Agency Producer
Jeroen Jedeloo
Executive Producers
Marcel Kornblum
Mark Pytlik
Editor
Nikaj Gouwerok
Music Arrangement
Metropole Orchestra
Music Remix
MassiveMusic
Digital Agency
Tribal DDB Amsterdam
Production Company
Stink
Project Managers
Richard Land
Christy Wassenaar
Planners
Niels Bellaar
Henk Rijks
Account Director
Sandra Krstic
Client
Philips

Nomination in Digital Design

Websites
PARTY
for Menicon

Magic
This is the brand site for Magic, Menicon's new contact lens series, which uses a new technology that enables the super thin 1mm container. We created the total brand communication, including the product name, packaging, communication design, PR solutions and adverts. The website runs a continuous reel of brand imagery. It includes information on the product, illustrations inspired by the product design and even several games featuring scenery composed of contact lenses.

Designers
Ayano Higa
Toshimitsu Tanaka
Art Director
Yoshihiro Yagi
Creative Director
Morihiro Harano
Technical Director
Qanta Shimizu
Interactive Director
Yusuke Kitani
Director
Takuya Demura
Programmers
Jun Kuriyama
Naoko Umeta
Flash Developers
Shinya Kobayashi
Shozo Okada
Minoru Sako
Qanta Shimizu
Miyuki Tsumagari

Copywriter
Haruko Tsutsui
Agency Producers
Tetsuji Nose
Koji Wada
Producer
Mitsuru Yamamori
Photographer
Takaya Sakano
Photography Director
Osamu Koiso
Sound Designer
Toru Sasaki
Advertising Agencies
Dentsu
Drill
PARTY
Production Company
Geek Pictures
Client
Menicon

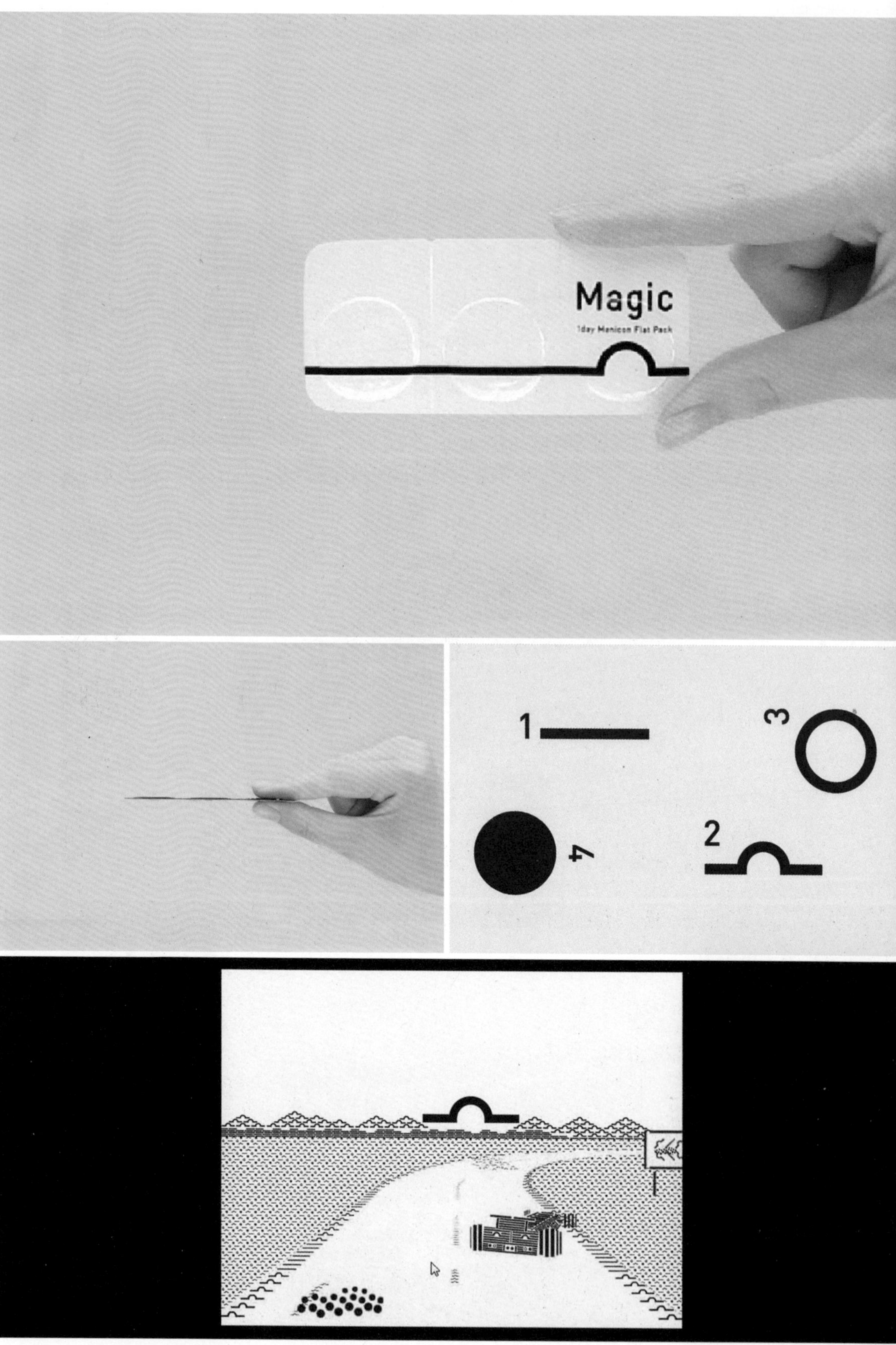

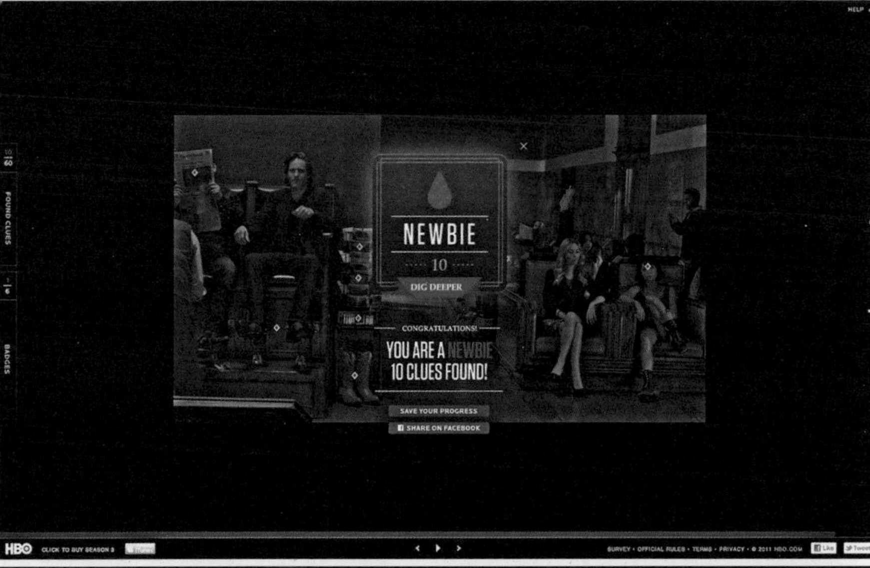

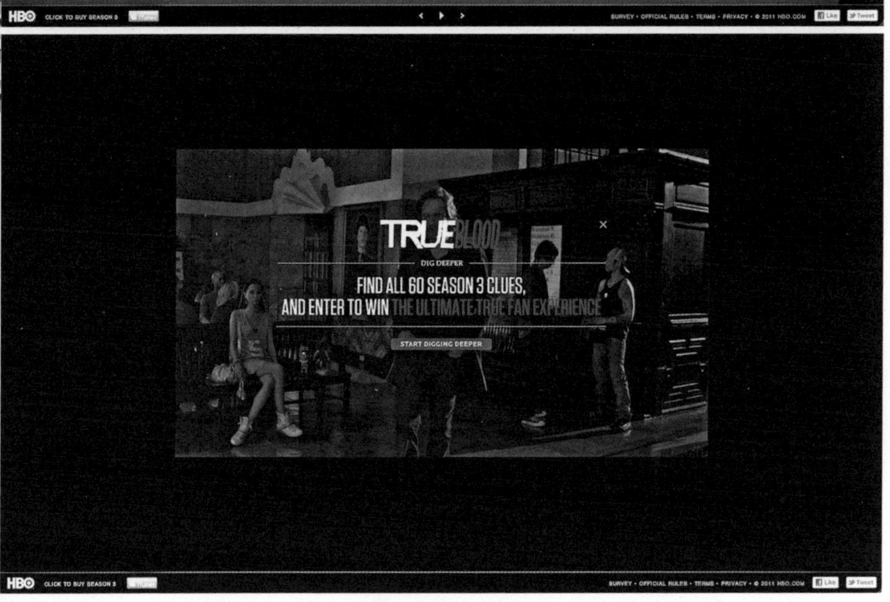

Nomination in Digital Design

Digital Design
BBDO New York
for HBO

Dig Deeper
'Dig Deeper' is an interactive film experience promoting HBO's hit series 'True Blood' season three on DVD, Blu-ray, and digital download. Our objective was to challenge fans to prove just how well they know their 'True Blood', by embedding clues in what at first appears to be a traditional commercial. It leads fans to a campaign site, where a custom player allows users to zoom deep into the film. There, fans discover 60 taggable clues embedded in the action. The more clues they tag, the more badges they earn that post directly to Facebook, elevating their fan status. This work was also selected in the 'Interface & Navigation for Websites & Digital Design' category.

Art Director
Marcel Yunes
Executive Creative Directors
Greg Hahn
Mike Smith
Chief Creative Officer
David Lubars
Director of Integrated Production
Brian DiLorenzo
Copywriter
Rick Williams
Director of Photography
Christopher Soos
Production Designer
Timothy Moen
Head of Interactive Production
Niklas Lindstrom
Director
Tim Godsall
Producer
Colleen O'Donnell
Line Producer
Mala Vasan
Executive Producers
Diane Hill
Holly Vega
Content Producer
Nicholas Gaul
Editor
Geoff Hounsell
Advertising Agency
BBDO New York
Production Company
Biscuit Filmworks
Digital Production Company
B-Reel
Editing
Arcade Edit
Sound Design
henryboy
Mixing
Sound Lounge
Account Executives
Leland Candler
Tara Deveaux
Austin Scherer
Client
HBO
Brand
True Blood

Nomination in Digital Design

Digital Design
Projector
for Intel

The Museum of Me
'The Museum of Me' is an interactive online experience that promotes Intel's smart new processor. Users create their own museum exhibits by connecting to Facebook. By visualising elements such as your close friends and most frequently used words, 'The Museum of Me' reveals who you are as a reflection of your Facebook activities. This virtual museum experience links to the core value of Intel: creating innovation in our digital lives from the inside. Users shared their museum photos on Facebook, which created a buzz and spread the campaign.

Designers
Mitsuhiro Azuma
Yuuki Nemoto
Hiroshi Takeyama
Takashi Yasuno
Interactive Designer
Ken Murayama
Design Director
Toru Hayai
Art Director
Masanori Sakamoto
Creative Director
Koichiro Tanaka
Technical Director
Seiichi Saito
Programmers
Hirohisa Mitsuishi
Hajime Sasaki
Writer
Lilia Silva
Music Composer
Takagi Masakatsu

Director
Eiji Tanigawa
Producer
Satoshi Takahashi
Video Producer
Keisuke Nishina
Music Producer
Yoko Hata
Production Manager
Yoshinari Hama
Creative Agency
Projector
Production Companies
DELTRO
MountPosition
Rhizomatiks
TAIYO KIKAKU
Project Manager
Shimpei Oshima
Client
Intel

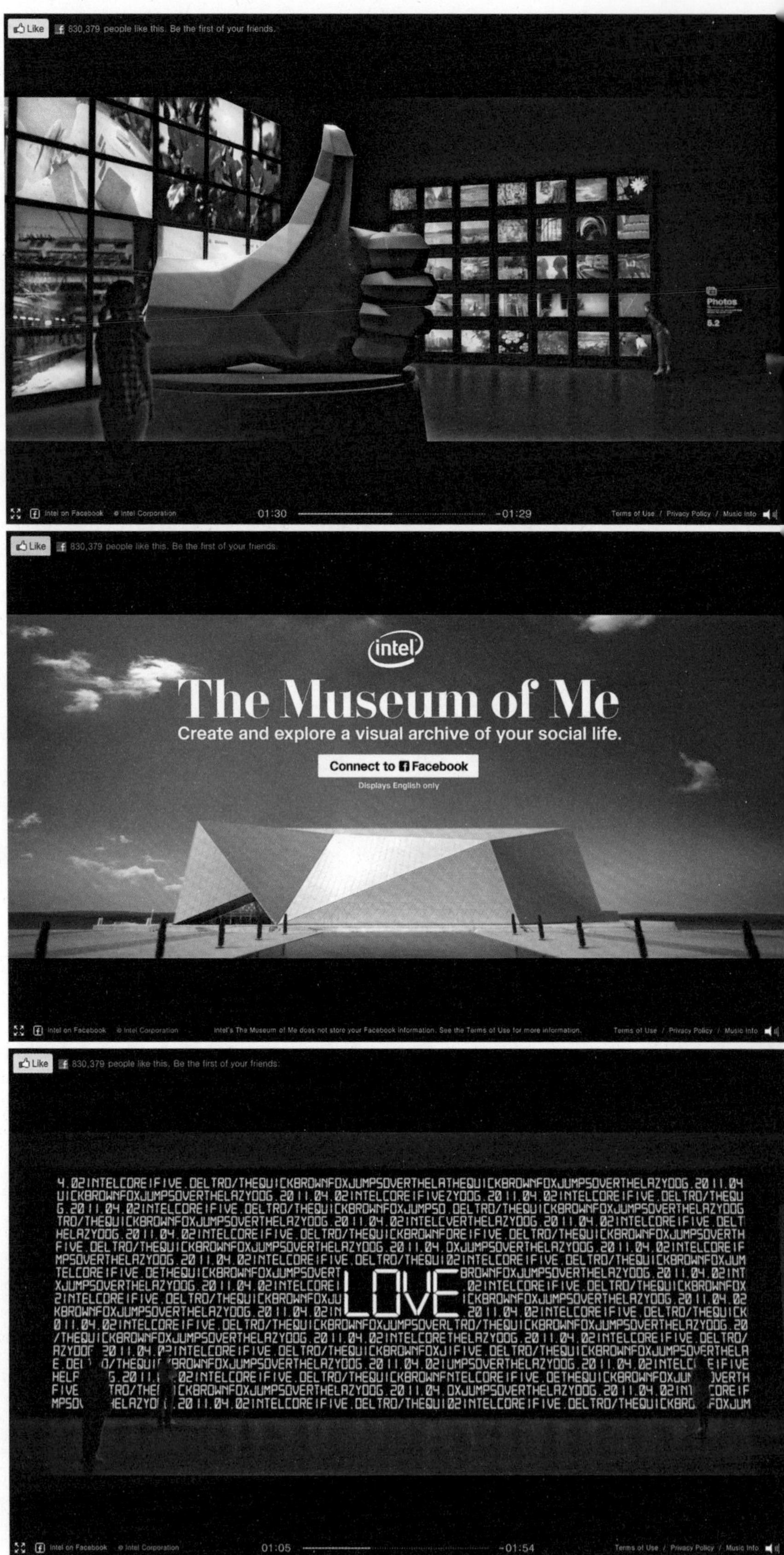

Nomination in Digital Design

Digital Design
Imagination
for Royal Dutch Shell

Pearl GTL Interactive Model
This interactive experience highlighted Shell's innovation in gas-to-liquids technology at the inauguration of the Shell Pearl GTL plant in Qatar, the crowning achievement of the Shell and Qatar Petroleum partnership. A 4.5m^2 scale model expresses the impressive size of the facility, the largest of its kind worldwide. A total of 1,600 Perspex blocks represent various technologies within the plant. Beneath these, 15 LCD screens play high-definition animations describing the GTL process. Twelve touchscreens surround the model presenting films and animations, helping audiences to explore the plant's story, its products and its people.

Creative Agency
Imagination
Client
Royal Dutch Shell

Brand
Shell

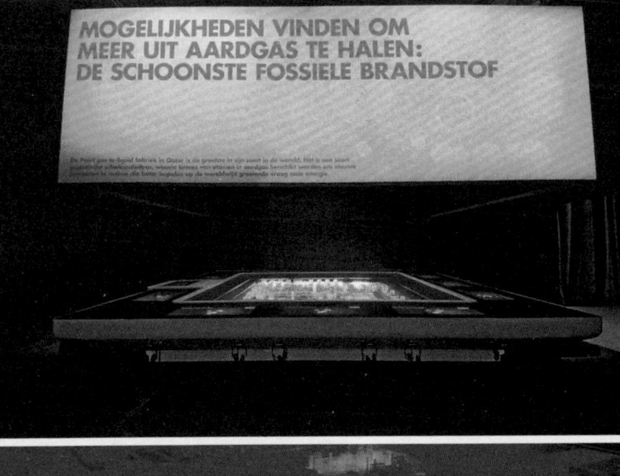

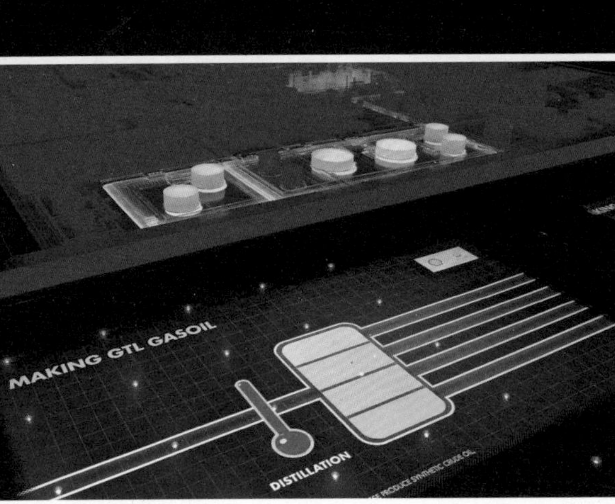

Nomination in Digital Design

Interface & Navigation for Websites
& Digital Design
The Mill Digital

Mill Touch

The Mill Digital has developed Mill Touch, an interactive, living portfolio, which visually illustrates its ever-expanding body of work. Executed from concept to launch in-house by our digital team, it is a rear projected, 5x3-foot interactive touch screen panel made entirely of switchable glass. Delve behind the scenes in real-time, perform text searches within the portfolio, explore content by manipulating a multi-million particle fluid simulation or use the virtual 'lens' apparatus to see before and after footage in real time. Come to our office and try it for yourself!

Designers
Audrey Davis
John Koltai
Design Director
Jeff Stevens
Art Director
Bowe King
Creative Director
Sheena Matheiken
Creative Technologists
Andrew Bell
Hai Nguyen
Colourists
Josh Bohoskey
DJ Miranda

Information Architect
Chris McKenzie
Digital Development Director
Andy Orrick
Producer
Kei Gowda
Executive Producer
Bridget Sheils
Digital Agency
The Mill Digital
Client
The Mill Digital

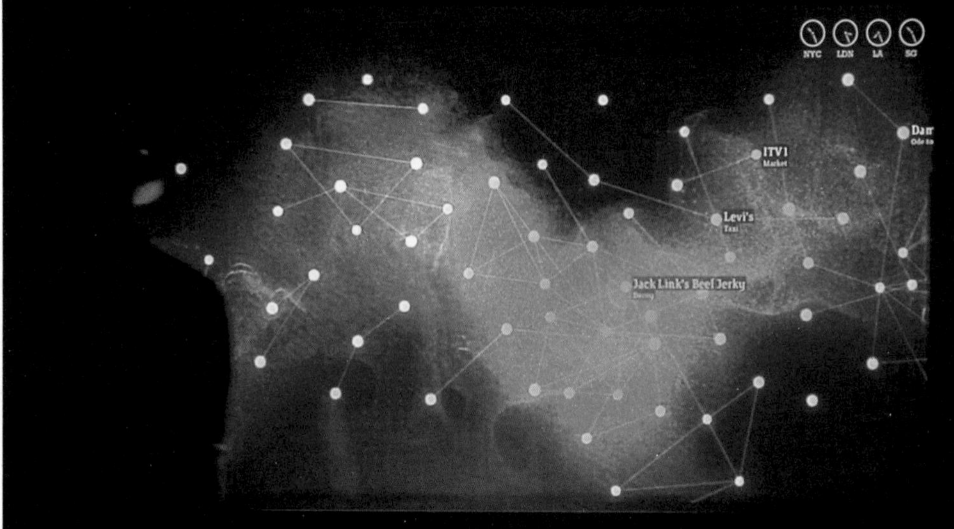

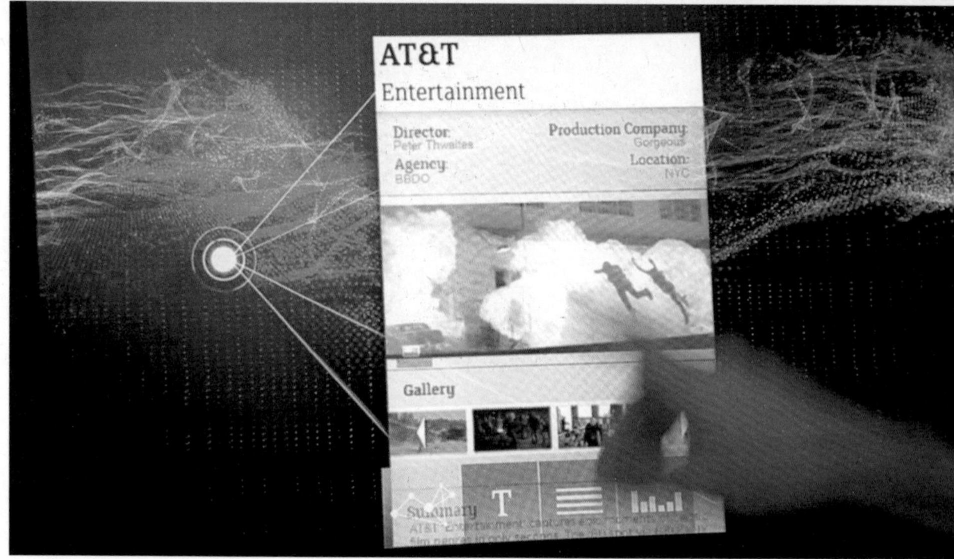

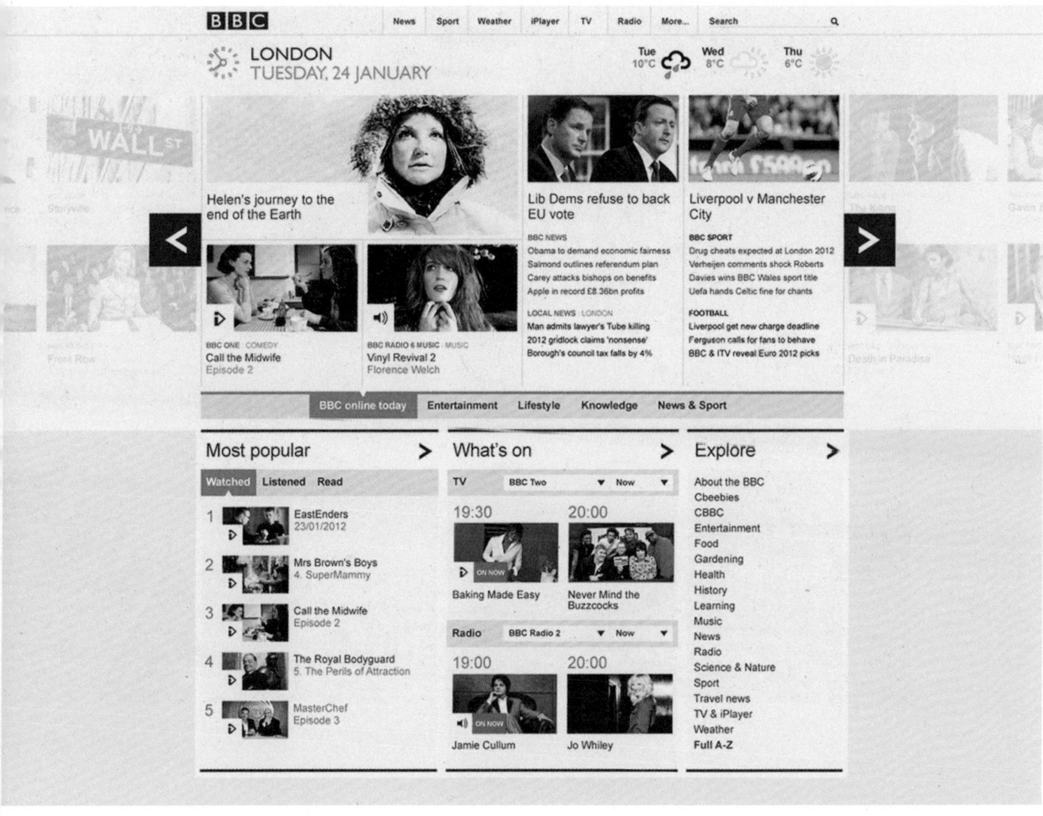

Websites
BBC

BBC Homepage
The homepage of the BBC website attracts nine million unique visitors each week. A dynamic carousel parades the breadth of BBC content, with simple filters enabling users to tailor the page based on their interests. Sliding 'drawers' reveal more or less detail from showcases of the most popular content, making it easier for people to explore the wealth of BBC Online.

Designer
Audrey Rapier
Senior Designer
David Ullman
Creative Director
Steve Gibbons
Executive Editor
Clare Hudson

Research Manager
Davie Taylor
Head of Product
James Thornett
Marketing Manager
Becky Bradley
Client
BBC

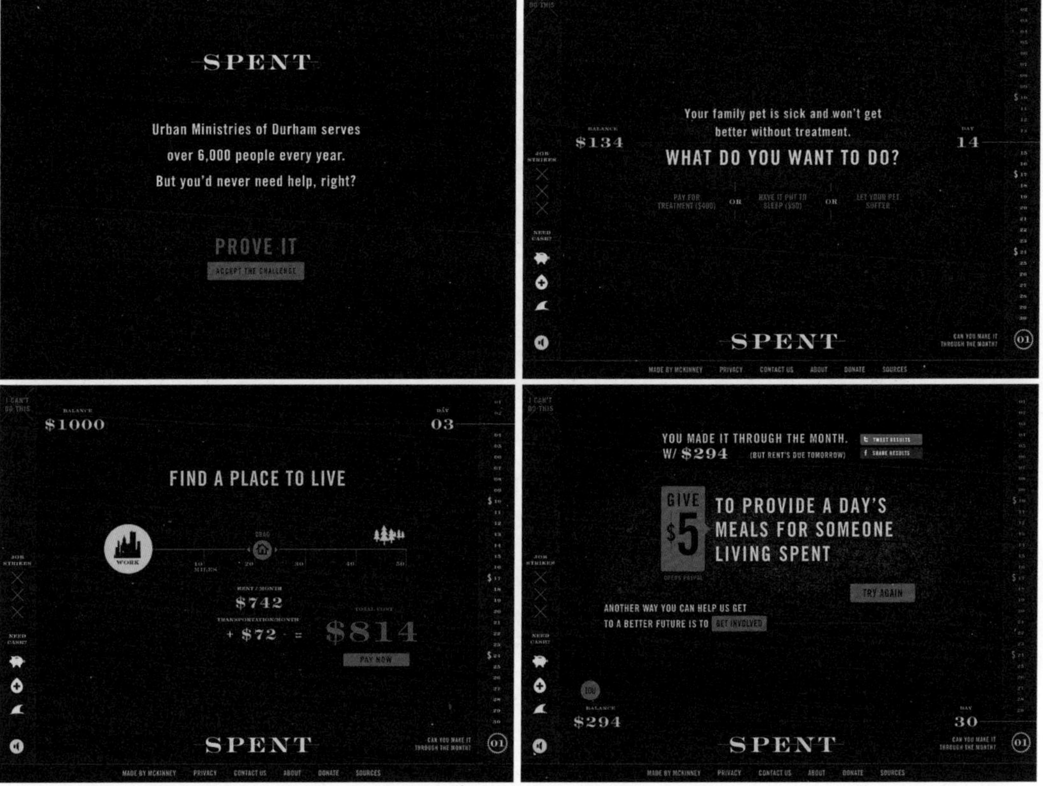

Websites
McKinney
for the Urban Ministries of Durham

Spent
'Spent' is a game that makes you prove you can pull yourself out of poverty. Make it through the month on $1,000, while facing some tough choices. Feed your family or keep the lights on? Lose a day's pay or send your sick child to school? In some challenges, you can avoid losing money by posting Facebook updates like: 'I can't pay all my bills this month. Can I borrow some money?' and 'We got evicted. Can we crash at your place?' Can you make it through the month and keep your dignity intact? Find out at playspent.org.

Designer
Able Parris
Art Director
Nick Jones
Chief Creative Officer
Jonathan Cude
Copywriter
Jenny Nicholson
Editor
Joseph Levinski
Agency Producer
Carmen Bocanegra
Programmers
Josh Barber
Matt Hisamoto
Illustrator
Karla Mickens

Sound Designer
Roger Lima
Communications Director
Janet Northen
Advertising Agency
McKinney
Project Manager
Lizzie Ruiz
Account Executive
Joel Richardson
Client
Urban Ministries of Durham

Websites
kempertrautmann
for edding International

Wall of Fame
For its 50th anniversary, pen manufacturer edding wanted to market to illustrators and creatives in the place where they spend most of their time: online. The Wall of Fame is an interactive live drawing board that features ten pens with which you can immortalise yourself. In the first six months alone, a collaborative piece of art was created consisting of more than 150,000 drawings by people from over 150 different countries. And the wall continues to grow.

Art Directors
Simon Jasper Philipp
Florian Schimmer
Stefan Walz
Associate Art Directors
Tobias Lehment
David Scherer
Creative Directors
Christoph Gähwiler
Simon Jasper Philipp
Stefan Walz
Gerrit Zinke
Copywriters
Christoph Gähwiler
Michael Götz
Samuel Weiß
Advertising Agency
kempertrautmann
Animation
LIGA_01
COMPUTERFILM
Interactive & Digital Production Company
demodern | digital design studio
Post Production
flavouredgreen/
PX Group
Sound Design
Supreme Music
Account Managers
Andrea Bison
Elisabeth Einhaus
Niklas Kruchten
Client
edding International

Digital Design
DDB Paris & unit9
for MINI France

MINI Maps
MINI France was launching its Facebook page and asked us to advise on the best way to bring to the network its global strategic idea: the art of entertainment. MINI France didn't want more passive likers; rather likers who were happy to be there, to share, and to be part of a vibrant and active digital MINI community. The MINI France likers we wanted were brand lovers, willing to discover a fan page offering a 'Be MINI' experience. MINI's Facebook page was to be like the MINI itself – nonconformist, eccentric and, above all, fun.

Art Directors
Alexis Benbehe
Pierre Mathonat
Motion Designer
Julien Taillez
Executive Creative Director
Alexandre Hervé
Technical Directors
Brice Aubert
Michael Paquereau
Copywriters
Alexis Benbehe
Pierre Mathonat
Digital Agency
unit9
Advertising Agency
DDB Paris
Communications Director
Estelle Suzenne
Account Executives
Paul Royer
Vincent Vannha
Account Manager
Florent Depoisier
Account Director
Vincent Léorat
Client
MINI France

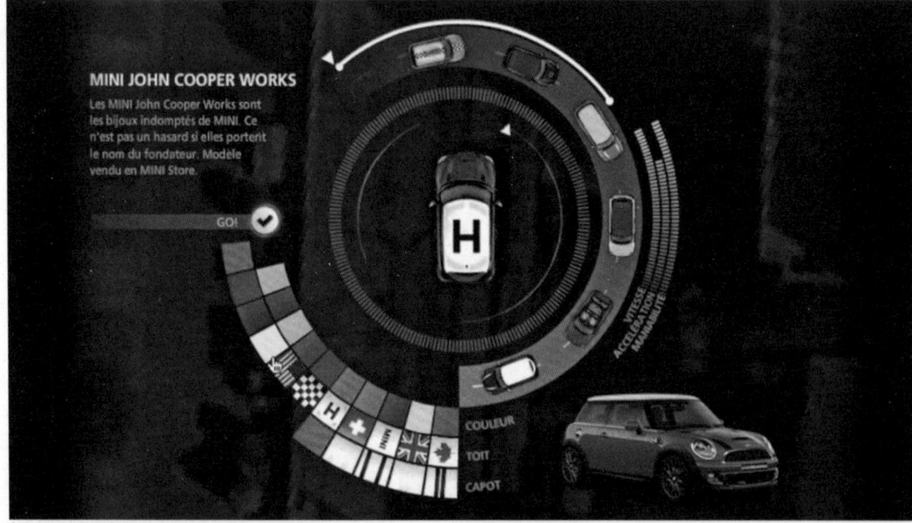

iPad 9:41 AM

theguardian Comment 5/8 Issues Sections Settings

Economic growth follows demand, so give people cash to spend

The chancellor's gamble hasn't paid off. An urgent shift in priorities is now needed if Britain isn't to slip back into recession

Simon Jenkins

Forget "It's the economy, stupid." Switch to "It's demand, stupid." If the 20th-century revolution in economics meant anything, it was that unless people go out and buy things, there will be no jobs, no incomes, no growth. Governments can worry about borrowing, lending, inflation, fiscal rectitude, whatever until the cows come home - but without demand there is recession.

This week's economic statistics are crystal clear. The recovery of the British economy from the recession of 2009-10 is not on track. Government policy is not going according to plan. Forecasts of a year ago, of slow but firm growth, have turned false. Banks have returned to seeking foreign funk-holes. Disposable income in the UK is at its lowest peacetime level since 1921. Services have now followed manufacturing and construction into stagnation. Shopping receipts fell last month by 0.6%, with the retail consortium reporting that "on all fronts, it is not good news".

« Previous 4/8
Children face one hammer blow after another | Polly Toynbee

» Next 6/8
Mark Lawson on Roald Dahl and JK Rowling

Economy
More in this issue

National
Rising prices could signal end of 'cheap chic'

Uplifting - or a vision of hell? Giant shopping centre opens its doors

Financial
US urges European leaders to avert crash

Comment
Economic growth follows demand, so give people cash to spend

On the website

12 September 2011
Alistair Darling's anger hardly seems to matter as the gloom descends

11 September 2011
Banking compound interests | Editorial

iPad 9:41 AM

theguardian Features 5/12 Issues Sections Settings

The Tate Modern at 10

It started with Louise Bourgeois's giant sculpture. Since then, Tate Modern's Turbine Hall has been filled with a succession of spectacular slides, sunsets and visions of the apocalypse. As the gallery turns 10, we talk to the artists who took on the commission of a lifetime

Olafur Eliasson's "The Weather Project" in the Turbine Hall of the Tate Modern. Photo by Dan Chung

Digital Design
The Guardian Design Team
for Guardian News & Media

Guardian iPad Edition
The brief for the Guardian iPad edition was to 'put the paper on the iPad'. It completely reworks the experience of reading a newspaper on an iPad. We created something that is a new proposition, different to other digital offerings. It works in either orientation and nothing is sacrificed. Instead of it being based on lists, breaking news, and the fastest updates, it's designed to be a more reflective, discoverable experience. This gives it the potential to have a design capable of responding to the news – just like a newspaper.

Designer
Barry Ainslie
Senior Designer
Andy Brockie
Creative Director
Mark Porter
Lead Developers
David Blishen
Martin Redington
Producer
Luke Hoyland
Executive Producers
Tara Herman
Katherine Le Ruez
Production Editor
Jack Arnott
Launch Editor
Merope Mills
Design Consultants
Matt Jones
Jack Schulze
Product Manager
Jonathon Moore
Design Group
The Guardian
Design Team
Client
Guardian News
& Media

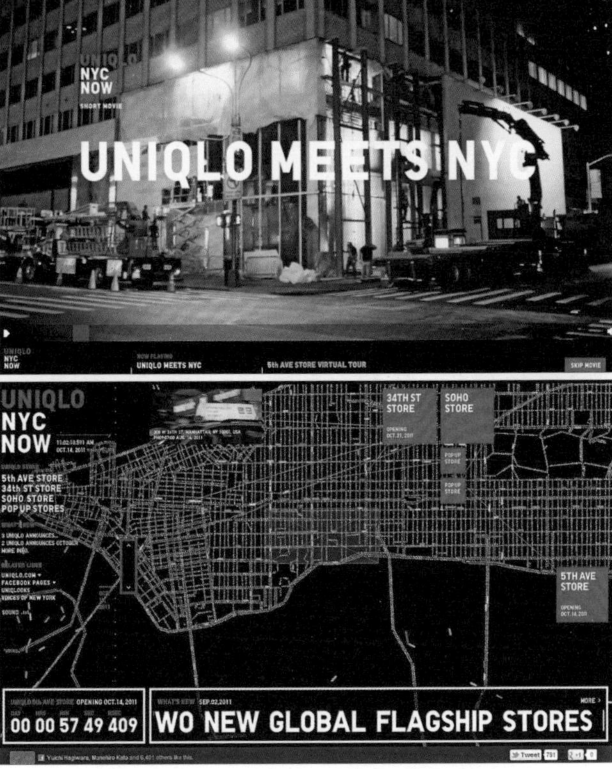

Graphic Design for Websites & Digital Design
mount
for UNIQLO

UNIQLO NYC Now
For the opening of UNIQLO's global flagship store, we sent a filmmaker to New York City to start shooting footage of day-to-day life in the city. He filmed how advertising for UNIQLO gradually increased in NYC every day. He stayed for 90 days, filming more than 4,600 cuts; of these, close to 1,000 were uploaded to the website, which was updated daily. 'NYC now' was adopted as a phrase to represent UNIQLO's spread all over the city through a variety of real-time information uploaded daily along a timeline on our website.

Designers
Hiroka Hasegawa
Jeong-ho Im
Art Director
Jeong-ho Im
Creative Director
Jeong-ho Im
Technical Director
Takeshiro Umetsu
Programmer
Hidekazu Hayashi
Flash Programmer
Takeshiro Umetsu
Producer
Yuichi Hagiwara
Design Agency
mount
Project Manager
Yuichi Hagiwara
Planners
Jeong-ho Im
Takeshiro Umetsu
Client
UNIQLO

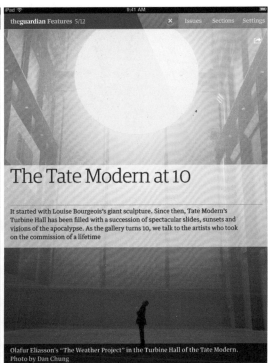

1

2

3

4

5

6

7

Jury Foreman
1. Angus Hyland
Pentagram London

2. David Tanguy
Praline

3. Martina Keller
Keller Maurer Design

4. Felix Ng
SILNT

5. Kate Moross
Breed London

6. Eike König
HORT

7. Lynn Trickett

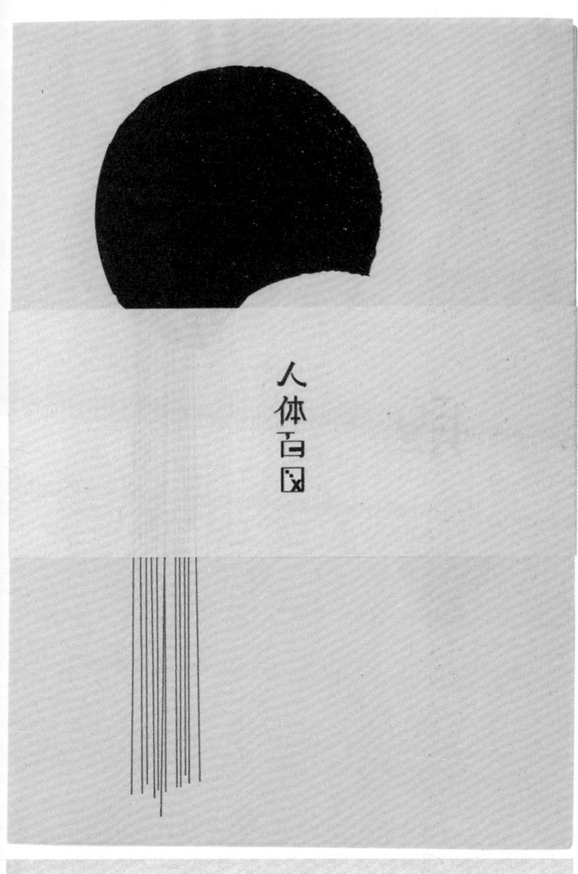

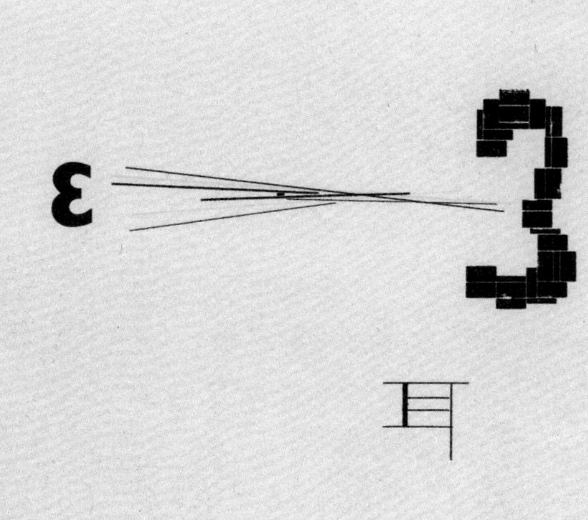

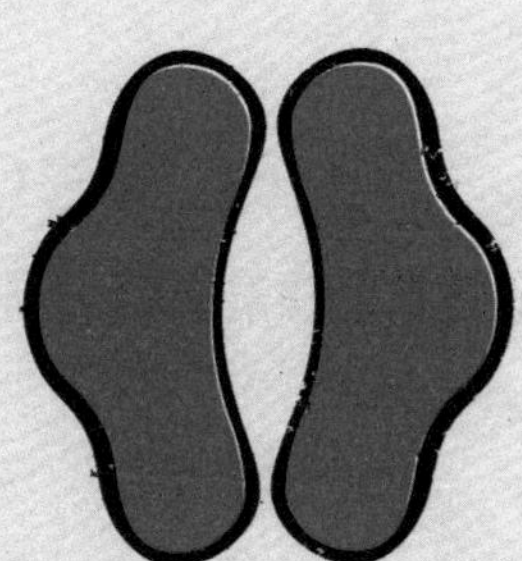

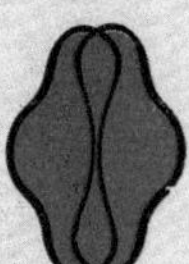

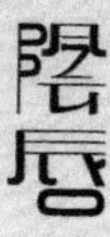

Yellow Pencil in Graphic Design

Catalogues & Brochures
Nippon Design Center
for GALLERY LETA

100 Graphics of Anatomy

The human body is a mystery. Everyone has one, and yet there are elements that remain unexplained. '100 Graphics of Anatomy' was made by pairing a word with a part of the body and a related visual image. While probing the line where the connection between the meaning and the form approaches the nonsensical, these works emphasise the beauty, danger and ambiguity of the body as a form. The collection of graphics on straw paper may make the subject an even greater mystery than it was originally, yet we hope you enjoy these interpretations of the body.

Designer
Daigo Daikoku
Art Director
Daigo Daikoku
Typographer
Daigo Daikoku

Design Agency
Nippon Design Center
Client
GALLERY LETA

Yellow Pencil in Graphic Design

Stamps
Gummo
for TNT Post

City of the Netherlands:
The Future in Motion
The Dutch Post Office asked Gummo to design a series of stamps on the theme of 'City of the Netherlands: The Future in Motion'. The stamps would celebrate Dutch architecture and feature five as yet unconstructed architectural projects. To show the plans to their full potential, we decided to transcend the limitations of a stamp's small, 2D surface by adding a 3D layer. We achieved this through the use of augmented reality. All you had to do was hold the stamp in front of a computer's webcam to see the buildings come to life in their full majesty and catch a glimpse of the Netherlands' future.

Designers
Mark Kuiper
Ingrid van der Meulen
Creative Directors
Hajo de Boer
Onno Lixenberg
Advertising Agency
Gummo
Digital Production Company
DPI Animation House
Account Handler
Sterre Jongerius
Client
TNT Post

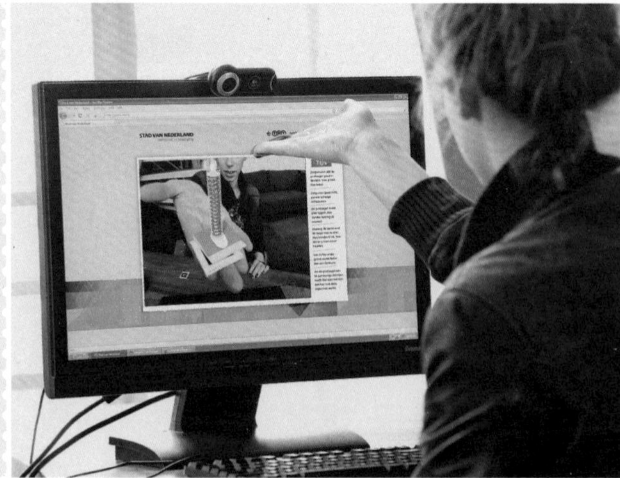

Yellow Pencil in Graphic Design

Posters
Ogilvy Malaysia
for Lego Singapore

Lego Posters

Using 97,096 pieces of Lego and three outdoor poster sites, we built posters entirely out of Lego. When viewed from the right position, each image within the frame formed a seamless continuation of the scene outside. Each poster also featured colourful Lego creatures interacting with the environment: the perfect way to show just how much more fun the world is with Lego.

Designers
Nicholas Foo
Too Jun Jie
Darshan Kadam
Inessa Loh
Art Director
David Stevanov
Creative Director
Eric Yeo
Executive Creative Directors
Robert Gaxiola
Gavin Simpson
Eugene Wong

Illustrators
Greg Rawson
David Stevanov
Andrew Tan Tsun Wen
Copywriters
Ross Fowler
Greg Rawson
Advertising Agency
Ogilvy Malaysia
Client
Lego Singapore
Brand
Lego

Nomination in Graphic Design

Integrated Graphics
Cosmos
for Koyama Kanamono

Architectural Hardware Company Graphics
Our aim was to present architectural hardware in a new and engaging way through striking illustrations of Koyama Kanamono's products. The graphics express quality through their weight and simplicity. Moreover, the textured, monotone finish used for the parts recreates the properties of the metal it represents. Overall, the graphics refresh perceptions of architectural hardware and promote Koyama Kanamono's goods as top-quality.

Designers
Atsushi Sugiyama
Yoshiki Uchida
Art Director
Yoshiki Uchida
Creative Director
Yoshiki Uchida

Design Agency
Cosmos
Client
Koyama
Kanamono

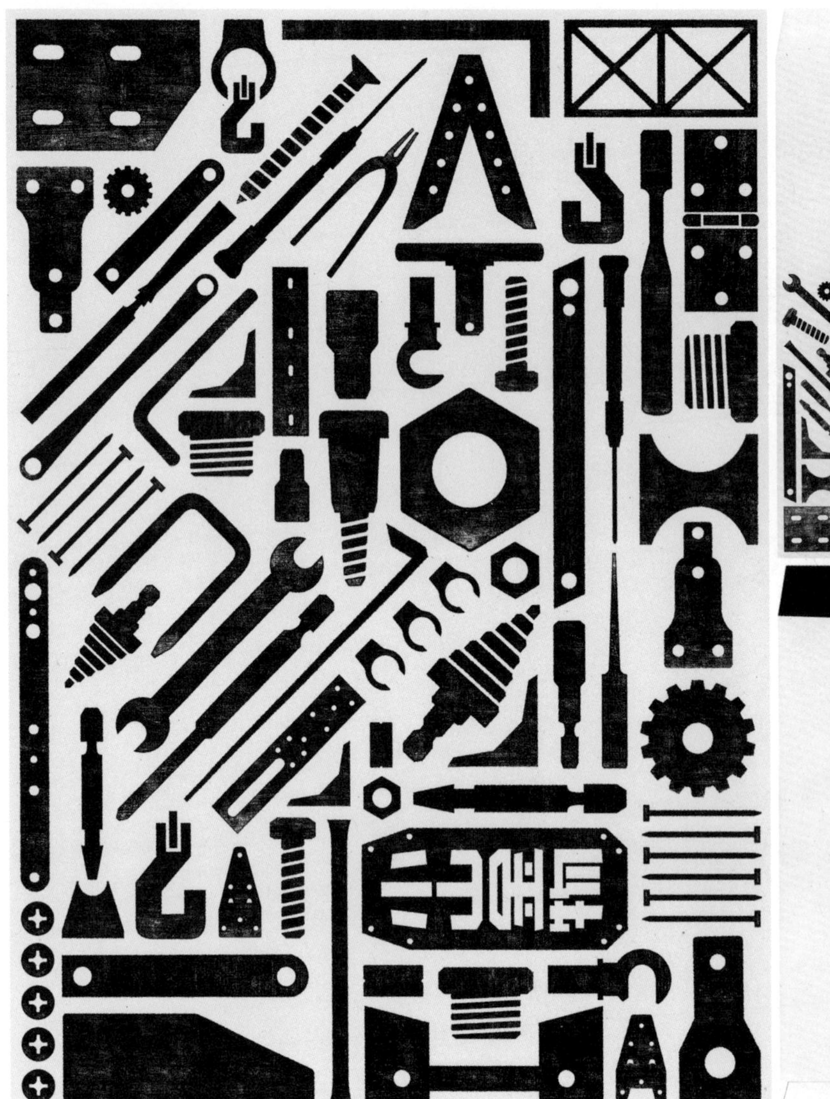

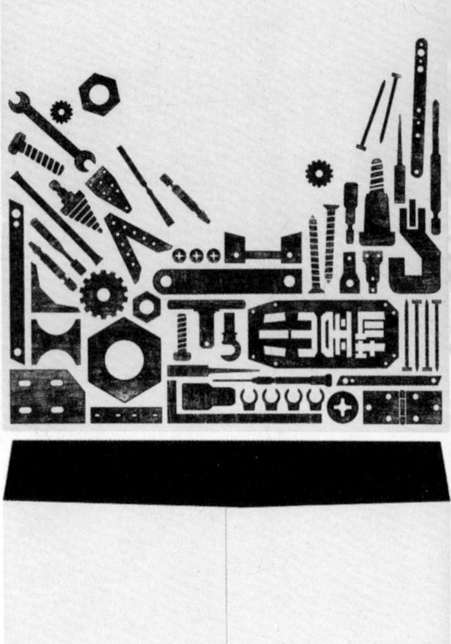

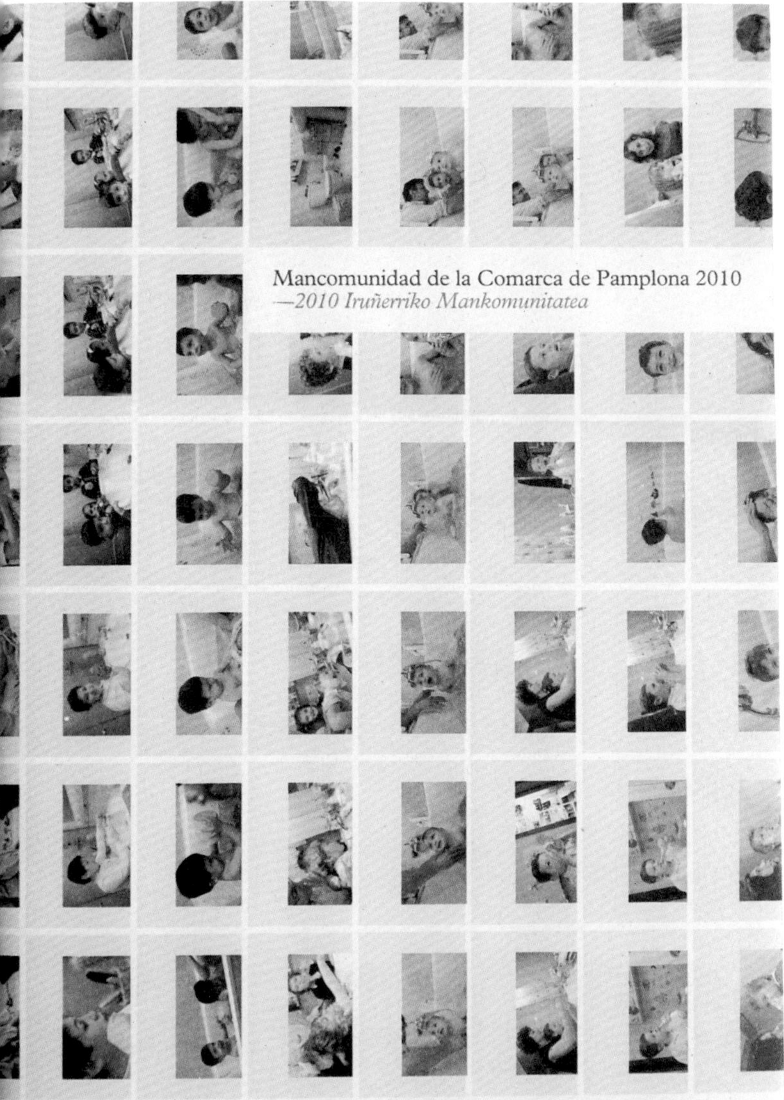

Mancomunidad de la Comarca de Pamplona 2010
—2010 Iruñerriko Mankomunitatea

Nomination in Graphic Design

Annual Reports
Errea Comunicación
for the Mancomunidad de Pamplona

Memoria Visual de la Mancomunidad de Pamplona
This report is a social and environmental study published annually by Pamplona's Commonwealth of Municipalities. It aims to improve the use of resources in the city. The report covers water usage, waste production, transportation and use of the riverside park. This edition presents the 2010 data through bold black and white graphics. We created a graphic story by showing how six families use resources in their daily lives, which put a human face on the statistics. The cover sleeve is a large folded poster with 350 photographs of the families. The photo gallery is structured using a gradient that moves from grey for urban transportation to green for the riverside park.

Designer
Nerea Armendariz
Art Director
Javier Errea
Photographer
Jesús Caso

Design Agency
Errea Comunicación
Client
Mancomunidad de Pamplona

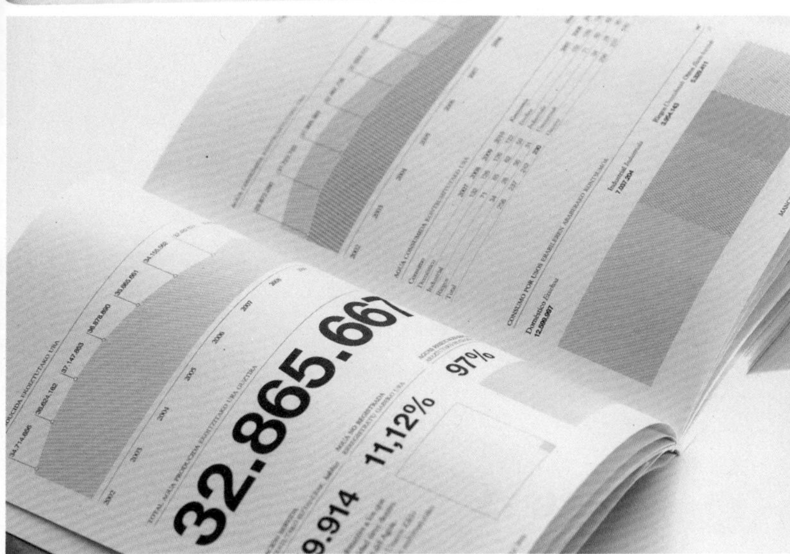

Nomination in Graphic Design

Catalogues & Brochures
Heine Warnecke Design
for Antonio Viani Importe

Viani Main Catalogue

Viani sources products from all over the world for delicatessen trading and top gastronomes. The Viani main catalogue presents these goods, combining clarity with aesthetics. Traders and gastronomes arrange their assortment of wares from more than 2,000 delicatessens shown on nearly 300 pages. Index cutting and coloured captions enable fast navigation. Complex binding, first-class materials, unusual feel, fine typography and brilliant pack shots create the right setting for the products.

Designers
Dirk Heine
Cord Warnecke

Design Agency
Heine Warnecke Design

Client
Antonio Viani Importe

Brand
Viani

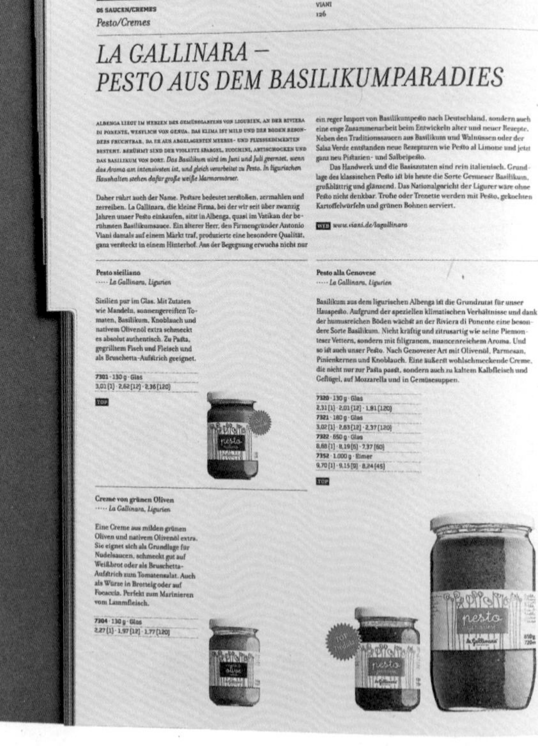

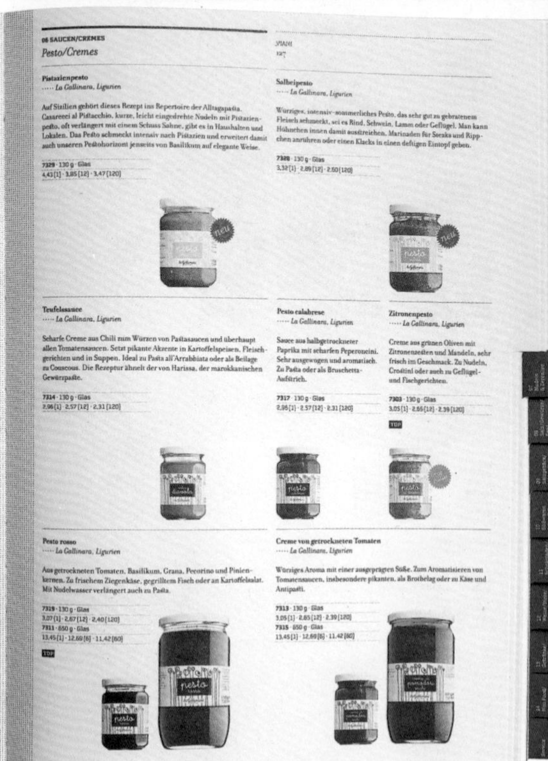

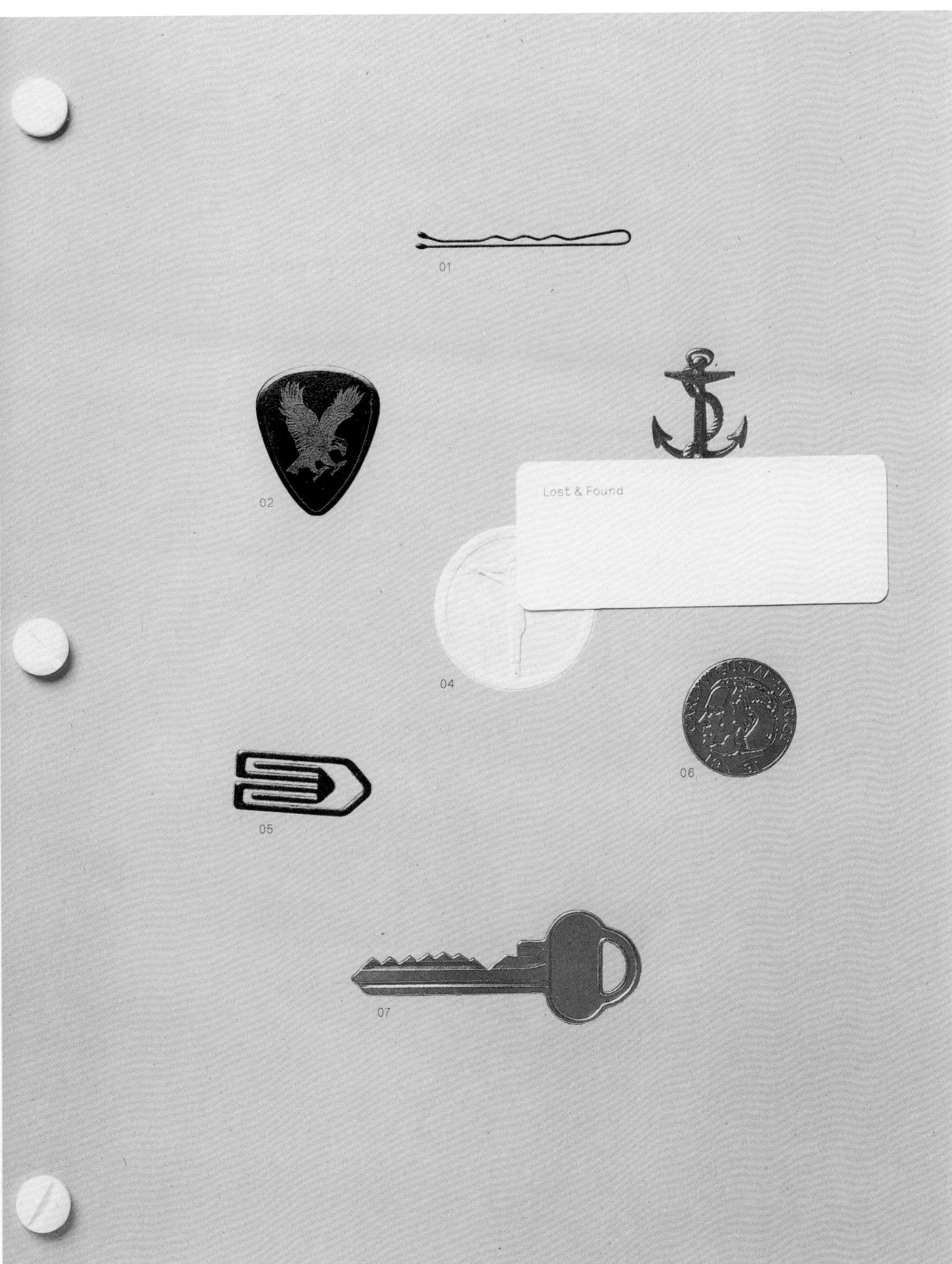

Nomination in Graphic Design

Catalogues & Brochures
Happy Forsman & Bodenfors
for Göteborgstryckeriet Printing House

Lost & Found
Göteborgstryckeriet is at the cutting edge of Sweden's printing houses. In 2011 it invested in a printing press for advanced foiling and embossing. We decided to communicate this to a select target group by creating a desirable object. Avoiding stereotypical imagery, we created a fictitious lost and found department at Göteborgstryckeriet. Using sophisticated techniques, tiny ordinary objects became extraordinary. The trompe l'œil publication caused a mail server crash at the printers, as hundreds of people ordered the book within less than an hour of its release.

Designers
Oskar Andersson
Gaioo Phunwut
Illustrator
Moa Pårup
Design Agency
Happy Forsman
& Bodenfors

Client
Göteborgstryckeriet
Printing House
Brand
Göteborgstryckeriet

Nomination in Graphic Design

Catalogues & Brochures
Nippon Design Center
for Yamate

Decoration Vegetable
Yamate trades in the delivery of fruit and vegetables to the food service industries. These brochures are both sales promotion tools and novelty magazines. We are suggesting to customers that they use our vegetable decoration, just like flower bouquets, on Japanese celebratory occasions.

Designer
Yasuhide Arai
Art Director
Yasuhide Arai
Photographer
Mikako Itou
Copywriter
Nobuhiko Suzuki
Stylist
Kyo Oba
Design Agency
Nippon Design Center
Client
Yamate

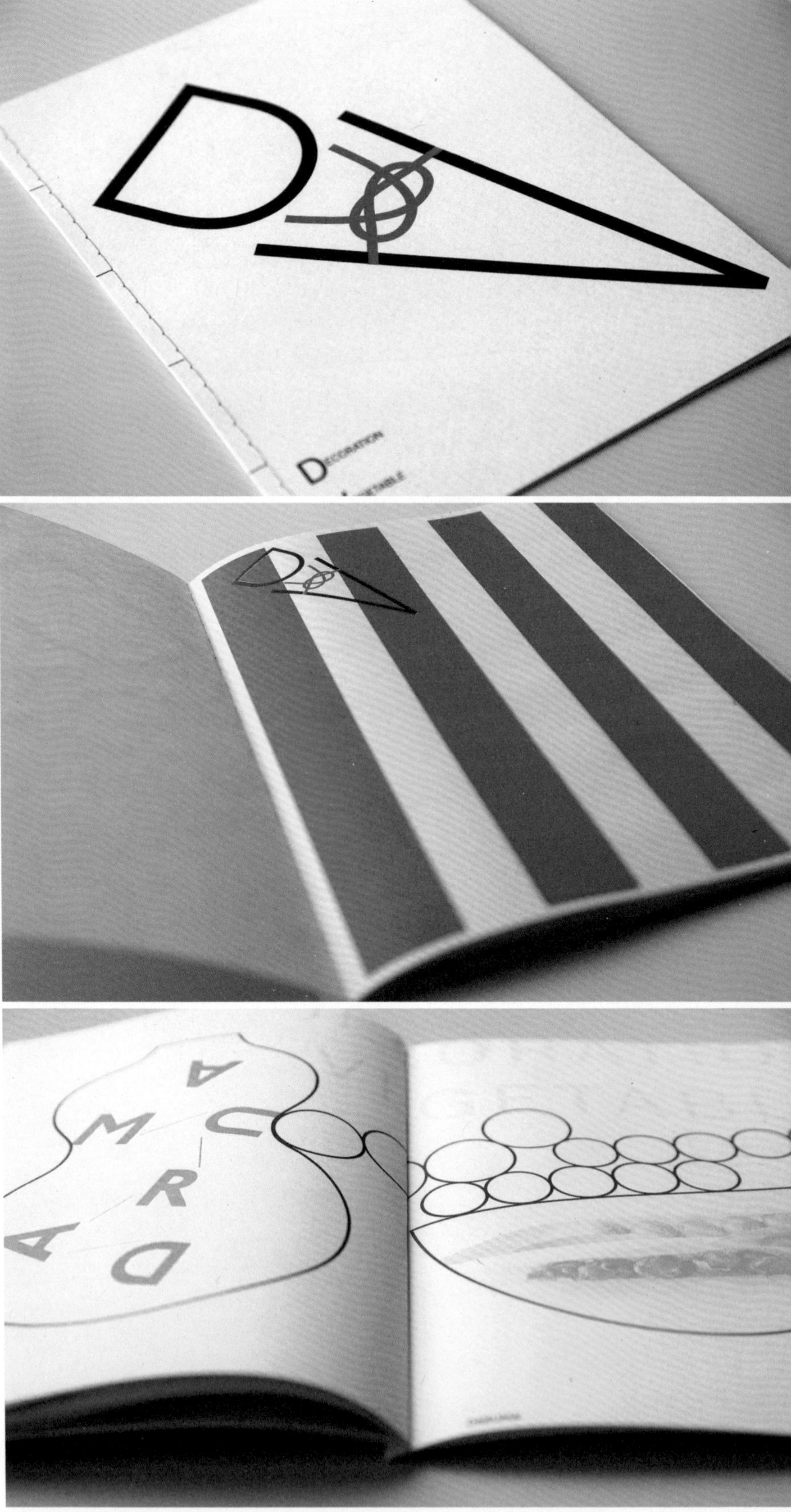

Nomination in Graphic Design

Catalogues & Brochures
SEA
for GF Smith

GF Smith Master Specifier 2011
The GF Smith Master Specifier was designed to reflect varying priorities when selecting paper. SEA focused its attention on the materials GF Smith offers, allowing their qualities to show beyond the imagery seen on previous selectors. Housed in a pale grey one-piece clamshell box, six books guide the user through the paper selection process. Print was kept to single colour and finishing to silver foil only.

Designers
Alex Broadhurst
Danny McNeil
Jimmy Smith
Creative Director
Bryan Edmondson

Design Agency
SEA
Brand Manager
John Haslam
Client
GF Smith

Nomination in Graphic Design

Calendars
Creative Juice Bangkok
for Tamiya

Tamiya Calendar
Plastic model kits producer Tamiya wanted to seize the festive period as an occasion to build a lasting bond with its customers. We designed this calendar, a premium gift that pulled more customers into the stores during the holiday season. It created brand interaction throughout the year, strengthening the connection between Tamiya and modelling enthusiasts.

Designers
Sermpan
Bunyalumlerk
Chittiporn
Chittapootti
Manasit Imjai
Kingkanok
Munkongcharoen
Chalermpun
Punjamapirom
Manamai Rodpetch
Tienchutha
Rukhavibul
Irada Sribyatta
Thirasak
Tanapatanakul
Nitipong Tancharoen
Kantaphat Witwasin

Art Directors
Tienchutha
Rukhavibul
Thirasak
Tanapatanakul
Executive Creative Director
Thirasak
Tanapatanakul
Advertising Agency
Creative Juice
Bangkok
Client
Tamiya

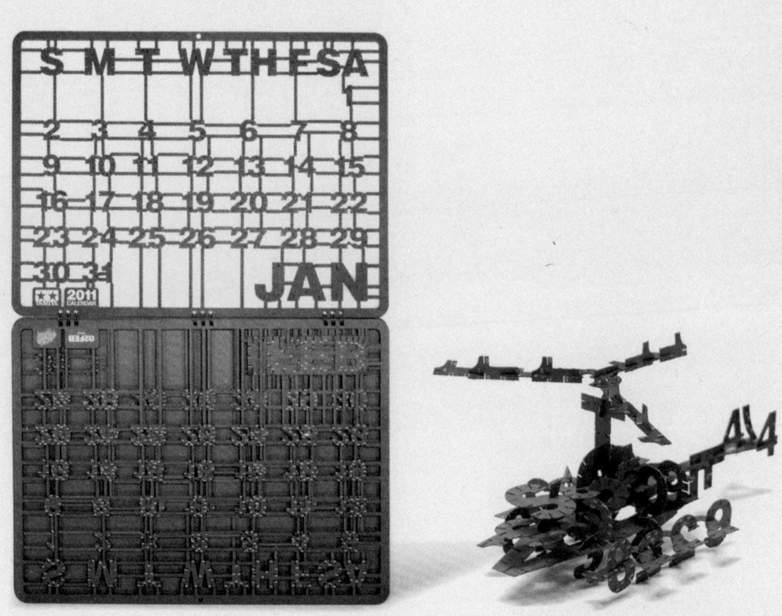

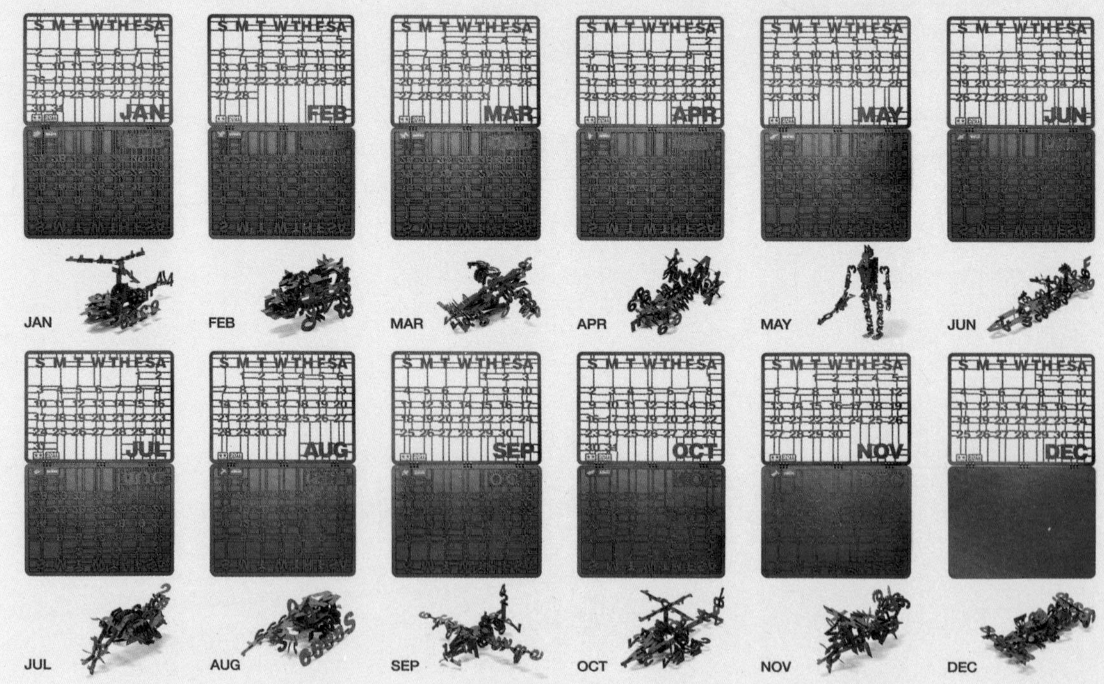

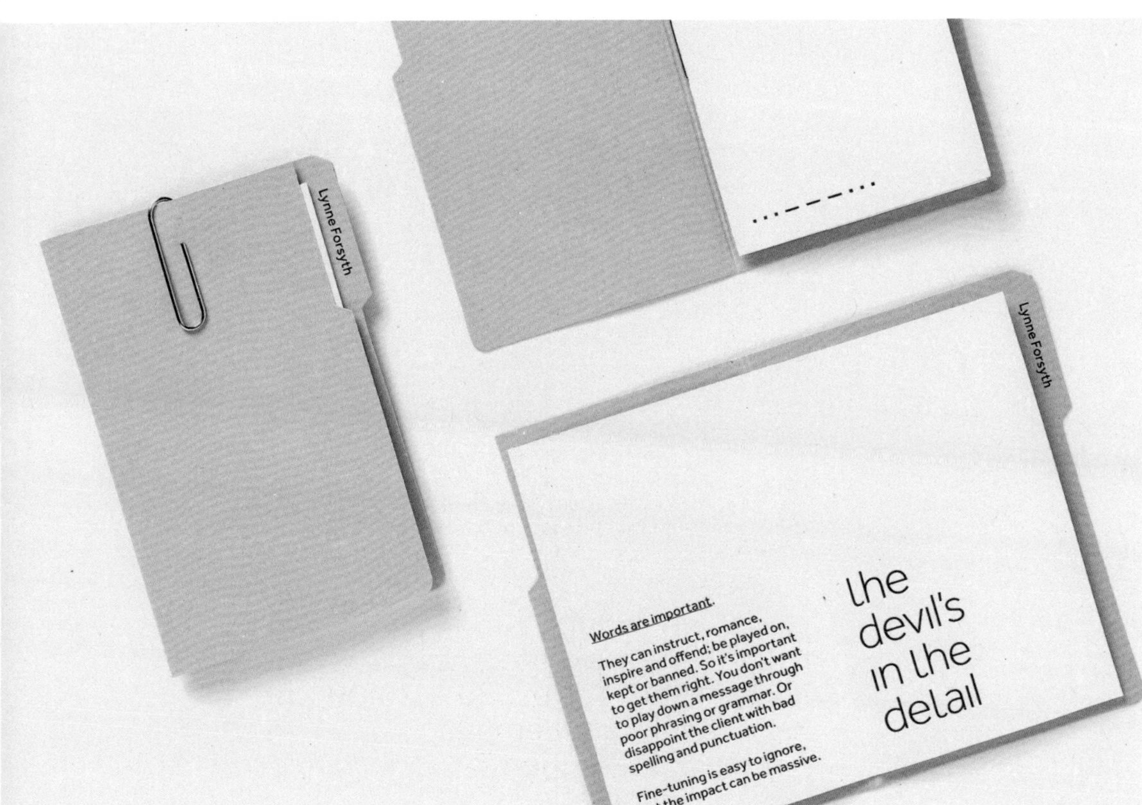

Nomination in Graphic Design

Direct Mail
Tayburn
for Lynne Forsyth

Lynne Forsyth Mailer
Lynne Forsyth is an editor and proofreader who needed something that would get the attention of agencies and could also be handed to people she met. Our solution was this direct mail piece: a brochure enclosed in a business-card-sized folder. Using well-known sayings and idioms that relate to accuracy and attention, it describes her role and the importance of words. Headlines have the cross from the t's and the dot from the i's removed, referencing this attention to detail.

Designer
Michael O'Shea
Creative Director
Malcolm Stewart
Copywriter
Michael O'Shea

Design Agency
Tayburn
Client
Lynne Forsyth

Nomination in Graphic Design

Greeting Cards & Invitations
Sigi Mayer
for Photographische Gesellschaft

Zeit-Zeugen Invitation
This is an invitation for a press conference. It was printed directly on the envelope which was sent to journalists. Inside was a blank newspaper, a symbol for filling the emptiness with information – information the journalists would receive at the press conference to fill the pages of their publications.

Designer
Sigi Mayer
Creative Director
Sigi Mayer
Copywriters
Werner Sobotka
Norbert Tomasi

Design Agency
Sigi Mayer
Client
Photographische Gesellschaft

Fülle die Leere.
Kommt und staunt!

Presse
Einladung.

Einladung zur
Pressekonferenz
am 14. Dez. 2011/10:00 Uhr
im Künstlerhaus
Zeit–zeugen
Fotografie in
Österreich seit (1945)
150 Jahre
Photographische Gesellschaft

150 Jahre Photographische Gesellschaft gegr. in Wien 1861

Die Photographische Gesellschaft ist die älteste Gesellschaft für Fotografie im deutschen Raum.
Sie wurde am 22. März 1861 in der Akademie der Wissenschaften in Wien durch Anton Georg Martin gegründet.
Sie beschäftigt sich mit der Förderung, Ausbreitung und Vervollkommnung der Fotografie.
Die Mitglieder treffen sich regelmäßig zum Informationsaustausch an der Höheren Graphischen Bundes-Lehr- und Versuchsanstalt in Wien.

Der Zweck der PHG ist die Förderung der Kunst und Wissenschaft der Fotografie und des Kommunikationswesens im weitesten Sinne des Wortes und aller mit diesen verwanten oder in Beziehung stehenden Disziplinen und Techniken.
Die PHG vereint Persönlichkeiten aus Kunst und Wissenschaft und stellt damit eine Organisation dar, die die gesamte Palette der Fotografie abdeckt.

Ende Mai 2011 war zum Auftakt des 150–Jahr–Jubiläums Österreich als Gastland in Zingst eingeladen, sich mit einem repräsentativen Querschnitt an den Fotoausstellungen zu beteiliegen.

Das inzwischen Internationale Fotofestival in Zingst an der Ostsee wurde innerhalb kürzester Zeit zu einem beachteten Zentrum der Fotografie.

Am 16.6.2011 hat die Photographische Gesellschaft, zusammen mit der Albertina ihre Jubiläumsausstellung "Die Explosion der Bilderwelt" feierlich eröffnet.

Hunderte Gäste waren Zeugen einer epochalen Ausstellung, die sich nahtlos in die Tradition der für die Fotografie so wegweisenden Ausstellungen von 1864, 1873 und 1901 eingereiht hat.
Gleichzeitig ist auch der Band "Die Explosion der Bilderwelt", der auf 200 Seiten die Geschichte der Fotografie in Österreich aufarbeitet, erschienen.

Unser nächstes Projekt zum 150–jährigen Jubiläum der PHG wird die Aussellung
"Zeit-zeugen Fotografie in Österreich seit (1945)"
im Künstlerhaus sein.
Die Stellung der Photographischen Gesellschaft in der Vergangenheit und in der Zukunft soll durch diese Schau in der Branche und in den Medien stärker ins Rampenlicht gerückt werden.

Gezeigt werden Exponate von Fotografen aus drei Generationen.

Ikonen wie Ernst Haas, Inge Morath, Harry Weber, Franz Hubmann, Elfriede Mejchar, Heinz Simonis führen die Liste von 140 Fotografen an.
Die Künstler der Sechzigerjahre sind ebenso vertreten, wie die Aktionisten der Sechziger- und Siebzigerjahre mit Hermann Nitsch, Rudolf Schwarzkogler, Günter Brus und Heinz Cibulka, der Wiener Gruppe mit Valie Export, und vielen anderen, die in den folgenden Jahrzehnten bekannt geworden sind, wie Elfie Semotan,
Margret Wenzel-Jelinek, Gerhard Trumler, Gerhard Heller, Horst Stasny, Alfred Seiland, Gerhard Sokol, Andreas Bitesnich
u.v.a. Bedeutende Fotografen werden neben einer gezielten Auswahl von trendweisenden jungen und aufstrebenden Fotokünstlern der Gegenwart zu sehen sein.

Gemäß der Vielfalt der Fotografie wird auch die Stereoskopei mit den modernsten 3D-Techniken, sowie Video vertreten sein.

Umgesetzt wird dies in einer völlig unkonventionell konzipierten Ausstellung, die die Buntheit und Vielfältigkeit der fotografischen Ausdrucksweisen zur Geltung bringt.

W. Sobotka

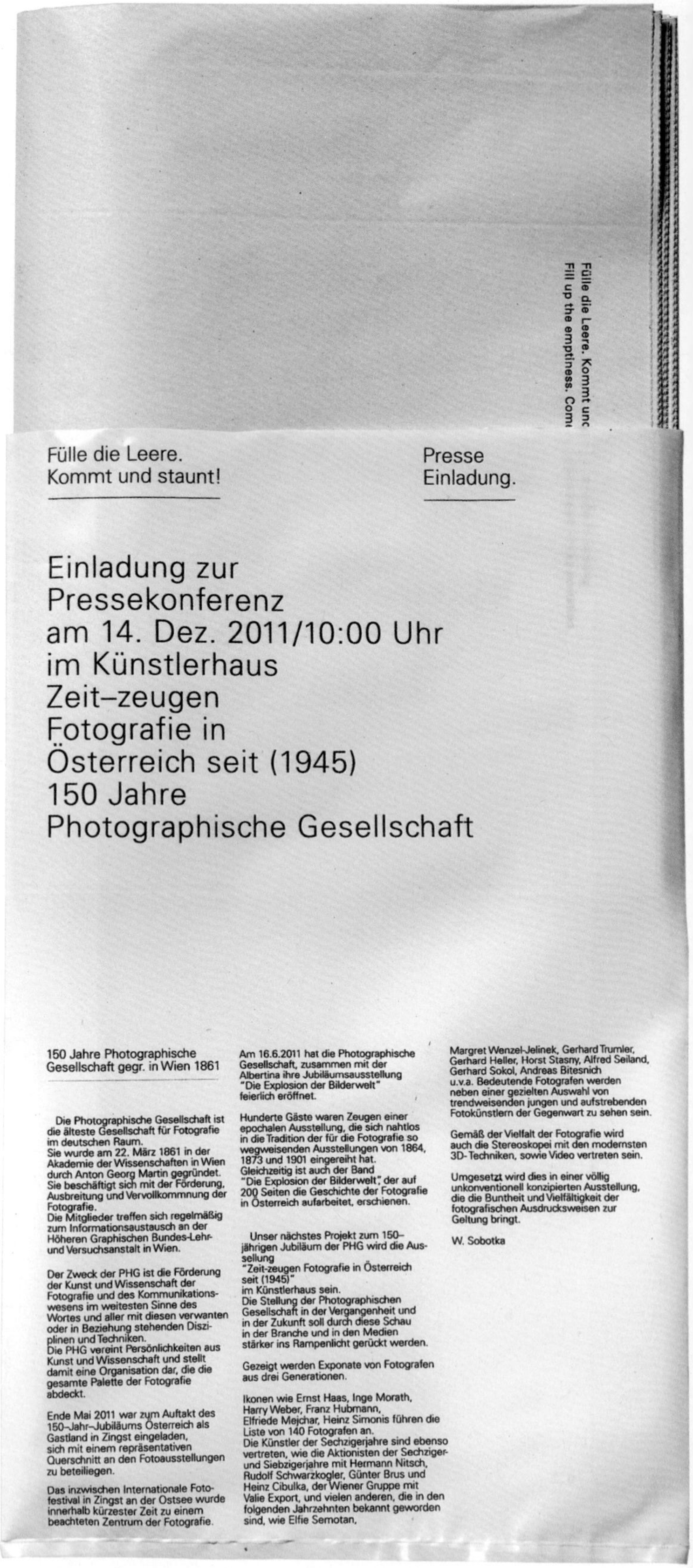

Nomination in Graphic Design

CD, DVD & Record Sleeves
Jason Smith
for Airecords

Ai032LP: Time to Exit

'Ai032LP: Time to Exit' was the final release from London-based record label Airecords. Jason Smith of Airecords wanted the release to visually symbolise the end of the label. Belgian artist Roa was commissioned to illustrate Jason's vision. The spring release coincided with the Chinese New Year of the rabbit, an animal Roa is famed for painting. The outside sleeve shows what seems to be a sleeping rabbit. Flip it over to reveal the animal's skeleton. The inner sleeve shows further stages of decay, while the marbled vinyl represents the animal's blood, celebrating the life and death of Airecords.

Designer
Jason Smith
Client
Airecords

Nomination in Graphic Design

CD, DVD & Record Sleeves
SPREAD
for Commmons & Mirai Records

Tadashii Soutaiseiriron
This is our CD cover design for 'Tadashii Soutaiseiriron', the album by Japanese rock band Theory of Relativity. The band asked themselves questions around the theme of 'What is the correct theory of relativity?' and the sound grew from there. The resulting music was reworked by ten musicians. For our cover design, we used expressions and diagrams examining the same questions. A red and green check sheet, a popular memory aid amongst Japanese students, is attached to the sleeve. Listeners can join in the fun by solving the mystery hiding in the diagrams and lyrics.

Designers
Hirokazu Kobayashi
Haruna Yamada
Art Directors
Hirokazu Kobayashi
Haruna Yamada
Illustrator
Etsuko Yakushimaru

Design Agency
SPREAD
Clients
Commmons
Mirai Records

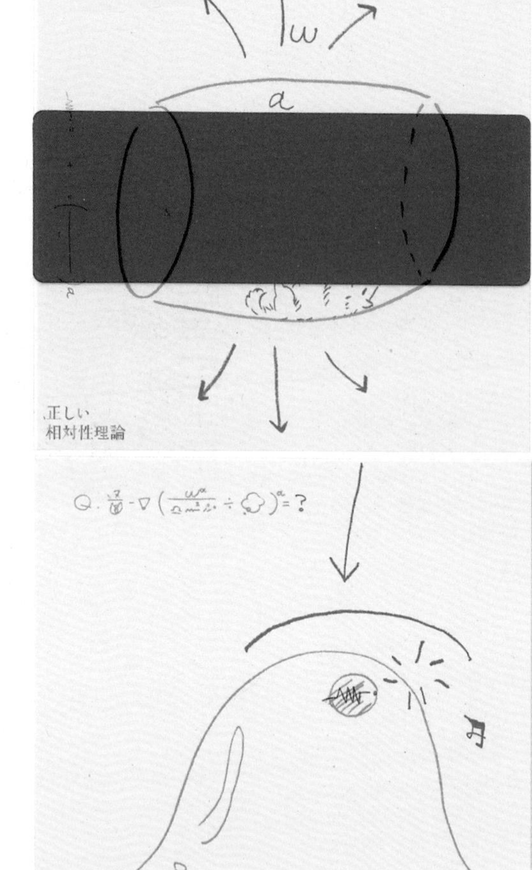

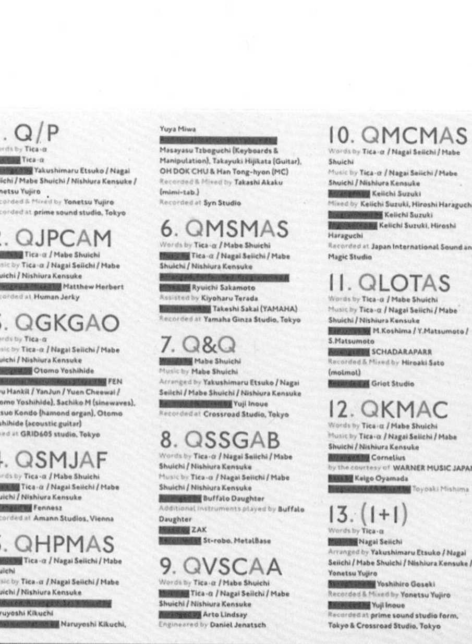

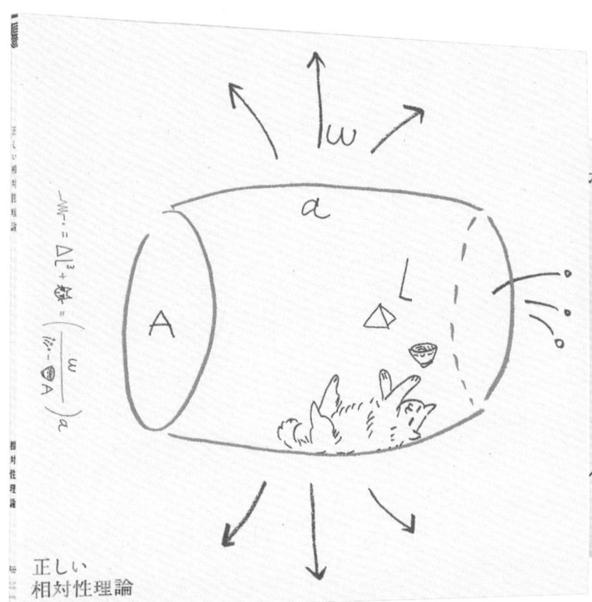

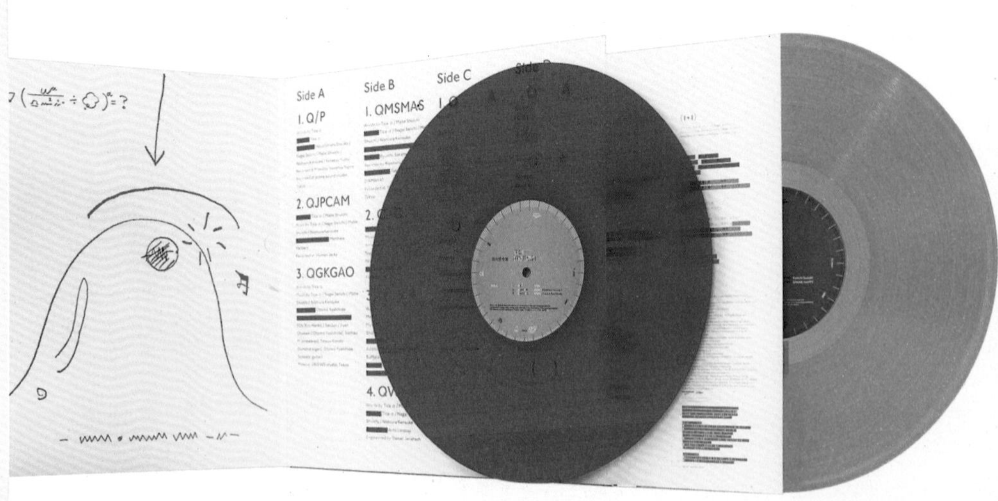

Nomination in Graphic Design

Applied Print Graphics
Magpie Studio
for Gavin Martin Colournet

Gavin Martin Colournet Poster Tubes
Award-winning printer Gavin Martin Colournet is always looking to raise its profile within the design industry. Its postal tubes presented an untapped opportunity as a mobile advertising canvas. Using the long thin canvas as a virtue, we adorned the tubes with a selection of images from baguettes to baseball bats. Carried under arm and inevitably left around design studios, the tubes become a humorous conduit for printed proofs, standing out in the sea of unmarked tubes from the competition.

Designers
Aimi Awang
Tim Fellowes
Will Southward
Creative Directors
David Azurdia
Ben Christie
Jamie Ellul

Design Agency
Magpie Studio
Brand Manager
Phil Le Monde
Client
Gavin Martin
Colournet

Nomination in Graphic Design

Applied Print Graphics
This Ain't Rock'n'Roll
for The Brixton Pound

The Brixton Pound

The Brixton Pound (B£) is the world's first local currency in an urban area. It's designed to support independent Brixton businesses and encourage local trade and production. It's a complementary currency working alongside pounds sterling. Brixton heroes, urban art and architectural detail combine on these notes to reflect the dynamic past and present of one of London's most vibrant areas. Balancing expected currency motifs with state-of-the-art production techniques, these notes are both an advert for Brixton's amazing diversity, and two-fingers to the pedestrian paper the rest of us have to carry in our wallets. Need to borrow a Ziggy anyone?

Designers
Clive Russell
Charlie Waterhouse
Printer
Paul Neal
Creative Agency
This Ain't Rock'n'Roll

Printers
Orion Security Print
Project Manager
Susan Tomlinson
Client
The Brixton Pound

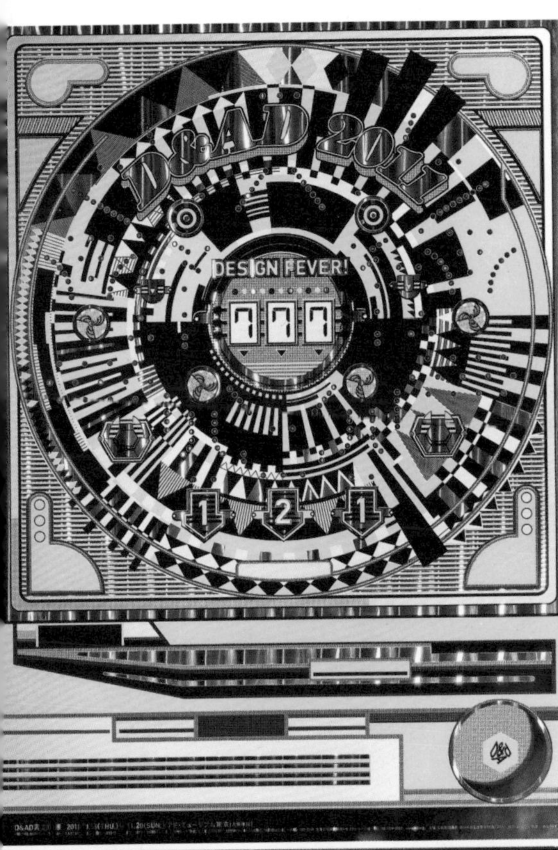

Nomination in Graphic Design

Posters
Dentsu Tokyo
for the Yoshida Hideo Memorial Foundation

Design Fever!
We created these posters for the 2011 D&AD Exhibition at the Advertising and Design Museum of Tokyo. We used visuals inspired by the Japanese game pachinko to embody the idea of 'Design Fever'. We created four different posters with themes ranging from outer space to moe anime.

Designers
Takuya Iimura
Minami Otsuka
Art Director
Yoshihiro Yagi
Creative Director
Yuya Furukawa
Photographer
Honoka Sueyoshi
Copywriter
Haruko Tsutsui

Agency Producers
Shinya Tamura
Yoshiko Tomita
Advertising Agency
Dentsu Tokyo
Client
Yoshida Hideo
Memorial Foundation

Nomination in Graphic Design

Posters
Three & Co.
for Complice

Complice Posters

People change their hairstyles with a cut or dye when they want to reinvent themselves. Hair salon Complice is the best place for that. Their hairdressers respect the wishes and opinions of customers and can give them great satisfaction with their expertise. In these posters, we refer to change not only on the outside but also on the inside by using the image of carving or peeling fruit on a plate.

Designer
Masaki Fukumori
Art Director
Masaki Fukumori
Photographer
Keisuke Nishitani
Artists
Masaki Fukumori
Mitsuhiro Minamitsuji
Copywriter
Hiroyuki Hayashi
Stylist
Mitsuhiro Minamitsuji
Design Group
Three & Co.
Client
Complice

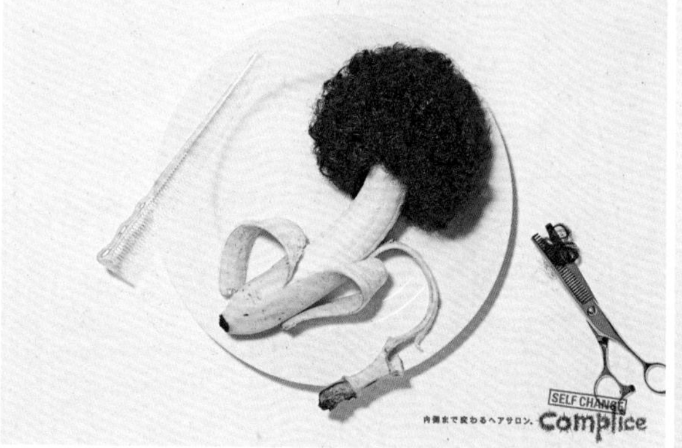

Nomination in Graphic Design

Logos
Wolff Olins
for Current TV

Current TV Identity

Current TV came to Wolff Olins in 2010 looking to reassert its reputation and direction within traditional news. The media company's viewer-generated content platform was beginning to feel competition from digital news platforms and video-sharing sites, so it needed to send a powerful message that would disrupt the traditional category of news. The resulting logo – a black and white flag in motion – now defines the brand as bold and alive. It stands apart in a category full of colourful symbols, expressing a brand with a strong point of view.

Designer
Chris Sherron
Senior Designers
LA Hall
Mads Poulsen
Creative Director
Jordan Crane
Executive Creative Director
Todd Simmons
Production Director
Kris Pelletier
Strategic Director
Sam Wilson
Design Agencies
GHAVA Motion Graphics
loyalkaspar
Branding Agency
Wolff Olins
Account Manager
Alicianne Rand
Client
Current TV

Nomination in Graphic Design

Logos
The Partners
for Tomorrow

Tomorrow
Tomorrow is a new online-only newspaper launched in 2012. It aims to bring integrity and responsibility to breaking news without compromising speed of delivery. The perpetually moving logo is based on the turning pages of a newspaper – tomorrow's news every day.

Designer	Design Agency
Tim Brown	The Partners
Creative Director	**Client**
Robert Ball	Tomorrow

Nomination in Graphic Design

Wayfinding & Environmental Graphics
Heatherwick Studio & Mode
for Swire Properties

Pacific Place
As part of a brand overhaul comprising architecture and visual identity, Mode collaborated with Heatherwick Studio to design the new branding and site-wide signage system for Pacific Place, Hong Kong's pre-eminent lifestyle destination. Central to the project was Heatherwick Studio's dynamic architectural approach, driven by a 'fluid and organic' aesthetic, which unites all the individual areas within the complex. The signage and supporting brand identity echoes the fluidity and organic form of the architecture, bringing visual cohesion to all areas.

Designers
Jennifer Chen
Fergus Comer
Virginia Lopez
Frechilla
Darrell Gibbons
Neil Hubbard
Alex Jones
Craig Miller
Andrew Taylor
Filipe Valgode
Tom Yu

Creative Directors
Phil Costin
Thomas Heatherwick
Design Agencies
Heatherwick Studio
Mode
Client
Swire Properties
Brand
Pacific Place

Integrated Graphics
Ground Tokyo
for KDDI

iida Integrated Graphics
Japanese mobile phone brand iida is renowned for its innovation and attention to detail. A high quality, integrated format is applied to the design of the tools for the device's features to stand out, because each iida product is of exceptional design.

Designer
Daisaku Nojiri
Art Director
Daisaku Nojiri
Creative Director
Daisaku Nojiri
Photographers
Hiroshi Harada
Satoshi Iwai
Hiroya Kitai

Copywriter
Junpei Watanabe
Advertising Agency
Ground Tokyo
Client
KDDI
Brand
iida

X-RAY iida.jp

LIFE > PHONE iida

KDDI株式会社

X-RAY

携帯電話は、ここにまったく新しいデザインを手に入れました。深みのある透明感をまとうボディを通して浮かび上がるプリント基板や集積回路といった電子部品。それらの形や色、配置にいたるまで、内部の構造までもデザインすることによって生み出された、これまでにない存在感を放つ携帯電話。それがX-RAYです。カタチをデザインするのではなく、携帯電話としての自然な姿が表面に現れてくるような、まるで裸のようなデザイン。計算されたボディの透明度と艶、そして色が、深い質感と高級感を叶えました。

もうひとつ、X-RAYが叶えたのは、美しさとハイパフォーマンスの両立。処理速度を大幅に向上させる高速CPUが快適な動作を実現。世界196の国と地域で通話できるGSMも標準装備し、アクティブに活動の幅を広げるあなたの毎日を、様々な最新のスペックでバックアップします。

Integrated Graphics
Blast
for Arjowiggins Creative Papers

Keaykolour Branding & Marketing
We created this brand identity as part of our 'Colourful Life' marketing campaign – a campaign to rejuvenate and relaunch Keaykolour paper to a worldwide designer audience. The identity featured a distinctive brand marque, which we recreated using innovative print and finishing techniques, as well as animation for video and online. The campaign followed the creation of three original artworks using Keaykolour, each finding an inspiring and different way to work with the paper. Marketing collateral included posters, art prints, viral films, a website and launch exhibitions in London and Paris.

Designers
Dan Bown
Lisa Jung
Creative Director
Colin Gifford
Illustrator
Ian Wright
Copywriter
Maf Bishop
Developer
Gary McClumpha

Design Group
Blast
Production Company
Spicer & Moore
Client
Arjowiggins
Creative Papers
Brand
Keaykolour

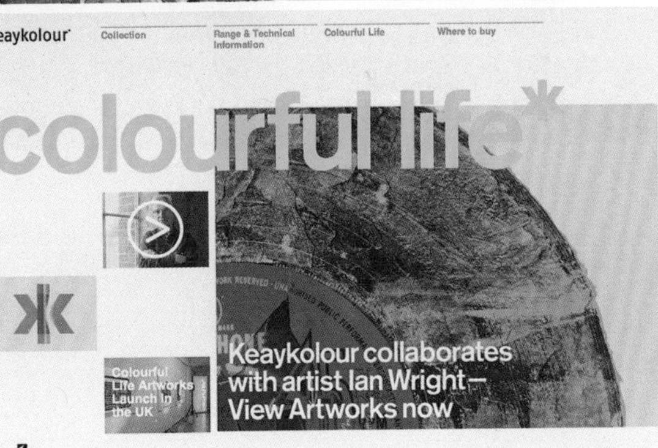

Integrated Graphics
Oktan Stavanger
for Sola Betong

The Concrete Crew
Sola Betong is a small regional cement producer based in western Norway. Cement is what you make of it; we chose to make art. A distinctive aspect of Sola Betong is its employees. They have a very positive mentality and are extremely engaging. We wanted to highlight the upbeat and sassy employees as the company's honest and genuine public face. Consequently, we produced 'The Concrete Crew'. We cast each employee in concrete, their own product, and created an art exhibition for clients, businesses, the public, media and, most importantly, the employees.

Designer
Anya Aasebø
Art Director
Anya Aasebø
Film Editor
Nina Børke
Web Producer
Jon Arne Tjelta
Copywriters
Inge Kvivik
Ingrid Milde
Elisabeth Rongved

Advertising Agency
Oktan Stavanger
Project Manager
May-Britt Skjøveland
Account Handler
Frode Midttun
Client
Sola Betong

Integrated Graphics
AGI Spain
for Alliance Graphique Internationale

Identity for AGI Congress and Open
The identity of the AGI Congress and Open is based on the typographic modular system SuperVeloz, designed by Joan Trochut in the first half of the 20th Century. Having borrowed from history, we faced the challenge of creating a fresh and distinctive visual language. We created a personalised AGI SuperVeloz Alphabet based on the initials of each speaker. When enlarged, the initials work as illustrations. We pared down type and colour to let them shine, transforming the series of initials into the focal part of the campaign.

Designers
Vicky Cabrera
Ana Lacour
Pablo Martín
Pedro Ponciano
Rafa Roses
Astrid Stavro
Maggy Villarroel
Art Directors
Pablo Martín
Astrid Stavro
Creative Directors
Mario Eskenazi
Pablo Martín
Astrid Stavro
Patrick Thomas

Typography
AGI Spain
Design Agency
AGI Spain
Project Manager
Patrick Thomas
Clients
AGI Spain
Alliance Graphique Internationale

Integrated Graphics
Buddy
for Plymouth University, Faculty of Arts

Changing Perceptions
'Cabinet' was an exhibition of works by 12 architects and designers, associates of the Plymouth City Museum who had unprecedented access to its archives and collections. The identity needed to reflect the artists' aims to challenge stereotypical public perceptions, questioning our cultural heritage and the relationship between the arts and public institutions.

Designers
Will Day
Mark Girvan
David Jones
Creative Directors
Mark Girvan
David Jones
Copywriters
Lisa Desforges
David Jones

Design Agency
Buddy
Client
Plymouth University, Faculty of Arts

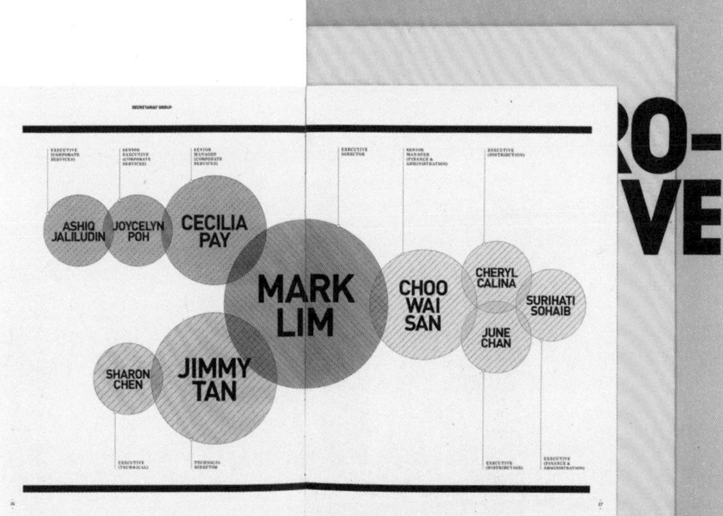

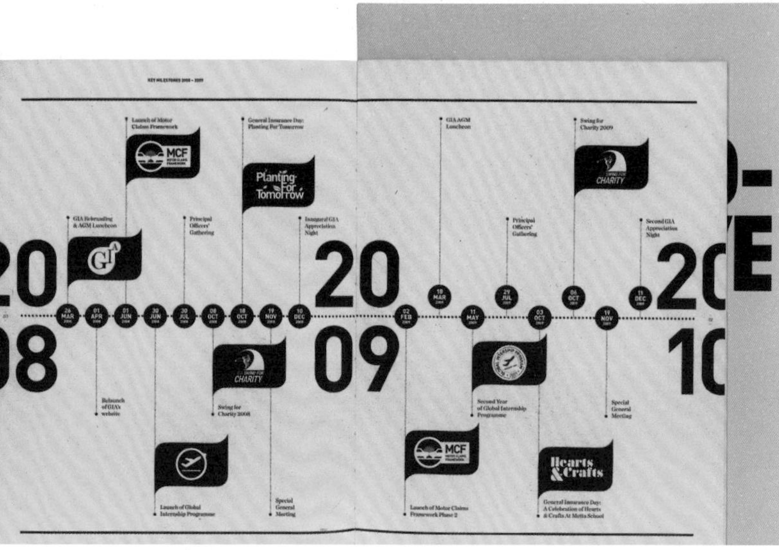

Annual Reports
&Larry
for the General Insurance
Association of Singapore

The Progressive Years
Following a rebranding exercise and the implementation of successful outreach activities and internship programmes, the past three years were instrumental in depicting the growth and progress of the General Insurance Association of Singapore. The company had made tangible leaps and bounds, so we decided to use this as the central design theme. Three distinct chapters were carved out in paper of different size and colour to visually depict GIA's significant progression over the years. Bound together with exposed thread-sewn binding, the result is a visually interesting and intriguing expression of an otherwise standard corporate document.

Designer
Lee Weicong
Creative Director
Larry Peh
Writer
Lua Ai Wei

Design Agency
&Larry
Client
General Insurance Association of Singapore

Annual Reports
Tayburn
for The Scotland Yard Adventure Centre

The Yard Annual Report 2010
The Yard is a children's charity based in Edinburgh. They provide a safe, stimulating and friendly environment for children with additional support needs. The annual report is the charity's major fund-raising document, used here to bring the essence of The Yard to life. The report is put together like a scrapbook, capturing the texture and touch of the different materials it uses, as these textures play an important role in helping the children who take part. Each spread is different and tells the children and staff's stories first hand, to feel as honest and inspiring as they are.

Designer
Judith Reid
Design Director
Michael O'Shea
Creative Director
Malcolm Stewart
Artworker
Kevin Woolard
Copywriter
Celine Sinclair

Production Manager
Nikki West
Design Agency
Tayburn
Client
The Scotland Yard Adventure Centre
Brand
The Yard

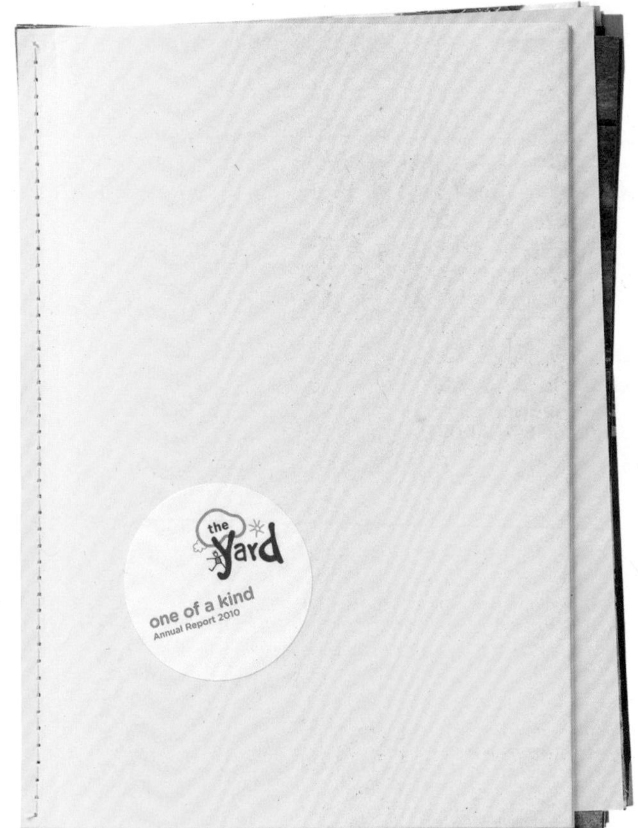

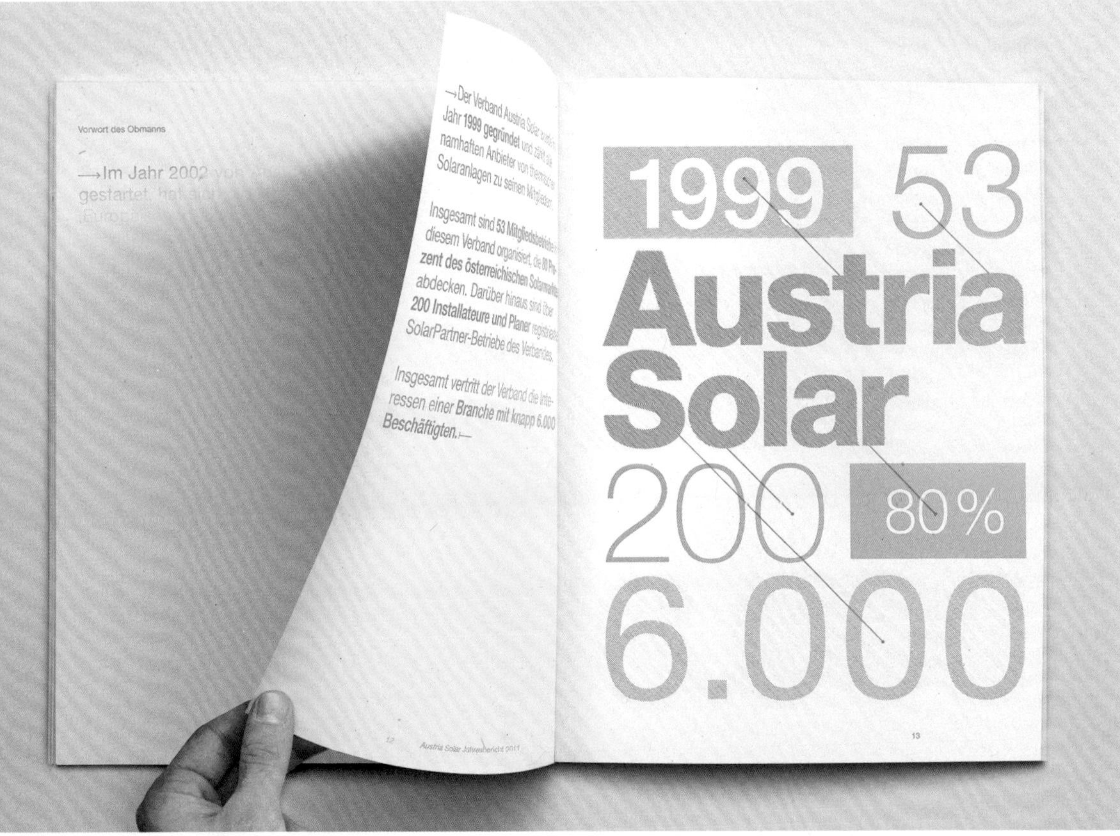

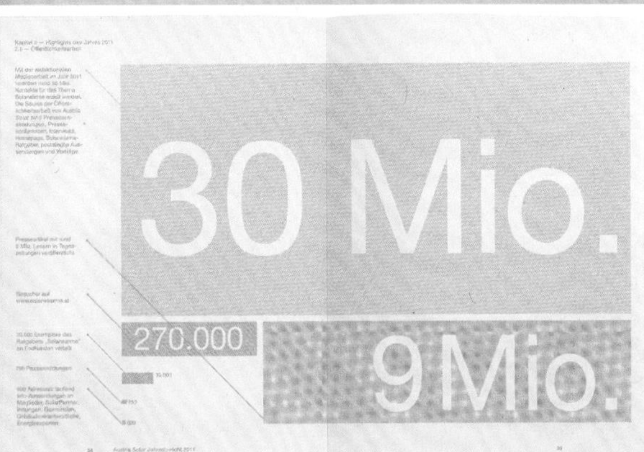

Annual Reports
Serviceplan München
for Austria Solar – Verein zur Förderung der Thermischen Solarenergie

The Solar Annual Report 2011
Solar energy is the main business of our client Austria Solar. That's why we thought about how we could put this energy to paper. The result: the first annual report powered by the sun. Its content remains invisible until sunlight falls on its pages.

Designer
Mathias Nösel
Art Director
Matthäus Frost
Creative Directors
Christoph Everke
Cosimo Möller
Alexander Nagel
Copywriter
Moritz Dornig
Print Producer
Melanie Dienemann
Advertising Agency
Serviceplan München

Account Handler
Diana Günder
Brand Manager
Roger Hackstock
Client
Austria Solar – Verein zur Förderung der Thermischen Solarenergie

Catalogues & Brochures
A Beautiful Design
for The Browsing Copy Project

For Browsing Only
The Browsing Copy Project focuses on unloved books – those that remain on the shelves unsold. These books were collected from local bookstores, then designers from around the world were invited to use them as canvases to express their creativity and give the books a second life. The 'before and after' results are documented. Only 300 copies were printed and circulated around the world's good bookstores, shops and design studios, just for people to browse. 'For Browsing Only' is not for sale. The condition of the books and the places they've been are documented on the website www.browsingcopy.com.

Designer
Roy Poh
Creative Director
Roy Poh
Photographer
John Nursalim
Copywriter
Roy Poh

Design Agency
A Beautiful Design
Client
The Browsing
Copy Project

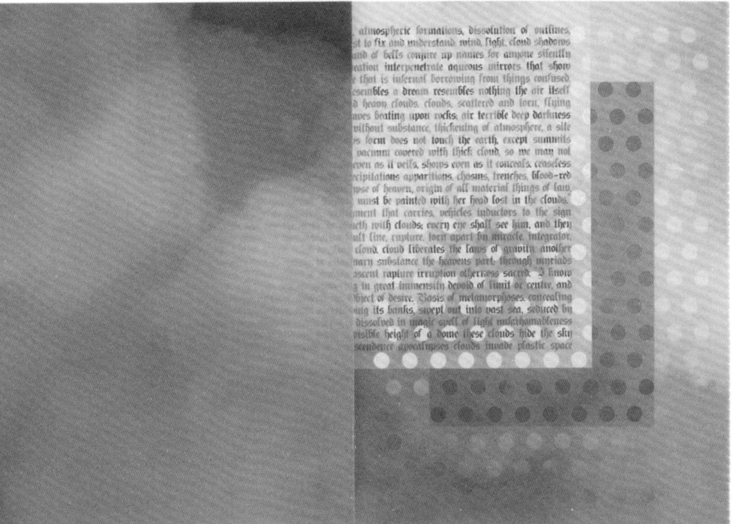

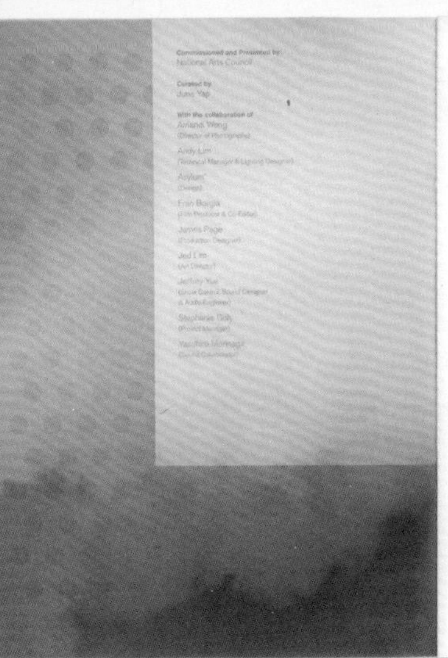

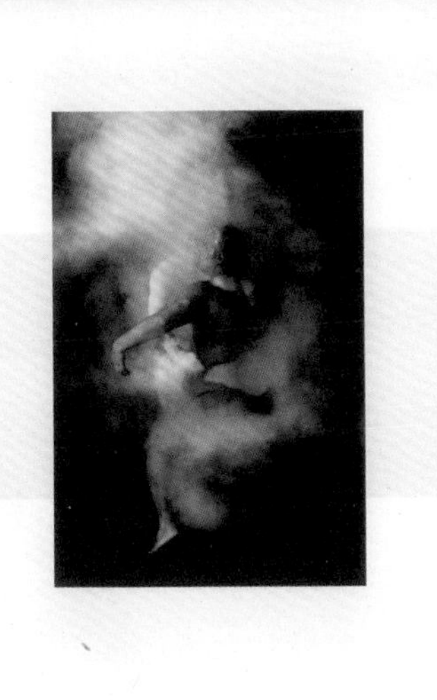

Catalogues & Brochures
The Asylum
for the National Arts Council Singapore

The Cloud of Unknowing
Commissioned by the National Arts Council, artist and filmmaker Ho Tzu Nyen was selected to represent Singapore at the 54th Venice Biennale 2011. His artwork, 'The Cloud of Unknowing', is an audio and visual installation piece sited in an old church, exploring the multiple roles of the cloud within art. Ho's exploration of the cloud is carried through with this accompanying catalogue. The catalogue, meant to recreate the qualities of a cloud, features film stills of Ho's current and past work and essays on a variety of translucent and lightweight paper stock, finished with rough edges.

Designer
May Chiang
Design Director
Cara Ang
Creative Director
Chris Lee

Design Agency
The Asylum
Client
National Arts Council Singapore

Catalogues & Brochures
Jäger & Jäger
for Nils Holger Moormann

Moormann Trade Fair Brochure
We designed a moleskin-style brochure for Moormann furniture to use at the trade show Salone Internazionale Del Mobile 2011. The brochure shows the new as well as the entire existing furniture collection. Dimensions were displayed using icons. Visible dimensions are highlighted in red, while grey is used for furniture combinations and sizes that are not shown.

Designers
Olaf Jäger
Regina Jäger

Design Agency
Jäger & Jäger

Marketing Manager
Nicole Christof

Client
Nils Holger Moormann

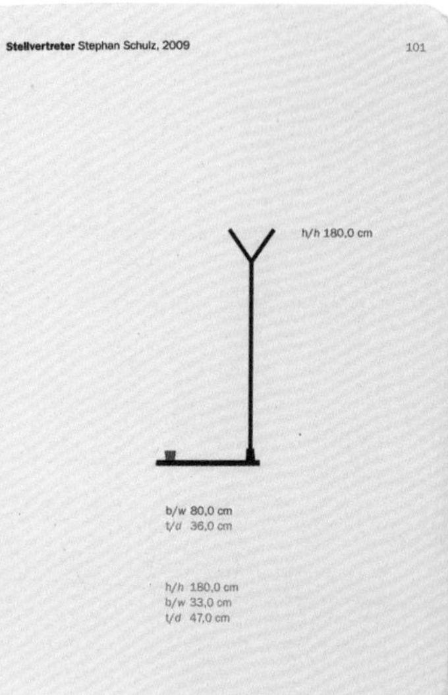

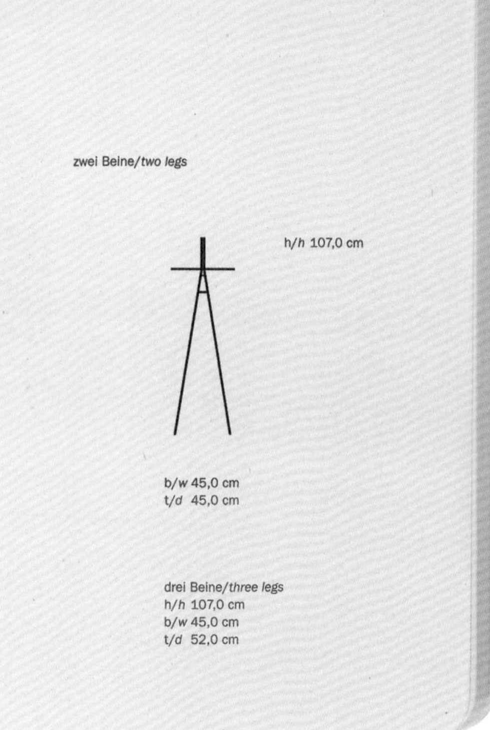

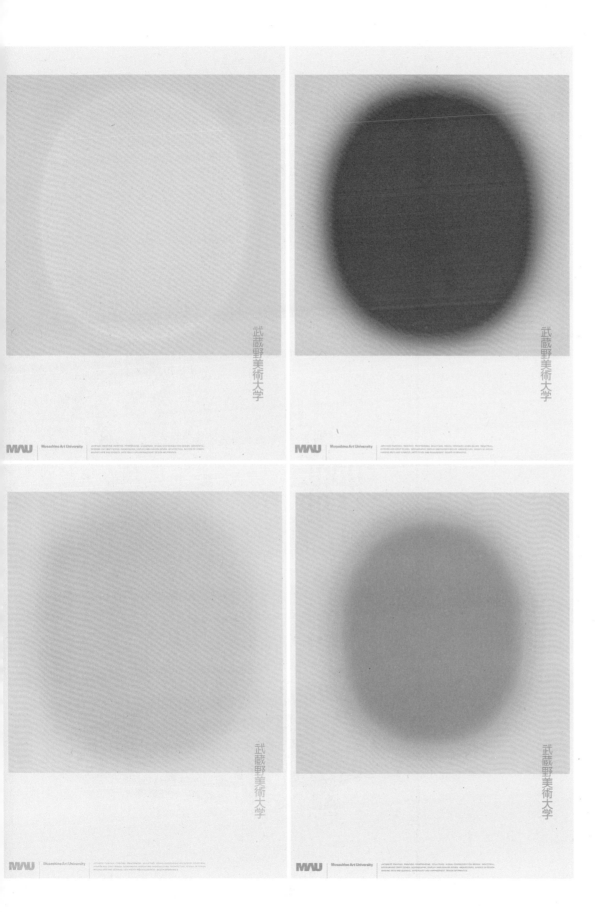

Catalogues & Brochures
Nippon Design Center
for Musashino Art University

Musashino Art University 2012 Brochures
When designing these brochures for the Musashino Art University, our aim was to emphasise the role of the university as a venue for creative activity. To represent the diversity and potential of artistic expressions, we used ovals with soft gradations printed in a variety of beautiful colours.

Designers
Daigo Daikoku
Takao Minamidate
Art Director
Daigo Daikoku
Photographer
Akitada Hamasaki

Design Agency
Nippon Design Center
Client
Musashino Art University

Catalogues & Brochures
Designers United

Designers United Work & Extensions
We published this 380-page monograph on the occasion of the exhibition 'The Gestalt Effect/ Work & Extensions of Designers United'. The exhibition was held at the Macedonian Museum of Contemporary Art from 31 May to 31 July 2011 and curated by art historian Thouli Misirloglou. The bilingual (English/ Greek) publication consists of six books, each focusing on a different topic: culture; forms and logos; illustrations; typography; Volvo Ocean Race; and contributor texts. The publication includes previously unseen works as well as new works designed and produced especially for the exhibition.

Designers
Dimitris Koliadimas
Dimitris Papazoglou
Creative Directors
Dimitris Koliadimas
Dimitris Papazoglou

Design Group
Designers United
Client
Designers United

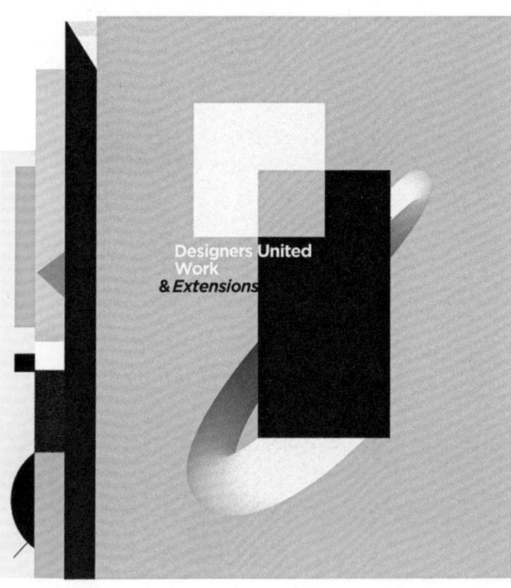

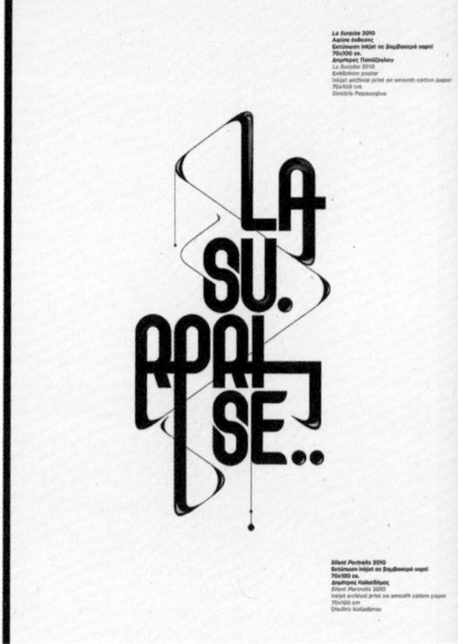

Catalogues & Brochures
TGG Hafen Senn Stieger
for Typotron

Typotron-Heft 29: Drei Weieren
This is the 29th edition of the Typotron series, a cultural publication by Typotron, a printing factory in St Gallen, Switzerland. It's about the Weieren, a recreation area with three lakes close to the town. With lots of pictures and text by a local author, it illustrates the seasons there. The constant in the series is the format, but we wanted the pictures to be large. The solution was a special binding. Each season has a poster; these are folded and bound together, so that you can open them fully and still flip through the pages. For the typography we used Allegra, a font by Jost Hochuli.

Designers
Dominik Hafen
Stieger Roland
Bernhard Senn
Type Designer
Jost Hochuli
Photographer
Stefan Rötheli
Copywriter
Liana Ruckstuhl

Design Agency
TGG Hafen
Senn Stieger
Print Production
Typotron
Client
Typotron
Brand
Typotron-Heft

Catalogues & Brochures
Kinetic Singapore
for holycrap.sg

Renn Lim by Renn Lim
This catalogue features an eight-year old's irreverent artwork and scribbling. It acts as a peek into his inaugural self-titled art exhibition 'Renn Lim by Renn Lim'. Created as a limited-edition keepsake for visitors to the exhibition, the catalogue features an art canvas, housing a myriad collection of his art. Visitors take home an individual art piece, which the artist hand-painted and inked, and a booklet and cards showcasing miniature replicas of his original drawings and his interesting choices of medium (receipts, ticket stubs, etc).

Designer
Pann Lim
Art Directors
Claire Lim
Pann Lim
Creative Director
Pann Lim
Illustrator
Renn Lim

Photographer
John Nursalim
Copywriters
Aira Lim
Claire Lim
Design Agency
Kinetic Singapore
Client
holycrap.sg

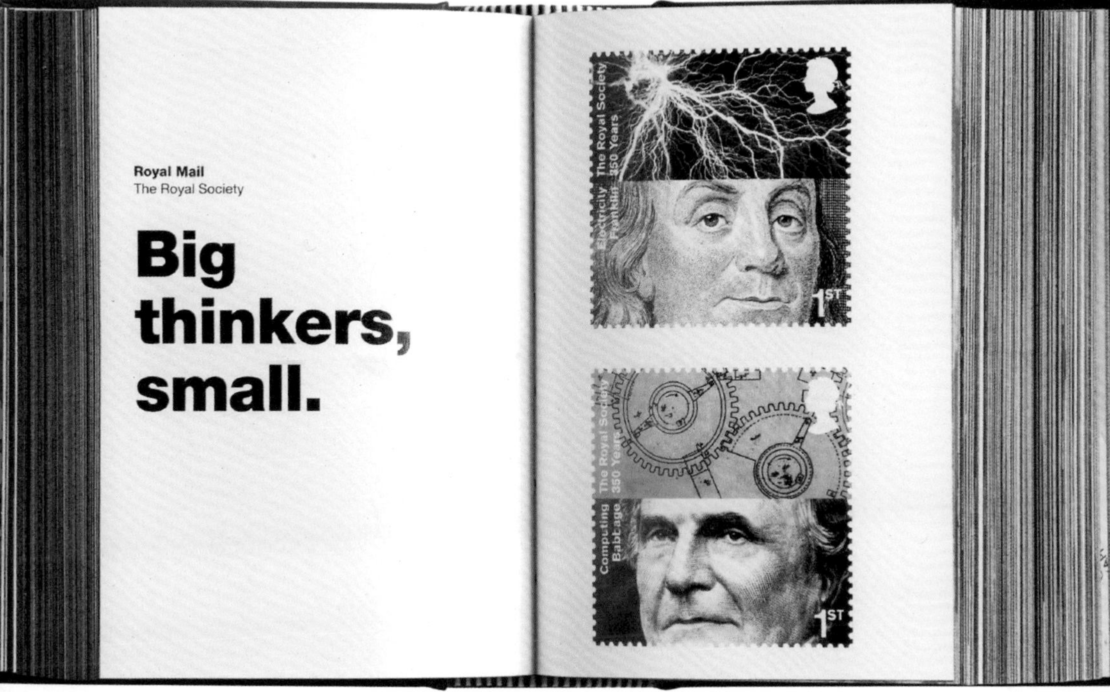

Royal Mail
The Royal Society
Big thinkers, small.

Catalogues & Brochures
hat-trick design

In Brief
To celebrate our tenth anniversary, we decided to produce a small book, 'In Brief'. The aim was to showcase and celebrate some of our work from the past ten years. Each project comes with a very brief description, written by Nick Asbury, as we felt that the work should speak for itself. The book opens with a quote by Elmore Leonard: 'I try to leave out the parts that people skip'. This is closely followed by the four-word foreword: 'Briefs aren't. Ideas are'.

Designer
Alex Jurva
Creative Directors
Gareth Howat
Jim Sutherland
Copywriters
Nick Asbury
Gareth Howat
Jim Sutherland

Design Agency
hat-trick design
Client
hat-trick design

Greeting Cards & Invitations
hat-trick design

Cocktail Party Invitation

We wanted to create an invitation for our ten-year anniversary cocktail party; to produce something that would get noticed and played with. We produced a series of small cards, which were fastened together using a cocktail stick. There were ten different cards, one for each year of business. Each card showcased items you normally associate with cocktail sticks, such as olives, sausages and cherries. Using the cocktail stick to fasten the cards together meant recipients had to interact with the invitation.

Designer
Laura Bowman
Creative Directors
Gareth Howat
Jim Sutherland
Illustrator
Laura Bowman

Design Agency
hat-trick design
Client
hat-trick design

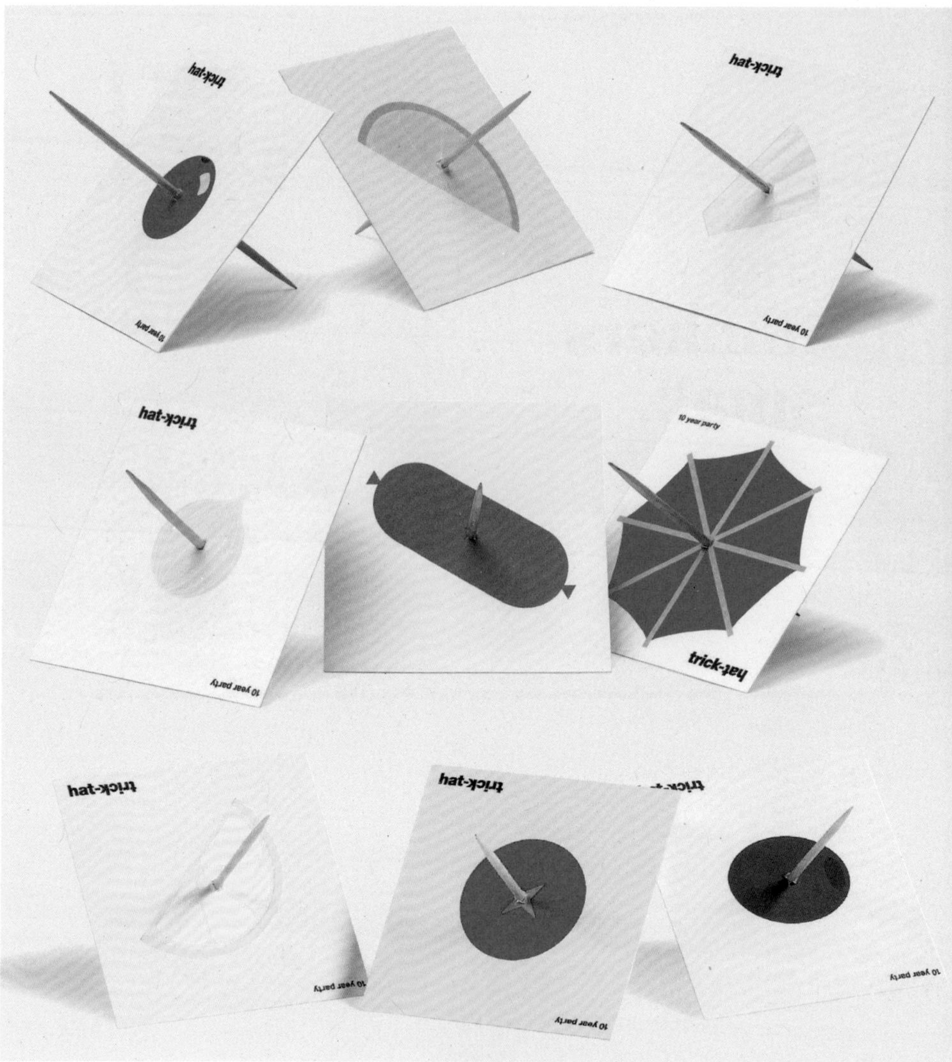

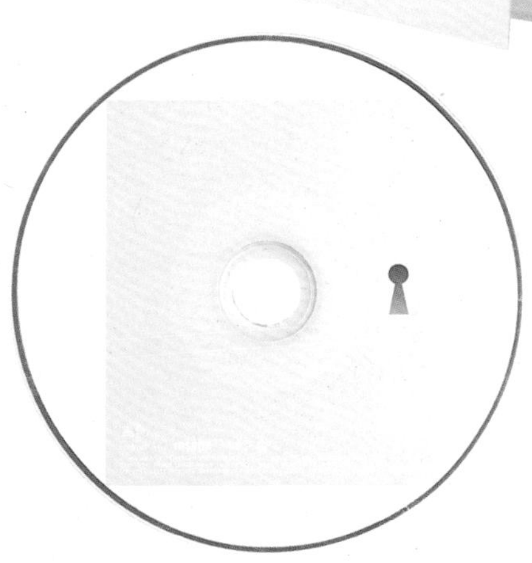

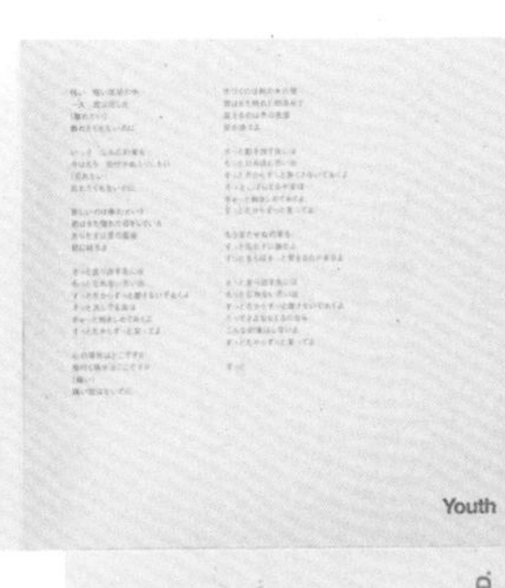

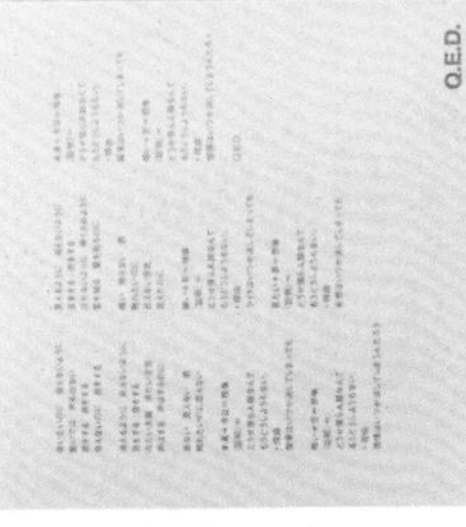

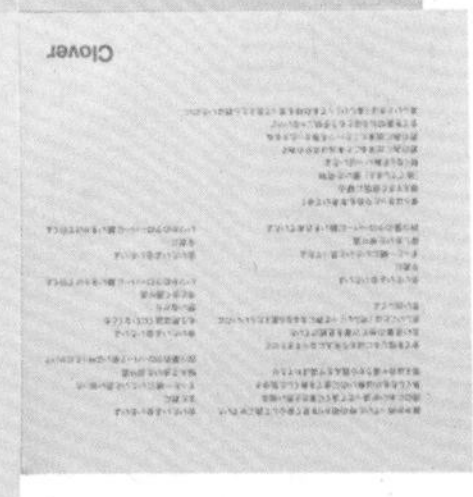

CD, DVD & Record Sleeves
Norio Tanaka
for Warner Music Japan

androp door
We designed this record sleeve for the album 'door' by Japanese band androp. The sleeve comprises eight pages (one for each track). Each page features a square hole in the centre. These represent eight doors. To emphasise the concept of simplicity and minimalism, the band's logo is embossed in lacquer on the back of the album in the basic, prescribed font. The lyrics booklet follows the design of the overall package. Each page is printed with the lyrics of one of the songs. The door visual extends to the CD itself, on which a door is printed in both gloss and matte finish, with the design featuring a single keyhole.

Designer
Norio Tanaka
Art Director
Norio Tanaka
Record Companies
Respire
unBORDE

Clients
Respire
unBORDE
Warner Music Japan

Stamps
hat-trick design
for Royal Mail

Royal Shakespeare Company Stamps
In these six stamps, hat-trick design captured the drama and energy of the Royal Shakespeare Company over its five decades. The stamps had to portray key productions while giving a sense of the groundbreaking, often avant-garde nature of the RSC's work. To that end, hat-trick researched stills from iconic plays and actors that held their intensity at a small scale. Resonant quotes and play titles were then applied by illustrator and typographer Marion Deuchars, in her energetic style. The Queen's head and value are a contrasting bright red – a nod to the RSC's famous red theatre seats and logo.

Designers
Marion Deuchars
Tim Donaldson
Gareth Howat
Jim Sutherland
Creative Directors
Gareth Howat
Jim Sutherland
Illustrator
Marion Deuchars
Photographers
Nobby Clark
Ellie Kurttz
Angus McBean

Design Manager
Catharine Brandy
Design Agency
hat-trick design
Photography
Joe Cocks Studio
Collection
Head of Design & Editorial
Marcus James
Client
Royal Mail

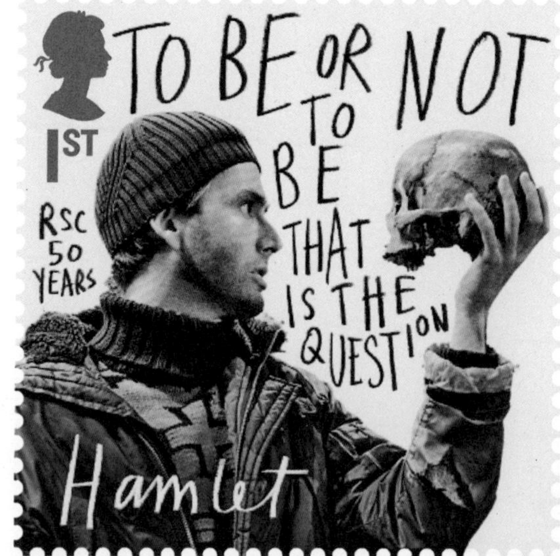

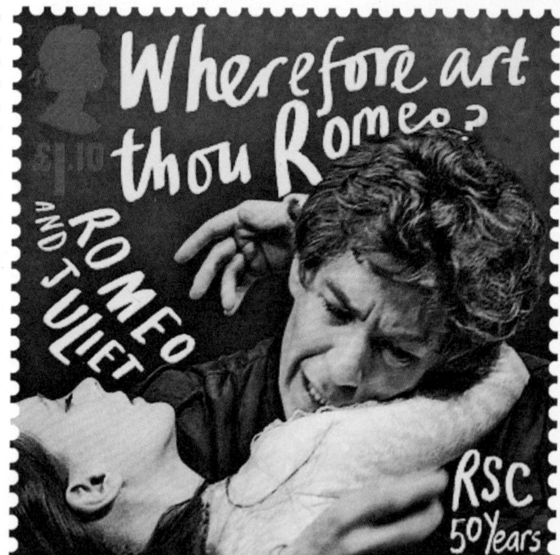

Stamps
GBH
for Royal Mail

FAB: The Genius of Gerry Anderson
Stamps and Products
GBH designed six stamps and a miniature sheet to celebrate puppet master Gerry Anderson's pioneering Supermarionation work. The stamps featured iconic scenes and characters within white borders evoking a 60's style TV screen, with programme logotypes laid across the bottom of the frame like film titles. Micro-lenticular print technology was introduced on the stamps to create an illusion of movement that showed the famous Thunderbirds launch sequence when tilted. A presentation pack featured an informative interview with Gerry Anderson and a history of his work.

Designers
Mark Bonner
Harry Edmonds
Russell Saunders
Creative Director
Mark Bonner
Illustrator
Gerry Embleton
Photographer
John Edwards
Writers
Chris Bentley
Stephen La Riviere
Stamp Design Manager
Catharine Brandy
Products Design Manager
Alastair Pether
Head of Design & Editorial
Marcus James
Editorial Manager
Helen Cumberbatch
Design Agency
GBH
Client
Royal Mail

Stationery
Pearlfisher
for Josh Wood

Josh Wood Stationery
Pearlfisher created the new brand identity and tone of voice for king of colour Josh Wood, one of the hair and beauty industry's foremost trendsetters. The identity has been expressed across stationery and printed materials, whilst also setting the tone for bringing the brand to life within the interiors of Josh Wood's London Atelier. Pearlfisher's identity design takes the form of a stylish master's signature in muted natural colours. This is punctuated by bright bursts of fluorescent colour through a set of three perfectly drawn O's to signify perfection and balance.

Designer
Poppy Stedman
Design Director
Poppy Stedman
Creative Director
Natalie Chung
Creative Partner
Karen Welman
Strategic Director
Yael Alaton
Design Agency
Pearlfisher
Client
Josh Wood

Applied Print Graphics
Hakuhodo
for The Asahi Shimbun

Massaging Circulation
The Asahi Shimbun is Japan's leading daily newspaper. It enjoys the second largest circulation in the world, which has fallen in recent years due to the increasing popularity of online news sites. The Asahi Shimbun decided to fight this decline. It printed the 'Massaging Circulation' ad, featuring a diagram of acupressure points. Cut out... slip on... and knead. Easy enough for anyone to deliver a great massage. The 'Massaging Circulation' ad connected families in ways digital media couldn't. Tweets, blogs and e-zines mentioned the ad, 75% of readers responded positively, and subscriptions stopped falling for a whole month.

Designer
Kayo Maeyama
Art Director
Kayo Maeyama
Creative Director
Takayoshi Kobayashi
Illustrator
Kayo Maeyama
Copywriter
Takayoshi Kobayashi

Producer
Mitsuki Kyo
Advertising Agency
Hakuhodo
Client
The Asahi Shimbun

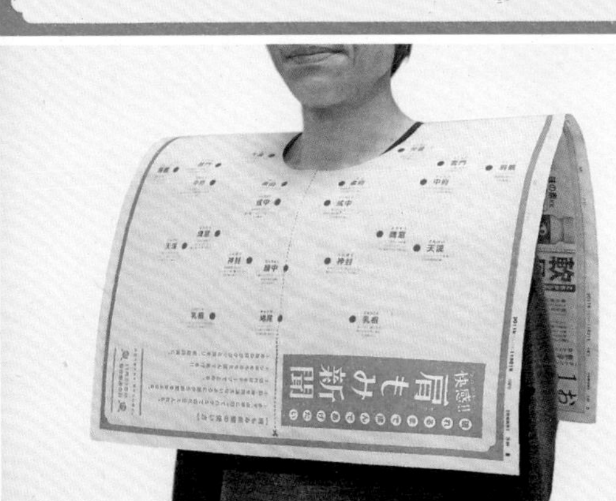

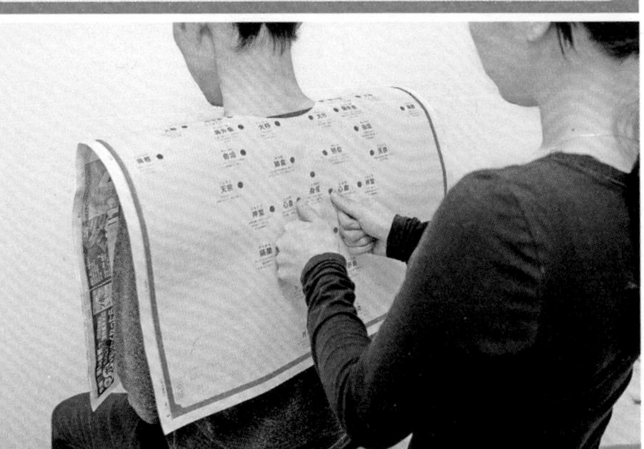

Applied Print Graphics
Imprimerie du Marais

Notebook#1
As our print shop turned 40, we started thinking of a fresh way to illustrate our second generation's know-how. Our idea stemmed from our daily involvement in creative production, and the challenges faced in print design. We produced a boxset of notebooks, each designed by a different studio and given a contemporary edge to traditional printing techniques such as embossing, hot foiling, silkscreen printing and stitched binding. Here comes 'Notebook#1', the joint product of eight creative agencies' flair and of our craft as printers.

Designers
Brogen Averill
Robert Boon
Johannes Breyer
Sebastian Fischer
Magnus Helgesen
Philipp Hubert
Camilla Kovac
Diedrich
Joe Kwan
Xavier Majewski
David Moritz
Gaute Tenold Aase
Julian Zimmermann
Creative Director
Mélody Maby
Printer
Jacky Przedborski

Creative & Art Direction
Imprimerie du Marais
Design Agency
Wahaus
Creative Agencies
Deutsche & Japaner
Grandpeople
Inventory Studio
Studiowill
Visiotypen
Paper Supplier
Arjowiggins
Creative Papers
Client
Imprimerie du Marais

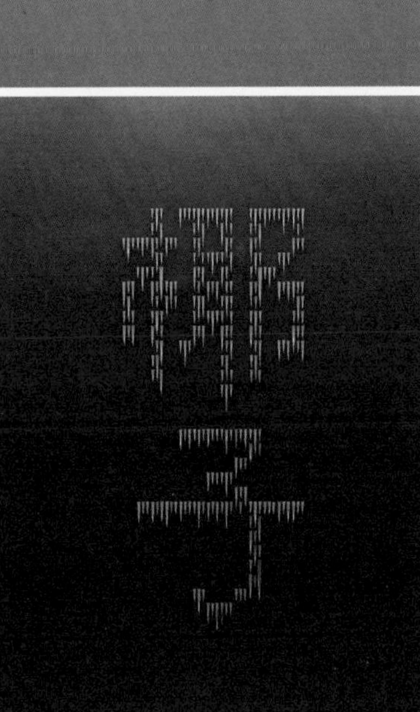

Posters
Roots
for The B Team

Durian / Pineapple / Coconut
In Malaysia, although local fruits are plentiful, they are seldom written about or celebrated in local culture. We designed a series of hand-crafted posters for three common local fruits – durian, pineapple and coconut – for an exhibition called 'Makanlah Buah-buahan Tempatan'. The audience connected instantly with the posters by recalling their forgotten love for the fruits. The posters evoked memories of the fruits' distinct characteristics, such as skin texture, colour and taste. These are elevated in the posters through the use of colours and paper cut techniques.

Designer
Jonathan Yuen
Art Director
Jonathan Yuen
Creative Director
Jonathan Yuen
Design Agency
Roots

Client
The B Team
Brand
Makanlah
Buah-buahan
Tempatan

Posters
Dowling Duncan
for Kodak

The Kodak Instamatic Posters
This is a series of posters designed as part of a programme by Kodak Design Strategy and Branding to reinvent the company's Instamatic camera. The posters introduced the 'reborn' camera, while clearly demonstrating and underlining Kodak's rich heritage in the instant camera field.

Designer
Gary Williams
Creative Directors
John Dowling
Rob Duncan
Copywriter
David Begler

Design Agency
Dowling Duncan
Client
Kodak

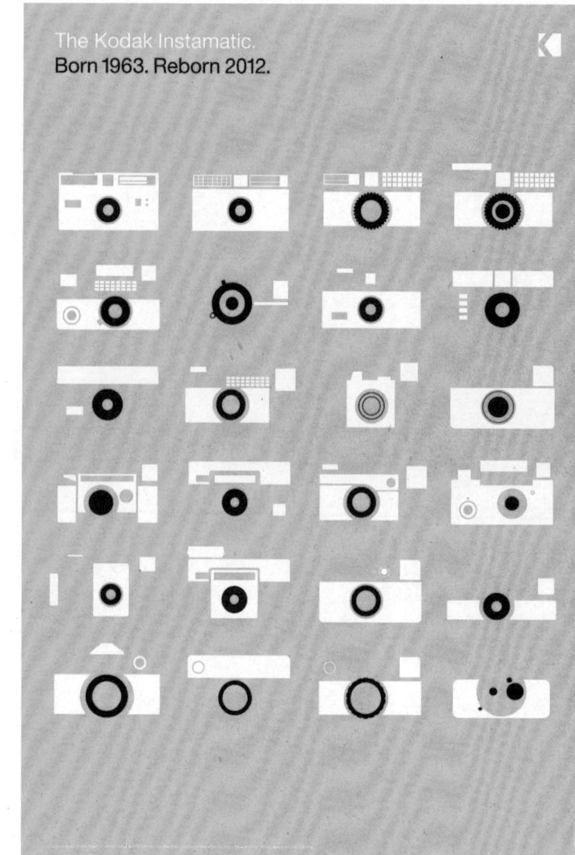

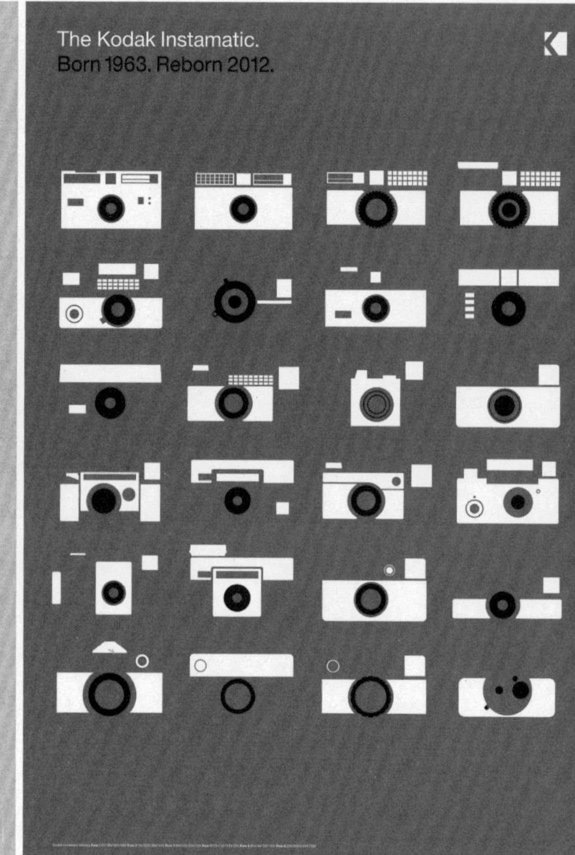

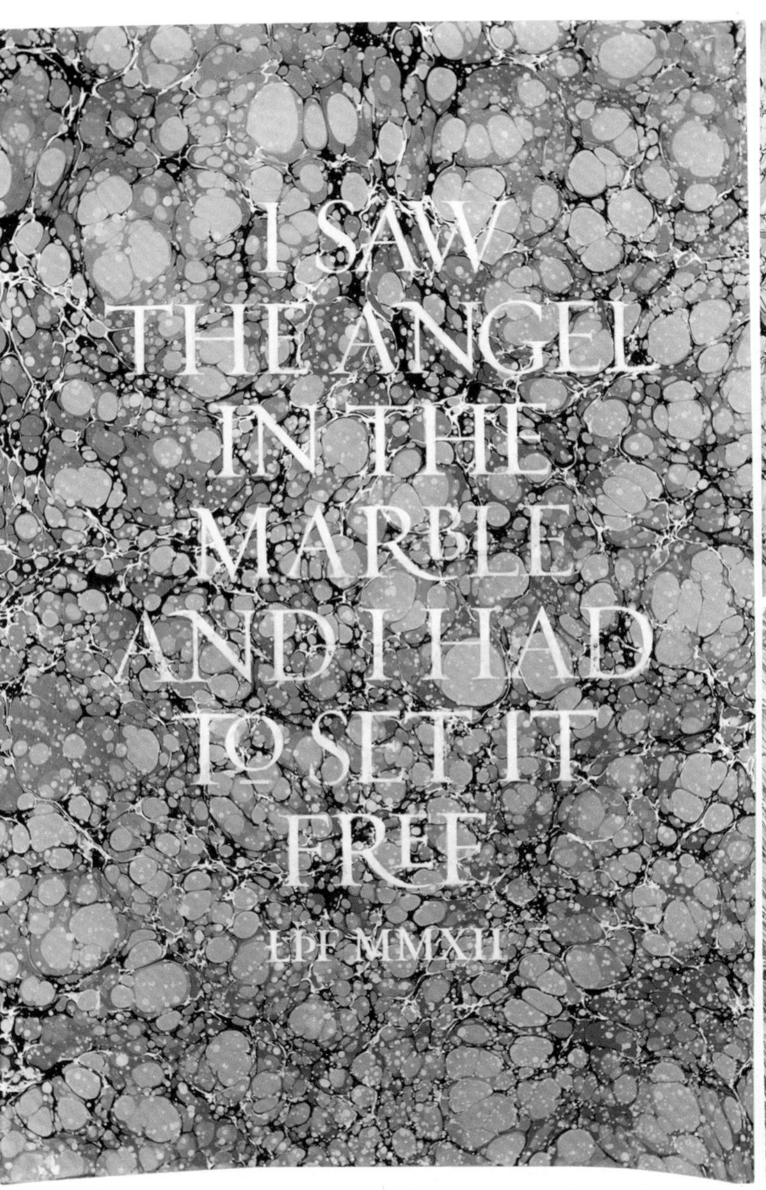

Posters
Music
for the Leeds Print Festival

Marbled Posters
As the Leeds Print Festival celebrates all forms of the printing process, virtue was made of an age-old practice that was dying out, yet one which had an emotional connection with people of all ages through their early school years: marbling. Using a tinted UV varnish, a typographic message was sealed onto blank paper, so when the marbling process began, the inks marbled everywhere but the sealed area. Hidden in the stock, the famous Michelangelo quote was revealed: 'I saw the angel in the marble and I had to set it free'.

Designers
Edward Johnson
Craig Oldham
Jordan Stokes
Marbling Artist
Jemma Lewis
Curator
Amber Smith

Production Manager
Matthew Beardsell
Design Agency
Music
Printers
AS For Print
Client
Leeds Print Festival

Posters
The Jupiter Drawing Room Utopia
for BirdLife

SOS Festival Posters
These posters were displayed at BirdLife's stand at the 'Oceans of Life' photographic exhibition. The week-long exhibition took place at the Iziko Museum and was in support of BirdLife's annual Save Our Seabirds Festival.

Designer
Steven Tyler
Copywriters
Jonathan Pepler
Gerhard Pretorius

Advertising Agency
The Jupiter Drawing Room Utopia
Client
BirdLife

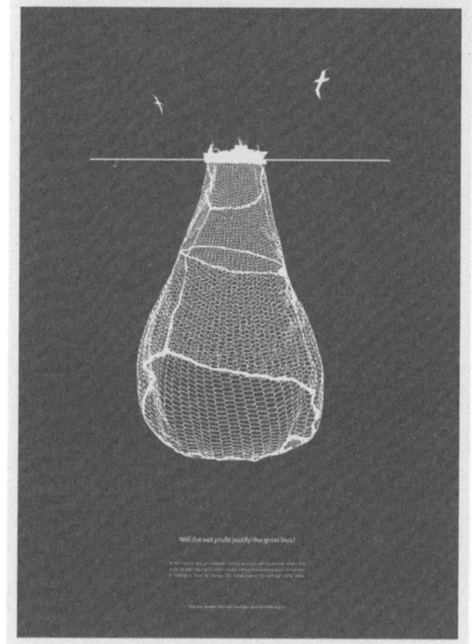

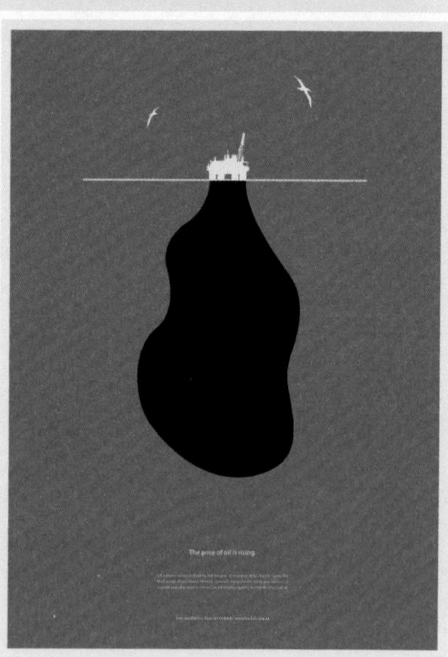

Posters
Serviceplan München

1m² of Curiosity: the Do-it-yourself Recruitment Posters

Serviceplan needs creatives who are searching for ideas everywhere and who are challenged by every blank sheet of paper. In order to communicate this message, we created posters that only revealed their messages when someone started doodling on them. Hung up on the blackboards of design universities, our series of illustrated messages addressed our target group: creatives with endurance and a wild imagination.

Designers
Fernando Santos Silvestrin
Manuel Wolff

Graphic Designer
Aletta Grolman

Creative Directors
Maik Kaehler
Christoph Nann

Copywriter
Michael Pilzweger

Chief Creative Officer
Alexander Schill

Advertising Agency
Serviceplan München

Client
Serviceplan München

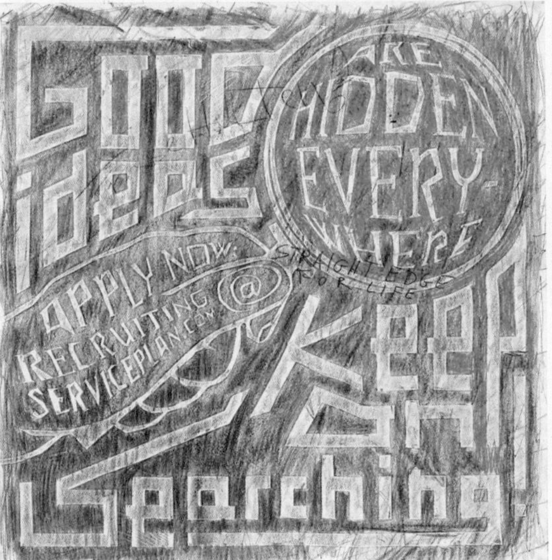

Logos
The Allotment London
for White Logistics & Storage

White Logistics & Storage Identity
The haulage industry is so commodified that skill, knowledge and dedication to service often go unnoticed. White Logistics wanted to change this and to grow their business. Our brief was to develop a brand proposition and identity that would communicate White's drive and passion, and put them on the map in the minds of potential customers. Research showed that White Logistics genuinely make a difference by going that extra mile to solve customers' challenges. This is expressed through the new straight forward 'black and white' problem solving attitude and visual expression.

Designer
James Backhurst
Creative Directors
James Backhurst
Michael Smith
Paula Talford
Animator
George Alexander

Design Agency
The Allotment London
Account Director
Paul Middlebrook
Client
White Logistics
& Storage

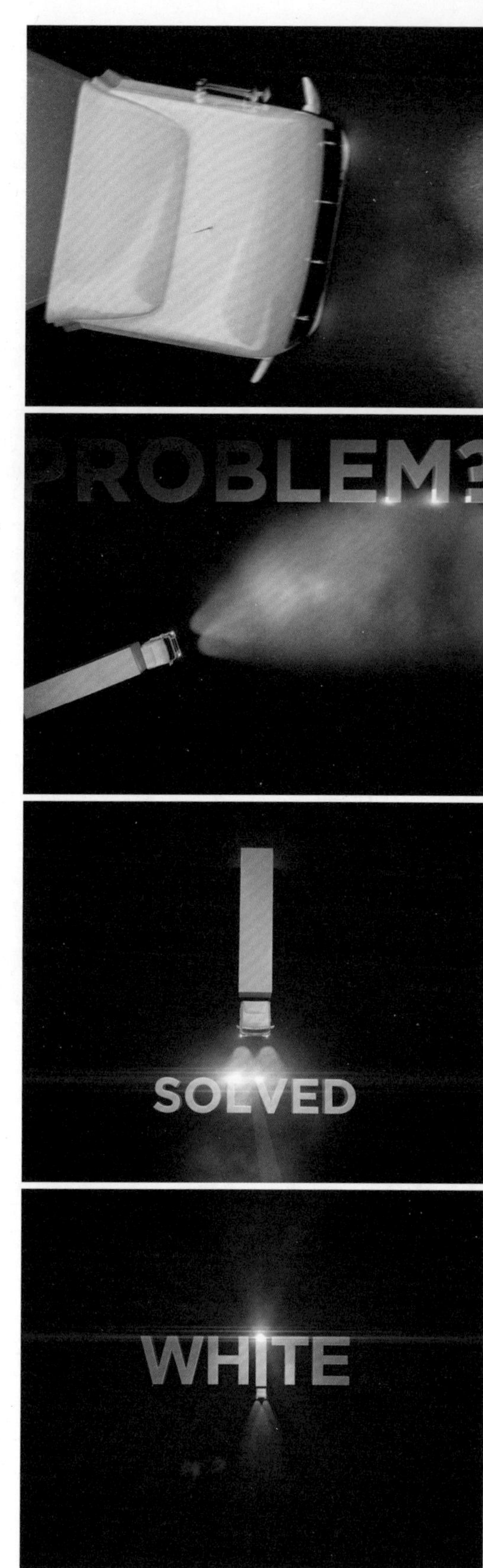

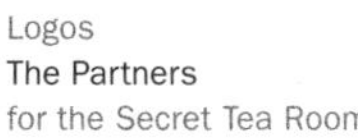
Logos
The Partners
for the Secret Tea Room

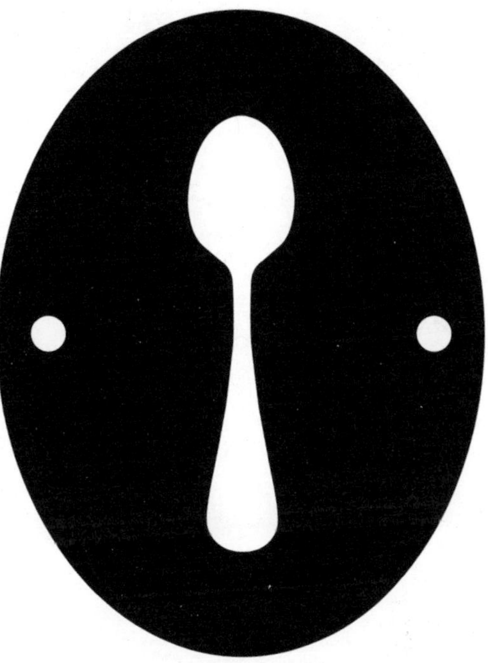

Secret Tea Room
This is a logo for the Secret Tea Room, a small, vintage-inspired tea room hidden in the heart of London's Soho. Find it if you can...

Designer
Leon Bahrani
Creative Director
Stuart Radford

Design Agency
The Partners
Client
Secret Tea Room

Point of Sale
McCann Erickson Malaysia
for Lotus Cars Malaysia

Lghtwght
Lotus sports cars owe their ultimate performance to their light weight. This philosophy of doing more with less influences the way the cars are designed and built – a minimalistic approach that is distinctly Lotus. Staying true to this philosophy, we designed a poster using the same materials that go into building the cars. Our aim was to showcase the technological brilliance and simplicity in design that are the hallmark of every Lotus. The poster became part of an innovative display at a Lotus road show, featuring a stripped down Lotus Exige S suspended in mid-air.

Designers
Vince Lee
Jerome Ooi
Art Directors
Ean-Hwa Huang
Vince Lee
Jerome Ooi
Executive Creative Directors
Ean-Hwa Huang
Szu-Hung Lee
Copywriters
Randy Lee
Szu-Hung Lee
Kevin Teh

Advertising Agency
McCann Erickson Malaysia
Account Handler
Sharon Hew
Marketing Manager
Oh Kah Beng
Client
Lotus Cars Malaysia
Brand
Lotus

LGHTWGHT
USNG AN ALMNUM CHSSIS INSTD OF STEEL
RDCES WGHT BY 50% W/OUT CMPRMSNG
STRNGTH. TKNG YOU FRM 0–100KM/H IN
4.1 SECS. A FACT NT TO B TKN LGHTLY.
DO MRE W LESS.

Wayfinding & Environmental Graphics
Moon Communications Group
for The Darling

The Darling
After creating the brand identity and tone of voice for The Darling, our brief was to extend those elements into the physical environment of the hotel. The architectural design featured wedges cut into the main form of the building, so we applied that technique to our bespoke typeface. The result was an elevated wayfinding design that literally leans out to greet you. We also wrapped the glass exterior of the building in oversized prose that was intriguing to read, either in part or in its entirety.

Designer
Andrew Smith
Senior Designer
Yuna Choi Moon
Creative Director
Anthony Donovan
3D Artist
Grant Hendren
Senior Copywriter
Julie Rath Faktor

Design Agency
Moon Communications Group
Account Directors
Samantha Jenkins
Joanna Peasland
Client
The Darling

Wayfinding & Environmental Graphics
45 Gradi
for The Walt Disney Company Italia

Interior Graphics for The Walt Disney Company Italia
We were asked to develop environmental and way-finding graphics for the new headquarters of The Walt Disney Company Italia in Milan. We had to keep the interior graphic design, as well as the building's identity and signage, as clean and minimal as possible. The solution was to create sober, delicate graphics and signage in line with the contemporary interior, without compromising Disney's friendly spirit. We managed to combine the playfulness of the Disney universe with an elegant institutional language, and created artwork that interacts with its environment.

Designer
Anton Stepine
Creative Directors
Marina Cattaneo
Silvia Grazioli

Design Agency
45 Gradi
Client
The Walt Disney Company Italia

Wayfinding & Environmental Graphics
Linnett Webb Jenkins
for Park Walk Primary School

Park Walk Primary School Graphics
Our brief was to develop graphics for the reception, atrium, corridors, lift entrances and lift shaft of Park Walk Primary School in Chelsea, London. We wanted to give the school a distinctive visual language in line with its desire to inspire pupils as well as educate them. We used illustrations of animals as close as possible to actual size, giving the children a sense of scale. The overlapping outline is a visual game: where do the animals start and finish? The black and white pictogram style allowed us to produce and apply the graphics relatively inexpensively, maximising the available budget.

Designer
Tim Webb-Jenkins
Illustrator
Tim Webb-Jenkins
Architects
Alex Bailey
Tim Bushe
Richard Walker
Design Agency
Linnett Webb Jenkins
Account Handler
Sophie Linnett
Clients
Park Walk
Primary School
Royal Borough
of Kensington
and Chelsea

Wayfinding & Environmental Graphics
Ogilvy & Mather Colombia
for Mattel

Hotwheels Loop
Mattel wanted to communicate the Hotwheels experience to both parents and kids, with a very limited budget. Hotwheels seemed like a brand that had done it all; our challenge was to create something fresh yet simple. We designed a special billboard structure and placed it at a strategic place, an overpass bridge on one of Bogotá's main highways. This reproduction of a real scale track captivated the imagination of both children and their parents. It transformed an ordinary overpass bridge in Bogotá into a brand experience. Clearance took months and tons of paperwork.

Designer
Daniel Mora
Art Directors
Andres Lopez
Camilo Ruano
Creative Directors
Diego Cardenas
Mauricio Guerrero
Executive Creative Director
Juan Jose Posada
Chief Creative Officer
John Raul Forero
Photographer
Javier Crespo
Copywriter
Julian Gutierrez

Producers
Leonardo Miranda
Freddy Rivero
Advertising Agency
Ogilvy & Mather Colombia
Contractors
Vallas Modernas
Art Buyer
David Alvarado
Account Director
Fabio Quiroga
Client
Mattel
Brand
Hotwheels

Wayfinding & Environmental Graphics
dn&co.

dn&co. New Studio Graphics

The company dn&co. is a property marketing and design agency. We recently moved to London's West End, the heart of our client base, and the new studio needed to match our bold aesthetic and big ambitions, and make an impression on the neighbourhood. Capitalising on our uniform graphic frontage, large lit-up ceiling signage delivers a playful take on street level branding. A thick black line directs upstairs past chunky wooden wayfinding and eventually ends in our motif: the ampersand. In essence: concise, confident and healthily irreverent for the standard.

Designers
Connie Dickson
Simon Yewdall

Creative Directors
Ben Dale
Joy Nazzari

Design Agency
dn&co.

Contractors
Standard 8

Client
dn&co.

1

2

3

4

5

6

7

Jury Foreman
1. Theseus Chan
Work

2. Jon Hill
The Times

3. Becky Smith
Twin Magazine

4. Miguel Buckenmeyer
Buckenmeyer & Co

5. Mario Garcia
Garcia Media

6. Jaime Perlman
Vogue Magazine

7. Patrick Burgoyne
Creative Review

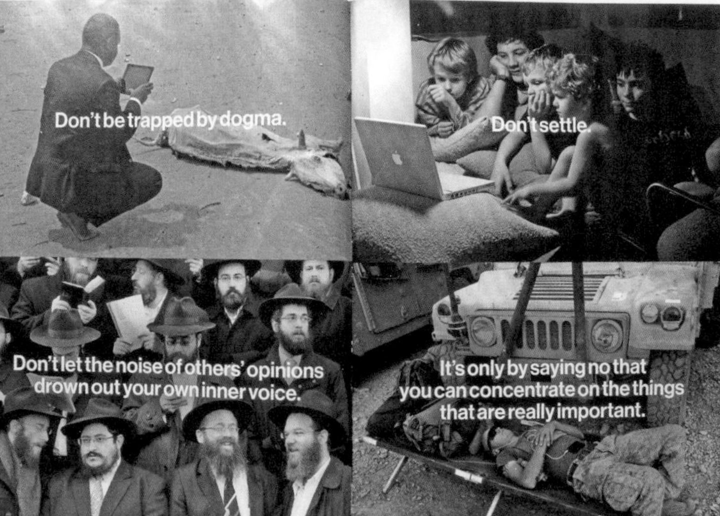

Yellow Pencil in Magazine & Newspaper Design

Entire Magazines
Bloomberg Businessweek

Steve Jobs 1955–2011
Official word of Steve Jobs' death reached 'Bloomberg Businessweek' as the staff of 40 was finishing a regular issue. The regular issue was scrapped and the staff spent all night finalising this special issue. The issue provides an in-depth look at the man behind all the products the world admires.

Art Directors
Jennifer Daniel
Robert Vargas
Designers
Evan Applegate
Shawn Hasto
Chandra Illick
Maayan Pearl
Kenton Powell
Lee Wilson
Design Director
Cynthia Hoffman
Creative Director
Richard Turley
Director of Photography
David Carthas

Picture Editors
Donna Cohen
Karen Frank
Jamie Goldenberg
Emily Keegin
Diana Suryakusuma
Publishing Company
Bloomberg
Project Manager
Emily Anton
Client
Bloomberg Businessweek

Nomination in Magazine & Newspaper Design

Entire Magazines
New York Magazine

9/11: One Day, Ten Years
For our special issue on 9/11, we chose an encyclopaedia format and a design scheme that allowed us to provide a full consideration of that world-changing day and its aftermath. The event, of course, was one of history's most photographed; the photo department played that familiar symphony in a new and surprising way, using many images that had never been seen before. The magazine's design was a rich, modern take on the reference form, with extensive marginalia adding depth and nuance.

Art Director
Randy Minor
Deputy Art Director
Hitomi Sato
Associate Art Director
Josef Reyes
Designers
Raul Aguila
Claudia de Almeida
Bianca Jackson
Design Director
Chris Dixon
Publisher
Larry Burstein
Illustrators
Kevin Hand
Henry Obasi
Photographers
Michael Ackerman
Bill Biggart
Yoni Brook
Alain Buu
Anthony Camerano
Eric Draper
Aristide Economopoulos
Nathan Harger
Emilie Lemakis
Ryan McGinley
Ben Melger
Lyle Owerko
Nelli Palomäki
Joseph Rodriguez
Timothy Schenck
Joe Tabacca
Larry Towell
Stephen Wilkes

Photography Director
Jody Quon
Editor in Chief
Adam Moss
Photo Editor
Leonor Mamanna
Senior Photo Editor
Lea Golis
Associate Photo Editor
Roxanne Behr
Design Agency
MGMT Design
Client
New York Magazine

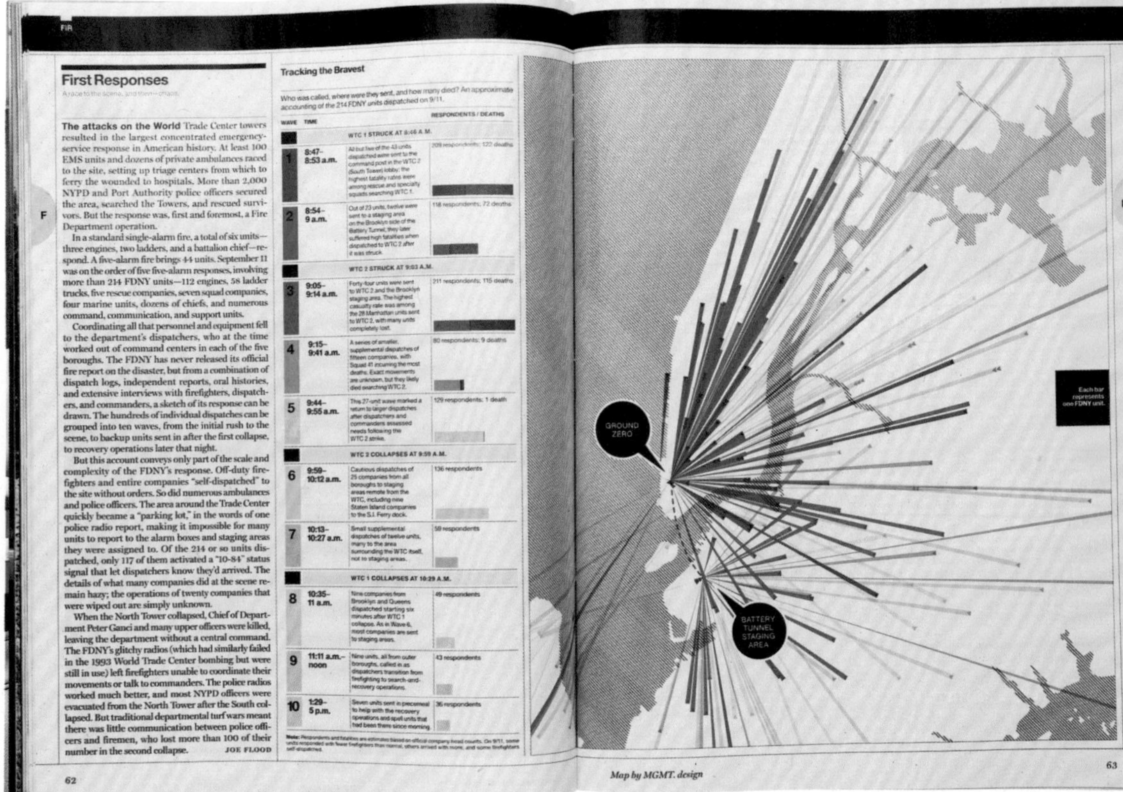

First Responses

A race to the scene, and then—chaos.

The attacks on the World Trade Center towers resulted in the largest concentrated emergency-service response in American history. At least 100 EMS units and dozens of private ambulances raced to the site, setting up triage centers from which to ferry the wounded to hospitals. More than 2,000 NYPD and Port Authority police officers secured the area, searched the Towers, and rescued survivors. But the response was, first and foremost, a Fire Department operation.

In a standard single-alarm fire, a total of six units—three engines, two ladders, and a battalion chief—respond. A five-alarm fire brings 44 units. September 11 was on the order of five five-alarm responses, involving more than 214 FDNY units—112 engines, 58 ladder trucks, five rescue companies, seven squad companies, four marine units, dozens of chiefs, and numerous command, communication, and support units.

Coordinating all that personnel and equipment fell to the department's dispatchers, who at the time worked out of command centers in each of the five boroughs. The FDNY has never released its official fire report on the disaster, but from a combination of dispatch logs, independent reports, oral histories, and extensive interviews with firefighters, dispatchers, and commanders, a sketch of its response can be drawn. The hundreds of individual dispatches can be grouped into ten waves, from the initial rush to the scene, to backup units sent in after the first collapse, to recovery operations later that night.

But this account conveys only part of the scale and complexity of the FDNY's response. Off-duty firefighters and entire companies "self-dispatched" to the site without orders. So did numerous ambulances and police officers. The area around the Trade Center quickly became a "parking lot," in the words of one police radio report, making it impossible for many units to report to the alarm boxes and staging areas they were assigned to. Of the 214 or so units dispatched, only 117 of them activated a "10-84" status signal that let dispatchers know they'd arrived. The details of what many companies did at the scene remain hazy; the operations of twenty companies that were wiped out are simply unknown.

When the North Tower collapsed, Chief of Department Peter Ganci and many upper officers were killed, leaving the department without a central command. The FDNY's glitchy radios (which had similarly failed in the 1993 World Trade Center bombing but were still in use) left firefighters unable to coordinate their movements or talk to commanders. The police radios worked much better, and most NYPD officers were evacuated from the North Tower after the South collapsed. But traditional departmental turf wars meant there was little communication between police officers and firemen, who lost more than 100 of their number in the second collapse. JOE FLOOD

Tracking the Bravest

Who was called, where were they sent, and how many died? An approximate accounting of the 214 FDNY units dispatched on 9/11.

Wave	Time		Respondents / Deaths
	WTC 1 STRUCK AT 8:46 A.M.		
1	8:47–8:53 a.m.	All but five of the 43 units dispatched were sent to the command post in the WTC 2 (South Tower) lobby; the highest fatality rates were among rescue and specialty squads searching WTC 1.	209 respondents; 122 deaths
2	8:54–9 a.m.	Out of 23 units, twelve were sent to a staging area on the Brooklyn side of the Battery Tunnel; they later suffered high fatalities when dispatched to WTC 2 after it was struck.	118 respondents; 72 deaths
	WTC 2 STRUCK AT 9:03 A.M.		
3	9:05–9:14 a.m.	Forty-four units were sent to WTC 2 and the Brooklyn staging area. The highest casualty rate was among the 28 Manhattan units sent to WTC 2, with many units completely lost.	211 respondents; 115 deaths
4	9:15–9:41 a.m.	A series of smaller, supplemental dispatches of fifteen companies, with Squad 41 incurring the most deaths. Exact movements are unknown, but they likely died searching WTC 2.	80 respondents; 9 deaths
5	9:44–9:55 a.m.	This 27-unit wave marked a return to larger dispatches after dispatchers and commanders assessed needs following the WTC 2 strike.	129 respondents; 1 death
	WTC 2 COLLAPSES AT 9:59 A.M.		
6	9:59–10:12 a.m.	Cautious dispatches of 25 companies from all boroughs to staging areas remote from the WTC, including new Staten Island companies to the S.I. Ferry dock.	136 respondents
7	10:13–10:27 a.m.	Small supplemental dispatches of twelve units, many to the area surrounding the WTC itself, not to staging areas.	59 respondents
	WTC 1 COLLAPSES AT 10:29 A.M.		
8	10:35–11 a.m.	Nine companies from Brooklyn and Queens dispatched starting six minutes after WTC 1 collapse. As in Wave 6, most companies are sent to staging areas.	49 respondents
9	11:11 a.m.–noon	Nine units, all from outer boroughs, called in as dispatchers transition from firefighting to search-and-recovery operations.	43 respondents
10	1:29–5 p.m.	Seven units sent in piecemeal to help with the recovery operations and spell units that had been there since morning.	36 respondents

Note: Respondents and fatalities are estimates based on official company head counts. On 9/11, some units responded with fewer firefighters than normal, others arrived with more, and some firefighters self-dispatched.

62

Map by MGMT. design

63

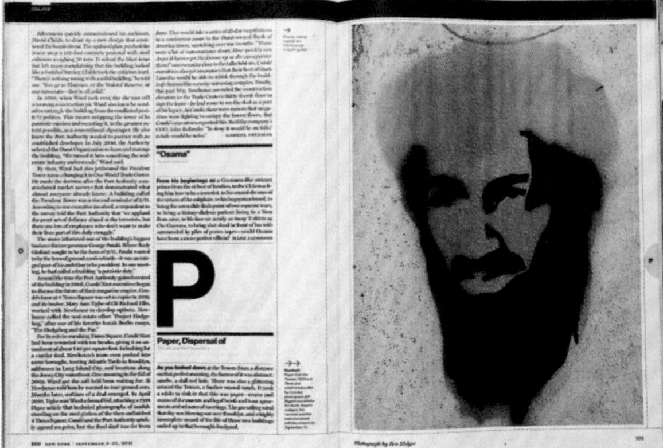

Exposed: WIKILEAKS' SECRET BUNKER p.34

INSIDER TRADING The black market in body parts p.94

YOUR LIFE TORN OPEN

We mean you . We're glad we caught you at home at Road in Clapham (we would ring you on 07956 but why disturb you?). Hope you're enjoying life as head of at . You must be terribly busy as director of (headquartered at Street), especially as you still hold 40 shares in the company, even if they only have a nominal value of . Don't forget to file your next tax return for And Media Ltd by 18 May 2011, but we're sure has that in hand. Hmm, just

We're printing these personal details only on your copy of WIRED – promise. We just wanted to show how easily we could find all sorts of data about you legally from public sources, from the electoral register to Companies House. Now just enjoy our cover story, by Steven Johnson, Andrew Keen and Jeff Jarvis, on life after privacy. And don't worry, we're not storing these details: we're destroying them once we've printed this copy. Though you know they'll still be out there somewhere, don't you?

The maveri behind the WORLD'S BIG CREDIT-CARD FRAUD p.122

Plus WIRED GEAR DIY sports cars + Portable power Cutting-edge axes

UK EDITION
The future as it happens

MAR 11 £3.99 wired.co.uk
03>
9 771758 833011

IDEAS **TECHNOLOGY** DESIGN **BUSINESS**

Nomination in Magazine & Newspaper Design

Magazine Front Covers
Wired

Wired March 2011 Cover
For our March 2011 cover story, we wanted to examine the new meaning of privacy in a socially networked age. So we built a research team with a brief to search the open internet for information about a number of our subscribers at random, as well as a few dozen public figures, from politicians to commentators. We then used an HP digital printer to produce high-quality individual covers for these readers, with their data displayed in a conversational style, warning them about the extent to which their private data was now public.

Art Director
Andrew Diprose
Photographer
Nick Wilson
Stylist
Tanja Martin
Picture Editor
Steve Peck

Publishing Company
The Condé Nast Publications
Client
Wired

Nomination in Magazine & Newspaper Design

Magazine Front Covers
The New York Times Magazine

What Happened to Air France Flight 447
For our cover story on 'What Happened to Air France Flight 447', we started to research existing photographs of the ocean, when it occurred to us that one of Tom Sandberg's waterscapes was a perfect evocation of an expanse of sea that the story's author, Wil S. Hylton, described as 'impenetrable as a shield of diamonds'. Even though Sandberg's picture was taken off the Canary Islands, on the other side of the Atlantic Ocean from where Flight 447 was found, we confirmed with experts that the sea near the crash site is in fact usually calm, as it is in our cover image. A small centred floating headline, without any other article deck, allowed us to convey the daunting nature of a search in a vast and endless body of water.

Art Director
Gail Bichler
Deputy Art Director
Caleb Bennett
Designers
Sara Cwynar
Hilary Greenbaum
Drea Zlanabitnig
Design Director
Arem Duplessis
Photographer
Tom Sandberg
Director of Photography
Kathy Ryan
Editor in Chief
Hugo Lindgren
Deputy Photo Editor
Joanna Milter
Associate Photo Editors
Stacey Baker
Clinton Cargill
Amy Kellner
Luise Stauss
Publishing Company
The New York Times Company
Client
The New York Times Magazine

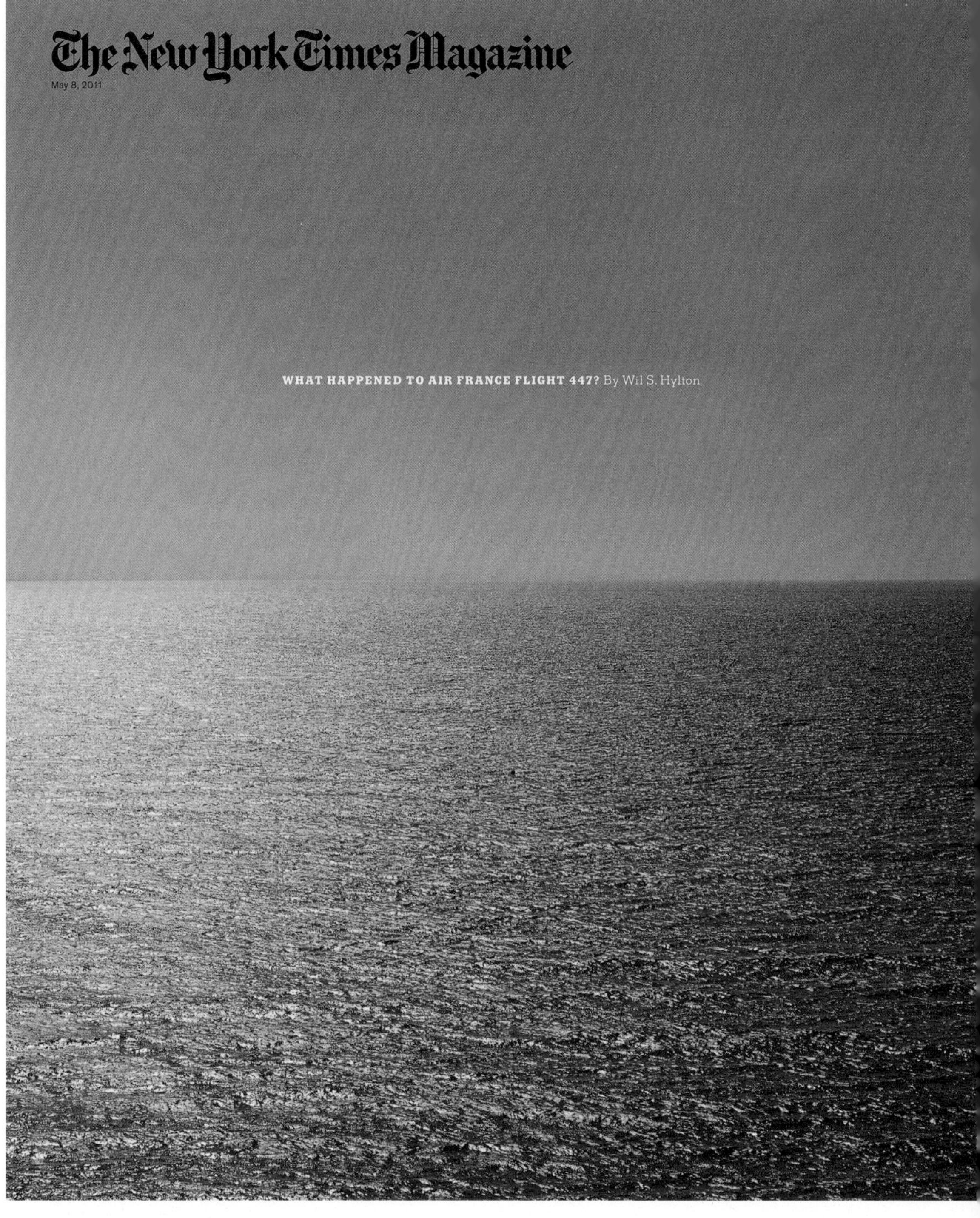

The New York Times Magazine
May 8, 2011
WHAT HAPPENED TO AIR FRANCE FLIGHT 447? By Wil S. Hylton

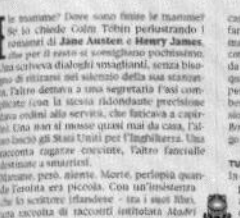

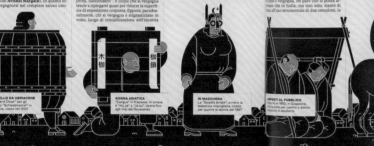

Nomination in Magazine & Newspaper Design

Magazine Sections
Il Sole 24 ORE

RANE
'RANE' is the cultural section of 'IL', supplement of 'Il Sole 24 ORE', the leading economics newspaper in Italy. The brief was to create a section with its own bold language. The tone of the articles is provocative and challenging; the visuals reflect this attitude. The foremost inspirations for the project were futurist magazines like 'Lacerba' and 'Dinamo Futurista'. The name 'RANE' is quoted from the medieval poem 'L'acerba' by Cecco d'Ascoli. Starting from there, the challenge was to elaborate a more modern language, using typography, infographics and visual storytelling.

Art Director
Francesco Franchi
Designers
Micaela Bonetti
Francesco Muzzi
Typographer
Christian Schwartz
Editor in Chief
Christian Rocca

Executive Editor
Roberto Napoletano
Editors
Guido Furbesco
Antonio Sgobba
Publishing Company
Il Sole 24 ORE
Client
Il Sole 24 ORE

Entire Magazines
SILNT
for Anonymous

Bracket Vol. 03: Education
'Bracket' is conceived as a publication that features everything in between: ideas, voices and processes that are overlooked and under-appreciated. The collection contains eight volumes on craft, hunger, ethics, spirit and failure. In each issue, we survey individuals from around the world on critical issues that surround our creative profession. The interviews are unedited and uncensored. 'Bracket' is also available online as a free digital download at www.brckt.com.

Art Director	Writer
Felix Ng	Robert Urquhart
Designers	Design Agency
Felix Ng	SILNT
Chloe Seet	Publishing Company
Editor in Chief	Anonymous
Germaine Chong	Client
Editor	Anonymous
Chloe Seet	

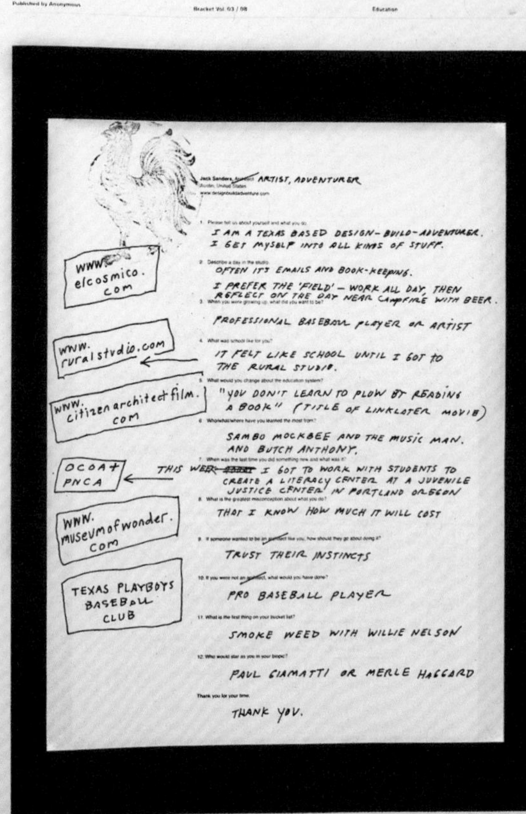

EDUCATION

BIANCA CHANG
CRAIG OLDHAM
JACK SANDERS
JASPER MORRISON
JOCELYN GLEI
JOHN JAY
KENYA HARA
KIRBY FERGUSON
KYLE BEAN
MAKOTO AZUMA
MASASHI KAWAMURA
NICOLE LAVELLE
SARAH TEMPLE
STEVE HELLER
TIMOTHY GOODMAN
XAVIER ENCINAS

ROBERT URQUHART

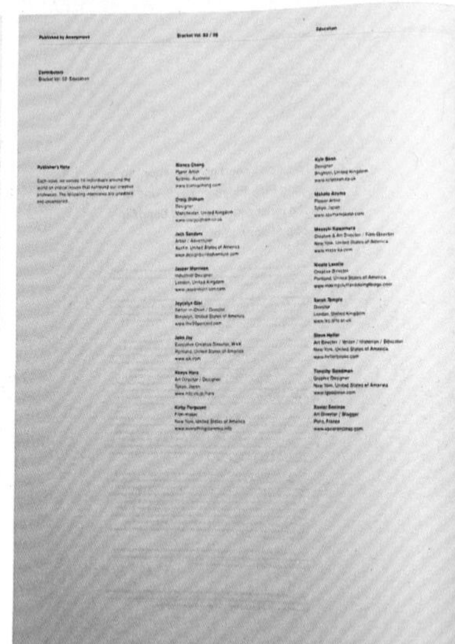

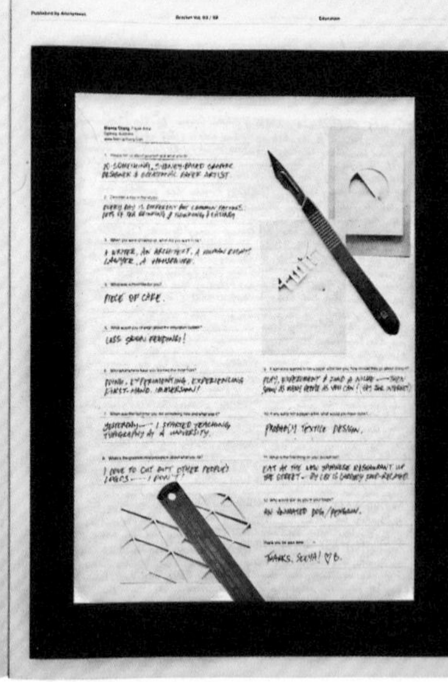

Entire Magazines
The Church of London

Little White Lies Issue 38: Another Earth
'Little White Lies' is an independent movie magazine that uses cutting-edge writing and design to get under the skin of cinema. Each issue takes a new film as its thematic blueprint. Issue 38 explored 'Another Earth', in which protagonist Rhoda is confronted by the existence of another world. The idea of duality – exploring parallel dimensions and reflections – was therefore a key visual theme. Two fully inverted print editions were produced (content, photographic and illustrative imagery included), employing a bespoke mirrored feature typeface.

Designer
Angus MacPherson
Creative Director
Paul Willoughby
Illustrators
Lauren Gentry
Kai & Sunny
Editor
Matt Bochenski

Creative Agency
The Church of London
Publishing Company
The Church of London
Client
The Church of London

Entire Magazines
Mash
for Meat & Livestock Australia

Chef's Special Latino Edition
After many trips to Latin America, this project was dear to us. We hired an old Mexican beach shack, threw a party, and invited Australia's best Latino chefs, a mix of young guys running taco trucks and old abuelas. Mash decorated the beach house and created Mexican inspired pottery and hand-painted tiles. A multitude of fabrics and crockery made for a beautiful array of colour. Finally, Australia realised there's another option to Tex Mex! The magazine is laden with bright illustrations, naive in style like Mexico City's sign writers – a true insight into the flavours and sites of Latin America.

Designer
Darren Song
Creative Director
James Brown
Illustrators
James Brown
Pat Mehbrei
Photographer
John Laurie

Stylist
Simon Bajada
Design Agency
Mash
Client
Meat & Livestock Australia

O-N-E C-U-T W-O-N-D-E-R-S

BRADD JOHNS (EXECUTIVE CHEF)
CROWN PLAZA – ADELAIDE

SERVES 6

STICKY BEEF SHORT RIB, WATERMELON, GINGER, RADISH, CORIANDER SALAD

2kg beef Short Ribs

MASTER STOCK
4lt chicken stock / 60g ginger, sliced not peeled / 6 cloves garlic, smashed
3 star anise / 2 lemongrass, smashed / 40g coriander seed, toasted
the zest of 4 oranges / 400ml Shaoxing Rice Wine / 500ml light soy / 300g palm sugar
— Combine all ingredients (except ribs), bring to the boil and allow to infuse overnight. Split the Short Ribs into individual bones and braise until soft. — Remove from the braising liquid and reduce down to half. — Return the ribs to the master stock and continue reducing, periodically spooning over the ribs to form a glaze.

WATERMELON SALAD
watermelon, cut in large cubes / breakfast radish, shaved into discs
fresh coconut, shaved / spring onion, finely sliced / pickled ginger / coriander, picked

NUM PLA DRESSING
fish sauce / ginger, chopped / chilli, chopped / lime juice / palm sugar
— Vacuum pack the watermelon with a couple of tablespoons of num pla dressing.

TO SERVE
— Remove watermelon from vacuum and mix with the rest of the ingredients.
— Artfully place the melon and other salad ingredients, lean two of the ribs against a cube and top with coriander, toasted rice and num pla dressing.

60

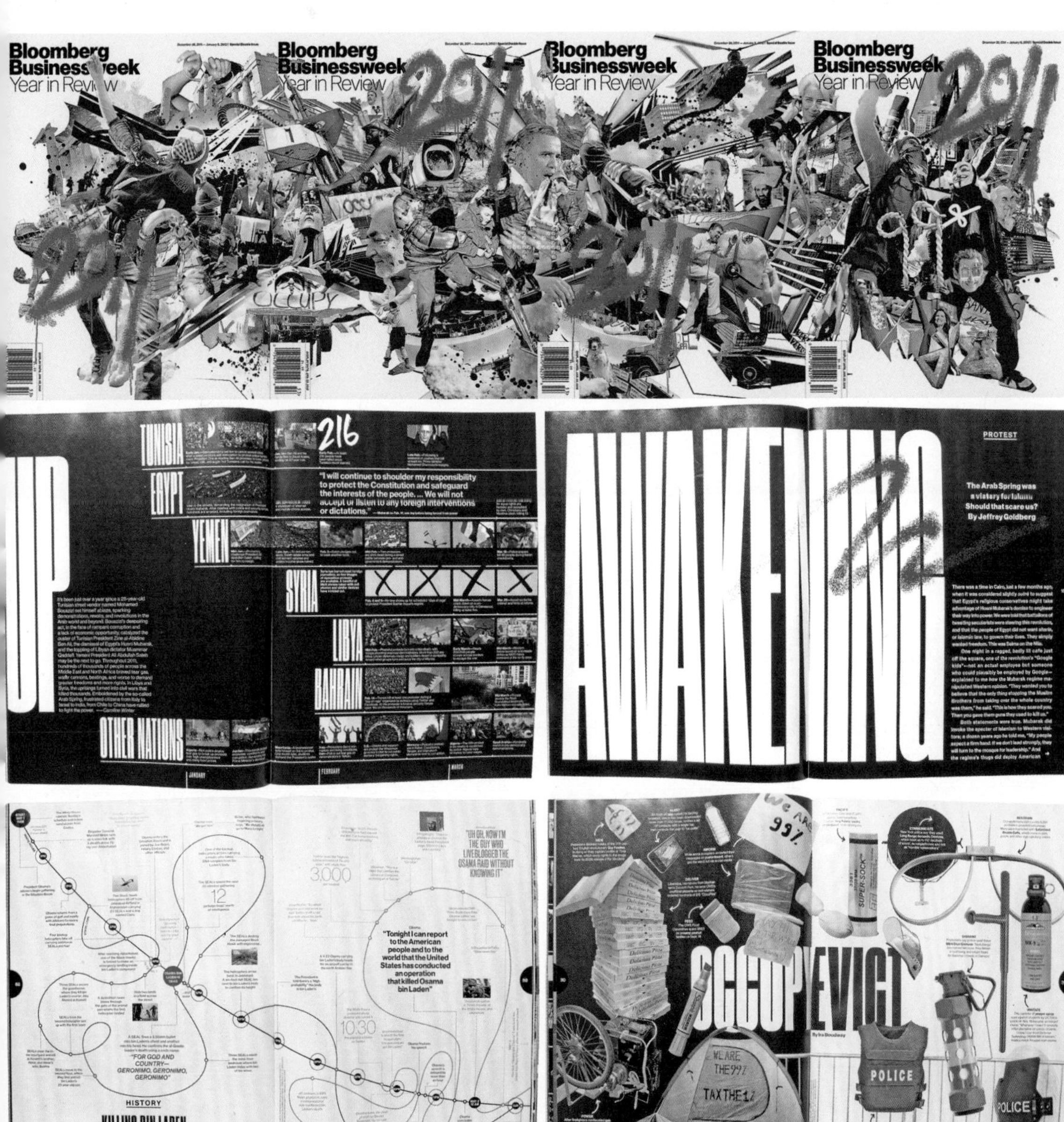

Entire Magazines
Bloomberg Businessweek

2011 Year in Review
It was a year of struggling economies, dysfunctional politics and open revolts. The 'Year in Review' issue chronicles the decline of the West and the rise of the rest. We released a set of four front covers that join together to make a single illustration reflecting a year of protest and pain.

Art Directors
Jennifer Daniel
Robert Vargas
Designers
Evan Applegate
Shawn Hasto
Chandra Illick
Tracy Ma
Maayan Pearl
Kenton Powell
Lee Wilson
Design Director
Cynthia Hoffman
Creative Director
Richard Turley

Director of Photography
David Carthas
Picture Editors
Donna Cohen
Jamie Goldenberg
Emily Keegin
Diana Suryakusuma
Publishing Company
Bloomberg
Project Manager
Emily Anton
Client
Bloomberg Businessweek

Entire Magazines
Carl's Cars

Carl's Cars Fall 2011 Issue
The cover with the muscle man is a tribute to the now unfashionable muscle cars. The spread with the chair is a story about an ice race in Sweden. The spread with the red car is about Sweden's Ferrari – SAAB Sonett. Other stories not shown: interview with actor Ryan Gosling (a 'Carl's Cars' trademark is a reprint of the interviewee's driving licence along with a signed car drawing); and Volkswagen New Beetle Coupé test drive down the Karl Marx Strasse in Berlin. The magazine finishes with a visit to the grave of John Z DeLorean.

Art Director	Publishing Company
Stéphanie Dumont	Carl's Cars
Creative Director	Client
Stéphanie Dumont	Carl's Cars Magazine
Editor in Chief	
Karl Eirik Haug	

Entire Magazines
Buffalo Publishing

Buffalo Zine
'Buffalo Zine' is a new editorial project based in Madrid and London: a publication on arts, aesthetics and self-expression. The focus is on featuring new talents and timeless icons from a personal, intimate perspective, with a punk wink and a hint of poetry. We named it a zine because of its free spirit. The form is as free as the content, and each issue will have a different format and design. But Buffalo is not even a zine. It wants to be an object. Homemade, like good bread, and created with joy, love and devotion, like a diary or an orchard. Something to own.

Art Directors
Adrián González
David G Uzquiza
Designer
David G Uzquiza
Creative Director
Adrián González

Editor in Chief
Adrián González
Publishing Company
Buffalo Publishing
Client
Buffalo

Magazine Front Covers
Wired

Wired May 2011 Cover
A five-minute shoot with an impatient and very busy Alan Sugar sounds like art director hell, specially when it's to illustrate a feature based on failure. For the May 2011 issue, 'Wired' took the conventions of cover design and turned them on their head; cropping through the face, misprinting a double masthead and running visible colour bars all gave the printers a nightmare – but the readers loved it.

Art Director
Andrew Diprose
Photographer
Peter Beavis
Picture Editor
Steve Peck

Publishing Company
The Condé Nast Publications
Client
Wired

Magazine Front Covers
Maison Moderne Publishing
for Ville de Luxembourg

City Mag
'City Mag' is the Ville de Luxembourg's official monthly publication. Its design is distinguished by two features. First, it is delivered in magazine format, unfolds into newspaper format, but has a magazine-quality feel. Second, its bold masthead changes for each edition – the first name of that month's cover star becomes the masthead title. Consistency on the cover is maintained by the photographic style and the subheading, 'City Magazine Luxembourg'. Browse all editions at www.citymag.lu.

Art Directors
Vera Capinha
Heliodoro
Maxime Pintadu
Designer
Stephanie Poras
Creative Director
Guido Kröger
Chief Creative Officer
Mike Koedinger
Photographer
Julien Becker
Production Director
Rudy Lafontaine
Editor in Chief
Duncan Roberts
Editor
Cynthia Schreiber
Managing Editor
Deborah Lambolez
Publishing Company
Maison Moderne
Publishing
Communications
Director
Marc Gerges
Client
Ville de Luxembourg

Magazine Front Covers
The New York Times Magazine

New York Times Magazine: The Illustration Cover Series

We commissioned illustrator Tim Enthoven for our cover story, 'The Human Swap'. The work brought visual scale to a piece on the complexities of negotiations for the release of Gilad Shalit – an Israeli soldier held prisoner, and released in exchange for 1,027 Palestinian prisoners. Tim illustrated all 1,028 figures by hand. For our Education Issue, we commissioned Will Bryant to draw doodles over a fun, hot-pink backdrop, to communicate the youthful zest in the issue's theme. We then added Dan Cassaro's sticker illustrations – resembling those in elementary school – on the cover and throughout.

Art Director
Gail Bichler
Deputy Art Director
Caleb Bennett
Designers
Sara Cwynar
Hilary Greenbaum
Drea Zlanabitnig
Design Director
Arem Duplessis
Illustrators
Will Bryant
Dan Cassaro
Tim Enthoven
Photography Director
Kathy Ryan

Editor in Chief
Hugo Lindgren
Picture Editors
Stacey Baker
Amy Kellner
Joanna Milter
Luise Stauss
Publishing Company
The New York Times Company
Client
The New York Times Magazine

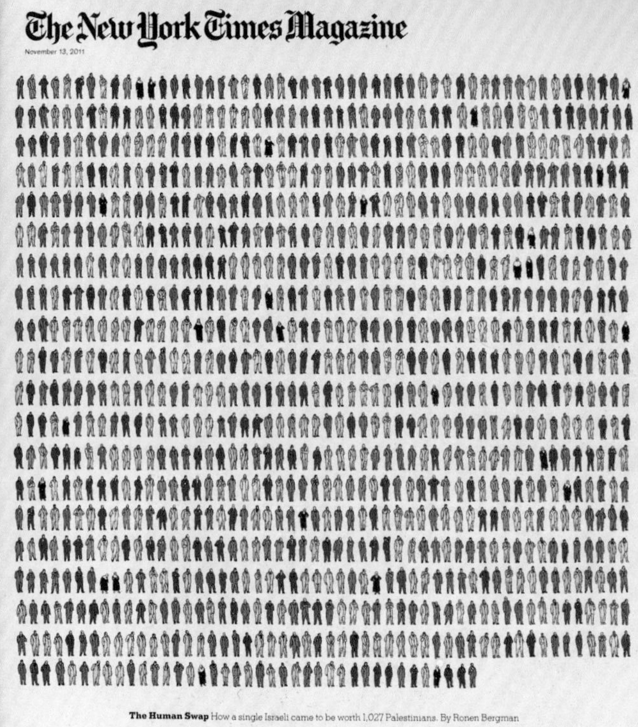

Magazine Front Covers
Bloomberg Businessweek

Bloomberg Businessweek Cover Series
Our goal is to design original, surprising covers each week that make people pick up the magazine. We strive for something that looks a little removed from what people traditionally perceive an American business magazine to look like, yet something accessible to anyone passing a newsstand.

Art Directors
Jennifer Daniel
Robert Vargas
Design Director
Cynthia Hoffman
Creative Director
Richard Turley
Director of Photography
David Carthas

Publishing Company
Bloomberg
Client
Bloomberg Businessweek

Magazine Front Covers
News International
for The Sunday Times

The Sunday Times Magazine:
Space Shuttle Cover
This cover needed to illustrate that the space shuttle and all it represented had come to an end. It had to be different and stand out from what else was going to be published. In addition, we wanted to convey what was going to happen to the shuttle in retirement. We thought of it becoming a museum piece or an object in an art gallery, which is when Fiona Banner's harrier jet installation at Tate Britain came to mind. We replicated her installation, with the shuttle replacing the jet – we did a rough Photoshop sketch and then sent it to a 3D artist who photographed the space and rendered the shuttle.

Art Director
Alyson Jane Waller
Image Manipulator
Colin Thomas

Publishing Company
News International
Client
The Sunday Times

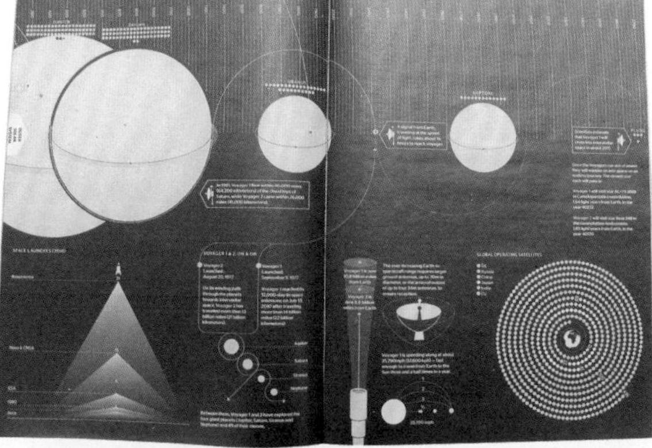

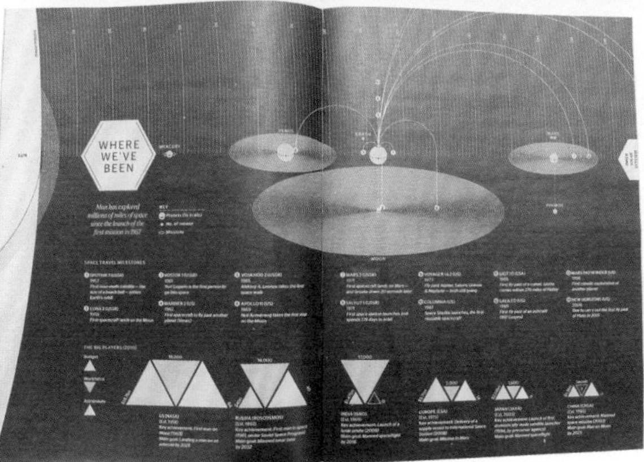

Newspaper Supplements
The Times

Eureka
Eureka is the monthly science magazine of newspaper The Times. It seeks to bring the wonders of science to a wider audience. Eureka has tackled complex subject matter from string theory to the Large Hadron Collider, making them accessible with clear and playful art direction.

Art Director
Matt Curtis
Designer
Fraser Lyness
Picture Editor
Madeleine Penny

Publishing Company
The Times
Client
The Times

1

2

3

4

5

6

7

Jury Foreman
1. Mary Lewis
Lewis Moberly

2. Alba Rosell
Bendita Gloria

3. Sarah Moffat
Turner Duckworth
San Francisco

4. Shaun Dew
Dew Gibbons

5. Chris Zawada
TAXI Vancouver

6. David Beard
BRANDHOUSE

7. Fred Gelli
Tátil Design

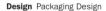

Yellow Pencil in Packaging Design

dBOD
for Heineken

Heineken STR Bottle

How do you make a mass-market product desirable in up-market environments? Usually, it's only the beer in the bottle that consumers seek out. But what if the bottle could become an experience in itself? STR, with its premium, minimalist aluminium design, is the world's first UV reactive bottle. The bottle looks amazing, feels amazing and reveals the Heineken Star Trail when under UV light. The STR bottle was first distributed in a bespoke 3D capsule to trade partners. Today it can be seen lighting up high-end nightclubs and bars around the world.

Designers
Stephane Castets
Glenn Docherty
Creative Directors
Ramses Dingenouts
Pascal Duval
Merien Kunst
Design Agency
dBOD
Creative Agency
iris Worldwide

Account Directors
Matt Atherton
Evelyn Hille
Brand Director
Mark van Iterson
Client
Heineken

Yellow Pencil in Packaging Design

LOVE
for Diageo

Johnnie Walker 1910 Special Edition Bottles
Diageo asked us to create a special edition range of whiskey bottles that celebrates the launch of the world's first whiskey embassy, the Johnnie Walker House in Shanghai. Johnnie Walker has a long and distinguished history in China. Our records show that it landed in Shanghai in as early as 1910. We used this heritage as our inspiration, fusing Scottish and Chinese cultures by creating a set of willow patterned, white porcelain square bottles that commemorate Johnnie Walker's pioneering ambition and epic voyage across continents and oceans.

Design Director
Chris Myers
Creative Director
Dave Palmer
Illustrator
Chris Martin
Production Manager
Dani Hawley
Creative Agency
LOVE
Manufacturer
Wade Ceramics
Account Manager
Kat Towers
Client
Diageo
Brand
Johnnie Walker

Johnnie
Walker

Nomination in Packaging Design

Pentagram London
for Cass Art

Cass Art Pads
This is a line of 25 paper pads for the artist materials supplier Cass Art. Each design emphasises the materiality of the product. The coloured paper pad is adorned with a target made from hand-cut coloured paper; the marker pads are decorated with lines drawn by marker pens; the tracing paper features a traditional draughtsman's technique of parallel motion; and the layout pad is patterned with blocks drawn with ballpoint and pencil.

Designers
Fabian Hermann
Alex Johns
Zara Moore

Design Director
Angus Hyland

Design Agency
Pentagram London

Client
Cass Art

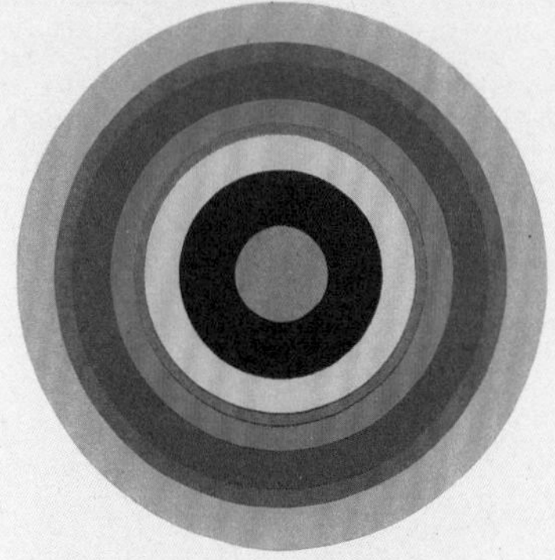

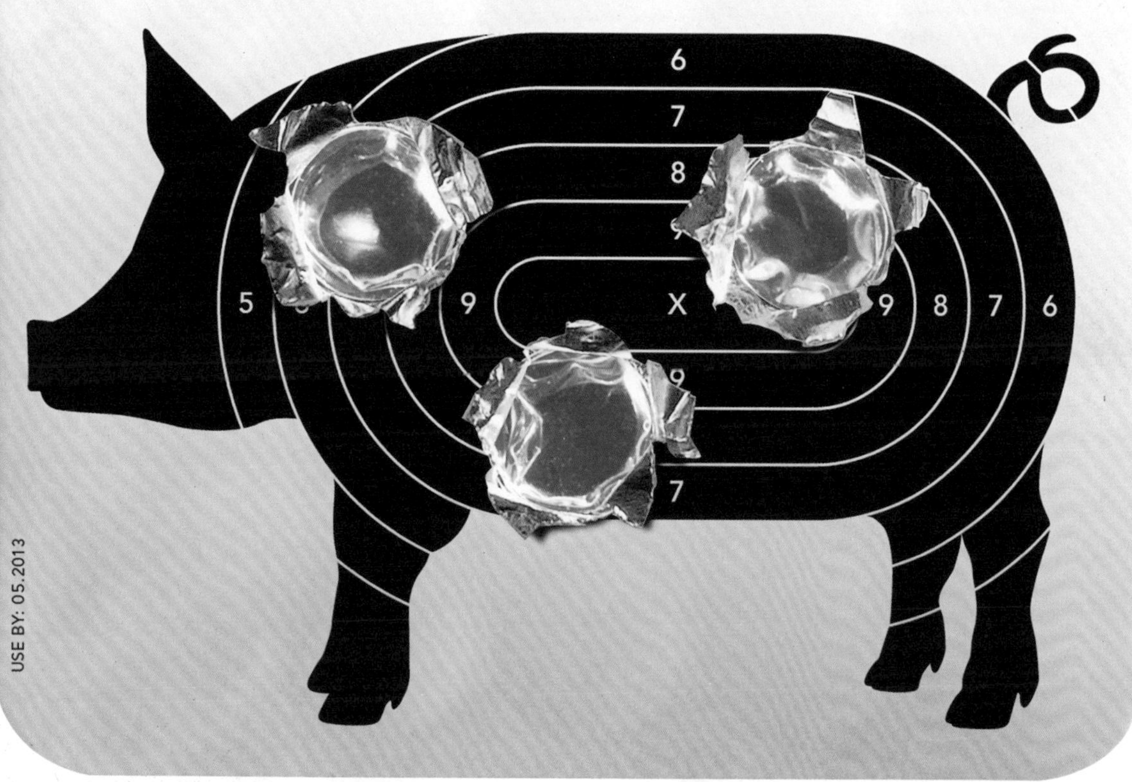

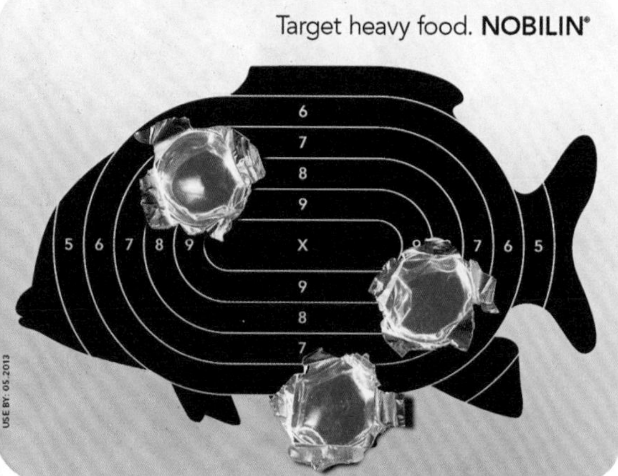

Nomination in Packaging Design

BBDO Proximity Berlin
for Medicom Pharma

Target Heavy Food
Nobilin aids digestion. By printing targets with different animals on the back of the blister pack, we demonstrated how the product works in a simple and playful way: every pill targets heavy food in your stomach.

Designers
Lukas Liske
Daniel Schweinzer
Art Director
Daniel Schweinzer
Illustrator
Daniel Schweinzer
Copywriter
Lukas Liske
Chief Creative Officers
Jan Harbeck
David Mously
Wolfgang Schneider
Agency Producer
Michael Pflanz
Advertising Agency
BBDO Proximity Berlin
Account Manager
Guelcan Demir
Marketing Manager
Rene Steinbusch
Client
Medicom Pharma
Brand
Nobilin

Packaging Design
Designers Anonymous

Warm Red
The brief was to create a bespoke Christmas gift for our clients, suppliers and friends. The gift needed to be desirable, demonstrate our creative thinking and have reference to design. We came up with a bespoke gift box based on an enlarged Warm Red Pantone chip. The colour split between the red and white conceals the join between lid and base. Inside is a bottle of mulled red wine, with a message on the label referencing the Warm Red colour chip.

Designers	Branding Agency
Darren Barber	Designers
Christian Eager	Anonymous
Creative Directors	**Client**
Darren Barber	Designers
Christian Eager	Anonymous

*
Add a touch of colour to your cheeks this season, with a glass (or two) of mulled wine.
Warmer wishes from Designers Anonymous®

Packaging Design
gürtlerbachmann
for Closed

The Four of Woolga
We designed the packaging for four pairs of wool socks, one for each member of the family: father, mother, child and baby. Customers received a wool sock package for free with every purchase of €50 in a Closed store. The four boxes can easily be stacked into each other, like the Russian Matryoshka dolls.

Designer
Veronika Kieneke
Executive Creative Director
Uli Gürtler
Illustrator
Veronika Kieneke
Copywriter
Matthias Hardt

Advertising Agency
gürtlerbachmann
Production Company
Produktionsbüro Romey von Malottky
Project Manager
Anna Lorenzen
Client
Closed

Packaging Design
The Collective
for De Bortoli

Este
Este is the passion of an award-winning Australian winemaker who wanted to create a premium sparkling wine that was the antithesis of traditional champagnes, by rejecting the usual glitz and slickness of the category. The client wanted to reflect his unconventional 'garagiste' winemaking style, which involves small quantities made with minimal intervention. The packaging had to have a sense of utilitarian rawness, so everything was designed to be assembled in the winemaker's shed: the logotype was hand-stencilled; the corks individually stamped; and the muselet secured with a cable tie.

Designer	Client
Margaret Nolan	De Bortoli
Creative Director	Brand
Margaret Nolan	Este
Design Agency	
The Collective	

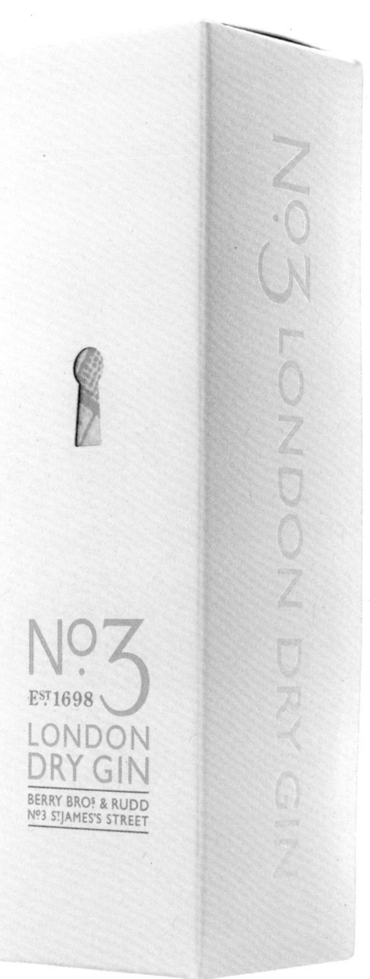

Packaging Design
BRANDHOUSE
for Berry Bros & Rudd

No.3 Gin
Berry Bros & Rudd have famously resided at No.3 St James's Street for over 300 years. The brand reflects this rich heritage, encouraging the consumer to discover the history behind the iconic address. The bottle structure is based on original gin bottles shipped from Holland with a tipped-in aged-metal key, wrapped in an original 17th Century map of the location, and housed in a luxurious die-cut and embossed gift box. Every element of the identity is based on threes, from the trefoil in the top of the key, to the key itself, the repeat of the logo around the foiling and the branded copy.

Designers
Pip Dale
Bronwen Edwards
Keely Jackman
Creative Director
David Beard
Typographer
Bronwen Edwards
Design Agency
BRANDHOUSE
Strategic Director
Gabriel Collins
Project Manager
Crispin Reed
Brand Managers
David King
Luke Tegner
Client
Berry Bros & Rudd
Brand
No.3 Gin

Packaging Design
The Chase
for Royal Mail

Royal Mail Collectibles
Royal Mail continues the popularity of its collectibles with these replica mail vans. These fine pieces aren't toys; they are metal-cast models, very detailed, and aimed at collectors aged 14+ who know their historic stuff. So that's exactly where the brief directed us: lots of accurate scaled down information, blueprint drawings and technical specs.

Designers
Harry Heptonstall
Mika Shephard
Creative Director
Richard Scholey
Illustrator
Graeme Jenner

Design Agency
The Chase
Client
Royal Mail

Packaging Design
BRANDHOUSE
for SABMiller

St Stefanus
St Stefanus beer originates from the Augustinian order in Ghent and is brewed according to traditional principles dating back to 1295. All iconography and typography is inspired by the St Stefanus Monastery in Ghent. The logo is based on library manuscripts, and the crown visual taken from a stained glass window. The beer is brewed with three different yeasts and refermented in the bottle, enabling consumers to drink it at varying stages of maturity according to personal taste. Each bottle of beer has a cellar releasc date and signature giving consumers the knowledge that they are drinking a truly handcrafted, premium drink.

Designers
Chris Nokes
Hamish Shand
Creative Director
David Beard
Typographers
Peter Horridge
Hamish Shand
Copywriter
Anna Hamill
Design Agency
BRANDHOUSE
Production Manager
Alexa Cohen

Project Manager
Crispin Reed
Strategic Directors
Gabriel Collins
Anna Hamill
Brand Managers
Eva Velclova
Nicolas Versloot
Client
SABMiller
Brand
St Stefanus

Packaging Design
Scholz & Friends Berlin
for 3M Deutschland

3M Earplugs Volume-Down Packaging
The task was to develop an original promotional packaging solution that immediately conveyed the product value of 3M's Solar Earplugs. The product is targeted at end users frequently requiring effective noise protection, such as musicians and festival-goers. We turned the purpose of the earplugs – to reduce noise – into an original package design. The container's cap looks like the volume knob of a hi-fi system; when opening it to reach the earplugs, one is turning down the volume. Overall, 5,000 units were produced.

Designers
Sebastian Frese
Ralf Schroeder
Nils Tscharnke
Art Directors
Sebastian Frese
Ralf Schroeder
Creative Director
Robert Krause
Executive Creative Director
Matthias Spaetgens
Chief Creative Officer
Martin Pross

Agency Producer
Benito Schumacher
Advertising Agency
Scholz & Friends Berlin
Account Manager
Josef Hoehnow
Client
3M Deutschland
Brand
3M

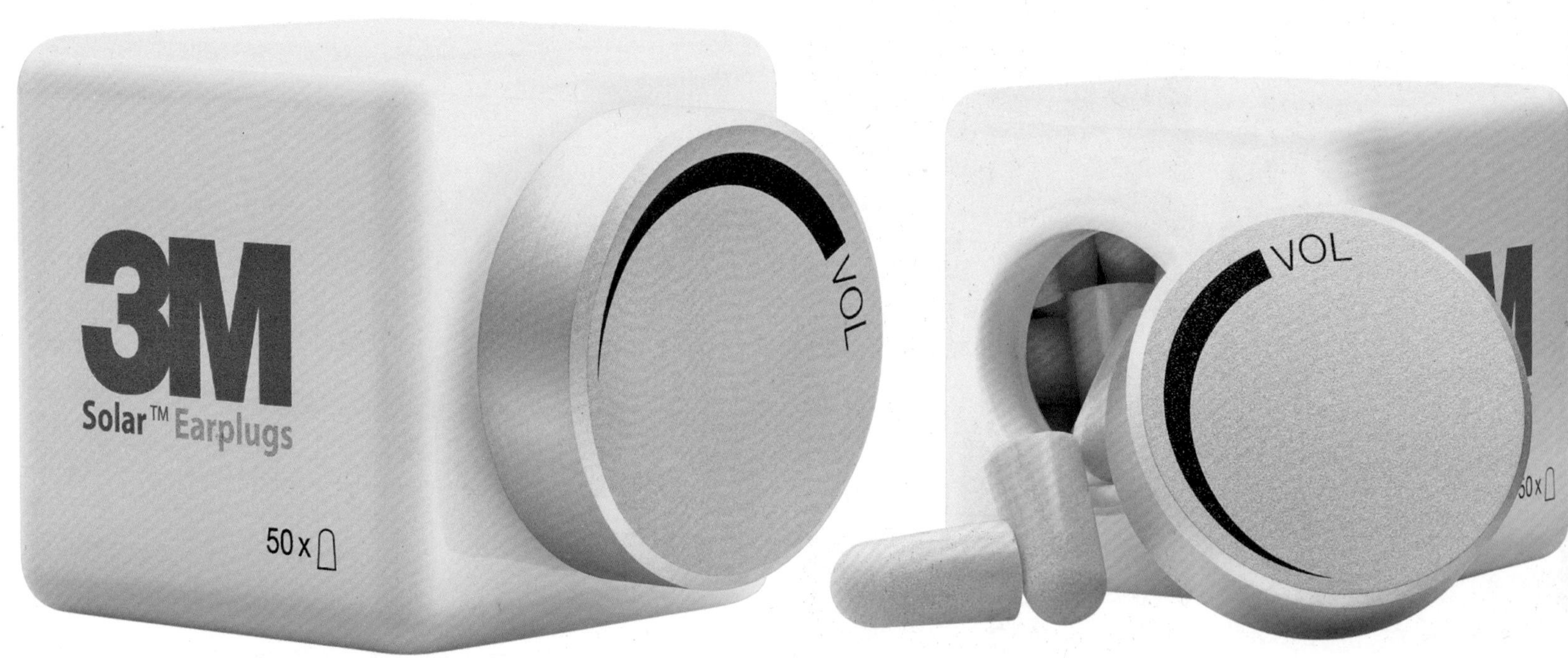

Packaging Design
Designers United
for G Papazoglou & Co

Col & Extra Acrylic
This is new packaging design for G Papazoglou & Co, a supplier of ceramic tiles and kitchen and bathroom fixtures, located in Greece. These two new products are industrial acrylic adhesive mortars, ideal for the facing of vertical surfaces and flooring with any type and size of ceramic and granite tiles.

Designers
Dimitris Koliadimas
Dimitris Papazoglou
Creative Directors
Dimitris Koliadimas
Dimitris Papazoglou

Design Group
Designers United
Client
G Papazoglou & Co

Packaging Design
Stranger & Stranger
for Truett Hurst

VML
A brief came in requesting a bottle design for a biodynamic wine made in the Truett Hurst winery in California. The winemaker, Virginia Marie Lambrix, uses biodynamic methods. She talked about powdered cow horn, phases of the moon and tea. We thought: witchcraft. Using a woodcut print look, the result is beautiful with spooky overtones. Very now.

Designer
Cosimo Surace
Creative Director
Kevin Shaw
Design Agency
Stranger & Stranger

Client
Truett Hurst
Brand
VML

Packaging Design
Ena Cardenal de la Nuez
for Do Not Say No

Do Not Say No
The major challenge in designing packaging for a franchise specialising in small gifts for women was the name: Do Not Say No. We didn't dare convince the owners to change it, so we asked ourselves the following question: what object would one never say no to? The answer came right away: a gift! We decided to create packaging with a shape as nice and simple as a gift box. We designed a series of boxes wrapped in transparent cellophane with a logo sticker on top. It's a gift you certainly can't say no to.

Designer
Ena Cardenal de la Nuez
Illustrator
Ena Cardenal de la Nuez

Design Agency
Ena Cardenal de la Nuez
Client
Do Not Say No

Packaging Design
LAQA & Co

LAQA & Co Nail Polish Pen
LAQA & Co is a start-up cosmetics brand. When designing our packaging, we wanted to stand out but also to stand for something. More than beauty, we aim to provide inspiration for young women with alternative role models – young artists. We decided to use our packaging as a canvas for these artists, featuring commissioned work, and sharing profit with them on each product sold. Product colour is used to inspire each piece of art, which can also hang on someone's wall.

Designer
Georgina Hofmann
Creative Director
Georgina Hofmann
Illustrators
Carol Del Angel
Pomme Chan
Géraldine Georges
Richard Grainger
Nazario Graziano
Katie Kirk
Soo Lee
Hazel Nicholls
Tatiana Plakhova
Paul Price
Cindy Rodriguez
James Roper
Amy Ross
Martin Sati

Print Producer
Deborah Nall
Client
LAQA & Co

Packaging Design
Leo Burnett Chicago
for Allstate

Mayhem Red
We were asked to create packaging for a private label wine that Allstate insurance executives could use as a relationship builder with business partners. The bottle needed to be both a conversation piece and a high-quality wine. Over the past year, Allstate has enjoyed huge success with its popular 'Mayhem' campaign. We kept the humorous tone to create 'Mayhem Red' – the most dangerous wine in the world. The bottle tells the story of a wine that has been to hell and back, surviving wildfires, car accidents, explosions, theft and personal injury to make it to your table.

Design Directors
Brian Loehr
Alisa Wolfson
Art Director
Mikal Pittman
Executive Creative Directors
Jeanie Caggiano
Charley Wickman
Chief Creative Officer
Susan Credle

Copywriter
Britt Nolan
Content Producer
Veronica Puc
Advertising Agency
Leo Burnett Chicago
Client
Allstate

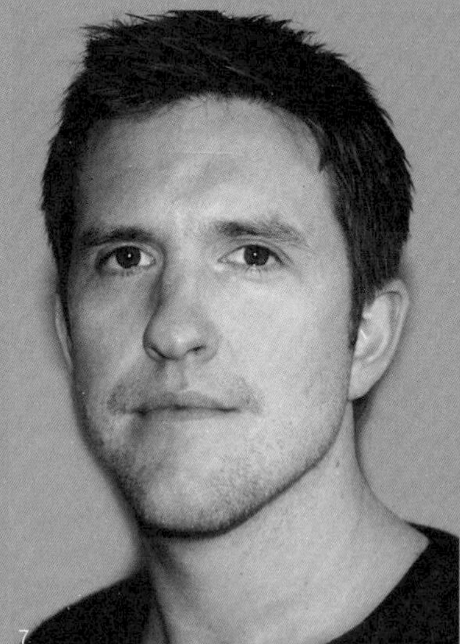

Jury Foreman
1. Marko Ahtisaari
Nokia

2. Carola Zwick
Weissensee School
of Art / Studio 7.5

3. Kazuko Koike
Kitchen

4. Dee Cooper
Decide Consulting

5. Tomoko Azumi
t.n.a. design studio

6. Patricia Moore
MooreDesign
Associates

7. Samuel Wilkinson
Samuel Wilkinson
Design

Yellow Pencil in Product Design

Furniture Design
Edward Barber & Jay Osgerby
for Vitra

Tip Ton
Tip Ton defines a new chair typology: a solid plastic chair with a tilt action that allows movement between two sitting postures: relaxed and forward-leaning. From a normal position the user can tilt the Tip Ton forward towards a table or desk where it then stays in place, a function of the chair's shaped skids. The movement Tip Ton enables, until now the preserve of mechanical office chairs, promotes comfort and increases circulation, which is proven to enhance concentration. Tip Ton makes this seating concept possible in a form that's lightweight, stackable and incredibly durable.

Designers
Edward Barber
Jay Osgerby
Client
Vitra

Yellow Pencil in Product Design

Interactive Design for Products
Nokia Design
for Nokia

Nokia N9
Nokia N9 is defined by the elegance and simplicity of one gesture: the swipe. Swiping from any edge takes you home so you can easily move between activities, rather than demanding you be buried in accurate targeting of tiny icons. This allows you to be more present with the people and the world around you. This interaction is also complemented by beautiful hardware. The seamless plastic unibody and curved glass set new standards in product making with a clear focus on reduction and craftsmanship. Overall, Nokia N9 offers a truly exceptional smartphone experience.

Design Agency
Nokia Design
Client
Nokia

Nomination in Product Design

Consumer Product Design
Apple Industrial Design Team
for Apple

iPad 2
The iPad 2 is the next generation of Apple's magical device for browsing the web, reading and sending emails, enjoying photos, watching videos, listening to music, playing games, reading ebooks and much more. It has a sleek, anodised aluminium rear housing and a glass front screen, available in either black or white. It features Apple's new dual-core A5 processor and stunning graphics.

Designers
Jody Akana
Bart Andre
Jeremy Bataillou
Daniel Coster
Daniele De Iuliis
Evans Hankey
Julian Hönig
Richard Howarth
Jonathan Ive
Steve Jobs
Duncan Kerr
Shin Nishibori
Matthew Rohrbach
Peter Russell-Clarke
Christopher Stringer
Eugene Whang
Rico Zörkendörfer

Design Group
Apple Industrial Design Team

Client
Apple

Nomination in Product Design

Consumer Product Design
Whipsaw
for Livescribe

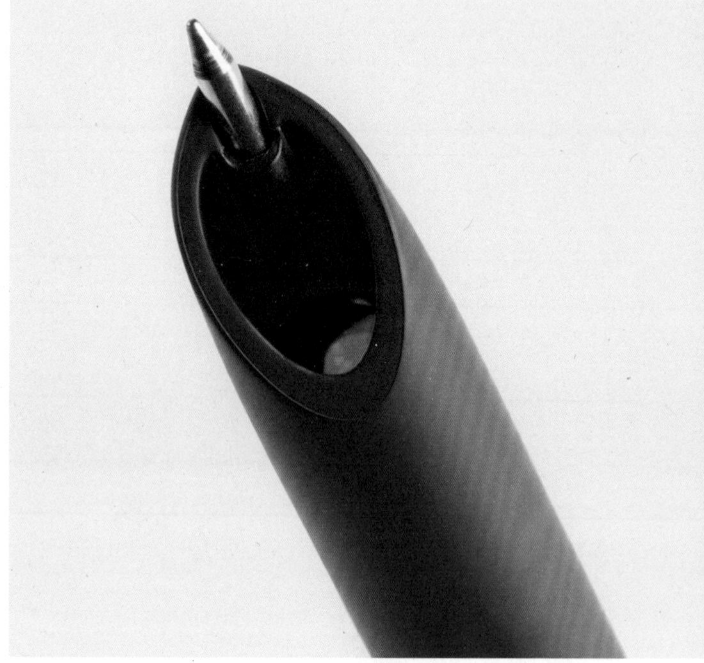

Echo Smartpen
The Echo Smartpen is a pen computer used for handwriting capture, audio recording, and other learning applications. The pen has a camera on its tip that records a micro dot pattern on Livescribe 'dot paper' while you are writing. This allows you to go back to a note later, tap on it, and hear the audio recording from the exact time of writing the note. This enables students to read their notes and listen again to a lecture simultaneously. Echo is the first product to combine all four modes of communication (reading, writing, speaking and listening) in a simple pen and paper format.

Designer
Dan Harden
Design Agency
Whipsaw

Client
Livescribe
Brand
Echo

Nomination in Product Design

Consumer Product Design
Edge of Belgravia

Edge of Belgravia Ceramic Onyx Knives
The Ceramic Onyx Series gives you the complete range of cutting-edge blades, with elegantly designed handles that express confidence and distinction. The Ceramic Onyx Chef's Knife is the centrepiece of the range. The futuristic, angular yet soft touch handle is testament to its innovative and bold design.

Designer
Christian Bird
Design Group
Edge of Belgravia

Client
Edge of Belgravia

Nomination in Product Design

Consumer Product Design
Ammunition
for Barnes & Noble

NOOK Simple Touch
NOOK Simple Touch is designed to replicate the immersive reading experience of a paperback book. The device has a six-inch screen, surrounded by a black bezel, with just one obvious button. There's no traditional touchscreen, instead the e-reader uses zForce technology to locate the position of the user's finger above the screen. At only 7.48 ounces, the NOOK is sleek but durable enough to fit in a jacket, pocket or purse. Its ergonomic, contoured design with rounded corners and soft-touch back makes it comfortable to read for extended periods of time, even with just one hand.

Designer	Design Group
Tim Tan	Ammunition
Design Director	Client
Robert Brunner	Barnes & Noble

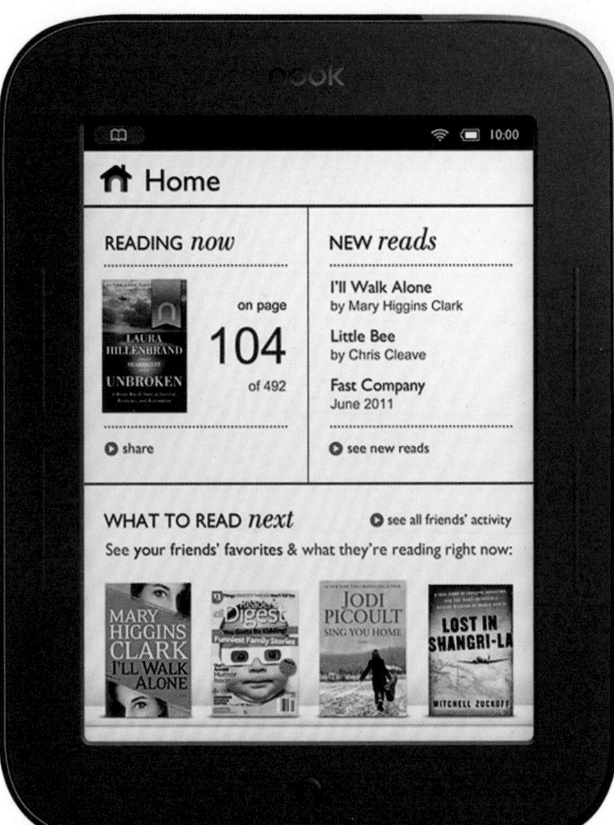

Nomination in Product Design

Furniture Design
Goodmorning Technology
for Luceplan

Archetype
With its simple, archetypal 50s silhouette, the Archetype lamp conceals a revolutionary concept and a technological heart. A warm-light LED is inserted between the external shell in painted aluminium and the internal transparent polycarbonate diffuser. It has an E27 fitting that permits direct attachment of the fixture to any standard bulb socket. Besides the 'basic' version, a supplementary kit is also available with ceiling rose, cable and socket in coordinated colours.

Designers
Nille Halding
Mads Kjøller Damkjaer
Lars Thomsen

Design Agency
Goodmorning Technology

Client
Luceplan

Consumer Product Design
No Picnic
for Propellerhead

Propellerhead Balance
This product brings iconic software brand Propellerhead into the real world, and establishes design assets for future hardware products. 'Balance' is a two-in/two-out audio interface for recording and playback. Interaction faces the user on the top-side instead of the common short-side. With colour-coded inputs for all the gear, instruments are always connected and ready to record. Equally large knobs for speakers and headphones acknowledge that music makers of today are as likely to create on their laptop with headphones on, as on a dedicated workstation.

Designers
Thomas Mach
Annacarin Neale
Design Agency
No Picnic

Project Manager
Jonas Westius
Client
Propellerhead

Consumer Product Design
Apple Industrial Design Team
for Apple

iPad 2 Smart Cover
The iPad 2 Smart Cover provides screen protection while maintaining a thin and lightweight profile. Designed with a self-aligning magnetic hinge, which makes it easy to attach and remove, the Smart Cover automatically wakes iPad 2 when opened and puts it to sleep when closed. It has a soft microfibre lining to help clean the screen, and folds into a stand for typing or viewing videos. It is available in vibrant polyurethane and rich leather.

Designers
Jody Akana
Bart Andre
Jeremy Bataillou
Daniel Coster
Daniele De Iuliis
Evans Hankey
Julian Hönig
Richard Howarth
Jonathan Ive
Steve Jobs
Duncan Kerr
Shin Nishibori
Matthew Rohrbach
Peter Russell-Clarke
Christopher Stringer
Eugene Whang
Rico Zörkendörfer
Design Group
Apple Industrial Design Team
Client
Apple

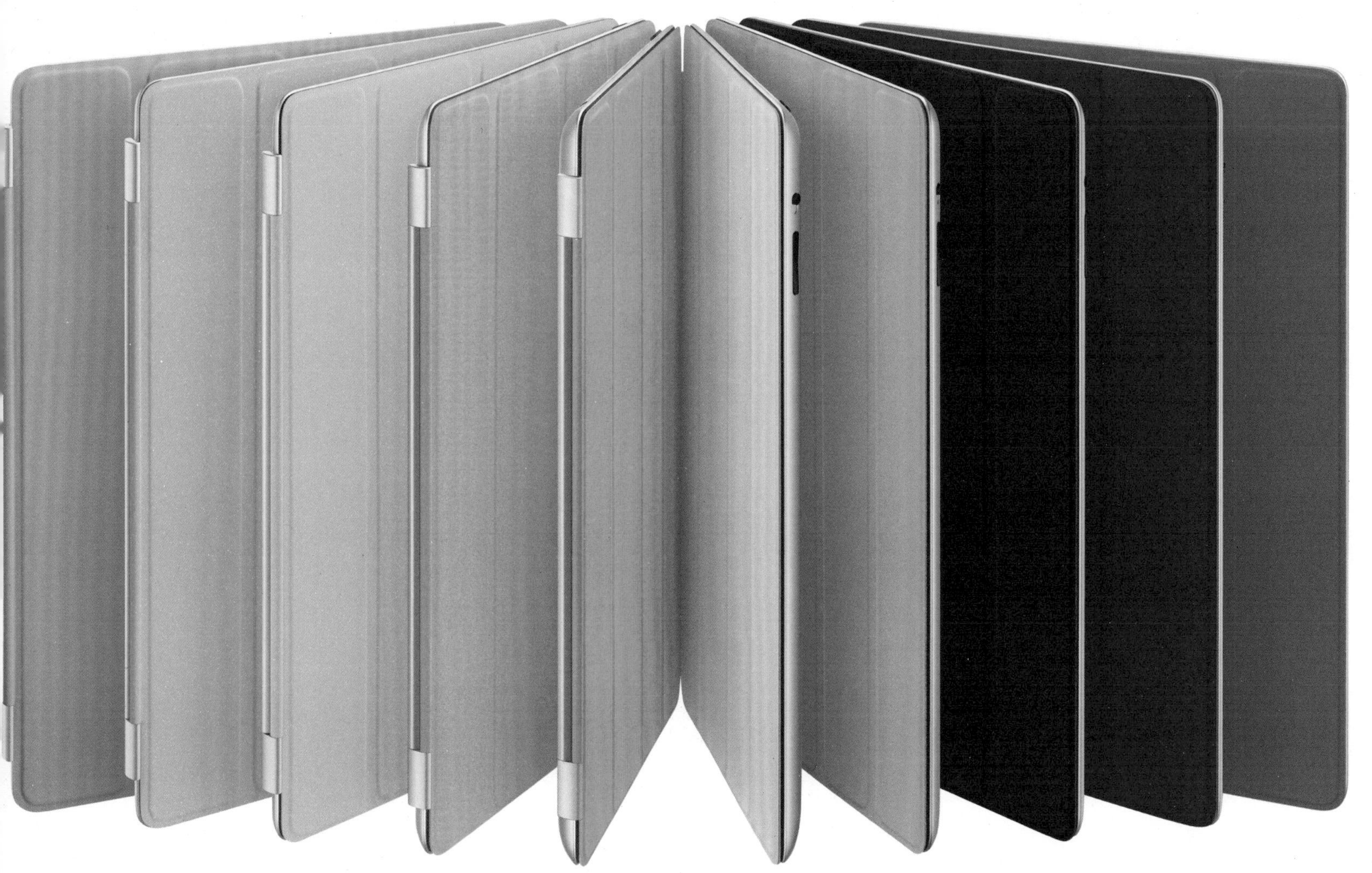

Consumer Product Design
Nokia Design
for Nokia

Nokia Lumia 800
Nokia Lumia 800 is optimised through quality, craftsmanship and consideration of every detail. The plastic unibody, moulded glass, incredible display, vibrant colours and inbox accessories all attest to the design ethos of 'less but better'. Designing the hardware from the inside-out led to an entirely new construction technique where the internals are assembled into a one-piece polycarbonate body through the window opening – much like a ship in a bottle. All additional openings are machined for added precision. The Nokia Lumia 800 is produced in four amazing colours.

Design Agency
Nokia Design
Client
Nokia

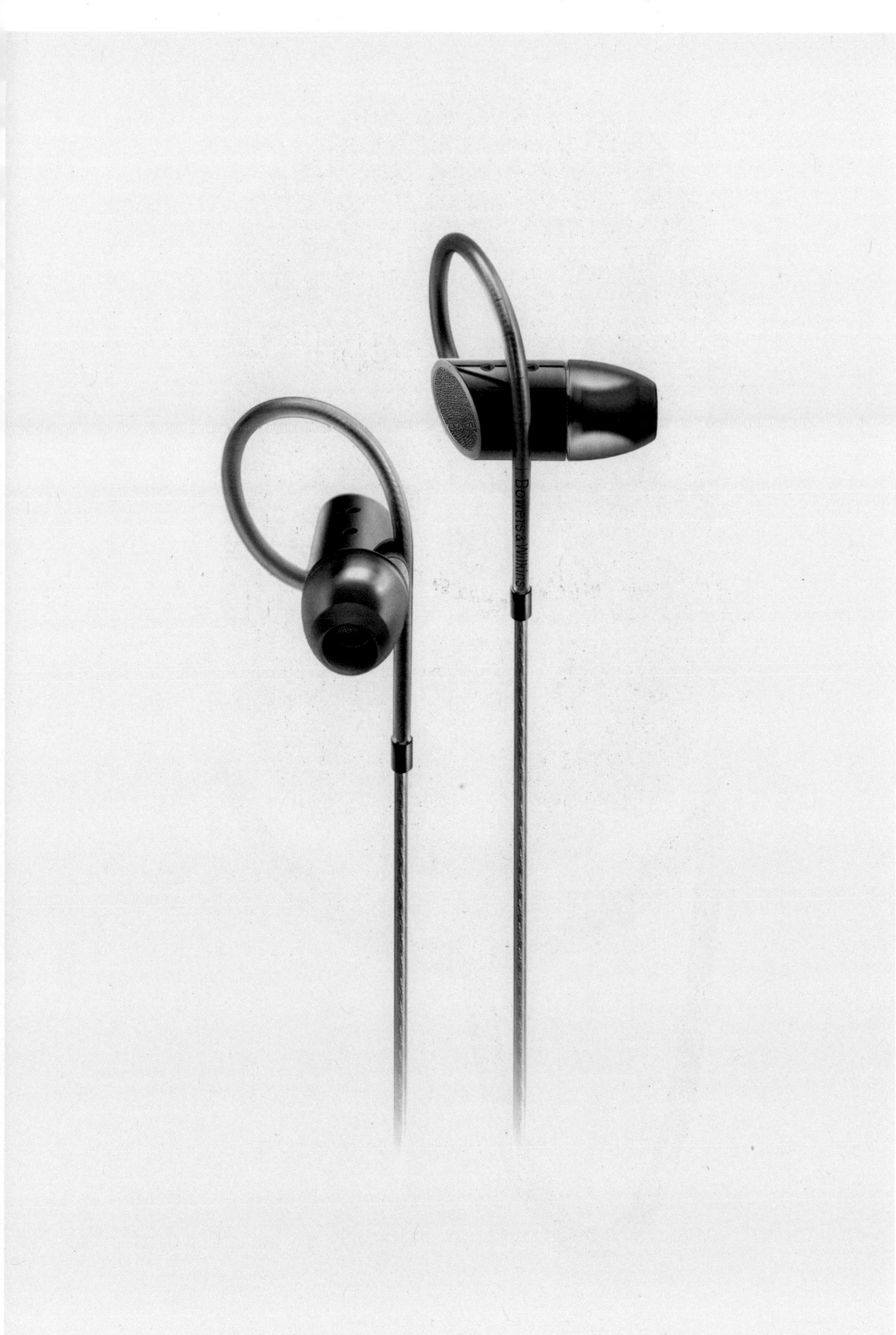

Consumer Product Design
Native Design
for Bowers & Wilkins

Bowers & Wilkins C5 In-Ear Headphones
Bowers & Wilkins's first in-ear headphones deliver tangible experience enhancements in terms of fit and acoustic performance. The timeless design respects and reflects the quality of the brand. Innovative design features such as the 'secure loop' provide unparalleled comfort and stability through an adjustable, compliant fit to the ear concha. The rear of the unit houses a micro porous filter, which helps ensure a smooth and natural musical reproduction. The ultra-compact C5 in-ear headphones deliver world-class audio quality to music lovers on the move.

Designers
Doris Bölck
Jesper Brehmer
Seongmin Hwang
Simon Matthews
Liam O'Brien
Design Directors
Marcus Hoggarth
Morten Warren
Technical Designers
Stuart Nevill
Doug Standen

Project Managers
Natalie O'Hara
Chris Wolfe
Design Agency
Native Design
Client
Bowers & Wilkins

Consumer Product Design
fuseproject
for General Electric

GE WattStation Wall Mount
The GE WattStation wall mount is an electric vehicle charger for easy installation and use in a home or office garage. With a subtle and user-friendly design, the WattStation can fit into any environment with ease. The user interface keeps the interaction clear. There is convenient cord storage built into the perimeter of the unit, while a simple power button ensures zero energy is consumed between charges. GE's Smart Grid technology enables the station to charge in record time. The residential WattStation works to make it as easy as possible to own an electric vehicle and reduce your carbon footprint.

Designers
Matt Malone
Josh Morenstein
Pichaya Puttorngul
Matt Swinton
Design Director
Yves Behar

Design Agency
fuseproject
Client
General Electric

Consumer Product Design
Hövding

Hövding
Hövding is a collar for cyclists, worn around the neck. The collar contains a folded up airbag that only comes out in case of an accident. The airbag is shaped like a hood, surrounding and protecting the cyclist's head. The trigger mechanism is controlled by sensors which pick up the abnormal movements of a cyclist in an accident. The collar, which is the visible part of the product, is covered by a removable shell that can be changed to match the cyclist's outfit. Further shell designs are being launched.

Designers
Terese Alstin
Anna Haupt

Industrial Design Company
Hövding

Client
Hövding

1

2

3

4

5

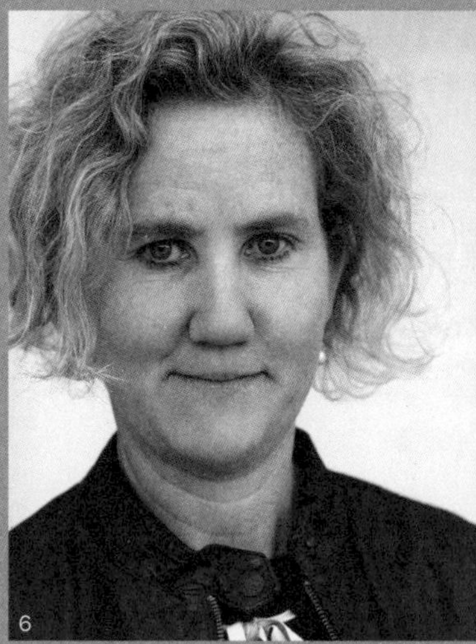
6

7

Jury Foreman
1. Morag Myerscough
Studio Myerscough

2. Matt Clark
United Visual Artists

3. Hei Yiyang
SenseTeam

4. Patrick McKinney
Ben Kelly Design

5. Tania Singh Khosla
tsk Design

6. Annabel Judd
The Victoria & Albert Museum

7. Conny Freyer
Troika

Yellow Pencil in Spatial Design

Installations
Leo Burnett Shanghai
for the Shanghai Qingcongquan Training Centre

The Distance Between Mother and Child
One million families suffer from autism in China. Due to the lack of awareness, parents with affected children have to confront the issue alone. We created an exhibition of living sculptures in Shanghai. A mother and her child, dressed in black, sat at two ends of a long netted cage, depicting the psychological distance between the autistic child and their parents. The event attracted the attention of over 120 media outlets. We reached an audience of over 50 million families, and the plight of autistic children was heard loud and clear.

Designers
Ken Lee
Chengtao Mu
Bonny Sheng
Forest Young
Design Directors
Gordon Hughes
Ken Lee
Handsome Wong
Amanda Yang
Forest Young
Creative Directors
Gordon Hughes
Amanda Yang
Forest Young

Producers
Christine Chen
William Huen
Copywriters
Dandan Lee
Jason Su
Amanda Yang
Advertising Agency
Leo Burnett Shanghai
Account Handler
Weiwei Chen
Client
Shanghai
Qingcongquan Training Centre

Nomination in Spatial Design

Installations
aberrant architecture
for FACT

The Social Playground
'The Social Playground' was part of 'Knowledge Lives Everywhere', an exhibition at FACT, Liverpool's Foundation for Art and Creative Technology. This giant interactive landscape was built in collaboration with local community groups in Liverpool. 'The Social Playground' is based around the British game of egg rolling, an Easter tradition that sees families decorating hard boiled eggs and rolling them down local hills. Aberrant's version invited visitors to explore and race wooden eggs down and around seven different structures, which represented and revealed work carried out by the various community groups.

Designer
Nicholas Wood
Design Directors
David Chambers
Kevin Haley

Architectural Studio
aberrant architecture
Client
FACT

Nomination in Spatial Design

Installations
AMV BBDO
for GE

Living Masterpiece
To demonstrate GE's commitment to helping reduce the National Gallery's carbon footprint, we created the world's first 'living' masterpiece. Using over 8,000 plants, we recreated one of the National Gallery's most famous paintings, Van Gogh's 'A Wheatfield, with Cypresses'. Over a four-month period the plants were grown and then installed onto a huge 22-metre site outside the gallery in Trafalgar Square, London. The installation was seen by over 60 million people over six months.

Art Directors
Mike Bond
Antony Nelson
Director
Jamie Maule-ffinch
Creative Director
Paul Brazier
Producers
Sam LeGassick
Ciara McGowan
Agency Producers
Chloe Robinson
Adam Walker
Copywriters
Bern Hunter
Mike Sutherland
Advertising Agency
AMV BBDO
Account Handlers
Amber Glenister
Tim Rogowski
Client
GE

Nomination in Spatial Design

Spatial Design
David Kohn Architects
for Artangel & Living Architecture

A Room for London
David Kohn Architects in collaboration with artist Fiona Banner were selected to design 'A Room for London', a temporary installation perched on top of the Queen Elizabeth Hall, Southbank Centre, London, throughout 2012. The brief was to create a room on one of the most visible sites in the British capital, where up to two people at a time could spend a night in an exemplary architectural landmark. Visitors to the room are invited to create their own narrative by recording their experience onboard. The room also hosts a guest programme of special visitors, artists, writers and cultural commentators.

Architects
Liz Betterton
Saya Hakamata
David Kohn
Tom McGlynn
Artist
Fiona Banner
Environmental Engineer
Max Fordham
Architectural Studio
David Kohn Architects
Digital Production Company
O Production

Structural Engineers
Price & Myers
Contractors
Millimetre
Cost Consultants
Boyden Group
Project Manager
Alex McLennan
Clients
Artangel
Living Architecture

QUEEN ELIZABETH HALL
PURCELL ROOM

Exhibition Design
6a architects
for the Design Museum

Wim Crouwel: A Graphic Odyssey
The prolific career of Dutch graphic designer Wim Crouwel was celebrated with a first UK retrospective at the Design Museum. The exhibition was designed by 6a architects. It spanned over 60 years of work, exploring Crouwel's innovative use of grids and typography, which earned him the moniker 'Gridnik'. The gallery was stripped back and opened up, allowing a 20-metre long table into the space, forming a subtle background to the works. The shifts of the table move visitors past, around and in between the pieces, reminiscent of Crouwel's use of three-dimensional space within two-dimensional design.

Architects
Andrew Dadds
Tom Emerson
Stephanie Macdonald
Owen Watson
Designers
Tony Brook
Natasha Day

Architectural Studio
6a architects
Client
Design Museum

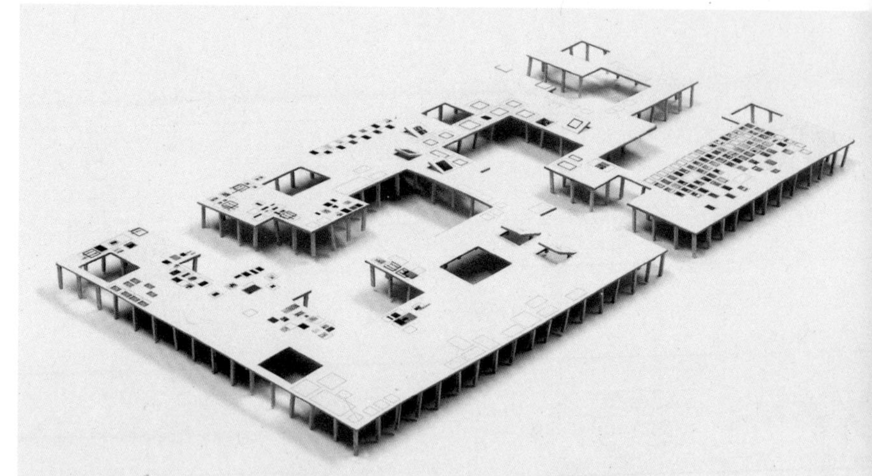

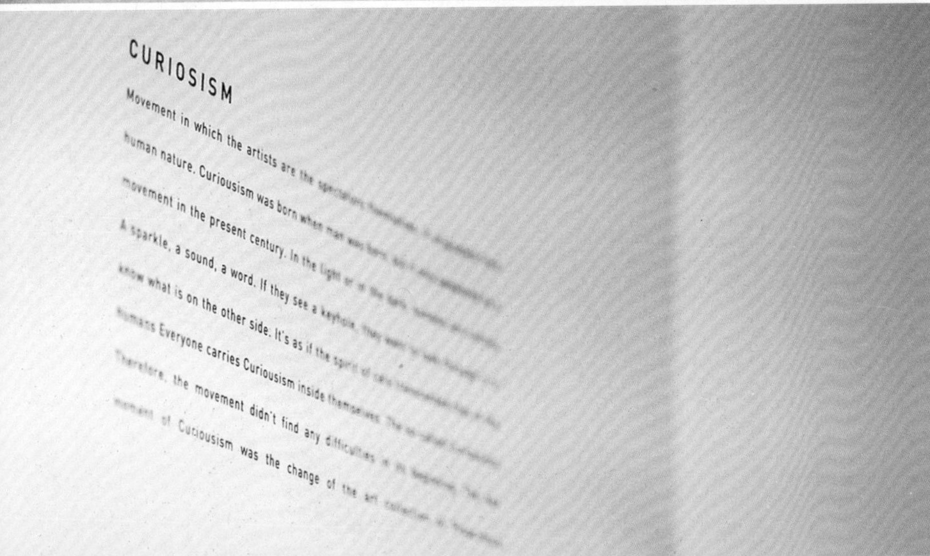

Exhibition Design
F/Nazca Saatchi & Saatchi
for the Pinacoteca Museum

Curiosism
After twelve years of being open to the public, the Pinacoteca Museum decided to change the permanent exhibition of its collection, closing the second floor of its building for a year. To prevent visitors being turned away and to feed the curiosity of those who passed by the museum, we created an artistic movement: Curiosism. For one year, we developed everything that a regular exhibition would have, such as installations, photo-essays, posters, a book about the movement, gifts sold at the museum shop and so on – all revolving around the theme of curiosity.

Creative Directors
Fabio Fernandes
Eduardo Lima
Directors
Jones+Tino
Head of Art
João Linneu
Executive Producer
Mario Peixoto
Illustrators
Fabricio Brambatti
Andre Maciel
Director of Photography
Andre Faccioli
Advertising Agency
F/Nazca Saatchi & Saatchi
Post Production
Pix Animation
Vagalume Studios
Sound Design
Satélite
Planner
José Porto
Account Handlers
Camila Hamaoui
Marcello Penna
Client
Pinacoteca Museum

Exhibition Design
Ab Rogers Design
for the Stanley Picker Gallery Kingston

A Day in the Life of Ernesto Bones
Echoing the cycle of art to life to art, 'A Day in the Life of Ernesto Bones' reflects on the place of narrative in design and exhibition as a creative process. The installation was produced under the auspices of the Stanley Picker Fellowship at Kingston University. Ab Rogers Design created an interactive, multi-sensory installation inspired by a story written by 24 creative collaborators. The Stanley Picker House contains his collection of art and sculpture, and was used as inspiration for the installation. The writers imagined that the house was the home of Ernesto Bones. Each of the writers was sent a photograph of an object from the Stanley Picker House and asked to write an hour of Ernesto Bones' day. The last two sentences of each piece were sent to the next writer to give the narrative coherence. Each completed text was then used as a design brief to define the concept for an object that became part of the installation.

Artists
Heston Blumenthal
Andrea Branzi
Lesley Bunch
Miranda Carter
Aric Chen
Susan Cohn
Michael Connor
Charlotte Cullinan
Michael Elias
Sara Fanelli
Shelley Fox
John Hegarty
Fergus Henderson
Daniel Hunt
Ben Kelly
Monica Narula
Jane Nisselson
Simon Ofield-Kerr
Helena Reckitt
Tom Scott
Adrian Searle
Deyan Sudjic
David Tanguy
Jane Withers

Curators
Michael Connor
David Falkner
Photographer
John Short
Design Agency
Ab Rogers Design
Sponsors
The British Council
THE DDSA
Clients
Beijing Design Week 2011
Stanley Picker Gallery Kingston

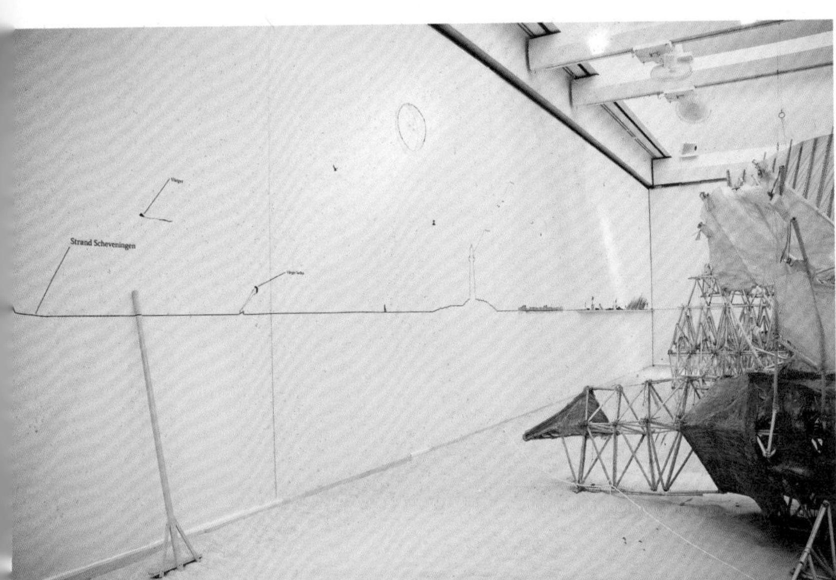

Exhibition Design
EARTHSCAPE
for the Oita Art Museum

Theo Jansen Exhibition

Theo Jansen's Strandbeesten are giant structures assembled from plastic tubes. When wind blows into them, their many legs move dexterously, enabling them to walk. Strandbeesten have traversed the oceans, from the Netherlands to the forests of Oita, Japan. We designed the exhibition showcasing them at the Oita Art Museum. The show was structured to allow visitors to vicariously experience the evolution of the structures. EARTHSCAPE added various features to the space using the earth itself from Scheveningen (the Beesten's home beach in the Netherlands), and Oita. Just as the natural scenery of Holland and Oita are connected by horizons, so are all living things connected. We symbolised these lines of connection with captions running between the show's entrance and exit, at a height of 145cm.

Designers
Yusuke Komatsu
Tomomi Takaoka
Design Director
Eiki Danzuka
Creative Director
Eiki Danzuka

Architectural Studio
EARTHSCAPE
Clients
Oita Art Museum
Oita Godo Shinbunsha

Installations

The Department of the 4th Dimension

for Sephora

Lucid Dreams at the Sephora Sensorium

The Sephora Sensorium is the world's first interactive scent museum. The multifaceted and interactive sensory experiences go beyond just the act and perception of sniffing perfume. The 'Lucid Dreams' experience – the finale – explores the physical act of smelling with an interactive mix of cinema, design and technology that creates visual stories based on how you sniff the fragrance.

Architect
Elena Manferdini
Designer
Justin Lui
Creative Director
Matt Checkowski
Interactive Designer
Gautam Rangan
Digital Designer
Ken Pelletier
Sound Designer
Patrick Cicero
Producer
Ron Cicero
Copywriter
Kate Cox
Director of Photography
Keith Dunkerley
Editor
Leander Rappmann
Design Agency
The Department of the 4th Dimension
Clients
Firmenich
Sephora
Brand
Sephora

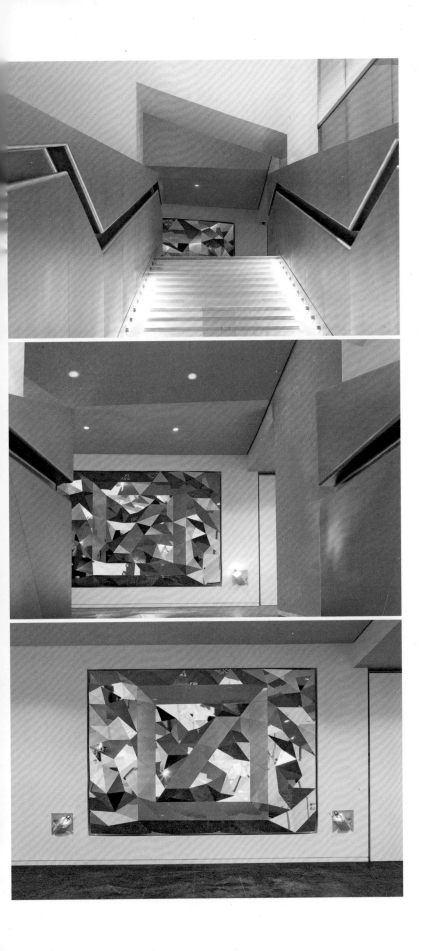

Installations
ART+COM
for Deutsche Bank

Anamorphic Mirror
This installation is situated at the end of a stairway leading up to the conference area in the headquarters of Deutsche Bank. It consists of a faceted mirror and blue light projected onto the opposite wall. Standing at the bottom of the stairs, visitors initially see seemingly random blue reflections on the mirror. Through their own movement, visitors then generate a filmic perception: what they see changes with every step. As they get closer, the blue light reflections begin to take shape, until they come together as the bank's logo upon the visitors the top of the stairs.

Architect
Jochen Gringmuth
Designers
Simon Häcker
Eva Offenberg
Creative Director
Joachim Sauter
Architectural Studio
Coordination

Design Agency
ART+COM
Project Manager
Gert Monath
Brand Managers
Christofer Habig
Michaela Luhmann
Client
Deutsche Bank

Installations
Scholz & Friends Berlin
for Siemens Electrogeraete

The Laundry Gallery
Siemens washing machines with anti-vibration design are extremely smooth and don't vibrate even during fast spin drying. This feature needed to be demonstrated to our high-earning and design-savvy target group. We built fragile sculptures out of familiar household items and placed them on the washing machines. Then we turned the machines onto the spin cycle. Eight of the sculptures were exhibited at a temporary art gallery in the centre of Berlin, the 'Laundry Gallery'. Posters, an online film and advertisements in local magazines announced the vernissage in advance.

Designer
Szymon Plewa
Graphic Designers
Philipp Bertisch
Susan Wesarg
Art Directors
René Gebhardt
Sebastian Kamp
Bjoern Kernspeckt
Creative Directors
Markus Daubenbuechel
Robert Krause
Mathias Rebmann
Florian Schwalme
Executive Creative Director
Matthias Spaetgens

Chief Creative Officer
Martin Pross
Copywriter
Stefan Sohlau
Advertising Agency
Scholz & Friends Berlin
Account Managers
Kerstin Seidel
Mehibe Tuncel
Client
Siemens Electrogeraete
Brand
Siemens

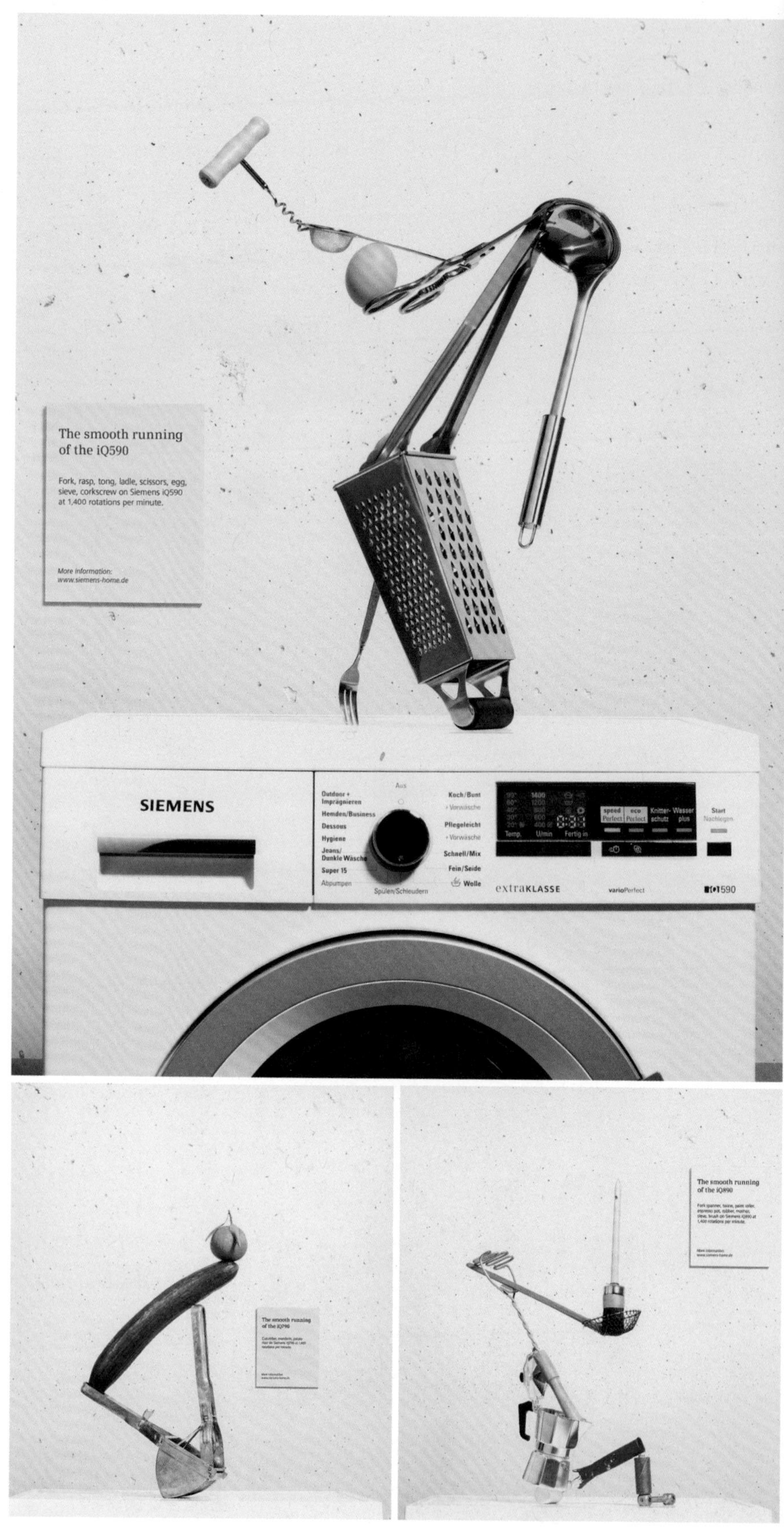

The smooth running of the iQ590
Fork, rasp, tong, ladle, scissors, egg, sieve, corkscrew on Siemens iQ590 at 1,400 rotations per minute.
More information: www.siemens-home.de
SIEMENS
extraKLASSE

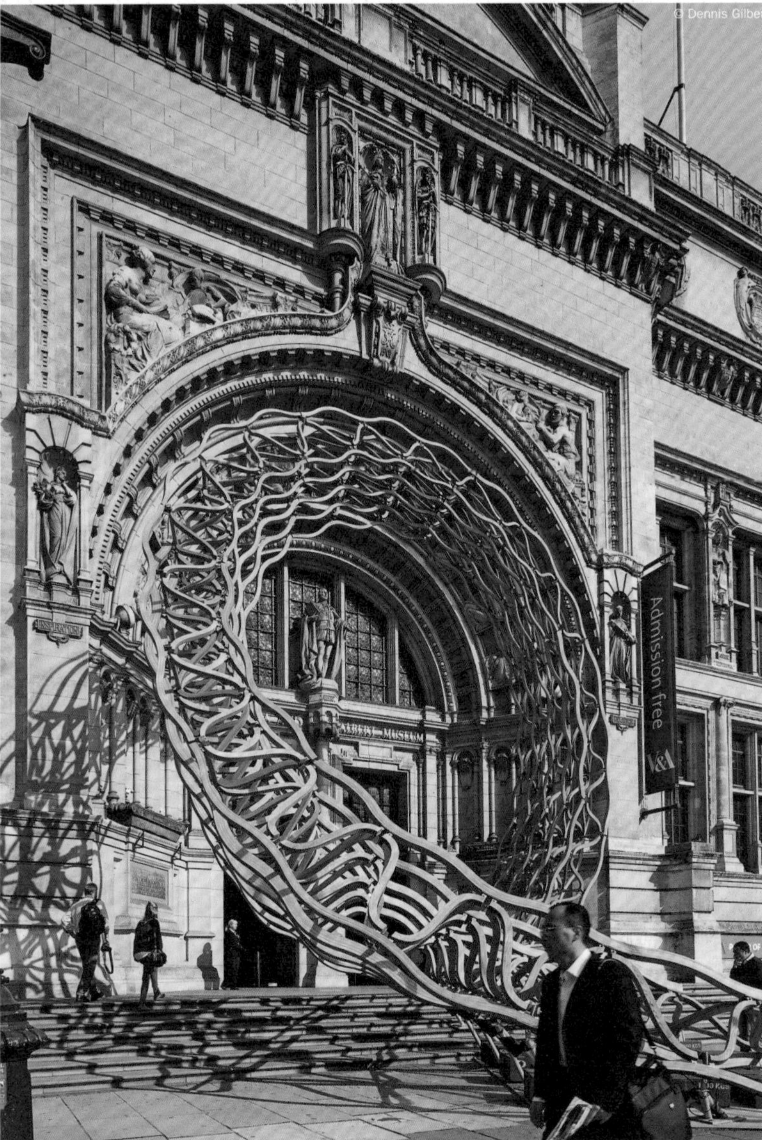

Installations
AL_A & Arup
for the American Hardwood Export Council & the London Design Festival 2011

Timber Wave
'Timber Wave' was installed at the entrance of the Victoria and Albert Museum for the London Design Festival 2011. The most ambitious commission of the festival to date, the 12m-high installation showcased the interest in design and making that is at the heart of the V&A's collections and London's creative industries. 'Timber Wave' was about taking the V&A out onto the street, and celebrating both the festival's residency at the museum and American red oak as a material. Techniques usually used in furniture making were applied at a vast scale. The repetitive motif reflects the decorative and didactic tradition of the V&A.

Design Agency
AL_A
Design Group
Arup
Builders
Cowley Timberwork
Lighting Scheme
SEAM Design
Lighting Manufacture
iGuzzini
Electrical Installation
PEI Delta
Specialist
Construction Advisor
Skanska
Timber Donors
Bingaman and Son Lumber
Coulee Region Hardwoods
Fitzpatrick & Weller
Frank Miller Lumber
Hermitage Hardwood Lumber Sales
Matson Lumber
Northland Forest Products
Pike Lumber

Clients
American Hardwood Export Council
London Design Festival 2011

Installations
United Visual Artists
for Cape Farewell &
the National Maritime Museum

High Arctic
An installation at the National Maritime Museum in London, 'High Arctic' invited visitors to explore a vast abstracted arctic landscape comprising sculpture, light and sound. Visitors discover 3,000 glaciers that will have melted by the end of this century and are confronted with the human impact on this environment over the course of history. Fragments of 'The Farewell Glacier', a commissioned poem by Nick Drake, work together with the visuals to create an immersive experience. The installation is based on the expedition of United Visual Artists creative director Matt Clark to Svalbard. Nick Drake was also part of the expedition, which was conducted in 2010 by climate foundation Cape Farewell.

Writer
Nick Drake
Sound Designers
Max Eastley
Henrik Ekeus
Programmer
Luke Malcolm
Design Agency
United Visual Artists

Stakeholder
Cape Farewell
Clients
Cape Farewell
National Maritime Museum

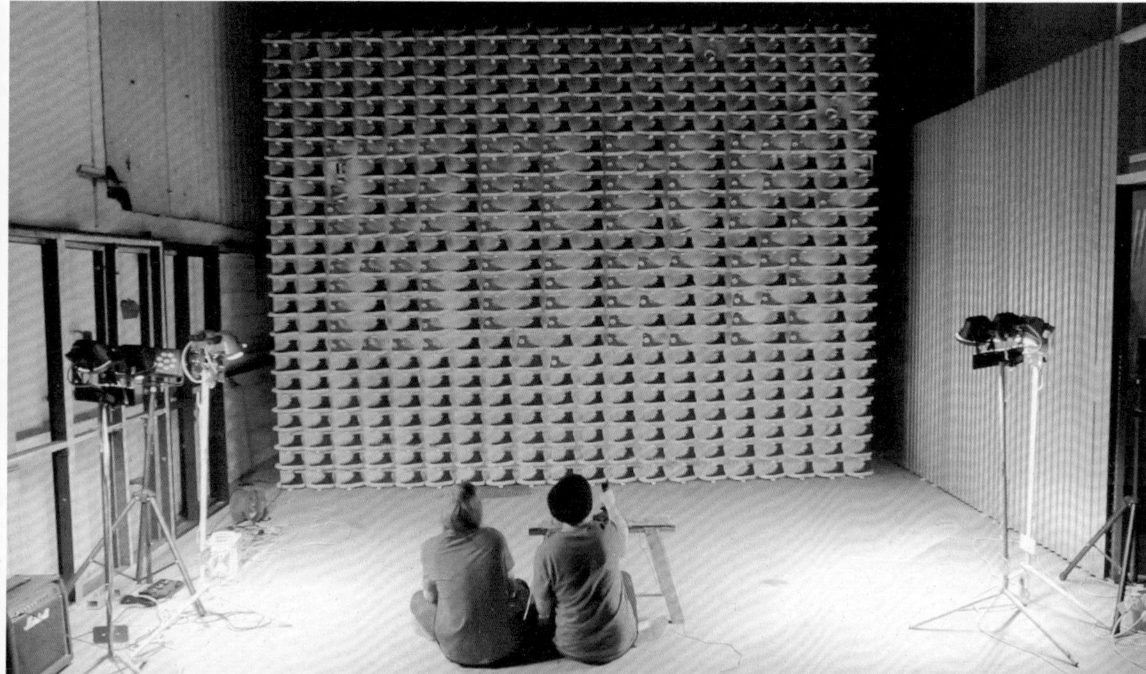

Installations
Checkland Kindleysides
for Converse EMEA

The Canvas Experiment
'The Canvas Experiment' was based on two ideas: 'a blank canvas for self-expression' and 'independent enough not to follow'. Converse is dedicated to enabling engaging brand experiences with an emphasis on music, art and events. Our idea was to use the shoes themselves as the vehicle for delivering one-off and exciting experiences. The Canvas is a fully-functional digital screen built out of 480 Chuck Taylors, each connected to a servomotor enabling 180-degree rotation. The shoes act as pixels, making it possible to render images and animations on what's effectively a low-resolution screen. The physical installation was first filmed in a warehouse and shared in Converse's social media and web channels. Then the installation went on the road to Converse retailers throughout Europe.

Designer
Martin Hammarberg
Art Director
Niklas Karlsson
Executive Creative Directors
Mark Chalmers
Tony Högqvist
Director
Karl Nord
Producers
Markus Björk
Patrik Sundberg
Executive Producer
Fredrik Heghammar
Copywriter
Patrick Gardner
Developers
Mattias Hallqvist
Mikael Lundmark
Technical Director
Björn Kummeneje
Director of Photography
Oskar Lundgren
Photographer
Alexander Radsby
Creative Agency
Perfect Fools
Design Agency
Checkland Kindleysides
Planner
Michael Aneto
Account Directors
Patrick Gardner
James Goode
Client
Converse EMEA

Installations
@radical.media
for Arcade FIre

Summer into Dust
'Summer into Dust' premiered at the 2011 Coachella Music Festival in Indio, California. Incorporated into the headlining performance of band Arcade Fire, the installation consisted of 1,500 balls designed with programmable and sound reacting LED lights that cascaded from the top of the 70-foot stage into the audience of 100,000 fans. The ball drop was timed with the final song and encore of the show. After the show the balls were switched into sound reactive mode so they could be taken away like spores.

Interactive Director
Chris Milk
Interactive Design Agencies
ESKI
Tangible Interaction
Production Company
@radical.media
Interactive Production Company
Moment Factory
Clients
Arcade Fire
Creators Project
Brand
Intel

Spatial Design
R2
for Casa do conto

Casa do Conto: House of Tales
Casa do Conto is an exceptional hotel established in a 19th-Century house in Porto, Portugal, which was rebuilt after a fire. Following a request from the client to reinterpret the destroyed ceilings featuring plaster angels and figures, R2 chose to take a more conceptual approach. R2 proposed that the client collected texts from authors who had experienced the house before the fire. Different typographic compositions were designed for each space.

Design Directors
Lizá Ramalho
Artur Rebelo
Architectural Studio
Pedra Líquida

Design Agency
R2
Client
Casa do Conto

JUST DO IT

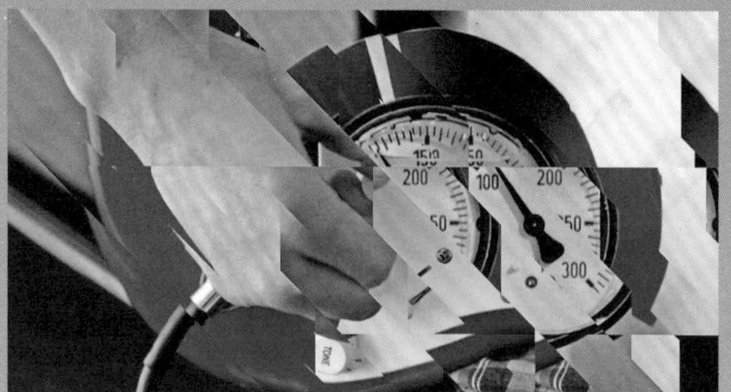

ABSOLUT

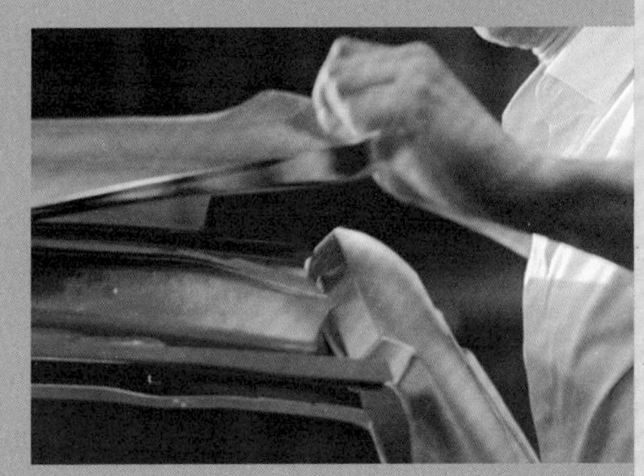

Crafts

PG
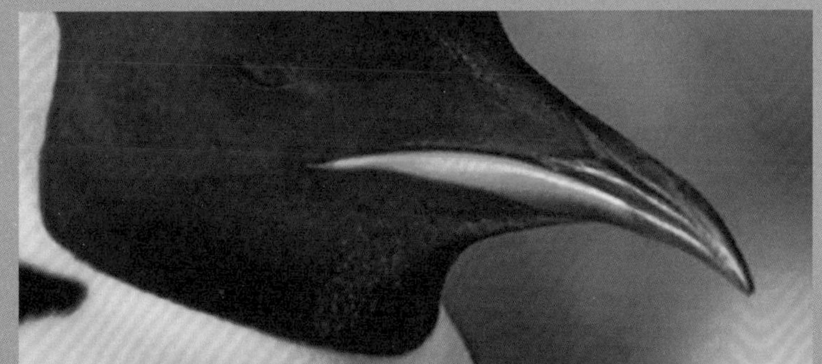
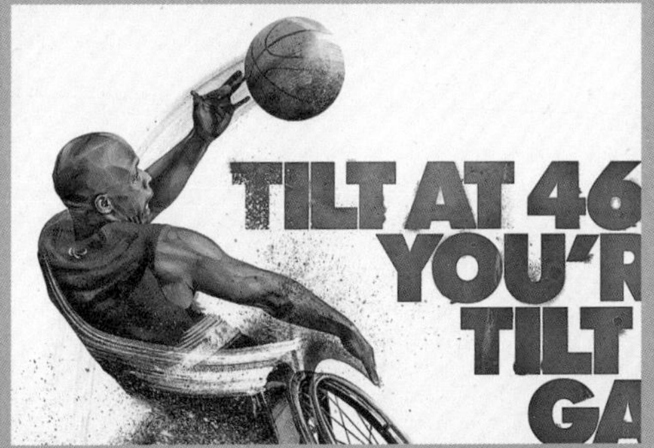
TILT AT 46
YOU'R
TILT
GA

MALAYAN TAPIR 1,500 - 2,000 AS OF LAST COUNT.
NILE LECHWE LESS THAN 40,000 IN THEIR NATURAL HABITAT.
ORANGUTAN NO MORE THAN 60,000.
QUAGGA PERISHED IN 1883.
RED RUFFED LEMUR THREATENED BY HABITAT LOSS, HUNTING AND PET TRADE.
SYRIAN WILD ASS NEVER SEEN SINCE 1927.
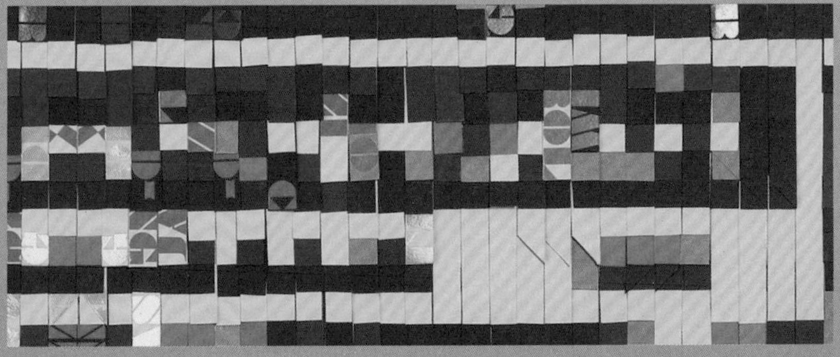
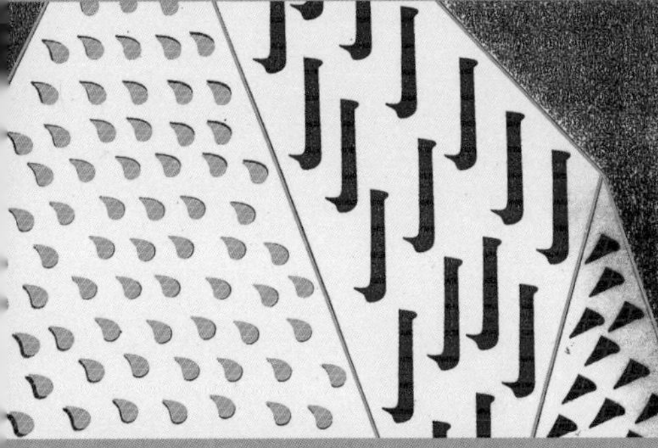

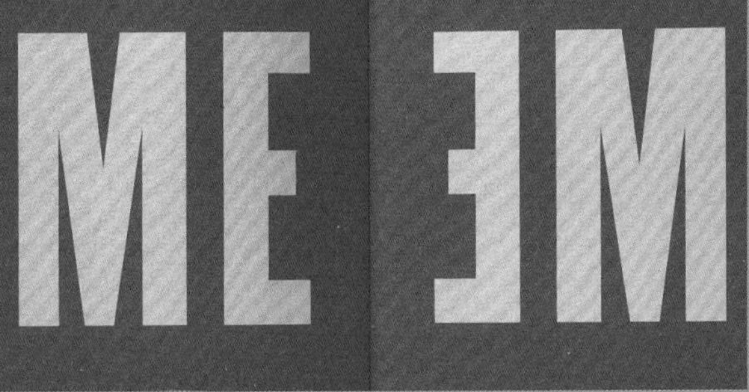
ME
ƎM

1

2

3

4

5

6

7

Jury Foreman
1. John Hegarty
BBH London

2. Souen Le Van
Marcel Paris

3. Matt Allen
The Red Brick Road

4. Yuya Furukawa
Dentsu Tokyo

5. Eva Stetefeld
Jung von Matt/Fleet
Hamburg

6. Martin Galton
VCCP

7. Menno Kluin
DDB New York

Yellow Pencil in Art Direction

Art Direction for Press Advertising
JWT Shanghai
for Samsonite

Heaven and Hell
The task was to produce print ads and outdoor communication for the Samsonite Cosmolite suitcase. The selling point is its ultra-durability. The creative idea is a vivid contrast between how 'heavenly' it is in first class for the passenger but 'hellish' down below where the suitcase is being handled. And yet the suitcase emerges sparkling after the torture.

Art Directors
Rojana Chuasakul
Danny Li
Haoxi Lv
Surachai
Puthikulangkura
Copywriter
Marc Wang
Illustrators
Surachai
Puthikulangkura
Supachai U-Rairat
Creative Directors
Hattie Cheng
Rojana Chuasakul
Executive Creative Directors
Elvis Chau
SheungYan Lo
Yang Yeo
Production House Producers
Somsak Pairew
Anotai Panmongkol
Advertising Agency
JWT Shanghai
Production House
Illusion
Account Handlers
Michelle Xiao
Lily Zheng
Maggie Zhou
Account Directors
Tom Doctoroff
Sophia Ng
Client
Samsonite

Art Direction for Poster Advertising
Marcel Worldwide
for Editions Points

Famous Speeches Collection:
Africa's Time Has Come

French publishing house Editions Points published its 'Famous Speeches' collection to underline the important role famous speeches have played in our past and consequently our present. This poster is part of a campaign to promote the collection with each ad featuring a line from a famous speech. Each letter has been designed to show an event, so when we read the entire title, we can chronologically see what the speech changed in history. Posters were placed on walls in strategic areas to make people aware of the impact these speeches still have today.

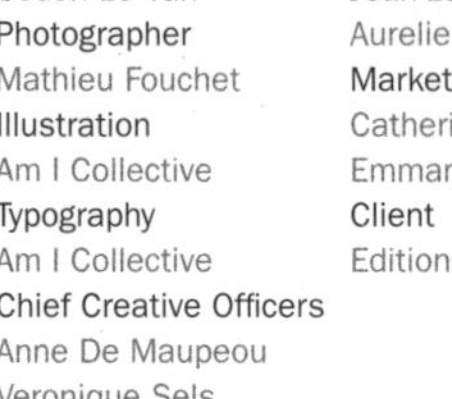

Art Directors
Romain Galli
Souen Le Van
Copywriters
Romain Galli
Souen Le Van
Photographer
Mathieu Fouchet
Illustration
Am I Collective
Typography
Am I Collective
Chief Creative Officers
Anne De Maupeou
Veronique Sels
Sebastien Vacherot
Advertising Agency
Marcel Worldwide

Project Manager
Cecile Henderycks
Account Director
Michel Kowalski
Art Buyers
Jean-Luc Chirio
Aurelie Lubot
Marketing Managers
Catherine Laupretre
Emmanuelle Vial
Client
Editions Points

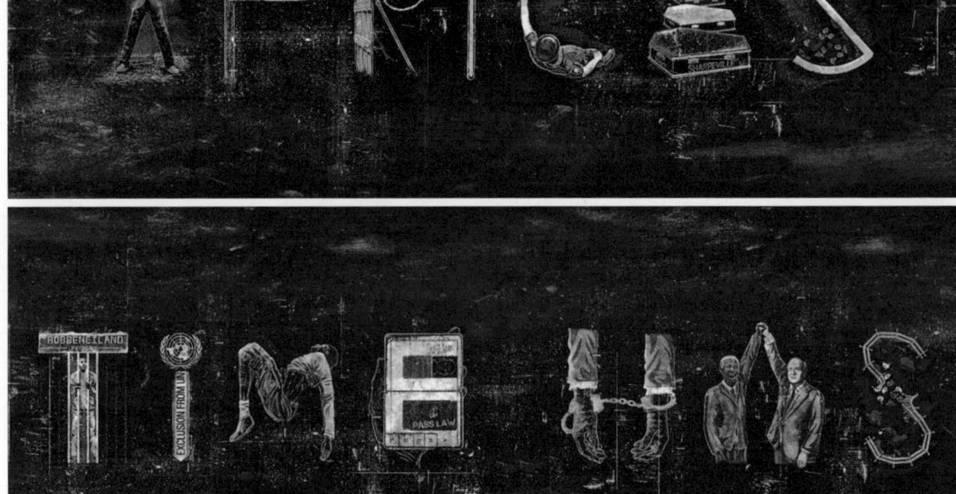

Art Direction for Poster Advertising
AMV BBDO
for GE

Living Masterpiece
To demonstrate GE's commitment to helping reduce the National Gallery's carbon footprint, we created the world's first 'living' masterpiece. Using over 8,000 plants, we recreated one of the National Gallery's most famous paintings, Van Gogh's 'A Wheatfield, with Cypresses'. Over a four-month period, the plants were grown and then installed onto a huge 22-metre site outside the gallery in Trafalgar Square, London. The installation was seen by over 60 million people over six months.

Art Directors
Mike Bond
Antony Nelson
Copywriters
Bern Hunter
Mike Sutherland
Creative Director
Paul Brazier
Director
Jamie Maule-ffinch
Producers
Sam LeGassick
Ciara McGowan

Agency Producers
Chloe Robinson
Adam Walker
Advertising Agency
AMV BBDO
Account Handlers
Amber Glenister
Tim Rogowski
Client
GE

Art Direction for Poster Advertising
Serviceplan München
for Barmer GEK

The Fat Posters
People eat too much fat. Health insurance company Barmer GEK asked us to make people aware of how much fat their food contains. We created posters made out of fat. In a complex chemical process, we extracted the fat from popular dishes and airbrushed it on white paper. The result: fat posters. The fat of one product for one poster – no more, no less.

Art Director
Roman Becker
Graphic Designer
Felix von Pless
Copywriter
Andreas Schriewer
Producer
Bianca Schreck
Programmer
Steffen Knoblich
Creative Director
Christoph Nann
Executive Creative Director
Maik Kaehler
Chief Creative Officer
Alexander Schill
Advertising Agency
Serviceplan München
Account Executive
Ines Herbold
Client
Barmer GEK

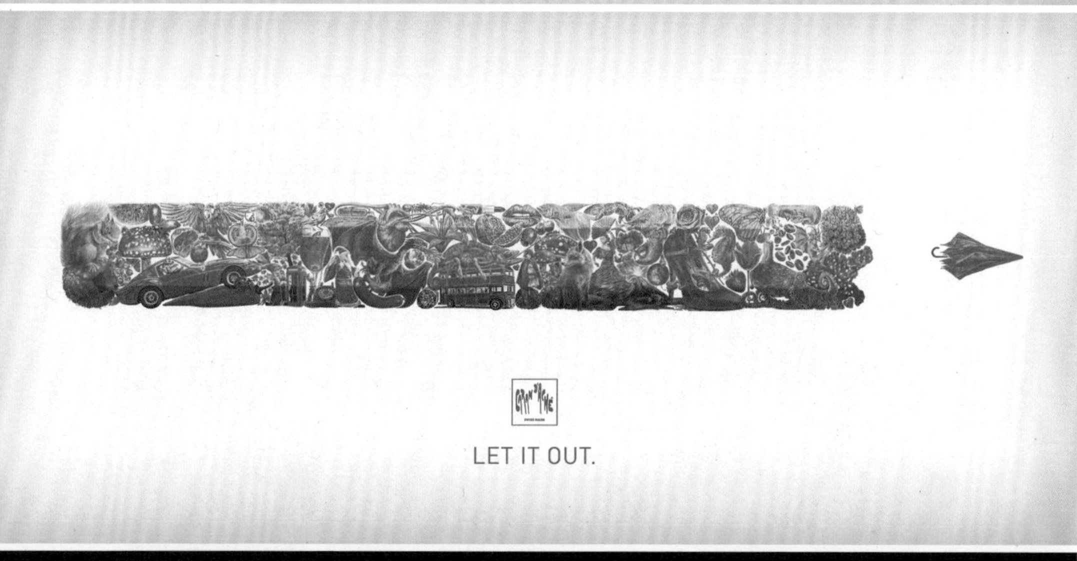

Art Direction for Poster Advertising
Wirz BBDO
for Caran D'Ache

Caran D'Ache Crayons – Let It Out

Caran d'Ache is Switzerland's oldest and largest manufacturer of wooden crayons. The brand is known to every child in the country, as well as their parents and grandparents. The crayons campaign shown here is a reminder to them all of what they love or used to love about Caran d'Ache: the sheer joy of creation, which anyone, no matter how advanced their skills, can relate to.

Art Director
Paul Labun
Illustrator
Isabelle Bühler
Typographer
Katja Schlosser
Creative Director
Philipp Skrabal

Advertising Agency
Wirz BBDO
Account Handler
Isabelle Jubin
Client
Caran D'Ache

Art Direction for Poster Advertising
Leo Burnett London
for Kellogg's

72,000 Flavours
When Kellogg's first begged Leo Burnett for an ad campaign to revive the fortunes of Rice Krispies Squares, we immediately set to work. Sorry, set off to work, we hadn't had much to do for a while and weren't going in till after lunch. After six or seven minutes' thought, we came up with the line: 'It's all lies, they're not even square'. This was presented by mistake to the client over the phone. He thought we said 'It's all wise, they're jolly good fare,' and approved it immediately. He was on holiday when these posters were made and we hope he likes them when he sees them here.

Art Director
Caroline Rawlings
Designer
Mark Denton
Copywriter
Chris Birch
Creative Director
Don Bowen
Executive Creative Director
Justin Tindall
Advertising Agency
Leo Burnett London
Project Manager
Gaynor Goldring
Planner
Olivia Heywood
Account Manager
Eric Schnabel
Art Buyer
Julie Hughes
Client
Kellogg's
Brand
Rice Krispies

BUY TWO - GET A FREE BOAT

It's all **LIES**
- they're not even Square!

Art Direction for Poster Advertising
Leo Burnett London
for Kellogg's

Buy Two, Get a Free Boat

When the annals of advertising history come to be written, surely this campaign for Rice Krispies Squares will recline proudly near the summit. Everything is exquisitely crafted, from the Squares themselves with their heat-inflated grains, artfully coagulated into rectangular cuboids in a factory just outside Salford, to the advertising campaign with its vibrant posters skilfully conjuring up an explosion in a graphics factory – all come together to leave campaigns for lesser confectionery products camped shivering in the foothills of Creativity, gazing wistfully upwards.

Art Director
Caroline Rawlings
Designer
Mark Denton
Copywriter
Chris Birch
Creative Director
Don Bowen
Executive Creative Director
Justin Tindall
Advertising Agency
Leo Burnett London
Project Manager
Gaynor Goldring
Planner
Olivia Heywood
Account Manager
Eric Schnabel
Art Buyer
Julie Hughes
Client
Kellogg's
Brand
Rice Krispies

Art Direction for Poster Advertising
Leo Burnett London
for Kellogg's

Actual Size

Rice Krispies Squares were invented in 1685 in Spitalfields by James Pryke, a confectioner distantly related to diarist Samuel Pepys. His secret recipe, written on parchment, was stored for many years in the British Museum. It was partially destroyed in a fire during the Blitz in the Second World War, and the only word that survived was the word 'Ryce'. Using only this ingredient, mixing it with some other stuff, then using a drawing of an oblong, Kellogg's painstakingly recreated Pryke's confection, then advertised them using these posters.

Art Director
Caroline Rawlings
Designer
Mark Denton
Copywriter
Chris Birch
Creative Director
Don Bowen
Executive Creative Director
Justin Tindall
Advertising Agency
Leo Burnett London

Project Manager
Gaynor Goldring
Planner
Olivia Heywood
Account Manager
Eric Schnabel
Art Buyer
Julie Hughes
Client
Kellogg's
Brand
Rice Krispies

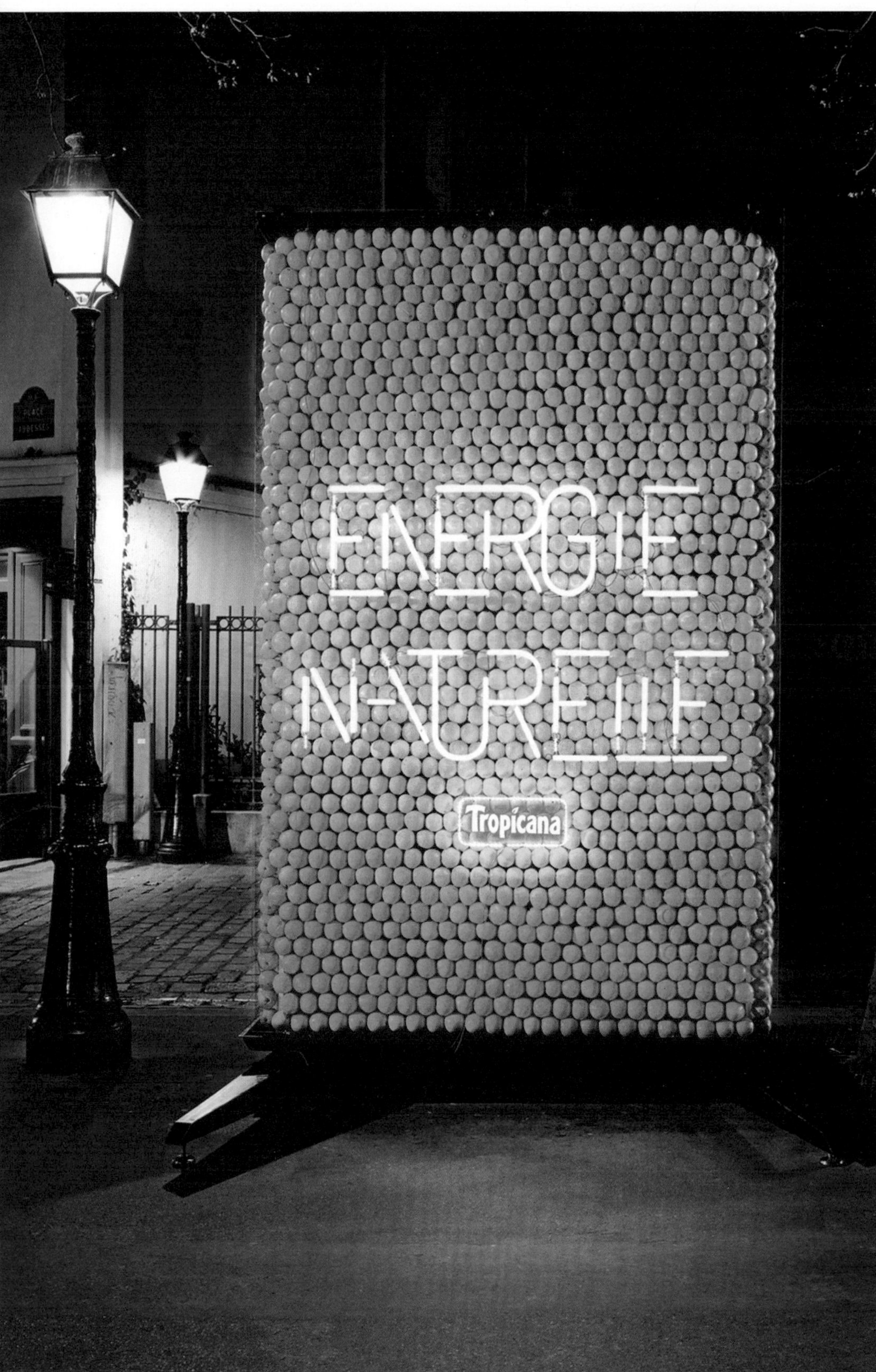

Art Direction for Poster Advertising
DDB Paris
for Tropicana

Tropicana Billboard Powered by Oranges
This billboard ad we created for Tropicana harnesses the energy from oranges to illuminate a neon sign that reads 'Natural Energy'. With several thousand spikes of copper and zinc, a lot of wiring and three months of testing, we managed to create a giant multi-cell battery powerful enough to light up the billboard. The custom build was produced by unit9 in collaboration with director Johnny Hardstaff, who created the accompanying 90-second film.

Art Directors
Alexander Kalchev
Siavosh Zabeti
Copywriters
Alexander Kalchev
Siavosh Zabeti
Production Designer
Alex Marden
Creative Directors
Alexander Kalchev
Siavosh Zabeti
Executive Creative Director
Alexandre Hervé
Director
Johnny Hardstaff
Executive Producer
Piero Frescobaldi
Agency Producers
Guillaume Cossou
Florence Gabet
Editor
Ed Cheesman
Advertising Agency
DDB Paris
Production Company
unit9
Account Director
Julie Regis
Client
Tropicana

Art Direction for Press Advertising
Y&R São Paulo
for Miami Ad School/ESPM

Letraset Ads
A good ad idea doesn't come that easy. To create a big campaign demands effort, hard work and dedication. We wanted to show that at Miami Ad School/ESPM you learn to create instead of just copying, so we reproduced classic 'Letraset' sheets with great all-time famous ads.

Art Director
Kleyton Mourão
Copywriters
Pedro Guerra
Roberto Kilciauskas
Illustrators
Gabriel Bueno
Kleyton Mourão
Print Producers
Elaine Carvalho
Rodrigo Cassino
Creative Director
Flavio Casarotti
Chief Creative Officer
Rui Branquinho
Advertising Agency
Y&R São Paulo
Planner
David Laloum
Account Director
Flavia Fusco
Art Buyer
Monica Beretta
Client
Miami Ad School/
ESPM

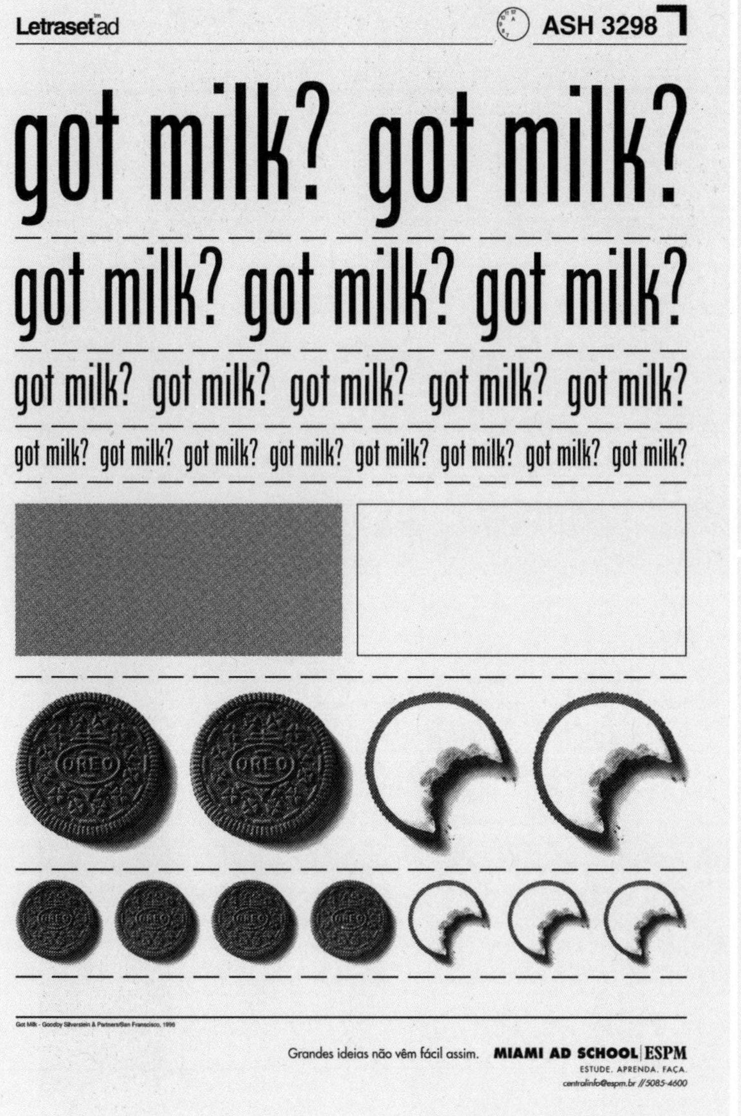

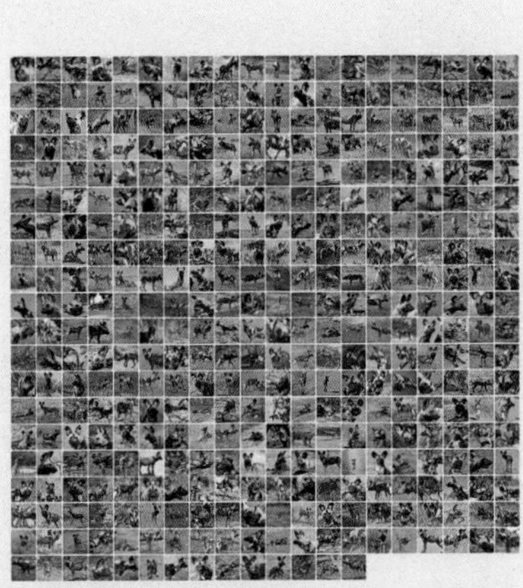

YOU ARE LOOKING AT EVERY WILD DOG LEFT IN SOUTH AFRICA.

YOU ARE LOOKING AT EVERY DUGONG LEFT IN AFRICAN WATERS.

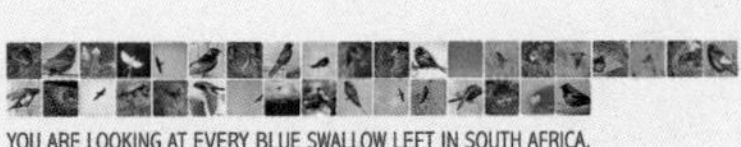

YOU ARE LOOKING AT EVERY BLUE SWALLOW LEFT IN SOUTH AFRICA.

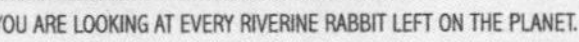

YOU ARE LOOKING AT EVERY RIVERINE RABBIT LEFT ON THE PLANET.

Art Direction for Press Advertising
TBWA\Hunt\Lascaris Johannesburg
for the Endangered Wildlife Trust

The Last Ones Left
The Endangered Wildlife Trust is a conservation group providing vital awareness about endangered species. Statistics have become prevalent in the mass of information people face every day, and are therefore easy to ignore. The public was no longer responding to the statistics the EWT was releasing. To increase the funds essential for wildlife conservation, we had to bring back the stopping power of statistics. We had to make people see the animals behind the information. From this insight came the idea of putting faces to the figures.

Art Director
Lizali Blom
Copywriters
Lizali Blom
Jared Osmond
Photographer
Mari Keyter
Creative Directors
Miguel Nunes
Adam Weber
Executive Creative Director
Damon Stapleton
Advertising Agency
TBWA\Hunt\Lascaris Johannesburg
Production Manager
Robert Mackenzie
Production Director
Craig Walker
Account Manager
Katiso Maarohanye
Account Director
Bridget Langley
Art Buyer
Sharon Cvetkovski
Client
Endangered Wildlife Trust

Art Direction for Press Advertising
Fred & Farid Paris
for the VF Corporation

Stunt
To illustrate the 'We are animals' concept, Wrangler sought stunt men and women to capture instinctive moments of life, while demonstrating the product's solidity. All photos were taken in real conditions and with no special effects.

Art Directors
Juliette Lavoix
Celine Moeur
Farid Mokart
Fred Raillard
Copywriters
Farid Mokart
Fred Raillard
Photographer
Cass Bird

Creative Directors
Fred & Farid
Advertising Agency
Fred & Farid Paris
Client
VF Corporation
Brand
Wrangler

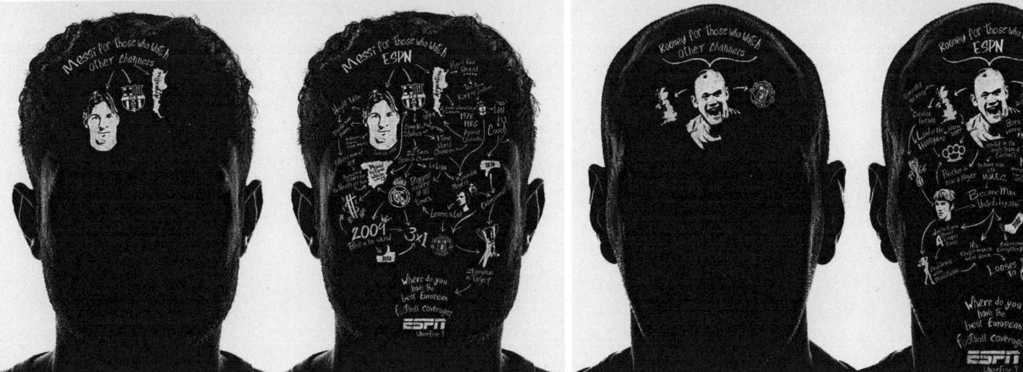

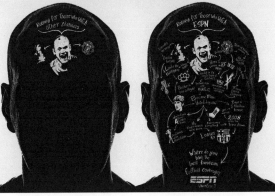

Art Direction for Press Advertising
Neogama BBH
for ESPN

Heads

We wanted to promote ESPN by comparing ESPN viewers to those who watch football on other channels. Other viewers have little information, while ESPN viewers have access to much more content. For the production, images were projected on a huge wall with chalk illustrations, and then photographed.

Art Directors
Fabio Astolpho
Pedro Utzeri
Copywriters
Eduardo Andrietta
Fernando Silva
Photographer
Bruno Cals
Creative Director
Marcio Ribas
Chief Creative Officer
Alexandre Gama
Illustration
LAB Burti
Advertising Agency
Neogama BBH
Art Buyers
Mariah Bayeux
Daniella Grandini
Vanessa Raad
Account Managers
Talitha Gomes
Fabio Losso
Diego Passos
Client
ESPN

1

2

3

4

5

6

7

Jury Foreman
1. Matt Lambert
FRIEND London /
Stink Berlin

2. Clare Donald
Euro RSCG London

3. Laura Gregory
Great Guns

4. Jamie Rockaway
Transistor Studios

5. Francois Chilot
Les Producers

6. Dulcidio Caldeira
Paranoid BR

7. Yoann Lemoine
ICONOCLAST / HSI

Yellow Pencil in Film Advertising Crafts

Animation for Film Advertising
Nexus Productions
for Chipotle

Back to the Start
Willie Nelson, Coldplay, Chipotle and director Johnny Kelly have joined forces with the Chipotle Cultivate Foundation to create 'Back to the Start', a short animated film highlighting the issue of sustainable farming. Chipotle founder Steve Ells met with Johnny Kelly in London to talk about his passionate efforts to source food on a more sustainable and ethical basis. Music legend Willie Nelson, well-known for his support of family farmers, was a perfect collaborator for the music, which features him covering 'The Scientist' by Coldplay. This film was also selected in the 'Use of Music for Film Advertising' category.

Character Animator
Gary Cureton
Set Animator
Matt Cooper
3D Previs Lead Artist
Mark Davies
Compositors
Alasdair Brotherston
John Taylor
Director
Johnny Kelly
Producer
Liz Chan
Executive Producers
Charlotte Bavasso
Cedric Gairard
Chris O'Reilly
Production Managers
Alistair Pratten
Claire Thompson
Production Designer
Graham Staughton
Director of Photography
Matt Day
Music Composers
Coldplay
Music Performer
Willie Nelson
Sound Designer
Barnaby Templer
Production Company
Nexus Productions
Music Arrangement & Supervision
Duotone Audio Group
New York
Advertising Agency
Creative Artists Agency
Client
Chipotle

Yellow Pencil in Film Advertising Crafts

Cinematography for Film Advertising
Delibistrot
for Nike

Addiction
To encourage the practice of running amongst young people, F/Nazca Saatchi & Saatchi created a hash tag for Nike entitled #coisadaboa (#thegoodstuff). The language of the campaign explores the addiction that running causes within its practitioners and the clear advantage it has over other addictions: it's good for your body. The campaign film uses stylistic techniques reminiscent of psychological thrillers to create a tense and eerie mood. The grayscale picture, uneven cinematography and manipulation of time and space work together to place the viewer in the restless shoes of an addict. A hoarse voice whispers: 'I have never met an ex-addict. Have a nice trip'. This work was also awarded a Yellow Pencil in the 'Direction for Film Advertising' category, and nominated in both the 'Editing for Film Advertising' and 'Sound Design for Film Advertising' categories.

Cinematographer
Andre Faccioli
Directors
Jones+Tino
Art Director
Rodrigo Castellari
Copywriters
Eduardo Lima
Pedro Prado
Creative Directors
Fabio Fernandes
Eduardo Lima
Head of Art
João Linneu
Agency Producers
Adriano Costa
Marcio Leitão
Editors
Ricardo Jones
Marcio Leitão
Production Company
Delibistrot
Sound Design
Satélite
Music Composition
No-Maddz
Advertising Agency
F/Nazca Saatchi
& Saatchi
Planner
José Porto
Account Handler
Marcello Penna
Client
Nike

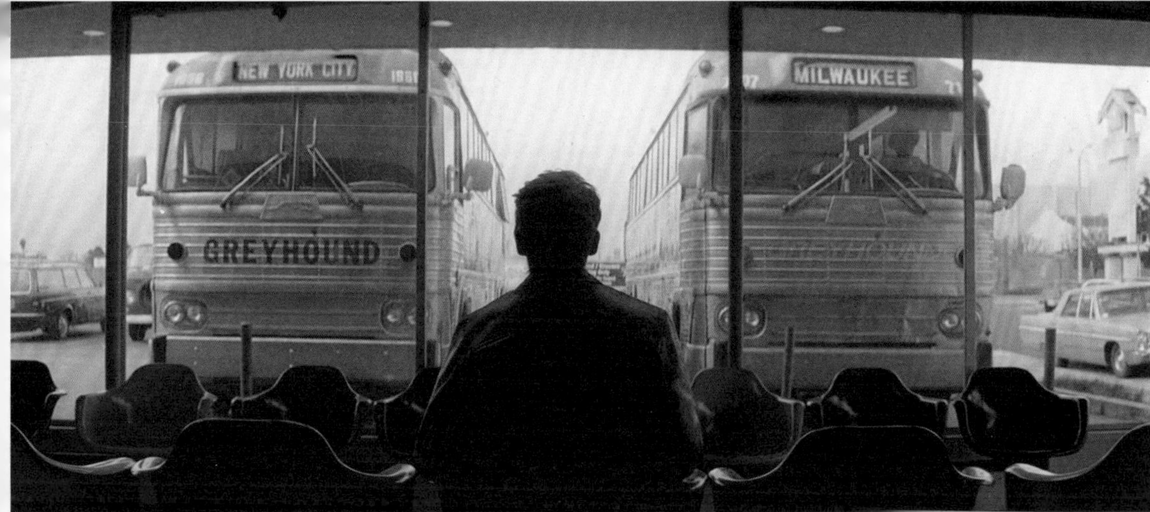

Yellow Pencil in Film Advertising Crafts

Cinematography for Film Advertising
MJZ Los Angeles
for Beam

Parallels
The bold choices we make, make us. The question is, which 'us' will we choose? In this latest anthem spot for Jim Beam, Oscar-nominated actor Willem Dafoe ponders that exact question. As a young man, Dafoe is at a crossroads, faced with a choice: to boldly leave his hometown of Appleton, Wisconsin, and head for the bright lights and long odds of an acting career in New York City; or to stay put, and let fate play a leading role in deciding his future. This ad was also nominated in the 'Direction for Film Advertising' category and selected in the 'Production Design for Film Advertising' category.

Director of Photography
Emmanuel Lubezky
Director
Dante Ariola
Copywriters
Todd Beeby
Josh Greenspan
Creative Directors
Josh Greenspan
Jason Koxvold
Chief Creative Officer
Kevin McKeon
Producer
Natalie Hill
Executive Producers
Jeff Scruton
David Zander
Agency Producer
Sherri Levy
Production Designer
Christopher Glass
Editor
Adam Pertofsky
Production Company
MJZ Los Angeles
Visual Effects Company
The Mill New York
Editing
Rock Paper Scissors
Sound Design
Human
Advertising Agency
StrawberryFrog
Account Director
Sherri Chambers
Client
Beam
Brand
Jim Beam

Yellow Pencil in Film Advertising Crafts

Direction for Film Advertising
Blink
for Alberto Culver

Pageant
This film depicts a scandal at the annual pageant in the village of Pliktisijiteur. Here young men compete for the title of Mr Plikt with traditional rounds of Talent, Swimsuit and Beauty. The foundations of this dull, rural community are rocked when our main character Luke deviates from the hair norm with the help of VO5 Extreme Style. He is banished forever but not before he gets the girl and they run off into the sunset together. The whole ad is set to an Eastern European folk cover of Cameo's 1986 classic 'Word Up!'. This ad was also awarded a Yellow Pencil in the 'Use of Music for Film Advertising' category, and nominated in the 'Cinematography for Film Advertising' category.

Director
Adam Hashemi
Art Director
Mike Insley
Copywriter
Harry Stanford
Creative Director
Dominic Gettins
Executive Creative Director
Mick Mahoney
Producer
Ben Mann
Agency Producer
Jo Charlesworth
Cinematographer
John Lynch
Editor
Leo Scott
Music Arrangers
John Greswell
Christopher Taylor
Sound Designer
Andy Humphreys
Production Company
Blink
Advertising Agency
Euro RSCG London
Client
Alberto Culver
Brand
VO5

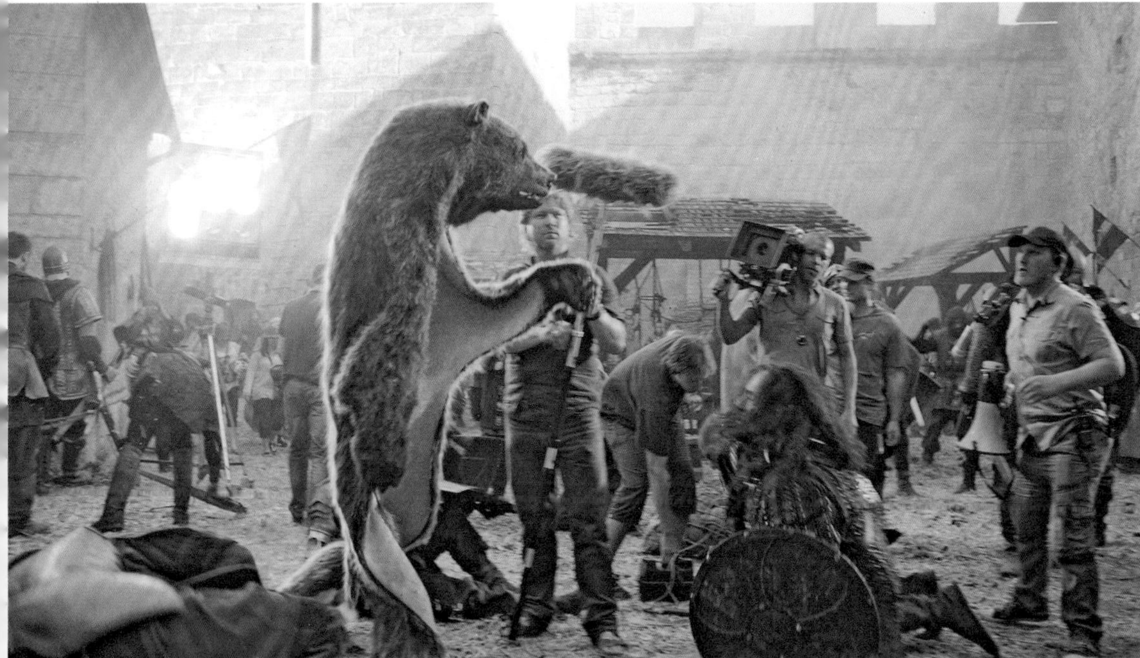

Yellow Pencil in Film Advertising Crafts

Direction for Film Advertising
Soixante Quinze
for CANAL+

The Bear
In this ad for CANAL+, a bearskin rug explains what it takes to become a great Hollywood director. The ad was also awarded a Yellow Pencil in the 'Editing for Film Advertising' and 'Special Effects for Film Advertising' categories, and nominated in the 'Production Design for Film Advertising' category.

Director
Matthijs van Heijningen
Art Director
Eric Astorgue
Copywriter
Jean-Christophe Royer
Executive Creative Director
Stéphane Xiberras
Executive Producer
Yuki Suga
Agency Producers
David Green
Isabelle Menard
Music Producer
Eric Cervera
Production Designer
Jan Houllevigue
Director of Photography
Joost Van Gelder
Editor
Jono Griffiths
Production Company
Soixante Quinze
Post Production
Mikros
Visual Effects Company
Mikros
Sound Design
GUM
Advertising Agency
BETC Paris
Planner
Clarisse Lacarrau
Client
CANAL+

Yellow Pencil in Film Advertising Crafts

Direction for Film Advertising
The Glue Society
for PepsiCo

Dip Desperado
Doritos is a sharing brand. But while its chips were flying off the shelves for social snacking, it seemed that consumers weren't buying Doritos dips to complete the experience. So we needed to put Doritos chips and dips together in the minds of consumers. We created a game around dipping chips into jars of salsa. To stand out in the app store, we did this in two ways. Firstly, we invented the Mexican sport of El Flicko – the art of flicking chips into salsa. Secondly, Esteban Ortega, the greatest chip-flicker who never lived, became the star of the commercial we subsequently produced.

Direction
The Glue Society
Art Directors
Jeremy Tribe
Tim Vance
Copywriters
Paul Knott
Tim Vance
Prabhu Wignarajah
Creative Director
Mark Fairbanks
Executive Creative Director
Paul Brazier
Producers
Jason Kemp
Suzy MacGregor
Digital Producer
Suzanne Melia
Editors
Adam Jenkins
Jeff Stevens

Production Company
Independent Films
Post Production
The Mill London
Digital Production Company
ACNE Production
Music Production
Human
Sound Design
750mph
Human
Advertising Agency
AMV BBDO
Planner
Tom White
Account Handler
Benedict Pringle
Client
PepsiCo
Brand
Doritos

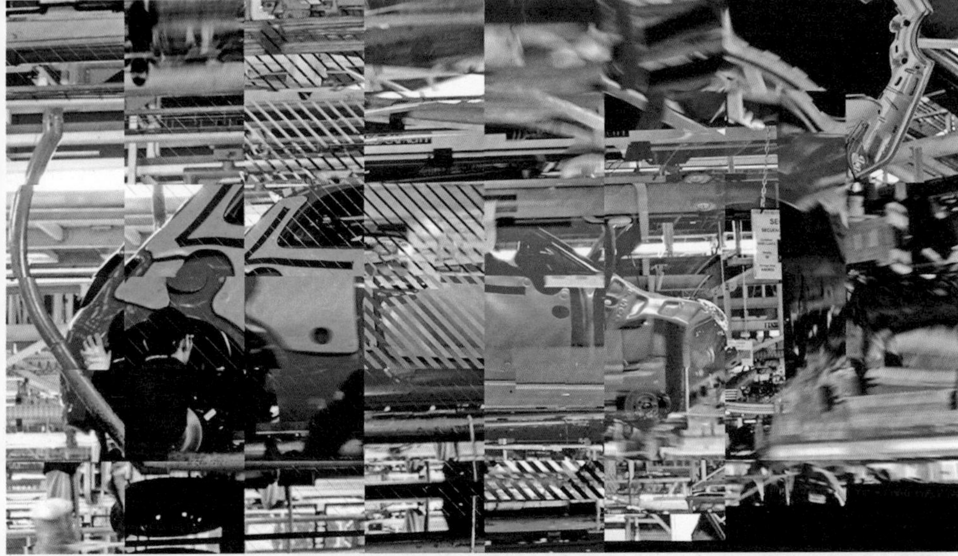

Yellow Pencil in Film Advertising Crafts

Editing for Film Advertising
Mirada
for FIAT USA

Get Ready
'Get Ready' launched the FIAT 500 in North America. The film features slick documentary-style footage of cranes, robotic arms and other factory machinery whose movements create a mechanical ballet. Editing techniques, such as split-screen action and cross cutting, emphasise the fast-paced energy of the spot. Director Mark Kudsi found inspiration in romantic comedies. Action intercuts between two characters preparing for a blind date with each other. Instead of 'boy meets girl', it's 'driver meets car'. Set to Vivaldi's 'Concerto in D Major', the track builds action within the spot.

Editors
Jeff Aquino
Fred Fouquet
Hoa Mai
Lenny Mesina
Director
Mark Kudsi
Art Director
Craig Smith
Senior Art Director
Jonathan Wu
Writer
Parag Tembulkar
Creative Directors
Craig Smith
Parag Tembulkar
Executive Producers
Scott Cymbala
Javier Jimenez
Agency Producers
Lorraine Kraus
Kristin Loudis
Line Producer
Anna Joseph
Director of Photography
Eric Schmidt
Visual Effects Producer
James Taylor
Compositor
Ash Wagers
Production Company
Motion Theory
Post Production
Mirada
Music Arrangement
MassiveMusic
Music Remix
The Glitch Mob
Advertising Agency
Impatto
Client
FIAT USA
Brand
FIAT 500

Yellow Pencil in Film Advertising Crafts

Production Design for Film Advertising
Stink
for TalkTalk

Homes within Homes
TalkTalk provides phone and broadband services for residential homes. It helps keep people connected to each other in a number of ways through email, Skype and phone calls. This commercial focuses on a number of homes where TalkTalk isn't available; it brings to life the longing and loneliness of the characters who live there. We then introduce TalkTalk into these unconnected homes, and see the emotional benefit that TalkTalk brings its customers. This ad was also selected in the 'Direction for Film Advertising' and 'Special Effects for Film Advertising' categories.

Production Designer
Kem White
Director
Adam Berg
Art Directors
Matt Collier
Wayne Robinson
Copywriters
Matt Collier
Wayne Robinson
Creative Director
Warren Moore
Executive Creative Director
Jonathan Burley
Producer
Ben Croker
Executive Producer
Blake Powell
Post Producer
Misha Stanford-Harris
Agency Producer
David Jones
Production Manager
Kate Wynborne
Director of Photography
Linus Sandgren

Animators
Martin Rhys Davies
Mike Mort
Kevin Walton
3D Artist
Alastair Hearsum
Special Effects
Duncan Malcom
Editor
Paul Hardcastle
Sound Engineer
Sam Ashwell
Production Company
Stink
Post Production
Glassworks
Animation
Evolution Studios
Creative Agency
CHI & Partners
Planner
David Jackson
Account Managers
Olivia MacLachlan
Susie Shing
Client
TalkTalk

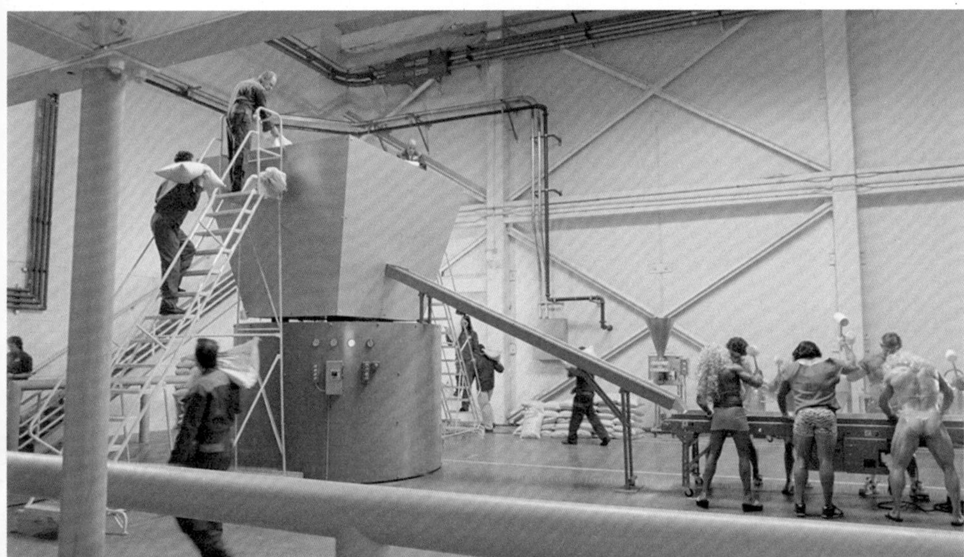

Yellow Pencil in Film Advertising Crafts

Production Design for Film Advertising
MJZ Los Angeles
for Hahn Super Dry

Super in. Super out.
In the Hahn brewery, superness is brewed into the beer at each stage of its creation. Barley is infused with the 'Knight Rider' song via huge speakers. The grain is pounded by body builders in Lycra, exposed to kung fu movies, churned by a monster truck DeLorean, mixed in an immense drum kit, poured over winning trophies, fermented in an Elvis-suited vat, and stroked by a smooth gentleman as it fills a glass panther before being approved by a CEO in a solid gold helicopter. As the Hahn Super Dry exits the factory, each bottle is capped by a uniformed ferret. Super goes in; super dry taste comes out.

Production Designer
Floyd Albee
Director
Tom Kuntz
Executive Creative Director
Micah Walker
Associate Creative Directors
Justine Armour
Ruth Bellotti
Agency Producer
Adrian Shapiro
Line Producer
Scott Kaplan
Editor
Gavin Cutler
Production Company
MJZ Los Angeles
Post Production
Eight VFX
Advertising Agency
Publicis Mojo
Account Director
Deanne Constantine
Client
Hahn Super Dry

Yellow Pencil in Film Advertising Crafts

Sound Design for Film Advertising
Factory Studios
for Unilever

PG Tips – Ahh
'Homemade' sound effects contribute to the cosy, familiar feel of Al and Monkey's house in this commercial. The rhythmic application of sound was used to create a tune for the duo's tea making ritual. The result is a memorable, warmly comedic ad that captures the essence of the PG brand. The organic sound design allows the commercial to convey its message wholeheartedly, without one word of dialogue uttered from either character.

Sound Designer
Sam Robson
Director
Garth Jennings
Art Directors
Jason Bottenus
Ben Middleton
Copywriters
Stuart Outhwaite
Ed Warren
Creative Directors
Stephen Butler
Ben Middleton
Stuart Outhwaite
Mark Waites
Ed Warren
Producer
Nick Goldsmith
Agency Producer
Mike Clear
Director of Photography
Simon Chaudoir

Editor
Dominic Leung
Sound Design
Factory Studios
Production Company
Hammer & Tongs
Post Production
Prime Focus London
Editing
Trim
Advertising Agency
Mother London
Planner
Britt Iverson
Client
Unilever
Brand
PG Tips

It's a wonderful world, watch it with us

Yellow Pencil in Film Advertising Crafts

Use of Music for Film Advertising
RKCR/Y&R
for the BBC

Wonderful World
This trailer features the BBC's David Attenborough as a voice over. As we hear his famously distinctive narration, we see the awe-inspiring shots of animals and nature that the BBC has broadcast over the years. However, when edited together over the music, we slowly realise that the words form the recognisable lyrics to Louis Armstrong's 'Wonderful World'. Aptly enough, we then see a caption that reads: 'It's a wonderful world, watch it with us'. This trailer was also selected in the 'Editing for Film Advertising' category.

Music Arranger
Nick Payne
Art Director
Paul Angus
Copywriter
Ted Heath
Executive Creative Director
Mark Roalfe
Agency Producer
Kate Woodhouse
Editor
Thomas Ioannou
Sound Designer
Gary Turnbull
Colourist
Ricky Gausis
Music Arrangement
The Works
Production Company
Red Bee Media
Post Production
MPC London
Editing
Thomas Ioannou Associates
Sound Design
Grand Central Sound Studios
Advertising Agency
RKCR/Y&R
Media Agency
BBC One
Account Director
Joshua Harris
Client
BBC
Brand
BBC One

Nomination in Film Advertising Crafts

Cinematography for Film Advertising
Smuggler
for Converse

History Made and in the Making
This film spans the epic history of Chuck Taylor and Converse for the past 100 years. By linking the shared spirit of rebellion and creativity of all those who've touched the brand, we wove a visual narrative of basketball, music, skate, dance and culture into a grand celebration of what makes this great brand iconic. No archival footage was used in this film. Each scene was carefully crafted as a period piece with great attention to detail. Only cameras available at that moment in history were used for each scene, giving the cinematography a rich, textured, gritty and authentic feel. This film was also selected in the 'Editing for Film Advertising' category.

Director of Photography
Linus Sandgren
Director
Brian Beletic
Creative Director
Ian Toombs
Executive Creative Director
Mike Byrne
Design Director
Kevin Lyons
Producer
Donald Taylor
Executive Producers
Brian Carmody
Patrick Milling Smith
Senior Producer
Niki Polyocan
Agency Producers
Andrew Loevenguth
Niki Polyocan
Visual Effects Producers
Baptiste Andrieux
Marsi Frey
Visual Effects Executive Producer
Shira Boardman
Production Designer
Brock Houghton
Head of Integrated Production
Andrew Loevenguth
Editor
Andrea Macarthur
Production Company
Smuggler
Advertising Agency
Anomaly
Account Director
Jill Ong
Client
Converse

Nomination in Film Advertising Crafts

Cinematography for Film Advertising
Stink
for Arla

Kitchen Odyssey
'Kitchen Odyssey' encourages consumers to reappraise their food decisions at times of weakness, inspiring them to make better ones. We took a very small moment and made it epic by introducing the spirit of adventure to whipping up an easy but delicious dinner. We worked with our director to create a classic narrative for this very tiny story. He used the technique of moving between the macro world and the real world to create tension. All the drama was kept in close-up. This ad was also selected in the 'Sound Design for Film Advertising' category.

Director of Photography
Stepan Kucera
Director
Martin Krejci
Creative Directors
Dan Norris
Ray Shaughnessy
Executive Creative Directors
Tony Davidson
Kim Papworth
Producer
Louise Gagen
Executive Producer
Blake Powell
Agency Producer
Anna Smith
Flame Artists
Jonathan Hairman
Tom Sparks
Editors
Filip Malasek
Tom Spark
Sound Engineer
Aaron Reynolds
Web Producer
Sarah Hiddlestone
Production Company
Stink
Post Production
Framestore CFC
Wave Studios
Editing
The Whitehouse
Sound Design
Wave Studios
Creative Agency
Wieden+Kennedy London
Account Director
Alice Von Oswald
Brand Manager
Thryth Jarvis
Client
Arla
Brand
Lurpak

Nomination in Film Advertising Crafts

Direction for Film Advertising
The Glue Society
for TMB

Panyee FC
This film tells the story of a group of kids from Thailand who followed their dream to start a football team, even though their island offered no flat surfaces. The film was shot entirely in local dialect and cast using children from Panyee itself. The story spread virally across the wider sports community, with two million views on YouTube, and through subsequent international news stories.

Direction
The Glue Society
Director
Matt Devine
Art Directors
Sanpathit Tavijaroen
Sompat Trisadikun
Park Wannasiri
Copywriters
Chanwit Nimcharoen
Puttipong
Pattanapongsagorn
Creative Director
Sanpathit Tavijaroen
Executive Creative
Director
Keeratie
Chaimoungkalo
Chief Creative Officer
Sompat Trisadikun
Producer
Alice Grant
Executive Producer
Michael Ritchie
Agency Producers
Sompetch
Nuntasinlapachai
Jirateep Sangsuwan

Cinematographer
Geoffrey Simpson
Editor
Daniel Lee
Sound Designers
Paisan Chamnong
Jirasak
Rungruengthanja
Production Company
Revolver
Advertising Agencies
Arc Worldwide Thailand
Leo Burnett Bangkok
Account Executive
Phatarada Tritiprungroj
Account Director
Suthasi
Sukpornsinchai
Client
TMB

For gifts you can't wait to give

Nomination in Film Advertising Crafts

Direction for Film Advertising
Blink
for the John Lewis Partnership

The Long Wait
This story follows a boy in the days leading up to Christmas. We see him wishing time away as he waits for the big day to arrive. But when he wakes on Christmas morning he ignores his own presents, and gets a gift he has crudely wrapped from his wardrobe. We realise he has been excitedly waiting to give the perfect gift to his parents.

Director
Dougal Wilson
Art Director
Matt Gay
Copywriter
John Long
Creative Directors
Ben Priest
Emer Stamp
Ben Tollett
Producer
Ben Link
Agency Producer
Matt Craigie
Production Company
Blink
Advertising Agency
adam&eve
Client
John Lewis
Partnership

Nomination in Film Advertising Crafts

Direction for Film Advertising
Academy Films
for Thomson & TUI Travel

Time for a Holiday
Faced with the challenge that consumers see no difference between Thomson and its competitors, we developed this campaign as a hard-hitting brand piece to establish Thomson as the category leader. In this ad, a small child reminds us of what's really important in life. We see shots of families and couples enjoying their holidays. The film has an effortless and natural beauty to it which is complemented by a musical rearrangement of 'Where is My Mind?' by the Pixies. This ad was also selected in the 'Cinematography for Film Advertising' and 'Use of Music for Film Advertising' categories.

Director
Martin De Thurah
Art Director
Stephen Reed
Creative Director
Gavin McGrath
Copywriter
Stephen Reed
Producer
Lucy Gossage
Agency Producer
Jonathan Chads
Director of Photography
Lasse Frank
Editor
Mikkel Neilsen
Music Composer
Guy Farley
Sound Designer
Aaron Reynolds

Production Company
Academy Films
Post Production
The Mill London
Sound Design
Wave Studios
Advertising Agency
Beattie McGuinness Bungay
Planner
Caroline Bermingham
Account Handlers
Aimee Luther
Andrew Milner
Brand Managers
Rebecca Edwards
Jeremy Ellis
Clients
Thomson
TUI Travel

Nomination in Film Advertising Crafts

Direction for Film Advertising
MJZ Los Angeles
for Xbox

Endangered Species
'Endangered Species' is a rallying cry for car lovers worldwide and a visceral illustration of something many have come to realise: the real world has become an unfriendly place for those who truly love cars. Economic concerns, environmental regulations, clogged motorways and a myriad of other restrictions all appear to threaten the very existence of the car enthusiast. Though the opportunities to have heart-racing experiences in the real world are becoming fewer and fewer, 'Forza Motorsport 4' offers a place to explore car passion freely, without fear of speed traps or other impediments. This ad was also selected in the 'Editing for Film Advertising' category.

Director
Nicolaï Fuglsig
Art Director
Rey Andrade
Associate Creative Director
Joe Rose
Chief Creative Officer
Scott Duchon
Executive Producers
Emma Wilcockson
David Zander
Senior Producer
Kate Morrison
Line Producer
Suza Horvat
Director of Integrated Production
Tom Wright
Director of Photography
Ben Serensin
Editor
Rick Russell
Production Company
MJZ Los Angeles
Post Production
The Mill Los Angeles
Editing
Final Cut Los Angeles
Advertising Agency
twofifteenmccann
Account Executive
Stephanie Scott
Business Directors
MaryBeth Barney
Peter Goldstein
Client
Xbox
Brand
Xbox Forza

Nomination in Film Advertising Crafts

Production Design for Film Advertising
trigger happy productions
for Hornbach Baumarkt

Every Change Needs a Beginning
A little run-down village somewhere in the middle of nowhere. For some reason the locals had forgotten how to use their hands. They started to consider them as totally useless. Until one day, a giant walnut full of tools and construction material appeared. The hands of the villagers came to life again and everybody set to work with a new enthusiasm. Every change needs a beginning. This ad was also selected in the 'Cinematography for Film Advertising' and 'Direction for Film Advertising' categories.

Production Designer
Marco Bittner
Director
Pep Bosch
Art Director
Hendrik Schweder
Copywriters
Guido Heffels
Sabina Hesse
Creative Directors
Guido Heffels
Myles Lord
Executive Creative Director
Guido Heffels
Producers
Miliane Nani Meimeth
Stephan Vens
Agency Producer
Kerstin Heffels
Director of Photography
Paco Femenia
Editor
Fabrizio Rossetti
Production Company
trigger happy productions
Post Production
El Ranchito
Editing
trigger happy productions
Music Agency
Sizzer Amsterdam
Sound Design
audioforce
Advertising Agency
HEIMAT Berlin
Planner
Franka Mai
Account Handlers
Matthias von Bechtolsheim
Mark Hassan
Maik Richter
Nicole Varga
Marketing Manager
Frank Sahler
Client
Hornbach Baumarkt
Brand
Hornbach

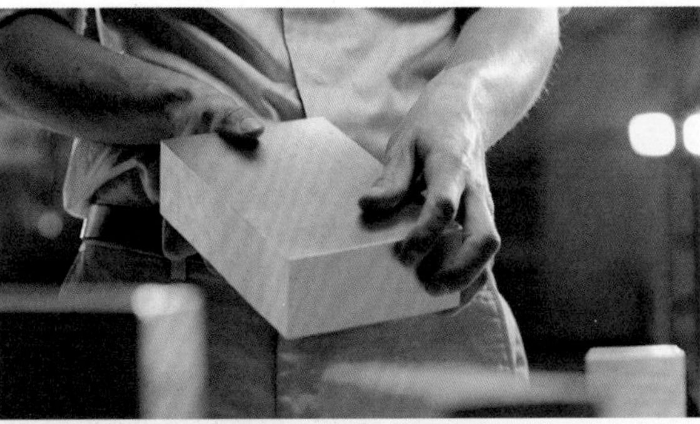

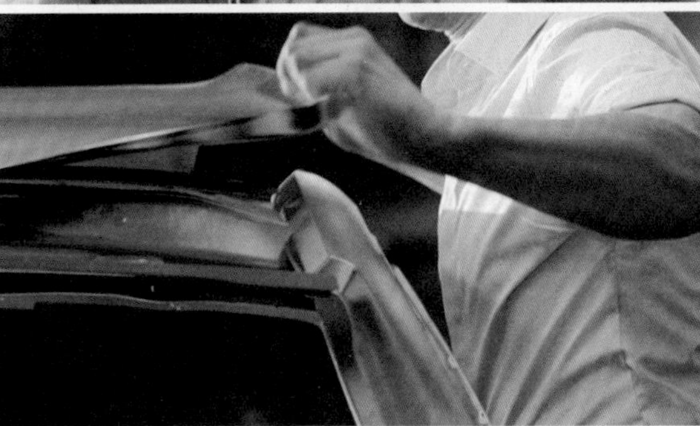

Nomination in Film Advertising Crafts

Special Effects for Film Advertising
Glassworks
for Audi

Manipulation
This spot demonstrates what is really possible within the realm of CG. It was a meticulous post process, modelling metallic materials in 3D to realistically mirror the movements of malleable materials being pushed and pulled. It gives the illusion of milling and crafting the separate elements out of aluminium. Being both 3D and 2D heavy, the ad required a high level of technical and creative expertise; the results are both realistic and mesmerising.

Special Effects
Duncan Malcolm
2D Artist
Duncan Malcolm
3D Artist
Nick Smalley
Director
Adam Berg
Art Director
Dan Bailey
Copywriter
Bradley Woolf
Creative Directors
Nick Kidney
Kevin Stark
Post Producer
Misha Stanford-Harris
Agency Producer
Ruben Mercadal
Director of Photography
Joost Van Gelder
Editor
Paul Hardcastle
Telecine
Ben Rogers
Post Production
Glassworks
Production Company
Stink
Sound Design
Factory Studios
Advertising Agency
BBH London
Client
Audi

Nomination in Film Advertising Crafts

Special Effects for Film Advertising
MPC LA
for DIRECTV

Hot House
The scene opens in a blazing house. A firefighter comes crashing through the wall and surveys the room. Just as the floor begins to give way beneath him, the shot freezes. We realise that a man lying on a bed has paused it with a remote control; he goes downstairs to view the underside of the collapsing ceiling and presses play. This was MPC LA's first project working with director Noam Murro, and he totally trusted the technical approach for the visual effects requirements of the shoot. The visual effects needed to be integrated in a location full of fire. Jittering light came from everywhere, smoke and debris filled the air... and of course the live-action fire had to be matched with a 3D generated stand-in that was capable of freezing! The key point was to obtain as much as possible in-camera and without motion-control, to see what really does happen when a house is engulfed by fire.

Visual Effects Supervisors
Franck Lambertz
Michael Wynd
Director
Noam Murro
Creative Director
Denise O'Bleness
Executive Creative Director
Todd Tilford
Chief Creative Officer
Tor Myhren
Executive Producers
Shawn Lacy
Colleen O'Donnel
Agency Executive Producer
Andrew Chinich
Post Producer
Andrew Bell
Director of Photography
Simon Duggan
Editor
Haines Hall
Telecine
Mark Gethin
Visual Effects Company
MPC LA
Production Company
Biscuit Filmworks
Advertising Agency
Grey HQ New York
Client
DIRECTV

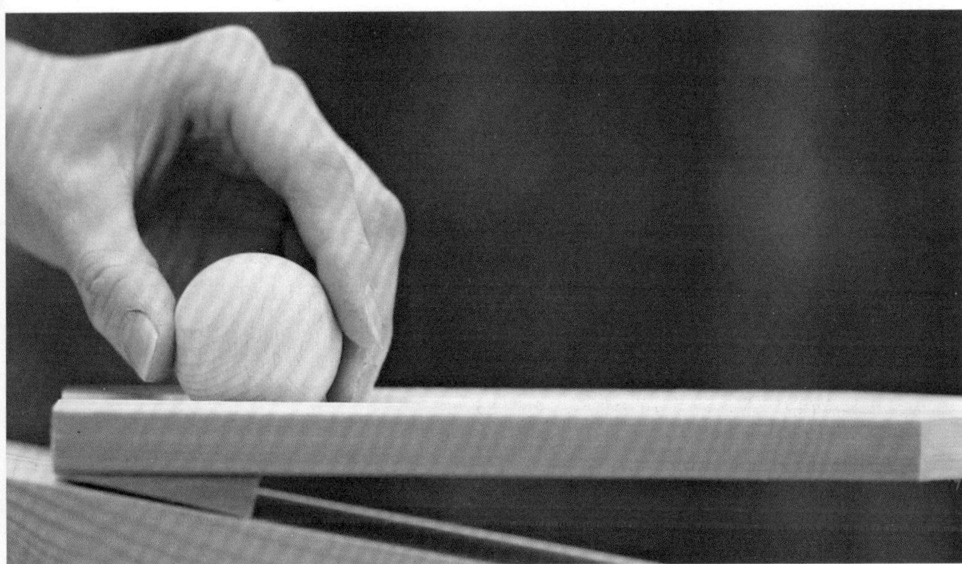

Nomination in Film Advertising Crafts

Use of Music for Film Advertising
Dentsu & Drill
for Docomo

Xylophone
This ad is for Touch Wood SH-08C, a mobile phone developed to increase awareness of forestry preservation. Like the product itself, the 44m long xylophone featured in the ad was made using only forest-thinning materials, which are a funding source for forestry preservation.

Music Composer
Johann Sebastian Bach
Director
Seiichi Hishikawa
Art Director
Jun Nishida
Copywriter
Noriko Yamada
Creative Director
Morihiro Harano
Producers
Hideyuki Chihara
Toshifumi Oiso
Agency Producer
Ayako Yoshinoya
Cinematographer
Eitaro Yamamoto
Editor
Hitoshi Kimura
Sound Designers
Kenjiro Matsuo
Mitsuo Tsuda
Production Companies
Drawing and Manual
Engine PLUS
Sound Design
Invisible Designs Lab
Advertising Agencies
Dentsu
Drill
Client
Docomo
Brand
Touch Wood

Nomination in Film Advertising Crafts

Use of Music for Film Advertising
Tribal DDB Amsterdam
for Philips

Obsessed with Sound

Philips Sound designs products for real music lovers, people to whom every single detail in music matters. Our job was to demonstrate that Philips is 'obsessed with sound' and claim that you can hear every detail with the brand's audio products. We collaborated with the Grammy Award-winning Metropole Orchestra and recorded a specially composed piece in 55 separate music tracks. On the site, which can be accessed through Facebook, viewers can experience the music video as a whole, played by the entire orchestra, and are invited to single out each musician to hear every detail.

Music Composers
Berend Dubbe
Sonja van Hamel
Orchestra Conductor
Jules Buckley
Director
Rob Chiu
Art Director
Bart Mol
Copywriter
Pol Hoenderboom
Executive Creative Director
Chris Baylis
Technical Director
Jan Willem Penterman
Executive Producers
Marcel Kornblum
Mark Pytlik
Agency Producer
Jeroen Jedeloo
Designer
Robbin Cenijn
Director of Photography
Matias Boucard
Creative Technologist
Ian Bauer
Editor
Nikaj Gouwerok
Music Arrangement
Metropole Orchestra
Music Remix
MassiveMusic
Production Company
Stink
Digital Agency
Tribal DDB Amsterdam
Project Managers
Richard Land
Christy Wassenaar
Planners
Niels Bellaar
Henk Rijks
Account Director
Sandra Krstic
Client
Philips

Nomination in Film Advertising Crafts

Use of Music for Film Advertising
Euro RSCG London
for Reckitt Benckiser

Vinyl
Apparently, there is a difference between the time it takes men and women to climax. To overcome this, Durex developed Performax Intense. The commercial uses a pair of record decks and 'Let's Get It On' by Marvin Gaye to highlight this difference and what the product does. The female record plays the track too slowly, while the male one plays it too quickly. However, through the DJ's skills, they are brought together to sync up perfectly, leaving both sides to make beautiful music together. This commercial was also selected in the 'Sound Design for Film Advertising' category.

Music Composers
Marvin Gaye
& Ed Towsend
Directors
Si & Ad
Art Director
Fabio Abram
Copywriter
Braulio Kuwabara
Creative Director
Brendan Wilkins
Executive Creative Director
Mick Mahoney
Agency Producer
Katy Dell
Sound Designer
Jack Sedgwick
Production Company
Academy Films
Advertising Agency
Euro RSCG London
Client
Reckitt Benckiser
Brand
Durex

Nomination in Film Advertising Crafts

Use of Music for Film Advertising
Droga5
for PUMA

Faas Lab
To launch PUMA's Faas running shoe, Droga5 recruited the world's fastest band from the world's fastest country. We highlighted the fun in running by way of a talented Jamaican band. The members – Rocker, Flex and Groove – made their music while on the move (with occasional 'encouragement' from the world's fastest man, Usain Bolt).

Directors
Fredrik Bond
Jim Gilchrist
Art Directors
Jesse Juriga
Dan Treichel
Associate Creative Director
Scott Bell
Executive Creative Directors
Ted Royer
Nik Studzinski
Creative Chairman
David Droga
Producer
Dana May
Executive Producer
Sam Kilbreth
Head of Integrated Production
Sally-Ann Dale
Music Composition
No-Maddz
Music Arrangement
Beacon Street Studios
Production Company
MJZ New York
Post Production
MPC LA
Editing
Spotwelders
Visual Effects Company
Charlex
Sound Design
Nylon Studios New York
Advertising Agency
Droga5
Account Director
Nick Phelps
Client
PUMA
Brand
Faas

Blam Blam

Autograph

Recording

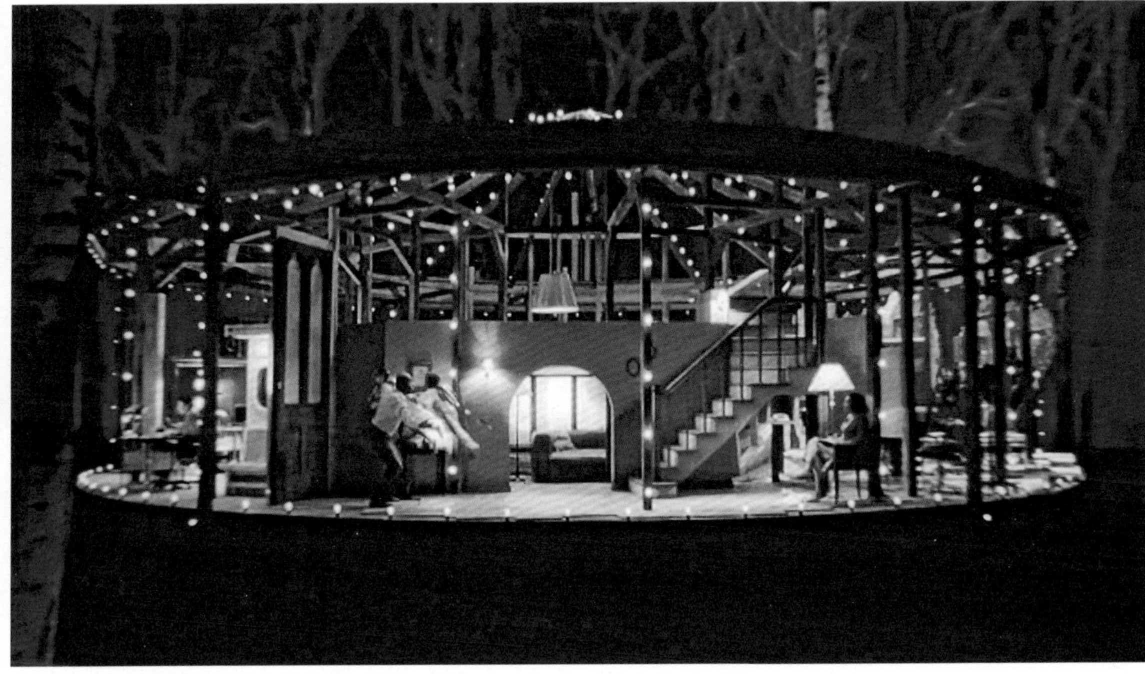

Production Design for Film Advertising
Partizan
for Nationwide

Carousel
In this ad a carousel illuminates each stage of people's lives, to represent how Nationwide puts people at centre stage. The ad brings a sense of calm in a magical world. A friendly, human world came across through the abundant use of different craft techniques.

Production Designer
Gregg Shoulder
Director
Eric Lynne
Art Directors
Anna Carpen
Max Weiland
Copywriters
Anna Carpen
Max Weiland
Creative Director
Johnny Leathers
Producer
Miranda Johnstone
Agency Executive Producer
Lou Hake
Agency Producer
Emily Hodgson
Director of Photography
Chris Doyle
Animation Director
Victor Haegelin
Editor
Dominic Leung
Production Company
Partizan
Post Production
MPC London
Advertising Agency
18 Feet & Rising
Account Handlers
Andrew Barnard
Adrienne Little
Brand Manager
Sandeep Grewal
Senior Brand Manager
Paul Hibbs
Head of Brand Marketing
Alastair Pegg
Customer Strategy & Marketing Director
Andy McQueen
Client
Nationwide

Production Design for Film Advertising
Loducca
for MTV Brasil

Balloons
This ad is a retrospective covering the most memorable events, facts and characters in music history. We produced it to celebrate MTV's 21st anniversary in Brazil, and to reinforce the brand's concept: 'The music never stops'. This ad was also selected in the 'Use of Music for Film Advertising' category.

Production Designer
Daniel Semanas
Director
Dulcídio Caldeira
Art Directors
Dulcídio Caldeira
André Faria
Guga Ketzer
Copywriters
Dulcídio Caldeira
André Faria
Guga Ketzer
Producer
Karina Vadasz
Executive Producers
Ana Luisa André
Egisto Betti
Sid Fernandes
Director of Photography
Alexandre Ermel
Animator
Daniel Semanas
Illustrator
Daniel Semanas
Music Composer
Gioachino Rossini
Sound Designers
Fernando Forni
Hilton Raw
Advertising Agency
Loducca
Account Executive
Sabrina Spinelli
Account Director
Carmen Assumpção
Planners
Isabella Mulholland
Mariana Quintanilha
Client
MTV Brasil

Animation for Film Advertising
weareflink
for ŠKODA

Curriculum Vitae
Created for use by ŠKODA's HR department, the film is an engaging demonstration of the company's commitment to its people. An applicant is preparing his CV; the pages of the CV begin to construct and animate a 3D paper world that eloquently tells the story of an employee, and illustrates the benefits the company offers. Iconic landmarks form a backdrop to show the global reach and huge range of opportunities that the company offers.

2D Artists
Stefan Galleithner
Martin Sächsinger
Christian Schnellhammer
3D Artists
Nils Engler
Alex Heyer
2D & 3D Designer
Philipp von Preusschen
Compositors
Markus Gratl
Alexander von der Lippe
Art Directors
Kristina Ambrozova
Lauren van Aswegen
Copywriter
Igor Paleta
Creative Directors
Tereza Sverakova
Niko Tziopanos
Executive Creative Director
Hermann Waterkamp
Producers
Karsten Müller
Tini Schwarz
Executive Producers
Andreas Lampe
Florian Sigl
Agency Producers
Vaclav Sladek
Katrin Wilken
Cinematographer
Roman Jakobi
Visual Effects Supervisor
Moritz Gläsle
Direction
weareflink
Production Company
Bakery Films
Music Composition
Supreme Music
Advertising Agency
Leagas Delaney Praha
Client
ŠKODA

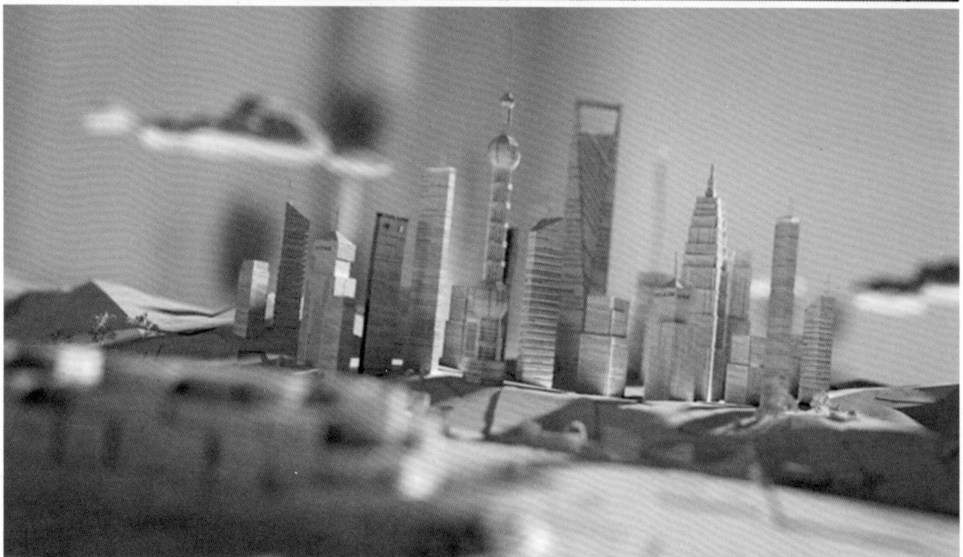

Animation for Film Advertising
Framestore
for Coca-Cola

Siege
Framestore created this entirely CG 60-second film for Coca-Cola's 2011 Super Bowl outing. 'Siege' is an epic battle of good versus evil, set in a fantasy world where a huge army of fire-warriors storm a peaceful mountain village belonging to the good creatures of Coca-Cola. Seemingly outnumbered, the defenders pull off an unexpected victory using their secret weapon: a bottle of Coca-Cola buried within a giant ice dragon. The film uses a rich and painterly visual style to tell a story filled with grandeur and humour.

Lead Animator
Mike Mellor
Directors
Fx & Mat
Creative Directors
Sheena Brady
Hal Curtis
Executive Creative Director
Chris O'Reilly
Producer
Isobel Conroy
Executive Producer
Julia Parfitt
Post Producer
Sarah Hiddlestone
Agency Producer
Lindsay Reed
Visual Effects Supervisor
Diarmid Harrison-Murray
Computer Graphics Supervisor
Simon French
Lead Compositor
Russell Dodgson
Effects Lead
Martin Aufinger
Crowd Lead
Visual Effects
Johnny Han
Telecine
Simon Bourne
Music Arranger
Robert Miller
Animation
Framestore
Visual Effects
Framestore
Production Company
Nexus Productions
Post Production
Framestore
Advertising Agency
Wieden+Kennedy Portland
Music Arrangement
Stimmung
Client
Coca-Cola

Animation for Film Advertising
Digital District
for WWF

Threads
With 'Threads' we wanted to show that everything is connected on this planet: the earth, trees, animals and the six billion human beings living on it. We are all responsible for any disruption in the thin line that connects us all. If we are not careful, we could cause a disaster for everyone and everything in our fragile ecosystem. We are all connected. WWF for a living planet.

Animator
Mato Atom
Director
Mato Atom
Art Director
Victor Alvarado
Copywriter
Fernando Carrera
Creative Directors
Victor Alvarado
Fernando Carrera
Executive Creative Directors
José Montalvo
Miguel Angel Ruiz
Producer
James Hagger
Agency Producer
Juan Pablo Osio
Animation
Digital District
Post Production
Digital District
Music Arrangement
Human
Sound Design
Human
Advertising Agency
Ogilvy & Mather Mexico
Account Handler
Alfonso Alcocer
Brand Manager
Jatziri Pérez
Marketing Manager
Mira-Bai Simón
Client
WWF

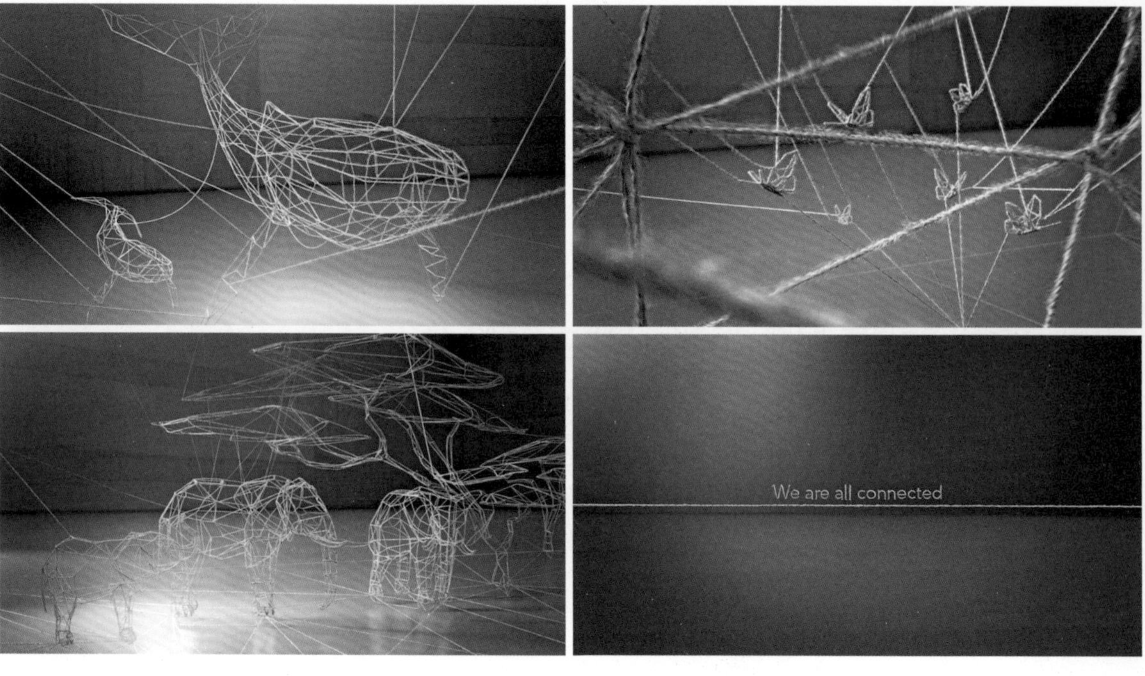
We are all connected

Animation for Film Advertising
Dvein
for Terminix

Flying Monsters
In this ad for pest control company Terminix, flying monsters swoop down on an unsuspecting neighbourhood, crashing through houses and destroying everything in their path. In the end, it is revealed that the monsters are a visual metaphor for termites and the havoc they wreak.

Directors
Fernando Dominguez
Teo Guillem
Art Director
Pete Voehringer
Copywriter
Steve Grimes
Creative Directors
Steve Grimes
Julia Melle
Pete Voehringer
Executive Creative Director
Shon Rathbone
Producer
Michael Neithardt
Executive Producers
Adina Sales
Esther de Udaeta
Agency Producer
Jaime Roderer
Animation
Dvein
Visual Effects Company
Vando
Post Production
Vando
Editing
Dvein
Sound Design
HECQ
Advertising Agency
Publicis Dallas
Client
Terminix

Termites are monsters.

Animation for Film Advertising
Sehsucht
for Vorwerk Kobold Wuppertal

Mite City
This film is about the history of a city: the City of Mites. From the first settlements to the mega metropolis, we trace the evolution to its inevitable demise.

3D Artists
Philip Broemme
Chris Hoffmann
Helge Kiehl
Hannes Weikert
Art Director
Thomas Knuewer
Copywriter
Dennis Krumbe
Creative Director
Thomas Knuewer
Executive Creative Director
Stefan Wuebbe
Post Producer
Bey-Bey Chen
Animation
Sehsucht
Advertising Agency
Kolle Rebbe
Account Handler
Jan Kowalsky
Client
Vorwerk Kobold Wuppertal
Brand
Vorwerk

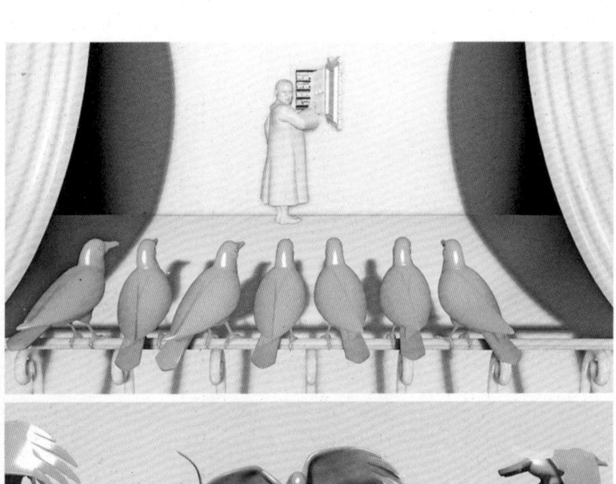

Animation for Film Advertising
Marcel Worldwide
for France 24

The Birds
French news channel France 24 is popular in the Arab world, and was a major source of information during the Arab Spring of 2011. To illustrate this, we represented Ben Ali, Mubarak and Gadhafi in an ad referencing Hitchcock's famous movie 'The Birds'. In this ad, more and more blue birds continue to observe the three dictators before finally overthrowing them.

Animators
Christophe Alenda
Joane Baz
Lionel Caruana
Axelle Cheriet
Director
Philippe Grammaticopoulos
Art Director
Souen Le Van
Copywriter
Martin Rocaboy
Chief Creative Officers
Anne De Maupeou
Veronique Sels
Sebastien Vacherot
Agency Producers
Cleo Ferenczi
Pierre Marcus
Producer
Hervé Lopez
Music Composer
Christophe Julien
Production Company
Mr. HYDE
Sound Design
WAM
Advertising Agency
Marcel Worldwide
Account Manager
Cecile Henderycks
Account Director
Anne de Maupeou
Brand Manager
Alain De Pouzilhac
Client
France 24

Animation for Film Advertising
Elastic
for Nestlé Waters

Nature's Fix
A ragtag team of forest creatures aims to get people hooked on Arrowhead sparkling water, aka Nature's Fix, a habit made with three natural ingredients – spring water, fruit essence and bubbles. In one film the forest animals and their goods are threatened in a face-off with the authorities. Another shows a bear learning to hustle. The third shows the bear and a squirrel finding a major kink in their supply chain – they are totally out of bubbles.

Animators
Lindsey Butterworth
Frantz Vidal
3D Artists
Paulo De Almada
Adam Carter
Martin Furness
Andy Lewis
Computer Graphics Artist
Max Ulichney
Compositor
Shahana Khan
Director
Andy Hall
Art Director
David Waraksa
Associate Creative Director
Don Marshall Wilhelmi
Executive Creative Director
Craig Markus
Producer
Heather Johann
Executive Producer
Jennifer Sofio Hall
Production Manager
Andrea Kaye
Director of Integrated Production
Jonathan Shipman
Sound Designer
Stephen Dewey
Sound Engineer
Steve Rosen
Production Company
Elastic
Advertising Agency
McCann New York
Strategic Directors
Gary Bonilla
Erica Yahr
Account Executive
Christiane Basagolti
Business Directors
Richard Donohoe
Emily Giordano
Client
Nestlé Waters
Brand
Arrowhead Brand
100% Mountain
Spring Water

The Raid

The Kingpin

The Lab

Animation for Film Advertising
Psyop
for Twinings

Sea
This commercial shows the journey of a woman as she sails through turbulent waters to calmer seas and returns to her former self. What is unusual about the production of this spot is that for the final layer above all CG passes, Psyop used traditionally trained artists to digitally paint over every single frame and create the painterly style.

Animators
Todd Akita
Sashdy Arvelo
Jacob Frey
Minor Gaytan
Yvain Gnabro
Chris Meek
Dan Vislocky
Art Director
Simon Rice
Copywriter
Diane Leaver
Creative Directors
Paul Brazier
Paul Kim
Kylie Matulick
Producer
Yvonne Chalkley
Executive Producer
Neysa Horsburgh
Editor
Brett Nicolletti
Animation
Psyop
Direction
Psyop
Production Companies
Psyop
Smuggler
Visual Effects Company
Psyop
Advertising Agency
AMV BBDO
Planner
Michael Lee
Account Handler
Louise Davidson
Client
Twinings

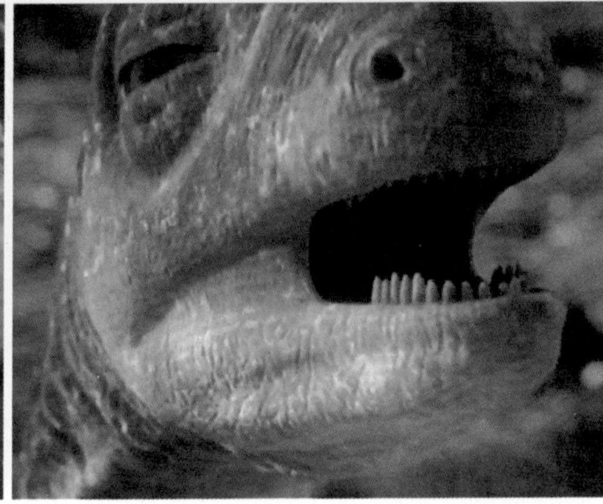

Editing for Film Advertising
Thomas Ioannou Associates
for the BBC

Big Moments
This trailer starts with the BBC's Morecambe and Wise singing their famous theme 'Bring Me Sunshine'. After the first line, we cut away from the comedy duo to see other recognisable BBC TV content. Edited together, all the characters (from Wallace and Gromit to Doctor Who to East Enders to creatures from 'Walking with Dinosaurs') appear to be singing the song with near-perfect lip-sync. After the caption 'When it's worth watching, watch it with us', Eric and Ernie conclude the piece by dancing off into the distance.

Editor
Thomas Ioannou
Directors
Paul Angus
Ted Heath
Art Director
Paul Angus
Copywriter
Ted Heath
Executive Creative Director
Mark Roalfe
Producer
Ella Littlewood
Agency Producer
Kate Woodhouse
Music Arrangers
Eric Morcambe & Ernie Wise
Editing
Thomas Ioannou Associates
Production Company
Red Bee Media
Advertising Agency
RKCR/Y&R
Account Director
Joshua Harris
Client
BBC
Brand
BBC One

Editing for Film Advertising
Final Cut London
for Audi

Audi A1 'Oomph'
Audi A1 'Oomph' was influenced by a video that director Sam Brown had previously made for Jay-Z. Playful vignettes featuring oversized Audi technology demonstrate the key features of the car, which are intercut with abstract symbolic elements to create an energetic piece of work that has a strong sense of rhythm and purpose.

Editor
James Rosen
Director
Sam Brown
Creative Directors
Nick Kidney
Simon Pearse
Emmanuel Saint
M'Leux
Kevin Stark
Producer
James Howland
Agency Producer
Ruben Mercadal
Editing
Final Cut London
Production Company
Rogue Films
Post Production
The Mill
Advertising Agency
BBH London
Client
Audi
Brand
Audi A1

Editing for Film Advertising
Work
for Bacardi

Luck is an Attitude
Don't let it rain on your parade... This playful spot features two versions of a man's night out. The side-by-side shots show him on the one hand, submissive and reserved, and on the other spontaneous, opportunist and charming. The contrasting sequence of events shows that you need to have the right attitude to get lucky.

Editor
Bill Smedley
Director
Peter Thwaites
Editing
Work
Production Company
Gorgeous
Advertising Agency
Fred & Farid Paris
Client
Bacardi
Brand
Martini

Editing for Film Advertising
Spotwelders
for Nike

Throwdown
From basketball players to weightlifters, bike riders to rugby players, a seamless and dynamic edit shows amazing athletes doing amazing things around the world, challenging each other with a 'throwdown'.

Editor
Brad Waskewich
Director
Jake Scott
Art Director
Stuart Brown
Copywriter
Dylan Lee
Creative Directors
Ryan O'Rourke
Alberto Ponte
Producers
Michelle Abbott
Caspar Delaney
Jennifer Dennis
Executive Producer
Tracie Norfleet
Editing
Spotwelders
Production Companies
Black Dog
RSA Films
Post Production
The Mill Los Angeles
Advertising Agency
Wieden+Kennedy
Portland
Client
Nike

Editing for Film Advertising
Guillotine
for Volkswagen

The Word
This advert celebrates different, everyday Australians and the quirky little sounds of appreciation they make when they interact with their Volkswagens.

Editor
Alexandre de Franceschi
Director
Steve Rogers
Copywriter
Steve Wakelam
Creative Directors
Grant McAloon
Steve Wakelam
Executive Creative Director
Dylan Harrison
Producers
Brenden Johnson
Clare Seffrin
Pip Smart
Executive Producer
Michael Ritchie
Production Designer
Steven Jones-Evans
Director of Photography
Simon Duggan
Editing
Guillotine
Production Company
Revolver
Post Production
Fin Design & Effects
Advertising Agency
DDB Sydney
Planner
Nick Andrews
Client
Volkswagen

Editing for Film Advertising
Home Digital Pictures
for Fromageries Bel

Sensations
The adverts open on a man in a quiet kitchen. He is making himself a Boursin tartine. As soon as he tastes the cheese, we enter into his mind for a fast journey through his sensations. It's an amazing experience: sometimes strong; sometimes soft; sometimes crazy; a journey into the extreme pleasure; a constant progression until the final climax. Once the trip is over, the man has only one thing on his mind: eat another piece of Boursin to live this experience all over again.

Editor
Bruno Tracq
Director
Vernie Yeung
Art Director
Agathe Rattel
Copywriter
Remy Hadjadj
Creative Directors
Jorge Carreno
Robin De Lestrade
Editing
Home Digital Pictures

Production Company
Carnibird
Sound Design
The Shop
Advertising Agency
Y&R Paris
Client
Fromageries Bel
Brand
Boursin

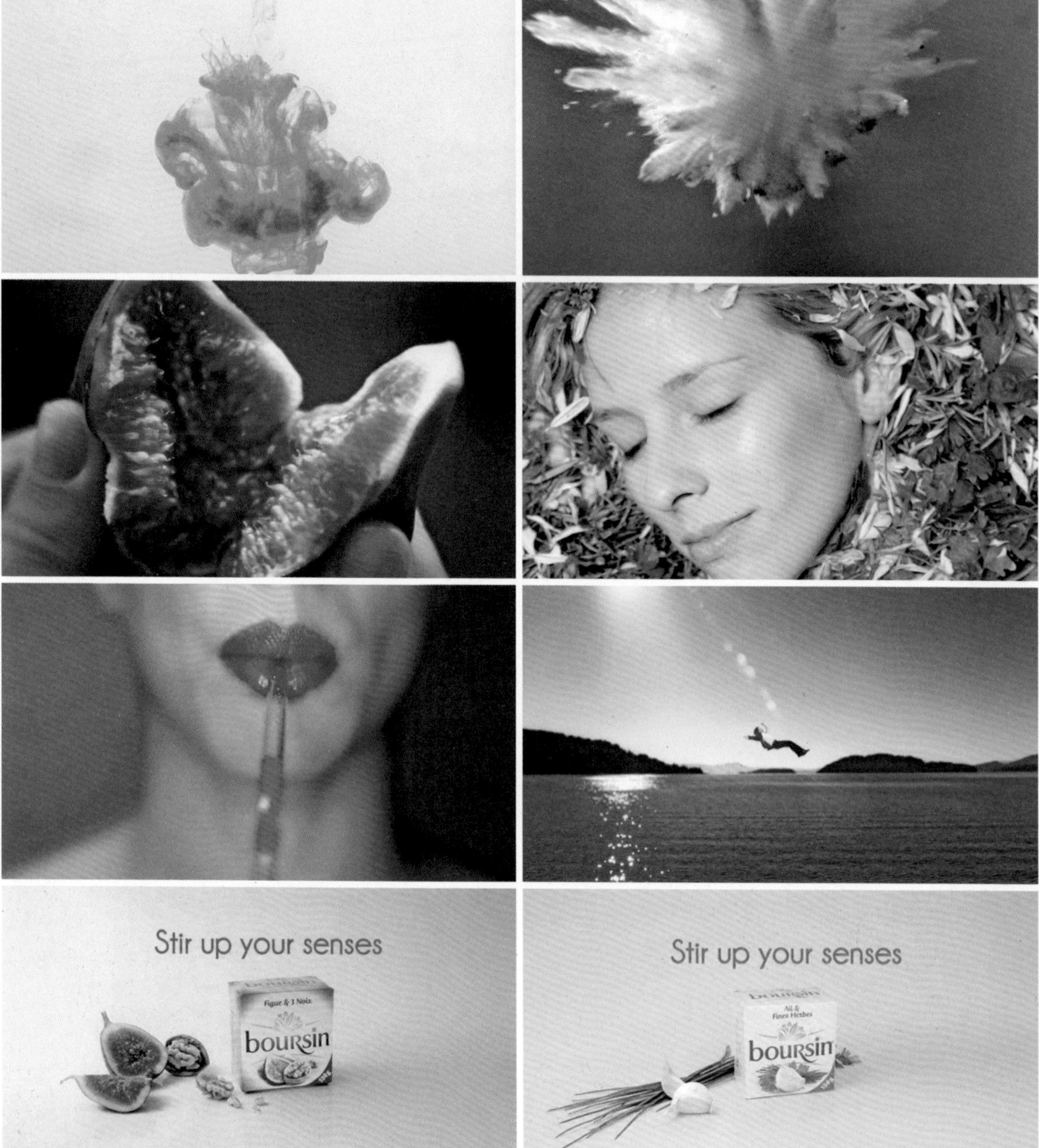

Figs & Nuts

Garlic & Herbs

Editing for Film Advertising
PosterBoy Edit
for adidas

Tomorrow Starts Now
MiCoach is a new shoe technology by adidas. It allows players to record their training data. This film was used to draw participants into the 'Get the Jersey Faster' challenge, a competition for football crazy kids to win a space in a national training camp by using MiCoach. The film tells the story of a boy making it into the camp, but in reverse – allowing us to showcase some amazing football action in a spectacular fashion.

Editor
Mark Paiva
Director
Mark Zibert
Creative Directors
Vesna Koselj
Lucio Regner
Executive Creative Director
Stefan Schmidt
Producer
Ulrich Kreis
Executive Producers
Stephan Fruth
Sabine Hackl
Post Producer
Andreas Rothenaicher
Agency Producer
Ilka Groeneweg
Director of Photography
Chris Mably
Editing
PosterBoy Edit
Production Company
Soup Filmproduktion Berlin
Advertising Agency
TBWA\Berlin
Marketing Manager
Markus Rachals
Client
adidas
Brand
MiCoach

Editing for Film Advertising
Cut+Run London
for French Connection

I Am the Suit
This was the second film of the Autumn/Winter advertising campaign for French Connection. For the campaign, films and print ads were staggered, with a constantly evolving message throughout the season digitally, in cinema, on TV, in print, outdoor and in store windows. Celebrating the power of clothes, each film is stylishly told from the point of view of a hero garment. Here, the hero garment is 'The Suit'.

Editor
Ben Campbell
Directors
Damien de Blinkk
Leila de Blinkk
Art Director
Alice Stein
Creative Directors
Richard Flintham
Dirk Van Dooren
Executive Producers
Abi Hodson
Chantal Webber
Agency Producer
Jack Water
Director of Photography
Marc Gomez del Moral
Sound Designer
Parv Thind
Stylist
Georgina Hodson
Editing
Cut+Run London
Production Company
Onesix7 Productions
Post Production
Wave Studios
Advertising Agency
101 London
Client
French Connection

Sound Design for Film Advertising
Stimmung
for Nike

Shine
The 'Basketball Never Stops' campaign celebrates a player's true love of the game and the desire to play no matter the time or place. The campaign included three films, and featured basketball greats LeBron James, Kevin Durant, Amar'e Stoudemire, Dirk Nowitzki and Sue Bird. The campaign premiered globally on the day NBA season is typically supposed to start. 'Shine' is the campaign's second film, featuring LeBron James. It speaks to the players who know that hard work and dedication are what the game is built on.

Sound Designer
Gus Koven
Director
Lance Acord
Art Director
Aramis Israel
Copywriter
Brandon Pierce
Creative Directors
Ryan O'Rourke
Alberto Ponte
Executive Creative Directors
Mark Fitzloff
Susan Hoffman
Agency Producer
Ben Grylewicz
Producers
Jennifer Dennis
Dale Nicholls
Editor
Biff Butler
Sound Design
Stimmung
Production Company
Park Pictures
Advertising Agency
Wieden+Kennedy Portland
Client
Nike

Sound Design for Film Advertising
Sonart
for X3 Productions

Star Wars Identities – Vader
'Star Wars Identities' is an international exhibition that delves into the legendary characters from the movies. This spot to promote it is a journey deep into the psyche of the greatest villain of all time: Darth Vader. The Rorschach-inspired animation consists of key moments from the Dark Lord's life, from childhood to his final act of… well, we won't spoil the ending. It's an original concept, but even the most casual fan can appreciate the audio and visuals pulled from the imagination of George Lucas.

Sound Designers
François Bélanger
Pierre-Hugues Rondeau
Art Directors
Martin Dupuis
Jean-Francois LeBlanc
Copywriters
Andrew Lord
Sebastien Maheux
Chief Creative Officer
Gaëtan Namouric
Agency Producers
Dominique Dufour
Eve Mathieu
Graphic Designer
Veronique Vigneault
Illustrator
Louis Hébert
Sound Design
Sonart
Animation
Fly Studio
Advertising Agency
Bleublancrouge
Client
X3 Productions
Brand
Star Wars Identities

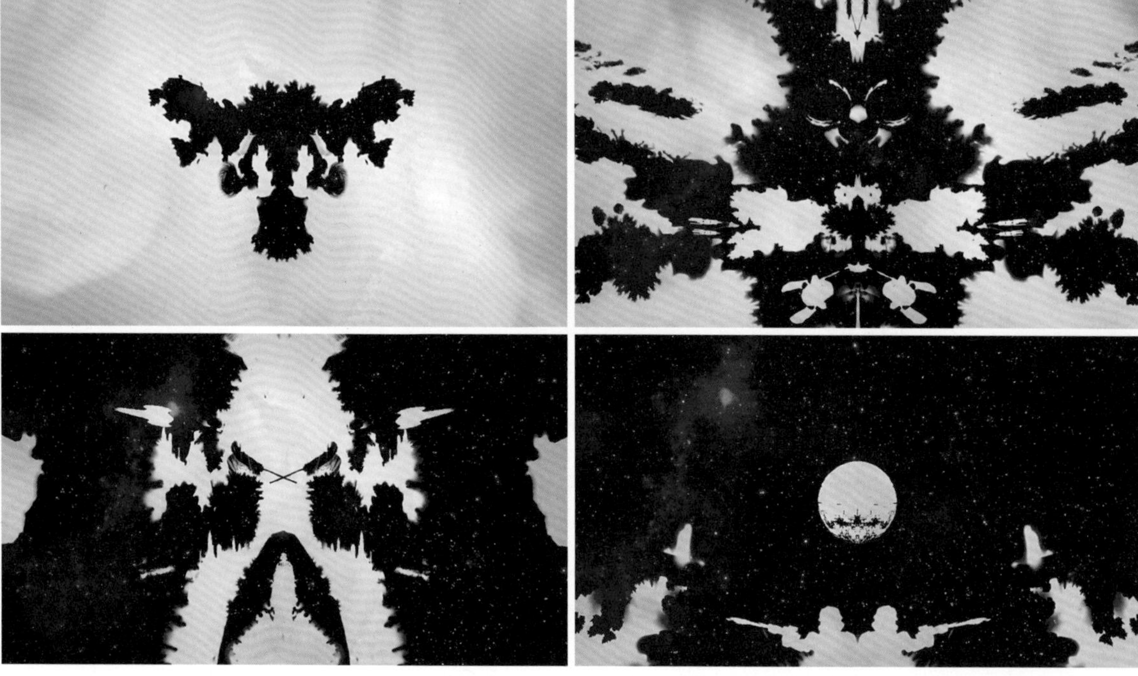

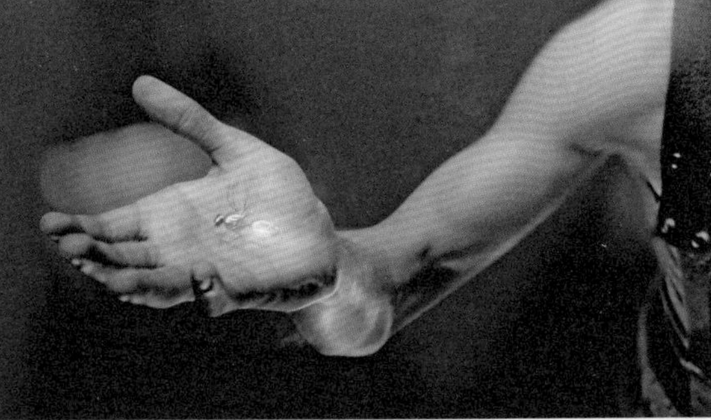

Ice Fly

Piano

Sound Design for Film Advertising
Stimmung
for the WM Wrigley Jr Company

Ice Fly / Piano
5 Gum is all about taking people to new heights of sensory stimulation. In 'Ice Fly', 5 Gum created a metaphorical world for its peppermint flavour through the use of a mysterious mechanical 'ice fly' that immediately freezes everything it comes in contact with. Later, when a swarm of the flies envelops our hero in a frosty cyclone, it takes him on the iciest ride of his life. In 'Piano', the tingling sensation of 5 Gum's spearmint flavor is illustrated by showing what it feels like to be suspended by the dozens of wires that make up an arena-sized piano-like device.

Sound Designer
Gus Koven
Director
Dante Ariola
Art Director
Isabela Ferreira
Executive Creative Directors
Frank Dattalo
Mike Roe
Chief Creative Officer
Dan Fietsam
Agency Producer
John Pratt
Editor
Andrea Mcarthur
Sound Design
Stimmung
Production Company
MJZ Los Angeles
Advertising Agency
Energy BBDO
Account Executive
Emily Kane
Client
WM Wrigley Jr Company
Brand
5 Gum

Sound Design for Film Advertising
Wave Studios
for French Connection

Trailer
A pile of clothes is thrown out of a window. A man slides down a banister. Another bounces on a bed in a grey suit. There's a girl holding a melting ice cream; a firework exploding; a Labrador running backwards; a safe full of gold. This ad was made to look like a trailer, featuring snaps of characters from a film that doesn't exist. Each character represents an item of clothing: The Suit, The Blouse, The Trouser, etc. In turn, they all have their own short films that you can watch to find out more. The sound was designed to give the ad the feel of a trailer. The executive creative director, Richard Flintman, wanted the sound to create sub plots and embed these individual characters and their stories in intrigue.

Sound Designer
Parv Thind
Directors
Damien de Blinkk
Leila de Blinkk
Executive Creative Director
Richard Flintman
Photographers
Damien de Blinkk
Leila de Blinkk
Head of Production
Anthony McCaffery
Editor
Ben Campbell
Sound Design
Wave Studios
Production Company
OneSix7 Productions
Creative Agency
101 London
Marketing Director
William Woodhams
Client
French Connection

Direction for Film Advertising
Nexus Productions
for Intel

The Chase
This ad for Intel's new Core i5 processor is a breakneck, all-action chase scene, the perfect showcase for the new processor's amazing capacity. With a dynamic mix of live action and animation, Smith & Foulkes used every trick in the action movie book and got some hot insider tips from their director of photography, Oliver Wood, of Bourne Trilogy fame, to create this thrilling spot. The result is a clever illustration of the Intel processor working at maximum capacity and showing just what the Core i5 can do.

Directors
Smith & Foulkes
Creative Director
Paul Foulkes
Producer
Tracey Cooper
Executive Producers
Charlotte Bavasso
Chris O'Reilly
Agency Producer
Kacey Hart
Director of Photography
Oliver Wood
Production Manager
Alistair Pratten
Visual Effects Supervisor
Ben Cowell
Editor
Paul Hardcastle
Sound Designer
Barnaby Templer
Production Company
Nexus Productions
Sound Design
Human
Advertising Agency
Venables, Bell & Partners
Client
Intel

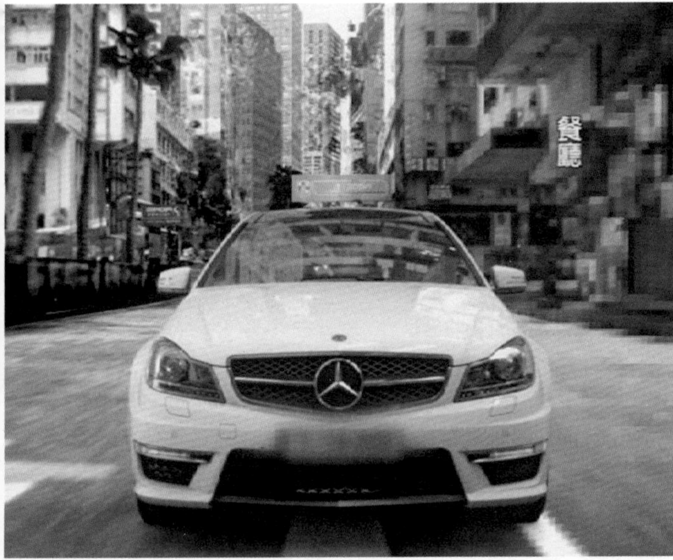

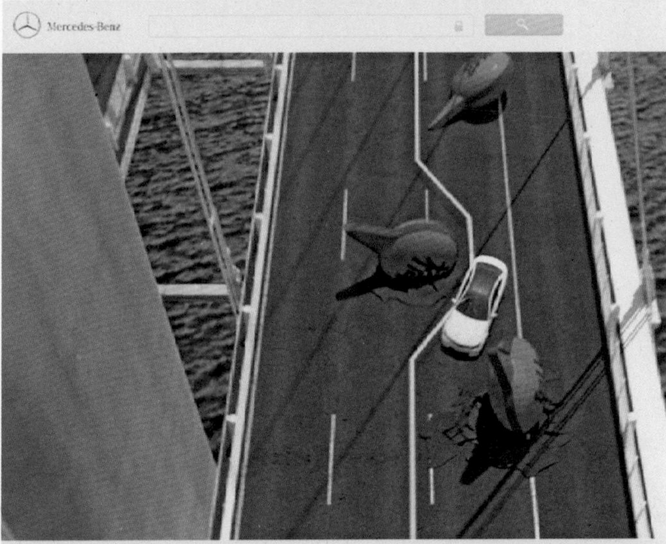

Direction for Film Advertising
RSA Films
for Mercedes-Benz

Escape the Map

Our interactive film brings Streetview to life in a strange, trans-media thriller. Viewers had to help a girl escape our virtual world to win a C63 AMG coupé. Everything was built in CG, apart from the characters and car interior. This enabled us to show the world constantly re-rendering in the same way Streetview does. We used photogrammetry to give our streets a glitchy and intentionally low-fi, dystopian feel. Electronic sounds were designed to complement the hyper-real 3D rendering of the virtual world. This helped to enhance the strangeness of the experience. This work was also selected in the 'Sound Design for Film Advertising' and 'Special Effects for Film Advertising' categories.

Director
Carl Erik Rinsch
Art Directors
Paul Knott
Tim Vance
Copywriters
Paul Knott
Tim Vance
Executive Creative Director
Paul Brazier
Production Director
Valentina Culatti
Interactive Director
Rob Corradi
Technical Director
Yates Buckley
Producer
Margo Mars
Digital Producers
Esther Cunliffe
Louise Tanner
Interactive Producer
Alessandro Pula
Agency Producer
Emmalou Johnson
Technical Designer
Silvio Paganini
Sound Designers
Tom Joyce
Anthony Moore
Production Company
RSA Films
Digital Production Company
unit9
Special Effects
Digital Domain
Post Production
Digital Domain
Sound Design
Factory Studios
Music Arrangement
11:59
Advertising Agency
AMV BBDO
Planner
Steve Mustarde
Account Handler
Nick Andrew
Client
Mercedes-Benz
Brand
C-Class Coupé

Direction for Film Advertising
Stink
for Diageo

Step Together
The latest film in Johnnie Walker's Global 'Keep Walking' campaign is a fable about the power of collective action. Set in a strange parallel universe, it tells the story of a young man who has to convince his entire village to walk with him to change their lives for the better.

Directors
Ne-o
Art Director
Diego Oliveira
Copywriter
Caio Giannella
Creative Directors
Justin Moore
Hamish Pinnell
Producer
Juliet Naylor
Agency Producer
Natalie Parish
Production Company
Stink
Advertising Agency
BBH London
Account Manager
Amy Duckworth
Account Director
Louise Barnard
Brand Communications Director
Anita Robinson
Client
Diageo
Brand
Johnnie Walker

Direction for Film Advertising
Biscuit Filmworks
for Jameson

Fire
When the Great Fire of 1789 reached his distillery, John Jameson devised a brilliant plan. But there was simply no time. So he devised another, less brilliant plan. In the end the not-so-brilliant plan saved the whiskey and, all of Ireland agreed, catastrophe was averted.

Director
Noam Murro
Art Director
Anthony DeCarolis
Copywriter
Erik Fahrenkopf
Creative Directors
Dan Glass
Jonathan Mackler
Chief Creative Officer
Mark Figliulo
Executive Producers
Shawn Lacy
Colleen O'Donnell
Director of Photography
Thomas Sigel
Editor
Brad Waskewich
Compositor
Chris Bankoff
Sound Designer
Tom Jucarone
Production Company
Biscuit Filmworks
Editing
Spot Welders
Post Production
Company 3
Visual Effects Companies
Method Studios
Los Angeles
Scanline
Music Arrangement
Human
Advertising Agency
TBWA\Chiat\Day
New York
Client
Jameson

Direction for Film Advertising
Imperial Woodpecker
for Playstation

To Michael
Video game characters are the heroes and stars of the gaming industry. In this epic live-action spot, we turn the tables by showing the most iconic heroes in gaming honouring the true hero, the one who makes it all possible for them: the gamer.

Director
Simon McQuoid
Senior Art Director
Ryan Dickey
Copywriters
Sam Bergen
Josh Fell
Associate Creative Directors
Sam Bergen
Josh Fell
Group Creative Directors
Mike Bryce
Jason Elm
Shannon McGlothin
Chief Creative Officer
Mark Hunter
Producers
Kristina Iwankiw
Marisa Wasser
Executive Producers
Scott Ganary
Doug Halbert
Stephen Venning
Director of Integrated Production
Vic Palumbo
Director of Broadcast Production
Victoria Guenier
Director of Photography
Jan Velicky
Editor
Steve Gandolfi
Music Composer
Robert Miller
Sound Designer
Andrew Tracey
Sound Mixer
Mark Meyuhas
Production Company
Imperial Woodpecker
Post Production
The Mill Los Angeles
Audio Post
Lime Studios
Editing
Cut+Run Los Angeles
Sound Design
Stimmung
740 Sound Design
Advertising Agency
Deutsch LA
Account Director
Matt Small
Group Account Director
John McGonigle
Chief Executive Officer
Mike Sheldon
Client
Playstation

Direction for Film Advertising
SONNY London
for Hyundai

Outsiders
This ad is centred around the reactions of inhabitants in an outré neighbourhood as a Hyundai ix35 passes by.

Director
Mattias Montero
Art Directors
Alex Bingham
Conrad Swanston
Copywriters
Alex Bingham
Conrad Swanston
Producer
Johan Lindstrom
Agency Producer
Mario Filio
Director of Photography
Kasper Tuxen
Editor
Patric Ryan
Production Company
SONNY London
Post Production
MPC London
Advertising Agency
M&C Saatchi London
Client
Hyundai

Direction for Film Advertising
Caviar LA
for K-Swiss

K-Swiss: MFCEO
In the 2010 campaign, K-Swiss signed the controversial fictional 'athlete' Kenny Powers to an endorsement deal. In the 2011 campaign, Kenny took over K-Swiss as MFCEO (Mother F***ing Chief Executive Officer) reshaping the company in his image and enlisting the world's baddest athletes to help him unsuck the sports world.

Director
Jody Hill
Copywriter
Matt Heath
Creative Directors
Barton Corley
Matt Murphy
Chief Creative Officer
Glenn Cole
Executive Producer
Michael Sagol
Agency Producer
Danielle Tarris
Designer
Jay Kamath
Editors
Matt Murphy
Graham Turner
Production Company
Caviar LA
Visual Effects Company
Animal
Editing
Final Cut Los Angeles
Advertising Agency
72andSunny USA
Brand Director
Matt Rohmer
Client
K-Swiss

Direction for Film Advertising
SONNY London
for Heineken

The Entrance
'The Entrance' sees the introduction of Heineken's new universal tag line, 'Open Your World', conveying the brand's worldly, open-minded and confident personality. Charming his way past a coterie of unexpected guests, the film's hero ends up on stage performing with The Asteroids Galaxy Tour.

Director
Fredrik Bond
Art Director
Alvaro Sotomayor
Copywriters
Carlo Cavallone
Roger Hoard
Executive Creative Directors
Mark Bernath
Eric Quennoy
Producer
Alice Grant
Executive Producer
Helen Kenny
Agency Producer
Tony Stearns
Editor
Tim Thornton Allan
Production Company
SONNY London
Post Production
The Mill London
Sound Design
Grand Central Studios
Advertising Agency
Wieden+Kennedy Amsterdam
Account Manager
Jasmina Krnjetin
Account Director
Clay Mills
Client
Heineken

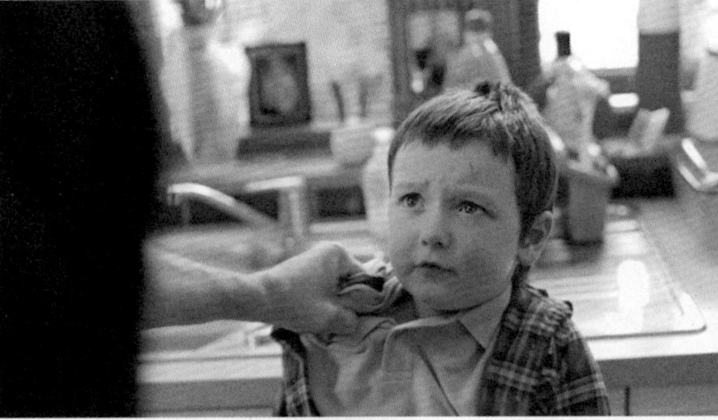

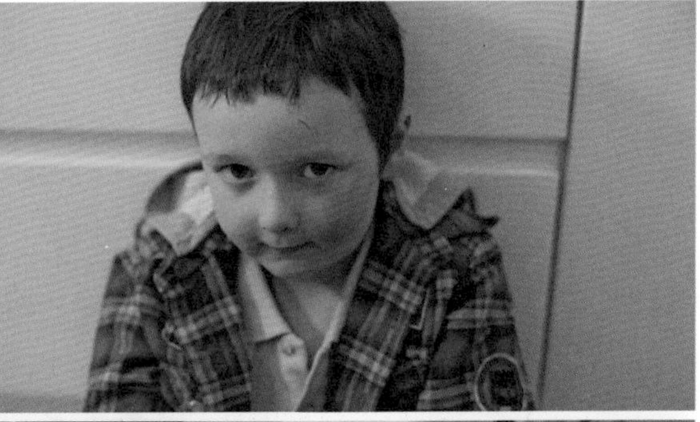

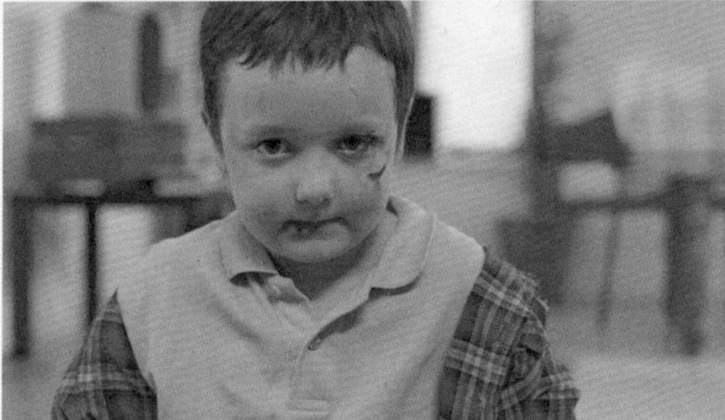

Direction for Film Advertising
Blinder
for the ISPCC

I Can't Wait
This commercial for the Irish children's charity ISPCC shows why a young boy might want to grow up quickly. It's not for the usual reasons; it's because he wants to fight for the rights of children like him. Throughout the commercial, the boy delivers a message in an unwavering monologue, while being beaten by an older person. The abuse gets progressively worse: the ad ends with the child bruised and cut, yet looking determinedly into the camera as he says his last line.

Director
Richie Smyth
Art Director
Des Kavanagh
Copywriter
Laurence O'Byrne
Creative Director
Colin Nimick
Producer
Glen Collins
Executive Producer
Michael Duffy
Agency Producer
Derek Doyle
Editor
John O'Connor
Production Company
Blinder
Editing
Windmill Lane
Advertising Agency
Ogilvy & Mather Ireland
Client
ISPCC

Direction for Film Advertising
Velocity Films
for First National Bank

Dog

Director Greg Gray's touching spot 'Dog' takes us on a young man's uplifting journey, as he navigates the cold, empty streets and back alleys of Cape Town – concluding with an unexpected twist on the idea that 'where there is help, there is a way'. The man's altruistic mission reflects First National Bank's proposition, 'How can we help you?'

Director
Greg Gray
Creative Directors
George Louw
Avi Pinchevsky
Executive Creative Director
Paul Warner
Producer
Helena Woodfine
Executive Producers
Peter Carr
Nicola Valentine
Agency Producer
Jill Lotriet
Production Company
Velocity Films
Advertising Agency
Metropolitan Republic
Client
First National Bank

Cinematography for Film Advertising
Somesuch & Co
for San Miguel

A Life Well Lived

Director Daniel Wolfe's incandescent gem is a textural montage of San Miguel from the 50s to the present. Wolfe's use of both digital and film gives delicate texture to the layers of era, character, sunsets and the iconic San Miguel bottle. 'A Life Well Lived' brings an emotional nostalgia to this historically revered brand. This film was also selected in the 'Direction for Film Advertising' category.

Director of Photography
Robbie Ryan
Director
Daniel Wolfe
Art Director
Marie Lanna
Producer
Nicky Barnes
Executive Producer
Sally Campbell
Editor
Tom Lindsay
Stylist
Hannah Edwards
Music Composer
Matthew Watson
Production Company
Somesuch & Co
Post Production
Framestore CFC
Sound Design
Grand Central Sound Studios
Advertising Agency
Saatchi & Saatchi London
Client
San Miguel

Cinematography for Film Advertising
@radical.media
for Levi Strauss

Legacy
'Legacy' was created to launch the global 'Go Forth' Levi's campaign. It conveys a powerful attitude of hope and optimism, speaking of young people's belief that both individuals and the greater collective can change the world. Using the words of American writer Charles Bukowski, Levi's calls upon all of us to make the world anew.

Director of Photography
Daniel Gottschalk
Director
Ralf Schmerberg
Art Director
Julia Blackburn
Copywriter
Antony Goldstein
Creative Directors
Eric Baldwin
Mark Fitzloff
Susan Hoffman
Tyler Whisnand
Jeff Williams
Producers
Donna Portaro
Sarah Shapiro
Executive Producer
Ben Grylewicz
Post Producer
Ryan Shanholtzer
Line Producer
Munir Abbar
Visual Effects
Robert Owens
Editor
Tommy Harden
Music Composer
Julianna Barwick
Sound Designer
Tommy Harden
Production Company
@radical.media
Advertising Agency
Wieden+Kennedy Portland
Account Handlers
Haley Mazza
Andrew Schafer
Client
Levi Strauss
Brand
Levi's

Cinematography for Film Advertising
Park Pictures
for Nike

Nike Chosen
Nike wanted to define 'Just Do It' through action sports for the first time. In this ad, top action sports athletes perform in the mother of all jam sessions and invite a new breed of athletes to take the stage and own the spotlight.

Directors of Photography
Lance Acord
Don King
Greg Schmidt
Dave Seaone
Director
Lance Acord
Art Director
Rob Teague
Copywriter
Cody Osborne
Creative Directors
Matt Murphy
Jason Norcross
Executive Creative Director
John Boiler
Chief Creative Officer
Glenn Cole
Producer
David Mitchell
Executive Producers
Jackie Kelman Bisbee
Mary Ann Marino
Justin Pollock
Agency Producer
Sam Baerwald
Editor
Chris Jones
Production Company
Park Pictures
Post Production
The Mill Los Angeles
Editing
Final Cut Los Angeles
Nike
Advertising Agency
72andSunny USA
Brand Manager
Megan Woods
Client
Nike

Cinematography for Film Advertising
@radical.media
for Pacific Standard Time

Ice Cube Celebrates the Eames
'Pacific Standard Time' was an exhibition celebrating LA art movements from 1945 to 1980. To introduce a whole new audience to the exhibition, we invited Los Angeles pop culture icons to pay tribute to the artists who inspired them. Ice Cube paired himself with the Eames to create new collaborative works.

Cinematographer
Danny Hiele
Director
Dave Meyers
Art Director
Stephen Lum
Copywriters
Evan Brown
Liz Cartwright
Creative Director
Jayanta Jenkins
Executive Creative Director
Patrick O'Neill
Agency Producers
Micah Kawaguchi-Ailetcher
Lacy Plunk
Chris Spencer
Producer
Hillary Rogers
Executive Producers
Jim Bouvet
Guia Iacomin
Richard O'Neill
Frank Scherma
Gaffer
Fritz Marx
Production Company
@radical.media
Advertising Agency
TBWA\Chiat\Day Los Angeles
Account Executive
Brienne Monty
Account Manager
Andrew Krensky
Account Director
Mike Litwin
Client
Pacific Standard Time

Cinematography for Film Advertising
Park Pictures
for Chivas Regal

Here's to Big Bear
'Here's to Big Bear' tells the tale of four friends getting on the wrong train home after a big night out. They wake to find themselves in the middle of the desert with no water, no money, and no idea how to get home. To achieve an authentic cinematic experience with big screen performances, Academy-award winning director Joachim Back was brought on board to direct. Filmed on location over ten days in the barren Atacama Desert, Chile, 'Here's to Big Bear' was beautifully captured by Joachim's right-hand man, director of photography Sebastian Blenkov.

Cinematographer
Sebastian Blenkov
Director
Joachim Back
Art Director
Russ Schaller
Copywriter
Ben Clapp
Executive Creative Director
Mick Mahoney
Producer
Tim Kerrison
Agency Producer
Jodie Potts
Editor
Russell Icke
Production Company
Park Pictures
Advertising Agency
Euro RSCG London
Client
Chivas Regal

Cinematography for Film Advertising
Logan
for Bethesda

Elder Scrolls IV: Skyrim
This spot for game publisher Bethesda was filmed in Prague over three days. Close to 100 extras, custom costumes and wardrobe, stunts, pyrotechnics, animals and children made the production a real challenge. It was shot on 35mm film in anamorphic format. Director Alexei Tylevich wanted to make the spot feel 'like a trailer for a feature film that doesn't exist yet'. We tried to make the world of the game feel as real as possible and capture the action in-camera, in contrast to the majority of game trailers, which rely heavily on CG. This ad was also selected in the 'Production Design for Film Advertising' category.

Director of Photography
Nicolaj Bruel
Director
Alexei Tylevich
Creative Director
Akira Takahashi
Executive Creative Director
Brendan DiBona
Executive Producer
Matthew Marquis
Post Producers
Albert Mason
Scott Siegal
Line Producers
Rich Kaylor
Kristyna Kodet
Production Designer
Jindrich Kocí
Designers
Heidi Berg
Diana Chang
Kenneth Robin
Gordan Waltho
Visual Effects Supervisor
Vincent Wauters
Flame Artist
Brandon Sanders
2D Artist
Reuben Corona
3D Artist
Benoit Vincent
Editor
Volkert Besseling
Music Composer
Michael Kadelbach
Head of Integrated Production
Lindsay Bodanza
Production Company
Logan
Advertising Agency
AKQA Washington DC
Account Executive
Paul Chang
Account Director
Ed Davis
Client
Bethesda

Cinematography for Film Advertising
Agile Films & O2 Filmes
for Microsoft

Hard Times
Brazil, October 2011. Microsoft reduces the price of the Xbox 360 by half, selling over 500 game consoles. We created this film to show the effect this had on Santa Claus: he came out losing since he was no longer getting Christmas letters. Our ad shows the hard life of an unemployed Santa. At the end of the ad we included a link inviting people to go on a site and 'save Christmas'. This ad was also selected in the 'Use of Music for Film Advertising' category.

Director of Photography
Will Humphris
Art Directors
Fred Siqueira
Mauro Villas-Bôas
Copywriter
Sandro Nascimento
Creative Director
Fred Siqueira
Executive Producers
Xanna D'aguiar
Paul Seymour
Music Composer
Louis King
Musical Director
Chris Jordão
Sound Designer
Matt Hauser
Production Companies
Agile Films
O2 Filmes
Advertising Agency
WMcCANN
Client
Microsoft
Brand
Xbox 360

Cinematography for Film Advertising
Goodoil Films
for the Commonwealth Bank of Australia

Human Bank
This commercial follows the journey of a young woman (representing the bank), played by Australian actress Claire van der Boom. She makes her way through the last century, pausing on significant moments in Australia's history. Scenes depict the might of the Commonwealth Shipping Line; the harsh conditions of the Broken Hill mines; the scars left by the 1939 Victorian bushfires; the tragedy of fallen Anzac troops on the battlefields of Gallipoli; and the national triumphs of sporting icons such as Donald Bradman, Cathy Freeman and the Australian team at the America's Cup.

Director of Photography
Russell Boyd
Director
Michael Spiccia
Art Director
Brian Gunderson
Copywriter
John Park
Executive Creative Director
Erik Vervroegen
Producer
Juliet Bishop
Agency Producer
Chris Moore
Production Designer
Annie Beauchamp
Editor
Bernard Garry
Production Company
Goodoil Films
Post Production
Fin Design & Effects
Advertising Agency
Goodby Silverstein & Partners
Client
Commonwealth Bank of Australia

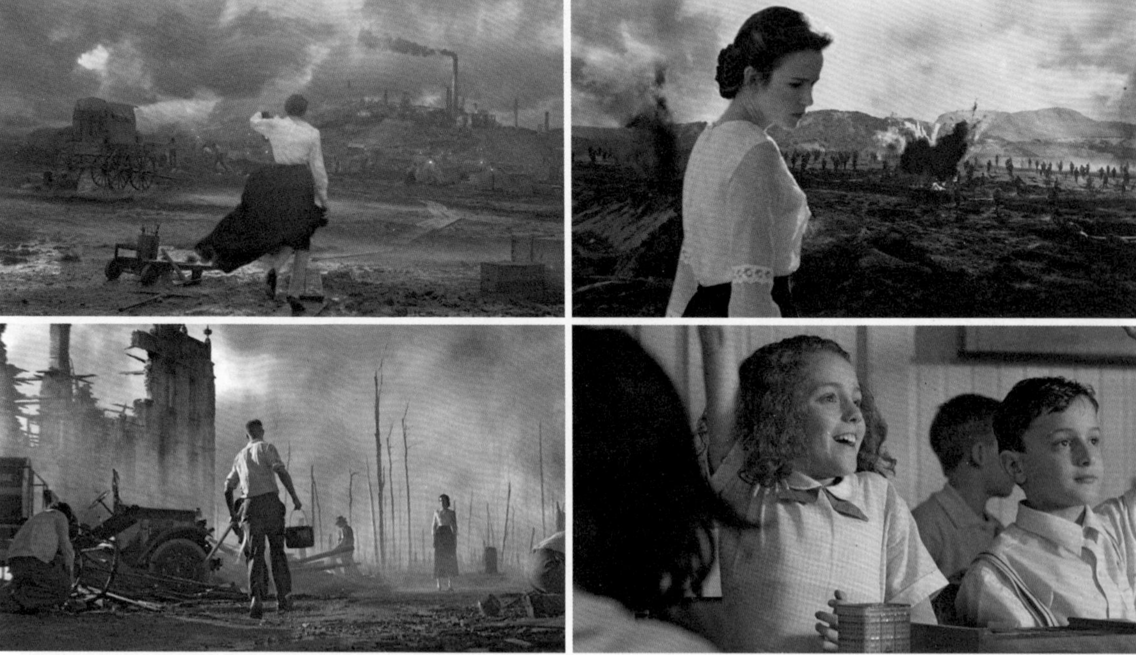

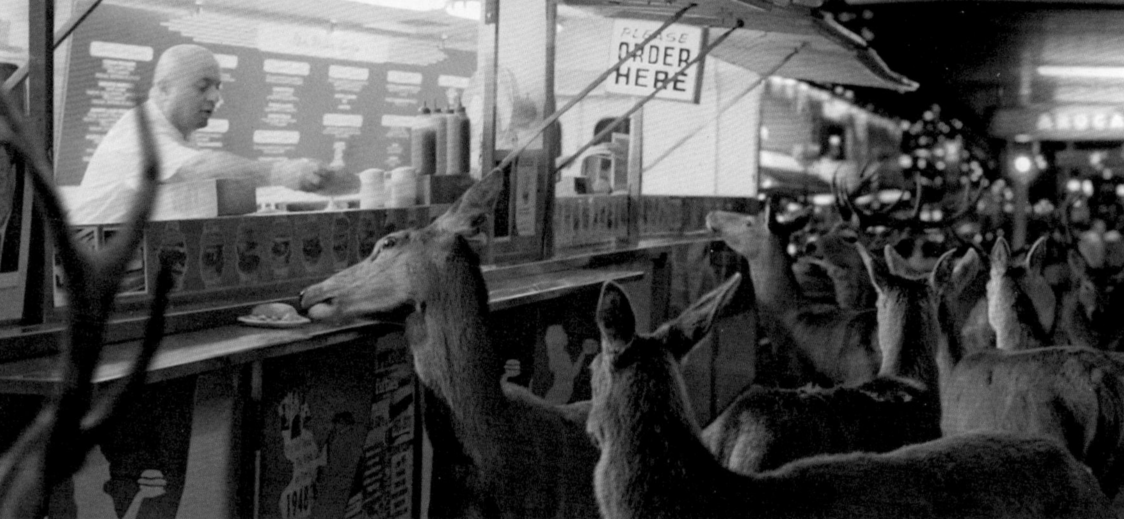

Cinematography for Film Advertising
Exit Films Melbourne
for Lion

The Nocturnal Migration
Head into the city on a busy Friday or Saturday night and you'll see that our behaviour isn't too different to that of migratory animals.
We never stay at one pub, house party or even music stage at a festival. We constantly move like a herd as the great migration of the night happens all over the country. Executing the idea was more than just bringing a brand icon to life. It was important that people could see themselves in the deer, from heading out for the night, strutting down the street and hitting a busy club to grabbing a kebab at the end of a great night. This ad was also selected in the 'Direction for Film Advertising' and 'Special Effects for Film Advertising' categories.

Director of Photography
Ellen Kuras
Director
Garth Davis
Art Directors
Corinne Goode
Guy Treadgold
Copywriter
Philip Sicklinger
Executive Creative Directors
Shane Bradnick
Warren Brown
Dylan Taylor
Producer
Karen Sproul
Agency Producer
Sue Hind
Visual Effects Executive Producer
Takeshi Takada
Visual Effects Supervisor
Colin Renshaw
3D Artists
Nick Angus
Sarah Collier
Nigel Haslam
Chris Rentoul
Malcom Wright
Compositor
Matt Chance
Editor
Jack Hutchings
Colourist
Warren Eagles
Flame Operator
Urs Furrer
Music Producer
Karl Richter
Sound Designer
Tone Aston
Production Company
Exit Films Melbourne
Post Production
Alt.vfx
Visual Effects Company
Alt.vfx
Advertising Agency
BMF Sydney
Planner
Simon McCrudden
Account Handlers
Tony Dunseath
Chris Kay
Brand Manager
Judy Fraser
Marketing Manager
Andy Disley
Client
Lion
Brand
Tooheys Extra Dry

Special Effects for Film Advertising
BUF
for the Réseau Ferré de France

Tomorrow on Track Today
Réseau Ferré de France builds the French rail network. Massive engineering works were undertaken in 2011, and train services were disrupted, so explaining why the works were necessary and who was carrying them out became key. The idea for the film came from a simple insight. Every day, Réseau Ferré de France carries out a wonder: upgrading the network while keeping it running for four million passengers. Produced with a mix of tilt shift footage and 3D modelling, the film creates a magical world where reality and fiction mesh, and a new and poetic interpretation of engineering works is born.

Special Effects
Marie Balland
Director
Thierry Poiraud
Art Director
Ivan Pierens
Copywriter
Thomas Stern
Executive Creative Directors
Ivan Pierens
Thomas Stern
Producer
Pascale Scetbon Pallatin
Post Producer
Elise Dutartre
Agency Producer
Annie Moysan
Director of Photography
Christophe Guyon

Sound Designers
Grégoire Couzinier
Thomas Couzinier
Production Company
Paranoid
Post Production
BUF
Music
Metronomy
Advertising Agency
W & CIE
Account Handlers
François Lamotte
Grégoire Weil
Brand Manager
Thierry Jankowski
Marketing Manager
Christophe Piednoel
Client
Réseau Ferré de France

Special Effects for Film Advertising
Animal Logic
for BUPA Health Australia

The Moment
Director Steve Rogers chose to cast a single actor to play two parts, with VFX marrying the dual performances into a single shot sans motion control. Animal Logic was given the challenge to seamlessly composite multiple preferred actions to a single plate with 2D match-moves of plates. Considering the differences of body doubles, we did a fair bit of rebuilding plates from out-takes and roto-ing extras and actors back in, with the odd morph for good measure!

Visual Effects Supervisor
Kirsty Miller
Visual Effects Producer
Sarah Hiddlestone
Director
Steve Rogers
Art Directors
Anthony Phillips
Lee Sunter
Copywriters
Andre Hull
Richard Williams
Creative Director
Ant Keogh
Producers
Sevda Cemo
Pip Smart
Executive Producer
Michael Ritchie
Director of Photography
Russel Boyd
Visual Effects Company
Animal Logic
Production Company
Revolver
Advertising Agency
Clemenger BBDO
Melbourne
Account Manager
Lesley Silverstone
Account Directors
Kirsten Darbyshire
Chris Howatson
Client
BUPA Health Australia

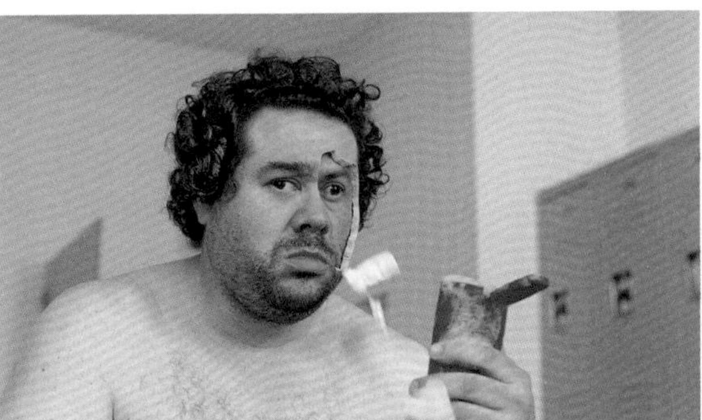

Special Effects for Film Advertising
The Mill Los Angeles
for Procter & Gamble

Motorcycle
'Motorcycle' takes a humorous look at how the scents of Old Spice can turn average guys into the manliest of men. With the scents of Old Spice, you can 'smell better than yourself'.

Director
Tom Kuntz
Art Director
Max Stinson
Copywriter
Andy Laugenour
Creative Directors
Craig Allen
Jason Bagley
Executive Creative Directors
Icaro Doria
Mark Fitzloff
Susan Hoffman
Guillermo Vega
Executive Producer
David Zander
Agency Producers
Ben Grylewicz
Lizzie Marcy
Line Producer
Scott Kaplan
Director of Photography
Philippe Le Sourd
Editor
Gavin Cutler
Visual Effects Company
The Mill Los Angeles
Production Company
MJZ Los Angeles
Post Production
The Mill Los Angeles
Advertising Agency
Wieden+Kennedy
Portland
Client
Procter & Gamble
Brand
Old Spice

Use of Music for Film Advertising
BBH London
for Yeo Valley

Yeo Valley
We created a love song to Yeo Valley's organic food and its methods of farming. We formed our very own boy band – The Churned – and filmed a pop promo of them singing on the actual farm. Complete with the moody opening, the slow-motion abs and even a beautiful Friesian. Add to that a catchy dance routine and an escaping chicken, and we had our ad.

Music Composer
Si Hulbert
Director
Jonathan Hopkins
Art Director
Martin Reed
Copywriter
Jonny Durgan
Creative Director
Rosie Arnold
Producer
Shirley O'Connor
Agency Producer
Sam Robinson
Editor
Sam Gunn
Production Company
Pulse Films
Post Production
Absolute Post
Editing
The Whitehouse
Sound Design
Wave Studios
Advertising Agency
BBH London
Planner
Simeon Adams
Strategic Director
Heather Alderson
Account Manager
Josie Robinson
Account Director
Mark Whiteside
Brand Communications Director
Ben Cull
Client
Yeo Valley

Use of Music for Film Advertising
101 London
for Avios

Fly
In this acclaimed spot for Avios, washing machines, barbecues and all manner of household objects skip, glide and pirouette across the skies in a subtle but mesmerising display. Ethereal electronica, in the form of 'Underwaters' by Leila Arab, adds to the otherworldly feel.

Music Arranger
Peter Raeburn
Production Company
HLA
Music Production Company
Soundtree Music
Advertising Agency
101 London
Client
Avios

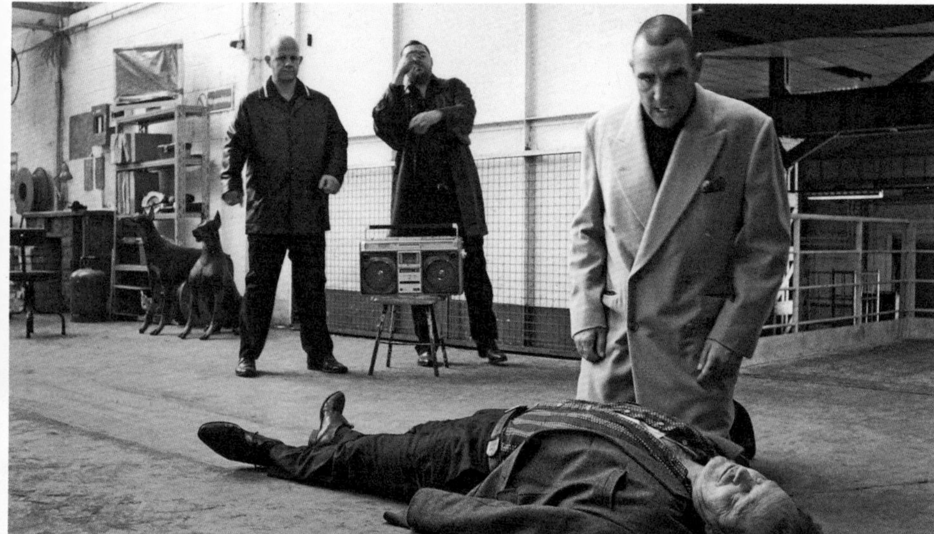

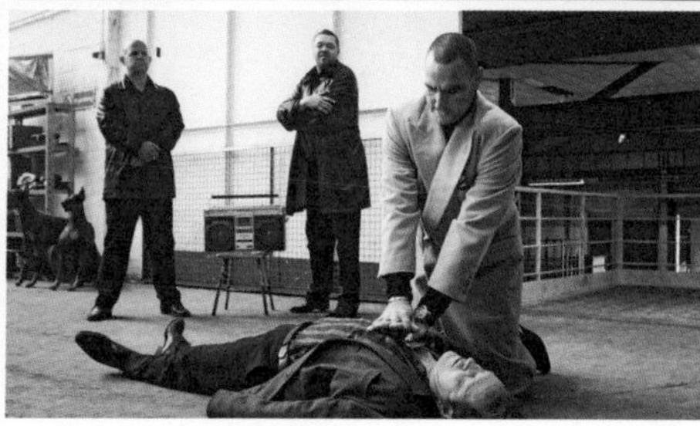

Use of Music for Film Advertising
Grey London
for the British Heart Foundation

Vinnie
Every year, 30,000 people in the UK collapse from cardiac arrest. To encourage more people to try CPR, the British Heart Foundation had news to convey: no kissing, just push hard and fast. The campaign starred hard man Vinnie Jones showing how simple hand-only CPR can be, to the iconic Bee Gees track 'Stayin' Alive' – the correct tempo to perform chest compressions.

Copywriter
Vicki Maguire
Creative Director
Vicki Maguire
Executive Creative Director
Nils Leonard
Producer
Wayne McClammy
Agency Producers
Jacqueline Dobrin
Daisy Mellors
Post Producer
Tom Johnson
Director of Photography
Fraser Taggart
Editor
Alaster Jordan
Production Company
Hungry Man
Post Production
The Mill London
Editing
The Whitehouse
Sound Design
Grand Central Sound Studios
Advertising Agency
Grey London
Planner
Simon White
Account Manager
Sophie Fredheim
Account Director
Camilla Ashenhurst
Client
British Heart Foundation

Use of Music for Film Advertising
Mother New York
for Sour Patch Kids

World Gone Sour
In October 2011 we premiered Method Man's lyrical tribute to Sour Patch Kids, the 'World Gone Sour' rap video, which spurred hip-hop enthusiasts to hype us across social networks. This ad uses behind-the-scenes clips of Method Man on-set to sustain momentum. The video travelled so far and fast that 25% of our initial launch day views hailed from major rap sites in Russia. Meanwhile, Facebook and Twitter shout-outs helped make 'World Gone Sour' YouTube's 'Most Favourited' video in October, garnering nearly 8,000 likes and well over a million views.

Creative Directors
Blaise Cepis
Jordan Chouteau
Paul Malmstrom
April Mathis
Allon Tatarka
Agency Producer
Emma Starzacher
Music Arrangement
Island Def Jam
Universal Music Publishing
Production Company
Hungryman
Advertising Agency
Mother New York
Strategic Directors
Krystal Plomatos
Shobha Sairam
Client
Sour Patch Kids

1

2

3

4

5

6

Jury Foreman
1. Bob Gill

2. Adrian Johnson
Adrian Johnson Studio

3. Dominique McMullan
The Leith Agency

4. Mr Bingo

5. Vic Lee
Vic Lee Prints of London

6. Eric Yeo
Ogilvy & Mather Phillipines

7. Mary Martin
AMV BBDO London
(not pictured)

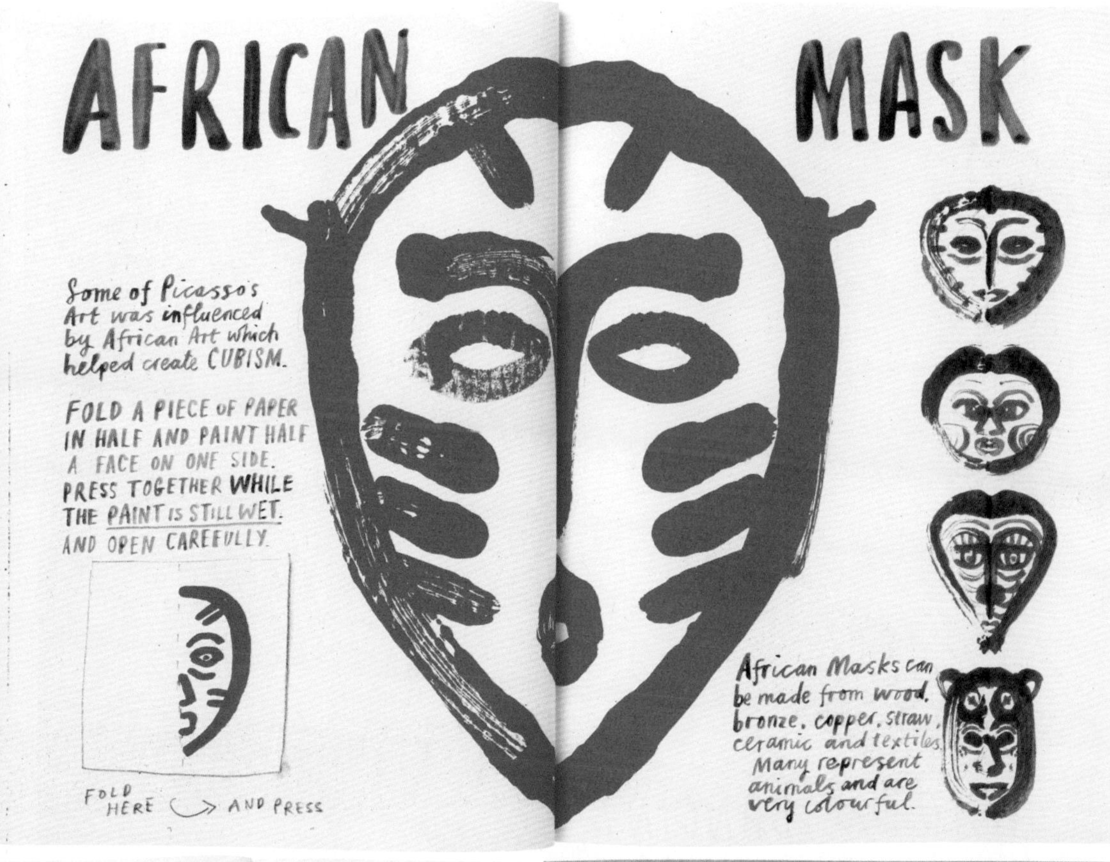

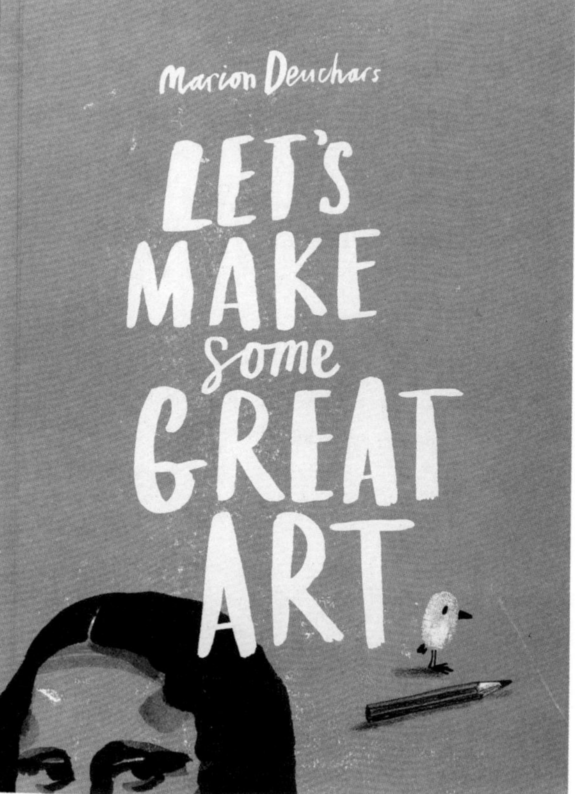

Yellow Pencil in Illustration

Illustration for Design
Laurence King Publishing

Let's Make Some Great Art
This book originated from a small promotional activity book for art material supplier Cass Art. The book was given away when someone purchased art materials in the children's department. One ended up at Laurence King Publishing and Laurence thought it was an idea worth developing into a book. The result: an interactive colouring and activity book. Marion Deuchars takes the broad canvas of art and fills it with drawings and activities that let the reader discover what art can be, how it can be made, what it can mean and what it has meant for people through the ages.

Illustrator
Marion Deuchars
Art Director
Angus Hyland
Designer
Marion Deuchars

Publishing House
Laurence King Publishing
Client
Laurence King Publishing

Yellow Pencil in Illustration

Illustration for Design
Shynola
for EMI & Virgin Records

Laura Marling – A Creature I Did Not Know
We created a bespoke special edition box to illustrate the story behind Laura Marling's third album. Laura wrote a poem called 'The Beast' specifically for this, which Shynola then used as a basis for the illustrations. The 12-inch vinyl was used as an anamorphic picture disc to represent the two sides of the beast, and also the dark and light themes running through the album. A guitar slide was included in the pack, which doubled up as a mirror to reveal the four illustrations on the vinyl. The pack also included a short film, acoustic performances, CD album format, lyrics and an illustrated book of the poem.

Illustrator
Shynola
Art Director
Alex Cowper
Record Companies
EMI
Virgin Records

Clients
EMI
Virgin Records

Nomination in Illustration

Illustration for Advertising
TBWA\Chiat\Day New York
for Pernod Ricard

Absolut Blank
We gave a new generation of multinational artists absolutely blank canvases in the shape of the Absolut bottle. They could fill them in however they wanted. These four pieces, each signed by the artist, are the results of our brief. The campaign re-established Absolut as a brand that not only believes in creativity, but also facilitates it, while making the bottle an icon again.

Illustrators
Fernando Chamarelli
Jeremy Fish
Sam Flores
Good Wives
and Warriors
Art Director
Teresa Rad
Creative Director
Hoj Jomehri
Chief Creative Officer
Mark Figliulo
Global Creative
Director
Sue Anderson
Production Director
Robert Valdes
Executive Producer
Darryl Hagans
Print Producer
Joni Adams
Advertising Agency
TBWA\Chiat\Day
New York
Project Manager
Christine Austin
Account Executive
Andrea Bohdan
Account Director
Geraldine Drpic
Client
Pernod Ricard
Brand
Absolut

Nomination in Illustration

Illustration for Advertising
McCann Erickson Worldgroup
for The London Organising Committee
of the Olympic and Paralympic Games

Sport Like Never Before

Our challenge was to overcome the misconception that Paralympic sport is not 'proper' sport and that it lacks the thrill of true competition. We needed to move it away from the 'don't pity me' visual language found at previous Games to focus on the sport and the athletes' abilities. Together with HelloVon, we reframed the Paralympics by showing it as an elite spectacle made even more thrilling because of the disability. HelloVon's broad strokes and attention to detail delivered a sense of motion and energy to a static format, allowing our subjects to be seen as the world-class athletes they are.

Illustrator
HelloVon
Art Director
Michael Thomason
Copywriter
Chloe Grindle
Typographer
Gary Todd
Executive Creative Directors
Simon Butler
Geoff Smith
Advertising Agency
McCann Erickson Worldgroup

Account Handlers
Simon Hill
Michael Grumbridge
Art Buyer
Sophie Chapman-Andrews
Marketing Manager
Jon Duckworth
Marketing Director
Greg Nugent
Client
The London Organising Committee of the Olympic and Paralympic Games

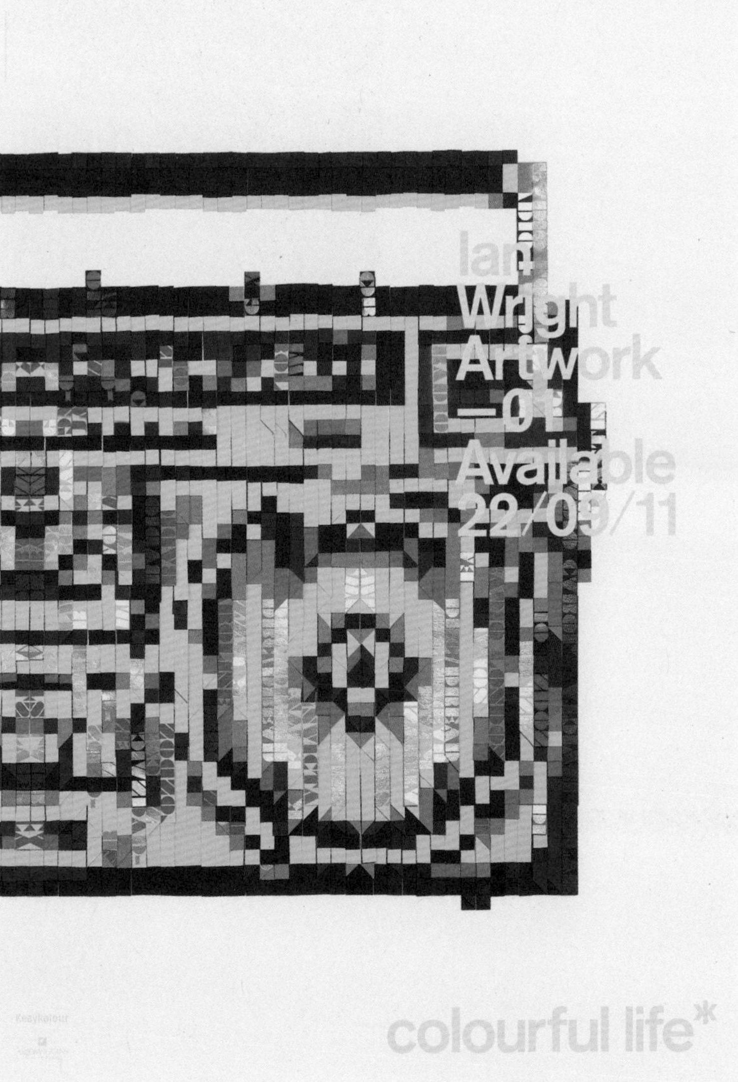

Nomination in Illustration

Illustration for Design
Blast
for Arjowiggins Creative Papers

Colourful Life
'Colourful Life' is a global marketing campaign created to relaunch Keaykolour paper, centred around a collaboration with illustrator Ian Wright. The campaign reflects the lifespan of the brand and Wright's creative and cultural life. The three artworks are based on Wright's musical influences, and each explores an innovative way to work with the paper. The artworks and the process of creating them reached a worldwide design audience through printed collateral, website, viral films and exhibitions in London and Paris.

Illustrator
Ian Wright
Designers
Dan Bown
Lisa Jung
Creative Director
Colin Gifford

Design Group
Blast
Client
Arjowiggins
Creative Papers
Brand
Keaykolour

Nomination in Illustration

Illustration for Design
BBDO New York
for Procter & Gamble

Million Emotions
Facial hair had become fashionable among young people in recent years, so Gillette needed to strike back. We came up with the strategy 'Your face has a lot to say. Don't hide it'. We created a storybook called 'The Man with a Million Faces', starring a funny, bearded cartoon character whose life is full of amazing situations that are lost in his beard. The objective was to show our target audience that when you have a beard, you lose facial expressivity.

Illustrator
Sameer Kulavoor
Art Directors
Raj Kamble
James Kuczynski
Designer
James Kuczynski
Copywriter
David Martin
Creative Director
Raj Kamble
Executive Creative Director
Toygar Bazarkaya
Chief Creative Officer
David Lubars
Production Manager
Rick Jones
Advertising Agency
BBDO New York
Account Executives
Henrie Clarke
Stephanie Petta
Cassi Pires
Client
Procter & Gamble
Brand
Gillette

He hit the jackpot.

Nomination in Illustration

Illustration for Design
Part of a Bigger Plan
for Louis Vuitton Digital

The Great Journey of Little Bag Charms
Part of a Bigger Plan created and produced this short animated online film for the release of Louis Vuitton's elegant new 'hot air balloon' bag charm.

Illustrator
Christian Borstlap
Art Director
Christian Borstlap
Animator
Manuel Ferrari
Creative Director
Christian Borstlap
Sound Designer
Rens Pluym
Producer
Daphne Litjens

Advertising Agency
Part of a Bigger Plan
Music Composers
The Dø
Brand Managers
Philippa Jenkins
Vincent Tajan
Client
Louis Vuitton Digital

Nomination in Illustration

Illustration for Design
The Church of London
for Google

The People Issue Cover
Every issue of 'Think Quarterly' features innovative cover artwork reflecting the issue's theme. 'The People Issue' celebrated the point at which society and technology come together to create new moments of possibility. A team of illustrators spent three days creating a giant piece of art, depicting characters interacting with technology. Every artist brought their own style, unified through using a marker pen. The artwork was split into many parts – each printed onto a cover and referenced on an accompanying gridded poster, giving the reader an appreciation of their place in the entire piece.

Illustrators
Ryan Chapman
Jasper Dunk
Daniel Frost
Matthew Hams
Yasmeen Ismail
Jean Jullien
Chetan Kumar
Paul Layzell
Maggie Li
Dale Edwin Murray
Dominic Owen
Hattie Stewart
Toby Triumph
Robbie Wilkinson
Paul Willoughby
Dan Woodger

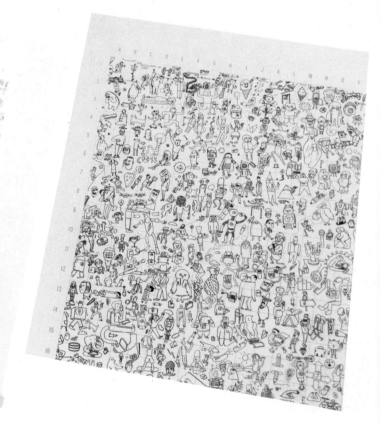

Designers
Anna Dunn
Angus MacPherson
Victoria Talbot
Creative Director
Rob Longworth
Creative Agency
The Church of London
Client
Google
Brand
Think Quarterly

Nomination in Illustration

Illustration for Design
Kinetic Singapore
for Fox International Channels

The A to Zs of Extinct and Endangered Animals

NatGeo Wild, a cable TV channel launched by the National Geographic Society, has rich animal-related content, and champions wildlife conservation. This poster aims to educate children on the importance of saving animals where many are fast becoming extinct and critically endangered. The familiar A to Z learning poster for children is recreated to feature extinct animals, which future generations are destined never to see, and endangered animals, which are likely to become extinct. The poster was placed in schools and community centres. It was also selected in the 'Illustration for Advertising' category.

Illustrator
Elen Winata
Art Directors
Pann Lim
Elen Winata
Designer
Elen Winata
Copywriter
Eugene Tan
Creative Director
Pann Lim

Design Agency
Kinetic Singapore
Account Director
Daniel Tan
Client
Fox International Channels
Brand
NatGeo Wild

Illustration for Advertising
JWT Vietnam
for United Pharma

Killer Sneeze
Decolgen Forte Pe is a pharmaceutical product that treats the symptoms of cold and flu. These illustrations explore the potential impact of a sneeze. They present a humorous take on the rainy season's most common ailments – cold and flu. The ads dramatise how even a little sneeze not only affects you, but also those around you.

Illustrators
Rizal Adman
Ho Hoang Quy
Andy Soong
Art Directors
Ho Hoang Quy
Andy Soong
Copywriters
Le Chi Nguyen
Hasnah Mohamed Samidin
Creative Director
Hasnah Mohamed Samidin
Executive Creative Director
Andy Soong
Advertising Agency
JWT Vietnam
Client
United Pharma
Brand
Decolgen Forte Pe

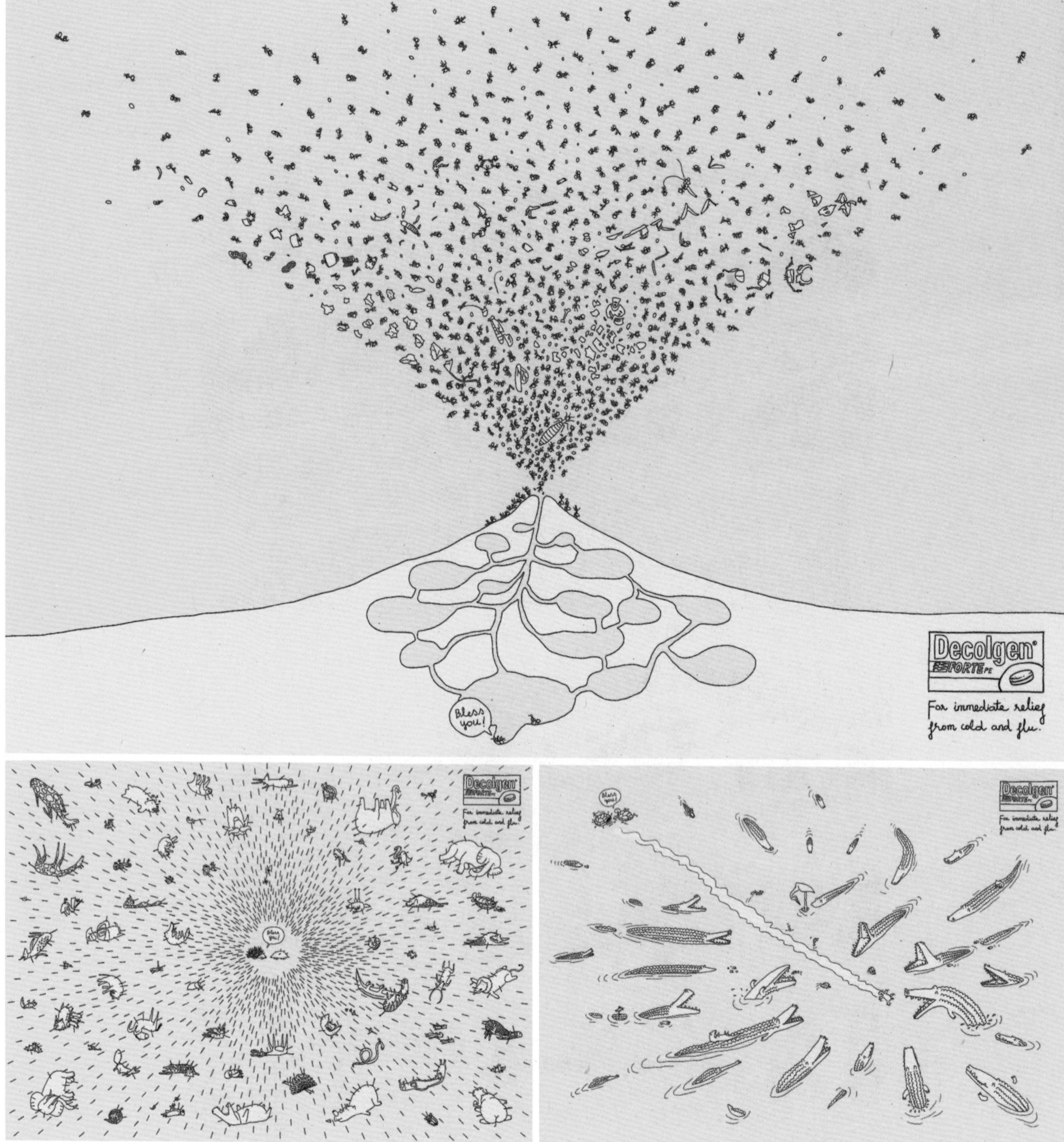

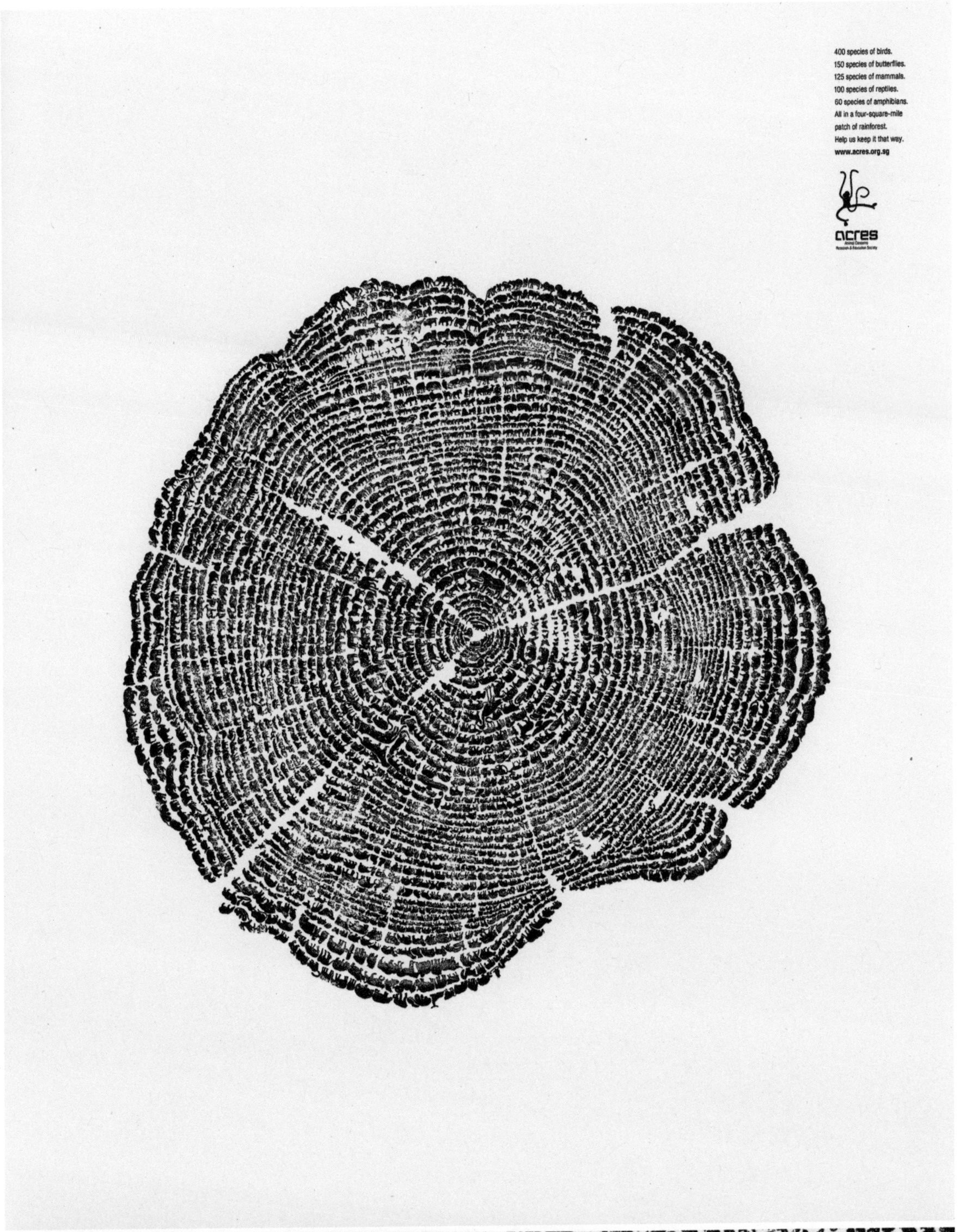

400 species of birds.
150 species of butterflies.
125 species of mammals.
100 species of reptiles.
60 species of amphibians.
All in a four-square-mile
patch of rainforest.
Help us keep it that way.
www.acres.org.sg

acres
Animal Concerns
Research & Education Society

Illustration for Advertising
DDB Singapore
for ACRES (Animal Concerns Research & Education Society)

Tree Rings
The lives of animals revolve around their living space. In order to convey this, we used a visual metaphor of tree rings. Each ring represents the ageing of a tree. By using animals to construct the rings, we communicated the idea that the longer we let a tree grow, the more wildlife it can sustain.

Illustrators
Aaron Koh
Gary Lim
Art Directors
Aaron Koh
Gary Lim
Copywriter
Khajrul Mondzi
Creative Director
Thomas Yang
Executive Creative Director
Joji Jacob
Chief Creative Officer
Neil Johnson
Digital Producer
Chris Ng
Advertising Agency
DDB Singapore
Account Manager
Rowena Bhagchandani
Client
ACRES (Animal Concerns Research & Education Society)

Illustration for Advertising
Brosmind
for Procter & Gamble

A Lot Can Happen Inside the Beard

There's a lot that happens when you grow a beard. It affects your social life, your career and your activities. This campaign dramatises this through elaborate beard illustrations.

Art Director
Raj Kamble
Copywriter
Paul Vinod
Creative Directors
Raj Kamble
Paul Vinod
Executive Creative Director
Toygar Bazarkaya
Chief Creative Officer
David Lubars
Illustration
Brosmind

Advertising Agency
BBDO New York
Account Executives
Henrie Clarke
Stephanie Petta
Cassi Pires
Art Buyer
Sara Gold
Client
Procter & Gamble
Brand
Gillette

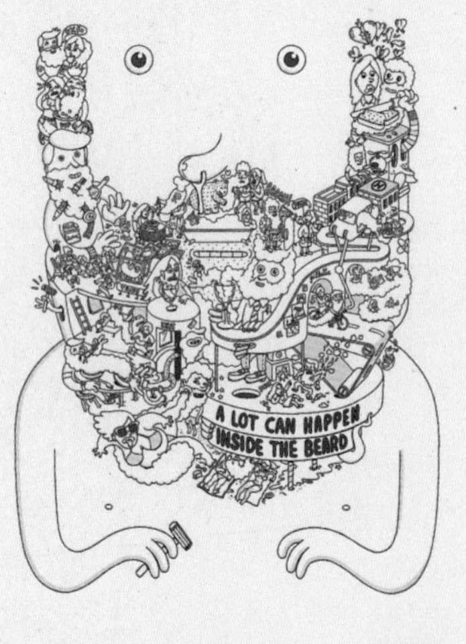

Acceleration

Cornering

Braking

PROUD SUPPORTER OF MOVEMBER

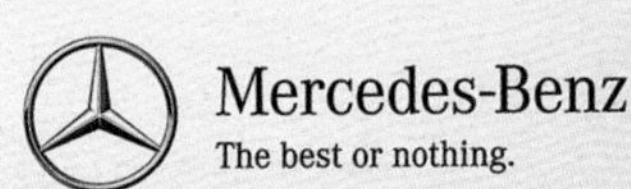
Mercedes-Benz
The best or nothing.

Illustration for Advertising
BBDO Canada
for Mercedes-Benz Canada

Moustaches
We wanted to let Canadians know that Mercedes-Benz is a proud supporter of Movember and prostate cancer research. Our solution: show how the accelerating, cornering and braking power of a Mercedes affects one's moustache. Karl Benz and his moustache would have been proud.

Illustrator
Steve Noble
Art Director
Dan Cantelon
Writer
Ryan Grosman
Creative Director
Linda Carte
Executive Creative Directors
Peter Ignazi
Carlos Moreno
Print Producer
Evan Dermit
Producer
Kay Izzard
Advertising Agency
BBDO Canada
Production Company
SGL Studios
Account Executive
Alex Potter
Account Directors
Adam Lang
Diana Nelson
Marketing Director
Jay Owen
Client
Mercedes-Benz Canada

Illustration for Advertising
CUE Art & Design
for Penguin Books Malaysia

The Pied Piper of Hamelin /
The Jungle Book / The Wizard of Oz
Everyone should be able to enjoy the timeless classics by Penguin books. For those who don't have time to read, they can now hear their favourite stories. We placed posters in popular bookstores and malls, catching the attention of shoppers where they already have an interest in buying an audio book, and a willingness to do so. The illustration style is a nod to classic picture books.

Art Directors
Joshua Tay
Siew Yuet Kie
Copywriters
Edward Ong
Andrea Yap
Typographer
Siew Yuet Kie
Creative Director
Gigi Lee
Executive Creative Directors
Edward Ong
Marcus Rebeschini
Illustration
CUE Art & Design
Advertising Agency
Y&R Malaysia
Client
Penguin Books Malaysia
Brand
Penguin Audiobooks

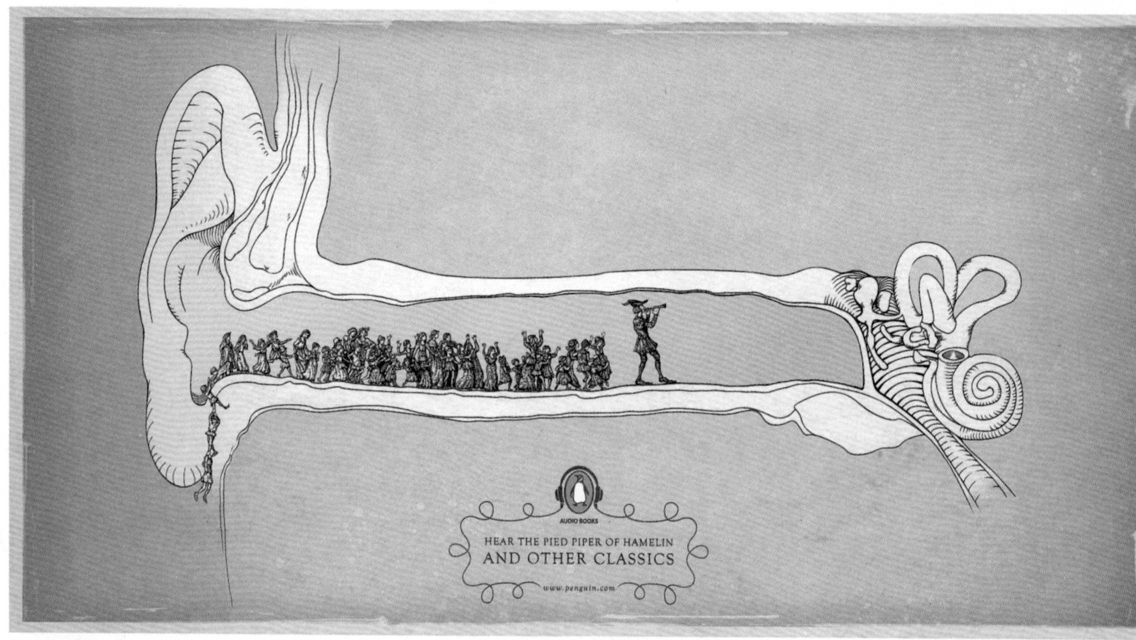

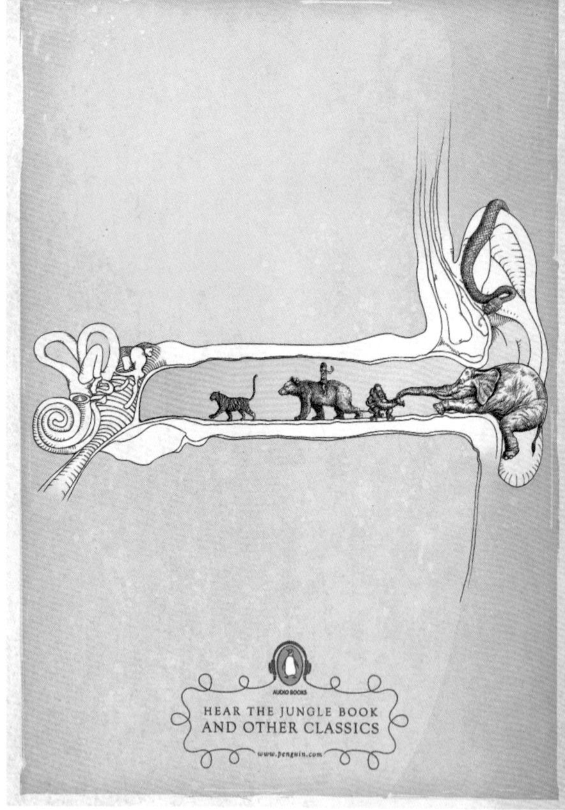

Illustration for Advertising
Ogilvy Malaysia
for Mattel Malaysia

Quick Draw Wins
The brief was to promote Pictionary, the game in which players guess words from drawings. We recreated the fun of playing Pictionary, where winning depends on how quickly you can draw, through ads featuring drawings. Guess them right and you'll get the message. These posters were placed in toy stores to help Pictionary stand out from the sea of games on the shelves.

Illustrators
Milx
Yee Wai Khuen
Art Directors
Tan Chee Keong
Gavin Simpson
Yee Wai Khuen
Designer
Lian Ee Wern
Copywriters
Adam Chan
Donevan Chew
Creative Director
Tan Chee Keong
Executive Creative Director
Gavin Simpson

Advertising Agency
Ogilvy Malaysia
Photography
Studio DI.
Account Executives
Joanne Lee
Amy Yep
Account Director
Sharon Khor
Client
Mattel Malaysia
Brand
Pictionary

Illustration for Advertising
Mudra Communications Delhi
for Philips Electronics

Flipped City

Philips wanted to show the benefit of their noise reduction headphones. No matter where you are or how noisy the place is, when you put your Philips headphones on you get cut off from the rest of the world. So we picked the three noisiest cities in the world – Mumbai, Tokyo and New York. We then did extensive research as to what kind of noise can be heard in each city. We used a heavy detailed illustration style with a lot of colour to show the chaos in each city.

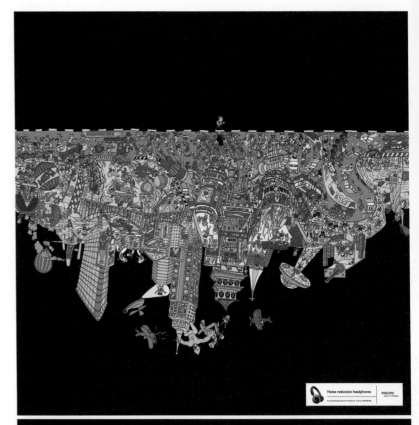

Illustrator
Satyam Patel
Art Directors
Satyam Patel
Raylin Valles
Copywriter
PUPU
Creative Director
Raylin Valles

Chief Creative Officer
Bobby Pawar
Advertising Agency
Mudra
Communications Delhi
Client
Philips Electronics
Brand
Philips

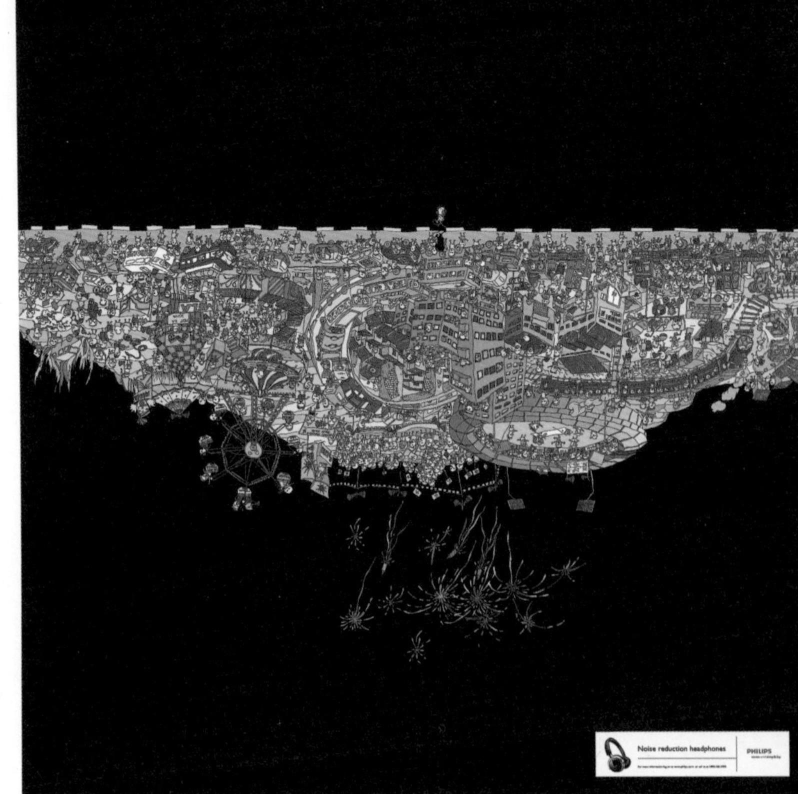

Noise reduction headphones
For more information log on to www.philips.co.in or call us at 1800-102-2929.
PHILIPS
sense and simplicity

Illustration for Advertising
DDB Philippines
for the Advance Paper Corporation

Fine China
We used the iconic blue china porcelain designs to illustrate the fine lines Monami 0.7 ball point pens can draw, creating photo real images and designs that are as detailed as the real thing.

Illustrators
Gomer Barce
Lester Bustarde
Cardy Santos
Art Directors
Gomer Barce
Lester Bustarde
Nina Fides Garcia
Cardy Santos
Copywriter
Joseph Ong
Typographer
Jas Saldariega
Executive Creative Director
Joseph Ong
Advertising Agency
DDB Philippines
Client
Advance Paper Corporation
Brand
Monami

Illustration for Design
Magpie Studio
for the Robert Horne Group

Imagine the Possibilities
Paper manufacturer Robert Horne was keen to catch the eye of the creative industries with the launch of its latest paper, Imagine. True to the paper's name, we wanted to create a promotional campaign that would fire the imagination of a design-savvy audience: to suggest that with imagination, anything is possible. We paired evocative thoughts on the nature of creativity with seemingly impossible illustrations to create a set of posters that would inspire and engage.

Illustrator
David Azurdia
Designer
David Azurdia
Creative Directors
David Azurdia
Ben Christie
Jamie Ellul

Design Agency
Magpie Studio
Account Director
Alex Wood
Client
Robert Horne Group
Brand
Imagine

Illustration for Design
Kinetic Singapore

Kinetic V5
Advertising is an exact science. Its results are measured with an array of precise apparatuses such as Key Performance Indicators and success metrics. However, unlike science, there are no set methods in achieving desired results. Our aim is to tell prospective clients that what worked yesterday may not work today; with every campaign, a new experiment is needed. Kinetic's website is a fanzine that blurs the lines between fact and fiction. It reflects what the agency does daily. Each page tells a story, blending in our history and philosophy in one frenzied publication.

Illustrators
Esther Goh
Jack Tan
Art Directors
Pann Lim
Jack Tan
Designers
Pann Lim
Jack Tan
Elen Winata
Copywriter
Joseph Davies
Photographers
Clay Kuok
Pann Lim
Jack Tan
Music Composer
Victor Low
Creative Technologists
Noel Chan
Edwin Toh
Creative Director
Pann Lim
Film Director
Desmond Tan
Design Agency
Kinetic Singapore
Client
Kinetic Singapore

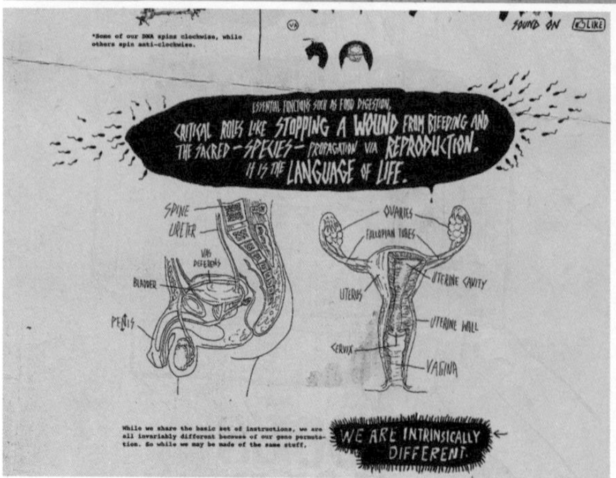

Illustration for Design
gürtlerbachmann
for Gruner + Jahr

Book of Poison
This high-quality book about poisonous plants describes what happens when beautiful flowers become evil. The book comes in a slipcase shaped like a skull, which is meant to warn children about poisonous plants. We used illustrations drawn in lino-style as well as evil little poems printed in their own scraggy typography to make the book interesting for adults too.

Illustrator
Veronika Kieneke
Copywriter
Claudia Oltmann
Creative Director
Reiner Fiedler
Executive Creative Director
Uli Gürtler
Advertising Agency
gürtlerbachmann

Production Company
Produktionsbüro Romey von Malottky
Project Manager
Katja Lesche
Client
Gruner + Jahr

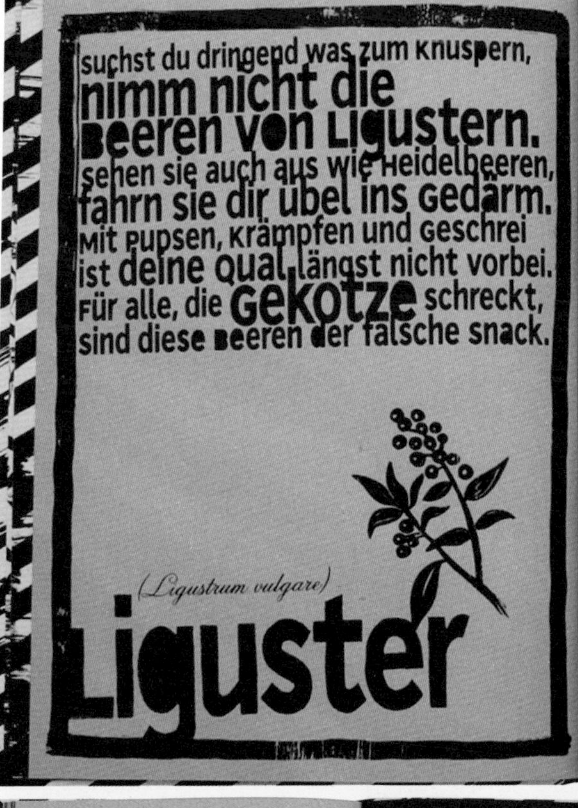

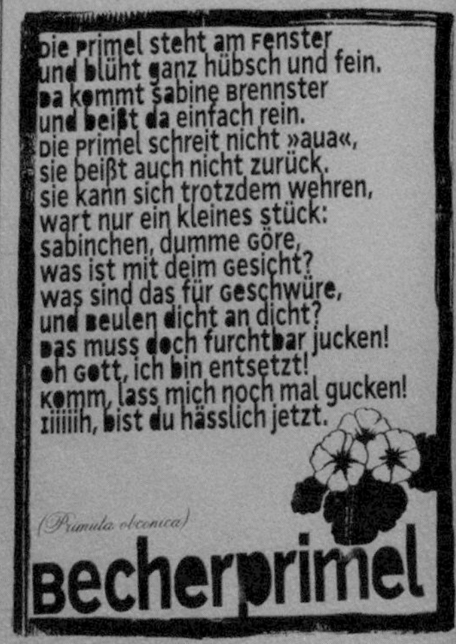

Illustration for Design
Dentsu Tokyo
for the Yoshida Hideo Memorial Foundation

The Ultra Asian
These pieces were created to promote the ADFEST 2011 Exhibition. We developed the concept of a 'life-sized Asian'. We wanted to show the history, culture, technology and trends of Asia becoming the flesh and blood of an Asian. A giant palm leads visitors into the exhibition hall, where they are welcomed by a giant Asian, who looks dynamic from a distance, but delicate at close range. Visitors could experience the Asian feel from the overall exhibition design while viewing the exhibited work. The number of visitors doubled, and the life-sized posters received a lot of praise.

Illustrator
Minami Otsuka
Art Director
Yoshihiro Yagi
Designers
Minami Otsuka
Kazuaki Takai
Copywriter
Haruko Tsutsui
Photographer
Takaya Sakano
Executive Creative Director
Yuya Furukawa

Advertising Agency
Dentsu Tokyo
Project Manager
Yoshiko Tomita
Client
Yoshida Hideo Memorial Foundation
Brand
ADFEST 2011

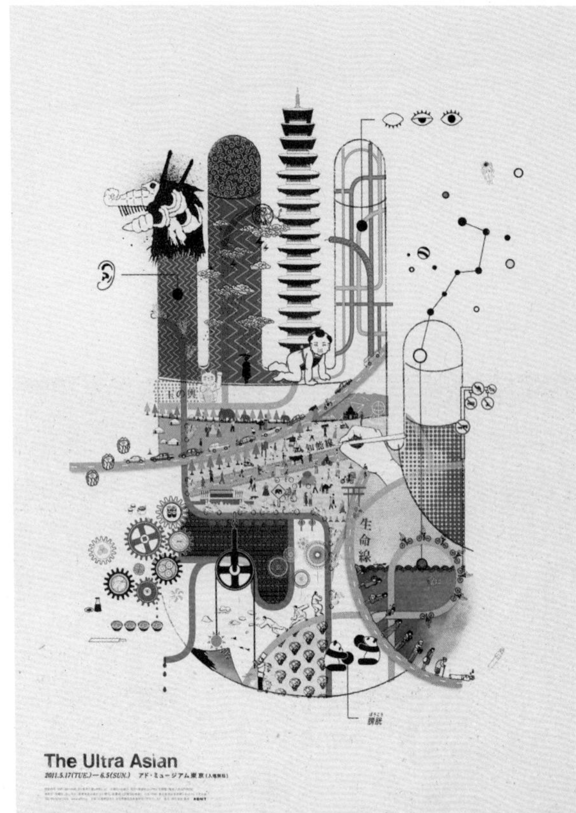

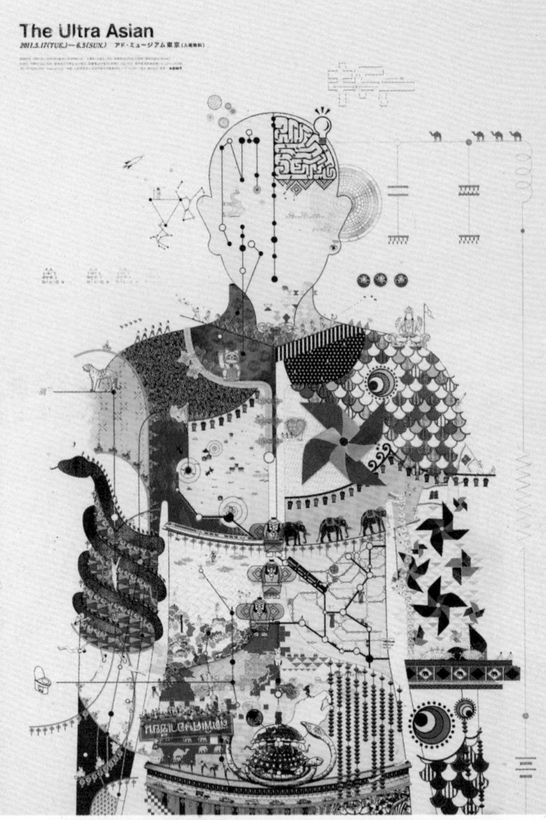

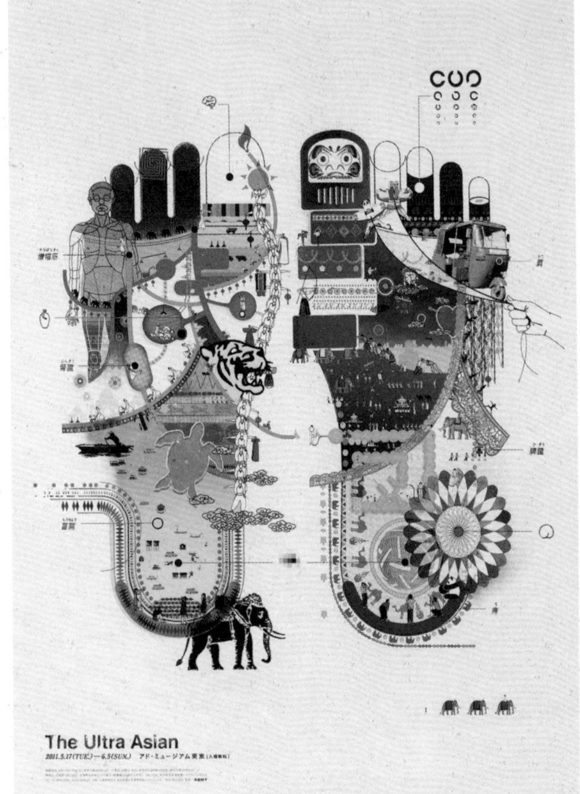

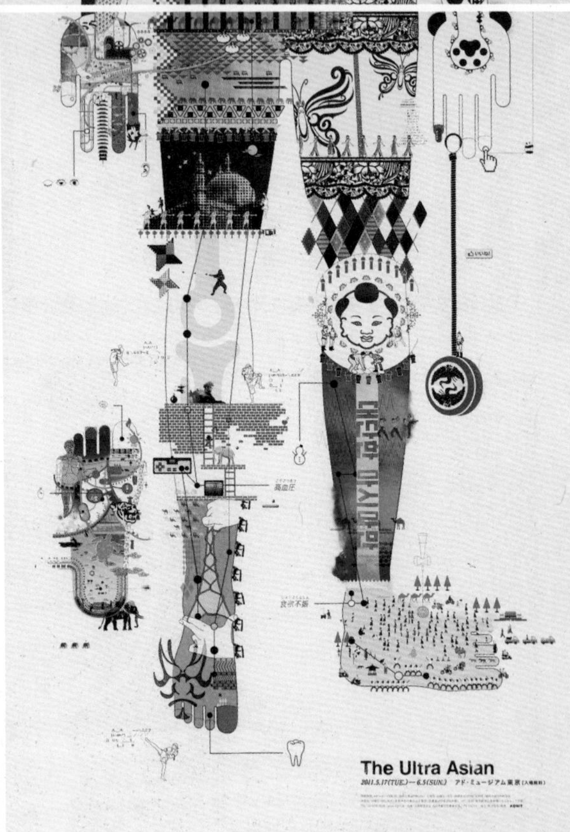

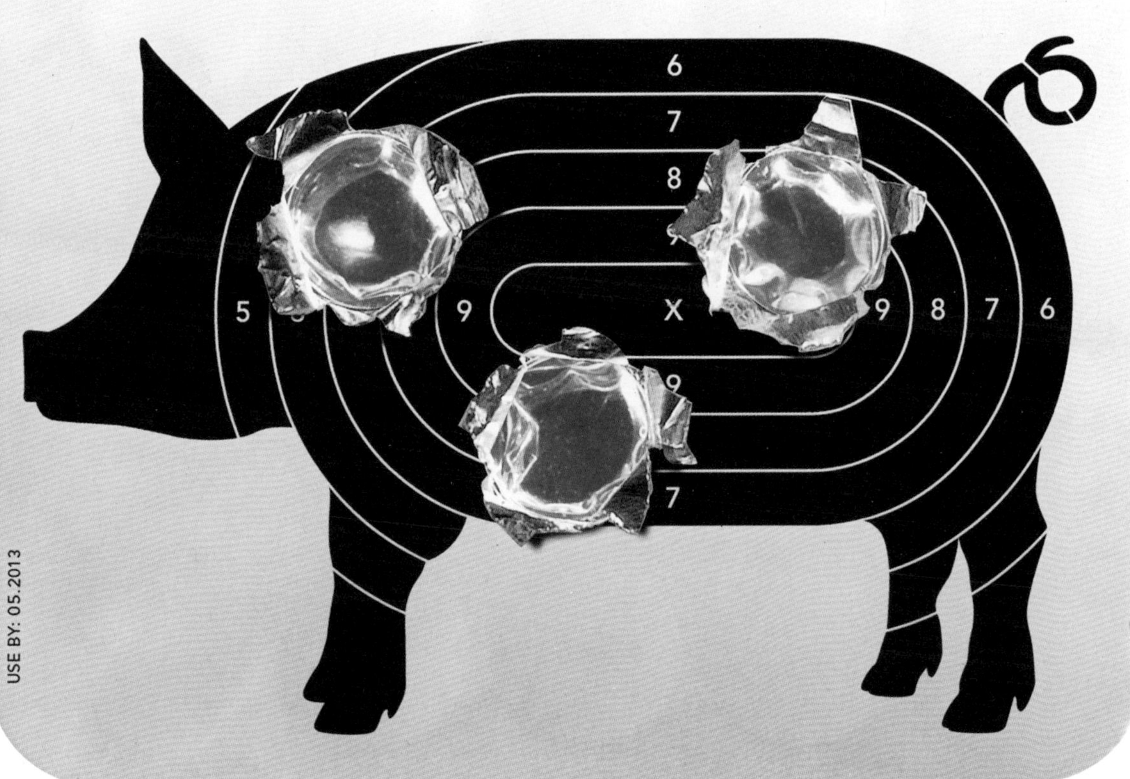

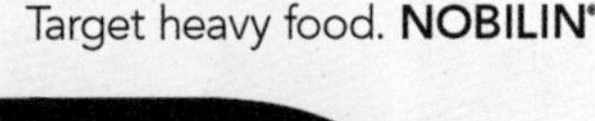

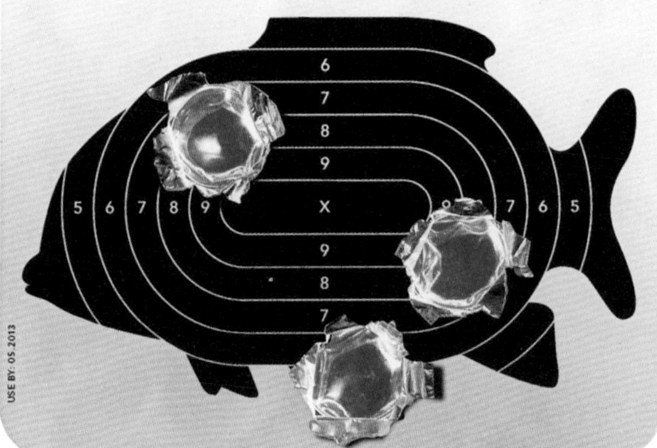

Illustration for Design
BBDO Proximity Berlin
for Medicom Pharma

Target Heavy Food
Nobilin aids digestion. By printing targets with different animals on the back of the blister pack, we demonstrated how the product works in a simple and playful way: every pill targets heavy food in your stomach.

Illustrator
Daniel Schweinzer
Art Director
Daniel Schweinzer
Copywriter
Lukas Liske
Chief Creative Officers
Jan Harbeck
David Mously
Wolfgang Schneider
Agency Producer
Michael Pflanz

Advertising Agency
BBDO Proximity Berlin
Account Manager
Guelcan Demir
Marketing Manager
Rene Steinbusch
Client
Medicom Pharma
Brand
Nobilin

Illustration for Design
Mash
for the Adelaide Festival 2012

The Adelaide Festival Barrio Illustration
Barrio, the nighttime venue for the 2012 Adelaide Festival of Arts, created a giant shanty town in the city centre. Mash worked to conceive a brand that would bring an instant makeshift community to the streets of Adelaide. The brand needed to capture all walks of life and help occupy a space that would change on a daily basis. Each element within the illustration refers to the acts, themes and stalls within the shanty Barrio town. The illustration shows how as a whole, it seems like a big mess, but together it makes for beautiful chaos.

Illustrators
Ryan Psaila
Minka Sicklinger
Designers
James Brown
Ryan Psaila
Dom Roberts
Creative Directors
James Brown
Dom Roberts

Design Agency
Mash
Client
Adelaide Festival 2012

Illustration for Design
Mash
for Boutinot

The Rude Mechanicals

Three of the finest boutique wine makers from Australia each created one wine for a new wine brand called The Rude Mechanicals. Wine traders Boutinot asked us to design a label for the three bottles. We wanted to take a surreal, tongue-in-cheek approach to the secret methods of winemaking and depicted two wine monkeys and the magical contraption they use to produce their wine. At one end birds fly out, growing grapes in their beaks as they fly, before dropping them into a funnel ready to be filtered and tapped into bottles. Hand drawn type was created as a part of the illustration to connect the writing with the imagery.

Illustrators
Jason Holley
Pat Mehbrei
Designers
Ryan Psaila
Dom Roberts
Creative Director
Dom Roberts

Design Agency
Mash
Client
Boutinot
Brand
The Rude Mechanicals

Illustration for Design
Arc Worldwide & Leo Burnett Malaysia
for the Dignity for Children Foundation

Punita

The Dignity for Children Foundation feeds and educates abandoned, homeless and refugee kids. They needed help raising funds. True success stories of kids with Dignity were hand-drawn on the cheap but much-loved school 'exercise books' familiar to every Malaysian. These were distributed in schools (to inspire kids with stories of their peers) and to the public. Sponsorship by banks, embassies and individuals increased. They also caught the eye of leading publisher Pearson Longman and collaboration on fully-sponsored mass production of these books is in progress.

Illustrators
Vivien Low
How Wei Zhong
Art Directors
Maria Alias
Miki Ho
Designers
Maria Alias
Vivien Low
Yap Win Shawn
How Wei Zhong
Design Director
Miki Ho
Copywriters
Jovian Lee
Petrina Shee
Shiang Fei
Typographers
Maria Alias
Vivien Low
How Wei Zhong
Advertising Agencies
Arc Worldwide
Malaysia
Leo Burnett Malaysia
Client
Dignity for Children
Foundation

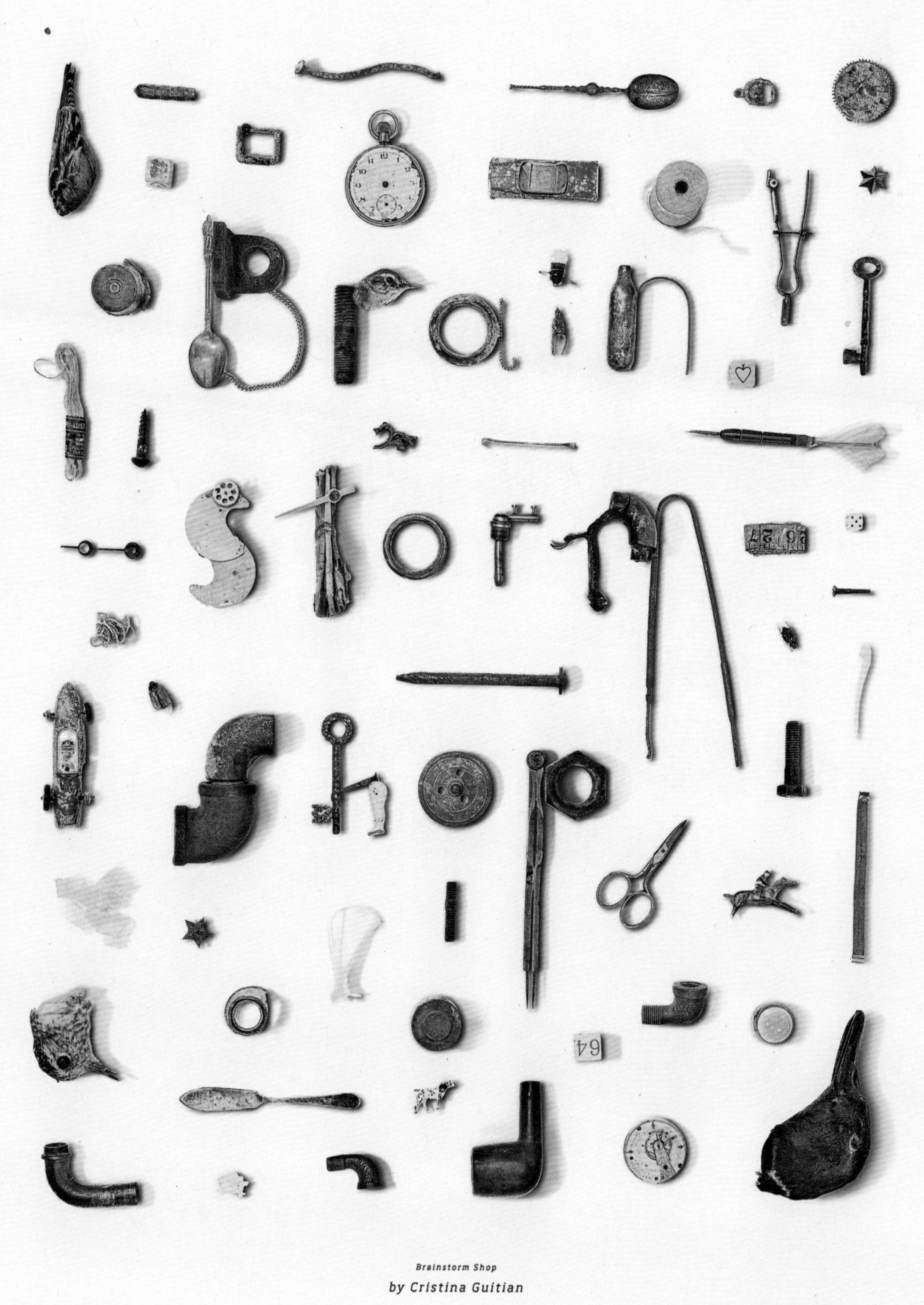

Illustration for Design
Brainstorm Shop

Brainstorm Shop Poster
Brainstorm Shop is a course run in conjunction with Miami Ad School/ESPM, São Paulo, where participants are taught to practice effective brainstorming methods, based on design thinking processes.
We created this poster to promote the course to the creative community. We believed in the power of a well-crafted poster, something that people would touch and hang on their walls. We commissioned an artist and asked for her view on the essence of the course: brainstorming. The outcome was an unbranded piece.

Illustrator
Cristina Guitian
Art Directors
Denis Kakazu
Marcelo Pena Costa
Photographer
Manuel Vazquez
Creative Directors
Denis Kakazu
Marcelo Pena Costa
Planner
Ivan Moreira
Clients
Brainstorm Shop
Miami Ad School/ESPM

1

3

4

5

6

2

Jury Foreman
1. David Stewart

2. Amanda Renshaw
Phaidon Press

3. Tim Bret-Day

4. Sophie Chapman-Andrews
McCann Erickson
London

5. Paulo Martins
Wieden+Kennedy
Amsterdam

6. Jigisha Bouverat
TBWA\Chiat\Day
Los Angeles

Nomination in Photography

Photography for Advertising
DDB UK
for Harvey Nichols

Daylight Robbery
This press and poster campaign is to announce the launch of the Harvey Nichols summer sale and remind people that they can get their hands on the most gorgeous fashion items at a fraction of their usual price. The campaign shows how getting your hands on those items at sale prices will feel like you've committed daylight robbery. It's a steal!

Photographer
Frederike Helwig
Art Director
Victor Monclus
Designer
Pete Mould
Copywriter
Will Lowe
Illustrator
Frederike Helwig
Creative Director
Grant Parker
Executive Creative Director
Jeremy Craigen
Head of Art
Grant Parker
Retoucher
Andrew Walsh
Advertising Agency
DDB UK
Project Manager
Sophie Simonelli
Account Manager
Charlotte Evans
Art Buyer
Sarah Thomson
Business Director
Paul Billingsley
Client
Harvey Nichols

Photography for Advertising
Leila & Damien de Blinkk
for French Connection

I Am The Collection
These adverts are part of the Autumn/Winter advertising campaign for French Connection. They followed on from a series of film ads celebrating the power of clothes, where each film was stylishly told from the point of view of a hero garment. Directed and photographed by Leila and Damien de Blinkk, films and prints were staggered, with a constantly evolving message throughout the season digitally, in cinema, on TV, in print, outdoor and in store windows.

Photographers
Leila & Damien de Blinkk
Art Director
Alice Stein
Creative Directors
Richard Flintham
Dirk Van Dooren
Executive Producers
Abi Hodson
Chantal Webber
Agency Producer
Jack Waters
Stylist
Georgina Hodson
Photography Agency
Webber Represents
Production Company
Onesix7 Productions
Advertising Agency
101 London
Brand Manager
William Woodhams
Client
French Connection

I Am The Blouse

I Am The Coat
French Connection

I Am The Suit
French Connection

I Am The Skirt

I Am The Blouse

52° 31′ 30.77″ N / 13° 23′ 52.14″ E

Krausnick Street 9 in 10115 Berlin, side wing second floor

Photography for Advertising
DDB Tribal Germany
for BSH Deutschland

Icebergs
Frozen freezer compartments waste a lot of energy and contribute to global warming. Or to put it straight: if you have icebergs in your fridge they are missing somewhere else. To dramatise this, we photographed frozen freezer compartments in a documentary style to make them look like arctic landscapes. And pointed out that a Bosch freezer with NoFrost-Technology prevents the ice from building up in the first place.

Photographer
Szymon Plewa
Art Directors
Mario Loncar
Veit Möller
Graphic Designer
Michail Paderin
Copywriters
Daniel Bödeker
Mario Loncar
Creative Director
Daniel Bödeker
Executive Creative Director
Bastian Meneses von Arnim
Chief Creative Officer
Eric Schoeffler
Advertising Agency
DDB Tribal Germany
Planner
Jonas Pöhlmann
Account Managers
Britta Posner
Azade Toygar
Art Buyer
Susanne Kreft
Client
BSH Deutschland
Brand
Bosch

Photography for Advertising
Ogilvy Johannesburg
for Multichoice M-Net

Nothing's Put On
KykNET is a South African TV channel broadcasting in Afrikaans. Launched by satellite operator DStv in October 1999, it has since become a local hit through its mix of actuality and reality shows presented by average South Africans instead of presenters or celebs. Thus the tagline 'Nothing's put on'.

Photographer
David Prior
Art Director
Renier Zandberg
Copywriters
Nico Botha
Mariana O'Kelly
Creative Director
Mariana O'Kelly
Executive Creative Director
Fran Luckin

Advertising Agency
Ogilvy Johannesburg
Account Handler
Caree Ferrari
Marketing Manager
Haddad Viljoen
Client
Multichoice M-Net
Brand
KykNET

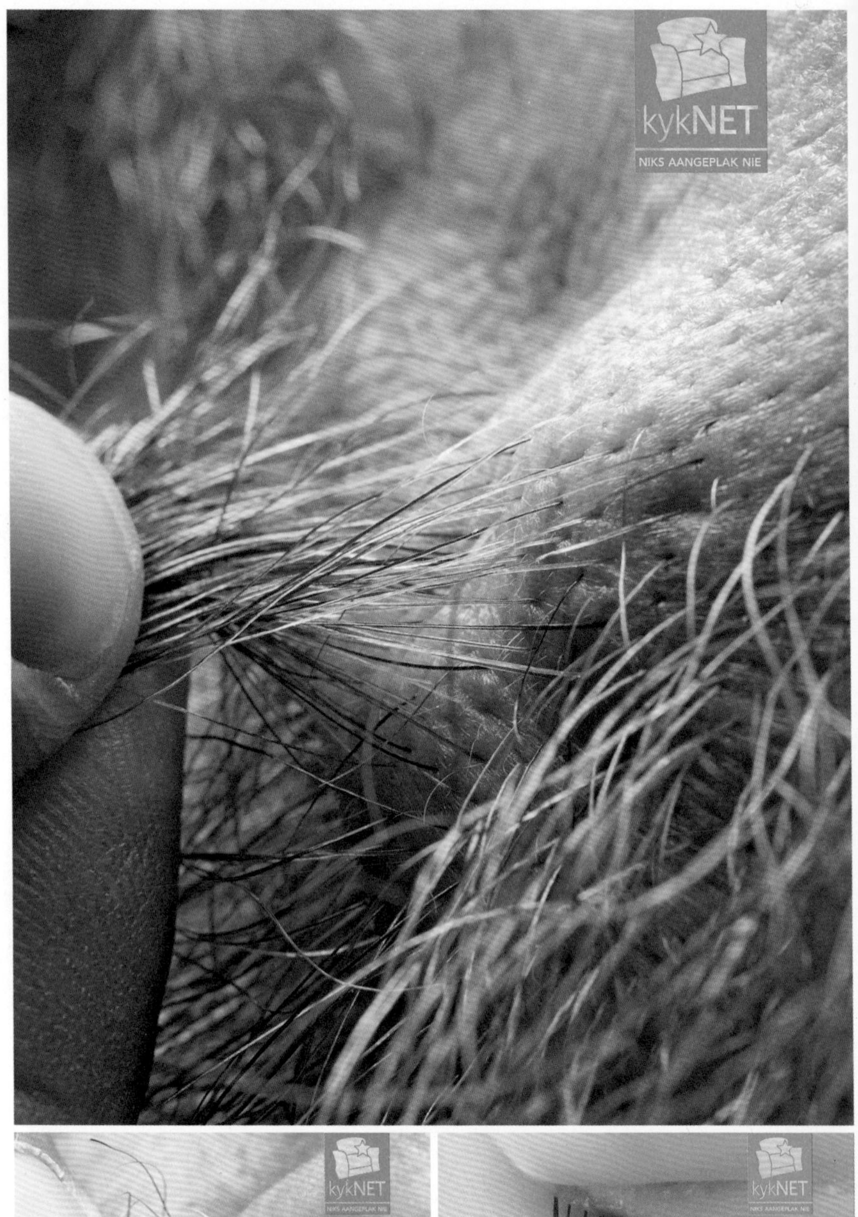

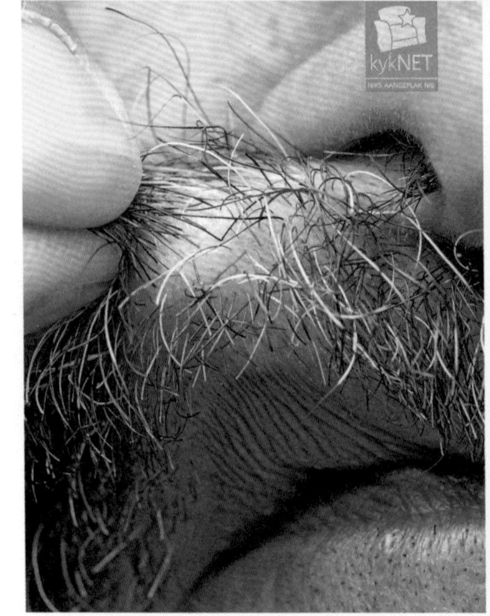

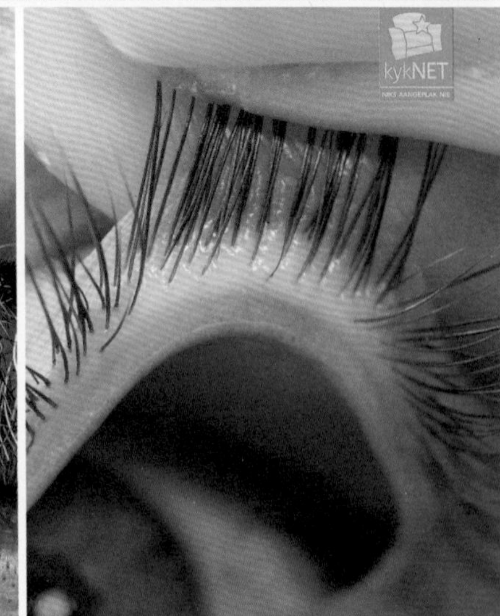

Photography for Advertising
4creative
for Channel 4

Top Boy
Our brief was to create a powerful single image that takes us into the heart of life on an East London estate, where violence, ambition and strength are rewarded. The solution was an arresting poster that alludes to the Top Boyness of it all, and the risks gangs take to rise to the top. Shot against the backdrop of an East London estate, the cast is standing on street furniture that forms the shape of a podium. In a two week campaign, the image was seen on 700 poster sites across London, Birmingham, Manchester and Bristol.

Photographer
Niall O'Brien
Art Director
Alice Tonge
Copywriter
Alice Tonge
Creative Director
Tom Tagholm
Producers
Shannane Lane
Ed Webster
Retoucher
Anna Watson-Smith
Advertising Agency
4creative
Marketing Manager
Laura Ward
Business Director
Kuba Wieczorek
Client
Channel 4

Top Boy
New drama starts Mon 31 Oct 10pm
BX55 DGX

Photography for Advertising
WE ARE Pi
for TEDx Amsterdam

Ideas United
We were tasked with the mission to unite a nation of TEDx Amsterdam fans. People follow TEDx Amsterdam to fill their brains with ideas, so we made brains from people. TEDx Amsterdam – Ideas United.

Photographer
Bill Tanaka
Designer
Bob Stel
Production Designers
Mathieu Gremillet
Altin Kaftira
Ernst Meisner
Creative Directors
Rick Chant
Barney Hobson
Production Directors
Kimia Farshidzad
Christel Hofstee
Executive Producer
Jamie Kim
Advertising Agency
WE ARE Pi
Models
Het Nationale Ballet
Nova Dance College
Strategic Director
Alexander Bennett
Grant
Brand Manager
Marian Spier
Client
TEDx Amsterdam

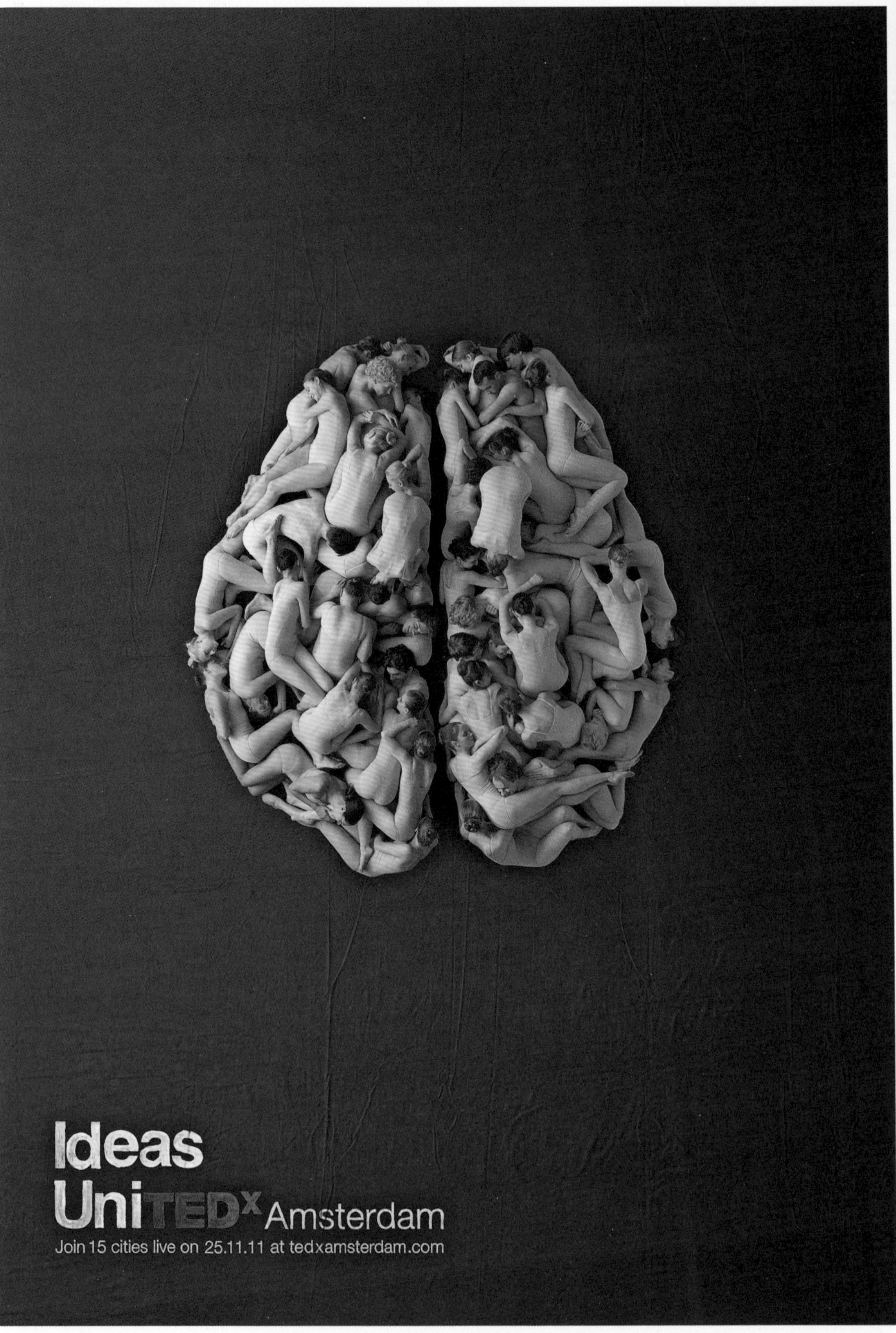

Ideas
UniTEDx Amsterdam
Join 15 cities live on 25.11.11 at tedxamsterdam.com

Photography for Design
This is Real Art
for Universal Music

Gee Up
This is the cover image for a 12-inch single. The image is in fact made up of two layers, to reflect layers of meaning in the music. The image was created by sandwiching two prints and photographing them using an infrared imaging scanner, more commonly used for art detective work.

Photographers
Adam Bainbridge
Pauline Beaudemont
Paul Belford
Creative Director
Paul Belford

Artist
Kindness
Design Agency
This is Real Art
Client
Universal Music

Photography for Design
David Stewart Photography
for Browns Editions

Teenage Pre-occupation Posters
Our objective was to make audiences aware of both a forthcoming book by British photographer David Stewart, and the publisher Browns Editions. Although the three A0 posters work individually, they have also been designed to interconnect, hinting at the aesthetic of the eventual publication. The posters were mailed to bookshops, galleries, museums and the press around the world to generate interest. Bookshops were encouraged to use the posters for point of sale.

Photographer
David Stewart
Designer
Aaron Easterbrook
Creative Director
Jonathan Ellery

Design Agency
Browns
Clients
Browns Editions
David Stewart Photography

Photography for Design
Hans Seeger
for Little Brown Mushroom Books

Conductors of the Moving World
In 1972, a delegation of Japanese police officials visited the US to study traffic in several cities. The unofficial photographer for the delegation was Inspector Eizo Ota. He produced a record of the group's travels, best described as forensic tourism. Using Ota's work as a starting point, author Brad Zellar plundered traffic manuals, haiku anthologies, Watergate transcripts and 'The Godfather' for inspiration. The result is a Zen travelogue through the America of 1972. From a large collection of C-prints, an assortment of 17 was added into individual volumes, making each book a singular work of art.

Photographer
Eizo Ota
Art Director
Hans Seeger
Author
Brad Zellar
Client
Little Brown Mushroom Books

A beautiful woman is sometimes said to stop traffic.
I was unfamiliar with this phrase.

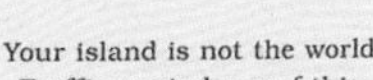

Your island is not the world.
Traffic reminds us of this.

To control your cow, put it in a larger pasture.

Here no bull can hide!

DATA IS THE COWBOY'S WHIP AND ROPE.

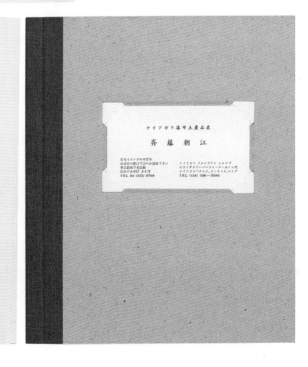

Photography for Design
Pool

Blow Up
'Blow Up' is the first collective publication by Pool. Each of the five artists at Pool developed a new series of images specifically for this project. The concept is based around capturing the collective ethos of Pool. Designed by branding and design agency Maud in collaboration with the members of Pool, this single, continuous work is unusual in that it can be separated into five individual elements, each printed on a different stock and each representing an artist within the group.

Photographers
Danny Eastwood
Simon Harsent
Christopher Ireland
Sean Izzard
Ingvar Kenne
Designer
Ben Crick
Creative Director
David Park
Executive Producer
Cameron Gray
Photography
Pool
Design Agency
Maud
Marketing Manager
Melissa Archer
Client
Pool

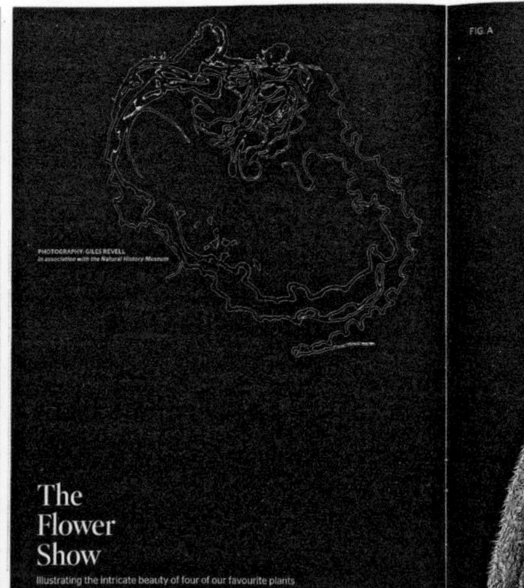

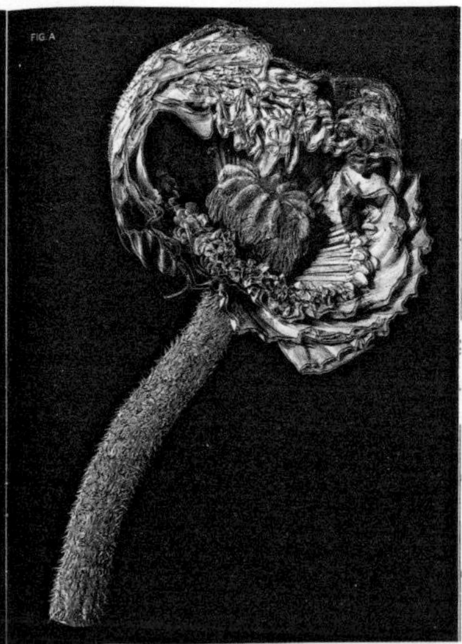

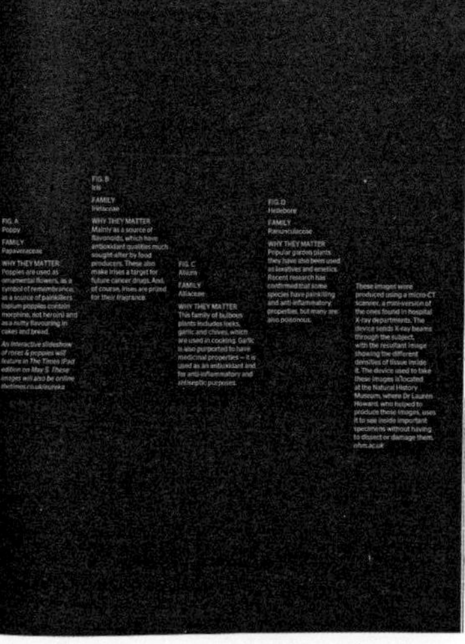

Photography for Design
Giles Revell
for The Times

Eureka: The Flower Show

The Times commissioned photographer Giles Revell to capture the intricate beauty of some of the UK's medicinal plants for its science magazine Eureka. In collaboration with Dr Lauren Howard at the Natural History Museum, Giles was able to produce micro-CT scanner footage in layers through each of the plants. Stills from the footage were featured in the May issue to coincide with The Times' Garden entry into the RHS Chelsea Flower show. The animated sequences of the rose and poppy footage appeared as an interactive slideshow in the paper's iPad edition and online.

Photographer
Giles Revell
Art Director
Matt Curtis
Picture Editor
Madeleine Penny

Production Company
Stella Pye
Photographers Agent
Client
The Times

1

2

3

4

5

6

7

Jury Foreman
1. Erik Spiekermann
Edenspiekermann

2. Alan Kitching
The Typography Workshop

3. Zoë Bather
Zoë Bather Creative

4. Kutlu Çanlıoglu
BBC World Service

5. Sonya Dyakova
Frieze Magazine

6. Rian Hughes
Device

7. Philippe Apeloig
Apeloig

Nomination in Typography

Typography for Design
Rikako Nagashima
for Dai Nippon Printing

Reconstructed Kanji: Ice & Snow
This is a commemorative poster for the centennial of a font called Shuei-tai, which 24 Japanese graphic designers were asked to design. We wanted to show a new expression of Shuei-tai, even though it's a traditional font with 100 years of history. We disassembled then reconstructed the Kanji characters for 'ice' and 'snow'. This was done in a way that maintained both their original meaning and the meaning the Kanji have in their new form.

Typographer	Designer
Rikako Nagashima	Rikako Nagashima
Art Director	**Client**
Rikako Nagashima	Dai Nippon Printing

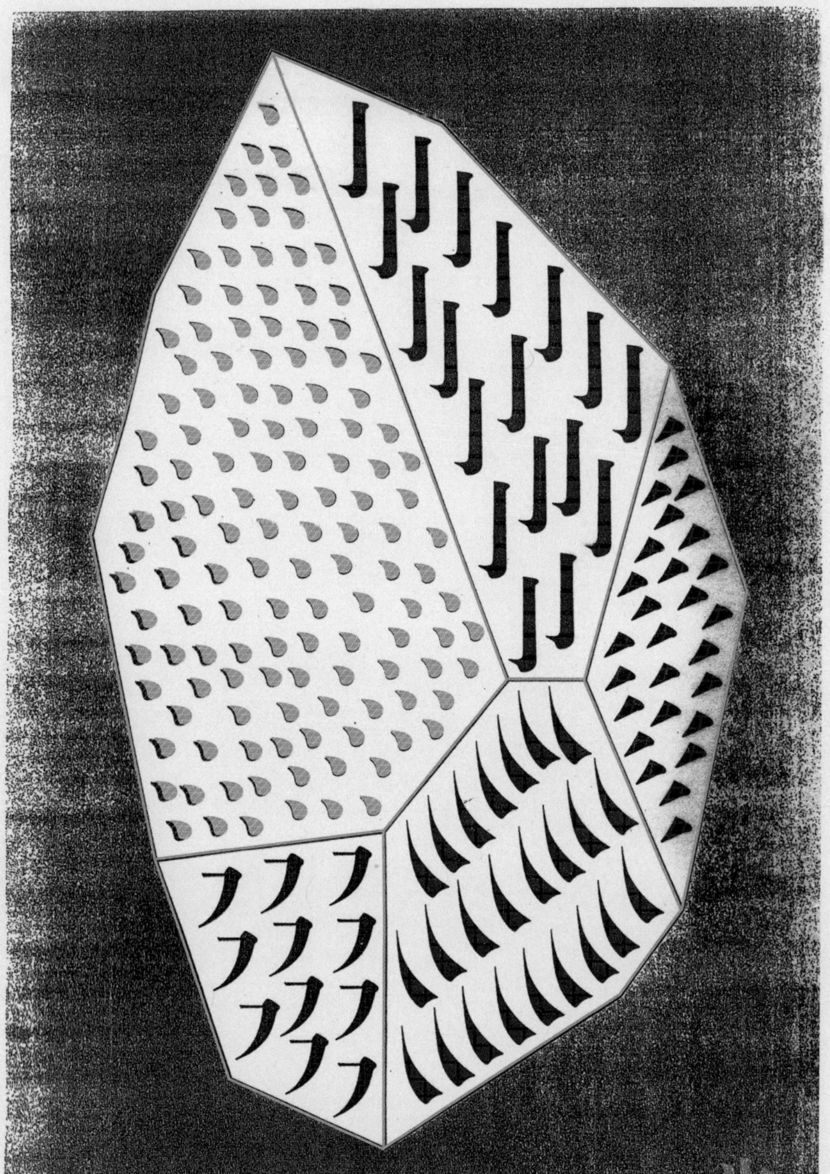

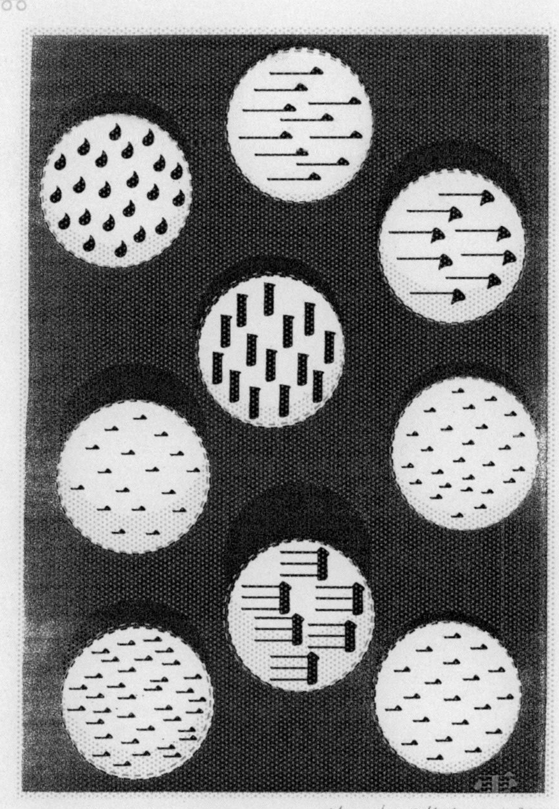

Nomination in Typography

Typography for Design
Eric Chan Design
for the CO-1 School of Visual Arts

CO-1 10th Anniversary Poster

Our task was to design a ten-year anniversary poster for an art school. We played around with the Chinese character 'ten years', using the traditional Chinese word 'ten' to replace the modern word 'ten'. We also replaced the word 'year' with the word 'link', which is pronounced the same way, to introduce the idea of continuity. This represents the ten years the art school has been supporting the development of students. We used a wooden frame as the main construction material for our poster. The frame is the foundation of a painting, which reflects the art school's supportive role to students.

Typographers
Eric Chan
Andries Lee
Art Director
Eric Chan
Photographer
Kitty Chan

Creative Director
Eric Chan
Design Agency
Eric Chan Design
Client
CO-1 School of Visual Arts

他們需要你的捐獻 orbis.org.hk
ORBIS
奧比斯

Typography for Advertising
Ogilvy & Mather Hong Kong
for ORBIS HK

Knots
The ORBIS Flying Eye Hospital saves the sight of thousands suffering from avoidable blindness all over the world. It's difficult to appreciate what it's like to suffer from a degenerative eye disease. To give people an idea, we created a type-driven poster with a barely legible message. The copy reads: 'Can't see, can't read, can't learn, can't see, can't read, can't learn. Don't let this be the story of a child's life'.

Typographer
Ben Yeung
Art Directors
Max Fung
Ben Yeung
Yvonne Yip
Copywriter
Buji Ng
Illustrator
Ben Yeung
Creative Directors
Buji Ng
Ben Yeung
Executive Creative Directors
Sandy Chan
Simon Handford
Advertising Agency
Ogilvy & Mather Hong Kong
Account Handlers
Tak Chi Lee
Paul Lam
Jessica Lau
Client
ORBIS HK

Typography for Design
AGI Spain
for Alliance Graphique Internationale

Identity for AGI Congress & Open

The identity of the AGI Congress and Open is based on the typographic modular system SuperVeloz, designed by Joan Trochut in the first half of the 20th Century. Having borrowed from history, we faced the challenge of creating a fresh and distinctive visual language. We created a personalised AGI SuperVeloz Alphabet based on the initials of each speaker. When enlarged, the initials work as illustrations. We pared down type and colour to let them shine, transforming the series of initials into the focal part of the campaign.

Art Directors
Pablo Martín
Astrid Stavro

Designers
Vicky Cabrera
Ana Lacour
Pablo Martín
Pedro Ponciano
Rafa Roses
Astrid Stavro
Maggy Villarroel

Creative Directors
Mario Eskenazi
Pablo Martín
Astrid Stavro
Patrick Thomas

Typography
AGI Spain

Design Agency
AGI Spain

Project Manager
Patrick Thomas

Clients
AGI Spain
Alliance Graphique Internationale

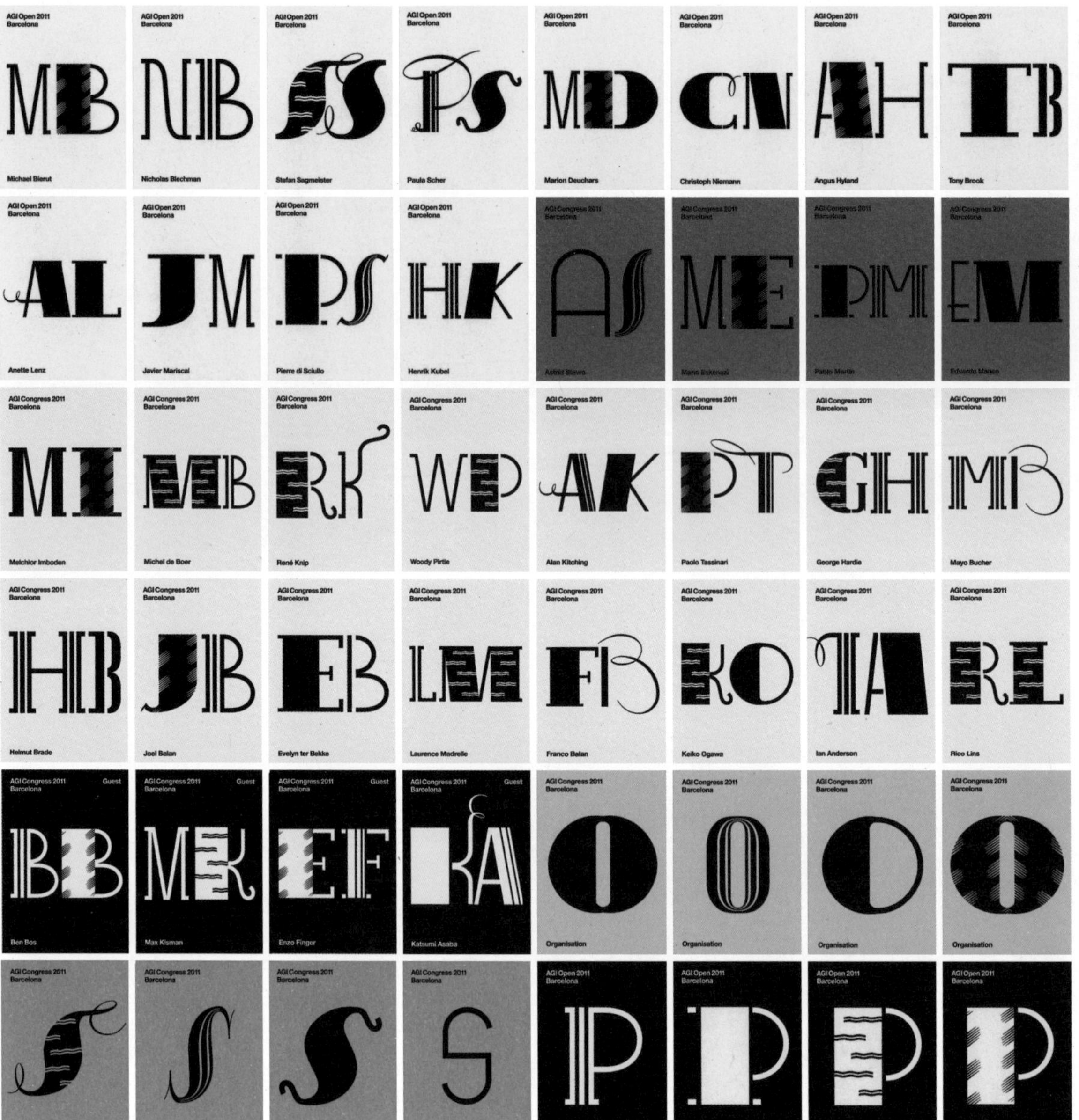

Works of

International Graphic Arts Show

Foil Stamping Machine

Gietz AG

U www.gietz.com
T +41 71 388 22 22
F +41 71 388 22 23

Engraving

hinderer+mühlich KG

U www.hinderer-muehlich.de
T +49 7161 9 78 22–0
F +49 7161 9 78 22–10

Sep. 16 — 21, 2011

Direction

Iwai Tsusho K.K.

U www.iwai-tsusho.com
T 03 5810 6361
F 03 5810 6363

Paper — Sappi Fine Paper Europe www.sappi.com

Foil — Kurz Japan Ltd. www.kurzjapan.com

Processing — Bihaku Watanabe Company www.bihaku-w.co.jp

Graphic Design — AD&D www.ad-and-d.jp

Typography for Design
AD&D
for Iwai Tsusho &
the Bihaku Watanabe Company

Works of International Graphic Arts Show
This poster for a graphic arts event was created as a demonstration of the stamping process. It illustrated the precision and productivity of stamping machines at the selling point.

Typographer
Ren Takaya
Art Director
Ren Takaya
Graphic Designer
Ren Takaya
Print Director
Katsuhiro Kagota
Print Producer
Hideyuki Watanabe

Design Agency
AD&D
Project Manager
Mitsuru Sato
Clients
Iwai Tsusho
Bihaku Watanabe
Company

Typography for Design
Tokyu Agency
for PIE International

Graphic Explanation in Advertisement
'Graphic Explanation in Advertisement' is a reference book for designers & students showcasing examples of graphic diagrams from manuals, magazines, brochures and other forms of advertisement. The typography design used on the cover was inspired by the diagrams inside. The reader has to follow the assembly instructions to form the letters.

Typographer
Tatsuki Ikezawa
Art Director
Tatsuki Ikezawa
Designers
Takemichi Chiba
Hiromi Fkui

Writer
Hiroyuki Nishio
Advertising Agency
Tokyu Agency
Client
PIE International

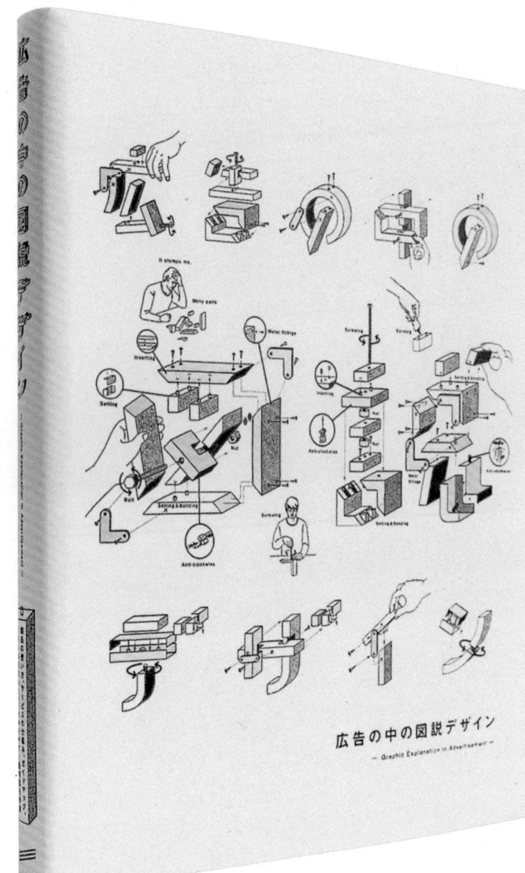

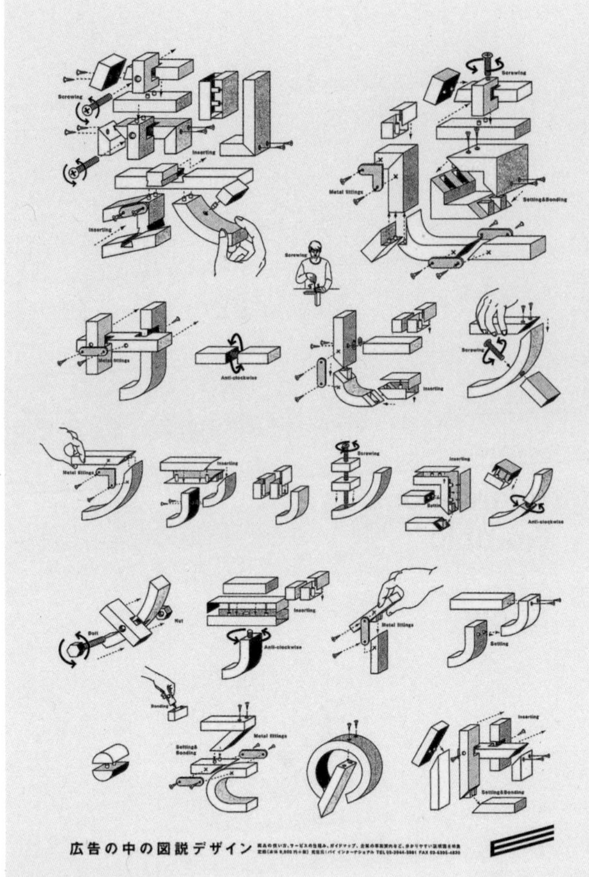

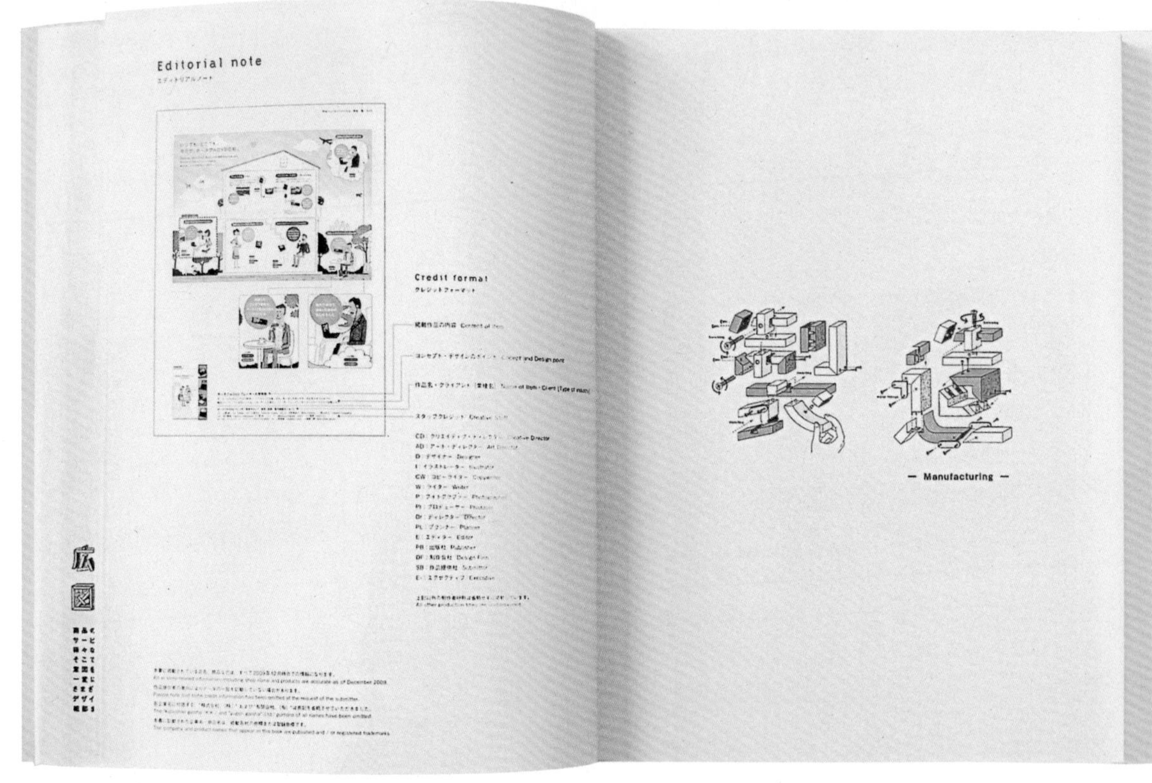

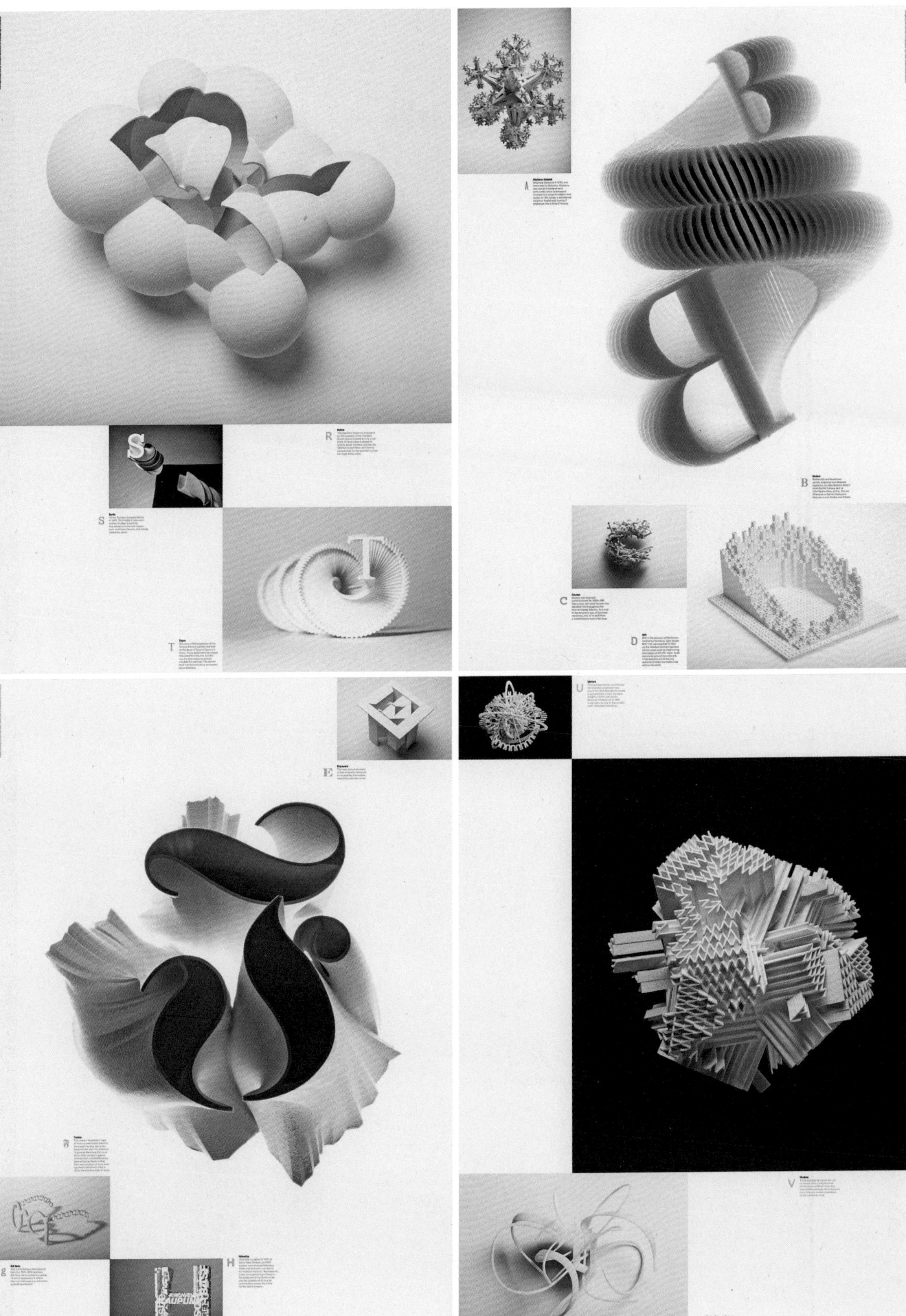

Typography for Design
johnson banks
for Ravensbourne

Arkitypo
The Arkitypo project came about when one of our clients, media and design college Ravensbourne, asked if we were interested in developing a research project to test and showcase their in-house 3D prototyping skills and technology. We suggested something typographic. We set ourselves the brief to develop a 3D 'alphabet of alphabets'. Each letterform is different; each in turn interprets its own alphabet. The final 26 were recorded in this set of posters.

Typographers
James Cooney
Tamara Elmallah
Michael Johnson
Pali Palavathanan
Dina Silanteva
Julia Woollams
Designers
James Cooney
Tamara Elmallah
Michael Johnson
Pali Palavathanan
Dina Silanteva
Julia Woollams

Creative Director
Michael Johnson
3D Modelling
Jon Fidler
Design Agency
johnson banks
Brand Manager
Jill Hogan
Client
Ravensbourne

Typography for Design
Loran Stosskopf Studio
for the Ecole d'Art de Mulhouse
& Les Presses du Réel

Faire Impression
This book is about the creation of French art schools in the 19th Century and their link with each region's industry. Mulhouse (Alsace) presents the story of these schools. Mulhouse was then renowned for its fabric printing industry. A drawing school was created to provide fresh designs. We used original students' drawings, found in the archives of the Fabric Printing Museum, to design the cover and title pages. Typography and pattern are merged down. The book size is the same as the annual books published by the Mulhouse Industrial Society. Fonts were designed by François Rappo, former typography teacher at the school.

Typographer
Loran Stosskopf
Type Designer
François Rappo
Art Director
Loran Stosskopf
Designers
Alexandre Chapus
Clara Sfarti

Publishing Company
Les Presses du Réel
Design Agency
Loran Stosskopf Studio
Clients
Ecole d'Art de Mulhouse
Les Presses du Réel

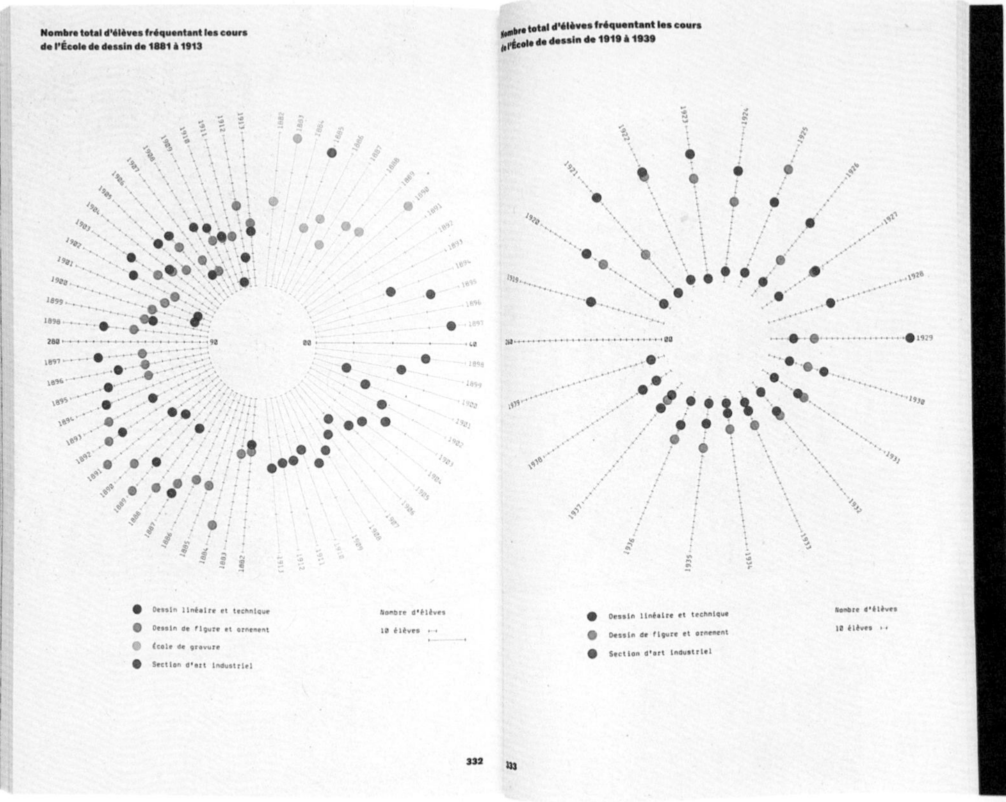

Typography for Design
Nokia Design & Brand Studio
for Nokia

Twenty-six Characters
'Twenty-six Characters' is an alphabetical journey around Nokia Pure, Nokia's new typeface. The book is a celebration of Nokia Pure's design story, its distinctive features and its value as a brand asset. It details how the typeface was designed with the user interface in mind, and how it was crafted into a contemporary typeface at the Dalton Maag foundry. This book is also design inspiration, a specimen sheet, a rough guide to typography and the tale of a global business undergoing radical change. All in all, it's a visual treat for type lovers, and the first step in establishing a visual language in which Nokia Pure can thrive.

Typographer
Bruno Maag
Designers
George Chevalier
Lewis
Samuel Clarke
Steve Foyle
Troy Hyde
Brody Larson
Tyrone Lou
Gisele Palatnik
Guilherme Schneider
Nuno Silva
Design Directors
Hugh Miller
Bradley Zimber
Copywriters
Lisa Desforges
Iván Mato

Creative Directors
Iván Mato
Lisbet Tonner
Editors
Aapo Bovellan
Chris Merrick
Type Design
Dalton Maag
Creative Agency
Nokia Design
& Brand Studio
Project Managers
Elisabeth Honerla
Tiina Ruohonen
Client
Nokia

Typography for Design
Toby and Pete
for Steve Back

Steve Back Logo
Our client wanted an eye-catching visual to head up his new self-promotional website. The brief was somewhat simple: 'I'd like my name to be fun and playful'. From this simple brief with many possible outcomes, we started to explore areas of childhood nostalgia. We eventually came to the solution of a brightly coloured jumping castle. We wanted the type to look fun enough to play on, so we made it interwoven and structurally quirky. We approached the design with the mindset that if we were to build this for real, it would actually work.

Typographers
Toby Pike
Piotr Stopniak
Creative Director
Steve Back

Design Agency
Toby and Pete
Client
Steve Back

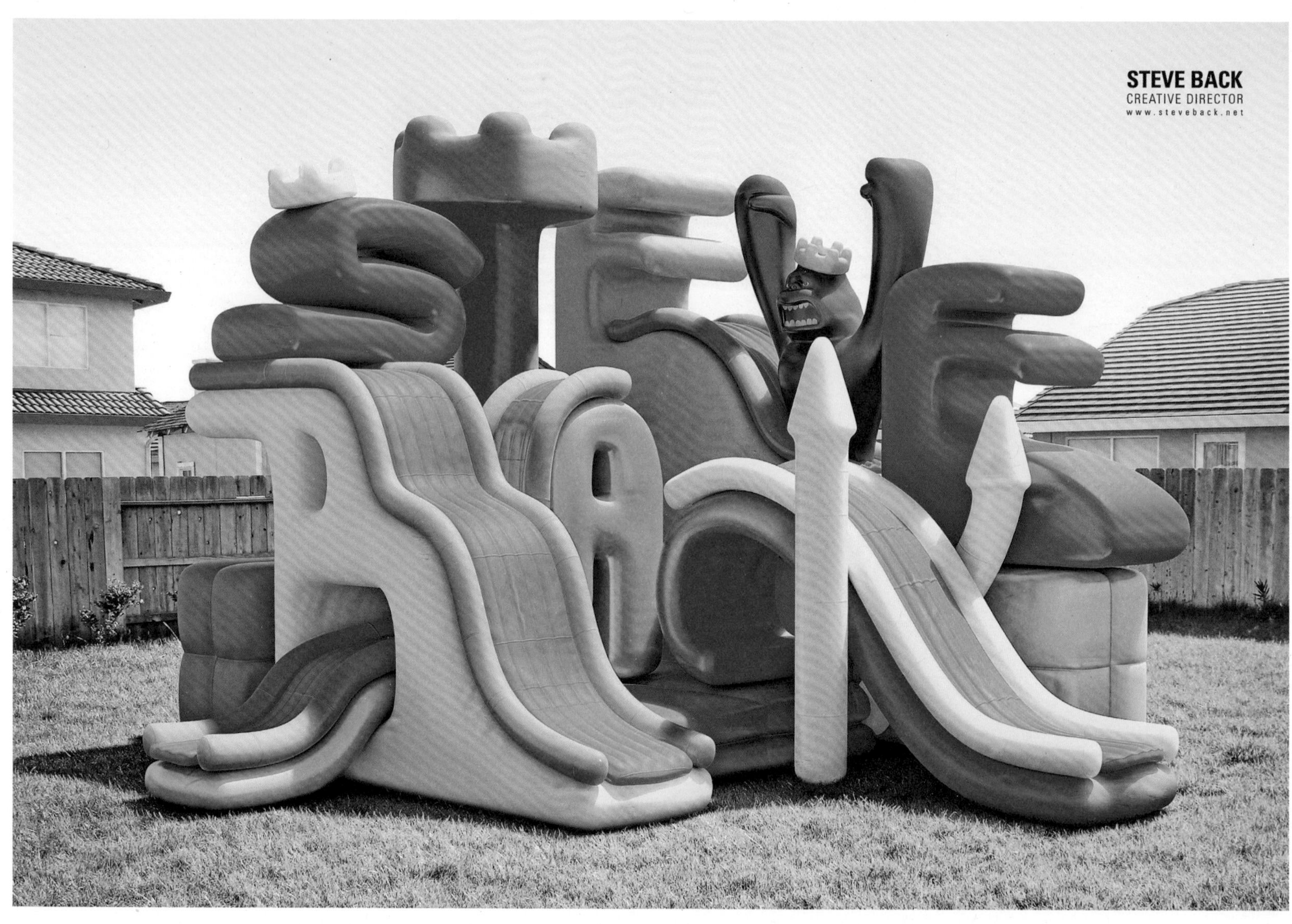

Typefaces
e-Types
for Berlingske Media

Berlingske
Berlingske is a customised typeface for the major Danish newspaper of the same name. In 2012 the Berlingske family was released to the public in a much larger version. The character set was extended with small caps, Greek, Cyrillic, Vietnamese, Latin extended, Greek extended and Baltic. Another 20 weights were also added to the original 15, plus multiple italics. Berlingske is a contemporary multi-purpose typeface that should grasp the wide-ranging needs of creatives, in both display and text, the web and print. A superfamily is born.

Typographer	Client
Jonas Hecksher	Berlingske Media
Design Agency	**Brand**
e-Types	Berlingske

må bruges i enkelte tilfælde, mener 23 procent af danskerne ifølge ny
er for at gøre tortur til en selvstændig forbrydelse i straffeloven.

dansker siger god for tortur

her-
ank-
n af.
atte
kere
isen

Noget af de
galt sidste gan
ber, var den p
ballade, hvor

Midt mellem tankernes vold og
intetheden

Ro. Det er himmelråbende simpelt, men hamrende svært. Træningen til et 24 timers meditationsmaraton er gået i gang på Østerbro, her ignorerer man alting for at opnå intethed, som avler frihed. Men det kræver hverken trommer af slangeskind eller haremsbukser.

De fire trin til meditation

EnlightenNext

Vær fuldstændig stille. Vær afspændt. Vær opmærksom. Lad alting være, som det er.

08. / AOK /
/ AOK / .09

1

2

3

4

5

6

Jury Foreman
1. Tim Riley
AMV BBDO

2. Ben Walker
Crispin Porter +
Bogusky London

3. Olivia Donaldson
Story UK

4. Dean Turney
Wild Colonial Boys

5. Graeme Hall
180 Amsterdam

6. Mary Wear

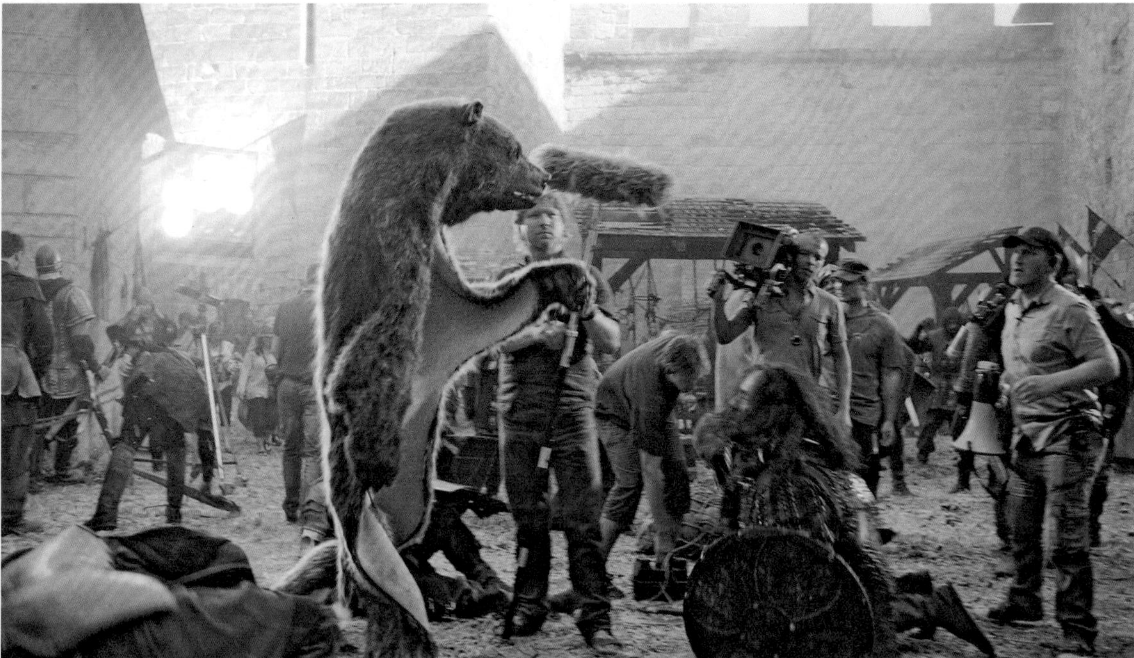

Nomination in Writing for Advertising

Writing for Film Advertising
BETC Paris
for CANAL+

The Bear
A bearskin rug explains what it takes to become a great Hollywood director.

Director
Matthijs van Heijningen
Copywriter
Jean-Christophe Royer
Art Director
Eric Astorgue
Executive Creative Director
Stéphane Xiberras
Executive Producer
Yuki Suga
Agency Producers
David Green
Isabelle Menard
Production Designer
Jan Houllevigue
Director of Photography
Joost Van Gelder
Music Producer
Eric Cervera
Editor
Jono Griffiths
Production Company
Soixante Quinze
Advertising Agency
BETC Paris
Visual Effects Company
Mikros
Post Production
Mikros
Sound Design
GUM
Planner
Clarisse Lacarrau
Client
CANAL+

Nomination in Writing for Advertising

Writing for Film Advertising
Grey London
for the British Heart Foundation

The Angina Monologues
Coronary heart disease is the biggest killer of women in the UK, yet breast cancer is seen as a bigger health threat. Women are constantly inundated with health scares – but what if we could make them engage with this unpleasant truth, by choice? We enrolled the nation's funniest women, led by Victoria Wood, and created 'The Angina Monologues', a comedy show and special TV event to raise awareness of heart disease amongst women. This hugely successful event saw Victoria Wood win 'Best Female Comedian' at the prestigious 2011 British Comedy Awards for her involvement in 'The Angina Monologues'.

Copywriters
Jo Brand
Katy Brand
Roisin Conaty
Jessica Hynes
Ria Jones
Vicki Maguire
Vicki Pepperdine
Joanna Scanlan
Isy Suttie
Victoria Wood
Art Director
Scott Bradley
Creative Directors
Dan Cole
Andy Garnett
Vicki Maguire
Executive Creative Director
Nils Leonard
Producers
Martin Dance
Hazel Stocker
Executive Producers
Lucy Ansbro
Simon Wells
Victoria Wood
Agency Producers
James Covill
Fran Mair
Leon McComish
Audio Producer
David Woolley
Advertising Agency
Grey London
Media Agencies
Drum
PHD
Planner
Nick Hirst
Account Manager
Sophie Fredheim
Client
British Heart Foundation

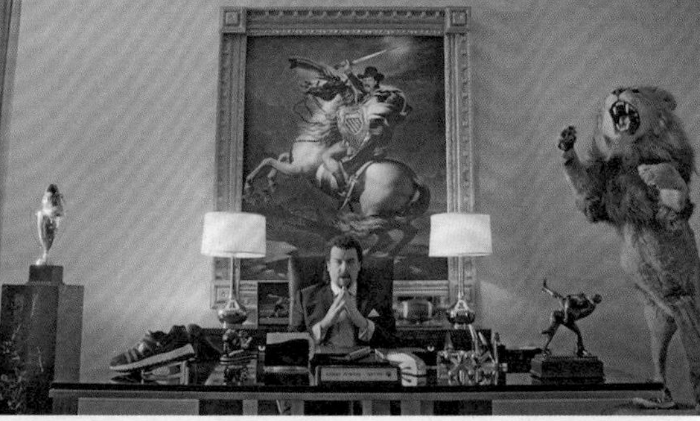

Writing for Film Advertising
72andSunny USA
for K-Swiss

K-Swiss: MFCEO
In the 2010 campaign, K-Swiss signed the controversial fictional 'athlete' Kenny Powers to an endorsement deal. In the 2011 campaign, Kenny took over K-Swiss as MFCEO (Mother F***ing Chief Exectutive Officer), reshaping the company in his image and enlisting the world's baddest athletes to help him unsuck the sports world.

Director
Jody Hill
Copywriter
Matt Heath
Creative Directors
Barton Corley
Matt Murphy
Chief Creative Officer
Glenn Cole
Executive Producer
Michael Sogol
Agency Producer
Danielle Tarris
Designer
Jay Kamath
Editors
Matt Murphy
Graham Turner
Production Company
Caviar LA
Advertising Agency
72andSunny USA
Visual Effects Company
Animal
Editing
Final Cut
Los Angeles
Brand Director
Matt Rohmer
Client
K-Swiss

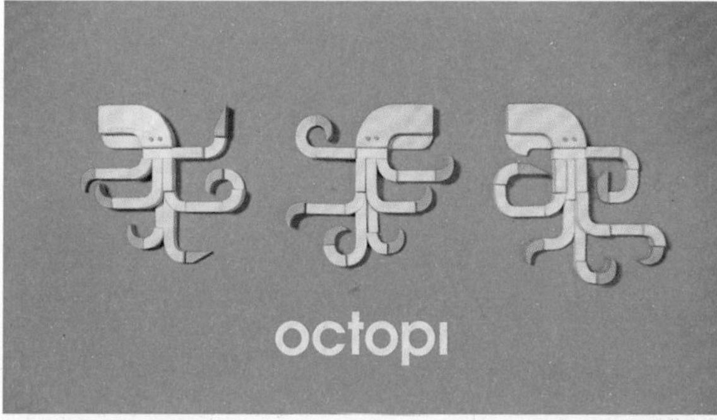

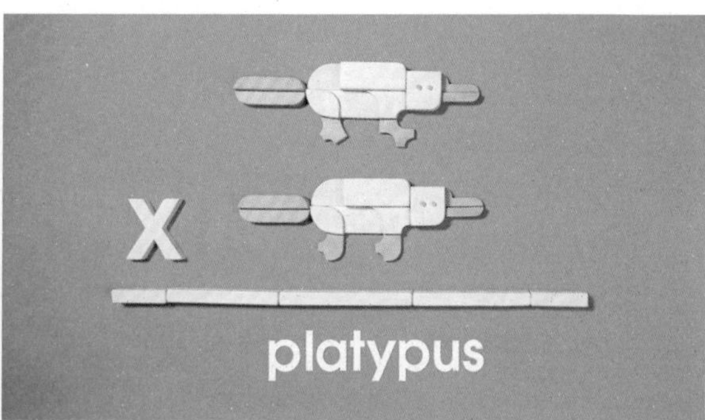

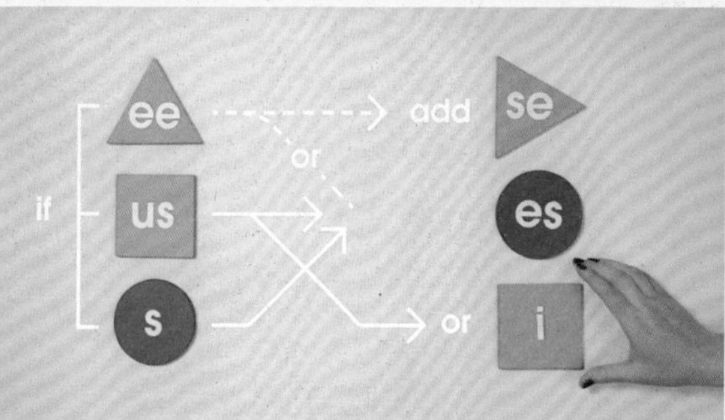

Writing for Film Advertising
Saatchi & Saatchi Los Angeles
for Toyota Motor Sales USA

Prius Goes Plural
The Toyota Prius is becoming a family. But what do we call them? Prii? Priuses? Prium? To dive deep into the nature of the plural, we created an educational music video that familiarised our audience with the complex nature of plurals – the plural of Prius being the subject of great debate. With this piece as a kick-off, we opened up the digital ballot boxes for our Prius fans to determine the official plural of Prius.

Art Directors
Zach Richter
Matt Titone
Copywriters
Nathan Dills
Andy Kadin
Creative Directors
Ryan Jacobs
Mike McKay
Todd St John
Executive Producer
Brigid Boyle
Agency Producers
Kait Boehm
Melissa Eccles
Tanya LeSieur
Charlie Maas
Animation
HunterGatherer
Advertising Agency
Saatchi & Saatchi Los Angeles
Post Production
Skyrmish
Sound Design
Lime Studios
Planner
Sara Bamossy
Account Handlers
Nicole Buckley
Keith Ellis
Client
Toyota Motor Sales USA
Brand
Toyota

Writing for Film Advertising
Grey London
for the British Heart Foundation

Vinnie
The British Heart Foundation wanted to get more people to have a go at CPR. They had news to convey: no kissing and just push hard and fast. This ad starred hard man Vinnie Jones showing how simple 'hand-only CPR' can be, to the iconic track 'Stayin' Alive' – which is the correct tempo to perform chest compressions. The film was the most shared video online during launch week.

Director
Wayne McClammy
Copywriter
Vicki Maguire
Creative Director
Vicki Maguire
Executive Creative Director
Nils Leonard
Producer
Nate Young
Agency Producers
Jacqueline Dobrin
Daisy Mellors
Post Producer
Tom Johnson
Director of Photography
Fraser Taggart
Editor
Alaster Jordan
Production Company
Hungry Man
Advertising Agency
Grey London
Post Production
The Mill London
Editing
The White House
Sound Design
Grand Central
Planner
Simon White
Account Manager
Sophie Fredheim
Account Director
Camilla Ashenhurst
Client
British Heart Foundation

Writing for Film Advertising
Clemenger BBDO
for the New Zealand Transport Agency

Ghost Chips
To tackle the problem of drink driving amongst young guys in New Zealand, we produced 'Ghost Chips', a film portraying our audience in a cool, aspirational way. We laced the content with catchphrases; some quickly became part of the Kiwi vernacular, giving our audience the tools they needed to speak up and stop their mates from drink driving. The campaign was a massive viral success, resulting in countless video mash-ups and the biggest New Zealand meme of the year.

Director
Steve Ayson
Copywriters
Mitch Alison
Brigid Alkema
Philip Andrew
Steve Ayson
Art Director
Brigid Alkema
Executive Creative Director
Philip Andrew
Producer
Larisa Tiffin
Agency Producer
Martin Gray
Editor
Peter Scribberas
Music Composer
Mahuia Bridgman-Cooper
Sound Engineer
Jon Cooper
Advertising Agency
Clemenger BBDO
Account Directors
Julianne Hastings
Linda Major
Brand Manager
Rachel Prince
Marketing Manager
Paul Graham
Client
New Zealand Transport Agency

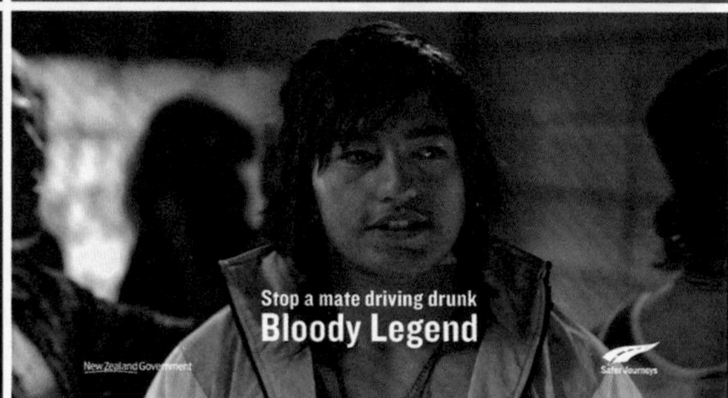

Writing for Film Advertising
BBDO New York
for AT&T

You've Got a Case
AT&T wanted to help young people prove to their parents that they deserve a new 4G smartphone this holiday season. But kids aren't always the best at winning arguments. Meet high-powered internet attorney Kent Wesley. Kent thinks you deserve an AT&T 4G smartphone, and he's here to prove it with 'You've Got a Case'. Using information from your Facebook profile and a panel of 'experts', Kent creates a personalised case video, twisting everything about you into a convincing argument for why you deserve a 4G smartphone from AT&T. If you've got Kent, you've got a case.

Director
Jonathan Krisel
Copywriters
Mark Anderson
Rick Williams
Art Directors
Danny Adrain
Marcel Yunes
Creative Directors
Arturo Aranda
George Ernst
Executive Creative Director
Greg Hahn
Chief Creative Officer
David Lubars
Executive Producer
Julian Katz
Agency Producer
Jeff Puskar
Interactive Producer
Clemens Brandt
Music Producer
Melissa Chester
Design Director
Brad Cohen
Director of Photography
Damian Acevedo
Production Company
Caviar LA
Interactive Production Company
The Famous Group
Advertising Agency
BBDO New York
Editing
Arcade Edit
Account Executives
Marc Burns
Kara Carpentier
Mallory Hartline
Maryeliza Massengill
Shannon Schmidt
Doug Walker
Client
AT&T

Writing for Film Advertising
Y&R New York
for Land Rover

Pathological Liar
Land Rover drivers experience a feeling of safety that drivers of other vehicles don't. That's why this pathological liar chooses to be in a Land Rover 4 while confessing to his girlfriend that he's not exactly who she thinks he is.

Director
David Shane
Copywriter
Julia Neumann
Art Director
Michael Schachtner
Creative Directors
Graham Lang
Guillermo Vega
Steve Whittier
Executive Creative Director
Kerry Keenan
Executive Producer
Ralph Laucella
Senior Producer
Mara Milicevic
Agency Producer
Jona Goodman
Director of Photography
Antonio Calvache

Editor
Jason Macdonald
Heads of Broadcast
Nathy Aviram
Lora Schulson
Advertising Agency
Y&R New York
Digital Production Company
O Positive
Post Production
Number Six Edit
Sound Design
Sound Lounge
Client
Land Rover
Brand
Land Rover 4

I never want children are great.

For all life's twists and turns:
Flexible financial plans.

I love my house now belongs to my ex-wife.

For all life's twists and turns:
Flexible financial plans.

I'm not interested in getting married in church is more romantic.

For all life's twists and turns:
Flexible financial plans.

She's my everything went wrong.

For all life's twists and turns:
Flexible financial plans.

I like working with you is impossible.

For all life's twists and turns:
Flexible financial plans.

You're the only woman I love a man now.

For all life's twists and turns:
Flexible financial plans.

Writing for Press & Poster Advertising
SPILLMANN/FELSER/LEO BURNETT
for SwissLife

Life's Turn in a Sentence
The SwissLife pension and life insurance solutions are flexible and adapt to life's twists and turns. So we created a headline campaign dramatising this, and pointing out that life sometimes does take unexpected turns.

Copywriters
Thomas Schöb
Simon Smit
Art Directors
Daniele Barbiero
Reto Clement
Executive Creative Director
Peter Brönnimann

Advertising Agency
SPILLMANN/FELSER/LEO BURNETT
Client
SwissLife

Writing for Press & Poster Advertising
Colenso BBDO Aukland
for Mars Petcare

Smart Puppies
We created this series of posters to promote the importance of Omega 3 in a dog's diet. Each one shows how smarter dogs solve complex dog problems via a flow diagram.

Copywriters
Dave Govier
Levi Slavin
Art Directors
Dave Govier
Levi Slavin
Creative Director
Levi Slavin
Creative Chairman
Nick Worthington
Designers
Kate Slavin
Levi Slavin

Advertising Agency
Colenso BBDO
Auckland
Account Manager
Dave Munn
Account Director
Karla Fisher
Client
Mars Petcare
Brand
Pedigree

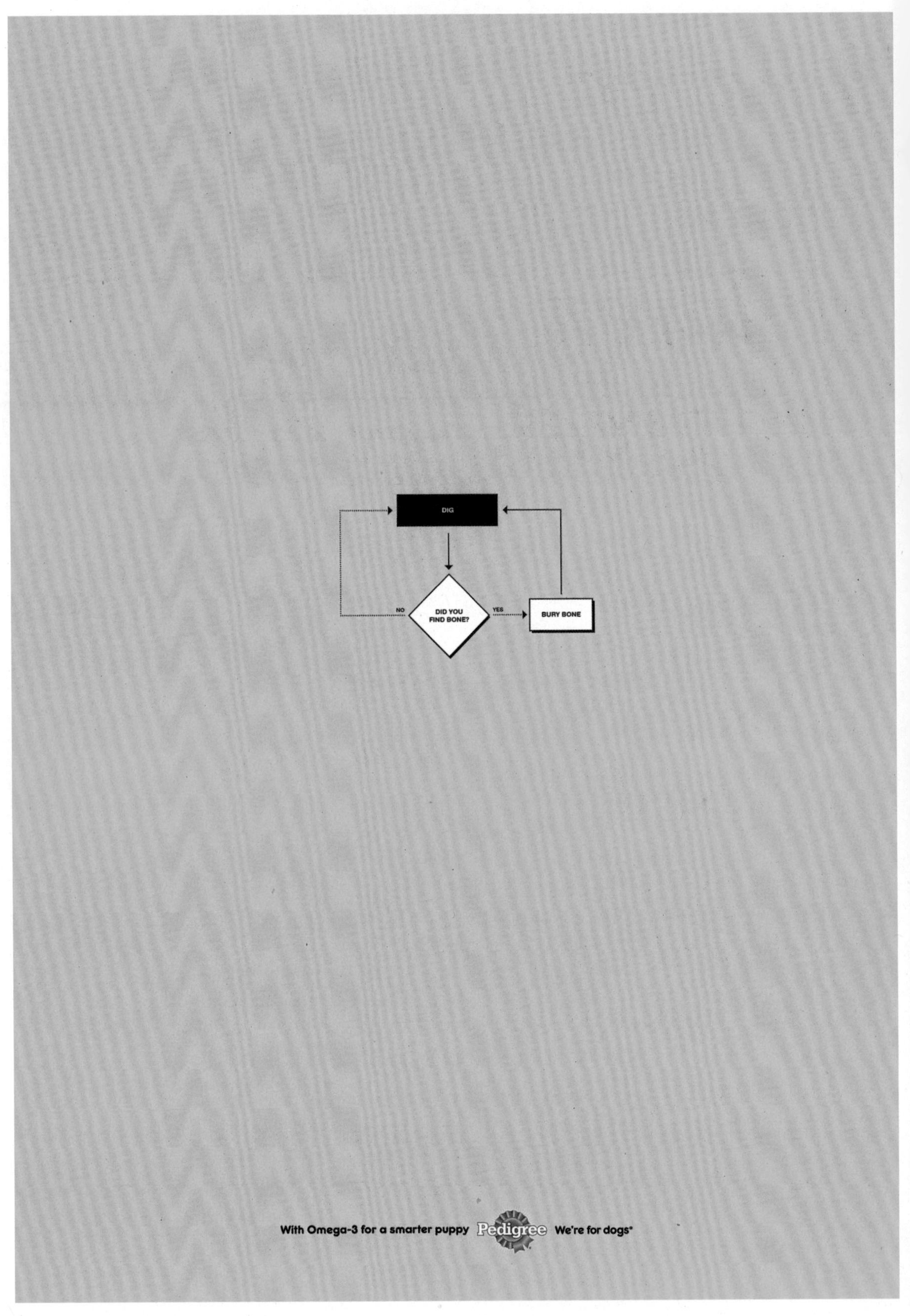

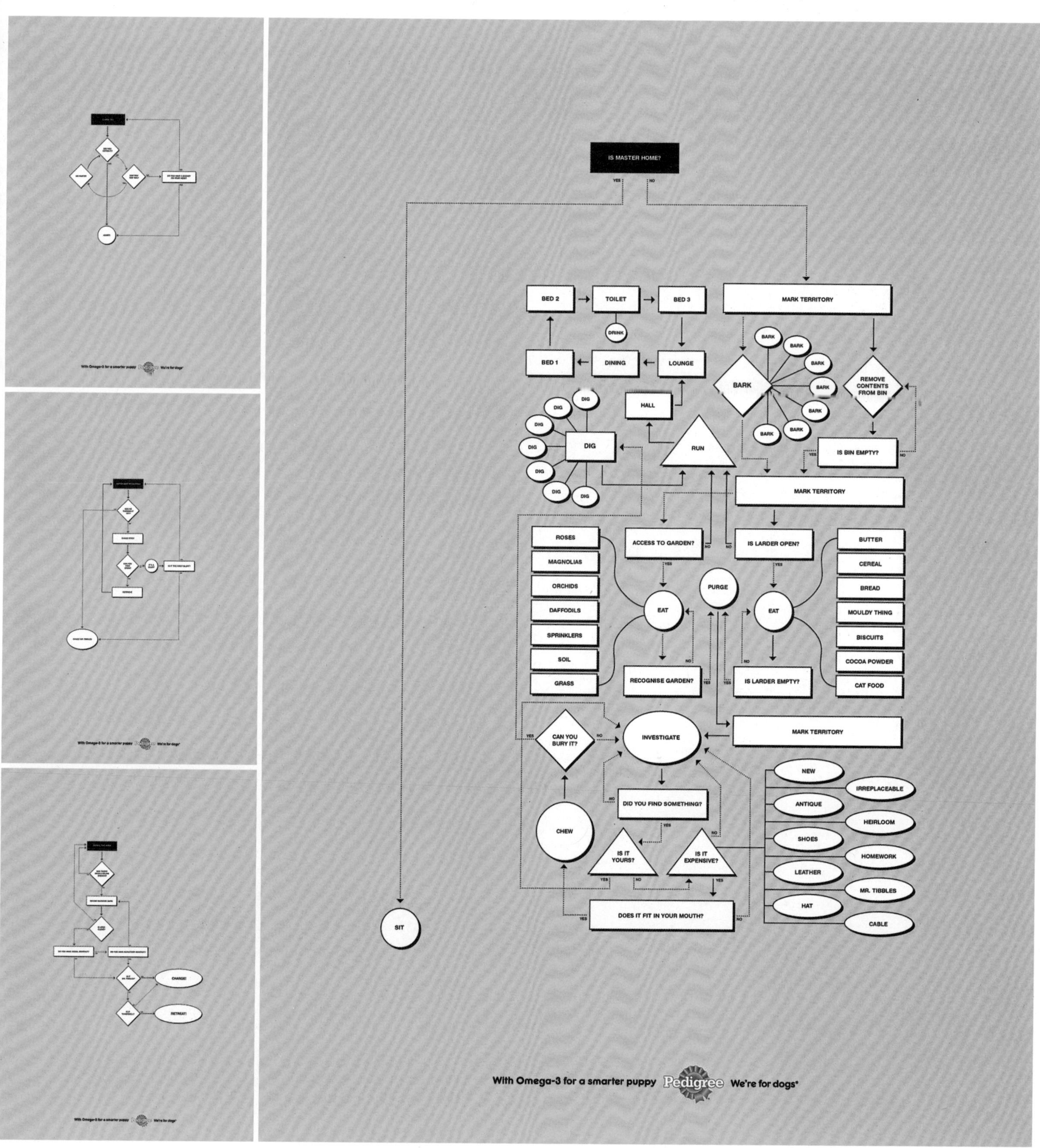
IS MASTER HOME?
YES
NO
BED 2
TOILET
BED 3
DRINK
BED 1
DINING
LOUNGE
MARK TERRITORY
BARK
BARK
BARK
BARK
BARK
BARK
BARK
BARK
REMOVE CONTENTS FROM BIN
HALL
DIG
DIG
DIG
DIG
DIG
DIG
DIG
DIG
RUN
IS BIN EMPTY?
YES
NO
MARK TERRITORY
ROSES
MAGNOLIAS
ORCHIDS
DAFFODILS
SPRINKLERS
SOIL
GRASS
ACCESS TO GARDEN?
NO
YES
EAT
PURGE
RECOGNISE GARDEN?
NO
YES
IS LARDER OPEN?
NO
YES
EAT
IS LARDER EMPTY?
NO
YES
BUTTER
CEREAL
BREAD
MOULDY THING
BISCUITS
COCOA POWDER
CAT FOOD
CAN YOU BURY IT?
YES
NO
INVESTIGATE
MARK TERRITORY
DID YOU FIND SOMETHING?
NO
YES
CHEW
IS IT YOURS?
YES
NO
IS IT EXPENSIVE?
NO
YES
NEW
IRREPLACEABLE
ANTIQUE
HEIRLOOM
SHOES
HOMEWORK
LEATHER
MR. TIBBLES
HAT
CABLE
SIT
DOES IT FIT IN YOUR MOUTH?
YES
NO
With Omega-3 for a smarter puppy
Pedigree
We're for dogs®

1

2

3

4

5

6

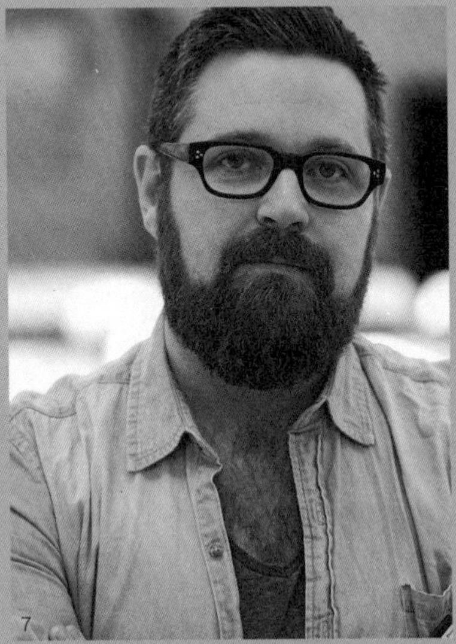
7

Jury Foreman
1. Jim Davies
totalcontent

2. Nick Asbury
Asbury & Asbury

3. Fiona Thompson
Wordspring

4. Anelia Varela
The Writer

5. Lisa Desforges

6. John Weich
Lemon Scented Tea

7. Christopher Doyle
Interbrand

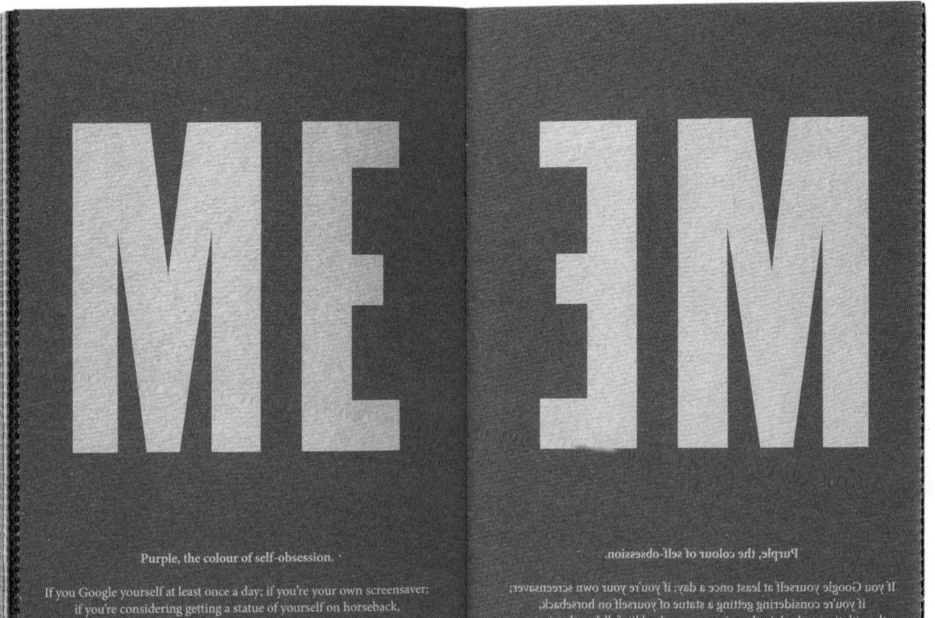

ME
Purple, the colour of self-obsession.
If you Google yourself at least once a day; if you're your own screensaver; if you're considering getting a statue of yourself on horseback, then it's time to look in the mirror – your backlit, full-length mirror – and admit that you might just be the tiniest bit purple.

Nomination in Writing for Design

Pentagram London

Today I'm Feeling Turquoise
'Today I'm Feeling Turquoise' is an attempt to do something that should have been done a long time ago: pairing up colours with their respective moods. The booklet is made up of double-page spreads of coloured paper sealed with a perforated edge. The reader selects a colour and tears open the perforations to reveal the mood it represents. We produced 'Today I'm Feeling Turquoise' to use it as Pentagram's 2011/12 holiday card – but it's much more than that. It's the first step on a journey to finally matching all the colours in the world with their corresponding moods.

Copywriters
Tom Edmonds
Naresh Ramchandani
Designers
Lucy Groom
Jeremy Kunze

Design Director
Domenic Lippa
Design Agency
Pentagram London
Client
Pentagram London

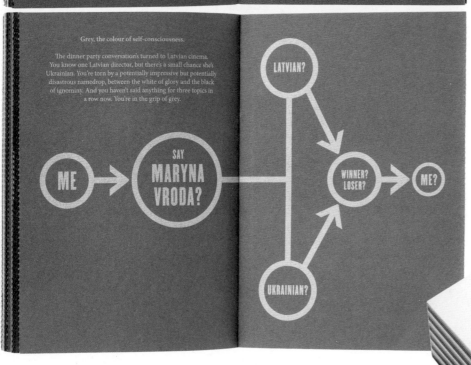

Writing for Design
venturethree
for Little Chef

Little Chef Menu
The new Little Chef was only going to be as good as the new Little Chef menu. The crack culinary team had reinvented the dishes. We had reinvented the brand. This was where it all came together: a wonderfully British menu from a wonderfully British brand.

Copywriters
Mr Blog/Nick Asbury
Joe Weir
Creative Director
Stuart Watson

Branding Agency
venturethree
Client
Little Chef

SORRY SACHETS
we only use Heinz bottles

Please tear here. Please tear here again. No, get a proper grip. OK, try using your teeth. That's it, give it a bite, then try again with your finger. Not too hard! Oh now look what you've done. Don't worry it'll wash off. It was mustard you wanted wasn't it?

Little Chef

FISH AND CHIPS
three words that mean so much

I love you fillet of hake. I love you crispy batter. I love you chips. I want to squeeze you lemon. You make me go all mushy crushy peas. We go together like bread and butter. Like salt and vinegar. Like ketchup on chips. Like tartare on fish. I love you fish and chips.

Little Chef

Writing for Design
Various Artists

byvariousartists.com
Various Artists is a design agency that was set up in April 2011. We needed a holding page for our website, but as all our work was under copyright with previous agencies, we couldn't show any of it. Instead, we chose one simple message – working with Various Artists will make you happy – and made it as engaging as possible. The words 'this' and 'that' all link to well-known, humorous or just plain crazy clips from YouTube that illustrate moments of complete joy or pure pain. To keep things fresh, the background colour changes periodically while you are on the site.

Copywriter
Simon Griffin
Designer
Adam Rix
Creative Directors
Simon Griffin
Adam Rix
Developer
Jono Brain
Creative Agency
Various Artists
Client
Various Artists

Various Artists is a new creative agency. We don't do this or this, but we do make you feel like this, this, this and this. We're great if you want to feel more like this, or like this, or even like that, but we'll never make you feel like this or this. And definitely not like that. This? Sure. This? Naturally. This? Comes as standard. Hey, if you want to feel like this we'll do it. We're all grown ups. But we try and stay away from this. That's just too far. If you'd like to see some of our work or find out more, you can use this, this, or this.

Various Artists

+44 (0)161 637 1125 hello@byvariousartists.com

Writing for Design
Here Design
for William Grant & Sons

William Grant & Sons Brand Ambassador Handbook
This handbook for the brand ambassadors of William Grant & Sons was created to combine sound advice with inspiring creativity and to capture the eclectic nature of the job. Our rule book for a role that has no rules contains an array of useful information, from how to avoid gout to how to say cheers in Azerbaijani, plus an inspiring tale about the golf sale man. Its creative, unbranded style captures the distillers' non-corporate and independent approach, and gives brand ambassadors permission to be just as imaginative on the job.

Copywriter
Lisa Desforges
Designer
Ashlea O'Neill
Creative Director
Caz Hildebrand

Illustrator
Ashlea O'Neill
Design Agency
Here Design
Client
William Grant & Sons

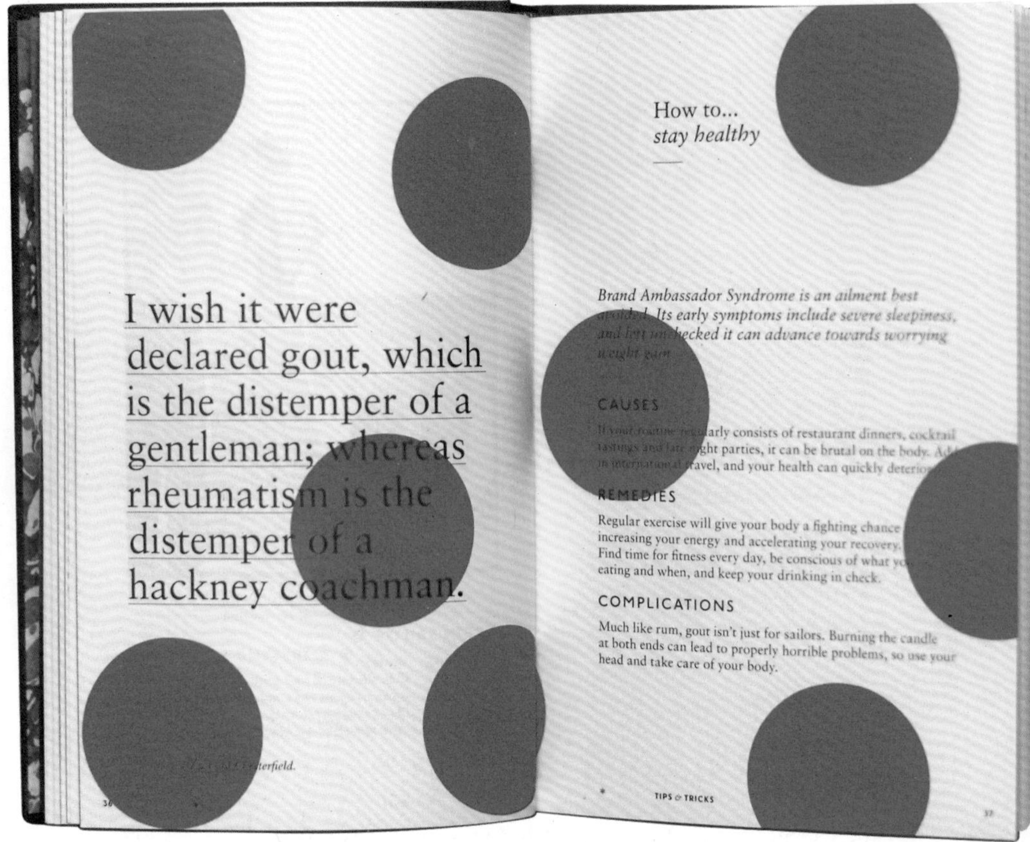

I wish it were declared gout, which is the distemper of a gentleman; whereas rheumatism is the distemper of a hackney coachman.
How to... stay healthy
Brand Ambassador Syndrome is an ailment best avoided. Its early symptoms include severe sleepiness, and left unchecked it can advance towards worrying weight gain.
CAUSES
REMEDIES
Regular exercise will give your body a fighting chance increasing your energy and accelerating your recovery. Find time for fitness every day, be conscious of what you eating and when, and keep your drinking in check.
COMPLICATIONS
Much like rum, gout isn't just for sailors. Burning the candle at both ends can lead to properly horrible problems, so use your head and take care of your body.
TIPS & TRICKS

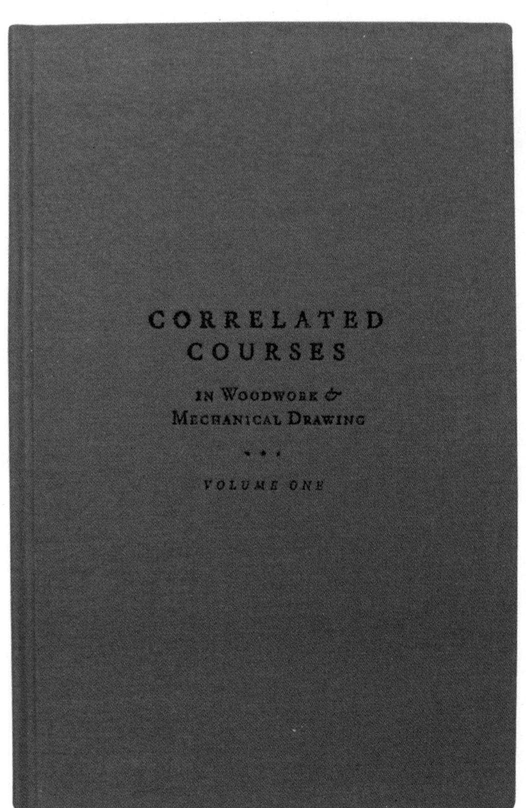

CORRELATED COURSES
IN WOODWORK & MECHANICAL DRAWING
VOLUME ONE

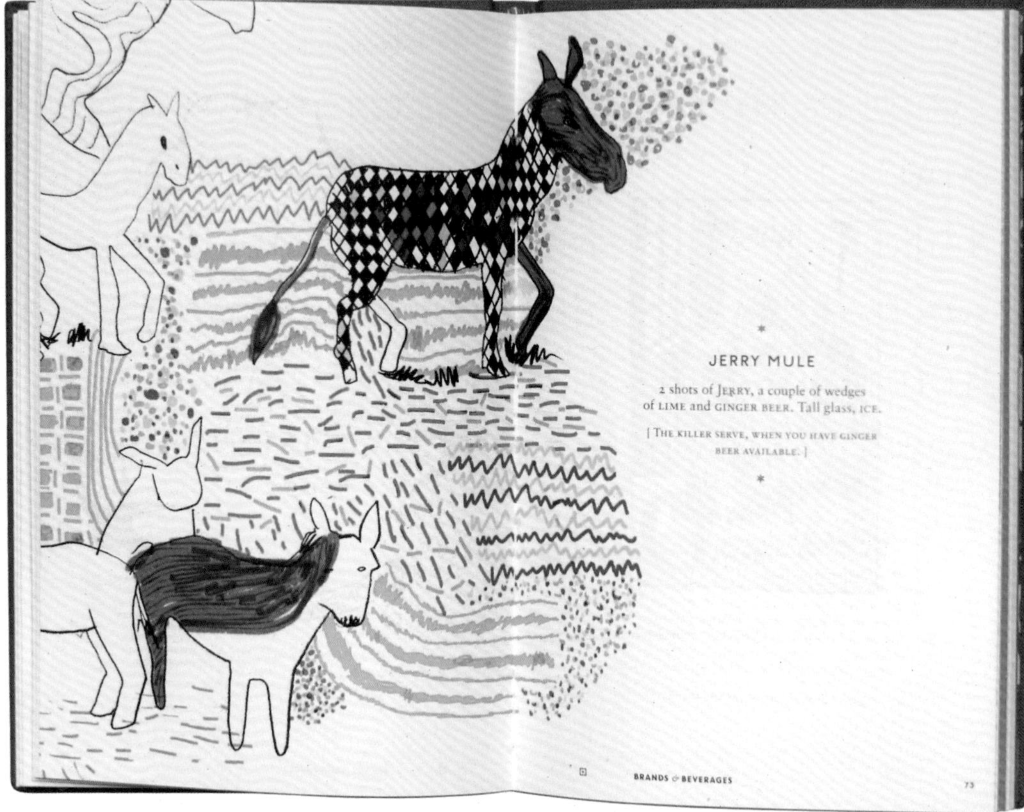

JERRY MULE
2 shots of JERRY, a couple of wedges of LIME and GINGER BEER. Tall glass, ICE.
[THE KILLER SERVE, WHEN YOU HAVE GINGER BEER AVAILABLE.]
BRANDS & BEVERAGES

Writing for Design
Interbrand Sydney
for Steve Bland

The Little Book of Photoshoppe Trickery
Steve Bland is The Great Blandini, Photoshop wizard and creative retoucher extraordinaire. He needed a promotional brochure that would show off his skills and knowledge, appeal to his industry and reflect his sense of fun and humour. 'The Little Book of Photoshoppe Trickery' features ten of Blandini's tricks plus some custom retouches such as 'sawing the lady in half'. The Victorian inspired type – painstakingly rendered with calligraphy pens and ink (yes, even the body copy!) – is a celebration of hand-crafted typography. It was a real labour of love (and magic).

Copywriter
Mike Reed
Designers
Diana Chirilas
Jefton Sungkar
Creative Director
Mike Rigby
Typographer
Jefton Sungkar

Branding Agency
Interbrand Sydney
Client
Steve Bland
Brand
The Great Blandini

THE MAGIC ERASER
Even for those as yet inexperienced in these arts,
spellbinding effects may be achieved by
employing this device, which in an instant causes
coloured backgrounds to vanish before your eyes.

SHADOW AND HIGHLIGHT
Transport a subject from light into darkness,
or vice versa, with this remarkable contrivance.
Revered by skilled retouchers, it renders clearly
to the eye that which was previously quite invisible.

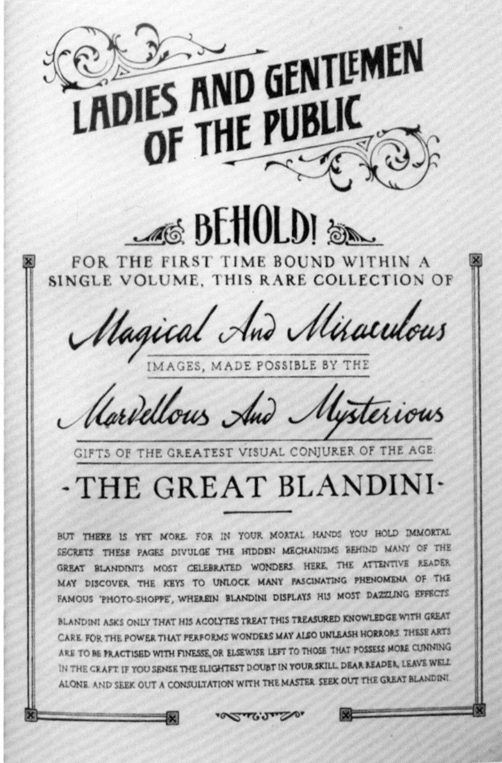
LADIES AND GENTLEMEN OF THE PUBLIC

BEHOLD!

FOR THE FIRST TIME BOUND WITHIN A SINGLE VOLUME, THIS RARE COLLECTION OF

Magical And Miraculous

IMAGES, MADE POSSIBLE BY THE

Marvellous And Mysterious

GIFTS OF THE GREATEST VISUAL CONJURER OF THE AGE:

· THE GREAT BLANDINI ·

BUT THERE IS YET MORE. FOR IN YOUR MORTAL HANDS YOU HOLD IMMORTAL SECRETS. THESE PAGES DIVULGE THE HIDDEN MECHANISMS BEHIND MANY OF THE GREAT BLANDINI'S MOST CELEBRATED WONDERS. HERE, THE ATTENTIVE READER MAY DISCOVER THE KEYS TO UNLOCK MANY FASCINATING PHENOMENA OF THE FAMOUS 'PHOTO-SHOPPE', WHEREIN BLANDINI DISPLAYS HIS MOST DAZZLING EFFECTS.

BLANDINI ASKS ONLY THAT HIS ACOLYTES TREAT THIS TREASURED KNOWLEDGE WITH GREAT CARE. FOR THE POWER THAT PERFORMS WONDERS MAY ALSO UNLEASH HORRORS. THESE ARTS ARE TO BE PRACTISED WITH FINESSE, OR ELSEWISE LEFT TO THOSE THAT POSSESS MORE CUNNING IN THE CRAFT. IF YOU SENSE THE SLIGHTEST DOUBT IN YOUR SKILL, DEAR READER, LEAVE WELL ALONE. AND SEEK OUT A CONSULTATION WITH THE MASTER. SEEK OUT THE GREAT BLANDINI.

Advertising Agencies

Animation

Architectural Studios

Branding Agencies

Brands

Clients

Design Agencies

Developers

Digital Agencies

Digital & Interactive Design Agencies

Digital Production Companies

Editing

Illustration

Interactive Production Companies

Lighting

Media Agencies

Mixing

Mobile Marketing Agency

Music